SUPERSEDED

The media's watching Vault!
Here's a sampling of our coverage.

....

"With reviews and profiles of firms that one associate calls 'spot on',
[Vault's] guide has become a key reference for those who want to know
what it takes to get hired by a law firm and what to expect once they
get there."
- *New York Law Journal*

"The best place on the web to prepare for a job search."
- *Fortune*

"Vault is indispensable for locating insider information."
- *Metropolitan Corporate Counsel*

"[Vault's guide] is an INVALUABLE Cliff's Notes to prepare for
interviews."
- *Women's Lawyer's Journal*

"For those hoping to climb the ladder of success, [Vault's] insights are
priceless."
- *Money Magazine*

"[Vault guides] make for excellent starting points for job hunters and
should be purchased by academic libraries for their career sections
[and] university career centers."
- *Library Journal*

Maybe a lawyer?
No, a doctor?
How about a computer scientist?

Come join our team at Fish & Richardson P.C. and you can be all three.

Don't drop the ball when it comes to pursuing all of your professional aspirations. With 300 attorneys in eight offices, Fish & Richardson has endless opportunities for you to use your knowledge of engineering or science in your law practice.

Don't lose sight of your dreams; at Fish & Richardson, we'll put all of your valuable skills to use. To find out more, check out our web site at **www.fr.com**.

Patents

Complex Litigation

U.S. International Trade Commission Proceedings

Trademarks & Copyrights

Corporate & Securities

International Regulatory Group

FISH & RICHARDSON P.C.

Intellectual Property | Litigation | Corporate

BOSTON | DALLAS | DELAWARE | NEW YORK | SAN DIEGO | SILICON VALLEY | TWIN CITIES | WASHINGTON DC

VAULT GUIDE TO THE
TOP 100
LAW FIRMS

VAULT GUIDE TO THE
TOP 100
LAW FIRMS

BROOK MOSHAN GESSER, J.D.,
MARCY LERNER, TYYA N. TURNER AND RON HOGAN

ACKNOWLEDGEMENTS

It takes a village to put together this book. Many thanks to Mike Baker, Lauren Capewell, Gerry Ferrara, Danielle Koza, Todd Kuhlman, Marshall Lager, Derek Loosvelt, Laurie Pasiuk, Chris Prior, Thomas Nutt, Kristy Sisko and Dan Stanco. A special thanks to Ed Shen for calming everyone down and Kelly Shore for designing this book with a smile on her face.

Thank you to the many law firm recruiting professionals and hiring partners who put up with our tight deadlines, frantic phone calls and repeated requests for information. Their commitment to this project is greatly appreciated year after year.

Thanks also to Matt Doull, Ahmad Al-Khaled, Lee Black, Eric Ober, Hollinger Capital, TBV Holdings, The New York City Investment Fund, American Lawyer Media, Globix, Hoover's, Glenn Fischer, Mark Hernandez, Ravi Mhatre, Ken Cron, Ed Somekh, Zahi Khouri and other Vault investors.

Many thanks to our loving families.

This book is dedicated to the nearly 12,000 associates who took time out of their busy schedules to complete our survey. This book would not be possible without their thoughtful, revealing and often hilarious survey responses. Many thanks!

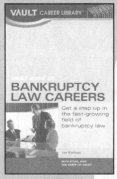

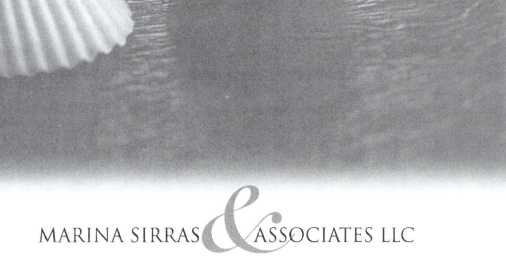

WINSTON & STRAWN

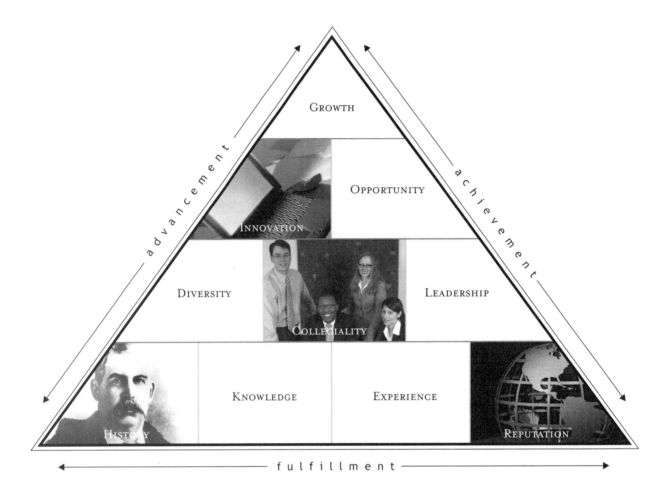

Winston & Strawn—150 years strong, globally connected, committed to diversity, technologically advanced. With unlimited opportunity, imagine the career you could build.

#1 in Best Firms to Work For

#1 in Retention

#1 in Offices

#1 in Partner/Associate Relations

#1 in Diversity for Minorities

Top 5 in Pay, Satisfaction, and Pro Bono

(Vault Guide to the Top 100 Law Firms, 6th Ed.)

WINSTON & STRAWN
Excellence, Experience, Ideals. Since 1853

CHICAGO | GENEVA | LONDON | LOS ANGELES | NEW YORK | PARIS | SAN FRANCISCO | WASHINGTON, D.C.

TABLE OF CONTENTS

The
Results are in...

Consider Jenner & Block's 2004 Vault rankings.
Out of nearly 150 firms we ranked...

JENNER & BLOCK, LLC

- #1 Pro Bono
- #1 Diversity for Gays and Lesbians
- #2 Overall Diversity
- #3 Diversity for Women
- #6 Best in Region—Chicago
- #9 Diversity for Minorities
- #10 Best 20 Law Firms to Work For

VAULT
TOP LAW FIRMS
2004

JENNER&BLOCK

THE VAULT 100: FIRMS 51-100   487

THE BEST OF THE REST
589

LEGAL EMPLOYER DIRECTORY   639

LEGAL RECRUITER FIRM DIRECTORY   683

APPENDIX 707

Use the most **targeted** job search tools for lawyers on the Internet.

Vault's Law Job Board and VaultMatch™ Resume Database

■ Law Job Board

The most comprehensive and convenient job board for legal professionals. Target your search by practice area, function, and experience level, and find the job openings that you want. No surfing required.

■ VaultMatch™ Resume Database

Vault takes match-making to the next level: post your resume and customize your search by practice area, trial experience, level and more. We'll match job listings with your interests and criteria and e-mail them directly to your in-box.

> the most trusted name in career information™

Find out more at www.law.vault.com

FOCUSED ON IP

picture losing MILLIONS over the

differences in a few PIXELS.

The technology inside this half-inch square is so advanced it takes a degree in electrical engineering to understand precisely where one patent begins and another ends. That's why the most innovative companies turn to Finnegan Henderson. With unsurpassed technical expertise, nearly 50 PhDs, outstanding trial lawyers, jury specialists, and decades of experience litigating to federal and state juries across the U.S., Finnegan Henderson can handle the most complex IP disputes. As one of the nation's most renowned litigation practices, we know that the real drama is in the details.

FINNEGAN
HENDERSON
FARABOW
GARRETT &
DUNNER LLP

INTRODUCTION

Welcome to the sixth edition of the *Vault Guide to the Top 100 Law Firms*, the most comprehensive, candid, up-to-date guide to the most prestigious law firms.

People will debate forever whether size matters, but at Vault we think it matters plenty – at least where our guide is concerned. This year, our guide is bigger and better, with law firm profiles and stats of more firms than ever before. In years past, we've ranked the top 50 law firms. Now we offer a ranking of 100 of the nation's top firms, complete with profiles incorporating quotes and opinions from thousands of associates. The guide also features stats for an additional 48 firms, with contact and salary information, office locations, notable perks, major practice areas and more, including the ever-popular "Buzz" section, in which associates offer observations about firms other than their own.

This year, a record number of associates participated in the Vault associate survey. We thought we'd never top last year's participation rate of over 9,500 associates, but an astounding 11,908 associates took time out of their busy schedules this year. We surveyed associates at over 140 of the most prestigious firms in the country and asked them to rank 149 law firms. Associates were invited to tell us what they thought of their peer law firms and were asked to score each firm based on its prestige. (Participants were asked only to rank those firms with which they were familiar.) We took those scores and calculated the Vault Top 100. We also asked associates to comment on and rank their own firm on subjects such as satisfaction, hours, compensation, diversity, treatment by partners and selectivity in hiring. As always, it's the associates who choose the Vault Top 100, not Vault editors or law firm management.

We're at it year after year, surveying associates and bugging law firm recruiting directors and hiring partners, for one reason: to provide lawyers and law students with an insider's view of what it's like to work at the nation's most prestigious law firms. But why do we bother ranking the Top 100 firms? Why does law firm prestige matter? A job is a job, after all, and many law firms not profiled in this guide pay as well as any firm on our list. Then again, prestige still counts for a lot. Working for a prestigious law firm means being exposed to a greater variety and volume of work, as well as more prominent and high-profile cases and deals. It can also mean working with some particularly gifted and accomplished lawyers from whom you can learn a great deal. Most importantly, working for a prestigious firm will give you instant credibility in the job market and mark you as someone to be taken seriously throughout your career.

Of course, prestige isn't everything, and to some jobseekers, prestige hardly matters at all. Choosing the right firm for you may mean looking beyond prestige to such issues as compensation, hours, perks, sophistication of the work, partnership chances, diversity and corporate culture. Our Best 20 Firms to Work For is where we rank the firms associates find most amenable to an enjoyable lawyerly existence.

Landing a position at the firm of your choice has never been more intimidating, with the nation in a recession and many firms drifting in and out of hiring freezes. And competition at law schools across the country has never been more daunting, with law school applications hitting record numbers as lawyers-to-be continue to flee an inhospitable job market. Those looking to join one of the prestigious firms profiled in this guide have their work cut out for them.

So get ready for those law firm interviews. Comb your hair, don your best navy blue suit, shine your shoes and practice that firm handshake. With the sixth edition of the *Vault Guide to the Top 100 Law Firms* at your side, we're confident that you have access to the best resource on the top law firms.

The Editors
Vault Inc.
New York, NY

THE STATE OF THE LAW

At least as far as the legal industry is concerned, 2002 sometimes felt like a repeat of 2001, only this time in overdrive. More attorney layoffs. Bigger drops in M&A and other financial action. Equally huge surges in bankruptcy and litigation work. More complaints about stingy bonus offerings and partners' tight clutch on the purse strings, coupled with an increased awareness of the competition over the jobs available in the tightening legal market. Add the shocking dissolution of a high-profile firm to the mix, and you've got quite a year. Here are some of the highlights.

Turn out the lights

Before we look at the ups and downs of 2002, we have to consider the stunning kickoff to 2003, when San Francisco-based Brobeck, Phleger & Harrison threw in the towel at the end of January, leaving 1,100 employees in 14 cities without jobs. The 77-year-old firm had bet heavily on technology during the booming 1990s, and clients like Cisco, Sun Microsystems and Nokia had helped fuel major expansion in that decade, making Brobeck the most profitable law firm in the Bay Area at the turn of the century. But the firm was entrenched too deeply in the new economy and unable to react to the tech sector's collapse in time to save itself. After a last-ditch effort to preserve the Brobeck infrastructure by negotiating a merger with Philadelphia's Morgan Lewis & Bockius fell through, swiftly followed by the defection of a top litigator (and about 20 other attorneys) to Akin Gump, the firm's leadership decided enough was enough.

The disbanding inevitably led to a recruiting frenzy, as competitors scrambled to acquire the firm's top attorneys and its blue chip clients. Morgan Lewis & Bockius picked up 150 Brobeck lawyers, while Paul, Hastings, Janofsky & Walker took on 41 attorneys in three California offices; other firms picking at Brobeck's bones included Heller Ehrman White & McAuliffe (which snagged the San Diego business/tech group), Mayer Brown Rowe & Maw (gaining an IT outsourcing practice), Weil, Gotshal & Manges and White & Case. Latham & Watkins also scored big, landing the assignment as Brobeck's bankruptcy counsel.

The high-profile dissolution overshadowed the closings of other law firms. Boston's Hill & Barlow and Lyons & Lyons of Los Angeles called it quits, as did Brobeck's local competitor, Skjerven Morrill, which more people might have noticed if it hadn't announced its closure the same week as Brobeck. The closings served as a grim reminder to attorneys of the shaky state of the economy, if they needed any further reminding after the recurring layoffs at firms in almost every major market throughout 2002. Many of the associates who responded to this year's survey complained that, in addition to eliminating benefits and perks, partners at their firms also saved money by skimping on annual bonuses – either reducing them outright or, in some cases, refusing to raise them despite substantial increases in firm revenue.

The numbers game

The mergers and acquisitions market continued to plummet in 2002. The top firm on *American Lawyer*'s M&A scorecard for the year, Sullivan & Cromwell, participated in two-thirds as many deals as it had in 2001. Even though one of those transactions, Pfizer's purchase of Pharmacia, was the biggest acquisition of the year at over $60 billion, S&C's deals last year still had a total value of little more than half of the ones from 2001; in fact, the firm's M&A 2002 track record would barely have been good enough for the top-ten list in 2001. Other big players in the scene were hit just as hard; Wachtell, the No. 1 M&A firm in 2001, saw the accumulative value of its deals nose-dive by approximately 70 percent the following year. (Things were just as bad for those acting as counsel to investment advisers; Dewey Ballantine still handled more transactions in that capacity than anybody else, but worked on half as many deals, worth only one-tenth the money.)

The IPO field was similarly soft. Skadden, Arps, Slate, Meagher & Flom was by far the leader among issuer's counsels judging by proceeds, but that was primarily on the strength of a single deal, a $3.89 billion offering for Travelers Property Casualty in March 2002. Bell, Boyd & Lloyd, which had counseled 15 IPO issuers in 2001, vanished off the radar screen, and the two firms that did the most IPO work, Vinson & Elkins and Wilson Sonsini, only represented a half-dozen corporations each. In a further indication of economic trends, Wilson's tech-heavy issuers attracted little more than one-quarter of the money that flowed to V&E's clients, like the $480 million raked in by Expressjet Holdings, the Texas-based owners of Continental Express.

Telecommunications breakdown

So what was hot in corporate law? Bankruptcy – and plenty of it. Just when most of us were just starting to comprehend the sheer magnitude of Enron's $63 billion Chapter 11 filing from the tail end of 2001, along came WorldCom's $103.9 billion collapse to completely blow our minds. And that was just the most prominent meltdown in the telecom sector, which also saw bankruptcy filings by Global Crossing, Adelphia, XO Communications and the Williams Communications Group. The numbers have become ridiculously huge: When a $61 billion insurer like Conseco goes under, the failings of aluminum merchant Kaiser ($3.3 billion) and software developer Genuity ($2.9 billion) seem almost immaterial in comparison. Genuity's counsel, Skadden Arps, has carved out the biggest niche among the debtor's counsel, taking on four more of the year's 20 biggest bankruptcies (including Kmart and US Airways), while Akin Gump is getting just as much work repping creditors committees, in the WorldCom proceedings as well as those for Kaiser.

Law and order comes to Wall Street

Litigation attorneys had plenty to do in 2002, often working on cases involving the very same companies that were keeping bankruptcy attorneys up late at night. The phrase "perp walk" entered the financial lexicon last summer as Adelphia CEO John Rigas and his sons were dragged off in handcuffs, a blunt symbol of the government's public commitment to getting tough on corporate crime. L. Dennis Kozlowski, former chief exec at Tyco, was indicted on sales-tax evasion charges and then again for swindling his company of $600 million. Andrew Fastow pled not guilty to 78 separate criminal counts in connection with his tenure as Enron's chief financial officer, while one of his subordinates admitted his guilt in conspiracy to commit wire fraud and money laundering. Of course, executives didn't wait until they were indicted to seek legal counsel; attorneys at A-list firms advised corporations and their current or former executives in connection with various preliminary investigations by federal and state authorities. Even lifestyle guru Martha Stewart came under scrutiny when she dumped her holdings in ImClone just before the stock plummeted; an SEC probe to determine whether her providential timing was the result of insider trading made headlines well into 2003, culminating in her indictment in early June both for the trade and her subsequent attempt at covering it up.

Investment banks also generated plenty of work for litigators and white-collar criminal defense attorneys, as the SEC – and New York Attorney General Elliott Spitzer, among other state prosecutors – conducted inquiries into whether they had artificially hyped stock offerings during the boom. A groundbreaking settlement in April 2003 cost 10 Wall Street firms a total of at least $1.4 billion and mandated several reforms in how investment banks will be allowed to tout IPOs in the future. Another prominent aspect of the settlement was the expulsion of two prominent technology analysts, Merrill Lynch's Henry Blodget and Jack Grubman of Salomon Smith Barney, from the securities industry for the rest of their lives. Shortly after that settlement, Frank Quattrone, the former head of Credit Suisse First Boston's technology-banking unit, was indicted by a federal grand jury on obstruction charges. He is accused of exhorting his staff to purge their files of old documentation despite his awareness of an SEC investigation of his department.

Pitt stop

The wave of corporate malfeasance led Congress to pass the Sarbanes-Oxley Act in the summer of 2002. In response to revelations of how companies had used questionable accounting techniques to hide their financial shenanigans, often with the help of outside auditing firms, the new law called for the establishment of an accounting oversight board to set new standards for corporate auditing. This board would prove to be the downfall of SEC Chairman Harvey Pitt, whose short tenure was marked by a series of political gaffes. Pitt, who had left a prominent position at New York's Fried, Frank, Harris, Shriver & Jacobson to take over the commission in 2001, was accused of strong-arming his fellow commissioners into accepting his nominee for the head of the oversight board, former CIA and FBI director William Webster. He was also accused of withholding information about Webster's participation in the audit committee of a struggling technology firm. The subsequent public controversy fueled long-running arguments that Pitt's close ties to the accounting industry made him an unsuitable champion for corporate reform. Pitt held on until early November and then buried his resignation announcement beneath a flurry of election night results. (Webster stepped down from the board shortly after.)

A GUIDE TO THIS GUIDE

If you're wondering how our entries are organized, read on. Here's a handy guide to the information you'll find packed into each entry of this book.

THE BUZZ

When it comes to other law firms, our respondents certainly like to dish! We asked them to tell us their opinions and observations about firms other than their own. We've collected a sampling of these comments in "The Buzz."

When selecting The Buzz, we included quotes representative of the common outsider's perceptions of the firms, even if (in our opinion) the quotes did not accurately describe the firm. We choose four Buzz comments for each firm: two in which associates had good things to say about the firm and two that were less complimentary. Hey, we're trying to be fair here!

Please keep in mind when reading The Buzz that it's often more fun for outsiders to trash than praise a competing law firm. Nonetheless, we have found The Buzz to be another valuable means of gauging a firm's reputation in the legal field, or at least to understand common misperceptions.

FIRM FACTS

Locations: A listing of the firm's offices, with the headquarters bolded. You may see firms with no bolded location. This means that these are self-proclaimed decentralized firms without official headquarters.

Major Departments/Practices: Practice areas that employ a significant portion of the firm's headquarters' attorneys as reported by the firms.

Base Salary: The firm's base salary at its headquarters. Base salary at other offices is given when available.

Uppers and Downers: Good points and bad points about working at the firm, as gleaned from associate interviews and surveys. Uppers and downers are the impressionistic perceptions of insiders and are not based on statistics.

Notable Perks: A listing of perks and benefits outside the norm. For example, we do not list health care, as every firm we surveyed offers health care plans.

Employment Contact: The person identified by the firm as the primary contact to receive resumes or to answer questions about the recruitment process. More than one contact is sometimes given. In some instances, we refer the reader to the firm web site.

Ranking Recap: New this year. A summary of all categories in which the firm ranked particularly well, including departmental, geographic, quality of life and diversity categories.

THE STATS

No. of attorneys: The total number of attorneys at a firm in all offices as of April or May 2003. Sometimes the number is an estimate.

No. of offices: The firm's total number of offices worldwide.

Summer associate offers: The firm-wide number of second-year law students offered full-time associate positions by the firm, compared to the firm-wide number of second-year law students who worked at the firm in 2002 as a summer associate.

Chairman, Managing Partner, etc.: The name and title of the leader of the firm. Sometimes more than one name is provided.

QUALITY OF LIFE METERS

Our meters are based on the responses to our survey by nearly 12,000 law firm associates. Survey participants were asked to rate their firm in a variety of categories on a 1 to 10 scale. The firm's score in each category is simply the average (mean) of the scores its associates gave in that area. We have highlighted the following categories for our meters:

Satisfaction: Associates rank their satisfaction with their firm on a scale from "unsatisfactory" to "entirely fulfilling."

Hours: Associates rank how they feel about their hours on a scale from "overwhelming" to "very livable." Please note the hours score is based on the subjective perceptions of associates, not on the actual hours they work.

Training: Associates rank their satisfaction with the level of formal and informal training their firm provides.

Diversity: Associates rank their satisfaction with all diversity issues, including the situations of minority group members, gays and lesbians, and women. Again, the diversity score is based on the subjective perceptions of associates, not on actual diversity statistics.

Associate/Partner Relations: Associates rank how well they feel they're treated and mentored by the partners at their firm.

Please note that firms that did not participate in our survey were usually not rated by our quality of life meters. In some cases, Vault contacted associates independently at firms that did not participate in our survey. If a representative sampling of associates completed our survey, the firm was rated by our quality of life meters, even if the firm did not participate in the survey.

THE PROFILES

You'll notice two types of firm profiles – long ones and short ones. What's the deal? Firms ranked No. 1 to No. 50 received long profiles, and shorter profiles were reserved for firms ranked No. 51 to No. 100. Both the long and short profiles are divided into three sections: The Scoop, Getting Hired and Our Survey Says.

The Scoop: The firm's history, clients, recent deals, recent firm developments and other points of interest.

Getting Hired: Qualifications the firm looks for in new associates, tips on getting hired and other notable aspects of the hiring process.

Our Survey Says: Actual quotes from surveys of current associates of the firm on topics such as the firm's assignment system, feedback, partnership prospects, levels of responsibility, summer associate program, culture, hours, pay, training and much more. Some profiles also contain brief "firm responses" to associate criticism or clarification of points of confusion expressed in the profile. Vault editors will often modify associate quotes to correct grammar or spelling.

BEST OF THE REST

In addition to the 50 long and 50 short profiles, we've also included information on additional law firms that did not make our Top 100 list this year.

"THE NATION'S STANDARD IN ATTORNEY SEARCH AND PLACEMENT"

With offices in Los Angeles, New York, Chicago, Miami, Austin and Washington, DC, BCG Attorney Search is the largest and most geographically diverse placement firm dedicated exclusively to permanent law firm attorney placements in the United States.

It is our core belief that it is better to do one thing exceptionally well than to do a multitude of things. All we do are permanent law firm attorney placements, and we are both confident about and highly committed to the work that we do.

ATTORNEY SEARCH

www.bcgsearch.com

THE VAULT PRESTIGE RANKINGS

Visit the Vault Law Channel, the complete online resource for law careers, featuring firm profiles, message boards, the Vault Law Job Board, and more. www.law.vault.com

VAULT CAREER LIBRARY

11

THE RANKING METHODOLOGY

TOP 100

This is Wachtell's year. Since we published the first edition of this book six years ago, some things remained constant year after year; Cravath, Swaine & Moore was always ranked No. 1 and Wachtell, Lipton, Rosen & Katz always No. 2. But now, for the first time, Wachtell has edged in front of Cravath, taking the top spot. But what does this change signify? Does it tell us anything profound about the state of the legal profession? It should be said that we at Vault think the change has more to do with an increase in name recognition for the diminutive Wachtell (fewer than 200 attorneys, compared with Cravath's nearly 500) than any decrease in the prestige of powerhouse Cravath. As far as we can tell, Cravath will always make the hearts of law students the world over go pitter-pat. But the one-office Wachtell has edged out Cravath in the New York regional rankings for years. It's nothing new that New York associates think Wachtell is the cat's meow. With the firm taking the top spot in the national ranking, it looks like associates around the country are coming to realize the extent of pint-sized Wachtell's prestige.

How does Vault come up with its list of the Top 100 firms in the country? The first step is to compile a list of the most renowned law firms in the land by reviewing the feedback we receive from previous surveys, consulting our previous lists, poring over legal newspapers, talking to lawyers in the field and checking out other published rankings. This year, our initial list was made up of 150 law firms, though we had to drop Brobeck pretty quickly after it broke up. (For more about Brobeck's collapse, see The State of the Law.) We asked the remaining firms to distribute a password-protected online survey to their associates. In total, 11,908 attorneys returned anonymous surveys to Vault. We heard from lawyers in New York, Los Angeles, San Francisco, Palo Alto, Chicago, Boston, Philadelphia, Houston, Dallas, Washington, D.C., Miami, Cleveland, Seattle, Orlando, Phoenix and Atlanta, among many other U.S. locations, not to mention London, Paris and beyond. The online survey asked attorneys to score each of the law firms on a scale of 1 to 10 based on how prestigious it is to work for the firm. Associates were asked to ignore any firm with which they were unfamiliar and were not allowed to rank their own firm.

We collected all the surveys and averaged the score for each firm. The firms were then ranked in order, starting with the highest average prestige score as No. 1 on down to determine the Vault Top 100. Remember that in the Top 100, Vault is not assessing firms by profit, size, lifestyle, number of deals or quality of service; we are ranking the most prestigious law firms based on the perceptions of currently practicing lawyers at peer firms.

Think it's easy getting 11,908 associates to take our survey? Think again. Lawyers are busy people, and many are stressed out as it is without having to take 30 minutes out of their day to work on a non-billable project – especially with the increased emphasis on racking up billable hours. Despite it all, an incredible amount of associates came through for us and helped us produce the Vault Top 100. Associates, many thanks for your insight and patience.

The Vault 100

2004*

The 100 most prestigious law firms

2004 RANK	LAW FIRM	PRESTIGE SCORE	2003 RANK	2002 RANK	2001 RANK	LARGEST OFFICE/ HEADQUARTERS
1	Wachtell, Lipton, Rosen & Katz	8.912	2	2	2	New York, NY
2	Cravath, Swaine & Moore LLP	8.850	1	1	1	New York, NY
3	Sullivan & Cromwell LLP	8.444	3	3	3	New York, NY
4	Davis Polk & Wardwell	8.209	5	4	4	New York, NY
5	Skadden, Arps, Slate, Meagher & Flom**	8.143	4	5	5	New York, NY
6	Simpson Thacher & Bartlett	7.844	6	6	6	New York, NY
7	Cleary, Gottlieb, Steen & Hamilton	7.731	7	7	7	New York, NY
8	Covington & Burling	7.517	8	10	14	Washington, DC
9	Latham & Watkins LLP	7.503	9	9	9	Los Angeles, CA
10	Weil, Gotshal & Manges LLP	7.438	10	12	13	New York, NY
11	Kirkland & Ellis	7.420	12	14	11	Chicago, IL
12	Shearman & Sterling	7.300	13	8	8	New York, NY
13	Paul, Weiss, Rifkind, Wharton & Garrison***	7.209	14	15	15	New York, NY
14	Williams & Connolly LLP	7.205	11	11	12	Washington, DC
15	Debevoise & Plimpton	7.157	17	16	18	New York, NY
16	Sidley Austin Brown & Wood LLP	7.090	16	17	16	Chicago, IL
17	Gibson, Dunn & Crutcher LLP	7.058	18	20	17	Los Angeles, CA
18	Arnold & Porter	7.006	19	23	21	Washington, DC
19	Wilmer, Cutler & Pickering	6.942	15	18	23	Washington, DC
20	White & Case LLP	6.892	20	19	20	New York, NY
21	O'Melveny & Myers LLP	6.860	22	21	19	Los Angeles, CA
22	Jones Day	6.857	21	29	30	Cleveland, OH
23	Hale and Dorr LLP	6.832	23	22	27	Boston, MA
24	Milbank, Tweed, Hadley & McCloy LLP	6.689	27	25	26	New York, NY
25	Ropes & Gray LLP	6.660	28	27	28	Boston, MA

NR = Not Ranked

* Vault rankings span two calendar years; they are dated as the second of these years. For example, our 2004 rankings are based on surveys completed in summer 2003 and apply to the 2003-2004 academic year.

** Skadden, Arps, Slate, Meagher & Flom LLP and Affiliates

*** Paul, Weiss, Rifkind, Wharton & Garrison LLP

2004 RANK	LAW FIRM	PRESTIGE SCORE	2003 RANK	2002 RANK	2001 RANK	LARGEST OFFICE/ HEADQUARTERS
26	Fried, Frank, Harris, Shriver & Jacobson	6.647	26	30	29	New York, NY
27	Morrison & Foerster LLP	6.595	24	24	22	San Francisco, CA
28	Dewey Ballantine LLP	6.508	29	34	31	New York, NY
29	Mayer, Brown, Rowe & Maw	6.487	34	31	25	Chicago, IL
30	Hogan & Hartson L.L.P.	6.399	30	35	39	Washington, DC
31	Willkie Farr & Gallagher	6.327	35	32	36	New York, NY
32	Clifford Chance LLP	6.283	25	28	33	New York, NY
33	Boies, Schiller & Flexner LLP	6.266	33	47	NR	Armonk, NY
34	Akin Gump Strauss Hauer & Feld LLP	6.252	36	49	43	Washington, DC
35	Cadwalader, Wickersham & Taft LLP	6.230	40	46	47	New York, NY
36	King & Spalding LLP	6.224	32	36	35	Atlanta, GA
37	Paul, Hastings, Janofsky & Walker LLP	6.162	42	40	41	Los Angeles, CA
38	Orrick, Herrington & Sutcliffe LLP	6.121	41	39	42	San Francisco, CA
39	Morgan, Lewis & Bockius LLP	6.119	48	38	34	Philadelphia, PA
40	Winston & Strawn	6.073	37	41	44	Chicago, IL
41	Proskauer Rose LLP	6.062	45	48	48	New York, NY
42	Cahill Gordon & Reindel LLP	6.030	43	42	50	New York, NY
43	Baker Botts L.L.P.	6.022	47	55	49	Houston, TX
44	Baker & McKenzie	6.015	39	44	45	Chicago, IL
45	Wilson Sonsini Goodrich & Rosati	5.998	31	13	10	Palo Alto, CA
46	Fulbright & Jaworski L.L.P.	5.990	49	45	NR	Houston, TX
47	McDermott, Will & Emery	5.892	50	51	NR	Chicago, IL
48	Munger, Tolles & Olson LLP	5.879	38	37	40	Los Angeles, CA
49	LeBoeuf, Lamb, Greene & MacRae, L.L.P.	5.831	53	53	NR	New York, NY
50	Chadbourne & Parke LLP	5.775	52	59	NR	New York, NY

The 100 most prestigious law firms

2004 RANK	LAW FIRM	PRESTIGE SCORE	2003 RANK	2002 RANK	2001 RANK	LARGEST OFFICE/ HEADQUARTERS
51	Jenner & Block, LLC	5.749	56	56	NR	Chicago, IL
52	Irell & Manella LLP	5.731	54	58	NR	Los Angeles, CA
53	Pillsbury Winthrop LLP	5.729	55	64	NR	San Francisco, CA
54	Alston & Bird LLP	5.636	66	89	NR	Atlanta, GA
55	Kaye Scholer LLP	5.626	57	60	NR	New York, NY
56	Cooley Godward LLP	5.614	46	33	32	Palo Alto, CA
57	Goodwin Procter LLP	5.581	58	61	NR	Boston, MA
58	Sonnenschein Nath & Rosenthal	5.580	59	67	NR	Chicago, IL
59	Dechert LLP	5.533	62	68	NR	Philadelphia, PA
60	Steptoe & Johnson LLP	5.514	51	50	NR	Washington, DC
61	Allen & Overy	5.510	NR	NR	NR	London, UK
62	Fish & Neave	5.434	63	66	NR	New York, NY
63	Howrey Simon Arnold & White, LLP	5.426	65	75	NR	Washington, DC
64	Heller Ehrman White & McAuliffe LLP	5.382	60	65	NR	San Francisco, CA
65	Vinson & Elkins L.L.P.	5.380	86	52	46	Houston, TX
66	Hunton & Williams LLP	5.342	70	82	NR	Richmond, VA
67	Holland & Knight LLP	5.332	69	76	NR	Tampa, FL
68	Coudert Brothers LLP	5.320	61	62	NR	New York, NY
69	Foley & Lardner	5.297	71	81	NR	Milwaukee, WI
70	Perkins Coie LLP	5.292	64	57	NR	Seattle, WA
71	Piper Rudnick LLP	5.235	68	69	NR	Chicago/DC
72	Stroock & Stroock & Lavan LLP	5.155	76	79	NR	New York, NY
73	Schulte Roth & Zabel LLP	5.135	81	84	NR	New York, NY
74	Testa, Hurwitz & Thibeault, LLP	5.093	67	63	NR	Boston, MA
75	Crowell & Moring LLP	5.082	72	78	NR	Washington, DC

Vault rankings span two calendar years; they are dated as the second of these years. For example, our 2004 rankings are based on surveys completed in summer 2003 and apply to the 2003-2004 academic year.

2004 RANK	LAW FIRM	PRESTIGE SCORE	2003 RANK	2002 RANK	2001 RANK	LARGEST OFFICE/ HEADQUARTERS
76	Kirkpatrick & Lockhart LLP	5.055	74	77	NR	Pittsburgh, PA
77	Greenberg Traurig, LLP	5.026	89	85	NR	Miami, FL
78	Fish & Richardson P.C.	5.022	92	NR	NR	Boston, MA
79	Patton Boggs LLP	5.012	77	72	NR	Washington, DC
80	Bryan Cave LLP	4.985	82	91	NR	St. Louis, MO
81	Bingham McCutchen LLP †	4.969	75 / 80	71 / 100	NR	Boston, MA
82	Fenwick & West LLP	4.918	73	70	NR	Palo Alto, CA
83	Pennie & Edmonds LLP	4.894	83	74	NR	New York, NY
84	Hughes Hubbard & Reed LLP	4.886	93	87	NR	New York, NY
85	Gray Cary Ware & Freidenrich LLP	4.838	78	73	NR	Palo Alto, CA
86	Dorsey & Whitney LLP	4.827	85	94	NR	Minneapolis, MN
87	Kelley Drye & Warren LLP	4.814	95	90	NR	New York, NY
88	Shaw Pittman LLP	4.777	84	80	NR	Washington, DC
89	Finnegan, Henderson, Farabow, Garrett**	4.771	91	97	NR	Washington, DC
90	Choate, Hall & Stewart	4.753	87	83	NR	Boston, MA
91	Baker & Hostetler LLP	4.723	79	93	NR	Cleveland, OH
92	Katten Muchin Zavis Rosenman	4.720	97	95	NR	Chicago, IL
93	Arent Fox Kintner Plotkin & Kahn, PLLC	4.711	88	NR	NR	Washington, DC
94	Mintz Levin Cohn Ferris Glovsky***	4.691	96	86	NR	Boston, MA
95	Kramer Levin Naftalis & Frankel LLP	4.683	NR	NR	NR	New York, NY
96	Thelen Reid & Priest LLP	4.659	100	NR	NR	New York, NY
97	Squire, Sanders & Dempsey	4.557	NR	NR	NR	Cleveland, OH
98	McGuireWoods LLP	4.533	99	98	NR	Richmond, VA
99	Wiley Rein & Fielding LLP	4.519	94	96	NR	Washington, DC
100	Preston Gates & Ellis LLP	4.509	NR	88	NR	Seattle, WA

† In last year's edition of this book, Bingham McCutchen had not yet merged and appeared as two separate firms in our rankings.

** Finnegan, Henderson, Farabow, Garrett & Dunner, L.L.P.

*** Mintz Levin Cohn Ferris Glovsky and Popeo, P.C.

REGIONAL RANKINGS

Sometimes all you care about is how a firm stacks up against its peer firms in a particular region of the country. That's where our regional rankings come in. We took only the votes from associates in each regional area to determine the regional prestige rankings. In most cases, firms that ranked high locally made the Vault 100 list, though the order of the firms in the regional ranking differs in some interesting ways from the order of the firms in the Top 100.

This year's regional categories are: Boston, California, Chicago, New York, the Pacific Northwest, Pennsylvania, the South, Texas and Washington, D.C.

New York

RANK	FIRM	SCORE	2003 RANK
1	Wachtell, Lipton, Rosen & Katz	9.158	1
2	Cravath, Swaine & Moore LLP	9.011	2
3	Sullivan & Cromwell LLP	8.622	3
4	Davis Polk & Wardwell	8.477	4
5	Skadden, Arps, Slate, Meagher & Flom*	8.090	6
6	Simpson Thacher & Bartlett	8.025	5
7	Cleary, Gottlieb, Steen & Hamilton	7.839	7
8	Paul, Weiss, Rifkind, Wharton & Garrison LLP	7.427	9
9	Debevoise & Plimpton	7.307	8
10	Weil, Gotshal & Manges LLP	7.280	10
11	Shearman & Sterling	7.062	11
12	Milbank, Tweed, Hadley & McCloy LLP	6.462	14
13	White & Case LLP	6.442	12
14	Fried, Frank, Harris, Shriver & Jacobson	6.403	15
15	Willkie Farr & Gallagher	6.387	13
16	Dewey Ballantine LLP	6.330	18
17	Boies, Schiller & Flexner LLP	6.156	16
18	Cahill Gordon & Reindel LLP	6.081	19
19	Proskauer Rose LLP	5.948	20
20	Clifford Chance LLP	5.824	17

Skadden, Arps, Slate, Meagher & Flom LLP and Affiliates

REGIONAL RANKINGS (cont'd)

California

RANK	FIRM	SCORE	2003 RANK
1	Latham & Watkins LLP	7.981	1
2	O'Melveny & Myers LLP	7.572	3
3	Gibson, Dunn & Crutcher LLP	7.451	2
4	Morrison & Foerster LLP	7.249	4
5	Munger, Tolles & Olson LLP	7.221	5
6	Irell & Manella LLP	6.904	6
7	Orrick, Herrington & Sutcliffe LLP	6.750	8
8	Heller Ehrman White & McAuliffe LLP	6.477	11
9	Paul, Hastings, Janofsky & Walker LLP	6.376	12
10	Wilson Sonsini Goodrich & Rosati	6.367	7
11	Cooley Godward LLP	6.098	9
12	Pillsbury Winthrop LLP	6.064	13
13	Fenwick & West LLP	5.712	14
14	Gray Cary Ware & Freidenrich LLP	5.643	NR
15	Manatt, Phelps & Phillips, LLP	5.336	NR

Chicago

RANK	FIRM	SCORE	2003 RANK
1	Kirkland & Ellis	8.574	1
2	Sidley Austin Brown & Wood LLP	8.188	2
3	Mayer, Brown, Rowe & Maw	8.059	3
4	Winston & Strawn	7.403	4
5	McDermott, Will & Emery	6.508	5
6	Jenner & Block, LLC	6.371	6
7	Baker & McKenzie	6.103	7
8	Sonnenschein Nath & Rosenthal	6.093	8
9	Piper Rudnick LLP	5.645	NR
10	Katten Muchin Zavis Rosenman	5.627	9

REGIONAL RANKINGS (cont'd)

Washington, DC

RANK	FIRM	SCORE	2003 RANK
1	Covington & Burling	8.369	2
2	Williams & Connolly LLP	8.343	1
3	Wilmer, Cutler & Pickering	8.061	3
4	Arnold & Porter	7.871	4
5	Hogan & Hartson L.L.P.	7.436	5
6	Akin Gump Strauss Hauer & Feld LLP	6.331	6
7	Steptoe & Johnson LLP	6.140	7
8	Patton Boggs LLP	6.042	NR
9	Howrey Simon Arnold & White, LLP	5.878	NR
10	Crowell & Moring LLP	5.824	8
11	Wiley Rein & Fielding LLP	5.693	10
12	Shaw Pittman LLP	5.663	9
13	Finnegan, Henderson, Farabow, Garrett & Dunner *	5.387	NR
14	Arent Fox Kintner Plotkin & Kahn, PLLC	5.383	NR
15	Dickstein Shapiro Morin & Oshinsky LLP	5.174	NR

* Finnegan, Henderson, Farabow, Garrett & Dunner, L.L.P.

Boston

RANK	FIRM	SCORE	2003 RANK
1	Ropes & Gray	8.291	1
2	Hale and Dorr LLP	8.212	2
3	Goodwin Procter LLP	7.284	3
4	Bingham McCutchen LLP *	6.454	5
5	Testa, Hurwitz & Thibeault LLP	6.165	4
6	Foley Hoag LLP **	5.900	6
7	Mintz Levin Cohn Ferris Glovsky and Popeo, P.C.	5.710	7
8	Fish & Richardson P.C.	5.591	10
9	Choate, Hall & Stewart	5.491	8
10	Palmer & Dodge LLP	5.372	9

* Last year's rank based on Bingham Dana before the merger with McCutchen, Doyle, Brown & Enerson.
** This year's rank based on last year's score in this category.

REGIONAL RANKINGS (cont'd)

Texas

RANK	FIRM	SCORE	2003 RANK
1	Baker Botts L.L.P.	7.977	1
2	Vinson & Elkins L.L.P.	7.413	2
3	Fulbright & Jaworski L.L.P.	6.956	3
4	Andrews & Kurth L.L.P.	6.081	4
5	Bracewell & Patterson, L.L.P.	5.925	5
6	Haynes and Boone, LLP	5.825	NR
7	Locke Liddell & Sapp LLP	5.703	NR
8	Jenkens & Gilchrist, A Professional Corporation	5.546	NR
9	Thompson & Knight LLP	5.515	NR
10	Gardere Wynne Sewell LLP	5.454	NR

Pennsylvania

RANK	FIRM	SCORE	2003 RANK
1	Morgan, Lewis & Bockius LLP	8.062	1
2	Dechert LLP	7.990	2
3	Ballard Spahr Andrews & Ingersoll, LLP	6.801	3
4	Drinker Biddle & Reath LLP	6.441	4
5	Reed Smith	6.367	NR
6	Pepper Hamilton LLP	6.323	NR
7	Blank Rome LLP	5.786	5
8	Buchanan Ingersoll Professional Corporation	5.671	NR
9	Duane Morris LLP	5.592	NR
10	Wolf, Block, Schorr and Solis-Cohen LLP	5.463	NR

REGIONAL RANKINGS (cont'd)

The Pacific Northwest

RANK	FIRM	SCORE
1	Perkins Coie LLP	7.977
2	Preston Gates & Ellis LLP	7.073
3	Davis Wright Tremaine LLP	6.609
4	Stoel Rives LLP	5.889

* Unlike other regional rankings charts, there is no historical comparison for the Northwest.

The South

RANK	FIRM	SCORE
1	King & Spalding LLP	7.900
2	Alston & Bird LLP	7.774
3	Troutman Sanders LLP	6.019
4	Kilpatrick Stockton LLP	5.947
5	Powell, Goldstein, Frazer & Murphy LLP	5.496

* Unlike other regional rankings charts, there is no historical comparison for the Southern region..

SOME OF US SEE FARTHER THAN OTHERS.

Lawyers with vision can spot hidden opportunity.

Davis Wright Tremaine LLP

Toll Free
1-877-398-8417
www.dwt.com

DEPARTMENTAL RANKINGS

Associates were allowed to vote for up to three firms in their practice areas and were not permitted to vote for their own firm. Associates who identified themselves as corporate attorneys were only allowed to vote in corporate-related categories (securities, business finance, etc.); litigators were only allowed to vote in the litigation category, and so on. We indicate the top firms in each area, as well as the total percentage of votes cast in favor of the firm. (Each associate surveyed chose three firms; the maximum percentage of votes per firm is 33.3 percent.)

This year's departmental categories are: Antitrust, Bankruptcy/Creditors' Rights, Corporate, Intellectual Property, Labor and Employment, Litigation, Mergers and Acquisitions, Real Estate, Securities, Tax and Technology.

Antitrust*

RANK	FIRM	% OF VOTES
1	Arnold & Porter	11.93
2	Howrey Simon Arnold & White, LLP	11.52
3	Cleary, Gottlieb, Steen & Hamilton	7.82
4	Jones Day	7.41
5(tie)	Hogan & Hartson, LLP	5.76
5(tie)	Skadden, Arps, Slate, Meagher & Flom**	5.76
6	Clifford Chance LLP	5.35
7	Gibson, Dunn & Crutcher LLP	4.94
8	Shearman & Sterling	4.12
9(tie)	Boies, Schiller & Flexner LLP	3.70
9(tie)	Kirkland & Ellis	3.70
9(tie)	Wilmer, Cutler & Pickering	3.70
10	Sullivan & Cromwell LLP	2.88

This is the first Vault ranking for Antitrust.
**Skadden, Arps, Slate, Meagher & Flom LLP and Affiliates*

DEPARTMENTAL RANKINGS (cont'd)

Bankruptcy/Creditors' Rights

RANK	FIRM	% OF VOTES	2003 RANK
1	Weil, Gotshal & Manges LLP	28.57	1
2	Skadden, Arps, Slate, Meagher & Flom*	17.43	2
3	Kirkland & Ellis	13.71	3(tie)
4	Milbank, Tweed, Hadley & McCloy LLP	5.86	3(tie)
5	Wachtell, Lipton, Rosen & Katz	4.29	4
6	Jones Day	3.71	6
7	Willkie Farr & Gallagher	3.43	5
8	Akin Gump Strauss Hauer & Feld LLP	2.29	8
9(tie)	Sidley Austin Brown & Wood LLP	1.14	NR
9(tie)	Simpson Thacher & Bartlett	1.14	NR
10(tie)	Bingham McCutchen LLP**	1.00	NR
10(tie)	Davis Polk & Wardwell	1.00	7
10(tie)	Fried, Frank, Harris, Shriver & Jacobson	1.00	NR

* Skadden, Arps, Slate, Meagher & Flom LLP and Affiliates
**Merger

Corporate

RANK	FIRM	% OF VOTES	2003 RANK
1	Cravath, Swaine & Moore LLP	18.53	1
2	Wachtell, Lipton, Rosen & Katz	14.54	3
3	Skadden, Arps, Slate, Meagher & Flom*	14.39	2
4	Sullivan & Cromwell LLP	11.38	4
5	Davis Polk & Wardwell	8.19	5
6	Simpson Thacher & Bartlett	5.45	6
7	Cleary, Gottlieb, Steen & Hamilton	3.57	7
8	Shearman & Sterling	2.41	8
9	Latham & Watkins LLP	2.26	9
10	Weil, Gotshal & Manges LLP	1.63	NR

* Skadden, Arps, Slate, Meagher & Flom LLP and Affiliates

DEPARTMENTAL RANKINGS (cont'd)

Intellectual Property

RANK	FIRM	% OF VOTES	2003 RANK
1	Finnegan, Henderson, Farabow, Garrett*	15.68	1
2	Fish & Neave	13.56	2
3	Fish & Richardson P.C.	12.83	3(tie)
4	Pennie & Edmonds LLP	5.25	3(tie)
5(tie)	Howrey Simon Arnold & White, LLP	4.46	9
5(tie)	Kirkland & Ellis	4.46	7
6	Morrison & Foerster LLP	4.13	5
7	Foley & Lardner	2.79	10
8	Irell & Manella LLP	2.51	NR
9	Wilson Sonsini Goodrich & Rosati	2.46	6
10	Weil, Gotshal & Manges LLP	2.40	NR

* Finnegan, Henderson, Farabow, Garrett & Dunner, L.L.P.

Labor & Employment

RANK	FIRM	% OF VOTES	2003 RANK
1	Paul, Hastings, Janofsky & Walker LLP	11.98	1(tie)
2	Littler Mendelson, P.C.	11.63	1(tie)
3	Proskauer Rose LLP	10.79	3
4	Morgan, Lewis & Bockius LLP	8.42	4
5	Seyfarth Shaw	8.19	2
6	Jackson Lewis LLP	6.88	NR
7	Epstein Becker & Green, P.C.	2.97	NR
8	O'Melveny & Myers LLP	2.25	7(tie)
9	Akin Gump Strauss Hauer & Feld LLP	1.90	6
10 (tie)	Alston & Bird LLP	1.78	NR
10 (tie)	Gibson, Dunn & Crutcher LLP	1.78	7(tie)

DEPARTMENTAL RANKINGS (cont'd)

Litigation

RANK	FIRM	% OF VOTES	2003 RANK
1	Cravath, Swaine & Moore LLP	8.68	1
2	Williams & Connolly LLP	7.37	2
3	Kirkland & Ellis	7.27	3
4	Paul, Weiss, Rifkind, Wharton & Garrison LLP	5.40	4
5	Skadden, Arps, Slate, Meagher & Flom*	5.24	6
6	Boies, Schiller & Flexner LLP	4.37	7
7	Davis Polk & Wardwell	4.32	5
8	Wachtell, Lipton, Rosen & Katz	3.63	8
9	Covington & Burling	3.25	NR
10	Jones Day	3.00	10

Skadden, Arps, Slate, Meagher & Flom LLP and Affiliates

Mergers & Acquisitions

RANK	FIRM	% OF VOTES	2003 RANK
1	Wachtell, Lipton, Rosen & Katz	25.82	1
2	Skadden, Arps, Slate, Meagher & Flom*	20.67	2
3	Cravath, Swaine & Moore LLP	16.87	3
4	Sullivan & Cromwell LLP	8.94	4
5	Simpson Thacher & Bartlett	5.71	6
6	Davis Polk & Wardwell	3.95	5
7	Shearman & Sterling	2.22	7
8	Cleary, Gottlieb, Steen & Hamilton	1.69	8
9 (tie)	Latham & Watkins LLP	1.16	10(tie)
9 (tie)	Weil, Gotshal & Manges LLP	1.16	9
10	Kirkland & Ellis	1.01	10(tie)

Skadden, Arps, Slate, Meagher & Flom LLP and Affiliates

DEPARTMENTAL RANKINGS (cont'd)

Real Estate

RANK	FIRM	% OF VOTES	2003 RANK
1	Skadden, Arps, Slate, Meagher & Flom*	8.36	1
2	Piper Rudnick LLP	6.69	2(tie)
3	Fried, Frank, Harris, Shriver & Jacobson	6.38	2(tie)
4	Paul, Hastings, Janofsky & Walker LLP	5.17	3
5	Cadwalader, Wickersham & Taft LLP	4.41	4(tie)
6	Sidley Austin Brown & Wood LLP	3.34	10
7	Mayer, Brown, Rowe & Maw	3.19	5
8	Stroock & Stroock & Lavan LLP	2.74	6
9(tie)	Latham & Watkins LLP	2.28	7(tie)
9(tie)	Shearman & Sterling	2.28	NR
10(tie)	Alston & Bird LLP	2.13	NR
10(tie)	Weil, Gotshal & Manges LLP	2.13	NR

Skadden, Arps, Slate, Meagher & Flom LLP and Affiliates

Securities

RANK	FIRM	% OF VOTES	2003 RANK
1	Sullivan & Cromwell LLP	14.70	1
2	Cravath, Swaine & Moore LLP	14.60	2(tie)
3	Skadden, Arps, Slate, Meagher & Flom*	12.86	2(tie)
4	Davis Polk & Wardwell	11.17	3
5	Wachtell, Lipton, Rosen & Katz	6.84	4
6	Cleary, Gottlieb, Steen & Hamilton	5.83	6
7	Simpson Thacher & Bartlett	5.60	7
8	Shearman & Sterling	4.44	5
9	Latham & Watkins LLP	2.93	9
10	Sidley Austin Brown & Wood LLP	2.09	10

Skadden, Arps, Slate, Meagher & Flom LLP and Affiliates

DEPARTMENTAL RANKINGS (cont'd)

Tax

RANK	FIRM	% OF VOTES	2003 RANK
1	Cravath, Swaine & Moore LLP	11.72	1
2	Cleary, Gottlieb, Steen & Hamilton	11.58	2(tie)
3	Skadden, Arps, Slate, Meagher & Flom*	9.12	2(tie)
4	Sullivan & Cromwell LLP	8.39	4
5	Davis Polk & Wardwell	6.80	3
6	Wachtell, Lipton, Rosen & Katz	6.66	5
7	McDermott, Will & Emery	4.05	6
8(tie)	Baker & McKenzie	3.76	7
8(tie)	Kirkland & Ellis	3.76	9
9	Shearman & Sterling	2.46	10
10	Simpson Thacher & Bartlett	2.32	NR

* Skadden, Arps, Slate, Meagher & Flom LLP and Affiliates

DEPARTMENTAL RANKINGS (cont'd)

Technology

RANK	FIRM	% OF VOTES	2003 RANK
1	Wilson Sonsini Goodrich & Rosati	16.79	3
2	Cooley Godward LLP	9.49	1
3	Fenwick & West LLP	6.57	5 (tie)
4	Morrison & Foerster LLP	5.84	4
5	Shaw Pittman LLP	5.11	5(tie)
6(tie)	Gunderson Dettmer Stough Villeneuve*	2.92	6(tie)
6(tie)	Milbank, Tweed, Hadley & McCloy LLP	2.92	NR
6(tie)	Mintz, Levin, Cohn, Ferris, Glovsky **	2.92	NR
7(tie)	Alston & Bird LLP	2.19	6(tie)
7(tie)	Arnold & Porter	2.19	NR
7(tie)	Finnegan, Henderson, Farabow, Garrett***	2.19	NR
7(tie)	Gray Cary Ware & Freidenrich LLP	2.19	6(tie)
7(tie)	Hale and Dorr LLP	2.19	NR
7(tie)	Mayer, Brown, Rowe & Maw	2.19	NR
7(tie)	Testa, Hurwitz & Thibeault, LLP	2.19	NR
7(tie)	Wiley Rein & Fielding LLP	2.19	NR

* Gunderson Dettmer Stough Villeneuve Franklin & Hachigian, LLP

**Mintz, Levin, Cohn, Ferris, Glovsky and Popeo, P.C.

***Finnegan, Henderson, Farabow, Garrett & Dunner, LLP

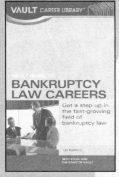

PICTURE
YOURSELF

@

Morgan Lewis
COUNSELORS AT LAW

Attracting and developing talented professionals who are committed to excellence is critical to our success. We offer our lawyers unparalleled opportunities for interesting work, a supportive and collegial environment and a promising pathway to career development and success. We have a diverse group of innovative thinkers who are passionate about the practice of law.

Picture *yourself* at Morgan Lewis and see what develops.

www.morganlewis.com

QUALITY OF LIFE RANKINGS

Visit the Vault Law Channel, the complete online resource for law careers, featuring firm profiles, message boards, the Vault Law Job Board, and more. www.law.vault.com

VAULT CAREER LIBRARY   33

QUALITY OF LIFE RANKINGS

METHODOLOGY

Associates were asked to rate their firm on a 1 to 10 scale for each of several quality of life categories. The firm's score in each quality of life category is simply the average of the scores its associates gave in that area. It is important to note that those firms without a high enough aggregate of associates completing the survey were ineligible to appear in these rankings.

THE BEST 20 FIRMS TO WORK FOR

Which are the best firms to work for? For some, this is a far more important consideration than prestige. To determine our Best 20 firms, we analyzed our initial list of 149 firms using a formula that weighed the most relevant categories for an overall quality of life ranking. Each firm's overall score was calculated using the following formula:

40 percent satisfaction

10 percent hours

10 percent treatment by partners

10 percent training

10 percent pay

10 percent diversity (with respect to women, minorities, and gays and lesbians)

5 percent retention

5 percent offices

Like our Top 100 rankings, our Best 20 is meant to be the subjective opinion of associates. By its nature, the list is based on the perceptions of insiders, some of whom may be biased in favor (or against) their firm.

BEST 20 FIRMS TO WORK FOR

Average score = 7.37

RANK	FIRM	HEADQUARTERS	SCORE
1	Winston & Strawn	Chicago, IL	8.475
2	Morrison & Foerster LLP	San Francisco, CA	8.287
3	Wachtell, Lipton, Rosen & Katz	New York, NY	8.142
4	Ropes & Gray	Boston, MA	8.062
5	Davis Polk & Wardwell	New York, NY	8.061
6	Jenkens & Gilchrist, A Professional Corporation	Dallas, TX	8.019
7	Alston & Bird LLP	Atlanta, GA	8.016
8	Haynes and Boone, LLP	Dallas, TX	7.973
9	Debevoise & Plimpton	New York, NY	7.965
10	Jenner & Block, LLC	Chicago, IL	7.961
11	Finnegan, Henderson, Farabow, Garrett*	Washington, DC	7.923
12	Fish & Richardson P.C.	Boston, MA	7.921
13	Hale and Dorr LLP	Boston, MA	7.907
14	Troutman Sanders LLP	Atlanta, GA	7.898
15	Gray Cary Ware & Freidenrich LLP	Palo Alto, CA	7.892
16	Orrick, Herrington & Sutcliffe LLP	San Francisco, CA	7.866
17	Jones Day	Cleveland, OH	7.838
18	Arent Fox Kintner Plotkin & Kahn, PLLC	Washington, DC	7.820
19	Cleary, Gottlieb, Steen & Hamilton	New York, NY	7.771
20	Allen & Overy	London, UK	7.770

*Finnegan, Henderson, Farabow, Garrett & Dunner, L.L.P

Top three firms to work for

1. Winston & Strawn

After two years in the No.-2 spot, preceded by stopovers in the No. 3 and No. 4 positions, Winston & Strawn has climbed to the top of the Best Firms to Work For list. The firm also earned top-three finishes in four quality of life categories: retention, pay, associate/partner relations and office space. Winston & Strawn insiders frequently cite the firm's "excellent client base" and "interesting, high-profile cases" as primary reasons for their high level of satisfaction.

Though the firm may have a reputation for being extremely formal, those who work at Winston & Strawn say, "The culture here is extremely friendly and laid back." According to an attorney in the Chicago office, "The culture is laid back, but very professional. Lawyers are very comfortable with one another, and socialize together frequently." "The firm culture is very friendly. Attorneys and staff on your floor who you don't even work with seem to make an effort to say hello in the halls and make small talk." "The people are great, which makes working much more pleasurable." In particular, the "partners and senior associates are all approachable and very social."

"As long as you do your best work" say insiders, "no one seems concerned with face time or other trivial matters. It's a very freeing place for people who have the discipline to work within that loose structure. Beyond that, there is a certain level of prestige associated with the firm that makes it a valuable place to work."

Managing Partner Jim Neis is gushing. "We are proud that our associates consider us among the very best firms to work for this year. In 2003 we mark our 150th anniversary, and we believe that our longevity stems in part from our strong culture and emphasis on teamwork and collegiality," Neis says.

2. Morrison & Foerster

Morrison & Foerster, last year's Best Firm to Work For, may have been edged out for first place this year, but this "collegial," "respectful" San Francisco firm is still tops to its associates. "Generally MoFo is a very laid-back place of business," "yet professional" at the same time. This dual nature results in an environment that is "not as hierarchical as other firms and very casual in dress, but at the same time very hardworking." Insiders characterize MoFo as "a meritocracy devoid of conflict or office politics," where everyone, including partners, is "relaxed, friendly, informal and accepting of differences in personality and lifestyle." It doesn't hurt to have "no emphasis on face time."

"The partners that I consider to be my mentors constantly check in with me to see how things are going and if I like what I'm doing. My experience is that they really try to keep us happy," shares an associate in the D.C. office. "The attitude appears to be that doing a great job for a client and providing quality work is more highly valued than face time." "It is hard to imagine a more ideal work environment," says a litigation associate. Another attorney praises the firm's "supportive and friendly" atmosphere, adding, "There is no lack of lawyers who are willing to lend an ear or to provide advice on both legal and personal issues." The firm "feels like a family once you've been here a while," a senior associate observes. A fellow insider says simply, "Working in this firm is highly satisfying."

3. Wachtell, Lipton, Rosen & Katz

"The culture is fairly intense" and there's "a sense of urgency about each matter," but Wachtell insiders seem to thrive on the excitement. "The work we do is very interesting, cutting-edge stuff that keeps associates very engaged," a second-year reports. Says another attorney, "If you enjoy fast-paced, front-page work and don't mind the attendant life complications, this is the place." "Wachtell is a special place to work. This is in large part due to the high level of responsibility given to associates, the interesting nature of the work, the firm's commitment to making it as easy as possible to do the work and the high level of compensation," says a corporate associate. "The work here is consistently challenging, satisfying and intellectually fulfilling."

But wait, there's more. Associates say they're privileged to "work hand-in-hand with incredibly smart, dedicated and experienced lawyers who treat you like an equal and involve you in every aspect of a matter." Other insiders happily report, "The firm offers unsurpassed responsibility for junior attorneys." "There's no other way to describe Wachtell than that it is a fun place to work. I am given tremendous amounts of responsibility, which in turn makes the learning process here extremely accelerated. I cannot imagine working anywhere else," states a fulfilled first-year.

John F. Savarese, chairman of the firm's recruiting committee, shares part of the secret to Wachtell's phenomenal success. "Our associates are a superb group of people whose talent and hard work are central to our success. We're delighted, therefore, that they've voiced so much enthusiasm for their experience at the firm. We aim, through our partner/associate ratio, relatively small size and close-knit work environment, to give our associates plenty of opportunities to shine on high-profile matters and to forge their own relationships with clients."

SATISFACTION

Average score = 7.26

RANK	FIRM	SCORE
1	Schiff Hardin & Waite	8.583
2	Wachtell, Lipton, Rosen & Katz	8.533
3	Morrison & Foerster LLP	8.500
4	Winston & Strawn	8.453
5(tie)	Debevoise & Plimpton	8.333
5(tie)	Jenkens & Gilchrist, A Professional Corporation	8.333
6	Alston & Bird LLP	8.148
7	Greenberg Traurig, LLP	8.143
8	Haynes and Boone, LLP	8.106
9	Fish & Richardson P.C.	8.102
10	Patton Boggs LLP	8.089
11	Morgan, Lewis & Bockius LLP	8.078
12	Jenner & Block, LLC	8.033
13	Arent Fox Kintner Plotkin & Kahn, PLLC	8.023
14	Davis Polk & Wardwell	8.010
15	Steptoe & Johnson LLP	8.000
16	Sedgwick, Detert, Moran & Arnold LLP	7.951
17	Orrick, Herrington & Sutcliffe LLP	7.950
18	Troutman Sanders LLP	7.943
19	Ropes & Gray	7.896
20	Williams & Connolly LLP	7.893

Top three in satisfaction

1. Schiff Hardin & Waite

Schiff Hardin & Waite may not have placed among the top 100 firms in the Vault survey, but its associates say they can – and do – get plenty of satisfaction from working there. Not even a top 10 contender in satisfaction last year, Schiff Hardin associates are ready to let the secret out about this Windy City mainstay. One associate states simply, "This is the best that a firm gets." Another associate isn't above bragging a little. "I think we have it much better here than at other similar firms," she says. With Schiff Hardin's "laid-back," "courteous, team-oriented," "professional" culture and "smart, creative" coworkers, it's not hard to understand why these attorneys like their firm. Associates really appreciate that the firm is "a place where you can be yourself" and "the unique character of the individual is valued," not to mention "the relationships between partners and associates," which "are healthy, constructive and respectful." "While other firms try to force people to socialize by sponsoring a myriad of after-work events, Schiff recognizes that people have a life and don't want it programmed for them 24-7. That being said, many people at the firm hang out with each other because they enjoy each other's company, not because it is expected."

As great as the atmosphere is, it's the "very challenging and rewarding" work and level of autonomy that insiders really crow about. Because "the firm does not require face time, attorneys are left to manage their own time and find their own work." Associates say they're excited to work at Schiff Hardin because the "ability to grow as a lawyer without being micromanaged," combined with flexibility "to practice in several different areas," affords "a significant amount of freedom to structure one's own career." Others say it is the "good balance between work and camaraderie" that makes Schiff Hardin & Waite a "great place to work."

2. Wachtell, Lipton, Rosen & Katz

The opportunity to work at the "congenial and professional" Wachtell is a lawyer's dream come true, insiders say. Where else can one find "an incredibly collegial and cooperative atmosphere" and a culture that "is very intense, yet surprisingly informal" all within the same firm? Furthermore, associates are privileged to "work hand-in-hand with incredibly smart, dedicated and experienced lawyers who treat you like an equal and involve you in every aspect of a matter." Associates are given early exposure to "big deals and cases that are headline news," and "the opinions of even the most junior associates are solicited and respected."

The "consistently interesting and challenging work," "terrific compensation" and "generous fringe benefits" are just some of the highlights of the Wachtell experience. "Close relationships with colleagues, including partners," is an element of life at the firm that's frequently cited by associates as one of the best aspects of working at Wachtell. And it's not just the attorneys. The caliber of everyone "from top to bottom, secretaries to partners, is nonpareil." Not surprisingly, the firm has a "very democratic culture, with thin lines between partners and associates and between lawyers and staff. There is a lot of firm pride, and that creates a friendly atmosphere." In the words of one wise associate, "We're in it together, so why not be nice?"

3. Morrison & Foerster

"Mofo is a place full of happy, well-adjusted lawyers and staff who take their work, but not themselves, seriously." Largely because "the variety and quality of work is astounding," and coworkers are "congenial and helpful," insiders deem work at Morrison & Foerster to be "as satisfying as it can be to work at a large firm." "Even as a junior associate, you are provided with many opportunities."

"Everyone here – partners, associates, secretaries and legal assistants – is very, very smart and enjoyable to work for and with." And the "casual and friendly" "open-door culture" fosters a "collegial environment where partners and associates regularly visit each other's offices to bounce ideas off one another." "Lawyers socialize to some degree, but there's no pressure to do so at the cost of family and friends." "Some groups socialize together a lot and are very close, but going home to your family is respected also." "There is a strong emphasis on family as many of the lawyers and staff have young children. As a result, many attorneys are understanding when family commitments require you to be away from the office during regular business hours." For those who'd rather unwind by going out after a long day at the office, there are "many formal and informal opportunities to socialize."

Remarks Morrison & Foerster Chair Keith Wetmore, "Quality of life isn't easy to achieve in the high-pressure world of a big law firm. We like to think that Morrison & Foerster offers the opportunity to do cutting-edge legal work in an environment that fosters teamwork, sharing and respect for the individual. So when our associates rank the firm highly in these areas we feel we're on the right track, and we find that very rewarding."

PAY

Average score = 7.79		
RANK	**FIRM**	**SCORE**
1	Wachtell, Lipton, Rosen & Katz	9.837
2	Winston & Strawn	9.281
3	Skadden, Arps, Slate, Meagher & Flom LLP and Affiliates	9.251
4	Irell & Manella LLP	8.952
5	Fish & Richardson P.C.	8.916
6	Sullivan & Cromwell LLP	8.815
7	Testa, Hurwitz & Thibeault, LLP	8.800
8	Orrick, Herrington & Sutcliffe LLP	8.755
9	Hale and Dorr LLP	8.710
10	Jenner & Block, LLC	8.700
11	Ropes & Gray	8.667
12	Shaw Pittman LLP	8.640
13	Haynes and Boone, LLP	8.625
14	Goodwin Procter LLP	8.583
15	Morrison & Foerster LLP	8.582
16	Gray Cary Ware & Freidenrich LLP	8.581
17	Jenkens & Gilchrist, A Professional Corporation	8.546
18	Gibson, Dunn & Crutcher LLP	8.500
19(tie)	Pennie & Edmonds LLP	8.444
19(tie)	Finnegan, Henderson, Farabow, Garrett & Dunner LLP	8.444
20	Chadbourne & Parke LLP	8.431

Top three in pay

1. Wachtell

"If Wachtell does not receive the highest scores in compensation, then it's clear that some very uninformed people are taking part in this survey," asserts a well-paid Wachtell associate. Well, that attorney can put his mind at ease because other Wachtellians say "no one else comes close" when it comes to salary. Associates at Wachtell – a happy bunch in general – rhapsodize about their firm's commitment to "paying a leading salary" and its "generous fringe benefits." It's not hard to understand why associates believe "from a financial point of view – as well as many others – it makes no sense to work at another big New York firm if you can work here." "The compensation here is terrific and shows that the firm values its associates. Our hefty bonuses should be a huge draw for anyone interested in working at a top-notch law firm in New York," a litigation associate states.

Who says associates are greedy? The associates at Wachtell know they're fortunate to be compensated at such a high level (especially in these difficult times) and are an appreciative bunch. "The firm is extraordinarily generous. People earn it, but still, the partnership does share, and that means a lot." One associate tells us, "The partners are very generous with this, even in bad economic times." Another insider exclaims, "With my bonus, I'm making more than even partners at lots of firms." In a word: Wow!

"Our commitment to be at the leading edge in compensation is part of that same desire to reward the outstanding contribution that our associates make to the firm," says John F. Savarese, chairman of the firm's recruiting committee.

2. Winston & Strawn

Winston & Strawn insiders agree: the "hours versus pay" are "hard to beat here." Winston & Strawn "pays you to work hard and rewards you when you do." "The firm is right on par with most as far as salary," insiders report. "However, they really reward performance and hours with very generous bonuses." Winstonites couldn't be happier. "Although I work hard and put in many hours, my current compensation very much exceeds any expectations I had when I joined the firm," says a very pleased midlevel. Associates are especially appreciative that "the firm is extremely fair and shares the wealth in good years." (This issue was a major sore spot for lawyers at other firms this year.) In the opinion of one elated senior associate, there's just "one word to describe the salary and bonuses: phat!"

Remarks Paul Hensel, Chair of Associate Programs, "We understand the importance in today's environment of providing a competitive and flexible compensation package that rewards our associates for their contributions to our firm's overall success."

3. Skadden, Arps, Meagher, Slate & Flom

No doubt about it, insiders say. "People come here for the money" because the compensation at Skadden is ""top dollar" and "can't be beat!" At a firm where first-years start at "$15,000 more than most other firms," it's little wonder associates feel a certain amount of pride in their fat paychecks. Skadden pays the "highest in the city. Need I say more?" As if that weren't enough for even the most avaricious associate, there are "also lots of perks, like a mentor/mentee budget and technology reimbursement." "Skadden's higher base pay is a godsend in this fragile economy. It allows us to live well in New York City and to enjoy life outside of the office," a first-year states. "Skadden pays well, especially compared to local firms in its regional offices," says a second-year. With an "unwritten policy of matching whomever pays the most," the firm's associates feel fortunate they "don't have to worry about compensation." Furthermore, associates are grateful that the firm "offered bonuses as long as you were relatively busy. Those who billed at least 1,200 hours qualified for their class' half bonus. Those who billed 1,600 hours qualified for their class' full bonus."

Executive Partner Robert C. Sheehan adds, "The competitive compensation, challenging work and collegial environment Skadden provides its associates are a reflection of our belief that the foundation of Skadden's success has always been the firm's ability to attract the best and brightest students the nation and the world have to offer."

TRAINING

Average score = 7.05

RANK	FIRM	SCORE
1	Testa, Hurwitz & Thibeault, LLP	9.450
2	Kirkland & Ellis	8.912
3	Hale and Dorr LLP	8.691
4	Davis Polk & Wardwell	8.688
5	Ropes & Gray	8.653
6	Finnegan, Henderson, Farabow, Garrett & Dunner, LLP	8.378
7	Cravath, Swaine & Moore LLP	8.344
8	Jones Day	8.324
9	Cooley Godward LLP	8.296
10	Goodwin Procter LLP	8.096
11	Fried, Frank, Harris, Shriver & Jacobson	8.085
12	King & Spalding LLP	8.026
13	Latham & Watkins LLP	8.018
14	Morgan, Lewis & Bockius LLP	7.960
15	Winston & Strawn	7.953
16	Bingham McCutchen LLP	7.933
17	Paul, Weiss, Rifkind, Wharton & Garrison LLP	7.917
18	Jenner & Block, LLC	7.900
19	Nixon Peabody LLP	7.867
20	Morrison & Foerster LLP	7.859

Top three in training

1. Testa, Hurwitz & Thibeault

For the second year in a row, Beantown's Testa, Hurwitz & Thibeault wins top honors in training. But that's no big surprise, since insiders regard the firm's training program as the "best in the country." The "training seminars are second to none," says a litigation associate. Others simply describe the firm's commitment to training as "awesome" and "incredible." "The firm puts a great deal of time and effort into professional development of its attorneys both through the review process and through in-house continuing legal education. There is also good support for seeking outside CLE." "Our training is far and away the best I have seen or heard of at any large firm. I find myself far ahead of my peers at other firms based largely on our training," a corporate attorney reports. "There are lunch trainings for different departments every day of the week," says an insider who "on average" attends "three trainings a week." According to one source, "Junior associate attendance at Friday lunch seminars is mandatory, trumping even billable work." "Testa continues to set the mark for associate training – especially valuable in an economy where almost no junior attorneys are getting the work experience they need to advance," comments a first-year. "We are all constantly learning from each other and from our professional development program," raves a colleague.

Managing Partner William Asher is justifiably proud of his firm's commitment to training. "Clients expect our lawyers at all levels of experience to be up-to-date with industry trends and current best practices. We create multiple opportunities every day for partners and associates to get together in formal and informal groups to learn from each other's experiences and to brainstorm creative solutions to the legal issues our clients face. Testa Hurwitz is a lifelong learning community, and involving associates in the creation and deployment of our intellectual capital is a core element of our firm culture," says Asher.

2. Kirkland & Ellis

Kirkland & Ellis has made its presence in the top three in the training category something of a tradition – for three years, the firm was ranked No. 1, and it held the No.-2 spot last year. Kirkland may not be No. 1 this year, but its training program still makes its associates' hearts go pitter-pat. "The firm offers regular classes in each practice area designed to keep the attorneys sharp," explains one associate. "This firm takes training very seriously and devotes a great deal of time and firm resources to it. The partners also try to ensure that cases are staffed leanly enough that associates get the opportunity to play an active role and not just handle document review and research," comments a third-year. Moreover, "the firm encourages all partners and senior associates to train junior associates on an informal basis " and "every attorney has a mentor."

"Kirkland has a number of formal programs used to train and update attorneys on recent legal developments and practices. These programs are actually very helpful and touch upon topics that actually come up in practice." "The firm spends many hours on both litigation and corporate training programs. The litigation training program culminates in a week-long mock trial with a real judge, jury and actors playing witnesses." One thing is clear: Whatever they're doing over there at Kirkland is working.

Hiring Chairman of the Chicago office, Linda K. Myers is justifiably proud of the firm's training efforts. "There are several unique aspects to the training received at Kirkland & Ellis," she says. "First, it's virtually all in-house. Every year our partners devote substantial time and effort in order to work directly with our associates in intensive training sessions. As a result, our associates reap the benefit of our partners' knowledge, experience, and successful practice tips. That's just invaluable. Second, the programs offered are not only comprehensive in terms of depth, but also quite varied in terms of topic, covering many areas of our practice including: corporate, litigation, intellectual property, bankruptcy and real estate. Third, it's not a one-shot deal. Programs are held throughout the year and all – regardless of seniority – are encouraged to attend."

3. Hale and Dorr

"Training is of the highest priority at Hale and Dorr," gush associates. "The formal training is exceptional, both in quantity and quality." "From first-year corporate boot camp to mock negotiations and monthly training meetings, there is a strong emphasis on training." The IP department holds "monthly high-level strategy discussions, monthly discussions regarding recent case law developments and biweekly e-mail updates about the Federal Circuit." For some associates, it's "the time the senior associates and partners make during the course of the work day that is the most valuable training." Indeed, "informal training is part of the firm culture. The firm stresses the importance of informal training to both associates and partners." Likewise, mentoring is a major component of the firm's overall training agenda. "Associates are assigned senior associate mentors within their departments, plus a senior partner mentor" to conduct performance reviews. But the fun doesn't stop there. Associates also get a "benchmarking mentor" who works with associates on their professional development goals.

Says Managing Partner Bill Lee, "We have always recognized that the training and development of our next generation of lawyers is critical to our clients and our institutional future. We consequently dedicated ourselves to ensuring the best formal and informal training for all of our lawyers. In many ways, it is the informal, day-to-day training that is the most important."

Be a better lawyer faster.

Why take a job where you'll be a six-figure file clerk? At Sutherland, you'll have challenging projects from the start, working one-on-one with the firm's partners for top clients. Visit our Web site to find out more about us and our wide range of specialties, from M&A to IP. Or contact Beth Miller at 404.853.8000 or beth.miller@sablaw.com, or Melissa Wilson at 202.383.0100 or melissa.wilson@sablaw.com.

Voted one of the "Best 20 Law Firms to Work for" in 2002 and 2003 and ranked as a top "Quality of Life" firm in 2004.

— Vault Guide to the Top 100 Law Firms

Sutherland
Asbill &
Brennan LLP

ATTORNEYS AT LAW

www.sablaw.com

Atlanta • Austin • Houston • New York • Tallahassee • Washington

RETENTION

Average score = 6.55

RANK	FIRM	SCORE
1	Winston & Strawn	8.781
2	Alston & Bird LLP	8.455
3	Schiff Hardin & Waite	8.409
4	Troutman Sanders LLP	8.024
5	Fish & Richardson P.C.	7.990
6	Finnegan, Henderson, Farabow, Garrett & Dunner, LLP	7.861
7	Wachtell, Lipton, Rosen & Katz	7.650
8	Sutherland Asbill & Brennan LLP	7.631
9	Hale and Dorr LLP	7.559
10	Ropes & Gray	7.493
11	Allen & Overy	7.429
12	Gray Cary Ware & Freidenrich LLP	7.407
13	Williams & Connolly LLP	7.385
14	Orrick, Herrington & Sutcliffe LLP	7.364
15	Jones Day	7.335
16	Morrison & Foerster LLP	7.286
17	Debevoise & Plimpton	7.250
18	Munger, Tolles & Olson LLP	7.226
19	Davis Wright Tremaine LLP	7.216
20	Blank Rome LLP	7.213

Top three in retention

1. Winston & Strawn

"I've now been here for almost five years, and virtually all of my friends remained at the firm this entire time and plan to be here for the long haul," one attorney happily shares. "People leave but not because of the work environment; departures tend to be driven by family decisions" such as "spousal transfers to different cities or terrific opportunities," often in government or "non-law firm jobs." "You don't hear about associates leaving Winston very often, and of those who do leave, many decide that they've made a mistake and return to Winston within a year." A senior associate reports having "no reason to leave." "The rate of attrition is so low that some partners are still working in what used to be midlevel associate offices," a litigation associate confides. "No one in the corporate department leaves," a senior associate tells us. A colleague echoes this sentiment: "We can't seem to get rid of anyone!"

So what is it that keeps Winston & Strawn associates at the firm? For many, it's "the friendly atmosphere among coworkers" and the opportunities to work on high-profile cases. "People here seem pretty happy."

Says Associate Programs Chair Paul Hensel, "Attracting and retaining top legal talent is essential to our long-term success. We've worked diligently to create a positive, yet challenging, atmosphere where our associates can develop their practices and build their careers."

2. Alston & Bird

There's no question in the minds of associates at Alston & Bird that it has "fairly low turnover for a firm our size." That's evidenced by the fact that "people really like working here and tend to stay for years and years." An insider offers an opinion on why that's the case. "Go anywhere else for the same or higher pay, and you are likely to find the same work, but rotten partners. We really do have good partners here," says an Atlanta associate. A fifth-year reports, "The only associates or partners I know who have left the firm do so either because a spouse has been relocated, they are retiring or to pursue another career. I have not known any attorney to leave here because they did not like the firm." "People who leave are generally moving to a new city or going into a different line of work." It may sound like a cliché, but insiders say, "People don't seem to leave this place once they get here – at least not for other law firms." It's not unusual for the few "who do leave for other firms" to "boomerang back within a couple of years."

Part of the firm's core strategy states, "Alston & Bird recognizes that its primary assets are its people, both professional and staff and is committed to a firm culture that makes it a better place to work than any other." Managing Partner Ben Johnson expands on how this belief affects the firm on an everyday basis: "Everybody understands that commitment: the managing partner, each practice group leader, each partner, each associate, our executive staff and each staff member. Each understands that he or she is a vital contributor and plays a vital role in whether we achieve the goal or whether we fall short. By stating this goal, we invite being judged against it. By knowing that we're constantly being judged against it, we all work a little harder to make it a reality."

3. Schiff Hardin & Waite

At Schiff Hardin & Waite, it's not just the lawyers who stick around for years. "Staff turnover is quite low," explains an insider. "Many staff members have hit 10-, 20- and 30-year anniversaries." That's quite an accomplishment. Also, "associate attrition is lower than in the more recent past, and I sense that it is similar or lower than at other large firms in the Chicago market," says an associate in the labor department. Further highlighting just how loyal folks tend to be at Schiff Hardin, one associate reports, "A good number of the corporate partners I work with were summer associates at this firm."

"From what I can see," says a second-year associate, "people have been here forever and some even return after leaving once." A third-year tells us, "Most of my class is still here, and those who have left have not left for other big firms in the city." Rather they've moved to a different city or changed careers.

ASSOCIATE/PARTNER RELATIONS

Average score = 7.91

RANK	FIRM	SCORE
1	Winston & Strawn	8.828
2	Schiff Hardin & Waite	8.826
3	Debevoise & Plimpton	8.806
4	Wachtell, Lipton, Rosen & Katz	8.762
5	Morrison & Foerster LLP	8.671
6	Jenkens & Gilchrist, A Professional Corporation	8.667
7	Steptoe & Johnson LLP	8.653
8	Arent, Fox, Kintner, Plotkin & Kahn, PLLC	8.625
9(tie)	Munger, Tolles & Olson LLP	8.606
9(tie)	Fish & Richardson P.C.	8.606
10	Allen & Overy	8.600
11	Latham & Watkins LLP	8.596
12	Gray Cary Ware & Freidenrich LLP	8.532
13	Baker Botts L.L.P.	8.513
14	Alston & Bird LLP	8.491
15	Davis Wright Tremaine LLP	8.460
16	Orrick, Herrington & Sutcliffe LLP	8.459
17	Palmer & Dodge LLP	8.450
18	Williams & Connolly LLP	8.444
19	Ropes & Gray	8.441
20	Perkins Coie LLP	8.438

Top three in associate/partner relations

1. Winston & Strawn

Associates know that how firm partners treat them can make their time at their firm either deeply satisfying or positively dreadful. Winston & Straw associates express warm regards for their "approachable, friendly" and "very professional" partners. "Not only are associates treated with respect, but we are mentored and dealt with as colleagues. That is, there's less of a hierarchy of authority than there is a hierarchy of expertise," says a corporate attorney. Insiders say instances of a partner displaying a "me partner, you associate" attitude are truly rare. Perhaps Winston partners hold their associates in such high esteem because they "realize the associates are truly the backbone of the firm." Indeed, "Partners generally are very appreciative of the associates' efforts and recognize the degree to which our work supports their practice," says a fourth-year. "I can pick up the phone and call any partner in any office to ask a question, and they warmly take my call," shares a senior associate. Partners are also known to "encourage associates to have a life outside of work and truly appreciate the extra efforts you put in when it is needed."

Managing Partner Jim Neis adds, "Winston & Strawn places great emphasis on mutual respect among all our people; we are particularly pleased that our partners and associates work so well together in providing exceptional client service."

2. Schiff Hardin & Waite

Schiff Hardin associates are feeling the love from partners, too. Mutual respect is "a very strong point here" because it encourages a positive "team culture." "The partners are very interested in assisting associates develop into skilled lawyers. The partners express this interest by providing associates challenging work assignments, formal training and opportunities to author articles, among other things." A fifth-year has nothing but praise for the firm's partners: "The partners I've worked with have uniformly exhibited a strong interest in making sure the associates receive training, experience and an appropriate amount of latitude to try to figure things out themselves." Associates say it is typical at the firm for a partner to ask for and take into account associate opinions, "even if we are new to the case or very junior." A corporate associate offers an example of how the partners take a personal interest in associates' development. A couple of partners, this attorney says, "have bent over backwards to help me seal some new client relationships of my own and nurture them as new clients. Both of them have gone out of their way to showcase these new clients as being mine, not in any way theirs, even though they helped me pull it off."

3. Debevoise & Plimpton

Respect is the name of the game at New York's Debevoise & Plimpton. "The level of respect and cordiality between partners and associates is very high," reports a Debevoise litigation associate. Associates appreciate that "partners are decent and show genuine concern," but don't seem surprised by such treatment. "The nice culture" is just "a way of life" at the firm. Insiders say there's "no screaming" at the firm and that the spirit of respect exhibited by partners "is catching" on throughout the firm. "My relationship with the partners I work with has been the highlight of a truly exceptional experience. Every senior attorney I've worked with has expressed – and demonstrated – a real interest in my professional development and sincere concern for my personal welfare," raves a second-year associate. What's more, they "genuinely are interested in associates' ideas and opinions."

Says Presiding Partner Rick Evans, "We believe our commitment to collegiality supports our commitment to provide the best in client service. It is great to have Debevoise recognized in this way."

OFFICES

Average score = 7.24

RANK	FIRM	SCORE
1	Winston & Strawn	9.297
2	Cleary, Gottlieb, Steen & Hamilton	9.022
3	Palmer & Dodge LLP	8.800
4	Preston Gates & Ellis LLP	8.733
5	Dewey Ballantine LLP	8.656
6	Thelen Reid & Priest LLP	8.579
7	Foley Hoag LLP	8.409
8	Hale and Dorr LLP	8.393
9	Arnold & Porter	8.304
10	Alston & Bird LLP	8.204
11	Wachtell, Lipton, Rosen & Katz	8.163
12	Bingham McCutchen LLP	8.079
13	Willkie Farr & Gallagher	8.016
14	Milbank, Tweed, Hadley & McCloy LLP	7.983
15	Stroock & Stroock & Lavan LLP	7.969
16	Troutman Sanders LLP	7.965
17	Greenberg Traurig, LLP	7.926
18	Davis Polk & Wardwell	7.925
19	Baker Botts L.L.P.	7.865
20	Sedgwick, Detert, Moran & Arnold LLP	7.864

Top three in offices

1. Winston & Strawn

Winston & Strawn's Chicago headquarters are "absolutely the most beautiful offices in the city." "Winston provides great offices with great views. It really makes a difference during long days." Insiders at the Chicago office agree. "Winston is the best-looking firm" most have ever seen. What makes Winston's office space so special? For one, the offices are "decorated very nicely." There's "great art, furniture [and] flowers everywhere you turn." It's so lovely that, according to a senior associate, "not a single person who has been here for the first time has failed to mention that the offices are incredibly beautiful and classy." "There's really no comparison to Winston's offices. They are refined, classy and functional," boasts one lawyer. Others consider the office space "elegant," but also "accommodating." D.C. associates are looking forward to moving to new offices "in the spring of 2005," and we're sure they'll be every bit as "nice and well maintained" as those in the Windy City.

Says Paul Hensel, Chief Administrative Partner, "We are proud that our firm consistently has received high marks in this category, and we continue to devote significant resources to providing a comfortable work environment for our attorneys and staff. This is one of the ways we can show our appreciation for our associates and their dedication to the firm and our clients."

2. Cleary, Gottlieb, Steen & Hamilton

Cleary Gottlieb associates are in awe of their "beautiful, stunning office space." "We have amazing views, large windows and lots of light," says a New York associate. Others are delighted by the "modern but warm" décor, "incredible views in all directions," the "wonderful, modern, bright common spaces" and proliferation of "great art" that populates the firm's "awesome space." And this is no run-of-the-mill artwork. "The office walls are adorned with one of the largest private collections of 20th and 21st century art, including works by Paul Klee, Jasper Johns, Ansel Adams, Ed Weston, Robert Rauschenberg and Roy Lichtenstein."

The vast art collection and other amenities make "it much more pleasant to spend time" working those long law firm hours. But it's the "light, airy, large private offices for associates" that attorneys rave about the most. Equally appealing is the fact that "associates have to share offices at most for only a couple of months." "Everyone gets his own office as soon as possible." Associates realize that such a perk "is pretty unusual for a large New York City law firm."

3. Palmer & Dodge

"We have brand new, beautiful office space," reports a senior associate at Boston's Palmer & Dodge, who adds, "I have heard many lawyers from other firms say that we have the nicest law firm office in Boston, and I think that is true." "Our new space is gorgeous," agrees a second-year. But the compliments don't stop there. This source, who has a whole laundry list of accolades, continues, "Everything is top of the line – posh and elegant. I am proud to have clients come to the office. The cafeteria is pleasant and spacious. My office is comfortable and efficient. The décor is modern and impressive." An equally enthusiastic but somewhat less effusive colleague simply says the firm has "the best office location in town."

Hiring Partner Elizabeth P. Seaman elaborates on why Palmer & Dodge associates are so pleased with the firm's office space. "We moved into brand new office space in the fall of 2001, located in the heart of Boston's lively Back Bay. Our offices were designed to provide a beautiful and comfortable work space, and the firm's lawyers, support staff and clients have been uniformly pleased with the results."

SELECTIVITY

Average score = 8.09

RANK	FIRM	SCORE
1	Wachtell, Lipton, Rosen & Katz	9.837
2	Munger, Tolles & Olson LLP	9.750
3	Covington & Burling	9.573
4	Cravath, Swaine & Moore LLP	9.526
5	Williams & Connolly LLP	9.500
6	Davis Polk & Wardwell	9.387
7	Sullivan & Cromwell LLP	9.319
8	Irell & Manella LLP	9.191
9	Gibson, Dunn & Crutcher LLP	9.122
10	Ropes & Gray	9.036
11	Cleary, Gottlieb, Steen & Hamilton	9.012
12	Simpson Thacher & Bartlett	8.910
13	Debevoise & Plimpton	8.905
14	Hale and Dorr LLP	8.904
15	Wilmer, Cutler & Pickering	8.855
16	Kirkland & Ellis	8.852
17	Morrison & Foerster LLP	8.784
18	Finnegan, Henderson, Farabow, Garrett & Dunner, LLP	8.714
19	Paul, Weiss, Rifkind, Wharton & Garrison LLP	8.702
20	Latham & Watkins LLP	8.676

Top three in selectivity

1. Wachtell, Lipton, Rosen & Katz

"Only the best and brightest" will do for the mighty Wachtell, Lipton, Rosen & Katz. Associates at Wachtell know they're part of a privileged few who make the cut. The firm looks "to hire candidates who excel in school. The combination of intelligence and hard work is what makes Wachtell successful, and we seek evidence of that in the transcript." Intelligence and "law review-caliber grades" may be the predominant criteria, but of course other factors play a part in determining if a candidate receives what one Wachetellian calls the "hardest offer in the city." "Independent," "highly engaged, very sharp people" with "interpersonal skills" "who are willing to speak their minds" are most likely to make the cut, as are "people from top law schools who show initiative, commitment to living in New York and living this lifestyle." Additionally, "law review is important," and "prior work experience between college and law school is good." An M&A attorney says the firm doesn't "always necessarily hire the biggest brainiacs" but does highly value the ability "to execute, to get things done and to make good, fast practical judgments."

2. Munger, Tolles & Olson

To score an offer from Los Angeles' Munger, Tolles & Olson, you've got to impress everyone at the firm. "Munger's idiosyncratic hiring process and extremely selective standards are well known" throughout the legal community. "After a typical on-campus and in-office interview process, the whole firm discusses and votes" on whether to extend an offer. "More than a handful of no votes means no offer." "The firm scrutinizes everything: grades, experience, clerkships, maturity, interview performance and so on" and "looks for candidates who have consistently demonstrated excellence in their past activities" and are "self-starters with extraordinary credentials." This exhaustive process is all part of Munger's pursuit "to hire the best people available." Successful candidates "need to be in the top 10 percent" of their class. But "just being at the top of your class is not enough" to get the nod at Munger, insiders say. Other factors that could get you noticed are a "clerkship, advanced degree or something fairly remarkable on the resume." Also, Munger pays close attention to candidates' recommendations. Aside from the usual credentials, the firm also keeps its eye open for candidates who possess a certain intangible "spark," or "ability to wow the firm."

"The cornerstone of our firm's success always has been to hire only the very best lawyers," notes Co-Managing Partner Greg Morgan.

3. Covington & Burling

Covington & Burling is looking for "only the top students at the top schools." "The firm has a very large population of Harvard grads," as well as attorneys from other Ivy League schools. Aside from the requisite high intellect, the firm looks for candidates who possess "some unique quality or experience they can bring to the practice of law," "a high degree of integrity" and the ability to "interact well with clients." The firm also places "a strong emphasis on writing" ability. "Covington expends considerable resources to make sure that it attracts and chooses the best associates that it can. It's rather staggering how much time and effort all the attorneys at this firm devote to the recruiting process," observes a litigator. "The firm hires or declines to hire after only one initial interview. There is no callback process." "Decisions to hire summer associates are based on a screening interview, a writing sample, resume, transcripts and references." According to a second-year associate, Covington "is harder to get hired at than virtually any other" firm. A midlevel describes the interview process as "rigorous" and confides that it "involves lengthy conversations with references."

Stuart C. Stock, the chair of the firm's management committee, notes, "Our lawyers at all levels and our clients appreciate the care and attention we have paid to the firm's hiring process over the years. We value having talented, diverse and interesting colleagues, and one of our principal priorities is identifying, recruiting and retaining such colleagues. Our lawyers have distinguished records from over 50 law schools in the U.S. and abroad."

PRO BONO

RANK	FIRM	SCORE
Average score = 7.30		
1	Jenner & Block, LLC	9.800
2	Debevoise & Plimpton	9.687
3	Arnold & Porter	9.392
4	Morrison & Foerster LLP	9.367
5	Winston & Strawn	9.254
6	Crowell & Moring LLP	9.250
7	Arent Fox Kintner Plotkin & Kahn, PLLC	9.244
8	Covington & Burling	9.222
9	Latham & Watkins LLP	9.113
10	Munger, Tolles & Olson LLP	9.065
11	Wilmer, Cutler & Pickering	8.976
12	Hunton & Williams LLP	8.954
13	Paul, Weiss, Rifkind, Wharton & Garrison LLP	8.952
14	Testa, Hurwitz & Thibeault, LLP	8.944
15	Foley Hoag LLP	8.905
16	Simpson Thacher & Bartlett	8.860
17	Schiff Hardin & Waite	8.826
18	Stroock & Stroock & Lavan LLP	8.818
19	Patton Boggs LLP	8.767
20	Palmer & Dodge LLP	8.750

Top three in pro bono

1. Jenner & Block

At Jenner & Block, pro bono "is one of our biggest, if not our biggest, selling points," and one that the firm's associates are truly excited about this year. That enthusiasm has propelled Jenner to the top of our rankings after landing in seventh place just a year ago. Associates praise Jenner's commitment, saying the firm "encourages pro bono work, rather than just tolerating it." Jenner & Block's dedication to public service is widely recognized outside the firm as well. Partner Thomas Sullivan participated on the Illinois advisory commission whose research on wrongful conviction and capital punishment inspired the governor to grant clemency to all the state's death row inmates; his work on that panel moved *The National Law Journal* to grant Jenner its 2002 Pro Bono Award. "Everyone here takes pro bono very seriously," and the firm offers "a wealth of institutional knowledge on how to represent pro bono clients," not to mention "great contacts to get interesting and varied work." New attorneys can apply for fellowships to work with public interest groups before officially joining the firm, and "junior associates have argued cases in trial and appellate courts, including first-degree murder cases and matters involving difficult constitutional issues. "If you want to do pro bono work at a large law firm in Chicago, there is no where else that is better than Jenner," rhapsodizes a first-year.

"Jenner & Block's pioneering pro bono program was once referred to as 'legendary' by *American Lawyer* magazine... partly, we think, because so many of our lawyers participate actively, from the chairman of the firm to the youngest associates," says Barry Levenstam, the Chicago co-chair of the firm's pro bono committee. "Of course, we are grateful for such recognition," adds the committee's Washington, D.C. co-chair, David DeBruin, "but a deep part of our culture is to dedicate a significant portion of our time to public service, whether in high-profile Supreme Court cases or ordinary child custody matters for indigent members of our communities."

2. Debevoise & Plimpton

The "best pro bono program in New York – hands down" advances a notch in our pro bono rankings, as Debevoise & Plimpton jumps from No. 3 to No. 2 this year. "Debevoise's commitment to pro bono work has been genuine, substantial and consistent for years." The firm has collaborated extensively with international activist groups such as Human Rights Watch, the Lawyers' Committee for Human Rights and the Committee to Protect Journalists. Debevoise's dedication includes working on "complex, time-consuming cases, as well as assisting lower-income residents with housing, social security benefits" and other needs. There is also "a strong commitment to working with asylum candidates and the arts." "A pro bono hour equals a paying client hour," and there's "no firm billing requirement" limiting the amount of pro bono work an attorney can perform. This policy leads one associate to suggest, "I honestly believe I could spend 80 percent of my time on pro bono for half a year and nobody would raise an eyebrow." Associates praise the firm for allowing them "to use any and every firm resource to zealously represent pro bono clients." "Even first-years are allowed – encouraged! – to take on personal pro bono projects." The firm's dedication to public service "seems to attract lots of people with progressive ideas, connections and willingness to do pro bono projects despite their heavy billable workload," creating a "self-perpetuating" legacy of excellence.

"The firm's pro bono work is an important and integral part of our practice. It is gratifying to have the pro bono efforts of so many of our lawyers recognized in this way," says Presiding Partner Rick Evans.

3. Arnold & Porter

Arnold & Porter "was founded by men who believed it was important not just to service the rich and the powerful, but to fight for the rights of the poor and the meek," and its current roster of attorneys strives hard to live up to that mandate. "Some firms talk a lot about their pro bono. This firm shows its commitment every day," including signing on "a full-time pro bono coordinator/social worker." "The upper echelons of the firm are constantly encouraging people to do more," and a first-year informs us that "a third of my clients since arriving here have been pro bono." "I was able to spend approximately 400 hours on pro bono matters last year," a midlevel proudly states. Since "the majority of attorneys devote substantial time every year" to some form of public service, "you're odd here if you don't have some pro bono work going on." The hard work doesn't go unnoticed. The firm was singled out by the D.C. Bar for its pro bono work in 2002, particularly for its active involvement with Ayuda, a local organization providing bilingual legal assistance in domestic violence, child support and immigration cases.

"Doing pro bono work – lots of it – is and always has been an important part of our firm's culture. We seek out a wide variety of pro bono opportunities to offer our lawyers, we have significant partner involvement in our pro bono program, and we provide institutional incentives – including treating pro bono work as billable for bonus purposes – to do pro bono work," notes Managing Partner James Sandman.

HOURS

Average score = 6.78

RANK	FIRM	SCORE
1	Troutman Sanders LLP	8.011
2	Jenkens & Gilchrist, A Professional Corporation	7.970
3	Davis Wright Tremaine LLP	7.886
4	Allen & Overy	7.781
5	Arent Fox Kintner Plotkin & Kahn, PLLC	7.667
6	Fulbright & Jaworski L.L.P.	7.631
7	Sedgwick, Detert, Moran & Arnold LLP	7.617
8	Haynes and Boone, LLP	7.615
9	Ropes & Gray	7.576
10	Davis Polk & Wardwell	7.564
11	Patton Boggs LLP	7.556
12	Winston & Strawn	7.516
13	Greenberg Traurig, LLP	7.482
14	Morrison & Foerster LLP	7.451
15	Sutherland Asbill & Brennan LLP	7.449
16	Steptoe & Johnson LLP	7.396
17	Perkins Coie LLP	7.354
18	Morgan, Lewis & Bockius LLP	7.353
19	Kaye Scholer LLP	7.345
20	Bryan Cave LLP	7.313

Top three in hours

1. Troutman Sanders

At Troutman Sanders, "there isn't any pressure for face time. From the start, people respect your ability to manage your own time," a Richmond attorney says. An Atlanta colleague remarks, "You never feel that someone is looking over your shoulder to make sure you're getting your time in." "Although there is an overall billing requirement, which is more than fair, the individual attorneys choose whether to stay late or go home." So "if you're here late or on the weekend, it's because you really have something you need to do," insiders say. Associates report that their 1,800-hour requirement is "very reasonable and the best deal in town." "The hours here are much more palatable as compared to those" worked by "my colleagues at other firms," a midlevel states.

Troutman Sanders' "major emphasis" is not on the amount of time an associate spends in the office, but rather "on the quality of the final work product," concurs a public finance attorney.

Furthermore, "the firm strongly encourages outside activities with a significant emphasis on community involvement." "I was told in my interview that if I billed 2,300 hours, I would get a lecture for working too much. They want us to be happy, and that means seeing us have lives outside the office," a second-year explains. "If I need to take time off or want to leave early or come in late for any reason, it's not an issue," shares a senior associate. A first-year tells us, "I expected that I might have to work lots of weekends and long hours, and that has not been the case."

2. Jenkens & Gilchrist

"Jenkens emphasizes a balance between work and leisure time." Because "many of the firm's partners have young families," they understand that while work is important, "there is more to life." "The firm encourages life outside work and has recently changed the compensation structure to be less dependent on billable hours," confides a litigation associate. "There is no face-time requirement, which makes the hours worked more meaningful. Also, there is a lot of freedom to set your own schedule, and hours that need to be done at night and on the weekends often can be done at home." "There is enough work to keep you busy, but you never feel like the other aspects of your life suffer." Best of all, "billable-hour goals are quite reasonable," and "weekend work is rare."

Says Chairman William P. Durban, "We are pleased to hear that our associates have rated us so highly in this area. Our associates are a very hard-working, motivated group. They came to Jenkens looking for the opportunity to do sophisticated and exciting work, and when you are doing work you enjoy, I guess it's always easier to invest the time that's needed."

3. Davis Wright Tremaine

Insiders at Seattle-based Davis Wright Tremaine say they're happy with the firm's "very humane billable expectations." A litigator in the New York office not only concurs that "the billable hours requirement is fairly reasonable," but adds, "It is lower than that of most large New York firms." DWT insiders appreciate how frank and direct the firm is when it comes to hours. "When they say 1,800, they mean 1,800. If you work more, you will be paid for it, but there's no expectation that you must do so," asserts a very pleased third-year associate.

Amazingly, a Seattle associate reveals, "The office is empty by 5:00 p.m., and almost nobody is here on a weekend." And associates can feel free to write their vacations into their calendars in pen, not pencil. "Vacations are supported, and partners will actually help out with clients while I am gone," a midlevel tells us. For a law firm, it's remarkable.

PART-TIME/FLEX-TIME

RANK	FIRM	SCORE
	Average score = 5.715	
1	Bryan Cave LLP	8.500
2	Jones Day	6.632
3	Sidley Austin Brown & Wood LLP	6.550
4	Mayer, Brown, Rowe & Maw	6.035
5	Orrick, Herrington & Sutcliffe LLP	5.895
6	Weil, Gotshal & Manges LLP	5.750
7	Kirkland & Ellis	5.421
8	Hunton & Williams LLP	4.778
9	Gibson, Dunn & Crutcher LLP	4.222
10	O'Melveny & Myers LLP	3.368

Top three in part-time/flex-time

1. Bryan Cave

Bryan Cave isn't just a legal star of the Midwest; its part-time program also makes it a star in the eyes of its associates. Insiders say they're pleased that attorneys "can craft your own flex-time program here to suit your needs." "Many corporate associates are on flex-time, and it seems to be working well," observes a full-time associate. An enthusiastic participant in Bryan Cave's part-time program states, "I switched to flex-time after I had my first child and have had a very positive experience. It has not affected the quality of the work I get or partners' willingness to work with me." An associate on a reduced-hours schedule of "approximately 1,600 hours a year" thinks the program "works out very well. I like the work, and you can't beat the pay." The program is considered "incredible and very equal and fair," and applies to "man or woman," says a male attorney. Determining salary and benefits for part-timers, this source adds, is as simple for an attorney as choosing the percentage of time he or she wants to work and multiplying "it by your required hours, pay, bonus hours, bonus amount [and] years of service. Everything is pro rata and, most importantly, respected."

2. Jones Day

A senior associate tells us that Jones Day doesn't have "a formal part-time or flex-time program." Instead, "the firm handles requests for a part-time schedule on a case-by-case basis," and "associates who work reduced hours negotiate a deal with the firm" regarding their schedules. However, "the firm is developing its part-time program," another insider says. Although the firm may not have formalized its part-time policy yet, associates are still quite pleased "that the firm

© 2003 Vault Inc.

permits part-time arrangements and is flexible about the sorts of arrangements it allows." A female attorney says the firm has been responsive to "meeting my needs and requests for an alternative work schedule so that I am able to balance my professional life with my family." Likewise, a New York associate is "very grateful" for the opportunity to work a reduced schedule "because it enables me to continue to practice law, which is very important to me, at a firm I care about very much, and still have time for my family." Sounds like the perfect arrangement.

3. Sidley Austin Brown & Wood

"The firm has been more than accommodating to my part-time schedule. I was skeptical at first but have had a very positive experience," a midlevel shares. An associate who experienced the birth of a child and death of a family member soon after joining Sidley reveals, "The firm has been nothing but generous with working with me to accommodate my increased needs and helping me maintain a manageable work schedule." Doing so has alleviated much of this associate's worries about balancing work and family obligations. A litigation attorney who admits being a litigator is not always conducive to working part time because litigation "generally requires round-the-clock availability" nevertheless praises the firm's willingness to make a part-time option available. "Sidley is very supportive of part-time and flex-time arrangements," this source says.

Use the most **targeted** job search tools for lawyers on the Internet.

Vault's Law Job Board and VaultMatch™ Resume Database

■ Law Job Board

The most comprehensive and convenient job board for legal professionals. Target your search by practice area, function, and experience level, and find the job openings that you want. No surfing required.

■ VaultMatch™ Resume Database

Vault takes match-making to the next level: post your resume and customize your search by practice area, trial experience, level and more. We'll match job listings with your interests and criteria and e-mail them directly to your in-box.

> the most trusted name in career information™

Find out more at www.law.vault.com

DIVERSITY RANKINGS

Visit the Vault Law Channel, the complete online resource for law careers, featuring firm profiles, message boards, the Vault Law Job Board, and more. www.law.vault.com

VAULT CAREER LIBRARY   65

VAULT CAREER LIBRARY

BEST 20 LAW FIRMS FOR DIVERSITY

Lawyers and firm management place increasing value on a diverse working environment. That's why, for the second year, Vault has devoted a special section to associates' rankings on diversity issues. Our diversity section includes separate categories for diversity as it relates to minorities, women, and gays and lesbians. To determine our Best 20 Law Firms for Diversity, we used a formula that weighed the three categories evenly for an overall diversity ranking.

It is important to remember that, like our other quality of life rankings, the diversity ranking reflects the opinions and perceptions of insiders.

BEST 20 LAW FIRMS FOR DIVERSITY

Average score = 7.260

RANK	FIRM	HEADQUARTERS	SCORE
1	Morrison & Foerster LLP	San Francisco, CA	8.951
2	Jenner & Block, LLC	Chicago, IL	8.662
3	Arent Fox Kintner Plotkin & Kahn, PLLC	Washington, DC	8.653
4	Arnold & Porter	Washington, DC	8.652
5	Davis Polk & Wardwell	New York, NY	8.381
6	Finnegan, Henderson, Farabow *	Washington, DC	8.352
7	Winston & Strawn	Chicago, IL	8.320
8	Cleary, Gottlieb, Steen & Hamilton	New York, NY	8.212
9	Powell, Goldstein, Frazer & Murphy LLP	Atlanta, GA	8.180
10	Preston Gates & Ellis LLP	Seattle, WA	8.102
11	Steptoe & Johnson LLP	Washington, DC	8.075
12	Ropes & Gray	Boston, MA	8.063
13	Debevoise & Plimpton	New York, NY	8.038
14	Orrick, Herrington & Sutcliffe LLP	San Francisco, CA	7.991
15(tie)	Alston & Bird LLP	Atlanta, GA	7.970
15(tie)	Gray Cary Ware & Freidenrich LLP	Palo Alto, CA	7.970
16	Fried, Frank, Harris, Shriver & Jacobson	New York, NY	7.946
17	Sedgwick, Detert, Moran & Arnold LLP	San Francisco, CA	7.887
18	Haynes and Boone, LLP	Dallas, TX	7.871
19	Heller Ehrman White & McAuliffe LLP	San Francisco, CA	7.867
20	Skadden, Arps, Slate, Meagher **	New York, NY	7.865

*Finnegan, Henderson, Farabow, Garrett & Dunner L.L.P
**Skadden, Arps, Slate, Meagher & Flom LLP and Affiliates

Top three in diversity

1. Morrison & Foerster

For the second year in a row, Morrison & Foerster's associates have placed their firm at the top of our diversity rankings. The San Francisco-based MoFo also repeats its achievement as the only firm to make the top three in each diversity subcategory: women, minorities and gays and lesbians. The presence of openly gay managing partner Keith Wetmore is frequently cited by associates as evidence of the firm's openness and tolerance, but the firm is more than just "a haven for gays." MoFo "makes a conscientious effort to maintain ethnic diversity" and "actively participates in minority student organizations' conferences." And female attorneys say MoFo has surpassed expectations, with "several women in firm management" and excellent opportunities for mentorship from women partners and senior associates. "For me," says one MoFo woman, "this is MoFo's biggest strength."

"Good policies alone will not create or maintain a diverse firm. Diversity requires that a firm care. And this is a firm that cares very much," says Chair Keith Wetmore. That much is clear.

2. Jenner & Block

Last year, Chicago's Jenner & Block just missed making the top 10 list when it came to diversity, but it's ridden a new wave of testimonials on its "absolutely improving" performance all the way into second place this year. "The firm is universally committed to increasing its number of diverse attorneys," and earned top marks for its commitment to gay and lesbian associates. Jenner & Block also landed the No.-3 spot for its treatment of women and made the top 10 list when it comes to minority diversity, as associates observe the ways in which "the firm is dedicating resources to improving diversity." Jenner is "quite mindful of these issues," and "we have been making great strides over the past two years." Bravo!

"A commitment to diversity in the courtroom and in the profession is a core value at Jenner & Block because we believe that encouraging diversity in our society as well as our nation's workforce is simply the right thing to do," says Managing Partner Robert L. Graham.

3. Arent Fox Kintner Plotkin & Kahn, PLLC

Washington's Arent Fox Kintner Plotkin & Kahn moves from fourth to third on our diversity list. The firm scores second when it comes to gay and lesbian diversity and also made the top 10 when it comes to our other diversity categories, providing ample support for an attitude shared by many associates: "All that seems to matter is an individual's ability as an attorney and their ability to work with others." That said, Arent Fox's associates have noticed that "the firm tries hard to hire, promote and mentor minorities." They also notice that "women often comprise the majority of summer associates" and figure prominently in recent partnership selections. "Women do great here," says one attorney, "even when they have children."

DIVERSITY FOR WOMEN

Average score = 7.45

RANK	FIRM	SCORE
1	Morrison & Foerster LLP	8.920
2	Davis Polk & Wardwell	8.808
3	Jenner & Block, LLC	8.583
4	Finnegan, Henderson, Farabow, Garrett & Dunner, L.L.P.	8.568
5	Arent Fox Kintner Plotkin & Kahn, PLLC	8.556
6	Steptoe & Johnson LLP	8.487
7	Powell, Goldstein, Frazer & Murphy LLP	8.473
8	Gray Cary Ware & Freidenrich LLP	8.446
9	Schiff Hardin & Waite	8.429
10	Preston Gates & Ellis LLP	8.407
11	Arnold & Porter	8.397
12	Greenberg Traurig, LLP	8.318
13	Debevoise & Plimpton	8.214
14	Alston & Bird LLP	8.175
15	Hogan & Hartson L.L.P	8.151
16	Jones Day	8.127
17	Stroock & Stroock & Lavan LLP	8.104
18	Ropes & Gray	8.090
19	Winston & Strawn	8.087
20	Seyfarth Shaw	8.080

Top three in diversity for women

1. Morrison & Foerster

Morrison & Foerster has come out on top again when it comes to promoting diversity for women, repeating its performance in last year's survey. "I picked MoFo because of its reputation for being woman-friendly," says one female associate, "and I have not been disappointed in the least. MoFo is a world apart in this category." Despite "certain realities that even a place like MoFo can't avoid, this firm is serious about respecting women" and "has truly achieved gender equality," with women occupying several management positions such as the litigation chair and the managing partner's desk in San Francisco. Additional junior female associates attest that when they seek advice from women partners, "they are more than happy to give it."

2. Davis Polk & Wardwell

New York's Davis Polk & Wardwell makes great advancements in associate recognition of its efforts towards women's issues with a second-place score in our survey. "Almost all of the senior attorneys I have worked with have been women," remarks one associate. Another notes that "the women here seem to be very happy and to experience no discrimination." Although one associate tempers her appraisal of the firm's "genuinely welcoming" attitude by suggesting "there are never as many women named to partner as men," a colleague observes "a higher proportion of female partners here than almost any of our competitor firms," with near-equal balance in the most recent incoming classes.

3. Jenner & Block

After falling off our top-10 list for women's diversity issues a few years back, Jenner & Block returns in full force, landing in the No.-3 position. "I feel completely comfortable with this office's treatment of women," says one associate. "Of course, it would be ideal to have more female partners, but there are several." Many of those who gave Jenner its highest marks in this category did so without elaboration, so the comments we received were often about what women at the firm feel remains to be accomplished. Some feel the firm "has not done an effective job of retaining more senior-level women attorneys," and hope for increased mentorship and commitment to part-time/flex-time scheduling as possible means of strengthening Jenner's performance in this category.

"At Jenner & Block, women attorneys serve in leadership positions on the policy committee and the management committee as well as in the firm's practice group management," says E. Lynn Grayson, Co-chair of the firm's diversity committee.

DIVERSITY FOR MINORITIES

Average score = 6.65

RANK	FIRM	SCORE
1	Winston & Strawn	8.639
2	Morrison & Foerster LLP	8.419
3	Arnold & Porter	8.375
4	Davis Polk & Wardwell	7.901
5	Finnegan, Henderson, Farabow, Garrett & Dunner, L.L.P	7.839
6	Troutman Sanders LLP	7.764
7	Arent Fox Kintner Plotkin & Kahn, PLLC	7.757
8	Haynes and Boone, LLP	7.753
9	Jenner & Block, LLC	7.750
10	Greenberg Traurig, LLP	7.737
11	Cleary, Gottlieb, Steen & Hamilton	7.731
12	Alston & Bird LLP	7.671
13	Fried, Frank, Harris, Shriver & Jacobson	7.600
14	Ropes & Gray	7.565
15	Steptoe & Johnson LLP	7.433
16	Paul, Weiss, Rifkind, Wharton & Garrison LLP	7.403
17	McGuireWoods LLP	7.393
18	Powell, Goldstein, Frazer & Murphy LLP	7.346
19	Hunton & Williams LLP	7.327
20	Shearman & Sterling	7.321

Top three in diversity for minorites

1. Winston & Strawn

Winston & Strawn jostles its way to the top of the minority diversity ranking, improving upon its third-place rating from last year. "The dialogue on diversity is ongoing here," one associate reports. "Change is occurring and will continue to occur, as senior management increasingly engages some of our more dynamic and open-minded junior partners in decision making." One such development cited by Winston associates is a program of scholarships for minority law students in cities where the firm has offices. Winston has "a respectably diverse composition" in its associate ranks, and an Asian-American attorney at the firm attests he has not received "particularly special treatment solely because I'm a minority. If special skills are brought to the table," such as fluency in foreign languages, "they are valued for what they are, not from where the skills originate."

2. Morrison & Foerster

Morrison & Foerster holds steady in the No.-2 spot for its commitment to minority issues. "MoFo's diversity is its strength," and "the firm tries hard here and succeeds" at creating a "very welcoming" environment. For many associates, MoFo is "one of the most ethnically diverse places I've ever worked," with attorneys at all levels participating in "in-depth awareness programs" and other diversity training. The firm also takes part in "various events held by local minority bar associations" and hosts a biennial Attorneys of Color workshop for associates. "I have never felt that being a minority at this firm meant that I was disadvantaged in any way," says one associate. "There are a number of minority partners and associates who I would feel comfortable seeking out if I needed advice."

3. Arnold & Porter

Arnold & Porter may have dropped a couple pegs on the diversity for minorities list this year, but it is still "one of the best firms in the country for minorities," associates say. Arnold & Porter's diversity is "outstanding," with "almost 50 percent" of the most recent summer associate class consisting of minority attorneys and "very high representation" throughout the associate roster. Arnold & Porter "aggressively recruits minorities" and "is actively trying to improve [its] efforts" through programs such as Minorities at Arnold & Porter (MAP) that assist in recruitment and mentorship.

DIVERSITY FOR GAYS AND LESBIANS

Average score = 7.71

RANK	FIRM	SCORE
1	Jenner & Block, LLC	9.654
2	Arent Fox Kintner Plotkin & Kahn, PLLC	9.647
3	Morrison & Foerster LLP	9.514
4	Arnold & Porter	9.185
5	Irell & Manella LLP	9.136
6	Heller Ehrman White & McAuliffe LLP	9.091
7	Cleary, Gottlieb, Steen & Hamilton	9.033
8	Orrick, Herrington & Sutcliffe LLP	8.923
9	Allen & Overy	8.919
10	Sedgwick, Detert, Moran & Arnold LLP	8.850
11	Debevoise & Plimpton	8.821
12	Preston Gates & Ellis LLP	8.739
13	Powell, Goldstein, Frazer & Murphy LLP	8.720
14	Chadbourne & Parke LLP	8.684
15	Wachtell, Lipton, Rosen & Katz	8.667
16	Finnegan, Henderson, Farabow, Garrett & Dunner, L.L.P.	8.650
17	Paul, Weiss, Rifkind, Wharton & Garrison LLP	8.564
18	Ropes & Gray	8.535
19	Milbank, Tweed, Hadley & McCloy LLP	8.488
20	Proskauer Rose LLP	8.446

Top three in diveristy for gays and lesbians

1. Jenner & Block

Jenner & Block must be doing right by its gay and lesbian attorneys. The firm has leapt from a seventh-place ranking on gay and lesbian diversity in last year's survey to the No. 1 slot this time around. "I couldn't ask for a better atmosphere in this regard," says one openly gay associate at the firm. "It's about ideal." The firm is "extremely committed and welcoming" and puts out a regular newsletter on gay and lesbian legal issues.

"Jenner & Block's commitment to its LGBT employees as well as the LGBT community has been reflected in the firm's *Equal Time* newsletter and featured in *American Lawyer* magazine and *Diversity & The Bar* magazine," says Paul Smith, managing partner of the firm's Washington,

D.C., office and co-chair of its Supreme Court practice. "This year, the firm also took the unprecedented step of volunteering to be included in the Human Rights Campaign's closely-watched Equality Index."

2. Arent Fox Kintner Plotkin & Kahn

Arent Fox Kintner Plotkin & Kahn may have slipped a notch in the rankings, but associates still believe "this is the place" when it comes to gay and lesbian diversity. The firm is "so welcoming I do not even know who all the gays and lesbians are," though the "many openly gay partners" have high visibility within the ranks. "I think we have more openly gay lawyers than minorities," one associate says, but "it is completely irrelevant," say others. "We all just work together and get along." "No one cares what your sexual orientation is here," another associate agrees. "People are valued for who they are and on the quality of their work."

3. Morrison & Foerster

"Our worldwide chair is an openly gay man," remarks one Morrison & Foerster associate. "What more need I say?" Once again, MoFo takes one of our top three slots for gay and lesbian diversity, as associates unite to express their belief that the firm is "very good about gay and lesbian issues" and "does not tolerate insensitivity." "I couldn't think of a more comfortable environment," says one openly gay attorney. "I was a little worried at first," another adds, "but no one here has ever done anything that makes me feel uncomfortable or like an outsider." The firm provides benefits for same-sex couples and even includes domestic partners in the staff directory. One attorney hopes the firm will go even further and "take the lead in new areas of gay rights," such as "offsetting tax penalties for domestic partnership."

THE VAULT 100: FIRMS 1-50

Wachtell, Lipton, Rosen & Katz

51 West 52nd Street
New York, NY 10019-6150
Phone: (212) 403-1000
www.wlrk.com

LOCATION

New York, NY

MAJOR DEPARTMENTS/PRACTICES

Antitrust
Bankruptcy
Corporate
Creditors' Rights
Executive Compensation & Benefits
Litigation
Real Estate
Tax
Trust & Estates

THE STATS

No. of attorneys: 193
No. of offices: 1
Summer associate offers: 15 out of 16 (2002)
Chairman: Richard D. Katcher
Hiring Partner: By committee

BASE SALARY

New York, NY
1st year: $140,000
2nd year: $150,000
3rd year: $165,000
4th year: $180,000
5th year: $195,000
Summer associate: $2,404/week

UPPERS

- Whopping paychecks
- Major prestige
- Loads of responsibility from the start

DOWNERS

- Little in the way of hand-holding
- "Long, difficult hours"
- No business casual dress code

NOTABLE PERKS

- Top-notch technology at your disposal
- Fully stocked kitchen on each floor with kitchen staff
- In-house birthday parties for attorneys
- Fro-yo machine

THE BUZZ
WHAT ATTORNEYS AT OTHER FIRMS ARE SAYING ABOUT THIS FIRM

- "The über-firm"
- "Hope you love your work more than your kids"
- "Overworked overachievers"
- "The gold standard"

RANKING RECAP

Best in Region
#1 - New York

Best in Practice
#1 - Mergers & Acquisitions
#2 - Corporate
#5 - Bankruptcy/Corporate Restructuring
#5 - Securities
#6 - Tax
#8 - Litigation

Quality of Life
#1 - Pay
#1 - Selectivity
#2 - Satisfaction
#3 - Best Firms to Work For
#4 - Associate/Partner Relations
#7 - Retention
#11 - Offices

Best in Diversity
#15 - Diversity for Gays & Lesbians

EMPLOYMENT CONTACT

Ms. Elizabeth F. Breslow
Director of Recruiting and Legal Personnel
Phone: (212) 403-1334
Fax: (212) 403-2334
E-mail: recruiting@wlrk.com

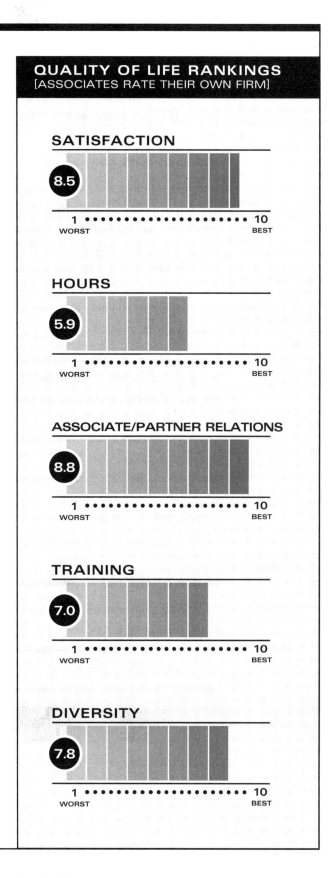

QUALITY OF LIFE RANKINGS
[ASSOCIATES RATE THEIR OWN FIRM]

SATISFACTION 8.5

HOURS 5.9

ASSOCIATE/PARTNER RELATIONS 8.8

TRAINING 7.0

DIVERSITY 7.8

THE SCOOP

While not a giant in size, Wachtell, Lipton, Rosen & Katz is nonetheless a true legal powerhouse. Known for handling big-time litigation cases and M&A deals and for providing its associates with bigger-than-big salaries, the firm is one of the most respected – and the wealthiest – in the nation.

Independent spirit

With 193 attorneys and just one office, Wachtell is certainly a standout in a legal market where many of its closest competitors have multiple locations and employ two times as many attorneys (or more). But Wachtell likes being different. Since its inception, the firm has prided itself on bringing a creative and sensible perspective to the practice of corporate law. For instance, the founders have sought to replace the hierarchical structure common to many top firms with a more collaborative environment by maintaining a one-to-one partner-associate ratio. The relatively small number of attorneys and even ratio means associates are given a great deal of responsibility from the get-go and partners stay very much involved with the work of the firm.

Unlike many of its competitors, Wachtell specializes in just a few key practice areas. In addition to the aforementioned corporate and litigation practices, the firm also has a strong creditors' rights practice. Real estate, tax, antitrust and executive compensation are other areas in which the firm concentrates. Moreover, Wachtell does not work with clients on a retainer basis. Instead, the firm chooses to take on a client based on the merits of each particular case or deal. This out-the-box thinking has paid off: Not only do Wachtell attorneys command high fees for their time, the firm's associates are the highest paid in the nation. Wachtell generally doesn't bill hourly rates as at most firms, but instead bases fees on a variety of factors, including the complexity of the deal and how well the firm handles the matter. Like investment bankers, the firm generally pockets a percentage of the value of the deals they negotiate.

Not a bitter pill to swallow

Early on, the firm established itself as a go-to player in the M&A arena. As a firm well grounded in what it takes to put two companies together, it actually makes sense that one of the things for which Wachtell has become best known is protecting hostile takeover targets. The strategy, devised in the early 1980s by firm co-founder Martin Lipton, enables a company to fend off a takeover by selling shares at a discount to its own stockholders other than the proposed buyer, thereby diluting the proposed buyer. While it may sound simple, the move, popularly known as the "poison pill," has been hailed for its ingenuity and has been used by many companies in various forms over the years.

Tough cases for a tough firm

The firm's most highly publicized case of late is its representation of Larry Silverstein, the leaseholder of the former World Trade Center. Insurers for the building complex dispute Silverstein's assertion that he's entitled to $7.1 billion in damages because the September 11 terrorist attack should count as two separate occurrences for purposes of the $3.546 billion policy on the properties. The firm is appealing a June 2002 ruling that a jury would have to decide whether the two planes crashing into the Twin Towers constituted one or two "occurrences." Co-founder Herbert Wachtell is a member of Silverstein's legal team. The firm's litigators are currently involved in representing a number of major securities firms and companies in responding to the recent wave of corporate governance and accounting investigations.

Mergers down, but it's all good

Thanks in large part to the $72 billion AT&T Broadband/Comcast merger, Wachtell enjoyed a banner year in 2001. That deal and others, such as the Wachovia/First Union merger, made Wachtell the leading legal advisor on M&A deals for the year, according to data from Thomson Financial. But that spectacular success proved impossible to repeat in 2002. Due in part to the stagnant economy and an industry-wide decline in large-scale deals, Thomson reported that Wachtell's rank in M&A fell to No. 10 in 2002. But don't throw a pity party for venerable Wachtell: The $60 billion worth of deals the firm advised on in 2002 is nothing to sneeze at, earning the firm a No.-2 ranking by Thomson Financial for completed M&A work.

Just because Wachtell doesn't have international offices doesn't mean the firm has a narrow worldview. The firm frequently consults with major firms in other countries when the interests of a client go beyond U.S. borders. And of course, Wachtell attorneys rack up their own frequent-flier miles helping clients in other parts of the world. One such recent case involved client Philip Morris, which sold its Miller brand of beer to South African Breweries in 2002.

A rumor is put to bed

While popular lore has it that the firm's founders – four New York University Law School classmates – banded together because opportunities in corporate law were scarce for Jewish attorneys, co-founder Lipton says the story "is something that has no truth whatsoever." In a June 2002 interview with *Global Counsel* magazine, Lipton describes the rumor as "one of those strange stories that get started," and takes on a life of its own.

Tellin' it like it is

Lipton, still an active member of the firm, continues to uphold the against-the-grain ideals he and his partners shared when they started the firm in 1965. In 2002 while many were pointing fingers but providing few solutions, Lipton became a leader of the chorus for post-Enron corporate reform. He authored a memo outlining his views on how corporate boards can improve communication and decision-making. His simple yet revolutionary observation: Corporate board members should devote more time to a thorough analysis of the companies they run.

Hooked up

When it comes to technology, Wachtell attorneys definitely have the hookup. Naturally all Wachtellians are outfitted with the requisite laptop, cell phone and PDA. But they also receive an in-home broadband connection and tech support, remote access to their desktop computers from anywhere in the world and training from in-house software specialists. It's no wonder Wachtell was ranked No. 1 in 2002 on *American Lawyer*'s Tech Scorecard for the second year in a row. While the firm provides nothing but the latest and greatest gadgets for its attorneys, it takes a surprisingly low-key approach to its web site. No fancy Shockwave graphics or even press releases touting the firm's successes. The site of this high-powered firm provides just the facts with a design so simple and clean, it's bordering on bland.

GETTING HIRED

"The hardest offer in New York"

One freshman attorney describes Wachtell as the "hardest offer in [New York]." Another recalls, "My Wachtell interview was the most difficult of all of my interviews, but I was impressed that the attorneys were more interested in determining whether I was a good fit for the place than in recruiting me and selling the firm." Everybody agrees on what goes into that determination. "You absolutely must have excellent grades, period," says a third-year associate. "Personality can tank you in the interview, but even the best personality and 'intangibles' will not get you a callback unless you have excellent, law review-caliber grades." "If you don't have stellar grades and law review, it will be almost impossible to get hired," a senior associate concurs, while another attorney chimes in, "Law journal work also appears essential if a candidate does not attend a top-three law school."

"We don't always necessarily hire the biggest brainiacs," an M&A associate counters. "The best associates here are very, very smart but not necessarily cerebral. You need to be able to execute, to get things done and to make good, fast, practical judgments." A senior litigator amplifies that assessment: "People from top law schools who show initiative, commitment to living in New York and living this lifestyle," he says, make the best candidates for that coveted Wachtell offer.

OUR SURVEY SAYS

This ain't no party

Wachtell's "very intense" offices are "quiet but congenial" and "surprisingly informal," despite the relentlessly formal dress code. "People here genuinely like each other and there are many close friendships," enthuses a third-year associate, "but very little socializing together outside the office." Though everybody agrees the mood is "not as social as it is at most firms at any time except dinner," they also say "the attorneys work well together as teams." A senior member of the corporate practice says firm pride "creates a friendly atmosphere. We're in it together, so why not be nice?"

"The collegiality between even the most senior partners and the most junior associates here continues to astonish me," a second-year marvels. Another associate avers, "You are treated as a colleague and a potential future partner from day one." "What matters most here," a bankruptcy attorney says, "is your dedication to consistently doing work of extraordinary quality. If you are good at what you do, you are valued, period."

Rise to the occasion

Attorneys at Wachtell regularly describe the firm as "a special place to work," and recognize that "enormous responsibility means accelerated growth." "There is no other law firm where I could have learned so much so fast," a junior associate avows. That said, the firm is a "baptism-by-fire" environment. "You learn by doing," explains a third-year, "which means that you are often asked to do things that you have never done before. To succeed here, you must be confident enough to accept those kinds of challenges." A midlevel litigator admonishes, "If you need to have your hand held, you came to the wrong place." Other colleagues paint not quite so harsh a picture. "There are other people in my department," reports one new recruit, "who are extremely helpful and go out of their way to answer questions. Sometimes they drop by just to see how I am doing." A senior attorney beams, "Wachtell lawyers love to talk shop, so it is not uncommon for the dinner conversation to include work. Wachtell lawyers never stop learning. We're intellectually curious and will take every opportunity to talk law, even without a formal environment."

Although Wachtell is, in the words of one second-year corporate attorney, "as close to perfection as you can get in a New York law firm," associates do have some recommendations for improvement, primarily centered on the need for more mentoring, especially of brand-new associates. "My mentors are wonderful and always available," says a woman in her first year with the firm, "but I know that other associates have not even met their mentors." She elaborates, "Some more senior associates do not understand that first-years need more guidance – or at least availability – from them. Partners are actually much better about this, and should encourage their senior associates to be more understanding of associates who are just starting out." A midlevel

litigator also wants a more formal mentoring system, claiming Wachtell "has become too large for this to occur naturally."

Wachtell women

Wachtell's associates view the firm as "extremely welcoming" of women, though some observe that "many women opt not to come here because they contemplate having a family, and the hours are quite long." Those women who do choose the firm "play an equal role" and are rewarded equally as well. "Considering the small number of women at the firm," a woman in her first year at Wachtell says, "there are quite a few female partners." She adds, "I feel that the other women are very supportive of each other and interested in making sure that we are happy." A second-year associate agrees, "The women that are here are tremendous role models. I have never felt my gender to be an issue." Associates have less to say about Wachtell's diversity in other arenas, cautiously remarking that "some of the most well-respected members of the firm are gay" and that "the firm hires and promotes the best people, regardless of race."

Working in the coal mines

"Nobody pretends that Wachtell is a lifestyle firm," but the long hours can be dismaying. "The life/work boundary should be more respected," says one rookie associate, "so that there is no macho attitude about staying all night and working all weekend." Another first-year counters frankly, "Working at Wachtell will be your life. You just have to be prepared to accept that fact." Even a senior attorney complains, "I work way too many hours. More every year." But, says another associate, "I rarely feel that I'm spending my time doing things that are unnecessary." And a third-year associate says it's not so hard to find a balance. "I've rarely had to cancel plans unexpectedly, and never had to cancel a vacation," she reports. "You are deeply involved in, and informed about, your matters, so you can better plan your time outside the office."

My big fat firm paycheck

Wachtell is "committed to paying a leading salary" and "consistently pays substantially more than anyplace else." Even in the current economic situation, associates describe the firm as "unbelievably" and "extraordinarily" generous, and call their salaries and bonuses "a major reason to come to this firm as opposed to the other top 10 firms in New York City." A senior associate proudly boasts, "I'm being paid better than contemporaries at other firms, and with my bonus, I'm making more than even partners at lots of firms." No wonder a midlevel litigator insists, "It makes no sense to work at another big New York firm, if you can work here."

Just don't expect to work in style. Wachtell's "functional" offices are "all business, no ostentation," "spartan and clean – nothing ritzy, but it gets the job done." Although "space is at a premium as the firm grows," and some incoming associates may have to share a room for a little while, the firm's attorneys have "very comfortable working arrangements" and no complaints.

Actually, says one sophomore associate, "The office space is under-appreciated" and "attractively appointed." A freshman attorney also singles out the "eclectic," "just amazing" art collection. "A lot of thought went into it," she notes approvingly.

Time for pro bono?

"No one is going to deter your from doing pro bono" at Wachtell, a source confides, "but no one is pushing it either." One first-year associate has had "a few very interesting pro bono matters," and another says, "Although associates are not always actively encouraged to take on pro bono work, those who do have all of the resources of the office at their disposal." Still, most point out that there just isn't enough time in the day to devote to non-paying matters. "The firm is encouraging about taking on pro bono matters, but the time commitment involved on top of regular work makes it tough for associates to sign on," shrugs a third-year associate. Moreover, the longer attorneys spend at the firm, the more it becomes "impossible to make time to do pro bono," a senior litigator opines.

2

Cravath, Swaine & Moore LLP

Worldwide Plaza
825 Eighth Avenue
New York, NY 10019
Phone: 212-474-1000
www.cravath.com

LOCATIONS

New York, NY (HQ)
London

MAJOR DEPARTMENTS/PRACTICES

Corporate
Litigation
Tax
Trusts & Estates

THE STATS

No. of attorneys: 466
No. of offices: 2
Summer associate offers: 68 out of 68 (2002)
Presiding Partner: Robert D. Joffe
Managing Partners: C. Allen Parker (Corporate) and
Richard W. Clary (Litigation)
Hiring Partners: Ronald Cami (Corporate) and Julie A.
North (Litigation)

BASE SALARY

New York, NY
1st year: $125,000
2nd year: $135,000
3rd year: $150,000
4th year: $170,000
5th year: $190,000
6th year: $205,000
7th year: $220,000
Summer associate: $2,500/week

UPPERS

- Cravath equals "instant credibility"
- Great training opportunities
- Sophisticated, high-level work

DOWNERS

- "Total commitment" to the firm expected
- Grim partnership prospects
- Shared offices

NOTABLE PERKS

- Back-up child care
- Discount at Tiffany's
- Subsidized gym membership (at Equinox, no less!)
- Free dinner and ride home after 8 p.m.

THE BUZZ
WHAT ATTORNEYS AT OTHER FIRMS ARE SAYING ABOUT THIS FIRM

- "Top sweatshop"
- "The firm that all firms strive to match"
- "The beast"
- "Big, bad and they know it"

RANKING RECAP

Best in Region
#2 - New York

Best in Practice
#1 - Corporate
#1 - Litigation
#1 - Tax
#2 - Securities
#3 - M&A

Quality of Life
#4 - Selectivity
#7 - Training

EMPLOYMENT CONTACT

Ms. Lisa A. Kalen
Associate Director of Legal Personnel and Recruiting
Phone: (212) 474-3215
Fax: (212) 474-3225
E-mail: lkalen@cravath.com

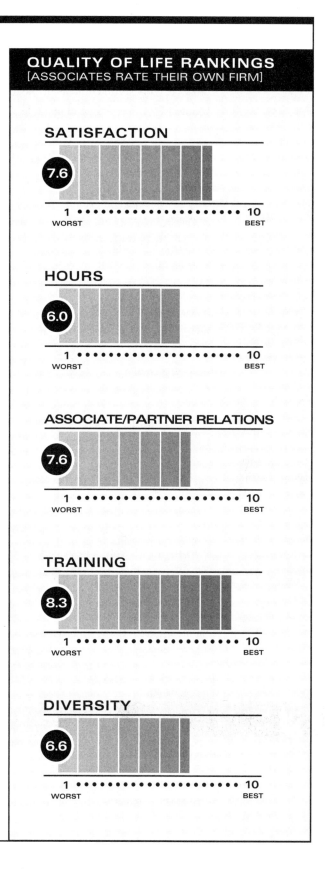

QUALITY OF LIFE RANKINGS
[ASSOCIATES RATE THEIR OWN FIRM]

SATISFACTION
7.6
1 WORST ··················· 10 BEST

HOURS
6.0
1 WORST ··················· 10 BEST

ASSOCIATE/PARTNER RELATIONS
7.6
1 WORST ··················· 10 BEST

TRAINING
8.3
1 WORST ··················· 10 BEST

DIVERSITY
6.6
1 WORST ··················· 10 BEST

THE SCOOP

Law students dream of working there. Lawyers covet the firm's giant salaries and massive prestige. High-profile clients throw themselves at the firm. Yes, New York's Cravath, Swaine & Moore LLP is a true legend in the legal community.

Model of a modern law firm

Cravath's roots extend back to 1819, when R. M. Blatchford founded a small law firm in New York City. After a merger with a firm in Auburn, N.Y., the firm became known as Blatchford, Seward & Griswold in 1854; it adopted its present moniker in 1954. The present-day structure of most law firms, in which junior associates strive for a place among the partners' ranks, owes much to the vision of Paul Cravath, whose guiding principles continue to influence the firm's modus operandi.

The Cravath system, which has now become common in the legal community, officially rejects merit-based compensation in favor of a lockstep structure in which associates' annual salaries and bonuses are determined strictly by seniority. Widely regarded as a compensation leader, Cravath's year-end bonuses for first-year associates were reported in December 2002 as $15,000, and the firm quickly matched the $17,500 figure announced by fellow New Yorker Sullivan & Cromwell.

With profits per partner consistently ranking near the top of the charts, partners at Cravath are a satisfied bunch. In 2000, for example, *American Lawyer* reported that the average take-home for Cravath partners was slightly more than $2 million.

Big, big business

Cravath has been providing counsel to titans of industry since the 19th century, when the firm represented developers of America's vast railroad network. Today approximately 260 attorneys staff the firm's corporate department. Modern corporate giants who turn to the firm for legal guidance include such heavy hitters as AOL Time Warner, Bristol-Myers Squibb, Vivendi Universal, Georgia Pacific and IBM. Cravath serves as a primary outside counsel to financial powerhouses J.P. Morgan Chase and Credit Suisse First Boston, and is also called upon by Salomon Smith Barney on a regular basis. The firm believes that a good attorney must possess an adequate legal foundation; in that spirit, junior associates rotate to different practice groups every 12 to 18 months, working on everything from commercial banking to securities offerings to mergers and acquisitions.

Cravath's name is attached to some of the most prominent mergers and acquisitions of the last decade. Although the M&A market has become somewhat diminished in recent years, Cravath can still be found working behind the scenes on many of the biggest deals. The firm was legal adviser to international forest products specialist Weyerhauser in its $6.2 billion merger with competitor Willamette Industries in January 2002. That August, Cravath acted as American counsel for

PricewaterhouseCoopers in the sale of its global business consulting and technology services unit, PwC Consulting, to IBM for $3.5 billion in cash and stock.

Although Cravath has only one foreign outpost, in London, more than one-fourth of its largest clients are based outside the United States. The firm is active in Canada, where it won an intense bidding war in February 2002 for the role of American co-counsel in the proposed $5.5 billion IPO of government-owned holding company Hydro One, whose subsidiaries supply much of Ontario with electrical service. Cravath also assisted Ballard Power Systems in its $155.9 million IPO in December 2002 and represented AT&T Canada two months earlier when it was bought out by a group of investors including AT&T and CIBC Capital Partners for $5.5 billion.

White-shoe pedal to the metal

The firm is currently representing car rental agency Hertz in federal and state litigation linked to the bankruptcy proceedings of competitor ANC Rentals. In an effort to bring its costs under control, ANC has tried to consolidate the physical operations of its two subsidiaries, National and Alamo, at airports across the United States by getting out of one agency's lease and having it share space with the other agency. Cravath has filed suits on behalf of Hertz against ANC and against those airports that have gone along with the plan, which its client views as anti-competitve.

Though not directly involved in any of the legal matters related to Enron, Cravath is defending Credit Suisse First Boston in a class-action lawsuit brought by frustrated Enron shareholders. CSFB is one of nearly three dozen defendants accused of helping the bankrupt energy firm hoodwink its investors by setting up off-the-books partnerships and hiding loans through offshore companies. Cravath filed a motion to dismiss on behalf of its client, but the motion was denied in December 2002. The case is pending.

Keeping busy for AOL

Cravath counseled Time Warner through its $165 billion merger with America Online in 2000, and the media giant continues to rely on the firm extensively for legal representation. In January 2002, Cravath lawyers were part of the team that filed a federal antitrust lawsuit against Microsoft on AOL Time Warner's behalf. The suit is the first by a company seeking damages against Microsoft after the 2000 ruling against the software developer. It claims that Microsoft's "anti-competitive and exclusionary" business practices enabled its web browser, Internet Explorer, to take substantial market share away from its biggest competitor, Netscape Navigator, which AOL had purchased in 1999.

Cravath also assisted AOL in an internal review of its accounting practices following an SEC probe into several advertising transactions and an investigation by the U.S. Attorney's office into other potential financial irregularities. The investigation turned up several questionable transactions tied to an executive vice president for business affairs, who was pressured to leave the company in August 2002.

Fancy footwork

In a departure from its usual cases, Cravath represented the Martha Graham Center of Contemporary Dance in an intellectual property case over who owned the rights to the famed choreographer's dances. The company's former artistic director filed a lawsuit over the claim that his status as Graham's legal heir entitled him to full ownership of all her works as well as the use of her name and original sets and costumes designed for the dance productions. A federal district court judge ruled against him on the trademark claims within a matter of months, and the copyright claims were ultimately resolved in the Center's favor in August 2002. The ruling confirmed Graham's transferral of rights for many of her dances to the Center before her death in 1991 and determined that the dance company also owned the rights to the works she had created while acting as its employee.

Running out of room?

Cravath is one of many Manhattan law firms that have begun to look outside city limits for backup office space in the aftermath of the September 11 attacks. The firm signed a lease in October 2002 for more than 15,000 square feet in a building in White Plains, N.Y., where competitor Davis Polk & Wardwell had already been operating an annex location for several months. The building, conveniently located a half-hour's train ride from midtown Manhattan, has its own backup generator and condenser water system, assets that should prove useful to keeping a business running after a natural or man-made disaster.

GETTING HIRED

Only the best

It doesn't get much more competitive than Cravath, so it stands to reason that "you don't get hired here unless you have outstanding grades from a highly competitive law school and strong interview skills." Moreover, associates say "the firm is looking for highly motivated individuals who will take initiative" and who are "not afraid of hard work or taking a large amount of responsibility early on." "The firm looks for very smart, motivated people who also have outside interests that make them interesting people. Once a candidate makes it to a callback interview, their resume and grades aren't as important as how well they will get along with the people who work here," says a litigation insider.

"The callback process consists of a day of interviews with partners and associates in the department in which the interviewee has expressed an interest. Usually, the interviewee is given a decision by the end of the day." According to a freshman, it's a simple matter of keeping your cool once you've made it to the callback stage. "Unless you bomb an interview, you'll be hired in most cases," but "if your GPA is borderline then it is possible you won't be." A junior associate shares this perspective: "I think the people who end up with offers tend to be people that were able to convince the partners that they love the law and love to work. Hobbies and extracurricular activities are fine, but only to the extent they do not interfere with your ability to work around the clock."

OUR SURVEY SAYS

Formal is good

Insiders say the culture at Cravath is "very formal." But many associates say they like it that way. "I do not view [the firm's formality] as a negative," insists a new associate. "It's formal because the lawyers are diligent and focused on their work." Another insider says, "Most prefer not to mix their social and professional lives, so when the work is finished, we go home." Many Cravath associates mention that formal doesn't necessarily mean unfriendly. "The firm's culture is formal, and lawyers do not tend to socialize together outside of work. However, the culture is respectful and friendly at work," suggests a first-year associate.

Cravath associates are proud of their firm and generally satisfied with the work they are doing. This pride in the Cravath name informs every aspect of the firm's culture. "The culture is one of excellence and merit. It is the work that matters more than belonging to the right group or club," says one insider. "I enjoy the responsibility, am impressed by my colleagues and partners and get much satisfaction from the prestige of the firm," declares a second-year associate. However, some insiders reveal they are frustrated by what they describe as a culture of secrecy. "Associates do not have a say in much, and decision-making is very secretive at the firm," confides a midlevel. That being said, some folks "like it that way. It wouldn't be the right fit for a very activist type who wants to influence the course of an institution."

All day, every day

New Cravathites should be prepared to work long and hard. "More often than not the work is seven days a week," says a tired first-year associate. Perhaps that's because "cases tend to be understaffed, so the workload is often excessive." "Working seven days a week becomes grueling, but at least the work is generally interesting," insists one source. Says a third-year insider, "The hours and the quality of work really go hand-in-hand. Although I would rather spend less time in the office, the significant amount of time corresponds with a significant amount of responsibility and challenging work." "The hours are long," chirps a midlevel, "but one cannot say that the firm ever misled anyone about that." A newcomer explains that what makes the long hours endurable is that "Cravath is not a face-time firm. When there is work to be done, you are expected to do it and do it better than any other firm however many hours that takes. Yet when business is calm, nobody expects you to hang around the office unnecessarily." "The hours can be long and the job can be a test of endurance," says a third-year. This source adds, "The difficult part is not so much the number of hours as it is their unpredictability."

Several associates point out that the down economy has them wishing for more work, rather than less. Laments a corporate associate, "Obviously, the work is exciting and intriguing when it's available. However, with the general slow down, there hasn't been a lot of very interesting work to go around, and the interesting work that is available seems to be given to a chosen few." One associate wearing rose-colored glasses suggests, "With hours generally down, I have noticed more interoffice socializing. And to think," it seemed "we all just didn't care to socialize with one another. Turns out, it was more a matter of lack of time to do so." A corporate finance attorney asserts, "The work is feast or famine. When things are busy, the work is incredibly challenging and satisfying, but there is very little feedback and little to no support or guidance from the partners. Thus, while the work is fulfilling, it is being done in a sink-or-swim environment."

We want our fair share

Cravath associates know their pay is "top of the market," and they know they shouldn't complain, but . . . Many associates contend that, considering Cravath's stellar reputation, associates "should be getting paid more than all other New York firms." A first-year whines, "I'm not eating Alpo anymore, but it would be nice if the firm matched Skadden's base [salary]." Another classmate complains, "Given the hours I work, I make about the same per hour as if I were working at McDonald's. It would be nice to be paid more, but I am thankful for my job." A corporate attorney tries to look on the bright side: "We are well paid, but I'm not ashamed to admit that, what with student loans and high apartment rents and needing to live close to the office given my hours, I could use more. Of course, I could also be unemployed, so that said, I'm very happy with my compensation." A litigation colleague offers this perspective: "For the hours that we work, the taxes in New York State and City and the cost of living in New York City, it makes absolutely no practical sense to work here. Why do we do it, then? In a word: vanity."

Some associates claim that, while "Cravath used to be a leader in the market," the firm "has developed a reputation for cheapness in recent years." "Most people were unhappy with 2002 year-end bonuses," reveals a litigation associate. Says another litigator, "I do not know of a single Cravath litigation associate who is happy with his or her pay – especially in light of understaffing and profits per partner well in excess of $2 million." A third-year asserts, "Our compensation should be somewhere in between Wachtell and the rest of the pack." On the other hand, says this same source, "It's a huge relief that there are no billable requirements and that bonuses are paid lockstep."

Of course, not everyone is complaining. A corporate associate says, "We are treated very well here in terms of salary and benefits," while one wisecracker insists, "It was much easier to complain when my banker friends were making twice as much."

Please work all weekend

Associates tell Vault that partners generally "act very cordially and politely toward associates." Respect is the name of the game. "I have been treated very well by all of the partners that I have worked with," raves a first-year lawyer. "They have taken the time, even when they don't have it, to explain the big picture to me. They teach me by giving me feedback on my work but also don't forget to compliment me when I do a good job."

Several associates, however, wish partners would show more consideration for associates' lives outside the office. "Partners generally treat associates with respect, but that respect is tempered by the expectation that all associates are willing to work 24/7 for months on end." A second-year tells us, "It is clear that at least some partners do not respect the personal time of associates. It is also clear that some partners and senior associates are very invested in Cravath's rigid social hierarchy." Other insiders agree that "partners treat associates with respect, but sometimes make irrational demands on short notice." Says a third-year, "The partners are generally not your friends, but they do treat associates with respect here."

Sit. Roll over. Give me your paw.

Cravathites go ga-ga over training at their firm. Raves a newbie, "There is no shortage of formal training. Also, the team system tends to lend itself to informal training, since there is an incentive for teams to help new associates become good associates." Insiders appreciate the training for "the topics covered, the material presented and the format of training sessions" and describe it as "high tech, detailed and top-notch." Litigators describe a special "formal litigation program" that is "very structured and comprehensive. We just built a beautiful courtroom used for training. All the partners get involved in the classes that are taught, and a lot of time goes into the preparation."

While formal training opportunities receive almost unanimous praise, some insiders maintain that "hands-on training really depends on the partner," with some insisting that "partners could be better in making a stronger effort to provide more feedback and guidance." Several insiders criticize the partnership for exhibiting "little interest in one-on-one mentoring or training." Still, associates are grateful for senior associates who take the time to help their junior counterparts.

Colorblind firm

"The meritocratic nature of things here means that race generally does not matter," says a minority associate. "Cravath seems to be very blind to diversity. If someone can do the work," says a corporate attorney, he or she gets the job. Insists a minority attorney, "There are certainly many faces of color here, but who are we kidding? Everyone has the same Ivy pedigree, so there isn't really a diversity of experiences. Nevertheless, Cravath makes an effort to reach out to and support minorities." A senior associate believes the firm is "actually very welcoming – works very, very hard – at hiring minority associates."

But "the firm has been unwilling to bend so far as to make minority partners just to claim friendliness to diversity." Others note with despair that there is "only one minority partner" at the firm. In the opinion of a litigator, "Hiring seems okay, but promotion prospects seem very bleak. Moreover, the lack of minority partners must make it nearly impossible for minority associates to obtain mentorship from minority members of the firm."

"Working seven days a week becomes grueling, but at least the work is generally interesting."

– *Cravath associate*

Sullivan & Cromwell LLP

125 Broad Street
New York, NY 10004
Phone: (212) 558-4000
www.sullcrom.com

LOCATIONS

New York, NY (HQ)
Los Angeles, CA • Palo Alto, CA • Washington, DC •
Beijing • Frankfurt • Hong Kong • London • Melbourne •
Paris • Sydney • Tokyo

MAJOR DEPARTMENTS/PRACTICES

Commercial Real Estate
Corporate & Finance
E-Business & Technology
Estates & Personal
Executive Compensation & Benefits
Financial Institutions
Litigation
Mergers & Acquisitions
Project Finance
Tax

THE STATS

No. of attorneys: 717
No. of offices: 12
Summer associate offers: 116 out of 116 (2002)
Chairman: H. Rodgin Cohen
Hiring Partners: Christopher L. Mann (NY); Robert H.
Craft (DC); Steven W. Thomas (LA); Scott D. Miller
(Palo Alto)

BASE SALARY

All domestic offices
1st year: $125,000
2nd year: $135,000
3rd year: $150,000
4th year: $170,000
5th year: $190,000
6th year: $205,000
7th year: $220,000
8th year: $235,000
Summer associate: $2,404/week

UPPERS

- Front-page work and prestigious clients
- Compensation leader
- Not as buttoned-up as you think they are

DOWNERS

- Unpredictable hours
- Need to improve retention of women
- Tight quarters for junior associates (NY)

NOTABLE PERKS

- Aeron desk chairs
- Subsidized gym memberships
- Free dinners and car rides home
- Cafeteria breakfast "is like a hotel brunch" (NY)

THE BUZZ
WHAT ATTORNEYS AT OTHER FIRMS ARE SAYING ABOUT THIS FIRM

- "All that and a bag of chips"
- "Old-school white shoe"
- "Has a hand in every high-profile deal"
- "Self-impressed in that New York way"

RANKING RECAP

Best in Region
#3 - New York

Best in Practice
#1 - Securities
#4 - Corporate
#4 - Mergers & Acquisitions
#4 - Tax
#10 - Antitrust

Quality of Life
#6 - Pay
#7 - Selectivity

EMPLOYMENT CONTACT

Ms. Nicole Adams
Assistant Manager of Legal Recruiting
Phone: (212) 558-3518
Fax: (212) 558-3588
E-mail: adamsn@sullcrom.com

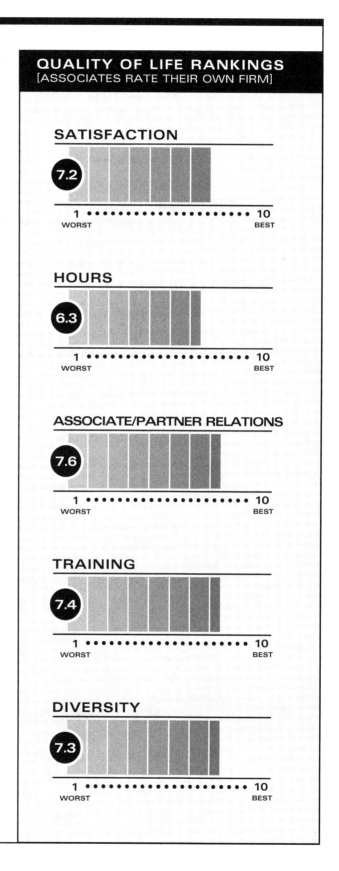

QUALITY OF LIFE RANKINGS
[ASSOCIATES RATE THEIR OWN FIRM]

SATISFACTION
7.2
1 WORST .... 10 BEST

HOURS
6.3
1 WORST .... 10 BEST

ASSOCIATE/PARTNER RELATIONS
7.6
1 WORST .... 10 BEST

TRAINING
7.4
1 WORST .... 10 BEST

DIVERSITY
7.3
1 WORST .... 10 BEST

THE SCOOP

The prestigious Sullivan & Cromwell is one of New York's grand, elite firms. Known for high-quality work and a strong international presence, S&C has been handling the bulk of Microsoft's work since 1992, including the various antitrust cases against the software giant.

Building America's corporate infrastructure

Since its formation by Algernon Sydney Sullivan and William Nelson Cromwell in 1879, Sullivan & Cromwell has made its reputation by being at the heart of blockbuster deals in the industrial, commercial and financial sectors. It had a hand in the creation of Edison General Electric in 1882 and US Steel in 1901, and represented numerous European investors who financed the building of America's railroads as well as the Panama Canal. By 1928, the firm had offices in Berlin, Buenos Aires and Paris to better serve the needs of its foreign clients.

Partners John Foster Dulles and Arthur Dean gave S&C a foothold in politics and international affairs. With that boost and the growth of markets in Europe, Asia and Latin America, the firm was able to continually expand its offices: London in 1972, Washington, D.C. in 1977, Melbourne in 1983, Los Angeles in 1984, Tokyo in 1987, Hong Kong in 1992, Frankfurt in 1995, Beijing in 1999, Palo Alto in 2000 and Sydney in 2001.

Show me the money

Responsibility for the lavish bonuses at the turn of the 21st century lies squarely on S&C's shoulders. The firm announced a $35,000 bonus for its first-years in 2000 and, when Cravath, Swaine & Moore raised the stakes to $40,000, S&C came up with the extra cash. But like many other top firms, Sullivan pulled in the reins the following year, dropping the first-year bonus to $20,000 (while dropping more than $50,000 in many senior associates' laps). It held back a little bit more in 2002, announcing in December that the first-year bonus would be $17,500, slightly above what Cravath was giving its freshmen. (Cravath ended up matching S&C.)

Public service pros

When it comes to public service, S&C takes its commitment seriously. The firm's pro bono practice group gives associates the opportunity to spend a full year working on pro bono cases under partner supervision. In September 2002, two associates at the firm secured the release of Lazaro Burt, who had spent 10 years in prison for a murder he did not commit. Spending the equivalent of 1,800 billable hours on investigating and litigating the case, the associates turned up eyewitnesses who had not testified at Burt's original trial and convinced the judge to vacate his murder conviction. On January 22, 2003, three associates and two partners, having made clemency presentations to the governor of North Carolina, obtained from the North Carolina Supreme Court a stay of execution of an inmate who had been scheduled to be executed on January 24, 2003.

Big deals

S&C more than holds its own in the high-powered world of mergers and acquisitions, pulling down the No.-1 ranking in the 2002 M&A league tables. Its name also pops up frequently in the annual "Deals of the Year" roundup in *Institutional Investor* magazine. The firm participated in 2002's largest M&A transaction when it advised Pharmacia on a $60 billion acquisition by Pfizer. The union solidified Pfizer's position as the world's largest and highest grossing pharmaceutical company and added such popular Pharmacia products as the arthritis medication Celebrex to Pfizer product offerings. The firm also represented P&O Princess, the cruise ship line (home of the "Love Boat"), in the $5.4 billion dual-listed company acquisition by Carnival Cruises. The aquatic acquisition was named "Deal of the Year" by *Euromoney* and *Financial News*. S&C also counseled Anthem in connection with its $4.2 billion acquisition of Tigron (the largest U.S. insurance deal of 2002) and online auction king eBay in a $1.5 billion acquisition of PayPal, an electronic payment service that was already handling 60 percent of the financial transactions related to eBay auctions, and assisted Cablevision in its sale of the Bravo cable network to NBC. Other major recent deals in which the firm played a role include the sale of Burger King by client Diageo; a merger between client Moore Corp. and its longtime rival, Wallace Computer Services, which created the third-largest printing company in North America; and Northrop Grumman's $11.8 billion purchase of TRW (where S&C represented TRW's financial adviser).

Although the IPO market was globally soft in 2002, S&C's outposts in Asia took part in some substantial deals. When the People's Republic of China decided to privatize the Hong Kong operations of the state-owned Bank of China, S&C acted as counsel on United States law to the underwriters led by the bank's affiliate, Goldman Sachs and UBS Warburg. The July 2002 offering on the Hong Kong Stock Exchange raised $2.5 billion. The firm also represented China Telecommunications Corp. in a $1.43 billion offering in New York and Hong Kong.

S&C coordinated defense efforts for a group of investment banks hit with lawsuits accusing them of rigging many of the "hot" technology IPOs between 1998 and 2000. Almost every investment bank you can think of has been named as a defendant, including Goldman Sachs, Merrill Lynch, Credit Suisse First Boston, Morgan Stanley and SG Cowen.

Scandalous litigation

Recent years have seen the firm's litigators at the forefront of newsworthy disputes. S&C's white collar team represented parties in some of the most recent high-profile corporate fraud to-dos, including Enron, Tyco and the sundry Wall Street research scandals, as well as assorted bribery, health care fraud and money laundering probes across the country.

In the Enron fiasco, S&C represented David Duncan, the former Arthur Andersen employee in charge of Andersen's auditing team for Enron. Andersen publicly gave Duncan the boot early in 2002, blaming him for the document-shredding frenzy that destroyed much of the potential evidence in the Enron case. Shortly afterwards, Duncan began cooperating with federal investigators and pled guilty in April 2002 to obstruction of justice charges. Although he could face a maximum sentence of 10 years in prison, it is expected that federal prosecutors will eventually argue for leniency, given Duncan's willingness to testify as a government witness in the obstruction trial against Arthur Andersen.

No to YES

S&C has been representing Cablevision in an antitrust case brought by the Yankees Entertainment and Sports Network, otherwise known as the YES Network (or just YES). The suit arises out of the failure of the parties to reach an agreement under which the YES Network's programming (which includes New York Yankees and New Jersey Nets games) would be carried on Cablevision's cable TV systems. S&C also handled the recent Cablevision negotiations with YES, which led to the signing of an agreement for Cablevision to carry YES in 2003. (To follow the latest news in the thorny history of the YES Network, the *New York Post* is your best bet.)

GETTING HIRED

"Last of the meritocracies"

Sullivan & Cromwell views itself as "the last of the meritocracies" and chooses associates accordingly. A senior associate lists four traits the ideal candidate possesses: "Analytical firepower, presentation skills, creativity in approach to problem-solving and an entrepreneurial instinct." Another veteran associate observes, "Associates tend to have a common denominator – sensible, professional, confident people with good judgment and good interpersonal skills."

Others suggest that's all well and good, but it's really all about the grades. "I believe that S&C is looking for a person who has both academic ability and the ambition to succeed," says a corporate associate. "Grades in law school are used as a measure of both of these characteristics." When another associate says the firm "looks at grades, grades, grades and pedigree, in that order," he isn't kidding. "The majority of associates come from one of the top 10 schools," observes a second-year, who adds encouragingly, "S&C seems to like to recruit one or two top students from a large number of second-tier schools."

Most S&C associates agree it has become harder to get in the door. "As the legal recruiting market has shifted to the buy side," an M&A associate says, "selectivity [has] increased. Gone are the days of 130 summer associates." "In this market, you have to be a superstar," another attorney says. "Most of us here wouldn't be here if we'd had to go through interviews this year."

OUR SURVEY SAYS

Cult of perfectionists

Despite S&C's attempts in recent years to transition to a more open and friendly environment, it continues to foster what associates frequently refer to as a "cult of perfectionists." But "once past the baggage that comes with working to such a high standard, the culture is fun and social and provides for a good community," says a midlevel associate. A freshman adds, "Outsiders often mistake professionalism for stuffiness or pompous formalism. In reality, virtually all attorneys here are down to earth people who are focused on doing a good job for the firm's clients."

"Young associates often make friends and go out together," a junior associate reports. "Young partners wear business casual. Everybody calls each other by first name. If you have a question, you knock on someone's door – they're all open." Another attorney has found "a surprisingly large amount of diversity among personalities – laid-back, super-casual dressers to suit- and suspender-wearing types, lively happy-hour-goers to quiet intellectual types." "We've got everything from reality TV alums to archetypal tools," a freshman litigator concurs. "We go out regularly and end up discussing work for less than 10 percent of the evening. Not bad for a bunch of lawyers." ("And the people here can drink anyone under the table," another first-year brags. "We just don't do it at work.")

"If a client needs you, they need you"

Sullivan & Cromwell "is not a place that cares about hours or face time," says one senior associate. "What matters is that you're around when people need you and you don't disappear on a deal. The flip side is that if a client needs you, they need you. It doesn't matter that you haven't had a weekend off in three months, doesn't matter that your mother's in town for the first time in years." Another corporate attorney chides, "You shouldn't expect to work on front-page M&A deals if you aren't ready to commit long hours. That said, partners and senior associates are generally very respectful and accommodating when you have personal engagements."

"Inevitably, in your first two years," one senior associate cautions, "you can be left waiting until 10 p.m. and then be asked to work all night." A midlevel litigator concurs, "It's not the number of hours, but rather the unpredictability of the hours that is so dissatisfying." One senior associate advises that the focus on hours is inappropriate: "In seven years, I have never heard a high number of billable hours used as a positive criterion for evaluating anyone." Indeed, associates typically never learn how many hours they bill (though they're free to make their own calculations, if they're interested.) Instead, "skill, creativity and care are the only ways to advance."

Strong working relationships

"Partners have great respect for smart, hard-working lawyers," says one S&C veteran. "I have worked with many partners on a one-to-one basis," reports one third-year associate. "Every partner I have come into contact with has been very respectful and open."

Trust and responsibility come quickly at S&C to associates who earn it. "I am somewhat alarmed at being asked on a conference call to leap in with comments on a $100 million matter," a second-year marvels. "There is no limit to what an associate can do here," a senior associate exults. "I can work in any business field, on any type of deal and take on whatever responsibility I can handle." Despite the occasional fits of existential doubt that are the lot of any lawyer, most S&C associates seem to accept – and enjoy – their lot in life. "Even during the weeks when I was working until 3 a.m. every night and getting only three or four hours of sleep," one attorney recalls, "I did not dread coming to work in the morning."

Leading the pack

With its "unwritten policy to match the top-paying firms," S&C keeps its attorneys largely satisfied. "Bankers got fired," a corporate attorney gloats. "We got a bonus." In fact, "this year, S&C upped the bonus announced by other New York firms," confirming the widespread opinion that the firm "leads the pack on bonus and salary," especially since, as one first-year says, "there are no minimum billables. From all accounts, there are no unwritten minimum billables, either." "In this economy, if you are complaining with all the money they give us," a young litigator says, "you are in a dream world." Several associates do harbor such fantasies, of course, if only fleetingly. "You always wish you had more," opines one first-year associate, "but I don't think I could do better at any other law firm." Another veteran attorney notes how the economic downturn has affected the firm: "Bonuses dropped significantly while hours, in litigation at least, stayed the same or increased significantly."

With that in mind, it can be difficult to tell sometimes whether associates who stay at S&C do so because they love their jobs or because, in the current market, they can't imagine or risk going anywhere else. "Many people have expressed desire to leave," one second-year associate reports. "Once the market picks up, I expect many attorneys to do so." But several within the firm view the comings and goings as healthy; as one senior attorney explains, "The turnover before year four is considerable – and it is designed to be. The firm hires up to 100 people a year to find a handful of partners. Opportunities for people who leave are considerable and have continued to be throughout the market downturn."

Working hard to make a difference in diversity

"[S&C chairman] Rodgin Cohen seems legitimately dedicated to improving the retention of women at the firm," says one first-year female litigator, but the firm still has "a long way to go," counters a senior female associate. "You see pockets of effort, but I don't feel a true firm-wide commitment to improving the situation." (The firm indicates that three out of the four litigation partners announced in November 2002 are women; in addition, S&C named a woman to the eight-partner committee that manages the firm in 2003.) Another veteran attorney says the firm's lower retention rate among women "may be because of the work-comes-first-no-matter-what attitude around here, which can be difficult for women with young children." Although "there is an active group of women partners (especially junior partners) who are devoted to making the firm more female-friendly," many associates still perceive that more work remains to be done despite improvements such as on-site child care and part-time scheduling options. "They are making an effort to provide opportunities for women associates to interact with the women partners and discuss issues of particular interest to women," says one associate, but "at this point, it's mainly just a reason for a cocktail party."

Minority recruitment is focused on by management as "a major issue" at S&C, though it is a difficult one. A senior attorney observes, "The firm basically does the right thing, but it's a slow process." The firm reportedly does an "outstanding" job when it comes to making gays and lesbians feel welcome. "I have spoken with a few gay associates who have come to S&C because of its reputation," says one attorney. Insiders say there are nine openly gay partners at S&C.

Beige, Currier & Ives and officemates

Most New York associates have an opinion about their office space. Most of those opinions, sadly, are negative. A "space crunch" has kept junior associates cooped together in the same space in two and threes for as long as two years. Many junior associates call offices "cramped." Complains one, "As a second-year, I share a small office, and the papers are beginning to build up." The wait for a single office, according to New Yorkers, is "growing." (The firm says that, by its calculations, the wait is now actually shrinking due to space reconfigurations.) As far as the décor goes, insiders term it "old and dark," "oddly faux Colonial," "beige" and "dreadful." The firm's fondness for Currier and Ives prints doesn't go over well; one associate snarks that they "do not inspire creativity." "There's a reason Ja Rule filmed his video in front of the Cravath lobby and not ours," observes one associate. On the bright side, the newer floors are said to be "much nicer." "I understand the firm ran out of the 18th century prints," jokes one associate. Not everyone obsesses about over-beige office space; "We're not going to win any design competitions, but the space works fine," comments one associate. S&C says the firm is taking steps to alleviate the wait for single offices and that the wait is now down to 18-24 months.

The lack of satisfaction with offices appears to be limited to New York. Associates in Washington praise the "beautiful artwork." And, boasts one attorney working overseas, "All European offices recently moved to new locales, so the offices in Europe are generally very modern and spacious."

4

Davis Polk & Wardwell

450 Lexington Avenue
New York, NY 10017
Phone: (212) 450-4000
www.dpw.com

LOCATIONS

New York, NY (HQ)
Menlo Park, CA
Washington, DC
Frankfurt
Hong Kong
London
Madrid
Paris
Tokyo

MAJOR DEPARTMENTS/PRACTICES

Corporate
Litigation
Tax
Trusts & Estates

THE STATS

No. of attorneys: 656
No. of offices: 9
Summer associate offers: 101 out of 101 (2002)
Managing Partner: John Ettinger
Hiring Partner: Gail Flesher

BASE SALARY

New York, NY
1st year: $125,000
2nd year: $135,000
3rd year: $150,000
4th year: $165,000
Summer associate: $2,400/week

UPPERS

- High-level, sophisticated work for prestigious clients
- Respectful and supportive of women
- Relaxed work environment with "courteous, pleasant" coworkers

DOWNERS

- Sharing offices
- Feedback hard to come by, due to overly polite culture
- Perception that firm drags its feet when it comes to bonuses

NOTABLE PERKS

- Moving expenses, including broker's fees
- BlackBerrys
- In-house cafeteria
- Four weeks paternity leave, as well as maternity leave

THE BUZZ
WHAT ATTORNEYS AT OTHER FIRMS ARE SAYING ABOUT THIS FIRM

- "Prestigious and classy"
- "Cheap"
- "Strong in all areas"
- "The whitest of white shoes"

RANKING RECAP

Best in Region
#4 - New York

Best in Practice
#4 - Securities
#5 - Corporate
#5 - Tax
#6 - Mergers & Acquisitions
#7 - Litigation
#10 (tie) - Bankruptcy/Corporate Restructuring

Quality of Life
#4 - Training
#5 - Best 20 Law Firms to Work For
#6 - Selectivity
#10 - Hours
#14 - Satisfaction
#18 - Offices

Best in Diversity
#2 - Diversity for Women
#4 - Diversity for Minorities
#5 - Overall Diversity

EMPLOYMENT CONTACT

Ms. Bonnie Hurry
Director of Recruiting & Legal Staff Services
Phone: (212) 450-4144
Fax: (212) 450-5548
bonnie.hurry@dpw.com

QUALITY OF LIFE RANKINGS
[ASSOCIATES RATE THEIR OWN FIRM]

SATISFACTION
8.0
1 WORST ... 10 BEST

HOURS
7.6
1 WORST ... 10 BEST

ASSOCIATE/PARTNER RELATIONS
8.3
1 WORST ... 10 BEST

TRAINING
8.7
1 WORST ... 10 BEST

DIVERSITY
8.4
1 WORST ... 10 BEST

THE SCOOP

Davis Polk & Wardwell isn't just considered one of the most polite law firms in New York, it's also one of the most prestigious. The New York-based firm has a highly admired securities practice, top-notch litigation and corporate departments and some of the highest revenues of any law firm in the nation. Add an incredibly prestigious client list to the mix, and you've got a very impressive firm indeed.

They brought GE to life

Davis Polk & Wardwell's roots in New York date back to 1849 and the formation of Bangs & Stetson. Francis Bangs achieved prominence for his willingness to take on William "Boss" Tweed's stranglehold over city politics, while Francis Lynde Stetson's reputation rests on his role as chief legal counsel to J. P. Morgan. It was Stetson who helped Morgan create General Electric by combining several smaller electrical companies. The firm continues to be at the center of significant transactions and court cases, such as the $81 billion Exxon/Mobil merger and the landmark $206 billion tobacco settlement with 46 states. Davis Polk continues to serve as a primary counsel to JPMorgan Chase & Co. to this day along with other financial powerhouses such as Credit Suisse First Boston and Morgan Stanley, not to mention high-powered corporations such as Comcast, Ford, Verizon Wireless, Bertelsmann, Aetna and Telefonica.

Each of the three partners whose names are enshrined in the firm's current moniker excelled in different practices in the early part of the 20th century. Litigator John Davis argued 141 cases before the Supreme Court; corporate lawyer Frank Polk led the American delegation to the peace conference that crafted the Treaty of Versailles; Alan Wardwell's expertise lay in banking, and he was also on hand in Russia during the 1917 revolution.

Comcast's busy year

Comcast, one of DPW's primary corporate clients, kept the firm very active with a variety of substantial transactions throughout 2002. As part of the finishing touches on Comcast's $53 billion acquisition of AT&T's broadband business, the largest deal completed in 2002, Davis Polk advised the cable giant on an exchange offer and consent solicitation for $11.8 billion of AT&T debt and a related offering of $3.5 billion in new notes, as well as a $12.8 billion credit facility. Davis Polk also represented Comcast in the $9 billion restructuring of Time Warner Entertainment and in its sale of cable systems in four western states serving 317,000 subscribers.

Going for broke

Like many top-ranking law firms, Davis Polk has been heavily involved in the legal proceedings surrounding Enron's bankruptcy and the subsequent allegations of corporate malfeasance. Its dual role in the matter included advising JPMorgan Chase & Co. on Enron's $1.5 million DIP financing and Arthur Andersen in connection with the SEC probe of Enron's accounting practices. The firm also acted as defense counsel in the criminal proceedings against Andersen, which was ultimately convicted of obstruction of justice in connection with the destruction of much of Enron's paper trail.

DPW also had a hand in another mega-bankruptcy case, the $6.5 billion collapse of financial services provider Conseco. The firm represents Bank of America, which at $2 billion is the lead unsecured creditor in the bankruptcy proceedings, which began in December 2002 in Chicago federal court.

Going ... going ... gone

Davis Polk provided defense counsel to A. Alfred Taubman, the former chairman of auction house Sotheby's, during his trial on charges of conspiring with rival Christie's to eliminate financial competition between the two firms by fixing the commission rates on their auctions between 1993 and 1999. While the former head of Christie's, Sir Anthony Tennant, avoided arrest by fleeing to England (where the extradition treaty with the United States does not extend to comeptition laws), Taubman was convicted in December 2002 and sentenced to a year and a day in prison.

Fingers in every pie

DPW combines preeminence in New York and around the world to a degree unsurpassed by any other firm. The firm's fingerprints were all over the December 2002 acquisition of Panamerican Beverages by Coca-Cola FEMSA, a $3.62 billion deal that made the latter company the largest soft-drink bottler in Latin America and the second-largest Coca-Cola bottler in the world. Not only did the firm act as legal adviser to J.P. Morgan Securities, the financial advisers for Panamerican Beverages, it also separately advised Coca-Cola FEMSA's lenders, Morgan Stanley and JPMorgan Chase & Co.

DPW's presence also looms large throughout the international finance scene. The firm advised the Royal Bank of Scotland Group in late 2002 on a series of financings that raised a total of $1.75 billion dollars. During that same period, the firm also counseled a group of financers on a $1 billion offering by Germany's Landwirtschaftliche Rentenbank and advised Banco Santander-Chile, the largest bank in Chile, on its exchange of $300 million worth of subordinated notes for a new batch of notes and a cash payment.

Davis Polk also scored a substantial victory in November 2002 on behalf of the European division of global trading company Nissho Iwai, which had hired the firm to litigate against Korea First Bank over the bank's failure to honor the terms of a revolving standby letter of credit the bank had issued to a financially insolvent company which owed Nissho Iwai $75 million. Although the bank claimed that the letter of credit's terms did not require it to continue making payments without reimbursement from the account party, the New York Court of Appeals upheld a series of lower court rulings in Nissho Iwai's favor and awarded the company an aggregate judgment of $95 million. The decision was expected to carry great significance for New York's financial markets, where revolving standby letters of credit are commonly used to arrange financing.

Yahoo for Yahoo!

Davis Polk picked up Yahoo! as a client in 2002, when the firm's London office advised the ubiquitous Internet company on its September acquisition of a 15 percent stake in Finnish wireless Internet portal Sonera zed. Although Yahoo! U.S. counsel in that transaction was provided by the company's usual law firm, the esteemed Skadden, Arps, Slate, Meagher & Flom, DPW must have done something right. Attorneys from the firm's New York and Menlo Park offices got the call to represent Yahoo! in its takeover of search engine developer Inktomi just a few months later. The $280 million deal is expected to close in 2003.

DPW can often be found at the center of big deals in traditional media as well. The firm advised financial information provider Multex.com on its acquisition by Reuters in early 2003, a buyout valued at $261 million, right around the same time it advised longtime client Comcast on the sale of cable systems in four western states serving 317,000 subscribers.

Pubs and private eyes

Despite the general downturn in public M&A activity in 2002, Davis Polk's large private equity practice remained quite busy. In one of the sector's largest deals, DPW advised Morgan Stanley's Princes Gates Investors III on its $2.9 billion acquisition of the Unique Pub Company and Voyager Pub Group. The firm also worked on Welsh, Carson, Anderson & Stowe's purchase of a majority stake in US Investigations Services for roughly $1.05 billion.

Talk about your real estate deals

Governors Island, a small island just off the southern tip of Manhattan, was a valuable defensive location for American forces in the Revolution and the War of 1812, after which it became a permanent U.S. Army base. In 1966, the Army gave the island to the Coast Guard, who abandoned it in the mid-1990s, at which point New Yorkers began to clamor for ownership. It took years of congressional haggling and legal negotiations, in which Davis Polk served as an advisor to the U.S. government, but President Bush finally authorized the sale of Governors Island to the city and state of New York in January 2003 for the princely sum of $1. (That's even more of a bargain when you consider that the Dutch colonists who bought the island from the Indians in 1637 shelled out two axe heads, a string of beads and a handful of nails with an approximate total value of $24.)

Davis Polk played a role in the sale of another New York institution – or half of it, anyway. The New York Mets had been co-owned by Fred Wilpon and Nelson Doubleday since 1986, but in August 2002 DPW advised Wilpon as he bought out Doubleday's half of the team for a reported $131 million.

GETTING HIRED

A first-year tells us, "While the firm has always been very selective, primarily recruiting top students at top law schools, this year the recruiting process seemed to get even more selective." Says a midlevel insider: "It doesn't matter if you're No. 1 in your class – if you're unpleasant or exhibit poor judgment, you're not going to get an offer." "Callback interviews – and we give out a lot more than most firms so it means less – generally come down to personality. If you are a geek or an intellectual snob, forget it – even if you have the grades to prove it." A corporate attorney concurs, noting, "Whereas most top law firms in New York give offers to 90-100 percent of those who get callbacks, here it is 30-50 percent."

Says a first-year: "During the interview process, it appeared that we were one of the few firms that did not automatically give offers to people who received a callback." "Personality and non-law experiences are important. Partners seem to appreciate working with people with varying interests and past experiences." According to a senior associate, "The litigation department is loaded with former federal court clerks, so much so that it seems almost a prerequisite to employment. However, I think that the firm hires from a wider range of law schools than its peer firms and places more value on relative class rank and academic accomplishments than it does on the law school attended."

OUR SURVEY SAYS

Inside the halls of Davis Polk

Insiders characterize Davis Polk as "friendly and caring." The firm is "a very comfortable place to work," filled with "smart, smooth," "social," "cordial and collegial" people. "While sometimes a bit formal, the firm culture is very friendly and considerate. The associates, in particular, are real team players," says a fourth-year. "For a firm that does such high-level, high-pressure work," says a first-year, "the culture is very collegial and friendly."

"We have a great time together without the whole fratty feeling that describes the socializing of associates at some other firms. I really can't say enough good things about the people here – with the rare exception, they are all very pleasant to be around," marvels another junior associate.

According to a Menlo Park attorney, "The culture is much less formal than the New York office, and lawyers tend to socialize outside of work quite a bit." Another California attorney finds the environment in the firm's West Coast office "professional, friendly and hard working." One New York attorney says, "The people here are the finest people working in the field of law. Unfortunately," says this associate, "the junior-level work is atrociously boring." "The people are really nice," and there is "no screaming," a fourth-year tells us. "However," this source adds, "people that are dissatisfied with you won't always tell you."

A senior associate has observed an element of "guarded pleasantry" within Davis Polk. This source elaborates: There are "no screamers, but sometimes there are awkward elevator moments, when people just don't seem to have the energy or the inclination to engage in small talk." Other elevator customs are quainter and more endearing. "One very odd example of Davis Polk's white shoe sense of dignity and respect is use of the elevators. It is an unspoken rule but one observed by almost everyone that one allows all women to enter or exit the elevators first and then the men are allowed to exit roughly in order of seniority (actually, how old you look and how well dressed you are!). It's a bizarre, anachronistic tradition, but still polite and gentlemanly nonetheless, and people seem to appreciate it."

The "humane" firm

The hours that attorneys keep "depend a lot on the practice group." However, associates say that on the whole "the hours generally seem more humane than comparable firms." What's more, associates say they "work only when needed, not just to bill." "Whenever I'm here late," says a fourth-year, "it's because I'm working on something interesting. And if I'm here, so are the senior lawyers and partners staffed on the same deal." A first-year says he has a "modest but steady flow of billable work and no one hassling me about it." Others report, "Hours have been great since the corporate side has been slow." Not everyone has it so easy. "I work quite a bit," says a fifth-year, "but they don't pay people $200,000 to work 9 to 5." The "firm's investment in technology makes working from home at night and on weekends possible."

Just give us our bonus and we'll all get along

Associates report that their pay is "really good, in line with other top-tier firms" and "just right." A second-year offers this perspective regarding the firm's pay structure: "Davis Polk may do it grudgingly but is committed to matching and maintaining the top pay in New York other than Wachtell. While few New York associates will forget how Davis Polk's partners tried to eliminate associate bonuses in 2001, Davis Polk never came close to not matching its competitor firms' pay, and I doubt it would ever try and get away with paying less." "We all cannot be Wachtell, but Davis Polk is where it should be every year. Of course, if any more preemptive memos come out saying 'no bonus this year,' revolt will ensue," warns a senior associate. A part-time attorney complains, "The part-time pay scale isn't ideal. It is an hourly scale based on billables and some non-billables rather than a salary." While "compensation always ends up competitive with peer firms," insiders do feel "there is a perception that we tend to lag, at least in announcing bonuses, and so on."

"I feel like a brat," says a somewhat contrite first-year associate, "but I did look jealously at other firms' summer stipends and technology bonuses. And paying the bonus as salary as Skadden essentially does would mean less tax [for the associates]." (The firm disagrees with that inspired fiscal analysis.) "Then again, no compensation is tied to hours billed, [which is] a definite plus." Partly "because hours are not tied to bonuses," the firm has been able to create "an environment of teamwork rather than competition."

Laid-back partners

On a whole, the partners at Davis Polk are "very respectful," "don't take themselves too seriously," "take into account your opinions and are open for new views and suggestions." A corporate finance associate considers the partners to be "friendly" and says they are "willing to pitch in when necessary." "Partners generally seem to treat associates well," notes a second-year, "though there seems to be less interaction between partners and associates than at our peer firms, both on work matters and socially." There's really no mystery on how to earn a partner's respect: "If you work hard, you get treated well," says a fifth-year. The only complaint of an associate in the tax department is that "sometimes associates are not included in meetings or in discussions that would help the associate plan his or her time and work efforts properly." Other than that, "partners generally give consideration to associates' ideas and comments relating to work projects." A freshman is full of praise for the partners. "The best relationships I've formed here are with partners, not with fellow associates," says this contact. This source continues, "Each of the partners with whom I've worked has taken pride in educating me about the task at hand, offering guidance for my work and showing appreciation when something goes well."

All the pro bono you can handle

A large majority of associates express approval for the firm's pro bono activities. "The firm is genuinely proud of its pro bono projects and devotes a tremendous amount of resources" to pro bono work. "There is one associate solely in charge of coordinating and facilitating the program." And associates tell us, "We get a pro bono 'new matters' e-mail every day. There is no shortage of pro bono work if you want to take something on." "Pro bono work, both corporate and litigation, is strongly encouraged at all levels," insiders say. But a corporate associate reports there is "little to none on the corporate side." A colleague in the corporate department backs up that claim. "I would estimate that 90 percent of the pro bono work here is done by the litigators," this contact says. (Wrong, says the firm: In 2002, litigators did 69 percent of DPW's pro bono, compared to 31 percent handled by corporate, tax and trusts and estate lawyers.)

Skadden, Arps, Slate, Meagher & Flom LLP and Affiliates

4 Times Square
New York, NY 10036
Phone: (212) 735-3000
www.skadden.com

LOCATIONS

New York, NY (HQ)

Boston, MA • Chicago, IL • Houston, TX •
Los Angeles, CA • Newark, NJ • Palo Alto, CA •
Reston, VA • San Francisco, CA • Washington, DC •
Wilmington, DE • Beijing • Brussels • Frankfurt •
Hong Kong • London • Moscow • Paris • Singapore •
Sydney • Tokyo • Toronto • Vienna

MAJOR DEPARTMENTS/PRACTICES

Antitrust/Sports Law
Corporate Restructuring
E-Commerce
Intellectual Property & Technology
Investment Management
Litigation
M&A, Banking & Finance
Mass Torts
Real Estate
Tax, Trusts & Estates
White Collar Criminal Litigation

THE STATS

No. of attorneys: 1,800
No. of offices: 23
Summer associate offers: 101 out of 106 (2002)
Managing Partner: Robert C. Sheehan
Hiring Partner: Howard L. Ellin

BASE SALARY

New York, NY
1st year: $140,000
2nd year: $150,000
3rd year: $170,000
4th year: $185,000
5th year: $200,000
6th year: $212,000
7th year: $220,000
8th year: $225,000
Summer associate: $2,400/week

UPPERS

- Great training opportunities and informal mentoring
- High-profile work
- Welcoming, supportive of gays and lesbians

DOWNERS

- Long hours
- Junior associates share offices
- Screamers

NOTABLE PERKS

- "Fantastic" gym with trainers & classes (NY)
- $3,000 one-time technology allowance and annual $1,000 allowances after second year
- Generous dinner allowances
- Month-long sabbatical after five years at firm

THE BUZZ
WHAT ATTORNEYS AT OTHER FIRMS ARE SAYING ABOUT THIS FIRM

- "When you think sweatshop, you think Skadden"
- "Brilliant lawyers"
- "The Machine "
- "Superstars"

RANKING RECAP

Best in Region
#5 - New York

Best in Practice
#1 - Real Estate
#2 - Bankruptcy/Corporate Restructuring
#2 - Mergers & Acquisitions
#3 - Corporate
#3 - Securities
#3 - Tax
#5 (tie) - Antitrust
#5 - Litigation

Quality of Life
#3 - Pay

Best in Diversity
#20 - Overall Diversity

EMPLOYMENT CONTACT

Ms. Carol Sprague
Director of Legal Hiring
Phone: (212) 735-3815
Fax: (917) 777-3815
E-mail: csprague@skadden.com

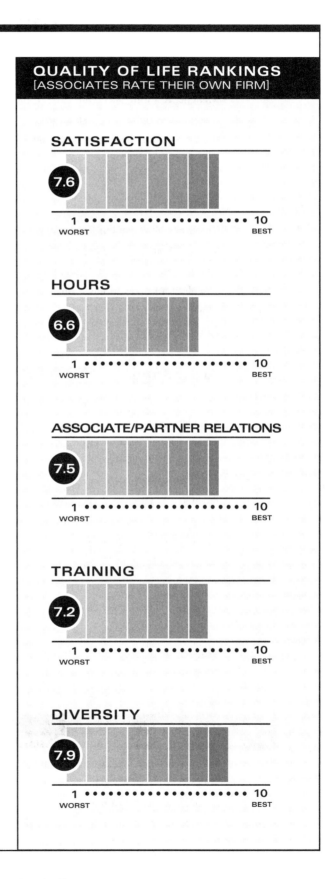

QUALITY OF LIFE RANKINGS
[ASSOCIATES RATE THEIR OWN FIRM]

SATISFACTION
7.6
1 WORST · · · · · · · · · · · · · · · · · 10 BEST

HOURS
6.6
1 WORST · · · · · · · · · · · · · · · · · 10 BEST

ASSOCIATE/PARTNER RELATIONS
7.5
1 WORST · · · · · · · · · · · · · · · · · 10 BEST

TRAINING
7.2
1 WORST · · · · · · · · · · · · · · · · · 10 BEST

DIVERSITY
7.9
1 WORST · · · · · · · · · · · · · · · · · 10 BEST

THE SCOOP

Armed with approximately 1,800 attorneys and 23 offices around the world, Skadden, Arps, Slate, Meagher & Flom has created one of the most respected full-service law firms in the world – not to mention the richest. These attorneys have practically turned litigation and M&A into an art. If there's a major lawsuit or M&A deal in the works, chances are Skadden Arps has a hand in the negotiations.

Beginnings

The firm was created in 1948 when co-workers Marshall Skadden, Les Arps and John Slate decided to leave their firm (the precursor to Dewey Ballantine) to start their own practice. They were just starting out and couldn't guarantee the firm's success, the partners told eager, young attorney Joseph Flom. Nevertheless, the opportunity excited him, and he became the firm's first associate. Flom's pluck paid off: He joined the partnership ranks in 1954. Partner Bill Meagher arrived in 1959, and in 1961 the firm adopted its current moniker.

Around the world in 23 offices

Looking now at the firm's international success, it may be hard to believe that for much of Skadden's existence it was a one-office firm. But it wasn't until 1973 that the firm opened its first branch office. "There was a partner we wanted to attract," explained Joseph Flom in a June 2002 interview with *Global Counsel* magazine, "but he would only go to a Boston office; so we opened one." A couple of years later, Skadden enticed a group of government attorneys to join its team by opening a Washington, D.C., office. After that measured start, the firm went on a tear, expanding rapidly stateside and abroad during the 1980s and 1990s. The firm continues its streak as the leading revenue producer among all U.S. law firms; in 2001, Skadden pulled in a hefty $1.225 billion, according to *The American Lawyer*.

Top of the charts

Corporate leaders at companies like Citigroup, Sears Roebuck, Merrill Lynch and Met Life call on Skadden when they need to bring in the big guns. And the firm doesn't fail to deliver. In June 2002, the firm played a major role in negotiating Bank One's $255 million purchase of Skadden client Polaroid. The king of instant film developing had been in bankruptcy proceedings prior to the deal, which gave Bank One a 65 percent stake in the company.

According to a 2002 Fortune 500 survey, Skadden represents 43 of the top 100 global companies. When looking at the entire Fortune 500, that figure more than triples to 154 companies. Of course, the foundation of its international reputation is built on its standing as a top firm in the U.S., where Skadden serves 53 of the top 100 companies and 168 of the leading 500 corporations. Continuing a streak that dates back to 1988, Skadden was first on *The National Law Journal's* "Who Defends

Corporate America?" list and *Corporate Counsel's* "Who Represents America's Biggest Companies?" list in 2002. Both publications survey leading U.S. companies regarding which firms they turn to for outside counsel. In 2002, Skadden was also the top U.S. M&A advisor based on total dollar value of the deals, according to Thomson Financial.

Let's make some deals

These days, failing corporations mean big business, and Skadden has come to the rescue of many beleaguered corporations as they undergo financial restructuring. The firm participated in the reorganization of British communications company NTL and will reportedly receive a $4 million reward for its efforts – a figure nearly twice that of the other firms involved. Skadden navigated retail giant Kmart through the rough waters of reorganization following its bankruptcy filing. The company emerged from bankruptcy in May 2003. Near the end of 2002, Skadden signed on to represent Massachusetts-based networking company Genuity Inc. in its quest for bankruptcy protection. Skadden also represented US Airways in its Chapter 11 restructuring. (US Airways emerged from Chapter 11 in March 2003.)

In addition to its expertise in the bankruptcy arena, Skadden is also known for its prowess in litigation and M&A. January 2003 found the firm fighting on behalf of client DaimlerChrysler. Former Chrysler Corp. investors filed a $13 billion suit charging that Daimler-Benz gained their approval for the merger through dishonest means. Compaq Computer Corp. sought Skadden's help in its highly publicized $25 billion merger with Hewlett-Packard Company. After many ups and downs – including the objections of board director Walter Hewlett – the firm was able to congratulate itself on a job well done when the merger was finalized in May 2002. Citigroup called on the firm in 2002 for assistance in its $5.8 billion acquisition of Golden State Bancorp, just as it had the previous year when it picked up Grupo Financiero for $12.6 billion.

On the move

Used to defending high-powered corporations, Skadden recently found itself in a position to which it's not accustomed. The firm was subpoenaed in connection with its representation of Enron. The court-appointed examiner in the Enron bankruptcy requested documents and testimony in February 2003 from attorneys at Skadden and 23 other firms in an effort to decipher the real numbers behind the energy company's doctored books.

Despite its top-tier status, Skadden is not immune to the occasional partner defection. Early in 2003, the firm experienced two such losses. It was reported by *The Lawyer* in January 2003 that partners Jonathan Pedersen and Vincent Pisano were leaving to join the New York office of Kirkland & Ellis. Pedersen, who had formerly headed Skadden's Hong Kong office, briefly became the subject of gossip in 2002 when he announced that he would leave Skadden to join another firm, only to rescind the announcement a few days later. Pisano's departure was equally noteworthy: He had spent 25 years with the firm, working with such clients as Drexel Burnham Lambert.

GETTING HIRED

Let's see some enthusiasm

"First and foremost," a senior associate advises, "a lawyer must be bright to be hired at Skadden. In addition, however, the person must be able to put the quality of the work product ahead of his or her desire for personal recognition." Another attorney emphasizes, "Have a personality; boring people don't cut it here. Also, be enthusiastic about the work; everyone we see is smart, so your enthusiasm for the job is of primary importance."

"I have seen lots of candidates called in for interviews but only the very, very best get offers," says a second-year associate. Skadden appears to view law school transcripts with less ruthlessness than some of its competitors. "The partners seem to look past GPA and school to find interesting and bright people," a new litigator observes. "We have our share of Harvard alums, but several of the partners went to Northeastern-type schools as well." A senior attorney calls Skadden "much more concerned with how and what you've done in school than where you went" and insists that "if you think an offer is assured because you went to Yale, you're dead wrong." "There are definitely some people here who were not academic standouts," says an M&A associate, but they must be "immensely personable and very capable practical lawyers." But that may already be changing. "With the market as tight as it is," a first-year notes, "the firm's emphasis on grades has really increased."

OUR SURVEY SAYS

Just call him Joe

"For a firm of Skadden's size and reputation," one senior attorney confesses, "the culture is very laid back." The "friendly, honest, busy" attorneys at Skadden are "very informal — even Joe Flom is just 'Joe.'" Moreover, there's "lots of fun to be had when serious work isn't being done." One freshman associate says she's found "the right balance between laid back and professional," and although the culture in some offices "tends to be cliquish," associates generally find Skadden "lives up to its work hard/play hard reputation." Another new arrival says, "It's very easy to be yourself here. The rumors that describe our office as cutthroat just aren't true."

Screamers and ghosts

Most of Skadden's partners, especially in New York, are "reasonable and helpful," except for a handful of "glaring and notable exceptions." The litigation practice, for example, "has its share of screamers and ghosts – those partners who head the case you work on but you have never met." Associates in Los Angeles say "lack of respect for an associate's personal time and weekends is like a virus" and that partners "don't care about your personal life or problems – so don't bother them." Other associates throughout the firm think of certain partners as "Jekyll and Hyde;" they can be "cordial in everyday relations but [have] no compunction about placing demands without regard to other commitments." But others insist that while "it's not a warm-fuzzy relationship" by any means, "partners are not demanding," and "you are treated appropriately and professionally."

The relationship is simple, says one litigator: "They pay us a ton of money, and in exchange we work hard on demand." The "intense" "roller-coaster ride" of a Skadden work schedule is "either crazy or dead," but the "unsurprisingly long" hours are commonly regarded as "a tradeoff for getting interesting, fast-paced deals." Even senior associates feel the pressure, reporting, "You are basically expected to be in the office at least until mid-evening even when the work is not piled up. When the work is piled up, you may as well have a cot in your office." Lately, however, since "the economy's down," "corporate work's been light for the most part." One rookie attorney notes gratefully, "I've pulled one all-nighter but am usually out by 7 p.m."

Deal central

"If you want to do deal-based corporate work, this is the place to be," Skadden associates acknowledge. "Whether working on a corporate takeover or an amicus brief to the U.S. Supreme Court," a midlevel associate elaborates, "the work provides constant stimulation." And not just for senior attorneys. "I have been exposed to top margin work from the day I arrived," boasts a first-year litigator. "Corporate work is very diverse," agrees a second-year. "You can get involved with a wide array of projects from securities offerings to venture capital financings to mergers and acquisitions."

"No one is interested in seeing you fall on your face," says one young associate, so Skadden offers first-years plenty of training, "so much that it is a bit overwhelming at times." The "extensive" sessions are "mandatory," and "if you don't show up for a training program, you hear about it." Although several more seasoned associates note the firm has recently begun providing midlevel training programs, most still view Skadden as "the kind of place that offers training if you want it, but also lets people spread their wings," with help always available. "The informal mentoring I receive as part of being on a deal team," says a sophomore associate, "is far better at teaching me the skills I need to develop to be successful." A veteran attorney agrees, "There is no better training than the work itself."

Lawyers first

"People matter" at Skadden, insists one senior attorney, and others will gladly tell you the firm "talks the talk about diversity, and seems to walk the walk – at least with respect to entry-level and lateral hiring." "When a minority lawyer walks into the room," one midlevel litigator comments, "most people see a lawyer first," and only note gender or ethnicity as an afterthought. "Women are treated very well here," agrees one young female attorney, though other women at the firm believe "it is very hard to work Skadden associate hours and raise a child." And there are "not enough female partners," especially in the corporate practice, where "there are several great candidates who are now eligible." At least one female associate thinks the problem might be that "women who want to get substantive work experience without having to act like fraternity boys" have difficulty attracting the mentorship of male partners, though it's widely acknowledged that "mentoring really happens" between female partners and associates.

The firm gets especially high marks for its "open, comfortable" treatment of gay and lesbian attorneys; some New York associates call Skadden "the best in the city in this respect." (Associates in other offices detect a less welcoming attitude.) "I have never encountered any difficulty with respect to my orientation," one openly gay attorney reports. "In contrast, as a summer associate I was paired with other out attorneys to serve as mentors, and the firm has a few vocal partners who ensure the firm takes tables at several community fund-raising events." The firm also hosts an annual "diversity dinner" to honor its gay and lesbian associates.

The sweet smell of success

New York associates love the "beautiful and well-kept" Skadden offices in Times Square's Conde Nast building, praising "everything from the waterfall in the lobby to our reception areas." Apart from universal frustration among junior associates about having to share "cramped" quarters for the first two years, the attorneys admire the "simple and modern" interior design and "daring" art collection. "Everything about the offices reeks of success," boasts one second-year. Attorneys in the firm's other offices echo the praise. A recent remodel in the Washington office "helps a lot," but a few associates still cringe inwardly at the "uniformly beige" décor. Some associates in Los Angeles dismiss their remodeling job as a switch "from Office Depot to IKEA," but others find the environment "comfortable and stylish without being oppressive or overbearing." But Beantown Skaddenites have few complaints; their "large windows" offer up the "best views in Boston."

Commitment to service

Skadden takes great pride in its pro bono program, and expects everyone to get involved. New associates often feel "peer pressure" to take on pro bono cases "within the first few weeks." A full-time coordinator "sends e-mails at least once a day" with fresh pro bono assignments available, and if there's an issue associates want to take on "and they don't have it yet, they will find what you want." Still, "when push comes to shove," several associates comment that "it can be difficult to fit in more than a few pro bono hours per month." "If it is a partner's pet project, you get support," cautions one attorney, "otherwise paying work is expected to take precedence."

Financial pacesetters

"People come here for the money," is one midlevel attorney's frank assessment, and Skadden doesn't disappoint. "Every associate at Skadden's peer firms thanks Skadden for locking in their bonuses in our base salary," one associate preens, while another rejoices that while "other firms are freezing salaries, so far Skadden has not done so." Junior associates find the high base pay "a godsend in this fragile economy," though attorneys who have been around for a while gripe that the firm "begins to lag behind" its competitors after the first few years, especially since it "slashed the pay raises" recently. Plus, "bonuses were sub-par this year," a senior associate complains. "I'm still bitter." He's not the only one; a second-year associate wants to know, "Why are bonuses so much less than the boom years when the reality is that [profit-per-partner] hasn't dropped?"

6

Simpson Thacher & Bartlett

425 Lexington Avenue
New York, NY 10017
Phone: (212) 455-2000
www.simpsonthacher.com

LOCATIONS

New York, NY (HQ)
Los Angeles, CA
Palo Alto, CA
Hong Kong
London
Tokyo

MAJOR DEPARTMENTS/PRACTICES

Bankruptcy
Corporate (M&A, Private Equity, Securities, Banking and Project Finance)
Executive Compensation & Benefits
Exempt Organizations
Intellectual Property
Litigation
Personal Planning
Real Estate
Tax

THE STATS

No. of attorneys: 681
No. of offices: 6
Summer associate offers: 83 out of 86 (2002)
Chairman: Richard I. Beattie
Hiring Partners: Paul Curnin and Marissa Wesely

BASE SALARY

New York, NY
1st year: $125,000
2nd year: $135,000
3rd year: $150,000
4th year: $170,000
5th year: $190,000
6th year: $205,000
7th year: $220,000
8th year: $235,000
Summer associate: $2,404/week

UPPERS

- Serious prestige
- "Almost fanatical" commitment to pro bono work
- Staffed by smart and talented colleagues

DOWNERS

- Grueling hours
- Lack of communication between partners and associates
- Over-crowding in NY office

NOTABLE PERKS

- Car rides home
- "The world's best cookies"
- Free Starbucks coffee
- Services of real estate attorney for home purchase

THE BUZZ
WHAT ATTORNEYS AT OTHER FIRMS ARE SAYING ABOUT THIS FIRM

- "Make sure to buy the vacation insurance – you'll be canceling yours soon enough "
- "Nicest of the Big Boys"
- "One of the best on all fronts"
- "Country club"

RANKING RECAP

Best in Region
#6 - New York

Best in Practice
#5 - Mergers & Acquisitions
#6 - Corporate
#7 - Securities
#9 (tie) - Bankruptcy/Corporate Restructuring
#10 - Tax

Quality of Life
#12 - Selectivity
#16 - Pro Bono

EMPLOYMENT CONTACT

Ms. Dee Pifer
Director of Legal Employment
Phone: (212) 455-2687
Fax: (212) 455-2502
E-mail: dpifer@stblaw.com

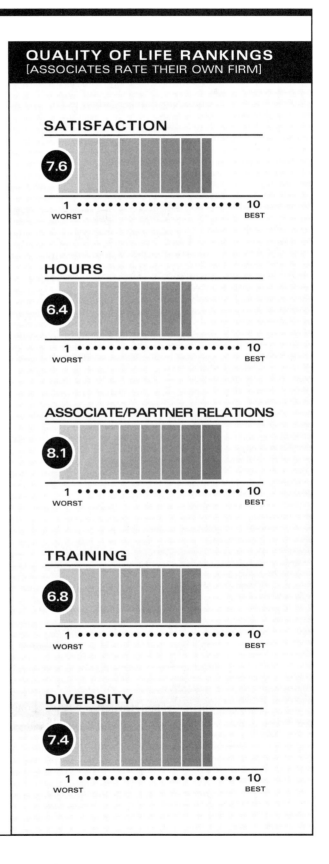

QUALITY OF LIFE RANKINGS
[ASSOCIATES RATE THEIR OWN FIRM]

SATISFACTION
7.6
1 WORST · · · · · · · · · · · · · · · · 10 BEST

HOURS
6.4
1 WORST · · · · · · · · · · · · · · · · 10 BEST

ASSOCIATE/PARTNER RELATIONS
8.1
1 WORST · · · · · · · · · · · · · · · · 10 BEST

TRAINING
6.8
1 WORST · · · · · · · · · · · · · · · · 10 BEST

DIVERSITY
7.4
1 WORST · · · · · · · · · · · · · · · · 10 BEST

THE SCOOP

Founded in 1884 by three Columbia University Law School grads, Simpson Thacher & Bartlett is one of the oldest and most revered Wall Street firms. With expertise in complex litigation, mergers and acquisitions, corporate governance, banking and capital markets and securities, the firm has established a reputation as one of the most sought-after corporate advisors. Plus, it's considered a firm with a healthy respect for courtesy and good manners.

In the beginning

Soon after its founding, the firm began to build a strong reputation among railroad and utilities companies. One of its early cases involved representing the Baltimore & Ohio Railroad in a suit against Western Union Telegraph Company. In 1895 the firm served as advisors during the formation of Brooklyn Union Gas, which continued to serve the New York City borough until it combined with Long Island Lighting Company to form Keyspan Energy in 1997. General Electric first retained the firm in the 1890s and has been a major client to this day. By the 1920s, the firm had become distinguished for its work as advisor on bond issues for bridge and other infrastructure projects and was a pioneer in the area of cooperative apartment complexes. In January 1952, Simpson Thacher assumed the role of general counsel to Manufacturers Trust Company. The firm subsequently handled Manufacturers Trust's merger with Hanover Trust, and then the union of Manufacturers Hanover Trust with Chemical Bank, Chemical Bank's absorption into Chase and Chase's coming together with JP Morgan.

Big deals, low profile

You're not likely to hear the name "Simpson Thacher & Bartlett" often on the nightly news, but the firm's attorneys are frequently the advisors behind the corporations featured in some of today's biggest headline-making business stories. Attorneys from Simpson advised Blackstone Capital Partners IV LP Group in raising a record $6.45 billion private equity fund, as well as assisting the Washington-based Carlyle Group in the creation of its latest venture capital fund in October 2002. The $600 million fund was one of the largest of the year. American Media and its parent, Evercore Capital Partners, have put their trust in the folks at Simpson quite a bit as of late. The firm advised Evercore on its January 2003 acquisition of Weider Publications, a publisher of health and fitness titles. The following month, a team of Simpson lawyers assisted Evercore in a $1.5 billion recapitalization of American Media. Around the same time, the firm was involved in another big media-related deal when clients Thomas H. Lee Partners, Bain Capital and The Blackstone Group purchased educational and trade publisher Houghton Mifflin for $1.65 billion.

The firm has the largest litigation department in New York and is the principal outside counsel to JP Morgan Chase, Accenture and Travelers and has conducted significant trials for each of these clients in recent years. Simpson Thacher is currently representing Swiss Re in its high-profile courtroom battle against World Trade Center leaseholder Larry Silverstein, as chronicled in Steven

Brill's latest book, *After*. The firm is also acting as counsel to the independent board members of drug company ImClone, which is under suspicion of providing inside information to former CEO Sam Waksal's family and friends, most notably Martha Stewart. Beleaguered telecom giant WorldCom has turned to Simpson for litigation assistance during its bankruptcy proceeding.

The public face of Simpson

If any one person can be considered the public face of Simpson, Richard Beattie would be it. Legal insiders consider the former Marine Corps fighter pilot and current Simpson chairman charismatic and high-spirited. (The sexagenarian is known to ride a Harley from time to time.) But mostly, he's revered for his skills at the bargaining table. Beattie was a player in such groundbreaking cases as the Kohlberg Kravis Roberts leveraged buyout of RJR Nabisco. Law isn't his only passion; another is the improvement of public education. In January 2003, Beattie was tapped by former IBM CEO Louis V. Gerstner as a member of the newly formed Teaching Commission, a task force of educators and business leaders created by Gerstner whose focus is improving the quality of teaching in public schools. As the founder of a similar organization focused on improving New York City's public schools, Beattie appears to be more than up to the challenge.

Honors abound

Simpson Thacher captured the No.-1 position on Thomson Financial's ranking of firms completing the most M&A deals in 2002: 52 transactions totaling $193 billion. Thomson also ranked the firm at No. 1 worldwide for equity issuances for U.S. issues. Then Simpson grabbed the No.-8 spot on *Corporate Board Member's* 2002 list of the top 20 firms corporations prefer to work with on national matters and tied for No. 20 on the magazine's list of the most admired firms. And it was the only New York law firm among the five finalists for *American Lawyer's* Best Litigation Department of the Year award. Additionally, Chambers & Partners ranked Simpson Thacher No. 2 in their survey of New York's top 10 firms and No. 1 in the following practice areas: antitrust, banking and finance, litigation, private equity (buyouts and investment) and private equity (fund formation). The *New York Law Journal* named a Simpson case involving school funding as one of the Top Cases of 2002 in its February 2003 issue. Simpson Thacher had previously garnered accolades and the 2001 Pro Bono Award for this case from *The National Law Journal*. The firm's hard work resulted in a victory for its client, the Campaign for Fiscal Equality, which argued that New York City's poorest children were receiving an inadequate education. But the initial ruling was overturned in June 2002. Simpson Thacher attorneys are representing the Campaign for Fiscal Equality in an appeal to the New York State Court of Appeals, which was argued in May 2003.

Things change, but not much

Although they do exist, lateral partners at Simpson Thacher are almost as rare as a long-term Hollywood marriage. It's well known that the firm is protective of its culture and prefers to create partners from the associate ranks rather than bring in partners from other firms. So it was big news

when two antitrust partners left Clifford Chance to join Simpson in February 2003. "It's the first time we've had more than one" lateral partner join the firm at the same time, Beattie said in an interview with *Legal Times*. So does that mean Simpson may abandon its bias toward homegrown partners? Not according to Beattie, who also told the reporter, "I don't see one or two carefully selected lateral partners as changing our culture."

GETTING HIRED

More than words

"We are looking for top candidates" who "have something more to offer than a great resume," a third-year associate explains to would-be Simpsonites. A colleague in the litigation department concurs, explaining, "Great grades with a big ego, no personality or no life outside of school or work is not typically well-received." Some, however, see things a bit differently. "Grades are key," says a midlevel, "which is a shame because being a good law school student does not necessarily translate into being a good lawyer." In addition, emphasis is placed on a candidate's school, with a top-10 school being the program of choice. "If you are from another law school, I think it can be very difficult," a litigation attorney tells us.

Other insiders tell us that Simpson Thacher "seems to appreciate candidates with an uncommon background," especially those who "have done something else besides law." A New York associate confides, "The callback interviews tend to be relaxed. I have the impression they are meant to establish if the candidate would fit in" at the firm because "law-related questions are rarely asked." "In this climate, we seem to be taking on the highest-qualified candidates; people who would have received an offer two years ago, don't get invited back for callbacks." A London associate reveals, "The firm is very choosy, especially when it comes to hiring laterals." Indeed, the picture seems somewhat bleak for lateral hires.

OUR SURVEY SAYS

Mostly work and a little play

"Simpson is an intriguing blend of fast-paced and cutting-edge legal work in an environment that retains a nice degree of civility," remarks a senior associate who may have a career as a copywriter should he decide to leave the law. A corporate attorney offers this summation: "The firm ranges from super-friendly to very formal and stand-offish. It is a huge firm so whoever you are, you can find your niche somewhere here." According to a litigation attorney, the culture at Simpson Thacher is "extremely friendly and collegial – almost but not quite to the point of being laid back." Others say the firm is "dignified," "traditional" and "appropriately formal." One source says

Simpson has a "somewhat rigid culture" in part because "attorneys have to log in and log out each day, and anyone at the firm can check to see whether you're in the office. But overall, people are friendly." Big Apple Simpsonites tell us the vibe at the firm is "friendly but not particularly social," possibly "because many attorneys have families they want to spend time with" or simply because "most people in New York City want to have a separate life outside the office." A first-year associate in New York sees the office environment in a different light, saying, "Simpson is pretty buttoned-up. While people cannot be described as formal per se, in their interactions with others at the firm generally people are aloof." "The Los Angeles office is friendly and fairly close. There are some very enthusiastic lawyers running the show here," gushes a happy second-year. In the London office, attorneys "socialize together fairly regularly – including the partners."

Good work if you can get it

Insiders say Simpson Thacher is the place for those desiring "challenging work for interesting and high-profile – and demanding – clients." A Londoner says, "Associates are given lots of responsibility and client contact from a very early stage but within a very good support structure." "Some groups, including mine, have been busy nonstop, while others have had very little work to spread around," confides a trusts and estates attorney. That has left some associates, especially those of a junior rank, with a desire for more work – or at least work that is more fulfilling. "I am still waiting for an assignment that puts my law degree to use," one first-year associate tells us. Says another freshman, "I am learning a lot and honing necessary skills. The cases are just not that interesting to me." Others are in awe of the quality of the work at Simpson. "Simpson gets lots of high-profile, *Wall Street Journal* front-page-type cases," a fourth-year shares. This source reveals, "There are pros and cons to this. The cases are exciting and have billions of dollars at risk, but they tend to be document intensive, drag on for years and ultimately settle because there's too much money on the line to risk an adverse jury verdict."

Bonuses: follow the leader

"Everyone wants to be paid more. I certainly do," admits an eighth-year associate. "But Simpson matches the top compensation of other big law firms, so you basically can't do any better." A second-year associate wisecracks, "We are paid well enough to have a very nice lifestyle – if we could get out of the office, that is." A freshman describes the compensation as "standard." However, this contact adds, "Considering the number of hours we work, the salary is insufficient." Many associates give Simpson Thacher credit for matching compensation given by other leading firms. But several complain that the firm is "more of a follower than a leader in the compensation area. They'll wait to see what their peer firms are doing on bonuses, say, and then match." According to a senior associate with a long memory, "Simpson made glaring mistakes in the past by not matching the bonuses given by its peer firms, but the firm now seems determined not to repeat those mistakes."

Despite such comments, the vast majority of Simpson associates give the firm high marks for compensation. A New York attorney explains the disconnect, saying that Simpson "always is the last to announce bonuses and tries to lowball the bonuses, only to cave and match the market long after other top law firms match." This "really rubs associates the wrong way," according to the source. However, an overwhelming number of associates feel "Simpson is up there with the top firms in terms of compensation." And at least one attorney is able to take the whole bonus thing in stride. "Who cares, as long as the check hits your account?"

Time management

No doubt about it. Life as a Simpson Thacher attorney means putting in long hours. And we do mean *long* hours. As is typical of life at a high-powered firm, hours tend to be "cyclical" and "unpredictable." According to a real estate attorney, hours can "fluctuate a lot, from leaving at 6:30 p.m. to working all night." A junior litigation attorney describes hours as "a roller coaster. One month you are swamped, the next there is a lot of downtime. Overall, though, the hours are very fair." A colleague echoes that sentiment, saying, "Some weeks are crazy, others are manageable. It's the nature of litigation and being an attorney." A second-year associate whose opinion of the hours isn't nearly as rosy, says, "I think the hours are crazy, and the firm does nothing to regulate it. They want you to bill, bill, bill, and they do not care what suffers as a consequence, whether it be your sanity, health, marriage or other relationships."

There is some disagreement as to the need to put in face time at the firm. Even though the slow economy means more manageable workloads for many lawyers, some Simpsonites complain that they "are still expected to spend long hours and put in face time at the firm, even if it just means sitting around surfing the Net." Most say they "don't feel any pressure to put in face time."

And speaking of the economy, several associates say they do have less work now, but none expresses anxiety about job security because of it. Reviews of the firm's part-time work options are mixed, with respondents saying everything from there is "enough flexibility and autonomy to make it work" to "assignments given to flex-time lawyers are the worst of the worst."

Working relationships

Insiders report, "Although there does not tend to be much overall camaraderie between partners and associates, individual interactions are usually pleasant and can be rather friendly," and "for the most part, partners tend to value associates' opinions and contributions." Los Angeles partners "are pretty great to work with, and most give a healthy amount of guidance and are very respectful of people at all levels," according to an associate in that office. "Like anything, it depends on who you work with," shrugs a noncommittal New Yorker. Another New Yorker confirms, "There are some great partners here," but adds, "for the most part, there is an 'us and them' mentality." Perhaps this is because "in some groups, junior associates work closely with partners, whereas in others – such as M&A – a fairly strict hierarchy is observed where junior associates might hardly ever meet the partner whose matter they are working on."

Pro bono fanatics

The firm's commitment to pro bono work is "a source of pride" for "many at the firm." The firm "encourages associates to work on pro bono matters," and associates happily report that "pro bono counts towards our billables." "In my experience, pro bono matters are given almost exactly the same respect as billable matters," shares a second-year. "Since corporate associates are slow in their other work, partners almost expect that they will take on pro bono projects with their down time. Partners are often deeply involved in pro bono cases as well." An Angeleno goes so far as to say management is "almost fanatical with their support for pro bono." Others are more critical, noting, "There is very little internal support to help one get involved." "The firm likes to give a lot of lip service regarding its dedication to pro bono work, but makes it clear that under no circumstances should paying clients take a back seat to pro bono clients," quips a corporate associate. Eager to provide its litigation associates with trial experience, Simpson Thacher has agreed to try a number of "trial-ready" cases on behalf of the New York City Corporation Counsel's Office.

Cleary, Gottlieb, Steen & Hamilton

One Liberty Plaza
New York, NY 10006-1470
Phone: (212) 225-2000
www.cgsh.com

LOCATIONS

New York, NY (HQ)
Washington, DC
Brussels
Frankfurt
Hong Kong
London
Milan
Moscow
Paris
Rome
Tokyo

MAJOR DEPARTMENTS/PRACTICES

Antitrust • Capital Markets • Corporate, Finance &
Infrastructure • International Sovereign Debt &
Privatization • Litigation • M&A • Real Estate • Tax •
Trusts & Estates • Workouts & Bankruptcy

THE STATS

No. of attorneys: 785
No. of offices: 11
Summer associate offers: 80 out of 80 (2002)
Managing Partner: Peter Karasz
Hiring Partner: Sheldon H. Alster

BASE SALARY

New York, NY
1st year: $125,000
2nd year: $135,000
3rd year: $150,000
4th year: $170,000
5th year: $190,000
6th year: $205,000
7th year: $220,000
8th year: $235,000
Summer associate: $2,404/week

UPPERS

• Prestigious international practice
• Strong commitment to pro bono work
• Respectful and supportive partners

DOWNERS

• Trouble retaining black attorneys
• "Randomness" of assigning process
• Scant review process

NOTABLE PERKS

• Fabulous cafeteria
• Wine and cheese on Fridays (NY)
• Free weekly Spanish lessons
• Free gym membership at fancy-schmancy
  Equinox (NY)

THE BUZZ
WHAT ATTORNEYS AT OTHER FIRMS ARE SAYING ABOUT THIS FIRM

• "Chic"
• "Easy to get lost in the crowd"
• "All-around great firm"
• "Overrated"

RANKING RECAP

Best in Region
#7 - New York

Best in Practice
#2 - Tax
#3 - Antitrust
#6 - Securities
#7 - Corporate
#8 - Mergers & Acquisitions

Quality of Life
#2 - Offices
#11 - Selectivity
#19 - Best 20 Law Firms to Work For

Best in Diversity
#7 - Diversity for Gays and Lesbians
#8 - Overall Diversity
#11 - Diversity for Minorities

EMPLOYMENT CONTACT

Mr. Jaime E. Martinez
Manager of Legal Recruitment
Phone: (212) 225-3163
E-mail: jmartinez@cgsh.com

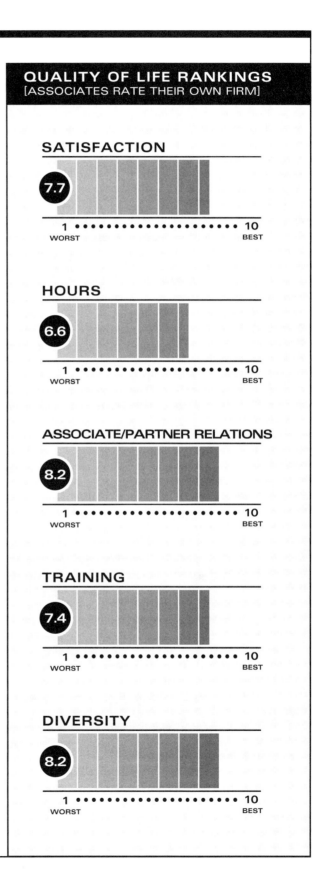

QUALITY OF LIFE RANKINGS
[ASSOCIATES RATE THEIR OWN FIRM]

SATISFACTION
7.7
1 WORST   10 BEST

HOURS
6.6
1 WORST   10 BEST

ASSOCIATE/PARTNER RELATIONS
8.2
1 WORST   10 BEST

TRAINING
7.4
1 WORST   10 BEST

DIVERSITY
8.2
1 WORST   10 BEST

THE SCOOP

Cleary, Gottlieb, Steen & Hamilton is known among New York law firms as the "quirky" one – and that reputation suits it just fine. From the beginning, the firm has desired to stand apart from the pack through its commitment to individuality and high ethical standards.

Bucking trends since day one

Cleary Gottlieb's founding partners walked away from successful careers at Root, Clark, Buckner & Ballantine in 1946, fed up with a competitive ethos that rewarded attorneys strictly on the basis of how much business they brought to the firm and how long they spent on their cases. The firm decided it would reward its associates strictly on the basis of seniority, a practice that has since become standard at many law firms.

The founding partners continued to excel in their new surroundings. George Cleary became known as one of the leading tax attorneys of his era, while Fowler Hamilton would eventually serve as director of the U.S. Agency for International Development under President Kennedy. George W. Ball, who also joined the Kennedy administration as an undersecretary in the State Department, was instrumental in building up Cleary Gottlieb's international practice, which began with a Paris office in 1949. The firm continued to build its European presence in Brussels and London over the years, then shifted its attention to Asia in the 1980s, opening offices in Hong Kong in 1980 and Tokyo in 1987. The firm returned its attention to Europe in the following decade, establishing outposts in Moscow, Frankfurt, Rome and Milan.

Today, the firm frequently provides the governments of foreign nations with counsel on international capital market transactions and has found especially fertile ground for this line of work in Latin and South America. It has represented Argentina in its efforts to resolve financial disputes brought about by the government's defaulting on several bonds after the national economy tanked during a 1998 recession that continued into the 21st century. Cleary advised the Chilean government on two multimillion-dollar bond issues in 2002; that same year, it began working with the Peruvian government on that nation's first international capital markets transactions in nearly eight decades, providing guidance on three deals that raised a total of $2 billion. The firm has also advised in debt offerings by Costa Rica, the Dominican Republic and Colombia.

The capital market scene

Cleary Gottlieb nabs its share of corporate capital market transactions as well. Within a two-week period beginning in late January 2003, shortly after being named the designated underwriters' counsel for Citigroup, the firm advised in the issuance of $2 billion in floating rate notes, another $2 billion in fixed rate notes and $1.1 billion in capital securities. Cleary also advised the main underwriter on those deals, Salomon Smith Barney, on a $30 million offering of equity-linked securities tied to American Express Group's common stock. The equity-linked security is a product developed by Cleary and Salomon that gives investors higher semi-annual returns than on standard bonds of comparable maturity, guaranteeing the payment of the full principal at maturity or, should the linked stock's price drop by an agreed-upon percentage, comparable shares of that common stock.

Outpacing the competition when it comes to competition

Cleary is recognized internationally as a leader in antitrust law (or, as they call it in Europe, competition), with a practice group that encompasses more than 100 attorneys, 20 of them partners, in Washington, D.C., and five European cities. The firm acted as antitrust counsel in four of the biggest mergers in recent years: the Dow/Union Carbide union, Alcoa's bond with Reynolds, AOL's purchase of Time Warner and Conoco's hookup with Phillips Petroleum. Other major clients in this practice group include ExxonMobil, Coca-Cola, General Motors, Merck, Benetton, American Express, British Airways and IMAX.

Cleary has represented IBM on European and international competition matters for several years, offering the technology giant counsel on its acquisitions of Sequent, Informix, PwC Consulting and Rational Software during a four-year period beginning in 1999. The firm has also been racking up significant victories against the antitrust authorities in the European Union, including a November 2002 ruling by Luxembourg's Court of First Instance that overturned the EU's attempts to revise the terms of a merger between Canal Plus and Cleary's client, Lagardere Groupe, two weeks after having given their union its seal of approval.

In June 2002, two separate groups gave the firm's efforts in antitrust and competition law top marks. London-based legal publisher Chambers & Partners named Cleary "Competition/Antitrust International Law Firm of the Year," while an *International Who's Who of Business Lawyers* survey ranked the firm's European competition practice first among U.S.-based firms.

Globalization in action

Cleary Gottlieb's M&A practice has equal renown, thanks in part to its carving out a niche for itself in the heart of the global banking market. In 2001, the firm played an advisory role in the merger of Allianz and Dresdner Bank AG, then followed up that deal in December 2002 by representing Crédit Lyonnais, the sixth-largest bank in France, in a 19.5-billion euro buyout by Crédit Agricole.

Cleary also scores big with its corporate clients. The Coca-Cola Company is just one of many clients the firm has advised on international deals, such as its January 2003 acquisition of Chaudfontaine Monopole's mineral water business. Cleary also represented Coca-Cola FEMSA, the Mexican bottlers of Coke and other soft drink products, in its 2002 merger with South American bottler Panamerican Beverages. The deal, valued at $3.6 billion, represented the largest merger in history between two Latin American corporations.

Fast food nation

Another Cleary client, McDonald's, relied on the firm to advise it during the negotiation of a joint venture with the owners of Fazoli's, a chain of mid-priced Italian restaurants. In addition to agreeing to help expand the restaurant in three new major U.S. markets, McDonald's purchased a stake in Fazoli's parent corporations with an option for full acquisition at a later date. From McD's to the King: Cleary helped a trio of private equity firms renegotiate the purchase of the Burger King restaurant chain. The investors had originally agreed to buy Burger King from spirits and wine distributor Diageo for $2.29 billion in July 2002, but the chain's weak performance brought all the parties back to the table, where Cleary was able to knock the price down to $1.5 billion by the end of the year.

From the heart

All these billion-dollar deals don't mean that Cleary has forgotten its commitment to serve the public. The firm is very active in pro bono work and waged successful efforts to obtain asylum for a number of political refugees in 2002, including six native Tibetans who fled persecution by the Chinese occupying government in their homeland. Cleary also provides free representation to New York's Legal Aid Society, the nation's largest provider of free legal services, and helped the Society arrange financing on the first office space that it will own rather than lease – a five-story building to be constructed in Harlem.

Insider deals

Cleary's litigators have been especially busy handling a deluge of securities-related matters and a sharp increase in securities enforcement work. In one such matter, the firm is representing defendants in what may turn out to be the sexiest insider trading case of 2003. Lehman Brothers' hotshot Internet analyst, Holly Becker, was accused by investigators from the Securities and Exchange Commission of colluding with her then-fiancé, hedge fund trader Michael Zimmerman, on several insider trades during the summer of 2000. Sources close to the investigation suggest that the couple may have taken advantage of a linkup between Becker's home computer and Lehman's computer network to funnel advance information to Zimmerman, allowing him to take profitable positions on tech companies like Amazon.com before her reports were released to the public. The couple was issued Wells notices by the SEC in January 2003.

GETTING HIRED

Getting in ain't easy

"Getting in the door is the biggest challenge" for prospective Cleary associates. The "rigorous" selection process is geared towards finding "brilliant, well-rounded, gracious, sophisticated, socially attuned, mature, self-motivated" candidates "who would thrive in the less structured Cleary atmosphere." During callbacks, an associate reports, "attorneys are not provided with an applicant transcript and are asked basically to figure out whether the applicant will fit in with the firm culture and will be a team player." One first-year attorney advises, "Once you get invited back, being polite and giving the impression that you're easy to work with is key." Other rookies stress the importance of the interview as well, suggesting, that "lunches are more important than prospective students may think" and that Cleary "make[s] more cuts on personality and fit than other firms."

Before you can dazzle them in the interview, though, you need the grades. "We take intellectual capability very seriously and have a fairly high grade standard," boasts a senior attorney. Cleary is "very grade conscious," another associate agrees, "and primarily tends to give offers to students from a handful of law schools." But "good writers" and "great thinkers" from any law school can stand a chance, especially if they score high on the three I's: "Interesting. International. Intellectual." Most Cleary associates can speak at least one foreign language, with Spanish, Portuguese and Korean "highly, highly regarded."

OUR SURVEY SAYS

Welcome to the island of misfit toys

Those in the know describe the Cleary vibe as "friendly but very focused" and "fairly chill." "We do have some strange birds here," says one associate, but most regard the "slightly off-beat" associates as "all brilliant yet not boastful," as well as "exceptionally friendly." Many associates attest to high attendance at New York's weekly wine and cheese parties, a frequent "meeting place to determine where to go next." Moreover, "a number of marriages were started here." In fact, says one midlevel associate, Cleary "should work harder on exporting the New York culture to other offices."

Reasonable workload

"Hard work fills your day," but "hours are long because the deals are exciting and top of the line." Though some associates assure us that "there is definitely work to be done, despite the economic downturn," those who have been in the trenches a while will tell you "the work hours have been quite reasonable over the last two years." Several sources report no face-time requirements. "Working from home is completely acceptable," says one litigator, "and everyone has a laptop and a BlackBerry to facilitate that." Another young corporate attorney knows several colleagues who "make it abundantly clear that they will not bill more than 50 hours a week" without drawing the ire of senior associates or partners.

A firm that takes care of its own

Cleary partners are "excellent teachers" who "expect and demand a very high level of work," but they also remember to "say please" and "try to keep you involved in the big picture instead of just assigning minutiae" to junior associates. "Information is shared freely and creative thinking is encouraged," with " an expectation that everyone is attempting to do their best work." A senior associate describes the mood as "intense and dynamic" but emphasizes that "very rarely do I feel an overriding stress or level of anxiety that I have heard about from associates at other firms." Another associate adds, "The regard for the associates is also evidenced in small ways," such as "the gourmet food always generously served at our training events."

In addition to the firm's "very highly evolved" training programs, "many upper associates and partners are available for talk and discussion on various issues if you take the initiative." One sophomore litigator says, "It is hard to find time to lunch with all the people trying to help you." But the "learn-by-doing" environment can be "nerve-wracking" at times, and freshly hired associates should "expect to be handed substantive work two days after arriving" with "very little spoon feeding." "Cleary is very much what you make of it," advises a second-year associate. "Those who are not self-motivated or independently resourceful don't flourish here."

Following the lead

Although some associates feel "market compensation in New York has fallen behind cost of living," most agree Cleary offers "top of the market" salaries. The firm "does not always lead the pack," but "we quickly match whatever is out there." Cleary's "strong policy against firing associates," coupled with the "tough economy," have younger associates staying put. "There has been very little attrition in my class," reports a third-year. But for those who have been around a bit longer, the appeal of an in-house counsel position or "teaching, joining the UN, working in government or for an NGO" often increases. "The firm is very slim on mid- and upper-level associates," one source confesses, and others suggest that the litigation group has a "major, major problem" hanging on to its associates.

Gold stars for diversity

Cleary "bends over backwards to provide a receptive environment for diversity issues," and is particularly well-regarded as "a haven" by gay and lesbian attorneys, whose domestic partners are "made to feel a part of the family" at all New York events. ("Some of the European offices," sources allow, "are more reserved and less welcoming.") "Working here as a summer associate was one of the chief reasons I felt comfortable coming out of the closet," says one first-year. Gay associates express feeling totally comfortable being out at the office; some attorneys even jokingly suggest that "pressure to be out" has "straight men walking around the halls wondering if they're gay, too."

The firm also rates well on its recruitment of women attorneys, with "as many or more women than men" in recent incoming classes. Keeping them around, however, has proven more difficult, according to one third-year, especially when professional and personal interests compete. "A lot of women still feel like they have to choose between making partner and having babies," she reports, and several others grumble that "no woman with children has made partner since 1995." Cleary has an "active" Women's Working Group to deal with such issues, although some worry that problems are relegated there "instead of being discussed and confronted among the entire firm." Still, the firm is widely viewed internally as "accommodating, understanding and flexible" when it comes to arranging schedules to balance career and family.

"Because of our firm's commitment to international work," boasts a junior litigator, "there are tons of lawyers with different backgrounds." Another associate praises the "astonishing level of Latino attorneys, particularly when one considers the high number of Latino partners," and colleagues consider Asian and South Asian attorneys to be "well-represented" among Cleary's ranks. All is not perfect; although Cleary is "better than most," it still has "difficulties retaining African-American attorneys," and "the partnership does not reflect the diversity of the associate base." Still, many associates seem to agree with a senior colleague who says, "The firm was one of the first to try to address issues affecting minorities in a formal manner." And progress is being made; the firm reports that it named another African-American attorney partner in 2002.

Have you done your pro bono yet?

Pro bono is "heavily emphasized" at Cleary, with hours on public service cases counting towards associates' billables (not that it matters, many point out, since the lockstep bonuses aren't tied to minimum hours). "I think Cleary is really outstanding on this," says a junior litigator, who sees a "great level of interest in pro bono activities among both the associates and the partners. It is definitely highly valued." "The firm has a pro-bono criterion for making partner," another associate reveals, as well as "a goal of exceeding 3 percent of billable hours devoted to pro bono" throughout the firm. "I have spent full days working on pro bono matters, and no one thinks of the work any differently," a first-year says. "Attorneys at the firm often ask each other about their pro bono work," says another associate. "It would be awkward to answer that I had [none]." Associates can even "turn down paying work" if they need the time to complete pro bono commitments.

Downtown delights

Cleary has the "coolest offices" in New York, a "beautiful, stunning" space with "amazing views, large windows and lots of light." Furthermore, even first-years can expect to have their own office within months, if not right away. "When I get bored," a freshman corporate associate says, "I just look at the sunset over the Statue of Liberty, kick my feet back and think that at 26 I'm probably working in the nicest office I'll ever work at in my life." Of course, you can't please everyone. A second-year associates asks, "Could somebody turn the heat on?"

Covington & Burling

1201 Pennsylvania Avenue, NW
Washington, DC 20004-2401
Phone: (202) 662-6000
www.cov.com

LOCATIONS

Washington, DC (HQ)
New York, NY
San Francisco, CA
Brussels
London

MAJOR DEPARTMENTS/PRACTICES

Antitrust • Arbitration/ADR • Communications •
Corporate, Securities, Insolvency & Real Estate •
Employee Benefits • Employment • Energy •
Environmental • Financial Restructuring • Food & Drug •
Health Care • Information Technology, Privacy &
E-Commerce • Insurance • Intellectual Property •
International Legislative • Litigation (Trial & Appellate) •
M&A • Patent Advice & Litigation • Sports • Tax •
Transportation • White Collar Defense

THE STATS

No. of attorneys: 508
No. of offices: 5
Summer associate offers: 49 out of 52 (2002, DC)
Managing Partner: Stuart C. Stock
Hiring Partner: Mark E. Plotkin & Paul V. Rogers

BASE SALARY

Washington, DC*
1st year: $125,000
2nd year: $135,000
3rd year: $150,000
4th year: $155,000
5th year: $165,000
6th year: $175,000
7th year: $185,000
8th year: $195,000
Summer associate: $2,400/week

*Base salary includes pension contribution for
Washington associates who received offers prior to
January 2000.*

UPPERS

• Commitment to pro bono
• Good working relationship with partners
• Low pressure to bill

DOWNERS

• Little communication from partners on state of
the firm
• Formality of the work environment
• "Uncertainty" regarding bonus system

NOTABLE PERKS

• "Liberal" car and dinner policies
• Bi-monthly happy hours
• Pre-tax metro cards
• BlackBerrys

THE BUZZ
WHAT ATTORNEYS AT OTHER FIRMS ARE SAYING ABOUT THIS FIRM

• "Still the big D.C. fish"
• "Snooty, elitist"
• "Intellectual"
• "Starched white shirts"

RANKING RECAP

Best in Region
#1 - Washington, DC

Best in Practice
#9 - Litigation

Quality of Life
#3 - Selectivity
#8 - Pro Bono

EMPLOYMENT CONTACT

Ms. Lorraine Brown
Director, Legal Personnel Recruiting
Phone: (202) 662-6200
E-mail: legal.recruiting@cov.com

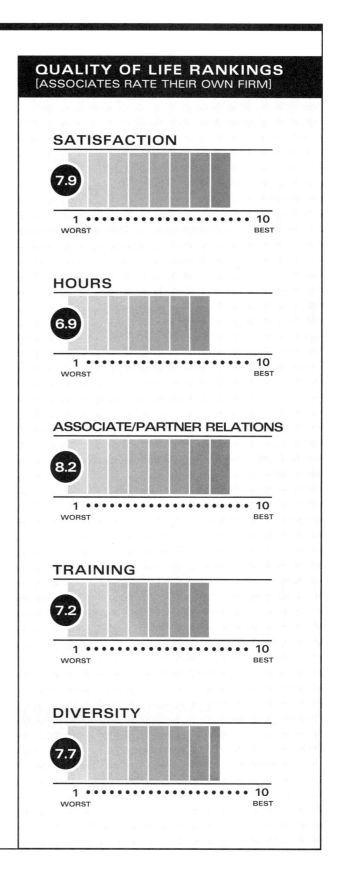

QUALITY OF LIFE RANKINGS
[ASSOCIATES RATE THEIR OWN FIRM]

SATISFACTION
7.9
1 WORST •••••••••••••••••• 10 BEST

HOURS
6.9
1 WORST •••••••••••••••••• 10 BEST

ASSOCIATE/PARTNER RELATIONS
8.2
1 WORST •••••••••••••••••• 10 BEST

TRAINING
7.2
1 WORST •••••••••••••••••• 10 BEST

DIVERSITY
7.7
1 WORST •••••••••••••••••• 10 BEST

THE SCOOP

Located just a stone's throw away from the White House and Capitol Hill, Covington & Burling has been a fixture in D.C. since 1919. The firm has made a name for itself not only among Beltway insiders, but also with Fortune 500 executives.

Washington versus Washington

As would be expected of a historic, well-connected D.C. firm, legislative and regulatory matters are a vital part of Covington & Burling's practice. Corporations from a variety of industries, including energy, environmental, transportation and health care, rely on the firm for its expertise in navigating regulatory hurdles. When the state of Washington needed an influential voice to represent its interests in our nation's capital, it turned to Covington for help. Legislators in the Evergreen State are hoping to cash in on a soon-to-be retired loophole that enables states to make excessive Medicare claims and then split the money with public nursing homes and hospitals. The state is seeking to gain $1.1 billion in federal Medicare reimbursements through the loophole for prior and coming years. Covington was hired to advocate on the state's behalf among the power brokers of Capitol Hill.

The firm has also represented individual government officials. Attorneys at Covington donated their time to counsel D.C. Mayor Anthony Williams during an investigation of his fundraising activities. The Office of Campaign Finance concluded in October 2002 that members of Williams' staff had violated fundraising rules and admonished Williams, but also noted that the mayor may have been unaware of the breaches and had already taken steps to prevent such situations in the future.

Big clients, big growth

The number of associates at Covington grew by 36 between April 2001 and April 2002, more than at any other D.C.-based firm. The partnership ranks also grew by seven during that time. This remarkable growth seems to be a function of the 84-year-old firm's strengths – corporate, litigation and regulatory work – which were often derided during the boom years of the 1990s as being too low-tech. Another mark of the firm's growth: Covington landed the No.-18 spot on *Corporate Board Member*'s 2002 list of the top 20 firms corporate counsel prefer to work with on national matters. This was Covington's first appearance on the list. It looks like the firm is anticipating an increase in business across the Pond, as well. At the start of 2002, the firm announced it had hired its first tax partner in the London office.

Here are just a couple of the deals and cases behind this tremendous growth: In January 2003, Covington & Burling negotiated a joint venture with Eli Lilly on behalf of its client, German pharmaceutical company Boehringer Ingelheim. The firm has signed on as counsel to the independent directors of communications provider Adelphia as the company undergoes an investigation of alleged financial misconduct by the family that owns and controls most of its stock. Covington also counts Brown & Williamson Tobacco Corp., Global Crossing, Gemstar and the American Automobile Association among its clients.

Covington can count the addition of former federal prosecutor Alan Vinegrad as another feather in its cap. Vinegrad, who cut his teeth prosecuting defendants in high-profile, racially charged cases like the assault of Haitian immigrant Abner Louima and the murder of Hasidic student Yankel Rosenbaum, joined the New York office's white-collar defense practice in December 2002.

Author, author!

There's at least one attorney at Covington who thinks lawyers have too much work – at least where lawsuits are concerned, anyway. Partner Philip K. Howard has authored several books on the increasingly litigious nature of American society and in 2002 formed Common Good, an organization dedicated to streamlining our legal structure. While improving the American legal system is likely to take quite a while, Howard has already succeeded in garnering media attention for his organization and attracting the likes of Paul Simon (the former U.S. Senator, not the music icon) and Newt Gingrich to the group's advisory board.

The work of another Covington attorney-turned-author received some attention he could have done without. The cover of Partner Stuart Eizenstat's January 2003 book, *Imperfect Justice*, angered some Swiss citizens and Americans of Swiss descent who felt the cover image of a swastika juxtaposed on the Swiss flag was misrepresentative of their country. Eizenstat's book details his efforts to gain reparations for art, money and other property taken from Jews during World War II and deposited in banks in Switzerland and other countries. Although he wasn't responsible for choosing the image on the cover and stands by the accuracy of his book, Eizenstat apologized for any ill feelings the image on the book jacket may have stirred up.

Helping hands

Covington's commitment to pro bono work has received numerous awards, including first place in *American Lawyer's* 2002 list of the top pro bono performers in terms of total hours and number of participants. The firm's top ranking is a reflection of its extensive pro bono program, which includes ongoing relationships with legal services agencies and representation of over 100 non-profit organizations. In July 2002, the firm held its second pro bono recognition reception, where more than 200 Covington attorneys were honored for giving at least 50 hours of pro bono service during the previous year.

The firm has taken up the cause of Richard Bourke, an Australian attorney who's in the States as a non-immigrant alien. Bourke came to the U.S. to work with a group that works to have death penalty sentences overturned. Bourke applied to take the bar as required of attorneys who are licensed elsewhere, but not in this country. However, the Louisiana State Supreme Court denied Bourke's request in June 2002.

Just no fax, ma'am

If you detest unwanted spam (and who doesn't?), listen up. The folks at Covington can feel good knowing they played a hand in bringing spammer Fax.com to justice. In a single week during June 2001, the firm received more than 1,600 unsolicited advertising faxes from the company. Covington filed a lawsuit under a federal law that prohibits sending faxes of this type, and in April 2003 won a court judgment awarding punitive damages against Fax.com. Partly based on Covington's suit, the Federal Communications Commission also admonished Fax.com and slapped it with a $5.38 million proposed fine in August 2002.

GETTING HIRED

If you're hoping to land a spot at Covington, you'd better have a stellar resume – even high achievers have a tough time getting a foot in the door. "This is one of the most competitive firms in the country. At my law school, which is generally considered among the top 10, you had to be on law review to get an interview," says a fourth-year. "Most associates here attended only a few schools: Harvard, Yale, Columbia, NYU, Stanford and Chicago. If you did not attend one of these schools and do well there, you have almost no chance of obtaining an interview," a third-year warns. "Covington hires summer associates based on their on-campus interviews and background checks," explains one insider. You won't get a second chance to make a first impression: There are no callbacks in the Washington office for summer offers. Expect the interview process to be "rigorous" if you're trying to break into the that office. "Covington expends considerable resources to make sure that it attracts and chooses the best associates that it can." "Lengthy conversations with references" are the norm. After summer offers are extended, a candidate is invited to "visit Covington to help him or her decide if they want to join us." Unlike the process for law students, Covington "requires three rounds of interviews for lateral hires" into upper-level positions.

OUR SURVEY SAYS

Somewhere between laid back and stuffy

"This is the classic old-school, white-shoe firm, and it shows for better and worse sometimes," observes a senior associate. A D.C. associate describes the atmosphere at the firm as "polite and reserved. People are nice," this source adds, "but the size of the office can make it difficult to meet colleagues with whom you do not work directly." "While no one is 'stuffy,' people are somewhat reserved generally," says another source in D.C. An attorney in the litigation department is more blunt: "Associates are too stiff and work-minded and not much fun." A New York associate dishes about the differences between the D.C. and New York offices: [The] "New York office is very friendly, laid back, informal. [The] Washington office is a bit more traditional and conservative."

"C&B is mostly quiet and genteel, but there are pockets of younger, more social associates." "The Covington reputation is for being uptight, but I have to say, after being here for three years, that really is not the case. Partners tend to be pretty relaxed [and] approachable, and associates are a pretty fun loving bunch."

Workin' and learnin'

Covington & Burling is the type of firm where "young associates can get serious responsibility early on, if they want it." A corporate attorney tells us that despite the slow economy, "our office has been busy, and the work diverse and interesting. This department is going places." In the opinion of one litigation associate, "There is an expectation that associates must accept some degree of dues-paying before they are allowed to take on meatier work. If a midlevel associate wants stand-up courtroom experience, for instance, then Covington is not the place to go." This source considers pro bono cases a good way to gain experience, but adds, "There is a point in one's career when one wants to be entrusted with such responsibilities with the firm's paying clients."

Views on formal training vary among the associates. One associate labels training opportunities as "virtually nonexistent," while another says the firm is "great about providing training opportunities, including CLEs and writing classes." "It varies by practice group." One attorney notes although "the firm has tried to implement a variety of formal and informal training programs for the corporate associates," it has been met "with varied success." "That's okay," most attorneys tell us, "because on-the-job training has been very good."

Time for work and play

"Make no mistake about it," says one insider, "associates have a lot of responsibility." That translates to "many hours" of hard work. Although the hours "ebb and flow" with little predictability, it isn't too hard to find Covington associates who think "the hours here are better than at most D.C. firms." Interestingly enough, several associates reveal, "There is no articulated emphasis on billing hours." In fact, according to a sixth-year, "If anything, the message as you get more senior is to bill less hours and make sure each product is of the highest possible quality." A first-year tells us, "The best thing about C&B is that you do not work long hours just to do it. There is no pressure to make 'face time' here. Many associates do not even reach 1,950 billable hours." Naturally, there are some Covington attorneys who disagree with these popular opinions. A midlevel says, "Those who are interested in making partner should probably bill a whole lot of hours." "The hours expectations are very high, no matter what the firm says to the contrary," confides one litigation attorney. A second-year counters: "Any pressure to bill a particular number of hours is entirely self-induced. I've never had anyone mention anything to me, and I did not hit the target this year." A senior associate suggests getting rid of "the billable hours benchmark. I think that most associates are committed to their work and would put the requisite effort into billable work regardless. Having the benchmark, however, is cause for anxiety in slow months."

Bonus watch

Attorneys in the firm's D.C. and New York offices report that salaries are "competitive." But some D.C. associates note, "Several other firms pay higher salaries." This from an associate who has a good news/bad news view of the compensation at Covington: "The salary level is, in my view, too high because it forces the firm to have high billing expectations. However, I realize that the firm must set its compensation at a competitive level. The bonus structure, however, is inadequate" because "in the last two years less than half of the associates have received bonuses." A content third-year shares, "We all make ungodly sums of money compared to the real world, but compared to other law firms," Covington pay is "about average." One attorney offers this comparison of Covington's salary and bonus structure to other area firms. "Starting at mid-level, associates do not receive the same compensation as their counterparts at the other major D.C. firms. While the base salaries are similar, other firms have bonuses that are either automatic or are easily achievable, while Covington's bonuses remain selective, subjective and difficult to achieve." This is a point of view shared by other associates, who say the bonus system is "murky" and "a mystery." U.K. attorneys, meanwhile, are tickled pink to be making "almost double the standard London rate."

No "us" and "them"

"Partners at C&B are not always a barrel of laughs," and "for the most part, there is no social interaction between partners and associates outside the office, and very little inside the office." However, associates express favorable views of the partnership overall. "There are very few, if any, 'screamers,'" and "partners are generally considerate of associates' time, particularly when it comes to family obligations and vacations." "In general, partners respect associates and indeed expect input from them. Voicing alternative or different views on the solution to a problem is encouraged." "Most partners are friendly, respectful and genuinely concerned with associate development. Open doors are the norm." Perhaps that is why "there is no feeling of 'them' and 'us' between the two groups." According to a third-year, "Partners here treat associates as colleagues, rely on them fairly heavily and provide them with significant responsibility. While there is often less explicit mentoring or teaching than I would like between partners and associates, you do learn from watching what the partners do." Most of the criticisms aimed at partners concern "poor communication at times about important issues like compensation and partnership prospects." Associates say this leaves them "in the dark on much [of the] decision-making." A San Francisco attorney who feels out of the loop complains, "We only hear about things like new partner hirings, for example, when the information is made public."

We love pro bono!

Associates rave about the firm's commitment to pro bono service and proudly crow about the firm's "two full-time pro bono coordinators who are very active in making sure associates have the opportunity to work on good cases" and its "active death penalty practice." Everyone does pro-bono [work] of some sort or another," a first-year tells us. Observes one senior associate, "The firm continues to promote pro bono work, almost to the exclusion of all else for more junior litigation associates." There is some disagreement, however, about whether pro bono work is billable, with associates in one camp saying the firm does not allow any portion of one's pro bono hours to count toward the billable hours requirement, and those in the other claiming, "Pro bono is treated exactly like billable work."

Latham & Watkins LLP

VAULT TOP 100

9

PRESTIGE RANKING

633 West Fifth Street
Suite 4000
Los Angeles, CA 90071-2007
Phone: (213) 485-1234
www.lw.com

LOCATIONS

Boston, MA • Chicago, IL • Costa Mesa, CA • Los
Angeles, CA • Newark, NJ • New York, NY • Reston,
VA • San Diego, CA • San Francisco, CA • Silicon
Valley, CA • Washington, DC • Brussels • Frankfurt •
Hamburg • Hong Kong • London • Milan • Moscow •
Paris • Singapore • Tokyo

MAJOR DEPARTMENTS/PRACTICES

Corporate (including Health Care, Venture & Technology
& Communications)
Environmental, Land & Resources
Finance/Real Estate
Litigation
Tax

THE STATS

No. of attorneys: 1,532
No. of offices: 21
Summer associate offers: 115 out of 120 (2002)
Chairman: Robert Dell
Hiring Partner: Tracy Edmonson

BASE SALARY

All domestic offices
1st year: $125,000
2nd year: $135,000
Summer associate: $2,400/week

UPPERS

- Laid-back California attitude permeates entire firm
- Widely beloved partners
- "A+ training"

DOWNERS

- First-years bitter as "summer stipend" turns into loan
- "It's starting to feel a little large"
- Billable hour target rankles

NOTABLE PERKS

- International office exchange program
- Annual weekend firm-wide meeting
- CLE reimbursement
- Soda for a quarter (not all locations)

THE BUZZ
WHAT ATTORNEYS AT OTHER FIRMS ARE SAYING ABOUT THIS FIRM

- "The Marine Corps of LA law firms"
- "Ultimate sweatshop"
- "Politically connected"
- "Frat boy atmosphere"

© 2003 Vault Inc.

RANKING RECAP

Best in Region
#1 - California

Best in Practice
#9 - Corporate
#9 (tie) - Mergers & Acquisitions
#9 (tie) - Real Estate
#9 - Securities

Quality of Life
#9 - Pro Bono
#11 - Associate/Partner Relations
#13 - Training
#20 - Selectivity

EMPLOYMENT CONTACT

Ms. Debra Clarkson
701 B Street, Suite 2100
San Diego, CA 92101
Phone: (619) 236-1234
E-mail: debra.clarkson@lw.com

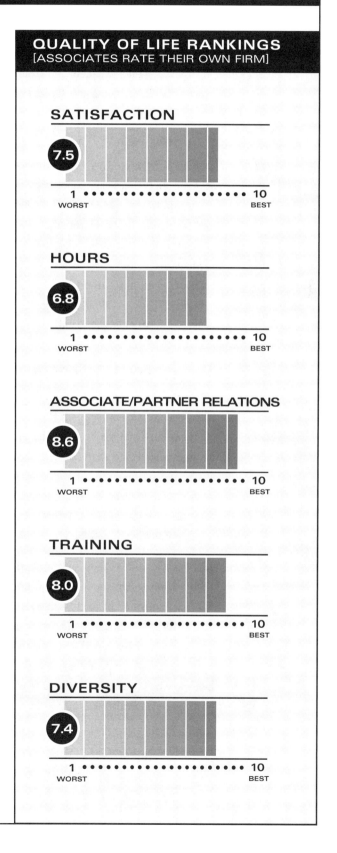

QUALITY OF LIFE RANKINGS
[ASSOCIATES RATE THEIR OWN FIRM]

SATISFACTION
7.5
1 WORST   10 BEST

HOURS
6.8
1 WORST   10 BEST

ASSOCIATE/PARTNER RELATIONS
8.6
1 WORST   10 BEST

TRAINING
8.0
1 WORST   10 BEST

DIVERSITY
7.4
1 WORST   10 BEST

THE SCOOP

Latham & Watkins is more than just the largest law firm in California. It's an international powerhouse with more than 1,500 attorneys in 21 offices worldwide, including five new European offices since 2001: Brussels, Paris, Hamburg, Frankfurt and Milan.

Big business is its business

Latham & Watkins was founded in 1934 by tax law expert Dana Latham and Paul Watkins, a specialist in business and labor law; legend has it they flipped a coin to decide whose name would go first on the letterhead. The firm has grown from 42 Los Angeles lawyers in 1969 to one of the global elite law firms. During the 1980s, Latham achieved a certain degree of notoriety for its work on high-yield debt structuring for Michael Milken and Drexel Burnham Lambert, but it also participated in other big deals of the era such as Kohlberg Kravis Roberts' takeover of RJR Nabisco, then the largest leveraged buyout in U.S. corporate history. Although the firm experienced some setbacks in the 1990s, it has thrived in recent years, landing a number of big deals and substantially expanding its international presence.

The best and the brightest

When it comes to lateral hires, Latham attracts high-profile names from both the public and the private sector. When William Baker, the former associate director of the Securities and Exchange Commission's enforcement division, joined the firm's securities litigation team in February 2003, he was the latest in a string of A-list hires that included the former general counsel for the Americas at Credit Suisse First Boston and a managing partner at the Virginia office of rival firm Wilson Sonsini Goodrich & Rosati. Latham's international hires inclued four leading antitrust lawyers from the Brussels office of Wilmer, Cutler & Pickering, the general counsel of Netherlands-based telecom KPNQwest and the managing partner of Lovells' Singapore office.

Another Latham partner with a Washington pedigree, former Deputy Secretary of the Interior David Hayes, spent a great deal of time in 2002 representing the Hearst Corporation in connection with its disposition of the massive Hearst Ranch, an 82,000-acre parcel surrounding Hearst Castle that includes 18 miles of California coastline. Hayes and his team are exploring an innovative combination of a sale and donation of a conservation easement over the ranch, and the transfer of some fee ownsership of coastal lands, to federal and state authorities so that virtually all of the lands will be preserved in perpetuity without development. The proposed transaction would be one of the largest ever of its kind.

I scream, you scream, we all scream for ice cream

Latham has served as legal adviser to Nestlé, the world's largest food company, in recent efforts to corner the ice cream market. After scooping up the American distribution rights to Haagen-Dazs in late 2001, Nestlé added a cherry to its sundae in June 2002 by moving to acquire a two-thirds ownership stake in Dreyer's Grand Ice Cream. The $2.6 billion deal could melt away, however, as the parties negotiate with the Federal Trade Commission to overcome its disapproval.

Leading LBOs

Dominating the rankings on LBO deals worldwide in *American Lawyer's* Corporate scorecard, Latham provided counsel on four of the top 20 LBO deals of 2002, including the Carlyle Group and Welsh, Carson, Anderson & Stowe's acquisition of Qwest Communications International's QwestDex telephone directory business for $7.05 billion, the largest leveraged buyout since RJR Nabisco, which Latham also worked on, in 1989.

Latham's no slouch in the corporate finance arena, either. In 2002, the firm represented the banks which arranged $2.4 billion in financing for Steve Wynn's new Las Vegas casino. The financing included $1 billion in bank financing, a $450 million IPO, a $370 million second mortgage rate offering and $188 million for a furniture, fixtures and equipment facility.

Play ball

Latham represented the National Football League in a legal dispute that pitted the league and the city of San Diego against a disability-rights activist who attempted to hold up play of 2003's Super Bowl XXXVII. The activist filed a request for an injunction to prevent the game from being played at Qualcomm Stadium, arguing that the city had failed to make promised modifications for disabled access and set aside tickets for disabled sports fans. The court denied the requested injunction, the kickoff went on as scheduled and the Tampa Bay Buccaneers defeated the Oakland Raiders.

Vroom, vroom

Latham scored an even clearer victory for AutoZone in January 2003 when it successfully defended the automotive retailer against federal antitrust charges. The $1 billion lawsuit was brought by a consortium of auto parts distributors who accused AutoZone of price discrimination. Latham was able to beat back the charges after a five-day trial followed by less than three hours of jury deliberation.

A chess game

Latham's famous clients aren't just corporate. The firm is also the American counsel to former chess champion Garry Kasparov and is representing him in a dispute with the First International Bank of Israel. The bank had fronted Kasparov and a group of investors $1.5 million to launch the "Kasparov Chess Online" web site in 1999. Though the site has proven unsuccessful, the bank wants to keep it running so it can recoup its investment, while Latham frames the bank's efforts as an attempt "to seize the name and likeness of Kasparov" for its own gain. In December 2002, a

Delaware court rejected the bank's efforts, rebuffing its request for a restraining order and calling the record in the case "far too thin."

Goin' bankrupt

Latham picked up a number of major bankruptcy cases in 2002. In February, the firm guided San Diego's Paragon Steakhouse Restaurants, part of a chain of restaurants stretching across 11 states, through its filing for protection from creditors while the company reorganized to cope with slackening business blamed on the recession and people's diminished interest in eating out after the terrorist attacks. Then, in September, the firm was appointed trustee for Consolidated Freightways and oversaw the auctioning of the trucking company's terminals two months later. Latham also advised Bank One, one of the debtor-in-possession lenders in United Airlines' bankruptcy. As the year drew to a close, the firm picked up one more bankruptcy client from among its own competition, as San Francisco law firm Brobeck, Phleger & Harrison threw in the towel and retained Latham to liquidate its assets.

Latham is providing defense counsel to a former vice president of AOL's business affairs unit in connection with probes by the SEC and the Department of Justice into a series of deals in 2000 and 2001 allegedly intended to generate misleading revenue figures for the media conglomerate's online advertising division. No criminal charges have been filed against AOL or any current or former executives as a result of the investigation. Several executives of the company with which former and current AOL executives are alleged to have colluded have entered guilty pleas on securities fraud charges and are cooperating with federal investigators.

Pro bono progress

Latham has made substantial advances in its pro bono practice over the past decade, when a 1994 survey ranked the firm in the bottom third of the nation's law firms when it came to pro bono hours. It now racks up awards for its public service work with regularity, including recognition by the American Bar Association with its 2003 Pro Bono Publico Award. In a current pro bono case, Latham is assisting in a class-action lawsuit against the California Youth Authority brought by former inmates of the juvenile detention system who claim they suffered physical and medical abuse and were incarcerated in substandard conditions where they were subject to sexual assault.

GETTING HIRED

"We are very picky," a senior M&A attorney testifies. "Certainly the most competitive of the national firms," another veteran concurs. Latham expects "the whole package" in its hires, but emphasizes academic stature above all other qualities. "If you didn't go to the right law school and graduate in the right percentage of your class," warns one insider, "your chances are next to nil." Furthermore, another source relays, "the GPA requirements have been going up steadily as the economy has slowed." Only "the best of the best" get offers, and "many law review types from top schools didn't make the cut." Likely candidates demonstrate "proven writing ability" and have often "clerked for at least one judge."

"Your accomplishments at school will get you in the door," a first-year says, "but to land the job, you've really got to be a mature, ambitious and vivacious person." The "smart, driven, normal" associates at Latham have survived a "rigorous" and "pretty exhausting" callback process, interviewing with up to seven associates in a single day. "Each person's comments must be considered and can have a sort of veto power," notes one insider. Another insider offers encouragingly, "If you're relaxed, have some fun and aren't cocky, chances are you'll do well. We like personalities, but personalities we can imagine having a few beers with."

OUR SURVEY SAYS

This ain't no party

A sophomore associate describes Latham & Watkins as "a very friendly firm that pretty much has something for everyone." But it is "not a party place," cautions a junior litigator, who adds there's "not much socializing between the lawyers once you're past the second year." A lawyer concurs, "As a junior lawyer we socialized together a lot. Now as folks have families and other priorities, there is less socializing. But my best friends – and my husband – are people I met at the firm." Other sources describe "a very strong frat boy culture" and warn of cliques within Latham. "Belonging to the in crowd in a department is crucial to have work assigned to you," a midlevel corporate attorney laments. "Not always but too often," a colleague agrees, "the good work is distributed on the basis of politics, not quality of work or merit."

"Latham is filled with type-A people," one first-year admits, "but some of the most bearable type-A's I've been around in my lifetime." A senior associate describes many of his colleagues as "people who claim to be slackers but work very hard." The firm's "serious and ultra-competitive" attorneys are "driven, yet more friendly than most." A second-year refers to "the vast majority" of Lathamites as "nice looking, athletic, well spoken and social," adding that the firm "does not have as much of an intellectual or even nerdy persona as a lot of law firms."

"I wish I had more hours!"

Latham "manages to combine a laid back attitude with enormous emphasis on hours," and "will push you as hard as you let them." But, a second-year reflects, "I do not think that Latham is a sweatshop and I have many friends at other firms who are much more disenchanted with the hours." A midlevel associate admits, "I work a little more than I would like, but about as much as I anticipated." The caseload has lessened somewhat in the last year, but that hasn't necessarily made associates feel more relaxed. "I was expecting to get here and have plenty of interesting

work to do," complains a first-year, "and instead, sometimes I sit around and do nothing all day waiting for an assignment." A junior associate observes "intense pressure to keep hours sky high for fear of being pushed out if you don't." A midlevel insider frets, "If I am out of the office, that means all that great work is getting away."

"I hate the feeling of always being on call," a second-year gripes. But a newly arrived associate counters that Latham is "very accommodating of personal schedules, and you have freedom in determining when you will do your work, as long as you get it done." One associate in San Diego seems to have it made. "I have been able to get in early, work hard during the day and leave at reasonable hours," he beams. "As long as I get my work done well, I have the freedom to surf in the early morning and get in a little before 9:00."

Summer stipend to-do

A midlevel associate describes the base salary as "fair," but calls the firm "stingy with bonuses." A first-year echoes the complaint that "bonuses have not necessarily been commensurate with firm earnings," while even a "more than satisfied" second-year has "a sense that bonuses this year were less generous than at some other firms." Another sophomore gripes, "The firm continues to make more money than ever, but bonuses are allocated right at market or below. The partners are not giving up any more money than they have to, regardless of how hard people are working."

Latham surprised many of its first-years when it informed them that the firm's bar stipends were no longer a signing bonus, but a salary advance, and docked their paychecks accordingly. "The removal of the summer stipends is a source of bitterness," says one affected freshman, "especially when the firm prides itself on what a banner year it had in terms of profits." Another rookie complains, "As a firm that prides itself in being open with its associates, it should have told us ahead of time that we were going to have to pay back the stipends before we accepted our offers to work here."

The value of teamwork

"Partners here truly treat others as their equals," marvels a Latham first-year. "At least until faced with a deadline," quips a senior attorney. But such cynicism is rare; Latham & Watkins received one of the highest rankings for associate-partner relations in this year's survey. "Reasonable and relatively grounded" partners "work right alongside the associates" and are "wonderful to work with on a daily basis." The firm also works hard to keep associates in the loop. "I've been surprised at some of the information on firm plans that has been revealed to me," says one Latham veteran. A few sources point out that it's in the partners' best interests to treat associates with respect, as associate reviews help determine the level of partners' annual bonuses.

Top-notch training

"In my time here," says one veteran corporate attorney, "Latham & Watkins has moved from adequate to top notch in training. The firm made it a goal and now really emphasizes it." Today, the firm offers "the best and most comprehensive training program of any firm," with "more formal training sessions than any one person can attend." ("I'd almost describe the training as overkill," one third-year exclaims.) But, says a junior associate, "I've found the informal training and mentoring to be even more valuable." A first-year agrees. "The lawyers are always eager to sit down with you," he reports, "so it's easy to learn by doing." A second-year associate tells us, "I have worked in the firm for less than six months and I have already appeared in court on a few occasions. I feel that Latham as an institution, and my officemates individually, are all concerned with helping me achieve growth in the law."

Get comfortable

"Lateral hires from other big law firms start here every month," one veteran corporate attorney boasts, "but in my years here, only one or two people have left Latham to go to another big firm." Another senior associate asks, "Why would you leave a well-paying job and one of the best law firms in the U.S. with no real prospect of getting a job elsewhere?" Others see "attrition at the midlevel ranks." A junior associate perceives that "it has become very difficult to make partner here in recent years."

Making the effort

"One big reason I chose Latham was the number and high profile of women partners," recalls a female associate in her second year with the firm. But a newly arrived woman has a less rosy view. "While it seems that women are treated on equal grounds as men," she says, "there is a lack of women among the higher associate ranks. Women are hired at equal, if not greater, numbers at the lower level, but they do not stay." A senior associate counters that Latham "is really trying to be receptive to addressing the particular issues facing female associates." Many associates feel "retention could be better," but "looks like it's improving." They feel much the same way about the firm's handling of ethnic diversity. "I feel like Latham is welcoming toward minorities, but its recruiting efforts could be stronger and more successful." Though the firm "welcomes a more diverse population," it "has not received many applicants." A senior litigator muses, "Few if any big firms have figured out the secret to minority retention and Latham is no exception."

In contrast, gay and lesbian associates find Latham "very welcoming," with one gay attorney in San Francisco having a "fantastic" experience. "I'm not pigeonholed as the gay attorney," he elaborates, "just totally accepted, as is my partner when he comes to events." Another gay associate in New York adds, "People judge you here by your work and commitment, not by your private life."

Weil, Gotshal & Manges LLP

767 Fifth Avenue
New York, NY 10153
Phone: (212) 310-8000
www.weil.com

LOCATIONS

New York, NY (HQ)
Austin, TX • Boston, MA • Dallas, TX • Houston, TX •
Miami, FL • Silicon Valley, CA • Washington, DC •
Brussels • Budapest • Frankfurt • London • Paris •
Prague • Singapore • Warsaw

MAJOR DEPARTMENTS/PRACTICES

Advertising • Antitrust/Competition Law • Business &
Restructuring • Business & Securities Litigation •
Capital Markets • Consumer Finance • Corporate •
Criminal (white collar crime) • First Amendment •
Institutional Finance • Intellectual Property • Labor and
Employment • Litigation & Arbitration • Media &
Technology • Mergers & Acquisitions • Private Equity •
Product Liability • Real Estate • Sports • Structured
Finance & Derivatives • Tax • Trade Practices &
Regulatory Law

THE STATS

No. of attorneys: 1,075
No. of offices: 16
Summer associate offers: 110 out of 129 (2002)
Chairman: Stephen J. Dannhauser
Hiring Partners: Todd Chandler, Helyn Goldstein, Josh
Krevitt and Rod Miller

BASE SALARY

New York, NY; Dallas, Houston, TX; Silicon Valley, CA
1st year: $125,000
2nd year: $135,000
3rd year: $150,000
4th year: $165,000
5th year: $190,000
6th year: $205,000
7th year: $215,000
Summer associate: $2,400/wk (NY, Silicon Valley)
Summer associate: $2,300/wk (Dallas, Houston)

Washington, DC; Boston, MA
1st year: $125,000
2nd year: $135,000
3rd year: $150,000
4th year: $160,000
5th year: $175,000
6th year: $190,000
7th year: $205,000
Summer associate: $2,400/week

UPPERS

- "Individuality is actually encouraged"
- "Best bankruptcy group in the country"
- Awesome New York location

DOWNERS

- "Hierarchy bordering on military"
- Limited dinner options
- Work allocation can be uneven

NOTABLE PERKS

- Technology stipend
- Monthly lottery for sports and concert tickets
- Four-week paid parental leave
- Firm and department retreats

THE BUZZ
WHAT ATTORNEYS AT OTHER FIRMS ARE SAYING ABOUT THIS FIRM

- "The best bankruptcy practice in the world"
- "Cheap"
- "Continues to impress and rise"
- "Sweatshop"

RANKING RECAP

Best in Region
#10 - New York

Best in Practice
#1 - Bankruptcy/Corporate Restructuring
#9 (tie) - Mergers & Acquisitions
#10 - Corporate
#10 - Intellectual Property
#10 (tie) - Real Estate

Quality of Life
#6 - Part-Time/Flex-Time

EMPLOYMENT CONTACT

Ms. Donna J. Lang
Manager of Legal Recruiting
Fax: (212) 735-4502
E-mail: donna.lang@weil.com

QUALITY OF LIFE RANKINGS
[ASSOCIATES RATE THEIR OWN FIRM]

SATISFACTION

7.1

1 • • • • • • • • • • • • • • • • • • 10
WORST   BEST

HOURS

5.8

1 • • • • • • • • • • • • • • • • • • 10
WORST   BEST

ASSOCIATE/PARTNER RELATIONS

7.3

1 • • • • • • • • • • • • • • • • • • 10
WORST   BEST

TRAINING

7.3

1 • • • • • • • • • • • • • • • • • • 10
WORST   BEST

DIVERSITY

7.4

1 • • • • • • • • • • • • • • • • • • 10
WORST   BEST

THE SCOOP

Weil, Gotshal & Manges boasts a multifaceted, international practice that just keeps getting stronger and bigger after 72 years. Long considered one of the premier bankruptcy firms in America, Weil has other impressive practices as well.

Bankruptcy king

When major corporations find themselves in a financial jam, they frequently turn to Weil Gotshal for help. The firm has been and continues to act as advisor to companies involved in some of the largest U.S. bankruptcy cases ever filed. The firm's roster of recent and current clients includes Enron, WorldCom, Global Crossing, Bethlehem Steel, Armstrong World Industries, Republic Technologies, Regal Cinema and Sunbeam, plus major creditors of KMart, US Air, United Airlines and Montgomery Ward. Weil's preeminence in the restructuring and finance area has helped it prosper during the economic downturn while other peer firms have suffered.

Notably, Weil's practice has continued to flourish despite the departure of Harvey Miller, the man credited with establishing the modern bankruptcy practice, to join an investment bank after more than 30 years at the firm. Legal insiders expected little to change as Miller had developed a strong stable of bankruptcy attorneys during his years at Weil and had already ceded leadership of the practice to two protégés: Martin Bienenstock, who leads the Enron matter, and Marcia Goldstein, currently heading up the WorldCom effort.

Diverse practice

Although the highly respected bankruptcy practice is probably Weil's most prominent calling card, the firm has more than 50 areas of specialty. From litigation to M&A to real estate and beyond, 2002 was marked by multiple Weil triumphs. Weil Gotshal obtained one of the largest non-punitive jury damage awards ever recorded on behalf of ExxonMobil in a licensing dispute involving technology related to the manufacture of polyethylene. Weil also advised General Electric in its acquisition of BetzDearborn's water treatment division from Hercules Incorporated. Finally, Weil's highly regarded IP practice scored major victories for Cisco Sytems, the Walt Disney Company, Intel and Samsung. These were just a few of the achievements that led *Global Counsel* magazine to name Weil its "Best Law Firm of the Americas" for 2002.

Happy holidays

Weil closed out the year and celebrated the holiday season by adding a few more deals to its stocking in December 2002. Weil attorneys were certainly jolly after negotiating the sale by French media and telecommunications giant Vivendi Universal SA of its U.S. and European publishing assets for approximately 3 billion euros. American Airlines breathed a sigh of relief when Weil successfully argued that the airline was not liable for termination of a contract between Lowestfare.com and TWA after American acquired TWA.

The sporting life

Baseball may be as American as apple pie, but it seems that Canadians have a soft spot for the sport as well. That's why 14 Canadian companies, all former owners of the Montreal Expos, enlisted Weil Gotshal's help in a July 2002 suit against several individuals who the former Expo owners claim conspired to shut the team down. In the arena of professional sports, Weil represented the NBA Players Association on behalf of energetic hoops star Latrell Sprewell after he choked his coach during a practice a few seasons back. The firm created a somewhat more substantial legacy years earlier when it won a landmark verdict for footballer Freeman McNeil, establishing NFL players' right to free agency. (It recently achieved a similar victory for the Arena Football League Players Association.) Today the firm represents the players' associations of the NFL, NBA and Major League Soccer, as well as a number of individual players and sports announcers. In addition, the firm is currently engaged in a major antitrust litigation against the NCAA on behalf of the pre- and post-season NIT college basketball tournaments.

Around the Weil in 80 days

During 2002 and 2003, expansion was the name of the game at Weil Gotshal. At a time when many law firms were making cuts or maintaining the status quo, Weil Gotshal entered new markets and beefed up existing offices. The first stop on the firm's worldwide expansion tour was Boston. Weil wooed several members of Hutchins, Wheeler & Dittmar's private equity team on the heels of news that Hutchins would merge with Nixon Peabody. Weil opened its Boston office with 17 attorneys in September 2002. The next stop was Paris, where the firm merged with Serra Leavy & Cazals, a top French M&A boutique with which Weil has worked on various matters over the years. The Paris office began operating under the Weil Gotshal name in January 2003. Finally, five attorneys migrated from the firm's Houston location to establish an Austin outpost in February 2003. This new office, led by former Texas Solicitor General Greg Coleman, specializes in appellate litigation. In the early 1990s, Weil Gotshal became one of the first major law firms to establish a Silicon Valley presence; the California office busily scooped up top legal talent from the defunct Brobeck, Phleger & Harrison after the firm bit the bullet in January 2003.

Computers are our friends

It only makes sense that a firm with strong ties to Silicon Valley would equip its attorneys with the most cutting-edge gadgets. In summer 2002, lawyers in Weil's Silicon Valley office were given Windows-driven Tablet PCs, laptop computers that can store handwritten notes in electronic form. After a successful test drive, firm managers are working on plans to give the computers to all the attorneys in the firm. The firm is also deploying wireless networks throughout its offices.

GETTING HIRED

"Weil seems to be increasingly selective. They're focusing more on grades and caliber of law school, while still looking for people who are smart – and not just book smart – accomplished and motivated," remarks an associate. The firm is said to value candidates who are "resourceful, analytical and confident and have good common sense." Additionally, it helps to have "a good and interesting personality such that attorneys would want to seek out that person to work on their projects." Although it's to be expected that most candidates attend Weil's choice schools, the firm also invites "some write-in candidates for in-office interviews." Says another insider: "If you're well organized, with a can-do attitude, you can get hired here. Where you went to school and grades are less important here than at other top-20 firms." In fact, a first-year remarks, "I am surprised at the large number of associates hired from second- and third-tier law schools, although admittedly these people typically have more personality than those from top-ranked law schools." But grades are important, no matter what school one attends. "We are very grade-conscious, so it can be difficult for talented lawyers with midlevel academics to even get an in-office interview," an insider confides.

OUR SURVEY SAYS

Friendly, but intense

At Weil Gotshal, "people take their work very seriously, but are also personable." According to an attorney in the Silicon Valley office, "Lawyers socialize a lot and laugh a lot in the office." It is a "very friendly environment, but you need to be able to handle high-pressure situations, too." The Dallas office is reportedly more laid back than the New York office. "We socialize more on an informal basis versus planned happy hours together on Friday afternoons. Everyone is friendly, but you need to make the effort if you want to get to know someone here." Another Dallas associate explains that while "the partners and associates are open, friendly, professional, [and] knowledgeable," they are "generally very busy. As such, there is limited fraternizing, except for an occasional lunch." An attorney in D.C. considers that office to be "laid back and friendly. Some of the lawyers socialize together after work and some don't – particularly older, married lawyers. It depends on you, really."

"WGM is really a meritocracy. So if you work hard, you will get ahead and you will be constantly challenged," a midlevel attorney asserts. "I think Weil will give you as much responsibility as you are willing to take on, which cannot be said of most other firms," says another contact. Others bemoan the "seriously inequitable distribution of work." A second-year offers an opinion about the work allocation system: "If you show you are willing to work hard and you'll do a good job, you tend to get more and more work piled on, while other associates are leaving at 6 pm and don't appear to have much to do. I think this is an overall complaint that a lot of people have at different firms in the city, but I'm struck by the fact that I hear a lot of associates in different departments here with different assignment systems having the same complaint."

Bonuses irk some

"Our salaries are fantastic," says one Weil insider, "but the firm is incredibly cheap with bonuses, especially in light of how profitable WGM is." Others confirm that the dissolution of the retention bonus is a sore spot among associates given the "great financial stability" of the firm. But many associates seem unfazed by the bonus situation. Weil pays "the same as other top New York firms," they tell us. "There have been some nickel-and-dime cuts due to the recession," admits a first-year, "but pay is still equal to or better than any firm I'm aware of." And a senior associate believes, "The compensation here is competitive with peer firms. There are very few firms that pay more."

Weil-ing away the hours

Associates at Weil Gotshal have some intense feelings about the hours they keep. Even among those who say the hours are more "a product of big firm life rather than Weil itself," there are many who are unhappy about the long days. "Our hours are no better and no worse than any other firm. That said, I think you'd be hard pressed to find an associate who didn't want to have more free time," observes an IP attorney. One attorney says the number of hours he works "varies from extreme dissatisfaction to relative satisfaction, with the caveat that when the hours are reasonable one begins to worry about being let go because there is not enough to do." "I work long hours, but because I like the work and the people, it is not an issue," says a first-year. A senior associate describes the hours as "very cyclical. Sometimes it's 15 hours a day, then it's back to eight to nine hours a day" depending on "what deals are going on." A bankruptcy attorney reports spending an "outrageous number of hours" working and "regularly billing 80 [hours] per week." Thus far, a first-year reports working "regular weekends and many 18-hour days, with a handful of nearly 24-hour days consecutively." A second-year offers these word of wisdom: The "hours are very long. Come in expecting and accepting that, and you'll be happier." Long days are now old hat to a fourth-year who explains, "The hours seem longest when you're a first-year. Every year after that, your hours will go up but it won't seem as bad, which goes to show that it's not just the number of hours, it's what you get to do."

Some insiders complain that firm management is overly focused on keeping billables up. "This firm never had a preoccupation with hours until the past few months. Now we get daily reminders about inputting time, and there is tremendous pressure to keep hours up. There seems to have been a switch in focus from pride in quality of work to caring only about hours and face time." A senior associate confirms that "recently, there is very strong pressure to bill hours."

Training regimens

"Weil provides a comprehensive training program, including a new associate orientation and ongoing training sessions within each department." "The training has really picked up over the last year or so," in part due to the availability of "numerous CLE opportunities on a weekly basis across all disciplines." "We have so many CLE classes and training programs, it is not even funny!" exclaims a first-year. According to a fourth-year, "The only thing missing is better training/mentoring on the business aspects of the firm, such as how to get and retain clients." "Overall the training is quite good," a second-year tells us. "However," adds this source, "training varies among the different groups within the corporate department." "A lot of the training is hands on since it is difficult to teach how to do a corporate transaction other than to simply do it. However, the firm has a couple of short seminars every month." "In the IP groups, beginning attorneys are assumed to have an extremely high level of knowledge here, such that you are not expected to need much training."

Partners: both snappy and kind

According to a first-year, "Most of the partners are friendly, but they're usually too busy to deal much with lower-level associates." A New York associate paints a nicer picture, saying, "Certain partners can be difficult and snappy at times, but most are very decent. On a basic level, I think we are treated as equals: They don't look down at us or expect us to address them by their last names, they want us to speak up when we disagree and are generally good at acknowledging our hard work." A litigation associate purrs that "partners I have worked with make every effort to include associates in higher-level strategy sessions and other more 'fun' aspects of litigation." The "treatment is fine" and there are "no screamers," says a Houston associate. "Partners at this office are very approachable and treat associates with respect," an attorney in the Dallas office tells us.

"Weil will give you as much responsibility as you are willing to take on, which cannot be said of most other firms."

– *Weil Gotshal associate*

11

Kirkland & Ellis

Aon Center
200 East Randolph Drive
Chicago, IL 60601-6636
Phone: (312) 861-2000
www.kirkland.com

LOCATIONS

Chicago, IL (largest office)
Los Angeles, CA
New York, NY
San Francisco, CA
Washington, DC
London

MAJOR DEPARTMENTS/PRACTICES

Bankruptcy
Intellectual Property
Litigation
Tax & Planning
Transactional

THE STATS

No. of attorneys: 913
No. of offices: 6
Summer associate offers: 51 out of 51 (2002)
Firm Administrator: Douglas O. McLemore
Hiring Partner: Linda K. Myers

BASE SALARY

Chicago, IL
1st year: $125,000
2nd year: $135,000
3rd year: $150,000
4th year: $165,000
5th year: $185,000
6th year: $195,000
Summer associate: $2,404/week

UPPERS

- "Unparalleled" training
- Prestigious name

DOWNERS

- Frustration over 2002 bonuses
- Mediocre record on racial diversity

NOTABLE PERKS

- $5,000 every year for CLE
- Free fruit and bagels for breakfast
- $10,000 stipend for first-years
- Dinner and car rides after 7 P.M.

THE BUZZ
WHAT ATTORNEYS AT OTHER FIRMS ARE SAYING ABOUT THIS FIRM

- "Litigation dynamos "
- "Macho sweatshop"
- "Top notch"
- "I'm 35 years old. Where has my life gone?!"

RANKING RECAP

Best in Region
#1 - Chicago

Best in Practice
#3 - Bankruptcy/Corporate Restructuring
#3 - Litigation
#5 (tie) - Intellectual Property
#8 (tie) - Tax
#9 (tie) - Antitrust
#10 - Mergers & Acquisitions

Quality of Life
#2 - Training
#7 - Part-Time/Flex-Time
#16 - Selectivity

EMPLOYMENT CONTACT

Ms. Norah Faigen
Attorney Recruiting Manager
Phone: (312) 861-8532
Fax: (312) 861- 2200
E-mail: norah_faigen@kirkland.com

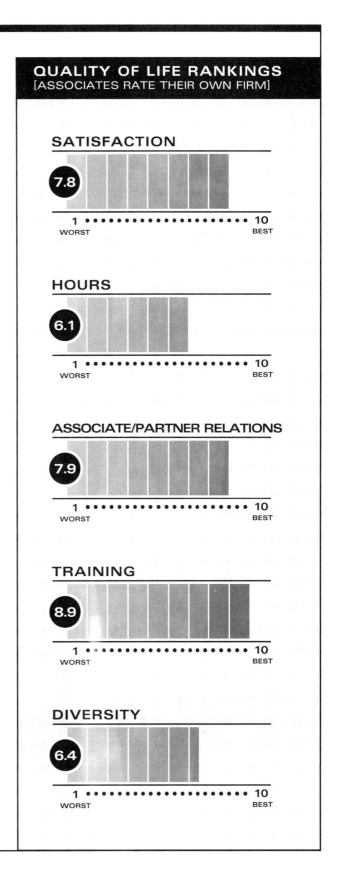

QUALITY OF LIFE RANKINGS
[ASSOCIATES RATE THEIR OWN FIRM]

SATISFACTION
7.8
1 • • • • • • • • • • • • • • • • • 10
WORST   BEST

HOURS
6.1
1 • • • • • • • • • • • • • • • • • 10
WORST   BEST

ASSOCIATE/PARTNER RELATIONS
7.9
1 • • • • • • • • • • • • • • • • • 10
WORST   BEST

TRAINING
8.9
1 • • • • • • • • • • • • • • • • • 10
WORST   BEST

DIVERSITY
6.4
1 • • • • • • • • • • • • • • • • • 10
WORST   BEST

THE SCOOP

For nearly 100 years, Kirkland & Ellis has been known for its ability to litigate and make deals. As one of the top firms in Chicago, Kirkland & Ellis is not only a leader in private equity, but also highly sought after as outside counsel to many of the Fortune 500.

Speak freely

Begun in 1908 by Stewart G. Shepard and Robert R. McCormick, Kirkland & Ellis soon built a reputation for its top-notch skills in the courtroom and later became known as a pioneer in the evolution of freedom of speech. A big part of that reputation was Weymouth Kirkland, who joined the firm in 1915. With the assistance of associate Howard Ellis, who also joined the firm in 1915, Kirkland successfully argued some of the firm's biggest cases of the day. By 1920, McCormick, grandson of *Chicago Tribune* founder Joseph Medill, had become so involved in the operations of the paper that he left the firm to publish the paper full time. When McCormick, outspoken in his views, found himself overwhelmed with accusations of defamation, he turned to Kirkland for help. Kirkland not only became chief counsel for the *Tribune*, but went on to serve this function for other newspapers as well. For his part, Ellis developed the fair comment defense, which is now a building block of American free speech.

Bankruptcy pays

Kirkland & Ellis is among the many firms involved in the mammoth Enron bankruptcy case. K&E was indirectly connected to Enron through its representation of partnerships allegedly set up to help officers of the embattled energy company make investments. Enron shareholders, however, thought that involvement was enough to hold the firm partially responsible for Enron's demise and filed a class-action suit against the firm. Kirkland received a present right before the holidays when the shareholder suit was dismissed in December 2002. Of the 12 defendants in the suit, Kirkland and Deutsche Bank were the only parties to be completely dismissed from the case.

Around the same time, financial services company Conseco filed for Chapter 11 bankruptcy protection, with Kirkland in the role of lead counsel. The case is likely to keep the firm busy for quite some time, not to mention bring in a hefty fee; Conseco's bankruptcy is the third largest (after Enron and WorldCom) in history. Smaller, regional companies also consider K&E a trusted advisor. Illinois-based Stations Holding (formerly Benedek Broadcasting) enlisted Kirkland's services during its 2002 bankruptcy. As if that's not enough, Kirkland is also representing United Airlines' parent company, UAL Corp., in its bankruptcy. Although the company didn't file until December 2002, UAL retained Kirkland's services shortly after the September 11th attacks.

We'll see you in court

On the litigation front, Kirkland & Ellis had a stellar year, racking up a number of high-profile victories in 2002. Two of those wins (on behalf of General Motors and Japanese manufacturer Kubota Corp.) were placed on *The National Law Journal*'s list of Top Defense Wins of the year. In the General Motors case, the automaker was sued for $100 million by the family of a woman who died when her SUV was hit head-on by a drunk driver. The plaintiffs argued that the woman would have survived had it not been for defects in the design of the GM vehicle. Kirkland attorneys argued that the impact, not the design, was responsible for the fire that killed the victim. The jury ruled in favor of GM on one of the claims in the suit; the company settled with the family on the others. In the Kubota matter, John Deere Co. sued Kubota for patent infringement. A team of K&E attorneys was able to prove their client did not infringe on John Deere's patent. Kirkland also secured courtroom victories for the Chicago Board of Trade, Discover Bank and Pioneer Corp. and two for Motorola.

European tour

Kirkland got 2003 off to a roaring start with a couple of big-money European deals that are sure to translate into hefty fees for the firm. In March, attorneys in the London office represented Bain Capital in its acquisition of paint company SigmaKalon. The acquisition, for which Bain paid nearly $1 billion, was its third purchase in three months. Kirkland represented the company in those acquisitions, as well. The U.K. office also played a major role in the management buyout of DB Capital Partners, the former private equity division of Deutsche Bank. The deal has an estimated value of $1.6 billion. Legal publishing company Chambers and Partners named Kirkland & Ellis "Private Equity International Law Firm of the Year" in 2002 and "U.S. Private Equity Law Firm of the Year" in May 2003. Of the top 100 law firms in the country, Kirkland was the third most profitable in 2001, according to a 2002 report by *American Lawyer*.

From the Golden Gate to Big Ben

In January 2003, K&E opened a San Francisco office. The office focuses on several practice areas, including IP and biotechnology litigation, corporate and private equity. Four Kirkland partners and 12 associates relocated to San Francisco to found the office. Kirkland's New York office scored a personnel coup when it lured two longtime partners from Skadden, Arps, Slate, Meagher & Flom's capital markets department and a senior corporate partner from Fried, Frank, Harris, Shriver & Jacobson. But the firm also lost partners in 2002 to local rivals Katten Muchin Zavis Rosenman and Jenner & Block. Kirkland also expanded its aforementioned thriving bankruptcy practice to its London office with the addition of a new partner. The firm lured well-known bankruptcy and restructuring attorney Lyndon Norley away from the London office of Cadwalader, Wickersham & Taft.

Starr power

In one of the firm's more unusual pro bono cases of late, former Whitewater special prosecutor and current K&E partner Kenneth Starr took up the plight of a South Carolina man who was arrested for disobeying the state's ban on tattooing. Ronald White had spent many years administering illegal tattoos, but was arrested, fined and sentenced to five years of probation in 1999 after footage of him giving a tattoo was aired on television. Starr challenged the state law, saying it violated White's artistic freedom. But the South Carolina State Supreme Court disagreed with Starr's argument, and in October 2002, the U.S. Supreme Court refused to hear White's appeal. Starr is also the man of choice for the Coalition of Free Trade, which retained the famous attorney early in 2003 to fight a state regulation banning California winemakers from shipping their products to consumers outside the state. Much of Starr's time, however, has likely been occupied by his challenge to a campaign finance bill backed by President Bush. Among other measures, the bill would abolish monetary limitations on individual contributions to national political parties.

GETTING HIRED

The hiring gauntlet

Kirkland "recruits well," brags a veteran attorney. "A number of associates have turned down Cravath offers to work here." The firm is "extremely selective, perhaps to a fault" and reserves its offers for "independent, smart, confident" candidates who "don't wait to be spoon fed." Associates describe Kirkland as "easily the most selective firm in Chicago" and "more concerned with school pedigree" than ever before. "Grades are important," one source drives home. "Period." In fact, some attorneys feel grades, and the "definite – and largely unfounded – bias towards Ivy League schools," have become overemphasized. Kirkland has "missed out on several great people just because of the school they went to or their grades," laments one midlevel litigation associate, echoing the concerns of many at the firm.

Others insist that the firm is "selective, but not elitist" and that Kirkland "will pass up candidates who have stellar academics but would not fit in socially." "A down to earth personality is very important," counsels one source. "K&E is a very social place, and you don't get anywhere in the firm by being rude." In addition to being "both book and street smart," you'll need "a little something extra" to fit in with the other "gregarious meat-eaters." "If you are smart but uncool," an associate warns, "Kirkland is not a place for you."

OUR SURVEY SAYS

Good luck making friends

K&E's "reasonably close-knit," "no-nonsense" associates are "generally laid back and friendly" one-on-one, but "formal and somewhat uptight in group settings." One associate cautions, "This is not a place where you come to make new social connections. If you came to the firm not knowing anyone in Chicago, it could be a problem." Others confirm Kirkland is "more a collection of lawyers than a firm," a "very professional but also somewhat cold" environment where professional and social bonds are rooted primarily in practice groups rather than the firm as a whole. "Corporate is uptight," says one source. "Bankruptcy is uptight but more friendly, younger."

The mood in other offices is somewhat lighter. "Kirkland's LA office is young, vibrant and friendly," says a midlevel associate. "I consider many of the lawyers in the firm to be friends first, colleagues second." New York is "tame and cordial but not relaxed," as recent expansion has made the office "less fun and generally a more stressful and competitive place to be." But "partners and associates frequently have lunch together," and the office is filled with "a lot of mavericks," many "quirky and even downright strange."

Ironman competition

K&E's "extremely inconsistent" workload may be a "total crapshoot," but more than one first-year has determined the firm is "not the sweatshop that many believe it to be." One rookie in the IP group notes "occasional spikes but mostly constant 50-hour weeks," and many report that they can work from home if they want. "You choose to work as hard as you want," stresses a midlevel associate. "Anyone who joins Kirkland thinking they won't be billing well in excess of 2,000 [hours] is kidding themselves," says a veteran associate, "and I don't think anyone lies to recruits about the fact that we work hard." Most are resigned to the situation. "If I have to put in long hours," runs the typical refrain, "it is because I am given responsibility that requires the work."

Others decry the "machismo about billing as many hours as is humanly possible," which makes it "hard to get out of the office without a total guilt complex." One source complains, "When you start to slow down you get bombarded with requests for more cases because clearly you have the time." An experienced bankruptcy attorney says partners "are good about letting you take vacation. But when you're in town," she adds, "your time is not your own." A junior associate pinpoints the problem: "We simply have too much work and not enough attorneys. As a result, the expectations of the amount of work each associate will do keep rising."

Grumble, grumble, grumble

"I expected to work hard," reports a veteran associate, "but not to be paid bonuses below market." He isn't alone. K&E associates feel "real pain and bitterness" over their bonuses, which one source points out as particularly frustrating given the increases in partner profits. "I have contributed lots of time and made lots of personal sacrifice for this job," another associate snaps, "while compensation has not reflected the firm's recent success due, in some part, to me." A new recruit gripes, "If we'd had a bad year, a polite e-mail explaining that would have made everyone feel better about the smaller bonuses. But the fact is that we had a stellar year, and while partner profits increased, associate bonuses dropped dramatically." Other associates complain succinctly that "they really screwed the associates this year" and "the wealth should be shared more."

Most feel the partners waited to see what everybody else gave out, then "lowballed bonuses because they could," but "people here expect way above market since they put in way above market hours." An associate points out, "They would never let us turn out work product that is at a level commensurate with the market." Furthermore, several second-years were shocked to discover that their original signing bonuses were being deducted from this year's bonus. "It was sneaky," says one, "and left us wondering why we weren't at some other big firm working the same hours and at least getting paid for it." (The firm insists that clerkship bonuses as well as the first-year stipend are additive to base salary and year-end bonuses, and that no such deductions were made.)

Train hard, work hard

At least one associate, however, feels "the compensation issue more than pales in comparison to the training that the firm so heavily invests in so as to make you a better trial lawyer." The firm's "outstanding," "unparalleled" formal training is "reason enough for Kirkland to retain its top ranking nationwide." Kirkland's Institute of Trial Advocacy (KITA), which brings nearly all the firm's litigation associates together for a week-long mock trial, is widely praised.

K&E associates also learn by doing, often and early. "I can't picture a better place to cut your teeth on some of the highest-end litigation as a first-year associate," says one rookie, "if you don't mind the intensity." A sophomore associate recounts, "Within my first few months of the firm, I got great deposition and even trial experience before a federal jury, not to mention at least three summary judgment motions and other heaps of great litigation training." A senior associate sees "no place better in the world to practice if one wants to do Chapter 11 debtor work. We have the best cases, and people are afforded a huge opportunity to learn and advance."

For many years, that opportunity, along with the competitive base salary, was enough to keep most associates at K&E, and "turnover in the New York office is extraordinarily low" still. But a senior attorney fears "a mass exodus may be brewing," and other sources hint that there's "always talk of who has one foot out the door."

Just be a stellar attorney

"Hiring is not a problem," says one female Kirkland associate. "Retention and promotion is." Other women at the firm agree "the firm hires and distributes work completely fairly with respect to gender," but "long hours have the effect of limiting the number of female partners, especially if they want to have children." "No one here cares if you are a man or a woman," one source insists. "Just be a stellar attorney." Some women, however, fear that means they need to be overly "aggressive," even "manly," to be seen as partner material. "I do not consider myself to be particularly sensitive when it comes to this issue," says one female associate, "and yet time and again I have been truly shocked by some of the attitudes" among male associates and partners.

The firm is less successful in attracting racial minority associates. The official attitude is that "merit is the only factor for success," but because Kirkland focuses on "certain academic credentials regardless of race," notes a senior African-American associate, "we compete for minority candidates who have a lot of options and don't always choose K&E." Other sources concur the firm "could work a lot harder to recruit minorities." The firm notes that a Firmwide Diversity Committee was formed in 2001 to focus on these issues, and is making strides in this area, including but not limited to sponsoring diversity scholarships, attending minority job fairs and hosting panel discussions focusing on diversity issues.

Associates are highly reticent about discussing gay and lesbian attorneys at all. "Sexual preference is not an issue that generally comes up," says one of the few willing to address the subject, "and I don't see why it should be relevant." Despite indications that gays and lesbians do exist at Kirkland, not one respondent to our survey said they were out at work.

Shearman & Sterling

VAULT TOP 100 · **12** · PRESTIGE RANKING

599 Lexington Avenue
New York, NY 10022
Phone: (212) 848-4000
www.shearman.com

LOCATIONS

New York, NY (HQ)

Menlo Park, CA • San Francisco, CA • Washington, DC
• Abu Dhabi • Beijing • Brussels • Dusseldorf •
Frankfurt • Hong Kong • London • Mannheim • Munich
• Paris • Rome • Singapore • Tokyo • Toronto

MAJOR DEPARTMENTS/PRACTICES

Antitrust • Asset Management • Bank Finance •
Bankruptcy & Reorganization • Capital Markets •
Executive Compensation & Employee Benefits • Leasing
• Litigation • Mergers & Acquisitions • Private Clients •
Project Development & Finance • Property
Securitization & Derivatives • Tax

THE STATS

No. of attorneys: 1,000+
No. of offices: 18
Summer associate offers: 80 out of 80 (2002)
Senior Partner: David W. Heleniak
Hiring Partner: T. Robert Zochowski, Jr.

BASE SALARY

New York, NY
1st year: $125,000
2nd year: $135,000
3rd year: $150,000
4th year: $165,000
Summer associate: $2,538/week

UPPERS

• Challenging international work
• Respectable commitment to pro bono work
• Less strenuous hours in market downturn

DOWNERS

• Morale still low after 2001 layoffs
• Associate-partner disconnect
• "Renovations desperately needed" in NYC office

NOTABLE PERKS

• 4th-year retention bonuses
• Skybox at Madison Square Garden (NY)
• Posh dining room
• Rotations at international offices

THE BUZZ
WHAT ATTORNEYS AT OTHER FIRMS ARE SAYING ABOUT THIS FIRM

• "Top-rung lawyering"
• "They blew it"
• "Great international practice"
• "Would steal from grandma for more PPP"

RANKING RECAP

Best in Region
#11 - New York

Best in Practice
#7 - Mergers & Acquisitions
#8 - Antitrust
#8 - Corporate
#8 - Securities
#9 (tie) - Real Estate
#9 - Tax

Best in Diversity
#20 - Diversity for Minorities

EMPLOYMENT CONTACT

Ms. Suzanne Ryan
Manager, Professional Recruiting
Phone: (212) 848-4592
Fax: (212) 848-7179
E-mail: sryan@shearman.com

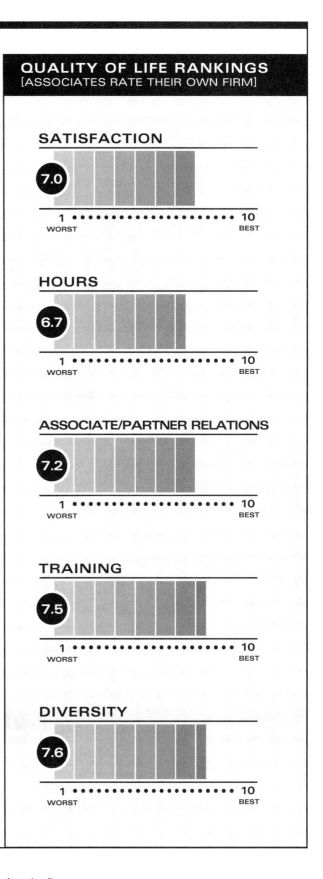

QUALITY OF LIFE RANKINGS
[ASSOCIATES RATE THEIR OWN FIRM]

SATISFACTION
7.0
1 WORST .... 10 BEST

HOURS
6.7
1 WORST .... 10 BEST

ASSOCIATE/PARTNER RELATIONS
7.2
1 WORST .... 10 BEST

TRAINING
7.5
1 WORST .... 10 BEST

DIVERSITY
7.6
1 WORST .... 10 BEST

THE SCOOP

Shearman & Sterling combines a venerable history in America with a strong contemporary international practice. The firm is one of the world's top M&A wheeler-dealers, reasserting itself in the last year after the layoff of approximately 80 associates caused a temporary blow to its prestige.

A long history of top clients

Shearman & Sterling opened for business in 1873, when Thomas Shearman and John Sterling broke ranks from the law offices of New York bar association head David Dudley Field to set up their own downtown firm headquartered in the Fourth National Bank Building. (The firm has since moved its Manhattan digs to a midtown skyscraper just blocks from Grand Central Station.) One of the firm's first significant clients was industrialist Jay Gould, whose takeover of the Union Pacific Railroad in 1875 was achieved with help from his new attorneys. Other early clients included Charles Osborn, cofounder of one of Wall Street's largest brokerages, railway magnates George and Donald Smith and various members of the Rockefeller clan.

Spanning the globe

Shearman has taken a slow growth approach to its non-U.S. offices since opening its first foreign branch in Paris in 1963, aiming to ensure that each office will blend in with the local cultures and display a true commitment to international practice. In the spring of 2002, the firm appointed Kenneth MacRitchie, a partner in the 30-year-old London office who initiated Shearman's English law practice in 1996, as the managing partner of that outpost and its 130-some attorneys. The firm has been on a European expansion spree of late; after acquiring most of the German law firm Schilling, Zutt & Anschutz in 2000, it has gone on to open new offices in Brussels, Munich and, most recently, Rome.

Shearman also has a strong presence in Asia, dating back to its arrival in Hong Kong in 1977. Additional outposts followed in Tokyo (1987), Beijing (1993) and Singapore (1995). The Hong Kong and Beijing offices work on the largest capital markets and M&A deals in Asia, as well as some highly innovative cross-border acquisitions. The firm established its Asian International Arbitration team in Singapore in 2002, representing clients in arbitrations throughout Asia as well as Asian clients in cases taking place in Europe and the Americas. High-profile representation in 2002 included acting for investors in arbitrations against the nations of Pakistan and the Philippines before the International Centre for Settlement Disputes, an affiliate of the World Bank.

Forever in blue jeans?

When legendary blue jean manufacturer Levi Strauss was seeking a new law firm, financial advisers Salomon Smith Barney and Bank of America recommended Shearman. The firm met the denim peddler's two most important conditions: It has a strong West Coast presence through its San Francisco and Menlo Park offices and a high-powered banking practice that could apply its expertise toward bringing down the jeans merchant's $1.8 billion debt. Shearman's first action for Levi's in late 2002 was to advise on the issuance of $425 million of senior notes to assist the company's refinancing.

Fidelity to Fidelity

Shearman also reeled in another hot client in 2002: financial services powerhouse Fidelity Investments. The switch offers Fidelity access to the expertise of Shearman partner Barry Barbash, who heads the firm's asset management group. Before joining the firm in 1998, Barbash ran the investment management division at the Securities and Exchange Commission, essentially overseeing regulation of the mutual fund industry.

Rising stars in project finance

Shearman's project finance practice group has been on a roll lately. In June 2002, the firm was named "Project Finance International Law Firm of the Year" by *Chambers Global*, then snagged *The Lawyer* magazine's "Projects/PFI Team of the Year" award less than a week later. And in February 2003, the hits continued: three separate magazines singled the firm's project finance group out for praise, with two of the awards citing Shearman's work on financing the new Wembley Stadium and an integrated petrochemical facility in Nanjing.

Bucking the M&A trend

The worldwide economic slump may have put a damper on the M&A scene, but Shearman didn't have any problem finding the biggest deals in Europe in 2002. The firm counseled Renault in the strengthening of its financial alliance with Japanese counterpart Nissan, who bought a $1.7 billion chunk of the French automaker in April. In October, it helped Swiss pharmaceutical firm Novartis sell off the international components of its National Beverages division, the makers of Ovaltine, to a British company for 272.5 million euros. It also represented Europe's largest insurer, Allianz AG, in a merger with Dresdner Bank and an increased investment in Banco Popular Español, while providing counsel to French broadband provider Louis Dreyfus Communications on several acquisitions of European telecom companies, including FirstMark, Kaptech and Belgacom France.

Shearman is no stranger to sweet American deals, either. The firm negotiated two substantial acquisitions for Cadbury Schweppes in 2002. First it counseled Cadbury's Snapple division on the $100 million purchase of the Nantucket Nectars brand, and it helped Cadbury take a $4.2 billion bite of the global chewing gum market with the purchase of Pfizer's gum division, which makes Dentyne, Trident and Chiclets. Shearman also counseled two longtime media clients on their latest acquisitions, assisting MTV's parent company, Viacom, in its buyout of the College Television Network and representing NBC in a $1.25 billion purchase of the Bravo network.

The firm has also staked out territory on the corporate side of major league baseball. After counseling John Henry and his co-investors in their acquisition of the Boston Red Sox (and the team's historic home, Fenway Park) for $660 million, Shearman helped Henry get rid of the team he already owned, the Florida Marlins, which he sold in February 2002 for $158.5 million. Then, in August, Shearman represented Nelson Doubleday when he sold his half of the New York Mets to co-owner Fred Wilpon for a reported $131 million.

Responding to tragedy

Shearman's New York office has provided extensive pro bono relief in the aftermath of the September 11 terrorist attacks. Attorneys at the firm represented Marmily Cabrera, who was originally denied survivor's benefits because regulations for the federal victim's compensation fund did not recognize her common-law marriage, and the parents of Cantor Fitzgerald employee John Willett, whose landlord refused to return the deposit on the lease he had signed the night before he died. Both cases were resolved successfully before heading to court.

Shearman attorneys are also doing their bit to promote law and order in Africa. The firm has provided legal assistance to the United Nations' special prosecutor's office for the international crime tribunal formed in response to the 1994 genocide in Rwanda, and have also conducted seminars for Rwanda prosecutors. In 2002, the firm collaborated with the International Bar Association and the Zimbabwe Law Society to investigate whether Zimbabwe's president, Robert Mugabe, was contravening his country's constitution in order to cling to power.

GETTING HIRED

Quick, now's your chance

Shearman is looking for "smart, personable, independent starters" and "hard workers." Insiders reveal that "exceptional international experience" or foreign language skills will land you in good stead, as will a "double background" of, say, an MBA to go along with your JD. The firm is "always desperate for Harvard, Yale and Stanford students," and lately the West Coast offices have been "trying very hard to improve recruiting" from U.C. Berkeley's Boalt Hall as well. "Just hit the middle of the pack in any top-10 law school," jests one senior associate, "and Shearman will be a safety firm in case Sullivan & Cromwell dings you." Still, a second-year corporate attorney insists, "We are all very book smart, with more than respectable academic credentials." Another concurs: "Shearman remains a prestigious firm and draws ambitious, talented people."

OUR SURVEY SAYS

The rebuilding continues

Shearman's offices may have a "veneer of gentility," but "an air of suspicion still pervades" in the "difficult transition" after the 2001 layoffs. "The firm needs to find ways to convince associates that there is a strong future ahead for the firm and for their careers," states one junior associate. "Many associates continue to worry that they will either be let go if the economy doesn't improve or be overloaded with work if the economy rebounds," says another. Though "many partners are great role models," associates feel "very little employee appreciation," and the "clear esprit de corps" of earlier years "is now long gone."

"Don't be fooled by the official business casual dress code," warns a first-year S&S associate. Despite the firm's public commitment to a relaxed fashion sensibility, this insider suggests there's a "very conservative" unwritten standard. "There is definitely a culture gap," a second-year corporate attorney concurs. "Older partners would like to see a return to business attire but younger partners and associates are very comfortable dressing down. Meetings often find people dressed across the spectrum."

It's a question of trust

Relationships with the partners can be "hit or miss." Some partners are "aloof" while others are "extremely accommodating." A midlevel associate gripes, "Partners mean to treat associates well. They just lack the people skills," while a senior attorney counters that despite the "them and us" mentality, partners "generally try to act fairly." "The real question," says one corporate attorney, "is whether the associates as a whole trust the partners as a whole," as "misinformation, rumor-mongering and speculation" leave many associates on edge.

A second-year corporate associate says many believe "attorneys in slow practice areas are being weeded out." (The firm cautiously reponds that "underperforming" attorneys "may" wind up on the outs "as a result of performance reviews.") Other sources say their colleagues aren't waiting to be asked to leave. "This office in particular," says one D.C. attorney, " has morphed from a place where good attorneys could make a career to a place with an 'up or out' mentality." Quite a few associates predict that "when the economy turns around, there will be an exodus from here."

"Feast or famine"

That's the phrase many Shearman associates use to describe their workload. "You either have nothing to do for weeks at a time or you're pulling 100-hour weeks," grouses a senior banking associate. "Hours have been uncomfortably long at least half the time I have been here," a securities attorney agrees. "It's frustrating to have little to do during the day or during the week," complains another member of the banking practice, "and have new assignments on Friday

afternoon to work during the weekend on a regular basis." An attorney in the M&A practice group says, "If you don't have enough work, you begin wondering when they are going to let you go."

Others take a more upbeat view of the "very slow" market, claiming it has made their hours "very nice" for the time being – "So much better than expected," as one freshman litigator puts it. "Weekends and vacations are ruined only when required," says a midlevel associate in San Francisco, who echoes reports from other sources that senior associates try to manage juniors' workloads equitably. "I have rarely been required to work on weekends," says a first-year corporate associate, "and my workload has been pretty steady since I started. Even when times are slow, there are so many training seminars and other activities to participate in that no associate should ever get bored working here."

Nothing to do, nowhere to go

Although many feel that working with senior attorneys on diverse cases provides "the best training that one gets at Shearman," others believe "more hands-on training and direct feedback between reviews would be welcome." A reduction in available work, says one associate, "has resulted in some midlevel attorneys not having the skills attorneys in their class years would have had in the past." Another associate comments, "The work distribution system sometimes results in assignments that are too challenging for junior associates, which is unfair to the client and not the best way to learn." Formal training is, as suggested above, available; in fact, associates praise the firm's commitment to training as "first-rate" and "strong, when it occurs," with sessions covering a variety of legal issues nearly every week.

Great chances for pro bono

With a full-time coordinator some associates describe as "arguably the best pro bono attorney in New York," S&S offers associates "numerous possibilities for pro bono work." At least in the New York office, "we've got more pro bono than we can handle" – everything "from hands-on litigation work and in-court representation to drafting constitutions and monitoring elections to advising international criminal tribunals."

Keeping pace with the market

When it comes to compensation, S&S insiders are, for the most part, content – even as they acknowledge that their salaries are "not the highest" and the firm is "never a trendsetter." A second-year associate summarizes, "The price is right." Many junior and midlevel associates find, as one third-year corporate attorney reports, "Shearman's retention scheme, on top of bonuses, puts us ahead." A junior associate on the West Coast also praises the policy. "I actually get paid more than my friends at California firms," the second-year explains, "because their bonuses are based on hours billed. In this economy, that means only 25-40 percent of the junior associates get bonuses, and those bonuses are still much lower than the New York market."

Down in the dumps

Despite the firm's Manhattan headquarters' "convenient location" and private dining room where attorneys can get "a four-course meal with linen service" on the cheap, few associates in New York have anything nice to say about their quarters. "The entire office is a dump," snaps one attorney, while another sighs, "The offices are an embarrassment, especially when entertaining visiting attorneys and clients." Others say the "ratty" décor, dominated by "a drab putty color," is "stuck in the '70s," singling out the "sad lobby art" and "coffee-stained carpets" for their opprobrium. "Too many associates are doubled up," say other associates, with third- and even fourth-years still sharing offices. "Hopefully," a first-year litigator says, "our coming expansion to a new floor will cure some of the problems." (The firm confirms that it has begun a refurbishing project in response to the Manhattan associate complaints.)

At least associates in D.C. find themselves in "quite comfortable" offices, "much roomier" than New York. Meanwhile, a second-year attorney in Germany has his own office "with a glass front and access to the patio," and a Londoner describes his office as "fantastic" with "lots of space." We don't think the New Yorkers are going to like that news one bit.

Paul, Weiss, Rifkind, Wharton & Garrison LLP

1285 Avenue of the Americas
New York, NY 10019
Phone: (212) 373-3000
www.paulweiss.com

LOCATIONS

New York, NY (HQ)
Washington, DC
Beijing
Hong Kong
London
Paris
Tokyo

MAJOR DEPARTMENTS/PRACTICES

Bankruptcy
Corporate
Employee Benefits & Executive Compensation
Entertainment
Environmental
Litigation
Personal Representation
Real Estate
Tax

THE STATS

No. of attorneys: 500
No. of offices: 7
Summer associate offers: 88 out of 88 (2002)
Hiring Attorney: Eric S. Goldstein

BASE SALARY

New York, NY
1st year: $125,000
2nd year: $135,000
3rd year: $150,000
4th year: $170,000
5th year: $195,000
6th year: $210,000
7th year: $220,000
8th year: $235,000
Summer associate: $2,400/week

UPPERS

- High-quality work
- Firm reputation
- Eclectic firm culture

DOWNERS

- Long hours
- Lower than expected bonuses
- Little feedback on assignments

NOTABLE PERKS

- Friday cocktail parties
- Subsidized gym membership
- Free BlackBerrys
- Drawings for free theater tickets

THE BUZZ
WHAT ATTORNEYS AT OTHER FIRMS ARE SAYING ABOUT THIS FIRM

- "Young and energetic"
- "Workaholics"
- "Litigation powerhouse"
- "Great despite abusive partners"

RANKING RECAP

Best in Region
#8 - New York

Best in Practice
#4 - Litigation

Quality of Life
#13 - Pro Bono
#17 - Training
#19 - Selectivity

Best in Diversity
#16 - Diversity for Minorities
#17 - Diversity for Gays & Lesbians

EMPLOYMENT CONTACTS

Ms. Patricia J. Morrissy
Legal Recruitment Director
Phone: (212) 373-2548
Fax: (212) 373-2205
E-mail: pmorrissy@paulweiss.com

Ms. Joanne Ollman
Legal Personnel Director
Phone: (212) 373-2480
Fax: (212) 373-2515
E-mail: jollman@paulweiss.com

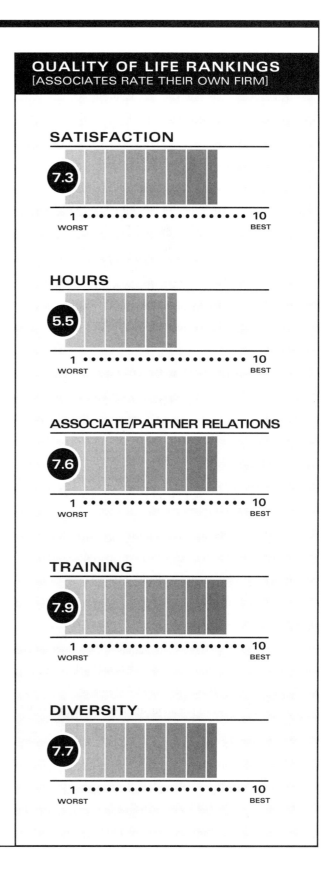

QUALITY OF LIFE RANKINGS
[ASSOCIATES RATE THEIR OWN FIRM]

SATISFACTION
7.3
1 WORST •••••••••••••••••• 10 BEST

HOURS
5.5
1 WORST •••••••••••••••••• 10 BEST

ASSOCIATE/PARTNER RELATIONS
7.6
1 WORST •••••••••••••••••• 10 BEST

TRAINING
7.9
1 WORST •••••••••••••••••• 10 BEST

DIVERSITY
7.7
1 WORST •••••••••••••••••• 10 BEST

THE SCOOP

A full-service firm with 128 years of experience, Paul, Weiss, Rifkind, Wharton & Garrison LLP is known for handling complex litigation and corporate matters, but is just as adept in entertainment, individual representation and other areas.

Partnership has its limits

In a move speculated to have been inspired by litigation resulting from accounting scandals at companies like Enron and Tyco, Paul Weiss became a limited liability partnership in January 2003. As opposed to the firm's previous status as a general partnership in which partners shared responsibility for malpractice claims, the new status means only partners directly involved in a case can be named in a claim related to it. The organizational change is one that Paul Weiss shares in common with several other major law firms, including giants like Cravath, Swaine & Moore; Sullivan & Cromwell; Cadwalader, Wickersham & Taft; and Latham & Watkins – all of whom have converted to limited liability partnerships in recent months.

That's entertainment

Companies and individuals in the entertainment industry consistently seek out Paul Weiss' expertise in a variety of legal matters. Time Warner Entertainment and Paul Weiss go way back. The firm counseled Warner Communications when it merged with Time Inc. in 1989. The firm then became involved in the creation of TWE, which combined the new company's various film, television and cable properties, and later negotiated the sale of a portion of TWE to phone giant AT&T. Paul Weiss' global relationship with the company came full circle in August 2002 when the firm helped AOL Time Warner regain full ownership of TWE. Attorneys in the firm's entertainment practice also represent New York City's Lincoln Center Theater, the New York Shakespeare Festival, the National Music Publishers' Association, Spike Lee and playwright August Wilson.

The urge to merge

Mergers and acquisitions is another area in which the name Paul Weiss is well regarded. Attorneys from Paul Weiss' New York office negotiated the pending acquisition of ProBusiness Services on behalf of client Automatic Data Processing Inc. In February 2003, the firm completed the $700 million acquisition of client Calvin Klein Inc. by Phillips-Van Heusen. On the cross-border M&A front, the firm enjoyed a banner year. Paul Weiss' relationship with Carnival Corp. has been smooth sailing. In a deal worth $5.3 billion, the firm's New York and London offices are representing the cruise line in its hostile takeover of Princess Cruises. The Carnival deal, as well as two others negotiated by the firm, made the Top 15 Global M&A Deals of 2002 as ranked by *The Deal*. Meanwhile, the firm's Hong Kong and New York offices are currently representing Hutchinson Whompoa in connection with the proposed acquisition of Global Crossing. Thomson

Financial also ranked Paul Weiss third among all law firms for Canadian mergers and acquisitions completed in 2002, including the firm's representation of Alberta Energy Co. Ltd. in a $16.8 billion merger with PanCanadian Energy.

Tackling the tough cases

The firm has a proven track record in white-collar defense. It successfully defended Senator Robert Torricelli against charges of accepting illegal campaign contributions, helping avoid any criminal exposure (though the associated publicity ultimately derailed his re-election campaign). At the same time, the firm has been helping ImClone founder Sam Waksal in connection with conspiracy, insider trading, perjury and other criminal charges arising from the federal investigation into sales of ImClone stock by members of Dr. Waksal's family and friends. Former Robertson Stephens tech stock analyst Paul Johnson has also called on the firm to clear him of charges leveled by the SEC. Johnson has been accused of not disclosing his ownership of stocks in companies being acquired while recommending the stocks of the companies doing the buying. Paul Weiss has countered that Johnson's actions were in accordance with SEC requirements.

Major corporations, directors, creditors and others connected to financially troubled companies frequently turn to Paul Weiss for guidance. For instance, the firm represents Citigroup in connection with the Enron case and various securities cases related to alleged issues involving research analysts. (It's also counseling Lehman Brothers on similar cases.) Paul Weiss advises the California Public Utilities Commission in the bankruptcy of Pacific Gas & Electric, California's largest investor-owned public utility and the largest public utility in U.S. history to file for bankruptcy. PG&E has sought to pre-empt California regulatory and environmental law, prompting the CPUC to object to the reorganization and propose an alternative structure. The firm also represents CPUC in connection with the state's $12 billion energy bond financing, believed to be the largest public financing offering in history.

Giving back

Community involvement is one of the guiding principles of the firm. Paul Weiss attorneys typically meet or exceed the guideline of 30 pro bono hours per attorney annually established in the Volunteers of Legal Service's Pro Bono Pledge. The firm well exceeded this standard in 2002, with 85 pro bono hours per lawyer. The firm has been active in death penalty, human rights and reproductive rights cases. The firm has also authored several amicus briefs, including one supporting affirmative action policies at the University of Michigan Law School. In March 2003, the firm prepared a brief on behalf of the Partnership for New York City supporting the Campaign for Fiscal Equity suit to provide quality education for students in poor New York City public schools. In a continuation of the pro bono services Paul Weiss attorneys provided following the September 11 terrorist attacks, a partner at the firm participated in the Mission Statement Drafting Committee of the Lower Manhattan Development Corporation. The committee worked to create

a mission statement that would serve as guideline for the creation of a memorial at the site of the former World Trade Center.

GETTING HIRED

Paul Weiss "operate[s] a very selective process, both at the screening and the callback stages." In the words of a sixth-year associate, "Our standards are very high." While those high standards aren't a new thing, "the current economic environment has made hiring at Paul Weiss even more competitive." "Most of the associates here are from top-10 law schools, but the firm does hire associates from other schools." Naturally "the firm wants to hire intelligent, capable individuals," but insiders say, "It is also looking for a personality fit." For candidates who have "the requisite academic qualifications, [the] interview process appears to be geared towards finding associates who have diverse interests and an interest in the law," according to a first-year. A fourth-year advises that during the interviews, candidates should "make friends with the partners. Associate reviews are appreciated, but they do not seem to be determinative." Some believe "the whole process is somewhat random and depends on how candidates 'click' with their interviewers." One junior attorney describes being "surprised to find that many candidates that I and other first- and second-year associates took to lunch were not receiving offers from the firm. I think the firm looks for people who are smart, well-rounded and would fit in to the firm culture."

OUR SURVEY SAYS

The many faces of Paul Weiss

A broad array of opinions about the firm's culture exists among Paul Weiss associates. Insiders say the firm's New York office is the type of place where "lawyers socialize and genuinely like each other." According to one midlevel attorney, Paul Weiss "has an eclectic, individualistic culture that can be at turns laidback, friendly or uptight." There are "brilliant people all around, and people that I'd love to spend time with outside of work – if only there were time!" "Everyone – from partners to secretaries – is on a first-name basis. It is rare to see closed office doors." Co-workers are "hardworking but down to earth," and there are "no excessive formalities" among attorneys. "Associates come from a variety of backgrounds and have a variety of interests, and most are not overly work-obsessed." "My department is very easy going and laid back, which is not the case with some of the other departments," confides a real estate attorney. A newcomer says the firm's reputation is known to be "laid back, friendly and social, but in reality people are very anal and uptight about their work, and somewhat cliquish." The folks at Paul Weiss "tend to be politically liberal."

All kinds of work

A litigation attorney gives the firm high marks for its "diversity of cases, great training, terrific pro bono opportunities and terrific support staff." Lest one get the impression that life at Paul Weiss is more play than work, this source goes on to say, "The firm culture is intense about work – everyone is a perfectionist – but also supportive of having outside interests. People are friends, do socialize and are supportive of one another's career choices." An attorney who recently joined the firm says, "I've been pleasantly surprised to find myself working with two partners on a few smaller cases. I have enjoyed the responsibility that comes with being the only associate on the case, and I've gotten a lot of experience." Things haven't gone as well for a more experienced associate. "I have gotten good experience, but on the most boring cases with the worst partners," sighs a fifth-year. A third-year finds, "My work varies and is sometimes quite interesting but can be tedious at times, depending on the task." An associate who's seen both sides says, "Depending on which practice group within the corporate department you are in, you may have incredible responsibility early or you may end up proofing other people's work for two years." An associate in the bankruptcy department appreciates the "combination of big-time cases/deals and smaller ones, where you can get more hands-on exposure. There are also plenty of opportunities to do pro bono work, if that's your thing."

Working for (and on) the weekend

On the whole, Paul Weiss associates are not very pleased by the number of hours they work, and many report difficulty balancing their work and personal lives. That said, insiders believe "the hours here are comparable to other big NY firms." "At times, I am unsatisfied with my life because of the number of hours that I am working. I think, however, that if I am going to be working these kinds of hours, I am happy that I am doing it here," reports a third-year. A second-year reports enjoying "the intensity of work and not being bored," but finds it difficult "to plan free time well, because I am constantly on call." A first-year concurs, stating, "When there isn't much work to do, it's a great life. When things get busy, however, there is no such thing as life outside the office." A senior associate gripes, "Good work is rewarded with more work." Working weekends is not uncommon, but "laptops make working from home a reality." Associates in some of the firm's smaller departments happily tell us that their hours are reasonable. However, "in the larger departments, the hours situation is entirely different." Says an associate in the corporate department: "I work hard and the economy is slow, I cannot imagine what life was like three or four years ago." A like-minded co-worker who finds the hours "grueling," is nevertheless happy to be at Paul Weiss because "in a down economy, it's good to be at a firm that is very busy." Another upside: There is "no 'face time' or 'busy work.'"

Bonuses viewed as bogus

"We tend to stay with the pack" in terms of salary, a second-year tells us. While the salary is "appropriate," a first-year believes "the firm too often follows other major firms, despite being

busier and more profitable." Insiders say, "Paul Weiss will never be the leader when it comes to compensation, but it always pays the market rate." There seems to be an undercurrent of "resentment that Paul Weiss could afford to pay higher bonuses," but did not. "We're obviously paid well compared to average folks, but are paid poorly compared to the hours we work and the firm's profitability. Bonuses have fallen over the past two years despite record profits." One annoyed associate boldly states, "As for bonuses, I think the partners were rather cheap, considering that they kept saying all year that we were turning away business and that they were having a banner year." Of course, there are also attorneys who are pleased with their salaries and think "the firm is great about keeping up with the market." "I think we are pretty much in line with other comparable New York firms," says a litigation associate. One tired corporate attorney is even willing to "settle for less money for more realistic hours."

Partners who show respect

"With some exceptions, the partners here treat you as respected colleagues. You are encouraged, even expected, to voice your views." However, "this is an area that varies, not surprisingly, a great deal from partner to partner." "In my experience," says a first-year associate, "the partners are entirely sociable at various firm functions and cocktail parties. They say hello when you pass them in the hallways, and most of them respect your vacations and personal life." "Some partners are moody and abusive, going so far as to yell at associates in front of clients," a litigation associate reveals. Insiders acknowledge the existence of a few not-so-nice partners, but most associates have never encountered any problems. Overall, the partners are "approachable and treat you with respect." "There are a few partners with reputations for treating associates harshly," admits a third-year. But this source adds, "It seems to me that even those partners have mellowed." "Depending on which practice group you are in, you may have no partner contact whatsoever," says a corporate attorney, who names the M&A group as an example. "If a partner isn't responding to you, it is usually just because [he's] too busy."

Dull offices, unbelievable art

Associates are lukewarm when it comes to their work environment. Insiders say the office space is "bland," with a design that "appears to have been done by committee." The space may be "functional" and "not very attractive, but it does the job." The major gripe is that "first-year associates share offices," which can "be distracting and annoying when it comes to the need for privacy." As second-years, associates graduate to private offices with windows. While the actual offices aren't very inspiring, we're told the artwork is "amazing." "There's a Wolf Kahn in the main lobby. And so many Walker Evans photographs," says one breathless art lover. Other niceties include "a kitchen with coffee, tea and a fridge" on "every odd-numbered floor," a new conference center and a renovated cafeteria.

"When there isn't much work to do, it's a great life. When things get busy, however, there's no such thing as life outside the office."

– *Paul Weiss associate*

Williams & Connolly LLP

The Edward Bennett Williams Building
725 12th Street, NW
Washington, DC 20005
Phone: (202) 434-5000
www.wc.com

LOCATION

Washington, DC

MAJOR DEPARTMENTS/PRACTICES

Corporate
Litigation
Tax

THE STATS

No. of attorneys: 200
No. of offices: 1
Summer associate offers: Because most summer
associates have judicial clerkships, formal offers are
only extended after clerks receive permission from
judges to request offers. Typically, all summer
associates who request offers are welcomed for
permanent employment.
Managing Partner: By Committee
Hiring Partner: Heidi K. Hubbard

BASE SALARY

Washington, DC
1st year: $140,000
2nd year: $150,000
3rd year: $170,000
4th year: $180,000
5th year: $190,000
6th year: $200,000
7th year: $210,000
8th year: $220,000
Summer associate: $2,400/week

UPPERS

- "You don't just join a case, you join a team"
- Early responsibility and trial opportunities
- Mentorship by brilliant partners

DOWNERS

- Drab offices
- Intense, stressful workload
- Lack of formal policies can leave you guessing

NOTABLE PERKS

- Free lunches
- Monthly socials on the rooftop deck
- Tickets to Orioles games
- Late night cab fare

THE BUZZ
WHAT ATTORNEYS AT OTHER FIRMS ARE SAYING ABOUT THIS FIRM

- "The best of the best"
- "Too much bark"
- "Elite shadow ops litigation commando team"
- "Stuffy and pompous"

RANKING RECAP

Best in Region
#2 - Washington, DC

Best in Practice
#2 - Litigation

Quality of Life
#5 - Selectivity
#13 - Retention
#18 - Associate/Partner Relations
#20 - Satisfaction

EMPLOYMENT CONTACT

Ms. Donna M. Downing
Recruiting Coordinator
Phone: (202) 434-5605
E-mail: ddowning@wc.com

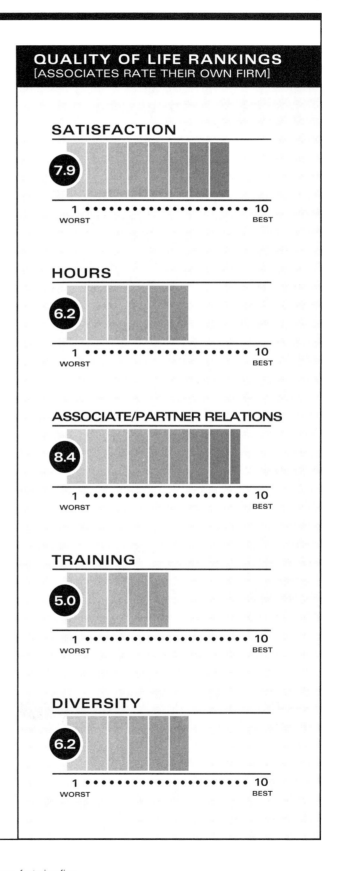

QUALITY OF LIFE RANKINGS
[ASSOCIATES RATE THEIR OWN FIRM]

SATISFACTION
7.9
1 WORST • • • • • • • • • • • • • • • • • 10 BEST

HOURS
6.2
1 WORST • • • • • • • • • • • • • • • • • 10 BEST

ASSOCIATE/PARTNER RELATIONS
8.4
1 WORST • • • • • • • • • • • • • • • • • 10 BEST

TRAINING
5.0
1 WORST • • • • • • • • • • • • • • • • • 10 BEST

DIVERSITY
6.2
1 WORST • • • • • • • • • • • • • • • • • 10 BEST

THE SCOOP

Williams & Connolly is a Washington, D.C. law firm that strictly adheres to the principle of discretion. Attorneys at this prestigious firm rarely speak publicly about cases, even for big clients like McDonald's or General Electric. The partners didn't even authorize an official web site for the firm until 2002. (Even then, the firm kept things subdued; press releases touting recent victories and new partners are conspicuous by their absence.)

Multifaceted founders

Williams & Connolly was founded in 1967 by Edward Bennett Williams and Paul Connolly, two attorneys who had earned strong reputations by defending high-profile clients like Jimmy Hoffa. Williams was regarded as one of the greatest litigators of his age – by no less an authority than U.S. Supreme Court Justice William Brennan – and his argument before the Supremes in favor of limitations on search and seizure of evidence in criminal cases helped set a new constitutional standard. But he was also a powerful figure in the world of sports who at one point owned both the Washington Redskins and the Baltimore Orioles. The firm's sports law practice continues to represent the Redskins, not to mention star athletes like Tim Duncan, Grant Hill and Chamique Holdsclaw.

Williams & Connolly has been a Washington insider since founding partner Joseph Califano brought the Democratic National Committee in as a client, and the firm's attorneys have frequently been called upon by the government. Partner Judy Miller served as general counsel at the Defense Department throughout the Clinton administration, while David Aufhauser was appointed general counsel of the Treasury Department in the spring of 2001 by George W. Bush. Later, when the original nominee to head the Securities and Exchange Commission's newly appointed oversight board, William Webster, was forced to resign amid a swirl of controversy, the SEC's commissioners named former Williams & Connolly partner Charles Niemeier the board's acting chief. Niemeier had been at the SEC since 2000, and was both the chief accountant of the enforcement division and chief counsel for the financial-fraud task force.

It's not surprising that Williams & Connolly's Washington connections have persuaded many A-list politicians to make the firm their legal adviser. The firm's star clients are U.S. Senator Hillary Rodham Clinton and former president Bill Clinton, for whom the firm has acted as counsel since 1992. But Williams & Connolly is a truly bipartisan law firm: it's currently representing Vice President Dick Cheney in a lawsuit alleging that he and other directors of Halliburton, where he served as CEO before running for office, inflated the value of the oil company's stock through fraudulent accounting practices.

Many of the firm's political clients rely on partner Robert B. Barnett, who has a thriving practice as an authors' representative. In addition to cutting a reputed $12 million deal for Bill Clinton's memoirs with Knopf, Barnett has lined up publishers for Lynne Cheney, Sen. Robert Byrd, William Bennett and former White House counselor Karen Hughes. He also reps an assortment of television news correspondents at every major network, including Sam Donaldson at ABC, Andrea Mitchell at NBC, Brit Hume at Fox News and Jeff Greenfield and Christiane Amanpour at CNN.

Fighting off the lawsuits

Edward Bennett Williams set a high benchmark for litigation prowess, but Williams & Connolly does its best to live up to that standard – and its best is definitely good enough. Just ask the board of directors at Wyeth Pharmaceuticals, makers of the contraceptive Norplant. Thousands of women had filed lawsuits against Wyeth beginning in 1994 over health complications they claimed were related to Norplant's surgically implanted silicone rods. In eight years of litigation, Williams & Connolly managed to settle more than 30,000 of the complaints for just $1,500 a plaintiff, got approximately 12,000 cases thrown out for failure to comply with discovery orders and had their lone trial defeat overturned on appeal. They effectively brought the matter to a close in August 2002 when a Texas federal court judge granted a summary judgment dismissing nearly all of the remaining claims.

Williams & Connolly has equal skill on the plaintiff's side of the courtroom. The firm represented the attorney generals of several states who chose to reject the federal government's resolution of its antitrust case against Microsoft and pursue further concessions against the software giant. A federal judge rejected the states' arguments in November 2002, endorsing the bulk of the original settlement. But those states that chose not to appeal the ruling received a windfall from their former adversary: Microsoft gave them $25 million to cover legal fees, plus an additional $3.6 million to pay for assistance in enforcing the settlement's terms.

Empowering the press

Williams & Connolly's association with *The Washington Post* dates back to founder Edward Bennett Williams' relationship with Ben Bradlee and Katherine Graham, and the firm has represented the paper on a number of matters. The firm helped the *Post* fight for access to law enforcement records in Prince George's County, Md., which county authorities had kept restricted from the public. The case began in 2000, when the paper was conducting an investigation into the unusually high police-shooting fatality rate in the county but was denied permission to examine case records or daily crime logs. The *Post* sued the county and obtained a favorable ruling in 2001, which was upheld in November 2002 by Maryland's Court of Special Appeals.

Williams & Connolly represents a number of other big media clients, like American Media, the publishers of five of the nation's top tabloids, including *The National Enquirer* and *The Weekly World News*. When the Federal Bureau of Investigation wanted to search American Media's headquarters in August 2002 after an anthrax scare at the Boca Raton office building, agents had to negotiate a precisely-crafted warrant and guarantee in writing that they would adopt a "hands-off" policy towards the company's network of confidential journalistic sources. Williams & Connolly also provides counsel to AOL Time Warner, and was retained in 2002 to represent the conglomerate in an ongoing joint investigation by the FBI and the SEC over a series of potentially illegal transactions by its online advertising division.

GETTING HIRED

Do you have what it takes?

"It's almost impossible to get a job here," says a senior litigator, but some younger Williams & Connolly associates offer some helpful tips. "Grades are a major consideration," agrees a junior litigator, "but they are not the only factor. You also have to have a good personality and truly be interested in what we do. In other words, you won't get hired if you're a jerk no matter how many A's you have, where you clerked or how intellectual you supposedly are."

"Williams & Connolly isn't really the place for late bloomers," a first-year associate advises, "meaning you've got to demonstrate that you'll hit the ground running." Another source suggests, "Accomplishment in other walks of life goes a long way in the interview process and with the Hiring Committee." Judicial clerks often seem to have an inside track to a job offer, but associates say the firm also places great value on "intangibles" such as "composure, poise, confidence and enthusiasm."

OUR SURVEY SAYS

Lambs in wolf's clothing

Williams & Connolly is "pretty laid back and friendly, considering that the majority of us are litigators," quips one second-year associate. The "tight-knit, clannish, cohesive" firm offers an "intense and fun" working environment where, as one source says, "the lawyering is very aggressive, but the culture is open and friendly." "Attorneys here take themselves and their work very seriously, but without sacrificing civility," a junior associate reports. "While there is a premium placed upon excellent work product and the hard work required to produce it, people here retain their sense of humor, friendliness and willingness to watch out for the more junior associates to make sure that they get good experience and feel part of the team." Partners regularly include associates in fun activities like "a cutthroat fantasy sports league, many friendly card games and happy hours," and daily free lunches further help create a "relaxed and easy" vibe.

Although some attorneys suggest that "W&C is becoming more and more just like any other big firm," for now the firm has "no set culture," with "no policies on dress or hours." One associate says, "While we are business casual, it's more the business side of casual, and people don't look askance if you are in a suit everyday." One junior associate says the office tone "makes you feel like a professional," and a midlevel colleague described the firm as "the best place to be a litigator, period."

All together now

Despite the lack of a minimum billables requirement, W&C is "far from your prototypical lifestyle firm," says a first-year associate. "We work a lot of hours for a non-New York firm," concurs a colleague, "but it really depends on how many cases you are working on and what stage each case is at." A senior litigator advises, "During trial, expect to work non-stop." Otherwise, a midlevel associate notes encouragingly, "When things are slow, most take advantage and get out of the office. There is no face time. Partners have better things to do." Other attorneys report that "the work you do here is always necessary and appreciated" and "the firm is quite sensitive about the hours that associates work." Says one grateful associate, "Partners seem to make an effort to prevent burnout by strongly encouraging time off when the pace of a case slows down."

"My interaction with the partners here has been surprisingly amicable," a corporate attorney reveals, "given the firm's reputation for being full of hard-asses." Williams & Connolly has "very little sense of hierarchy" and a "true team feel" among attorneys at every level of experience and seniority. "Partners and associates share the 'cool' work and the 'uncool' work," says a young litigator, "whether it's taking a deposition or reviewing a roomful of documents." Another attorney says, "Everyone here is treated as an adult who has something to contribute."

Put me in, coach, I'm ready to play

Associates get their chance to contribute very early on, as "W&C believes in experiential rather than classroom training." As one junior associate puts it, "The most intensive training I received was phone and computer training the first week." A midlevel litigator scoffs, "If you want hand-holding, this is not the place." Bravado aside, just about everyone agrees that "partners go out of their way to give as much experience to associates as possible," and that learning new skills in the middle of casework is "only scary the first time." "I did my first deposition within weeks of arrival," recalls one second-year. "Stressful? Yes. But did I learn more from the experience than 20 hours of classroom training on depositions? Yes."

"No second-year associate I know has the level of responsibility on interesting, large cases that I do," brags a young litigator. "The work is phenomenal," a third-year associate agrees. "Cases are second-to-none." A fifth-year recalls, "I thought I'd leave after two to three years here, but I've been pleasantly surprised by how much I enjoy the cases I'm working on."

Neutral on pro bono

Williams & Connolly "has a neutral attitude towards pro bono," says one associate. "The firm won't dissuade you from doing it, but won't persuade you either." Another attorney gamely suggests, "I think the firm will allow you to do as much pro bono as you want, as long as you finish up your other work, too." A midlevel associate adds, "It's not formally encouraged, but such formality is against the firm's culture." The firm replies that it makes a variety of pro bono opportunities available to associates, including established relationships with local public interest legal services providers.

So who needs bonuses?

Williams & Connolly pays "as much money as anywhere else," but don't get your hopes up at the end of the year, because the firm doesn't hand out bonuses. Then again, if none of the associates are bothered, why should you be? "We do not want bonuses," insists one attorney, "because it causes additional billing pressures that no one here wants." Another associate says, "My compensation is probably higher than associates in this region, even considering bonuses." But a senior litigator points out one possible downside to the no-bonus rule. "The disparity between those associates who work hard and those who don't means that the hardest-working associates are underpaid relative to the market," he explains, "and the associates who don't work hard are overpaid."

A slow trickle?

"Since I've been here," a second-year associate observes, "no one has left to go to another firm." Other colleagues agree that attorneys don't leave Williams & Connolly "unless it is to accept a plum government position or head for a new part of the country." But some sources say a retention problem is beginning to develop, "not as bad as New York, but getting there." A midlevel litigator elaborates, "Some surprising 'nos' and 'holds' on people up for partnership in the past couple of years have made senior associates unsure that they can succeed by doing good work." (Firm management counters that 25 of the 28 partnership candidates since 1998 were accepted.)

Slowly but surely

"W&C is a good place for women to work," says one female attorney. "However, we don't advertise it." A male colleague agrees that there "seems to be a genuine effort" to improve the firm's retention of its women associates, but "the actual results seem more limited." Though Williams & Connolly has been adding more women at the partnership level, a senior litigator notes that "the hours and demanding pace can cause women who wish to slow down some when they have children to leave." The firm's recruitment of minorities also "continues to improve," with three minority attorneys among the new partners of 2002. "We have done very well on adding African-American attorneys to the firm," notes one associate. "We are still lacking in other minority categories," she acknowledges, "but we're working on it." The firm says it does not inquire about sexual preference, which it considers a private matter, and the associates apparently agree ; there was virtually no commentary whatsoever about the subject in our survey.

"A little more sprucing up wouldn't hurt"

Williams & Connolly may have the "biggest associate offices in D.C.," but "sometimes it's a battle with office services to get them furnished with more than a desk and a chair."

Furthermore, one attorney complains, "The furniture is cheap and worn. The computers are a year or two out-of-date." (A firm-wide upgrade is in the works.) Associates don't like the "grayish-brown carpeting and mismatched art work" in the hallways any better. "I wouldn't call the surroundings drab," one shrugs, "but I do find them a bit plain." But some are determined to make the best of the situation. "The offices are fine," comments one associate. "Not ornate or luxurious, but it works."

Debevoise & Plimpton

919 Third Avenue
New York, NY 10022
Phone: (212) 909-6000
www.debevoise.com

LOCATIONS

New York, NY (HQ)
Washington, DC
Frankfurt
Hong Kong
London
Moscow
Paris
Shanghai

MAJOR DEPARTMENTS/PRACTICES

Corporate
Litigation
Tax
Trusts & Estates

THE STATS

No. of attorneys: 587
No. of offices: 8
Summer associate offers: 92 out 92 (2002)
Presiding Partner: Martin Frederic Evans
Hiring Partner: Michael J. Gillespie

BASE SALARY

New York, NY; Washington, DC
1st year: $125,000
2nd year: $135,000
3rd year: $150,000
4th year: $170,000
5th year: $190,000
6th year: $205,000
7th year: $220,000
8th year: $235,000
Summer associate: $2,400/week

UPPERS

- "Unparalleled commitment to pro bono"
- High-profile cases and name-brand clients
- Collegial work environment

DOWNERS

- Sharing offices
- "Hardly anyone in litigation makes partner"
- Lack of feedback/communication from partners

NOTABLE PERKS

- Subsidized cafeteria
- Bi-monthly lawyers' teas
- Free admission to the Whitney Museum (NY)
- Moving expenses, including broker's fees

THE BUZZ
WHAT ATTORNEYS AT OTHER FIRMS ARE SAYING ABOUT THIS FIRM

- "Happy associates"
- "Nicest sweatshop in the city"
- "Stuffy"
- "Great people, great culture"

RANKING RECAP

Best in Region
#9 - New York

Quality of Life
#2 - Pro Bono
#3 - Associate/Partner Relations
#5 (tie) - Satisfaction
#9 - Best 20 Law Firms to Work For
#13 - Selectivity
#17 - Retention

Best in Diversity
#11 - Diversity for Gays and Lesbians
#13 - Diversity for Women
#13 - Overall Diversity

EMPLOYMENT CONTACT

Ms. Ethel F. Leichti
Manager of Associate Recruitment
Phone: (212) 909-6657
E-mail: recruit@debevoise.com

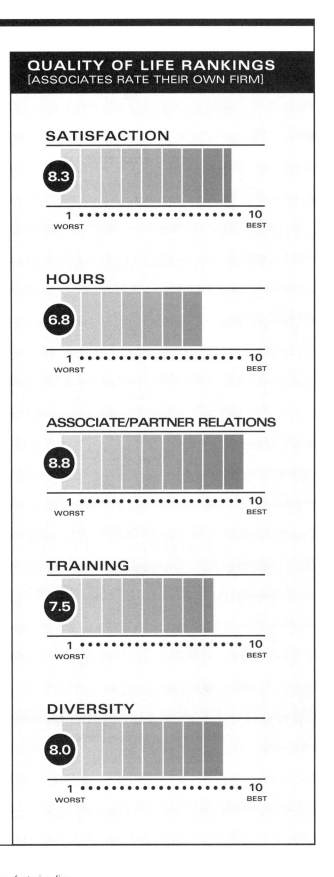

QUALITY OF LIFE RANKINGS
[ASSOCIATES RATE THEIR OWN FIRM]

SATISFACTION
8.3
1 WORST   10 BEST

HOURS
6.8
1 WORST   10 BEST

ASSOCIATE/PARTNER RELATIONS
8.8
1 WORST   10 BEST

TRAINING
7.5
1 WORST   10 BEST

DIVERSITY
8.0
1 WORST   10 BEST

THE SCOOP

Debevoise & Plimpton's prestigious corporate and litigation departments have always ensured the firm's reputation, while the pleasant firm culture makes it a favorite of humane lawyers with an academic bent.

Names and more names

Eli Whitney Debevoise, named after his cotton gin-inventing ancestor, convinced Olympic gold medalist (and Oxford-trained attorney) William E. Stevenson to leave the law firm where they both worked as associates and set up shop for themselves as Debevoise & Stevenson in 1931. Two years later, they were joined by Debevoise's Harvard Law School classmate, Francis T. P. Plimpton. Fellow Crimson alum Robert G. Page was added to the letterhead in 1935. After several more iterations, the moniker was shortened to its present form in 1981, on the 50th anniversary of the firm's founding.

The firm achieved early prominence through its handling of the bankruptcy of "Swedish Match King" Ivar Kruger in 1934; other early clients included Tampax and investment counselors Scudder, Stevens & Clark. Over the years, Debevoise has cultivated a prestigious client list, and its current clients include old-school outfits like American Airlines, DaimlerChrysler and Goldman Sachs as well as younger companies like Oxygen Media.

They keep their clients

Look at Debevoise's history and you'll notice that, even when its clients go through radical changes, their trust in the firm typically stays strong. American Airlines has been a client since the 1940s. Scudder, Stevens & Clark's association with the firm continued after its merger with Zurich Kemper Investments in 1997 and again after Zurich Scudder merged with Deutsche Bank in 2002. DaimlerChrysler is a client because Chrysler was a client right up until its $38 billion merger with Daimler-Benz. And the North American division of Swedish Match, the international tobacco-products conglomerate that grew out of Ivar Kreuger's original enterprise, instructed Debevoise in the summer of 2002 to file an antitrust lawsuit against competing snuff manufacturer US Smokeless Tobacco.

Bottoms up

Debevoise and Plimpton counseled telecommunications company Global Crossing during a government investigation into its finances and suits brought by frustrated shareholders. In the first three months of Global Crossing's bankruptcy, Debevoise was by far the largest biller, filing an application for more than $6 million in fees covering the months of February, March and April 2002.

Still finding the big money

When it comes to M&A work, Debevoise really did write the book – or at least four of its attorneys did. Meredith Brown and Paul Bird, co-chairs of the firm's M&A group, wrote 2001's *Takeovers: A Strategic Guide to Mergers & Acquisitions* with partners Ralph Ferrara and Gary Kubek. A few months after the book's publication, Brown was involved in yet another high-stakes deal, leading the team that advised Cogentrix Energy when they were almost acquired by Aquila. Bird, meanwhile, currently leads a team of lawyers working on a pending $3 billion stock merger between client Riverwood Holding and Graphic Packaging International Corp. Debevoise partners Stephen Friedman and John Vasily advised Prudential Financial on its merger with Wachovia; that deal, completed in early 2003, will create the nation's third largest brokerage firm with combined assets of $537 billion.

In the midst of the most severe recession in the advertising industry in six decades, Debevoise helped the world's largest advertising agency, Japan's Dentsu Inc., further consolidate its hold on the industry. When European ad agency Publicis Groupe S.A. decided to purchase the Chicago-based Bcom3 Group, Dentsu's lawyers cut a deal whereby Dentsu's 21 percent stake in Bcom3 became a 15 percent stake in the new venture, which brought into being the world's fourth-largest advertising holding company and second-largest media planning group.

A significant portion of Debevoise's involvement in M&A work comes through its representation of major financial institutions, like Merrill Lynch, who advise on corporate mergers. In 2002, the firm counseled Merrill through billion-dollar deals like Dynergy's sale of its Northern Natural Gas Co. division and Quest Diagnostics' purchase of Unilab. Debevoise also lent its expertise to Goldman Sachs in advising AT&T in the $72 billion sale of its broadband business to Comcast, and to Deutsche Bank Securities when the German bank advised Ocean Energy on its February 2003 merger with Devon Energy. And while that deal was being negotiated, a separate team of Debevoise lawyers represented a consortium of investors that paid 1.5 billion euros for Deutsche Bank's private equity unit.

Insurance pros

Insurers know they, too, can rely on Debevoise to help them close big deals. In January 2002, SNL Securities ranked Debevoise first in deal value and number of deals in insurance M&A transactions for the previous year. Shortly afterwards, *The American Lawyer* picked insurance industry practice co-chair Thomas Kelly as one of 10 attorneys named Dealmaker of the Year for his work bringing Principal Life Insurance Co.'s $1.85 billion IPO to market less than two months after the September 11 attacks.

But insurance companies also turn to Debevoise for its skills in litigating liability and discrimination cases. Longtime client MetLife sought the firm's assistance when it faced a lawsuit accusing the company of systematically denying proper coverage to African-American clients. The firm's attorneys were able to successfully settle the matter before trial, just as they had in similar cases for American General Life and Accident Insurance Co.

Welcome back

After a nine-year stint as the U.S. Attorney for the Southern District of New York, former Debevoise partner Mary Jo White came back to the firm in early 2002 to take charge of the litigation department. She didn't waste any time building up a caseload. Before the year was over, she'd been retained by Bristol-Myers to probe its sales practices and by Kansas-based Westar Energy to conduct an internal review prompted by a Department of Justice investigation into the utility company's finances. She was also hired by rival New York law firm Pillsbury Winthrop to defend it against a $45 million defamation suit brought by former partner Frode Jensen after the firm's chair and managing partner commemorated his departure with a press release highlighting "sexual harassment allegations…and a significant decline in his productivity." (The terms of the March 2003 settlement she helped negotiate were confidential but presumably included the public apology from Pillsbury acknowledging Jensen as one of its "most productive corporate partners.") High-profile cases like these should add spice to the memoirs White is purportedly contemplating.

The rest of the litigation department has it pretty busy, too. The firm is representing Universal Music Group and the Island Def Jam record label in connection with a criminal investigation of the rap music business, while helping Rosie O'Donnell in a dispute with the publishers of her defunct magazine. Debevoise is also the legal counsel for Tyco's ex-CEO, Dennis Koslowski, in all the civil and regulatory proceedings he faces.

Shanghai express

After a slow but steady start, Debevoise has ramped up its international practice in the last decade. In the firm's first 50 years of operation, it added only two new offices: Paris in 1964 and Washington, D.C. in 1982. But after testing the waters with a London branch in 1989, Debevoise took to global expansion with enthusiasm, adding a Hong Kong office in 1994, followed by a Moscow debut in 1997, then Frankfurt in 2001. The firm returned to China to establish a second office in Shanghai in late 2002.

GETTING HIRED

Top dogs

Want to work at Debevoise? Join the club. "Debevoise is competitive," shrugs an insider, "and the firm puts a great emphasis on law school grades. The firm, however, also highly values candidates with unique talents that are not law-related." In addition, the firm is "looking for people with energy, passion and warmth in their personalities." A first-year associate advises would-be candidates to be "ready, willing and able to take on anything." According to a fourth-year insider, "You generally have to come from a top law school and graduate at the top of your class. I think one of the problems with the hiring process is that it tends to be too snobby, ignoring otherwise qualified candidates because they did not go to the 'right' schools."

Although a senior associate notes remarks that Debevoise is "very focused on law school grades, more so than on journal activities, college performance and other resume items," other insiders tell us that "an interesting background or prior experience, pleasant personality and compatibility with the firm's overall 'nice guy' culture are also important."

OUR SURVEY SAYS

A civil practice

Insiders at Debevoise report that the firm culture is "fairly relaxed given the high-stress environment." Debevoisians are considered "friendly and relaxed" and are "courteous with juniors and staff." Moreover, "classes are sociable, but not so tightly knit as to result in cliques. Relationships between junior and senior associates are easygoing and informal." "The culture is wonderfully collegial during working hours. It's everything its reputation suggests. There doesn't seem to be much socializing outside of work, however," says a first-year associate. The firm's "weekly lawyers' tea provides an atmosphere for socializing and, while most lawyers are serious, everyone is extremely nice and friendly." "The work has been interesting throughout," a third-year associate shares, "and, far more importantly, my peers have been a joy."

Insiders reveal that the key to the good vibe at Debevoise is "the good balance between laid back and formal." In the opinion of a litigation associate, "Most partners and associates are congenial and respectful, although this is not the place where dynamic personalities are the norm. Think nice nerds with a slight 'I'm entitled to success' attitude." Some point out that there is a down side to all this civility. "Debevoise lives up to its reputation – for better or worse. It is civil and polite, as well as quiet and rather dull," says a first-year. However, that is not necessarily a bad thing. This source elaborates: "I think that even if I completely screwed up an assignment here, I would only be told perhaps that it was not my best effort or that it needed work. The message would still be clear, but a little sugar-coating goes a long way."

Nothin' to brag about, but we'll take it!

Most associates agree that they "can't complain about the money," although they're not doing cartwheels over it either. A second-year deems the salary "nothing special – just the usual New York deal. No complaints, but no bragging rights either." Maybe "Debevoise is not the market leader," concedes a senior associate, but the firm pays "the going rate – both salary and bonus – and matches the increases that their peer firms such as Cravath, Cleary and Davis Polk put in

place." Others agree that Debevoise's compensation is "totally commensurate with other big New York City firms" ("other than Wachtell"). "The compensation is competitive with other firms," a nit-picky freshman points out, "but Debevoise does not give the same perks that other firms do, such as gym membership. Whereas most firms subsidize nearly 100 percent of your gym fees, Debevoise does not."

It comes with the territory

Debevoise insiders work hard. "Leaving before 10 p.m. feels early," confesses one first-year associate. But many associates take the long hours in stride. "I'm not satisfied because I work way too much, but I have to expect to work more than I'd like," reveals a third-year associate. "It just goes along with being at a New York firm." A second-year who is "satisfied overall" admits, "That is because I am billing an average of 'only' nine hours a day, which is considered slacking these days."

Of course, some associates wearing rose-colored glasses express satisfaction with the long days. "For the most part," says a first-year associate, "my hours have been tolerable. I haven't lost many weekends, which I zealously guard. There is also flexibility within the hours required in a given day. That is, if I want to go to the gym in the afternoon and work later, there is nothing that prevents me from doing so." A second-year tries to find an upside in all the long hours: "There is no face-time culture, which is great. Hours are long, but this reflects that the firm has continued to receive good, steady work despite the downturn." A bankruptcy attorney credits the lack of face time to a focus on "the quality of work product, not the number of billable hours." A litigation attorney says Debevoise provides "a challenging work environment without pressure to work like a slave."

According to another litigator, "If you have a deadline, expect to work regularly after 10 p.m. for the week before the due date. But there's definitely room for downtime, depending on how many cases you are juggling and when and if they are active." This source adds, "If you can do your work without getting sucked into the subtle but powerful undercurrent of competition, you can definitely have a life. It's your choice. It's about creating your own boundaries and learning when to say no. Then again, if you want to be partner someday, you'll have to put in the serious time."

Are we at the same firm?

Viewpoints on the amount and effectiveness of formal training at Debevoise vary widely among associates. "Upon arrival, new associates are given extensive and excellent training in their area," remarks a bankruptcy associate. While a corporate finance associate reports, "Extensive training is provided by the firm," a litigator tells us there's "very little provided." The firm "could definitely use more time dedicated to litigation training," another litigator informs us. "We have a lot of training and CLE [classes] available to us," says an attorney in the tax department, but "some are not as good as others." A midlevel complains, "I am not being trained in areas within my specialty in which I am not already proficient."

Aside from the formal training program, "there is an advisory program with both associate and partner advisors for junior associates. The senior associates and partners give constructive feedback and advice." Some insiders report employing means other than formal classes to gain skills. "I've had a chance to work independently on a number of pro bono cases and accordingly have learned a lot," reports a first-year. "The hands-on training is most beneficial," asserts a second-year. This associate adds, "Here, the best way to be trained is to find a partner or an associate who will give you a fair share of responsibility."

Tell us what you think

"The level of respect and cordiality between partners and associates is very high," insiders say. In the experience of a second-year, "partners respect associates' lives outside the office, when possible, and genuinely are interested in associates' ideas and opinions." A first-year gives an equally glowing report: "The partners I work with demonstrate great respect toward associates at different levels. They are responsive and are considerate of the associates' time and schedule."

However, a number of associates say they'd love to receive more feedback from the partners. A third-year finds, "Most of the training – at least the effective training – is on the job, such as the partner or associate you're working with explaining why she completely rewrote your draft brief or why she's using a certain strategy in the litigation. Partners are spotty on this. Some explain, some don't." Consequently, "most feedback tends to come from associates." "Some partners give more satisfying work and feedback than others. There is not much consistency," says a third-year. A midlevel associate poses this rhetorical question: "Is it really respectful and/or professionally responsible not to tell an associate on a regular basis how she can improve her work?"

Doubling up

"The firm just recently moved in to entirely new polished offices," shares a first-year. "It now has extensive conference room space. As a result, however, associate offices are a bit small and people double up for longer than they did before." Associates should expect to share "for at least their first two years," insiders warn. Several find that to be a "cruel and unusual length of time." "Many fourth-year associates have internal offices or offices that will require them to take on a summer associate officemate," explains a lawyer, "and associates in classes below that are doubled or in interior offices." "Perhaps I'm being a little too critical, but I see no reason why as a third-year [associate] I'm still sharing an office. The firm moved office space a year and a half ago, and my class definitely got screwed. Who knows when I'll have an office to myself?" To make matters worse, says this source, "The partners couldn't care less." As for aesthetics, insiders admit the new space is "bright and airy, very pleasant" and a "very comfortable and modern work environment."

Sidley Austin Brown & Wood LLP

Bank One Plaza
10 South Dearborn Street
Chicago, IL 60603
Phone: (312) 853-7000

787 Seventh Avenue
New York, NY 10019
Phone: (212) 839-5300
www.sidley.com

LOCATIONS

Chicago, IL • Dallas, TX • Los Angeles, CA • New
York, NY • San Francisco, CA • Washington, DC •
Beijing • Geneva • Hong Kong • London • Shanghai •
Singapore • Tokyo

MAJOR DEPARTMENTS/PRACTICES

Bankruptcy • Business & Banking Transactions
Corporate/Securities • Employee Benefits
Employment & Labor • Environmental
Intellectual Property • Litigation • Real Estate
Tax • Trusts & Estates

THE STATS

No. of attorneys: 1,533
No. of offices: 13
Summer associate offers: 162 out of 172 (2002)
Chairs: Tom Cole, Chuck Douglas and Tom Smith
Hiring Partner: John Levi

BASE SALARY

All domestic offices*
1st year: $125,000
2nd year: $135,000
3rd year: $150,000
4th year: $160,000
5th year: up to $185,000
6th year: up to $195,000
7th year: up to $205,000
8th year: up to $210,000
Summer associate: $2,400/week

*Associate salaries in the New York office range
$5,000-$10,000 higher.*

UPPERS

• Well-organized mentorship program
• Unusually supportive and respectful partners
• Stable – no layoffs or pay cuts

DOWNERS

• Distribution of best work said to be uneven
• Merger brings more bureacracy
• Bonus program "not competitive"

NOTABLE PERKS

• Emergency daycare
• Free train/bus passes and parking
• Firm sports teams
• Weekly catered lunches (D.C.)

THE BUZZ
WHAT ATTORNEYS AT OTHER FIRMS ARE SAYING ABOUT THIS FIRM

• "Securitization powerhouse"
• "Not as impressed as I should be"
• "A fine institution"
• "Why did they merge?"

RANKING RECAP

Best in Region
#2 - Chicago

Best in Practice
#6 - Real Estate
#9 (tie) - Bankruptcy/Corporate Restructuring
#10 - Securities

Quality of Life
#3 - Part-Time/Flex-Time

EMPLOYMENT CONTACTS

Chicago
Ms. Jennifer C. Hernandez
Recruiting Manager
Phone: (312) 853-7495
Fax: (312) 853-7036
E-mail: jherna01@sidley.com

New York
Ms. Shana Kassoff
Recruiting Manager
Phone: (212) 839-8600
Fax: (212) 839-5599
E-mail: skassoff@sidley.com

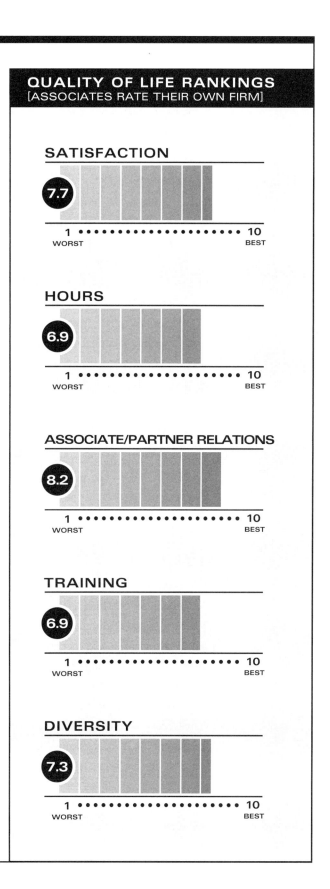

QUALITY OF LIFE RANKINGS
[ASSOCIATES RATE THEIR OWN FIRM]

SATISFACTION
7.7
1 WORST • • • • • • • • • • • • • • • • • 10 BEST

HOURS
6.9
1 WORST • • • • • • • • • • • • • • • • • 10 BEST

ASSOCIATE/PARTNER RELATIONS
8.2
1 WORST • • • • • • • • • • • • • • • • • 10 BEST

TRAINING
6.9
1 WORST • • • • • • • • • • • • • • • • • 10 BEST

DIVERSITY
7.3
1 WORST • • • • • • • • • • • • • • • • • 10 BEST

THE SCOOP

With more than 200 years of combined experience in the practice of law, Sidley Austin Brown & Wood has managed in a short period of time to combine two firms with disparate practices into a singular legal standout.

Two firms become one

Brown & Wood, founded in New York in 1914, rapidly became a leading advisor to investment banks and other financial institutions after its founding. A Chicago fixture since 1866, the strengths of Chicago's Sidley & Austin were primarily in corporate and regulatory law and litigation. Each firm had already expanded geographically in the U.S. and abroad. They also enjoyed successes in their respective specialties prior to their 2001 merger. But thanks to their recent partnership, Sidley Austin Brown & Wood has become a national player with a full-service practice. In addition to the aforementioned practice areas, Sidley also handles a substantial amount of antitrust, bankruptcy, trusts and estates, intellectual property and tax matters.

Roll out the welcome mat

The start of 2003 was a busy time as the firm welcomed several new lateral partners in various offices. The closings of California-based firms Brobeck, Phleger & Harrison and Skjerven Morrill afforded Sidley the opportunity to scoop up some local talent. News that nine Skjerven attorneys would become partners in Sidley Austin's San Francisco office was reported in February 2003 in *The Recorder*, a legal newspaper. The firm's Los Angeles office picked up two Brobeck partners. The D.C. office also added two antitrust partners from Powell, Goldstein, Frazer & Murphy.

Big-time clients

Sidley has helped accounting firm Andersen inch closer to ending the legal mess triggered by the Enron bankruptcy. In August 2002, Sidley attorneys negotiated a settlement in which Andersen Worldwide would pay $60 million to Enron creditors, investors and former employees. The agreement was reached in part because Andersen Worldwide, which coordinates work among Andersen's international offices, was considered less culpable for the energy company's falsified accounting records. Litigation is still pending against the U.S. arm of fallen Big Five accounting firm Arthur Andersen LLP. Sidley has been retained by some of the preferred and common shareholders of embattled cable concern Adelphia to represent their interests following the company's bankruptcy filing during the summer of 2002. As if that weren't enough, Sidley attorneys are also representing Charles Conaway, Kmart's former chairman and CEO. Conaway is a defendant in a shareholder lawsuit, as well as another related to Kmart's employee benefit plan. Additionally, he's being investigated by the retailer itself regarding his role in the company's bankruptcy.

In March 2003, attorneys in the firm's San Francisco office served as counsel to investment banks Goldman Sachs, Lehman Brothers and Morgan Stanley in a private placement deal with Fidelity Investments parent FMR Corp. The ability to cultivate such deals has helped Sidley make an impressive showing on Thomson Financial's 2002 year-end rankings of top legal advisors. In the U.S. debt and equity categories, the firm was No. 1 for both issuers and managers. Sidley also captured the top spot as advisor to issuers of asset-backed securities and second place as advisor to managers of mortgage-backed securities.

Strong medicine

A team of Sidley lawyers secured a huge victory for drug manufacturer Pharmacia in March 2003. Along with competitor Pfizer, the Searle division of Pharmacia was sued by the University of Rochester. The drug companies, which co-market the arthritis medication Celebrex, were accused of infringing on a patent held by the school. The Sidley legal team was able to prove that the school's patent is invalid. The firm is also representing Searle in a suit against law firm Pennie & Edmonds because P&E helped the University of Rochester obtain the patent that later became the basis of the suit. Searle was also a client of Pennie & Edmonds at that time.

High court maestro

Sidley has a nationally respected appellate practice headed by partner Carter Phillips, who has racked up more than 30 appearances before the Supreme Court over the course of his career. It was Phillips to whom the General Accounting Office turned in 2000 for advice when it sought access to files regarding Vice President Dick Cheney's involvement with Enron. Later that year, Microsoft tapped Phillips to lead the appeal in its infamous antitrust battle with the Justice Department. Some of Phillips' most recent high court appearances have been on behalf of Norfolk Southern Corp. and the Pharmaceutical Research and Manufacturers of America. In a November 2002 appearance, Phillips argued that, if allowed to stand, a verdict awarding $5.8 million in damages to six railway workers with asbestosis could bring about more litigation from workers who had been exposed to asbestos, but had not developed cancer. (The ruling was upheld by a 5-4 margin.) In January 2003, Phillips was at the Court again, this time arguing to disband Maine's prescription drug rebate program. The case is pending.

EEOC update

Sidley's battle with the Equal Employment Opportunity Commission, which began in 1999, continues. The commission has been investigating the demotion of 32 Sidley Austin partners to senior counsel and of counsel in 1999 (prior to the merger with Brown & Wood). An unknown insider tipped off the agency, alleging that some of the partners were demoted because of their age. It has also been alleged that the partners held little voting power, in effect making them employees and therefore subject to age discrimination laws. The firm inched closer to proving its case when a panel of judges ruled in late 2002 that the demoted attorneys were indeed partners. However, the

panel made no decision as to whether the partners held enough power within the firm to be considered employers. The case remains unresolved, as the EEOC continues to investigate the partner/employee debate.

GETTING HIRED

Candidates interviewing with Sidley undergo the "standard on-campus interview and callback" process. In one office, "the callback interview consists of meeting with three attorneys for 25-minute interviews, two of which are usually partners. After the interviews, two junior associates take the candidate to lunch, which gives the candidate an opportunity to ask questions in a more relaxed forum." (Interviews in other offices can be more extensive.) Insiders say the firm is highly selective, recruiting from only a few choice schools. "If you are not from one of the top 10 to 15 schools, you will probably need to be on law review to get a callback." A senior associate who helps interview candidates says, "I personally look for someone who is interesting to talk to and with whom I would enjoy working." Sidley "has a fairly firm grade cutoff, but there is some flexibility" if a candidate brings "other outstanding achievements" to the table. For instance, a midlevel confides, "There is a definite preference for clerks." "Sidley hires mainly from its summer associate class and does not seek as many lateral hires as other firms may. There is a definite view to hire associates who will remain at the firm and become partners," a fourth-year shares. Although some associates seem pleased that "the firm has become significantly more selective" since the merger, others feel "the firm is trying too hard to recruit based on school rather than on personality."

OUR SURVEY SAYS

Period of adjustment

Although the firm's merger was completed in May 2001, insiders tell us attorneys are still adjusting to the change and, as such, the culture is in flux. "The firm used to be a 'lifestyle firm' but that has long since passed. While the associates and partners are all still friendly, there is definitely a more uptight feeling," reports a junior associate. "It's a combination of quirky personalities – former Sidley [lawyers] and the frat-boyish former B&W [lawyers]. The cultural divisions are still evident. [It's] hard to know when and how the two cultures will coalesce." A midlevel finds the firm atmosphere to be "very strange since the merger. I have a few post-merger friends, but mostly the groups are separate."

The Los Angeles office is "friendly, but quite professional" and possesses "a very comfortable, team-oriented environment." "The associates don't go out in big groups to happy hours like at some other firms, but you can find a group of three or four people to go out with or have lunch with," says an attorney in the D.C. office. A like-minded officemate says, "Lawyers do not socialize much outside the office." "While I generally like the people here, it seems that this office is becoming more of a 'have or have not' kind of place. You either get a lot of great billable work or you find yourself scraping to get enough," says a nervous D.C. associate. "The people are great, but at times because of the economy the work can be boring or non-existent, which makes the days drag."

Base better than bonus

Sidley associates aren't ecstatic about their pay, but most believe "the compensation is competitive," while some even brag, "Sidley is at the top of the market." While "salary is where it should be," the sentiment that "bonuses are below market" was voiced by a number of Sidley associates. A corporate attorney explains, "The bonus is connected to billable hours and as a result, many people get nothing!" However, an L.A. associate reports receiving a small bonus "for almost hitting 2,000 hours." An opinion from the other end of the spectrum: "My compensation, with bonus, plainly exceeds all firms. Sidley's bonus plan, which is highly linked to hours, makes sure that if you bill a lot of hours, you will be making more than any comparable associate in the city," says a Chicago associate. A senior associate making upwards of $200,000 considers the pay "average for a large firm." Hey, that's nothing to sneeze at! Yes, this source admits, "'Average' is still pretty good."

Long hours, but some flexibility

A midlevel who considers her hours to be "pretty reasonable" says, "It can be hard to get enough billable hours. There has been more of a push in recent months to get the average hours up in the office." Other associates report that it's "difficult to manage the fluctuations in workload," and say they'd "gladly accept less pay for fewer hours." Hours can "fluctuate substantially between groups." A junior litigation attorney reports working "about nine hours or more a day" and "five to seven hours a weekend." "Sidley has been tremendous in giving me the opportunity to work from home at odd hours that allow me to spend more time with my young children," reports one very satisfied associate. While "there is a greater pressure to bill than there used to be," Sidley "provides everything you need to work out of the office, which makes things easier," according to a senior associate. A midlevel reports being "on a 'reduced-hours' schedule" and being "able to do quite a bit of work from home." "Sidley has as a goal that associates bill 2,000 hours, which, as long as it gets approved, includes all hours billed to pro bono matters." Associates cheerily say, "There is no 'face time' required here." A Chicago attorney tells us, "As long as you get your work done on time and done well, if you want to sneak out at 3:00 on a Friday, it is no problem."

A little more feedback, please!

"There are a couple of bad apples," but "most partners are respectful and collegial" and "will gladly stop what they are doing to answer questions, provide guidance or just shoot the breeze," insiders say. According to a Chicago attorney, "It's quite common to see associates and partners joking around at work." "Overall, I think that the partners are good with associates, and I think that there has been a push for more communication and feedback," says a litigation attorney. "Most are generous in giving general advice, although performance-related feedback – both of a formal and informal nature – is less frequently given." The topic of feedback is a recurring theme and one on which opinions are split. Many attorneys say they have been "fortunate enough to receive feedback" from partners on a regular basis. But the desire for the firm to "conduct reviews more often" is also noted by a fair number of associates.

On-the-job training

Associates couldn't muster much enthusiasm for the training they receive. "There is a litigation training program at our office, and I think that corporate people have training opportunities. But that's about it" for in-house, formal training, explains a midlevel. "Training is pretty good for junior associates, but is sparse for midlevel or senior associates." A seventh-year associate observes, "Opportunities for training are very frequent." However, this attorney believes, "The pressure for billable hours probably causes associates to pass up many of those opportunities." "One has to make one's own opportunities to learn new things," says an attorney in the appellate litigation department. At least some of the lack of formal training may be by design. "My own feeling is that Sidley believes in training-by-doing, as opposed to mock exercises and spending years watching others," says a litigation attorney who agrees with that philosophy. A third-year expresses hope that "training can be improved" because "there are holes in what I know how to do." A New York associate reveals, "There are repeated statements of intention to start a training program, but they never come to fruition." However, this source would prefer more hands-on training, including "more opportunities to get to speak in court and take depositions." Associates do note that "the firm created women's mentoring groups so that women across different practice groups could get together and have a group to go to with issues and/or problems."

Cramped, but functional

Work accommodations are a mixed bag, depending on which office you're located in. Offices in the firm's Los Angeles outpost "are very bright and open with a modern, but not cold, feel." An annoyed D.C. associate blows off a little steam: "I know that this new office is much prettier than our old place, but they really blew it when they had this building designed. There are no functional work rooms, the paralegal space is disgraceful and given all the boxes of documents that are carried around, the doors should swing both ways." However another Beltway attorney says the new digs are "overall, an improvement." Her only complaint: The new office space is "not as social as the old offices, which had an internal staircase and more of an open architecture." A Windy City attorney reveals that the Chicago office is "looking for new space." According to one Chi-town associate: "Boxes, piled four or five high, often line the hallways because storage – other than long-term records storage – is at a minimum. Storage for my own files often crams my office to the point where no one can use my chair to sit." But it's not all bad. The Chicago office provides "magnificent views of Lake Michigan." Associates in New York say their current space is "not as nice as" the firm's previous offices in the World Trade Center, which were destroyed in the September 11 attacks. "The space we are in now is fairly drab and boring" and "wholly uninteresting," with bathrooms that "need to be renovated."

Gibson, Dunn & Crutcher LLP

333 South Grand Avenue
Los Angeles, CA 90071-3197
Phone: (213) 229-7000
www.gibsondunn.com

LOCATIONS

Los Angeles, CA (HQ)
Century City, CA
Dallas, TX
Denver, CO
Irvine, CA
New York, NY
Palo Alto, CA
San Francisco, CA
Washington, DC
London
Munich
Paris

MAJOR DEPARTMENTS/PRACTICES

Antitrust
Corporate
Environmental
Financial Restructuring
International
Labor & Employment
Litigation
Public Law & Policy

THE STATS

No. of attorneys: 794
No. of offices: 12
Summer associate offers: 104 out of 114 (2002)
Chairman: Kenneth M. Doran
Chairman, Hiring Committee: Kevin S. Rosen

BASE SALARY

Washington, DC
1st year: $125,000
2nd year: $135,000
3rd year: $150,000
4th year: $165,000 ($170,000 - NY)
5th year: $185,000 ($190,000 - NY)
6th year: $195,000 ($205,000 - NY)
7th year: $205,000 ($220,000 - NY)
8th year: $210,000 ($235,000 - NY)
Summer associate: $2,404/week

UPPERS

- Assignment system promotes flexibility, responsibility
- Market dip brings decent hours
- High-profile litigation cases

DOWNERS

- Resentment over diminishing bonuses
- Inconsistent mentoring opportunities
- Struggling with diversity

NOTABLE PERKS

- Annual allowances for books, client development
- Picks up tab for just about any CLE course
- Triennial department-wide and firm-wide retreats
- BlackBerry, laptop, high-speed home connection

THE BUZZ
WHAT ATTORNEYS AT OTHER FIRMS ARE SAYING ABOUT THIS FIRM

- "Rising Washington star"
- "Vast right-wing conspiracy"
- "LA's Cravath"
- "Macho sweatshop"

RANKING RECAP

Best in Region
#3 - California

Best in Practice
#7 - Antitrust
#10 (tie) - Labor & Employment

Quality of Life
#9 - Selectivity
#9 - Part-Time/Flex-Time
#18 - Pay

EMPLOYMENT CONTACT

Ms. Leslie E. Ripley
Director, Professional Development & Recruiting
Phone: (213) 229-7273

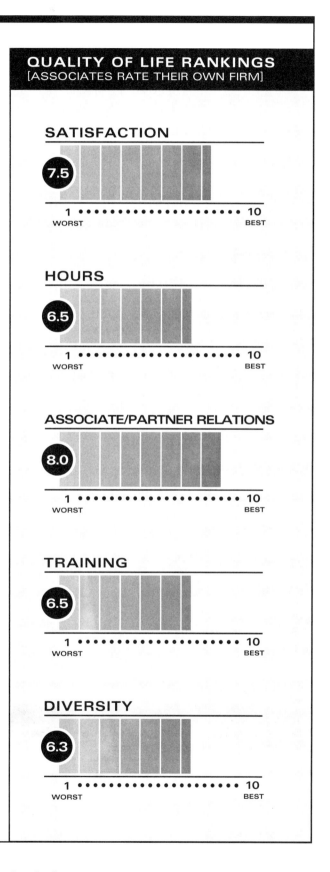

QUALITY OF LIFE RANKINGS
[ASSOCIATES RATE THEIR OWN FIRM]

SATISFACTION
7.5
1 •••••••••••••••••• 10
WORST   BEST

HOURS
6.5
1 •••••••••••••••••• 10
WORST   BEST

ASSOCIATE/PARTNER RELATIONS
8.0
1 •••••••••••••••••• 10
WORST   BEST

TRAINING
6.5
1 •••••••••••••••••• 10
WORST   BEST

DIVERSITY
6.3
1 •••••••••••••••••• 10
WORST   BEST

THE SCOOP

Gibson, Dunn & Crutcher is one of Los Angeles' "Big Three" firms, with more than a century's worth of experience in southern California and around the world. The prestigious firm has been associated with many a legal and political heavyweight. Stanford Law School valedictorian and future U.S. Supreme Court Justice Sandra Day O'Connor was offered a position as a legal secretary in 1952 – though she turned it down.

We love LA

Corporate attorney John Bicknell built a strong practice in Los Angeles in the latter half of the nineteenth century. By the time he teamed with Walter Trask in 1890, he had an impressive client list that included the Southern Pacific Railroad. The union of Bricknell and Trask started an unbroken chain of partnership that has, so far, culminated in Gibson, Dunn & Crutcher.

Friends of Dubya

Gibson Dunn has been in Washington, D.C., since 1977 and has cultivated a rich network of political connections. Former Republican congressman Richard Zimmer joined the firm in 2001 after leaving office, while a slew of Gibson attorneys resigned to take posts in George W. Bush's administration. Eugene Scalia, son of Supreme Court Justice Antonin Scalia, left for the Department of Labor, where he became the department's acting solicitor before resigning in early 2003 and returning to his old office. Theodore Olson, who led the team of Gibson Dunn lawyers that litigated on Bush's behalf after the ambiguous election in 2000, was rewarded for his successful efforts by an appointment to the position of solicitor general, representing the federal government's interests before the Supreme Court. Another attorney who worked on the Bush case, Miguel Estrada, was nominated to fill a vacancy on the D.C. Circuit Court of Appeals, generally viewed as a fast track to the Supreme Court. But Democrats, claiming that Estrada lacked relevant experience and concerned about his legal philosophy, refused to accept the nomination when they controlled the Senate; afterwards, they filibustered to prevent a confirmation vote from taking place.

The firm has also had its share of Democrat bigwigs, of course, including former congressman Mel Levine, who maintains offices in both Los Angeles and Washington, and retired partner Aulana Peters, who served as a minority commissioner on the Securities and Exchange Commission during the 1980s.

Hotshots

Gibson Dunn has another major player in senior corporate partner Andy Bogan, a 2002 "Dealmaker of the Year" according to *American Lawyer* magazine. The magazine also pegged Theodore J. Boutrous Jr., co-chair of the appellate law and media law practice groups, as one of its "45 Under

45" outstanding lawyers (selected for the January 2003 issue). Boutrous is a whiz at obtaining the reduction of damage awards against his clients, including the reversal of a $259 million verdict against DaimlerChrysler in October 2001 and a $222 million libel verdict against *The Wall Street Journal* in May 2000. He's also representing Ford in the appeal of a $290 million punitive damages award, and in early 2003 asked the Supreme Court to review the case.

In April 2002, Gibson Dunn's Dallas office welcomed William V. Dorsaneo, the attorney and law professor who wrote the book on litigation in the Lone Star State. We mean he *really* wrote the book, the 26-volume *Texas Litigation Guide*. (He also co-wrote the five-volume *Texas Civil Trial Guide* for good measure.) Dorsaneo is of counsel in the firm's Dallas office and heads the Texas appellate group in its litigation department.

Timothy Roake started out at Gibson Dunn as an associate in 1983, but left five years later and eventually became the chairman of the litigation group at Fenwick & West. In January 2003, he came back to the firm, joining the litigation group at the Palo Alto office. Roake is an expert litigator in intellectual property cases for technology companies and also has significant experience representing individuals and companies in SEC insider trading and accounting investigations.

Still doing the M&A deals

Gibson remains one of the nation's top M&A advisors. In the first quarter of 2003, it played a role in nine deals with a cumulative value of $8.96 billion. This followed a year in which it completed 89 deals worth more than $102 billion, the second-highest tally by a U.S. law firm in 2002 according to Thomson Financial. Among those was a transaction *The Deal* magazine called 2002's "Deal of the Year": Northrop Grumman's $13 billion purchase of TRW. The firm represented Northrop, the nation's fourth-largest defense contractor, in an acquisition process that consumed much of the year, beginning with a hostile takeover bid in February. After TRW accepted a $60-per-share offer in July, negotiations continued until mid-December.

Gibson also advised Dole Food Co., the world's largest fresh fruit producer, during a takeover bid by CEO David Murdock in September 2002. Murdock, who already owned 24 percent of the company's stock along with his family, was willing to pay $1.26 billion for the rest of the company. After months of legal haggling, Dole and Murdock eventually agreed on a final price tag of $1.43 billion in December 2002.

A full range of pro bono

Gibson Dunn has an active and varied pro bono practice, and was awarded honors as the 2002 Pro Bono Law Firm of the Year by Los Angeles' Public Counsel Law Center. Through the American Bar Association's Death Penalty Representation Project, the firm has taken on the defense of Texas death row inmate Darlie Routier. Routier was convicted of murder in 1997 for the stabbing deaths of two of her sons, aged six and five, but has always maintained that they were killed by an unknown intruder who attacked her as well. Gibson argued on her behalf in July 2002 to have key evidence retested in hopes of obtaining a new trial. In other pro bono news, the Los Angeles office collaborated with Bet Tzedek, a non-profit law center providing services for low-income tenants, in suing one of the city's worst landlords. (Gibson Dunn lawyers have frequently served on Bet Tzedek's board, including two past presidents.) The attorneys obtained an out-of-court settlement in March 2002, convincing the landlord to improve maintenance at 23 of his properties and pay $1 million in delinquent utility bills; they also got $200,000 for the tenants' rights group who acted as plaintiffs in the case.

In another rather unusual pro bono case, Gibson Dunn is defending several ethnic grocery stores in California's Santa Clara County against a lawyer who is waging a self-appointed battle against video piracy in the Indian film industry. State law allows individuals to sue vendors of pirated videos on the basis of deceptive or misleading advertising (because the bootleg copies were not manufactured by the production company on the label). This lawyer has sued 180 shops throughout the state which he accuses of selling unauthorized copies of hit Bollywood movies. Gibson has accused him of exploiting the law to prey on small storeowners for his own gain.

GETTING HIRED

Grade snobs and proud of it

Even Gibson Dunn's own associates admit that the firm's hiring committee are "grade snobs" when it comes to selecting new associates. "It's no secret that Gibson takes pride in the pedigree of its attorneys," says one midlevel attorney. Even prospective lateral hires are subject to the "strict" grade cutoffs, which have become "much higher than they used to be," as "the firm only looks to hire the top people from the top 20 schools." A second-year associate admits, "I know I would not have been hired here had I applied this year as opposed to a few years ago." Some associates find the grade requirements "silly and arbitrary," and believe they work "to the detriment of the culture of the firm." A midlevel associate grouses, "We turn away well-rounded, smart law students in favor of those who score higher on their Crim Pro exam." A senior litigator concurs, "The firm would rather hire a book smart but socially stupid lawyer than the best lawyer in the world who happened to get only B's in law school."

But "grades and intelligence aren't enough," sources insist. "Everyone who participates in recruiting gets a voice in the process," says one associate, "and recruits who would make difficult co-workers are generally not hired, fabulous resume notwithstanding." A first-year offers some encouraging words. "If they like you," she says, "they will roll out the red carpet and do some heavy recruiting." You may end up having lunch or cocktails with nearly every associate in the office before they make a final decision.

OUR SURVEY SAYS

Polo shirts, not stuffed shirts

Gibson's Washington, D.C., office "seems to have a reputation as a stuffy or stodgy place to work," generally considered "formal and very uptight" compared to the culture in other locations. But a first-year associate there offers, "I've found that senior associates and partners are generally nice, down-to-earth and quite willing to joke around." Another junior litigator concedes "the environment inside the office is a bit stuffy," but adds, "[It] is changing because many of the young partners and associates are more laid back." Much depends on which practice group you end up in. "The appellate practice group is more formal. They wear suits all the time," another litigator observes. "The partners that I work for, on the other hand, are much more laid back. They wear khakis and polo shirts."

Associates in other cities tell much the same story of a "somewhat formal, but friendly" firm culture. Palo Alto and the other Bay Area offices are "much less formal" and offer "a collegial, mutually supportive working environment" where "respect is the order of the day," while Dallas is "nerdy but nice." In New York, "people go out of their way to be friendly with everyone," despite "the underlying intensity and pace" of the office. Still, a second-year associate says, there's very little socializing after hours, "except for the requisite fratty group of guys that exists at every New York law firm."

"Younger associates have a dynamic social network with a propensity for happy hours and a definite work-hard, play-hard attitude," a midlevel associate suggests. "Partners tend to be very friendly but quite family-oriented, and a lot of the more senior attorneys tend to get their work done and go home." Another attorney clarifies, "Some associates socialize after work, but not as much as they used to." A midlevel associate calls the mood "sufficiently formal to give one the sense that something important is happening here. Though many of us are friends," he adds, "we are also professionals and conduct ourselves as such."

Team spirit

"Good associates are valuable commodities," a Gibson veteran says, "and the free market system here makes that very clear." Under the firm's assignment system, "you work with the people you want to work with – and if a certain crowd is not your style, you are free to switch to a different group, no questions asked." According to a senior litigator, "Partners for the most part view the associates as colleagues and not minions to do their work." A first-year associate shares, "I have experienced great working relationships with partners who will let you do more work above your level and give you more autonomy as you build their trust." Another young attorney agrees the firm "provides a surprising amount of opportunity to develop a well-rounded skill set as a practitioner. I am given as much responsibility as I am willing to take on."

Some associates are less enamored of the system, finding it "difficult to manage." "A junior associate does not have a particular supervisor or mentor to ensure that they have an appropriate amount of work," one source argues, and "you often have more than one senior associate or partner demanding your time." A first-year in Dallas muses, "This office location has a lot of trouble integrating new associates into ongoing work. These guys like to work with those they've worked with before, which is hard for new attorneys." And other sources describe the firm as "a place where you come to work, put in your hours and partners don't know much about what goes on in your life (nor do they care to ask) when you are not billing." A midlevel associate takes a more upbeat tack: "There is not much interaction, but what there is, is positive."

Welcome to the downturn

"The recession has arrived at our doorstep," and with it "inconsistent" hours for Gibson associates. "It can be four to five hours for days at a time," a midlevel associate reports, "then 12-14 hours for the next few days." A senior litigator adds, "Many people don't have enough work to keep things interesting, and those who are busy tend not to think that the work is challenging." But the overall attitude toward hours is rather cheery, all things considered, and many at Gibson consider it "possibly one of the only top firms in the nation where one is encouraged to lead a balanced lifestyle." (Firm officials point out that profits-per-partner have increased annually for several years running, indicating no shortage of work opportunities for partners and associates alike.)

A first-year says the time requirements are "probably shorter than a number of big New York law firms." "This office has more consideration for associates' lives than other firms in the city," agrees a litigator in Dallas. "I work too hard," says one masochistic midlevel associate, "but I largely have myself to blame. I have been repeatedly told to ease up, but the work is really interesting and the responsibility is high." A corporate attorney suggests, " I work more hours than I would prefer, but I also seek out the types of projects that I want, so my hours speak more to my own drive than demands placed on me." But "when it's slow," a second-year associate chirps, somewhat implausibly, "no one even cares if you show up."

Survival of the fittest

Gibson is "fabulous" about paying for outside CLE seminars but otherwise, associates say, training is "more superficial than substantive." Though the firm is "making more efforts" to offer in-house programs, including monthly practice group luncheons and "countless live presentations via the Web," word is you simply must learn to "fend for yourself." A third-year litigator says, "Mentors must be sought out. If an associate has an aggressive (but pleasant) personality, she will likely benefit from positive mentoring relationships. If not, she may feel somewhat adrift." A senior associate elaborates, "The firm as an institution simply has no interest in dedicating energy and resources to practice education, skills training or mentoring. Law students should be aware of this. The firm routinely poaches trained midlevels from other firms because the associates who start here directly from law school are usually gone by the fifth year." The firm points out that it has responded to some of these concerns and, for example, now has office training coordinator positions in every domestic office responsible for managing in-house and outside training opportunities for associates.

Several insiders confirm Gibson's "fairly high turnover rate" and remark that "midlevel associates have been leaving in droves." Senior associates are particularly hard on the firm. "I am consistently frustrated at the lack of firm attention on associate development, retention and morale," says one corporate attorney. Another alleges, " Gibson has been weeding out (i.e., laying off) associates at all levels. This is being done quietly and rather deftly, but the ax has been falling far and wide." (Other sources concur, noting a particularly strong shakeup to the roster in Palo Alto.) And a litigator complains, "There is not much homegrown talent. Many of the partners also joined the firm from elsewhere. In litigation particularly, the firm has headhunters on almost a constant lookout for midlevel and senior associate laterals." Optimistic associates point out that "the change in presidential administrations explains a lot" of the recent departures and suggest attrition is "probably not worse" than at comparable firms, while firm officials contend that midlevel lateral hiring levels have been "quite small" relative to the total number of associates.

The diversity project

Gibson Dunn has "no problem hiring women," several associates tell us. However, the small number of female partners makes for "limited" mentorship opportunities for women who join the firm as associates; some associates are particularly perturbed by the paucity of female litigation partners in the New York office. One female insider suggests, "The free market system rewards associates who are most outwardly aggressive. This tends to be men. A lot of the mentoring is informal and, while encouraged by the firm, is not reinforced much institutionally." But many insiders say the firm is "making a true commitment" to improve the retention of high-ranking female attorneys and "getting better every day." Gibson also has "spotty success" with its retention of minority associates, but has applied "added focus" to the issue, with "ad hoc diversity committees" in several offices. "New York is the strongest in this regard," suggests one insider. And though most of our sources believe Gibson generally avoids acknowledging the issue of sexual preference, one first-year notes, "There are more gay people at this firm than I would have ever imagined for a firm with such a conservative reputation."

Show us the money

Gibson's compensation is "in line with the market rate" for big New York firms, "above average" in D.C. and "tops in the Dallas market." But some associates complain that the firm "follows the market only because they have to" and that "bonuses have been shrinking for three years straight." A veteran insider elaborates, "Every year the firm seems to be having an unprecedented year and no upside is being shared with the associates." "The partnership claims that the bonuses did not need to be as high because they only need to give bonuses at market, and since the market went down, so did the bonuses," adds a litigator. "Of course, it's their money, but it seems like an odd way of rewarding the associates who worked so hard that 2002 was the firm's best year, despite the crappy economy."

Arnold & Porter

555 12th Street, NW
Washington, DC 20004
Phone: (202) 942-5000
www.arnoldporter.com

LOCATIONS

Washington, DC (HQ)
Century City, CA
Denver, CO
Los Angeles, CA
McLean, VA
New York, NY
London

MAJOR DEPARTMENTS/PRACTICES

Antitrust • Banking • Bankruptcy • Benefits • Corporate
& Securities • Environmental • Food & Drug •
Governmental Contracts • Intellectual Property •
Legislation • Life Sciences • Litigation • Public Policy •
Real Estate • Tax & Estates • Telecommunications •
Trusts

THE STATS

No. of attorneys: 700
No. of offices: 7
Summer associate offers: 69 out of 72 (2002)
Chairman: Michael N. Sohn
Hiring Partner: Claire Reade

BASE SALARY

Washington, DC
1st year: $125,000
2nd year: $135,000
3rd year: $145,000
4th year: $155,000
5th year: $165,000
6th year: $175,000
7th year: $185,000
8th year: $195,000
Summer associate: $2,400/week

UPPERS

• Strong on diversity
• Committed to pro bono
• Major D.C. prestige

DOWNERS

• Increasing focus on billable hours
• High hours threshold for attaining a bonus
• "Completely uncertain partnership track"

NOTABLE PERKS

• Drinks and snacks nightly in the Garden Room
• Profit sharing
• Subsidized cafeteria
• Pizza on Fridays

THE BUZZ
WHAT ATTORNEYS AT OTHER FIRMS ARE SAYING ABOUT THIS FIRM

• "Innovative D.C. firm"
• "Stodgy and old school"
• "Great work environment"
• "Nothing special"

RANKING RECAP

Best in Region
#4 - Washington, DC

Best in Practice
#1 - Antitrust

Quality of Life
#3 - Pro Bono
#9 - Offices

Diversity
#3 - Diversity for Minorities
#4 - Overall Diversity
#4 - Diversity for Gays/Lesbians
#11 - Diversity for Women

EMPLOYMENT CONTACT

Ms. Lisa Pavia
Manager of Attorney Recruitment
Phone: (202) 942-5059
Fax: (202) 942-5999
E-mail: Lisa_Pavia@aporter.com

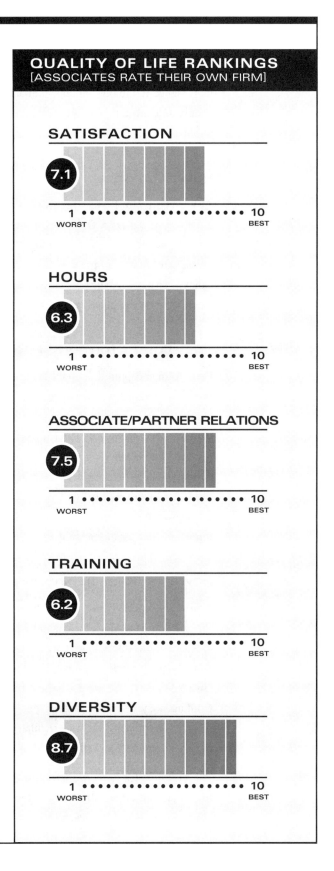

QUALITY OF LIFE RANKINGS
[ASSOCIATES RATE THEIR OWN FIRM]

SATISFACTION
7.1
1 WORST .... 10 BEST

HOURS
6.3
1 WORST .... 10 BEST

ASSOCIATE/PARTNER RELATIONS
7.5
1 WORST .... 10 BEST

TRAINING
6.2
1 WORST .... 10 BEST

DIVERSITY
8.7
1 WORST .... 10 BEST

THE SCOOP

Arnold & Porter, one of the vaunted "Washington Big Three" law firms, has no problem making its presence felt in our nation's capital. Not only does the firm represent the interests of powerful clients in a full range of practice areas, it is highly regarded by its peers for its commitment to public service.

Power brokers

Arnold, Fortas & Porter was formed shortly after the end of the World War II by three former members of Franklin Delano Roosevelt's administration: FCC Chairman Paul Porter, antitrust prosecutor and appeals court judge Thurman Arnold and Interior Undersecretary Abe Fortas. Fortas' name came off the letterhead in 1965, when Lyndon Johnson appointed him to the Supreme Court as an associate justice; two years earlier, he had impressed the court with his argument in the landmark case establishing a criminal defendant's right to an attorney.

The scooter formerly known as Ginger

Dean Kamen captured the public's attention in early 2001 with the secrecy surrounding his latest invention, originally codenamed "Ginger" or simply "IT." The device turned out to be a 65-pound motorized scooter, capable of speeds exceeding 12 miles an hour, with a unique gyroscopic steering system. The Segway Human Transporter, as it's officially known, could revolutionize commuting – except that many cities and towns currently ban the use of motorized scooters on their sidewalks. Arnold & Porter to the rescue. Kamen hired A&P to lobby federal regulators on his behalf. The firm's hard work paid off in August 2001 when the Consumer Product Safety Commission agreed the Segway was a consumer product rather than a motor vehicle. This categorization should make it much harder for municipalities to ban the scooter.

Powerful financial interests

A&P represented a consortium of trade groups and national banks in a federal lawsuit filed in 2002. The suit sought to block the enactment of a California law that would require credit card companies to tell customers how long it would take to pay off their balance if they make only the minimum monthly payments. Although lobbyists for the banks and credit unions had helped California lawmakers draft the legislation and made several suggestions that found their way into the final wording, they ultimately argued that the state law made unconstitutional encroachments on the federal government's right to regulate interstate lending. The U.S. District Judge presiding over the lawsuit agreed, and struck the law down in December 2002.

The firm litigates for consumers just as readily as it does for corporations. In August 2002, A&P filed a lawsuit on behalf of three elderly victims of macular degeneration – the leading cause of blindness in older Americans – over Medicare's refusal to provide coverage for a new treatment that might reverse the gradual deterioration of their eyesight. The suit specifically argues that the failure of the Department of Health and Human Services to honor a congressional deadline to institute an appeals process for Medicare coverage decisions denied the plaintiffs their constitutional right to make their case for getting the treatment approved.

Working for the public good

In addition to a wide range of pro bono opportunities within the firm (lawyers averaged 125 pro bono hours each in 2002), Arnold & Porter's D.C. office has two "loaned associate" programs – one at the Legal Aid Society, providing legal counsel and defense to those unable to afford it, and one at the Washington Lawyers Committee for Civil Rights and Urban Affairs, involving civil rights, worker's rights and housing cases. The firm has a long legacy of pitching in to protect civil liberties. As mentioned above, founding partner Abe Fortas won Gideon v. Wainwright, the Supreme Court case concerning the rights of criminal defendants, and in the 1950s Paul Porter was equally vigorous in the fight against McCarthyism. The firm contributed to another major civil rights case in 2002, assisting in the defense of Rabih Haddad, a Muslim activist who was detained by federal authorities shortly after the September 11 attacks. The government claimed that Haddad's charitable organization, Global Relief Foundation, was a front for funding terrorists and sought to close his deportation hearings to the public. A&P attorneys assisted the Center for Constitutional Rights in persuading a U.S. District Court judge that the secret proceedings violated Haddad's constitutional right to due process.

Breaking new ground

Arnold & Porter refuses to rest on its laurels, formally adding a sports practice group to its repertoire in June 2002. The announcement consolidated a practice that had existed informally within A&P for several years; the firm is chief counsel to the Los Angeles Lakers and represents the baseball commissioner's office on a number of financial and IP issues.

In early 2002, Arnold & Porter coaxed renowned pharmaceutical and product liability litigator Ian Dodds-Smith away from CMS Cameron McKenna to lead the firm's product liability practice from the London office. In addition to his own substantial track record in dealing with pharmaceuticals and biotech products, Dodds-Smith brought with him two partners and six associates. That August, A&P's Washington office trumpeted the addition of a four-member team to its patent litigation group. The four new partners, led by senior litigator Stan Lawrence, adds new depth in the chemical, pharmaceutical and biotechnology fields to the firm's established expertise in patent litigation.

Happy campers

You'll read a lot of upbeat remarks in Our Survey Says section of this profile, but we're not the only ones to observe how satisfied A&P's attorneys are with their work experience. *Working*

Mother magazine named the firm one of the "100 Best Companies for Working Mothers" in September 2002, the fourth time A&P had been so honored since 1996. A few months later, A&P became one of just three law firms selected by *Fortune* for its annual "100 Best Companies to Work For" list.

A&P's efforts to create a supportive working environment for a diverse range of associates have also been noticed by the Minority Corporate Counsel Association, which presented the firm with its 2002 Thomas L. Sager Award for its recruitment, retention and promotion of minority lawyers. It was the fourth consecutive year in which the MCCA had honored the firm for its hiring and retention practices.

GETTING HIRED

It's all about the summer

Although the consensus is that A&P is selective when it comes to bringing on new associates, most associates agree that the hard part is scoring a summer position. "Once a summer is hired during school, they almost always get an offer upon graduation," observes a third-year associate. It's the opinion of a junior associate that "in comparison with other prestigious law firms in D.C., you have a better chance finding a job here with a degree from somewhere outside the top 15 schools, assuming you have superb grades." A midlevel agrees with that assessment, saying, "Although Arnold & Porter is very selective, it tends to hire from a wide array of schools." The firm is also open to hiring "outside of the top-tier schools if a candidate has distinguished herself in other ways, such as a clerkship." "If you are from Harvard though, it's a lot easier to get in," a litigation associate maintains.

Insiders say Arnold & Porter is "looking to hire smart," but "not necessarily gunner types" "who learn fast and can work without a lot of guidance." "The firm wants smart people, but it is also very interested in getting people with diverse intellectual backgrounds and people that they think will fit in well with the firm culture."

OUR SURVEY SAYS

Room for everyone

The motto at Arnold & Porter could be "different strokes for different folks." The firm is "very individualistic," confides a midlevel associate. "There are some weirdos here, but that's what makes the place interesting. There is a wide spectrum of personalities. Everyone has a place." "A&P culture is one of the things I like best about the firm," says an associate in the government regulation group. "On the whole," continues this source, "everyone is treated with dignity and respect, from the housekeeping staff to the most senior partner. That tends to mask the hierarchy that is pervasive in big-firm culture. There's never any question about who gives orders to whom, but the egalitarian atmosphere makes them feel less like orders than instructions as to how to properly fit into the business."

Insiders disagree about whether the vibe at A&P is more "laid back" or "negative." Happy associates describe the culture as "friendly," "diverse, open, principled, professional but informal," "committed to pro bono," "unpretentious" and "social." Some frustrated associates, meanwhile, say they've witnessed a change in the last few years. "When I joined the firm several years ago," says an IP attorney, "the culture was informal, friendly and overall very positive. Since then, and especially recently, I've seen a dramatic change in the tone of the firm. The atmosphere has become negative and morale is at an all-time low." "The firm has a great reputation in the outside world," says a litigation attorney, "but working here is tough. A&P is obsessed with high billables and increasing profits per partner. It doesn't know whether it wants to be a D.C.- or New York-style firm."

I want a bigger bonus!

While some insiders are quite content with their compensation, many others see room for improvement in two main areas: bonuses and midlevel base salaries. First, bonuses. "We make the market rate in terms of salary, but we make little or nothing in bonuses," complains a first-year associate. "Friends at comparable firms make $30,000 to $70,000 more in bonuses than we do." Sighs a fourth-year associate, "We essentially have no bonus system unless you kill yourself and bill over 2,400 hours annually," while a senior litigator sniffs, "The bonus system makes little sense." The firm counters that its compensation system was designed with heavy associate input, noting that in 2002, all associates who had been with the firm for six months received bonuses ranging from $5,500 to $16,500, depending on seniority and regardless of hours billed.

According to several insiders, the "midlevel and senior associate pay is below market." "Let's face it," says a midlevel, "we're all overpaid. But the firm still doesn't pay as well as some other peer firms in D.C." "We have one of the lowest pay scales among the big firms," observes a corporate finance associate. "At the highest levels we make about $20,000 to $30,000 less than at comparable firms." Of course, not everyone sees reason to complain. A first-year counters, " I know of a few firms where people make a little more, but the trade-off for quality of life is well worth it." "Anyone who claims they don't make enough money here is just whining," states a very satisfied first-year.

Same old, same old

Like their counterparts at firms across the country, A&P associates are far from thrilled with their hours. "The work load seems to vary significantly among first-years. Some are extremely busy, while others are not," says a first-year associate. A midlevel associate agrees that in some cases, the "work is very unevenly divided." Insiders also say that the unpredictability of their hours can be stressful because "the hours range from not enough to far more than you want. Sometimes it is difficult to strike a good balance and maintain that balance over an extended period of time."

Some insiders say the hours are just fine. "Hours are going to be tough in any big law firm, but as far as large law firms go, you probably won't do better hours-wise anywhere else," a senior associate informs us. "We work hard, but it is possible to have a life," says a litigator, while a fifth-year happily reports, "I have worked fairly hard, but I have been compensated extremely well for doing so." "The firm – at least the IP practice group – is very flexible regarding schedules and allows for work at home," says an attorney in that group. "There are times that you may pull an all-nighter if something is due, but for the most part, the hours are reasonable. That being said, it is not unheard of for partners to insist that an associate bill eight to 10 hours a day on a consistent basis." (The firm reports that in 2002, the average associate had 1,790 billable hours and 1,957 hours of billable and pro bono work.)

A widening divide?

A senior associate tells us, "Partners and associates work well together. There is not a feeling that you are somehow lesser because you are an associate." "I am a lateral," says a D.C. associate, "and the partners here are much more respectful than at my old firm. I feel that I am an equal part of the team." While "there is, of course, some variation among partners," a sixth-year finds that "on balance, they treat associates respectfully and as valued professional colleagues." "I have never had a partner treat me with anything but total respect. I've heard of others who've had different experiences, but my impression is they're rare," shares an environmental attorney.

Other associates complain, "The partner/associate relationship is becoming increasingly polarized." "Partners are almost never rude and usually respectful. But they are almost never warm and usually disinterested in associates," remarks a first-year. A fourth-year laments the firm's "not-so-distant past. When I started here, the firm made real efforts to balance work and life and to make this a decent place to work. Now that the economy is bad," this contact adds, "the partners treat associates like they have them by the hair. We are frequently reminded that this is a business and that to stay competitive the firm has to make more and more money for the partners." A corporate attorney confides, "Associate/partner relations have declined since the great raise of 2000. Even though the partners have made more and more money, they look at associates with contempt and lament about how much they have to pay us."

The ups and downs of training

Insiders just can't agree on the value and extent of training at A&P. Maybe that's because training "varies greatly from associate to associate." One attorney confides, "I think that this is one of the weak points of the firm, at least in the litigation department. We've had no guidance on anything of substance." Meanwhile, another associate in the same class and office says the "litigation training is excellent." An associate in the antitrust group reports receiving "extensive training." "Formal training is good initially in some groups," says a fourth-year, but "informal mentoring is a joke. It happens for some people, but the norm is that most don't have informal mentors." Another fourth-year reports, "Access to training seems to depend upon having a close relationship with a partner. Access to training in certain departments is not uniform and based upon subjective criteria." "I cannot speak for other departments within the firm," says an attorney in the tax department, "but from what I can see the training is abysmal." The firm announced in March 2003 that it had hired a full-time director of professional development to improve training firm-wide.

Diversity: (almost) everyone is happy

Most Arnold & Porter associates believe the firm "does an excellent job" of hiring minority associates. "Like most firms," Arnold & Porter "aggressively recruits minorities," says a first-year. This source adds, "Like most firms, they are successful in terms of associates, but the partnership ranks just have not grown much in terms of minorities. But I don't know what else the firm can do." "Our diversity is outstanding. For example, our incoming summer associate class is almost 50 percent minority, and we have a relatively high percentage of minority associates." However, not everyone approves of the firm's record on racial diversity. "We have very few people of color and almost no partners of color," a litigation attorney sighs.

"From what I can see, there does not appear to be any glass ceiling or discrimination. There are many powerful women partners," says a male midlevel associate, while a female associates raves, "The climate here could not be better for women." Associates appreciate that working part time is a viable option, and several insiders mention the on-site day care facility, although a junior female associate reports, "It is next to impossible to get your kids into it. Of course, you don't find that out until after you sit on the waitlist for years." (A&P says it has added more space to the program in response to pressing demand.) "The firm is great about women if and only if you act like a man," says a female litigator. "In other words, if you can work 12-14 hours a day, this is a great place to be a woman." However, according to a senior associate, "this is a culture issue and not unique to the firm." A male associate observes, "The firm is a good place for women to work, but if they have limited schedules because of children, partnership will not likely happen."

Wilmer, Cutler & Pickering

2445 M Street, NW
Washington, DC 20037
Phone: (202) 663-6000
www.wilmer.com

LOCATIONS

Washington, DC (HQ)
Baltimore, MD
New York, NY
Tysons Corner, VA
Berlin
Brussels
London

MAJOR DEPARTMENTS/PRACTICES

Antitrust & Competition
Bankruptcy
Communications & Electronic Commerce
Corporate
Financial Institutions
International Aviation, Defense & Aerospace
Litigation
Securities
Tax
Trade

THE STATS

No. of attorneys: 541
No. of offices: 7
Summer associate offers: 50 out of 53 (2002)
Summer associate offers (NY): 4 out of 4 (2002)
Chairman: William J. Perlstein
Hiring Attorney: David P. Donovan
Hiring Attorney, New York: Paul Engelmayer

 THE BUZZ
WHAT ATTORNEYS AT OTHER FIRMS ARE SAYING ABOUT THIS FIRM

- "Big names, cool work"
- "Has grown too much too quickly"
- "I would hire them to defend me in a second"
- "Overrated"

BASE SALARY

Washington, DC; Baltimore, MD; Tyson's Corner, VA
1st year: $125,000
2nd year: $135,000
3rd year: $158,000
4th year: $168,000
5th year: $191,000
6th year: $201,000
Summer associate: $2,400/week

New York, NY
1st year: $125,000
2nd year: $135,000
3rd year: $158,000
4th year: $168,000
5th year: $191,000
6th year: $205,000
Summer Associate: $2,400/week

UPPERS

- Stellar pro bono practice
- Friendly, bright colleagues
- High-profile criminal and securities work

DOWNERS

- Grueling pace of multiple big cases
- Bonuses leave some dissatisfied
- Growing focus on billables

NOTABLE PERKS

- 401(k) matching
- Ping-pong room with Central Park view (NY)
- Subsidized cafeteria (DC)
- Emergency day-care (DC & NY)

RANKING RECAP

Best in Region
#3 - Washington, DC

Best in Practice
#9 (tie) - Antitrust

Quality of Life
#11 - Pro Bono
#15 - Selectivity

EMPLOYMENT CONTACTS

Washington, Baltimore and Tysons Corner
Ms. Mary W. Kiley
Lawyer Recruitment Administrator
Fax: (202) 457-4992
E-mail: JoinWCPLawyers@wilmer.com

New York
Ms. Marian Freed
Office Administrator
Fax: (212) 230-8888
E-mail: Marian.Freed@wilmer.com

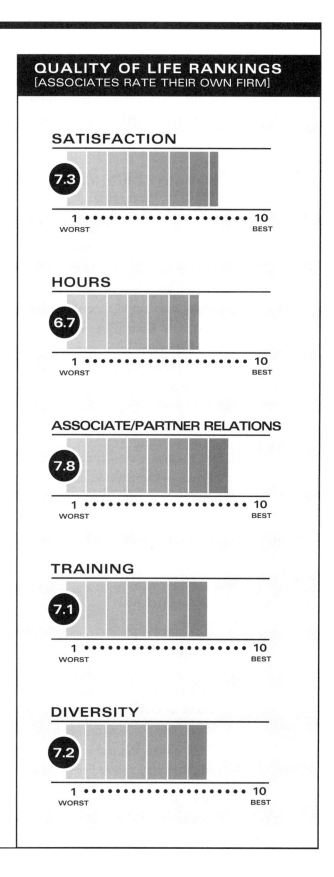

QUALITY OF LIFE RANKINGS
[ASSOCIATES RATE THEIR OWN FIRM]

SATISFACTION

7.3

1 ••••••••••••••••••• 10
WORST   BEST

HOURS

6.7

1 ••••••••••••••••••• 10
WORST   BEST

ASSOCIATE/PARTNER RELATIONS

7.8

1 ••••••••••••••••••• 10
WORST   BEST

TRAINING

7.1

1 ••••••••••••••••••• 10
WORST   BEST

DIVERSITY

7.2

1 ••••••••••••••••••• 10
WORST   BEST

THE SCOOP

Founded in Washington, D.C., in 1962, Wilmer, Cutler & Pickering didn't take long to become one of the region's three biggest firms. WCP now has more than 500 lawyers in seven offices, including three in Europe. It is highly regarded for its regulatory practices, but also admired for its fierce commitment to pro bono.

Eye of the hurricane

Pick any major corporate scandal from 2002, and chances are Wilmer, Cutler & Pickering will pop up in one context or another. Enron's outside directors hired the firm to conduct an internal investigation into the company's transactions with partnerships managed by its own employees. The resulting document, written by a team led by former Securities and Exchange Commission enforcement chief William McLucas, was deemed "scathing" by *The Washington Post*, and WorldCom's outside directors signed on for a similar review of that company's accounting issues. This time around, however, observers were skeptical of the firm's ability to produce a comprehensive report, as two of the imploded telecommunication company's funders, Salomon Smith Barney and its corporate parent Citigroup, had already retained WCP as their counsel for WorldCom-related litigation. The firm therefore said in court filings that its investigation would exclude WorldCom's dealings with investment bankers, focusing instead on the company's accounting fraud and governance issues.

WCP also represents Citigroup in the ongoing investigation by New York Attorney General Eliot Spitzer into whether Salomon's research division misled investors by publishing unduly hyped analyses of telecommunications stocks during the "Internet bubble" of the late 1990s. The firm is counseling another financial services giant, Credit Suisse First Boston, one of 55 investment banks charged in a broad securities lawsuit with inflating the price of shares in technology IPOs during that period.

Hiring power

As McLucas' presence on the roster indicates, the firm has little trouble attracting former government officials. In December 2002, a year after former solicitor general Seth Waxman joined Wilmer Cutler, his old assistant Paul Wolfson signed on as a counsel in the litigation practice. That same month, the firm snagged Peggy Kuo, former acting deputy chief of the Department of Justice, and ex-special counsel to the SEC Knute Salhus. Effective July 2003, Fannie Mae's former vice chair, Jamie S. Gorelick, will be joining WCP as a partner as well. The firm can also supply the government with capable attorneys: longtime partner William Kolasky returned to Wilmer in late 2002 after a stint in Justice's antitrust division.

Other attorneys (and recent law school grads) are drawn to WCP by its strong firm-wide commitment to mentoring. Senior attorneys at every level take part in the New Associate Working

Group, ensuring the smooth transition of new associates during their first six months at the firm. The group sees that new associates are given appropriate assignments, receive group feedback, are not over- or underworked and have opportunities to develop solid working relationships with partners.

Big clients

Check the client list for any of WCP's practice groups, and you'll find plenty of blue chip firms. Citibank, First USA, Salomon Smith Barney and Merrill Lynch have called on the firm for class-action defense, while the media practice receives regular instruction from AOL Time Warner, the Bell companies, Yahoo! and Disney/ABC. Bear Stearns benefited from Wilmer's expertise at corporate litigation in September 2002, when the firm's attorneys got a $164.5 million judgment against their client reversed. Although a jury had found the brokerage liable for not providing enough information to a non-discretionary client, the appeals court agreed with WCP that brokerages had very limited responsibilities to such clients and dismissed the case.

The firm represents the corporate interests of several sports teams, including two that play in its hometown: hockey's Washington Capitals and the Washington Redskins football franchise. WCP attorneys recently prevailed on behalf of Redskins owner Dan Snyder in arbitration proceedings instigated by his former business partner, who had made a failing bid to buy the team before Snyder broke away to put together his own successful bloc of investors.

Pro bono

WCP's pro bono work often takes its attorneys to the Supreme Court. In recent cases, the firm has persuaded the justices that the presidential line-item veto is unconstitutional and argued on behalf of the League of Women Voters in Arkansas in their effort to overturn the state's term limits. The firm also files numerous amicus briefs with the Supremes, buttressing Common Cause's stance on campaign finance laws and the American Geriatrics Society's position on physician-assisted suicide.

The firm recently provided pro bono representation in a nationally reported case, achieving a "stunning reversal" of a miscarriage of justice involving drug convictions of more than 10 percent of the African-American population of Tulia, Texas. All of the convictions were based on the uncorroborated testimony of an undercover agent with a questionable past – including an undisclosed arrest during his undercover operation for theft and abuse of office – as well as serious allegations of racism. After a contentious, week-long habeas evidentiary hearing, the WCP team, working with the NAACP Legal Defense Fund and another Washington law firm, persuaded state authorities to join in a request to the Texas Court of Criminal Appeals that all of the convictions be overturned.

Movin' on up

After months of negotiations, WCP signed a lease for new digs just two blocks away from the White House. The deal, completed in February 2003, is the largest private lease in the city's history, and calls for 524,000 square feet of office space in three buildings (including one still to be constructed) with an option for an additional 120,000 square feet. When the firm's new main building is completed in late 2006, plans call for the buildings to be linked internally, creating a block-wide complex.

GETTING HIRED

"If you're not in the top 5 percent to 10 percent in your class," warns one WCP insider, "you're wasting your time." The firm "likes pedigree," and is famous for its "very school-snobby" approach to recruiting. "Personality is nice," a third-year observes, "but pure intellectual horsepower is key." One midlevel associate says, "I've been frustrated that Wilmer wouldn't interview candidates from my alma mater unless they are in the top handful in the class." A junior litigator adds, "These days, they're even rejecting Harvard and Yale grads for getting too many Bs." Some at the firm also think a federal clerkship may be "almost mandatory," preferably at the Supreme Court level.

Though a few attorneys wonder if Wilmer Cutler "may be less selective than it was in the past because it is expanding its size," most consider the opposite to be true. "It has been more difficult to get hired here than during the boom years," says a senior regulatory associate. Even laterals are subject to the "grade-conscious" regimen, but, an antitrust attorney offers encouragingly, "they will consider accomplished laterals with expertise in their fields." Telecom, bankruptcy and securities law are the most highly sought after skill sets.

OUR SURVEY SAYS

Brainiacs in high gear

Just about everyone at WCP says things aren't how they used to be. "The firm likes to think it is friendly and laid back," but, runs the typical complaint, "is becoming more and more of a sweatshop." A senior associate confides, "The Wilmer way is something people still take seriously here, but the inherent friction between the older culture and the demands of the modern market is only growing." Long hours spent on complicated cases have resulted in "little informal socialization between partners and associates" and a culture that is "less friendly" – "not formal or uptight," says a second-year litigator, "but nobody socializes anymore." Another associate agrees, "You have to search to find Wilmer's social associates."

It's not impossible, however, to find more satisfied associates, who describe the firm as "a fairly quiet environment" and "a firm of intellectuals." A midlevel corporate attorney remarks, "You're equally likely to hear a discussion of last night's football game as you are to hear a discussion of a story on NPR this morning." A veteran litigator adds, "The culture places great value on intellect, idealism and integrity." He also describes the D.C. office as possessing a "sedate dignity." And a third-year associate enthuses, "I've never met a better group of people with whom to work. Even when work is heavy, the good company keeps it enjoyable."

"Watch the pros"

Relationships between partners and associates at WCP are guided by "a prevailing ethic of decent treatment," and "most partners are quite respectful." One midlevel associate says, "Partners command more respect, but they're colleagues at the end of the day." A few trouble spots do exist, however, particularly with lateral partners "who come from previous work environments that did not have the same culture." And a midlevel associate echoes the concerns of many when she suggests some partners "deal too ineptly with their own stress to be good to work with."

Associates respect partners so much that they'd love to spend more time with them. "The partners are at times too overwhelmed to provide as much mentoring as I would wish," says a second-year associate. Another sophomore agrees, "On-the-job coaching and training is minimal," but points out that "formal training is intensive." A corporate attorney concurs, "The firm is making substantial investments in training and we expect to see some dividends soon." In the meantime, "watch the pros," advises one litigator. "Several partners in the New York office came from the U.S. Attorney's office," this source explains, "and it's instructive to watch them run cases."

All we want is our fair share

Junior associates may consider their compensation package "very generous considering the quality of life the firm tries to maintain," but attorneys who have been around the block a bit suggest WCP is "not as competitive as [it] thinks." "Wilmer matches market," gripes one litigator, "but God forbid they should pay one penny more in a year where profits per partner were at an all-time record." One offended corporate attorney concedes that "both our 401(k) plan and vacation policies were above market in comparison with our peer firms," but reports "associates still believe that management is just taking money from our pockets to put into theirs."

They work hard for the money

The firm offers "an excellent compensation system for attorneys who work the required hours," says one source, "though the system is not really geared to reward associates who kill themselves for the firm by working, say, more than 2,500 hours a year." And the latter category appears to be growing ever since WCP "got slammed" by a cluster of high-intensity cases and investigations. "I am working much, much harder here than I ever expected I would," grumbles one third-year

associate. "I worked very hard last year," concedes another attorney, "but it was my own choice – I was able to work on several incredible projects." Despite the grinding pace, many associates feel "the firm acknowledges that they are asking a lot of us" and "is honest… as to how many hours it expects of associates." A senior associate puts it bluntly, "If you don't want to work hard, don't come to a big firm."

Slowly but surely

Diversity building is "a real work in progress" at WCP. Hiring of minority associates, for example, "has improved dramatically over the last year." One Latina associate endorses the firm's "enormous efforts," going so far as to call them "over the top." The change is particularly welcome in the New York office, which, according to an insider, "was all white" until very recently. A senior attorney in the corporate practice feels the need for continued changes, though, saying the firm still places "too much emphasis on law school and grades and not enough on other factors."

Women associates also believe the firm has room for improvement, suggesting that it is "clearly a male-dominated environment" where "middle-aged male partners are unbearably cliquish with other men." A midlevel litigator offers, "While I think the leadership is open to having women partners, I doubt they are willing to take very active steps to achieve that goal." Others concede that efforts are being made; 24 of WCP's Washington partners are women, which compares favorably to other D.C. law firms. But the continued lack of female partners in the New York office, and the perception that many current female partners "affirmatively eschew" mentoring younger associates, dampen their enthusiasm.

While a lesbian attorney at the firm does not see "an explicit goal of recruitment and support," she and other associates agree WCP is a "pretty gay-friendly" firm. "They do have gay partners," says one gay midlevel associate, "and try to give gay interviewees at least one gay interviewer." He also points out that the firm wrote an amicus brief in Lawrence v. Texas, the Supreme Court case involving a Texas law prohibiting consenting same-sex couples from engaging in sexual activities. "I am confident that being gay is not a problem here," he concludes.

That's a lot of pro bono you've got there

WCP offers associates an "overwhelming" number of pro bono opportunities, including many chances to work on high-profile amicus briefs. (In addition to the case mentioned above, the firm has also prepared briefs in the University of Michigan affirmative action case and the judicial battle over the McCain-Feingold campaign finance law.) Associates appreciate that a "very accessible and helpful" full-time pro bono counsel is on staff and that up to 150 pro bono hours can be applied toward billable hours requirements. Though some WCP attorneys claim "several associates were reprimanded for doing too much pro bono work this year," the firm strongly disputes the notion, and points out that it honored 11 lawyers for distinguished pro bono work in 2002, including the recipient of the firm's annual John H. Pickering Award.

"You're equally likely to hear a discussion of last night's football game as you are to hear a discussion of a story on NPR this morning."

— *Wilmer Cutler associate*

White & Case LLP

1155 Avenue of the Americas
New York, NY 10036-2787
Phone: (212) 819-8200
www.whitecase.com

LOCATIONS

New York, NY (HQ)
Los Angeles, CA
Miami, FL
Palo Alto, CA
San Francisco, CA
Washington, DC
32 other offices worldwide

MAJOR DEPARTMENTS/PRACTICES

Banking
Litigation/Intellectual Property
Mergers & Acquisitions
Projects/Leasing
Securities
Tax

THE STATS

No. of attorneys: 1,671
No. of offices: 38
Summer associate offers: 40 out of 41 (2002)
Managing Partner: Duane D. Wall
Hiring Partner: M. Elaine Johnston

BASE SALARY

New York, NY; Los Angeles, Palo Alto, San Francisco, CA; Washington, DC
1st year: $125,000
2nd year: $135,000
3rd year: $150,000
4th year: $170,000
5th year: $190,000
6th year: $200,000
7th year: $205,000
8th year: $210,000
Summer associate (New York, Los Angeles, Palo Alto): $2,403/week
Summer associate (Washington): $2,400/week

Miami, FL
1st year: $105,000
2nd year: $110,000
3rd year: $120,000
4th year: $140,000
5th year: $155,000
6th year: $165,000
7th year: $170,000
8th year: $175,000
Summer associate: $2,019/week

UPPERS

- Global reputation
- Pro bono stars
- New commitment to training

DOWNERS

- Mysterious bonus scheme
- Poor record on racial diversity
- Unpredictable schedules

THE BUZZ
WHAT ATTORNEYS AT OTHER FIRMS ARE SAYING ABOUT THIS FIRM

- "International powerhouse"
- "Painfully dull"
- "Strong New York and international firm"
- "Way past its prime"

NOTABLE PERKS

- Free on-site gym (NY)
- Generous summer associate lunch budget
- Sports tickets and museum passes
- Summer parties at New York landmarks

RANKING RECAP

Best in Region
#13 - New York

EMPLOYMENT CONTACT

Ms. Dana E. Stephenson
Director of Attorney Recruiting & Employment
Phone: (212) 819-8200
Fax: (212) 354-8113
E-mail: recruit@whitecase.com

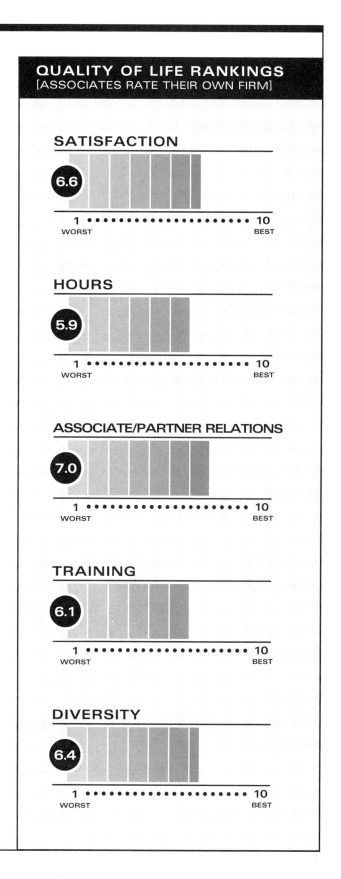

QUALITY OF LIFE RANKINGS
[ASSOCIATES RATE THEIR OWN FIRM]

SATISFACTION
6.6
1 WORST   10 BEST

HOURS
5.9
1 WORST   10 BEST

ASSOCIATE/PARTNER RELATIONS
7.0
1 WORST   10 BEST

TRAINING
6.1
1 WORST   10 BEST

DIVERSITY
6.4
1 WORST   10 BEST

THE SCOOP

White & Case is everywhere. The firm, which recently celebrated its 100th anniversary, has 1,600 lawyers in 38 offices all around the world. Besides global reach, White & Case is known for its antitrust, banking and corporate practices.

$500 and a dream

In May 1901, young attorneys J. DuPratt White and George B. Case threw in $250 each to found a law firm in New York. The firm flourished, in part thanks to its founders' relationship with Henry P. Davison, second-in-command at super-bank J.P. Morgan. One of White & Case's early clients was Bankers Trust. The firm helped Bankers Trust at its founding in 1903 and kept the bank as a client until it was bought out by Deutsche Bank in 1999.

White & Case continued to grow throughout the 20th century, working on high-profile cases for prestigious clients. The firm represented J.P. Morgan when the bank financed arms sales from U.S. military suppliers to France and Britain during World War I. The arms shipments were a great boost to the Allied war effort, and after the war DuPratt White was made a Chevalier of the French Legion of Honor, one of the highest honors the French government can bestow upon a non-citizen.

The firm began expanding globally in the 1960s. White & Case reopened its Paris office (which had closed during World War II). In 1971, the firm moved into London. New offices sprang up in Washington, D.C. (1974), Hong Kong (1978), Singapore (1983), Los Angeles (1986) and Tokyo (1987) on its way to its current global domination.

Representing a would-be president

Partner George J. Terwilliger III played an important role in the case of the century. Terwilliger was part of George W. Bush's legal team in Bush v. Gore, the challenge to the 2000 presidential election. Then-Vice President Al Gore asked for and was granted a recount of the votes in Florida. Bush's team challenged the recount ruling as unconstitutional; the U.S. Supreme Court agreed, handing the election and the presidency to Bush.

M&A work

One of White & Case's leading practices is M&A. The firm represented Nestle Waters in its purchase of Clearwater Group, the leading bottled water delivery firm in Russia, in March 2003. Moscow-based partner Eric Michailov led the White & Case team. The firm represented Triton, a private equity fund, in its $238.5 million purchase of fish food-maker Tetra from Pfizer. Frankfurt-based partners Markus Hauptmann and Annica Lindegren and New York partner Oliver Brahmst were Triton's lawyers on the deal, announced in January 2003. In August 2002, White & Case represented Four Seasons Health Care in its acquisition by Omega Worldwide.

They'll see you in court

White & Case also has a healthy litigation practice, with approximately 300 lawyers practicing litigation or arbitration worldwide. In 2002, the firm scored a victory for the Baltimore Ravens, who were sued for damages by an amateur artist who claimed he had contributed to the design of the team's newest logo. The plaintiff sought a percentage of the mucho bucks in profits that he said flowed directly from the logo itself, although White & Case partner Robert Raskopf argued that it was not the logo but "the fans, NFL brands and the power of professional football" that generated the revenue. Though one federal jury ruled in favor of the offended artist, a second jury, deciding the issue of damages, awarded the plaintiff a big fat nothing in August 2002.

The firm also secured a victory in September 2002 for its client, Gotham Partners LP, in Delaware Supreme Court. The court ruled that Hallwood Realty Corp. gained control of a real estate partnership by buying shares in the company in violation of the Hallwood's agreement with Gotham. The decision was said to strengthen protections for investors in limited partnership arrangements.

Musical chairs

White & Case has managed to add talent to the firm in the form of both familiar and new faces. In October 2002, the firm welcomed back Vincent R. FitzPatrick, who left White & Case for rival Dewey Ballantine in 1995. Joining FitzPatrick were partners Wayne Cross (of Geneva/NCH fame) and Robert A. Milne, who left White & Case as an associate with FitzPatrick in 1995. In January 2003, Mary J. Sotis joined the firm's intellectual property practice in Rome from the National Hockey League, where she had been group vice president of National Hockey League Enterprises. That same month, Ulf Kreppel, a partner at rival Allen & Overy, joined White & Case as a structured finance partner in the firm's Frankfurt office.

In February 2003, the firm added five partners from the now-defunct Brobeck, Phleger & Harrison. Kevin B. Fisher, William L. Harvey, Douglas M. Young and David F. Dedyo joined White & Case's San Francisco office while Maria K. Pum joined White & Case Los Angeles. One month later, Brobeck refugee Mark Lewis Mandel became a partner in White & Case's M&A practice in New York.

Back to the top of the pro bono heap

White & Case has renewed its commitment to pro bono law in recent years. The firm began its pro bono work during World War I by representing the Red Cross. James Stillwagon, head of the firm's corporate immigration practice, became full-time chair of the pro bono committee in May 2002, at a time when White & Case has rocketed to the top of pro bono rankings. The firm placed fourth in the *American Lawyer* pro bono rankings in 2002 and 2001. That's an improvement from the firm's ranking in 2000 (seventh) and a major jump over 1999, when White & Case came in at No. 48. Three White & Case attorneys in Los Angeles were honored for their efforts to improve public safety and the environmental record of the Los Angeles to Pasadena Gold Line light rail service that's currently under construction. Bryan A. Merryman, Mark E. Gustafson and Maria R. Harrington were honored by the LA City Council and the Mt. Washington Association, a homeowners' group concerned about the railway.

GETTING HIRED

Star search

White & Case, like many of its peer firms, is more selective now than in years past, due in large part to the sluggish economy. "The firm has been getting very picky due to the economy, with a lot of emphasis on grades," reports one insider. "A lot also depends on the interview and your ability to impress people." One White & Case associate has overheard talk about economic conditions changing the recruiting process at the firm – and not for the better. That source says that some at White & Case believe "because of the economy, they can recruit more selective candidates. This is lawyer-speak for candidates from top-20 schools. I thought the practice of not limiting itself to those schools was a strong point of the firm, not something that needed to be altered." "If you are at a good law school and a pleasant/interesting/lively person, you will get an offer from White & Case," observes one insider. "White & Case also hires people from second-tier law schools if they demonstrate intelligence and eagerness."

Those interested in White & Case should keep in mind its international reach; it makes the firm more likely to chase candidates with some kind of overseas experience or expertise. "Given the firm's international focus, language skills and time spent or interests abroad are highly valued and make for a more diverse group of people than at most other firms," says one source. The right background can even make up for less-than-stellar grades. "White & Case generally looks for someone with a well-rounded personality," says one contact. "They seem to require a good GPA, but solid work experience can gloss over some problems in a law school GPA."

OUR SURVEY SAYS

Is this thing on?

White & Case associates are divided on the firm's culture; some find the place laid back while others say the firm's drive to succeed gives lawyers an unfriendly edge. No matter what your experience, lay off the comedy. "Nobody seems to be able to tell when I am making a joke," says one would-be Carrot Top. "It's not that it's formal or stuffy here, it's just that nobody seems to expect a joke at any given time. The desire is to be laid back and friendly, but the partners' personalities can make it somewhat difficult to be loose." Even if you're not getting laughs, you can still make friends. "The firm is quite friendly," reports one associate. "An atmosphere of mutual respect and enthusiasm for the practice of law pervades. We frequently socialize together, going out for a beer after work or getting together for lunch."

Of course, a firm as big as White & Case doesn't have just one vibe. Says one insider, "There are six sections/departments in New York, and each one has its own flavor. They are all significantly different from each other. Banking tends to be pretty formal and hierarchy-oriented, project finance/leasing is markedly more laid back – just to give two contrasting examples." "People here are great, both in the corporate and litigation departments," says another contact. "There are jerks anywhere in the world, but in this firm people generally treat each other politely."

Some insiders complain the firm uses its associates like so much grist for the mill. "The firm claims to have a collegial culture, but the senior lawyers are only collegial when they want you to finish work quickly and then do more," gripes one source. "White & Case claims to have a collegial culture, but that simply is not the case," agrees another lawyer. "Unless people want work product from you, they act as if you do not exist."

It's a shame about that tidal wave

Like the overall culture, associate/partner relations at White & Case vary greatly. "It's a mixed grab bag at the firm," says a senior associate. "Some partners treat associates with respect. Others do not care." Associates seem to have picked up on the "do not care" vibe. "Most of the partners are human beings and treat associates as human beings most of the time," says one insider. "However, if a tidal wave suddenly killed all the associates, the reaction probably would be, 'That's awful. OK, let's go get more associates.'" "Rarely are partners disrespectful or mean to associates, but they certainly aren't friendly towards them," says another contact. Not all lawyers think the White & Case partnership is so cold-hearted. "The partners respect the associates, which is demonstrated both in daily interaction and through institutional measures," says an associate.

Working nine to five, plus a whole lot more

White & Case attorneys don't log more hours than the average big-firm lawyer, but that doesn't mean they're thrilled about their hours. "Hours are part of the bargain," says one insider. "Everyone knows it is not a nine-to-five job most days. That said, this is no sweatshop, and people are genuinely sensitive to the need to have a personal/family life. But when it's game time, you are expected to give it your all." Unpredictable schedules are a problem. "I certainly don't have much to complain about in terms of total number of hours," says one associate. "What gets to you is the erratic nature of it. You spend 15 hours a day for a whole month and then you have nothing to do for another month."

Be careful about picking up the phone. "The worst is when you have nothing to do all day, then the phone rings at 6 p.m. when you're ready to leave the office, and you're there until midnight but have only billed six hours." There are other horror stories as well. "While my hours are not always very high, I feel there is a lot of pressure to bill a lot of hours, even when the work is not there," complains one not-always-busy lawyer. "I feel this detracts from any benefit I might take away from having decent hours." At least one White & Case associate feels bound to his desk. "Work hours are the only kind of hours I have."

Bonus shenanigans

"Compensation is as good as at any big law firm," says one well-paid insider. "However, White & Case has a tendency to follow the others rather than being a leader. Especially on bonuses, they can be a bit cheap." The bonus structure is a source of confusion and complaint. Some dislike the firm's hours requirement. "The 2,000-billable hours requirement in order to receive the bonus is too high," says one associate. "The firm has low-balled on bonuses each of the past three years and has attempted – and failed – to mislead associates about the details of the three successive schemes each year," fumes another contact. "The way bonuses have been handled has been execrable."

The ire is shared. Says one source, "I am particularly not happy with the bonus situation in 2002. The criteria were unclear and I feel as though the firm was finding excuses not to pay anything but was too afraid to have it reported on Lawyer.com – hence the makeshift bonus policy that excludes most." Still others are just plain perturbed. "I cannot for the life of me fathom how this firm cannot pay a bonus to everybody and allocate bonuses on the basis of billed hours and claim that compensation is competitive with other firms that pay across-the-board bonuses," wonders one lawyer. "Can someone please explain this to me?"

Getting better at training

Some insiders feel that formal training at White & Case has gone from a weakness to a strength – or, at the very least, that White & Case holds its own. "This has historically been a massive problem at this firm," says a corporate lawyer. "However, it seems that there is an effort under way at the moment to improve this in the securities section. It is still very halting, and firm-provided training is only a small fraction compared to the self-training that I do here." Others are more positive. "The White & Case New York office provides over 200 on-site courses a year given by White & Case attorneys and outside providers," reports one insider. "The New York office has a full two-week core curriculum for incoming associates. And all U.S. attorneys can take unlimited PLI classes." Don't expect to be spoon-fed. "All the resources are there, you just won't get any kind of handholding at all and you will be unpleasantly surprised if you come in expecting it."

Diversity efforts

Insiders complain that despite the firm's efforts, White & Case has a problem common to big law firms: a lack of female partners. "There is a lack of diversity with respect to women in the partnership," reports one insider. "I am not sure if the reason for that is internal, societal or for reasons that are unique to women such as child rearing, personal fulfillment and so on. It has been brought to management's attention, although I am not sure what is being done about it. It is my belief that the firm is committed to making sure that they do what they can to correct this situation." Another source says diversity with respect to women is "great overall on the associate level – but when it comes to making partner in the New York office, women still lose out." Family issues may be to blame. "The firm is welcoming for single, driven women," says one attorney. "I understand that some women with families have had a different experience." "Women partners do not mentor women associates," sighs one insider.

Minority recruiting and retention seem to be issues, and some blame the firm for not following up. "The firm is committed to having a diverse group of associates," states one insider. "However, this diversity does not seem to extend to the partnership rank, especially in the New York office." Some complain that there's no formal diversity program at White & Case. "The firm seems to be lacking a pronounced recruiting, retention and mentoring program aimed at U.S. minority students," says one associate. White & Case "had a diversity consultant a couple of years ago to begin the process of diversifying," reports one associate, who divulged that a senior manager "disclosed at an associates' retreat that absolutely nothing had been done to follow up on this."

O'Melveny & Myers LLP

400 South Hope Street
Los Angeles, CA 90071-2899
Phone: (213) 430-6000
www.omm.com

LOCATIONS

Los Angeles, CA (HQ)
Century City, CA
Irvine, CA
New York, NY
Newport Beach, CA
San Francisco, CA
Silicon Valley, CA
Tysons Corner, VA
Washington, DC
Beijing
Hong Kong
London
Shanghai
Tokyo

MAJOR DEPARTMENTS/PRACTICES

Intellectual Property & Technology
Labor & Employment
Litigation
Tax
Transactions

THE STATS

No. of attorneys: 900+
No. of offices: 14
Summer associate offers: 115 out of 120 (2002)
Chairman: Arthur B. Culvahouse Jr.
Hiring attorney: Carla Christofferson

BASE SALARY

Los Angeles, CA
1st year: $125,000
2nd year: $135,000
3rd year: $150,000
4th year: $165,000
5th year: $185,000
6th year: $195,000
7th year: $205,000
8th year: $210,000
Summer associate: $2,400/week

UPPERS

• Collegial co-workers
• Challenging, sophisticated work
• Glamorous and prestigious clients

DOWNERS

• Increasing emphasis on billable hours
• Little in the way of formal training
• Big-firm bureaucracy

NOTABLE PERKS

• Paid parking (in most offices)
• Free wireless e-mail
• Subsidized attorney dining room
• Overtime meals

 THE BUZZ
WHAT ATTORNEYS AT OTHER FIRMS ARE SAYING ABOUT THIS FIRM

• "Old school Los Angeles"
• "One of the best"
• "O'Misery & Misers"
• "Very classy"

RANKING RECAP

Best in Region
#2 - California

Best in Practice
#8 - Labor & Employment

Quality of Life
#10 - Part-Time/Flex-Time

EMPLOYMENT CONTACT

Ms. Jacqueline Wilson
Recruiting Administrator
Phone: (202) 383-5300
Fax: (202) 383-5414
E-mail: jwilson@omm.com

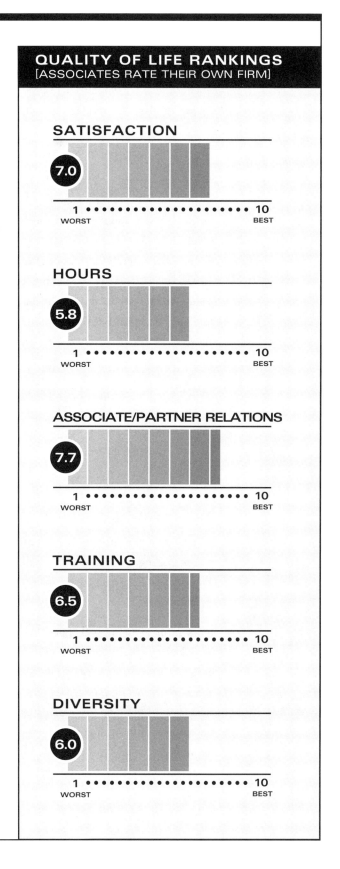

QUALITY OF LIFE RANKINGS
[ASSOCIATES RATE THEIR OWN FIRM]

SATISFACTION
7.0
1 WORST • • • • • • • • • • • • • • • • • • • 10 BEST

HOURS
5.8
1 WORST • • • • • • • • • • • • • • • • • • • 10 BEST

ASSOCIATE/PARTNER RELATIONS
7.7
1 WORST • • • • • • • • • • • • • • • • • • • 10 BEST

TRAINING
6.5
1 WORST • • • • • • • • • • • • • • • • • • • 10 BEST

DIVERSITY
6.0
1 WORST • • • • • • • • • • • • • • • • • • • 10 BEST

THE SCOOP

Founded in 1885 as Graves & O'Melveny, O'Melveny & Myers is the oldest law firm in Los Angeles. And like the fine wines produced in California, the firm keeps getting better with age. At 118 years old, O'Melveny is experiencing phenomenal growth and record profits per partner.

Two O's are better than one

During the summer of 2002, O'Melveny caught the merger fever that's been sweeping the legal industry. In July, the firm announced that it would merge with O'Sullivan LLP, a leader in private equity. By September, the firms had sealed the deal. The addition of O'Sullivan's 88 attorneys helped make O'Melveny the 18th largest firm in the country, according to a survey by *The National Law Journal*. But the merger announcement wasn't the firm's only big news in 2002. Earlier in the year, the firm gave notice to the legal community that it has moved into the upper echelons of big law, with its profits per partner jumping 33 percent to $940,000, giving it the third biggest jump among all firms for the year. The trend continued into 2003, with profits per partner increasing almost 18 percent to just over $1.1 million.

With two New York offices following the merger with O'Sullivan, the firm is looking to consolidate its Big Apple attorneys in one space. O'Melveny will consolidate its ranks in Times Square Tower sometime in 2004. Meanwhile, attorneys in the firm's D.C. office will soon occupy a new building on Eye Street near the White House. On the international scene, O'Melveny also recently expanded its presence in Asia, announcing the addition of a 10-attorney Beijing office in December 2002.

An appeal-ing practice

O'Melveny has a thriving appellate practice headed by partner Walter Dellinger. A true D.C. insider, Dellinger served as acting solicitor general and assistant attorney general during the 1990s. Dellinger and his group are frequently called upon to represent Fortune 500 companies in bet-the-company cases.

In one of its more unusual appellate cases, O'Melveny is representing footwear company Nike in a freedom of speech case. A lawsuit was filed against the company by a California citizen who alleges that misleading statements concerning its plants in Asia were made by CEO Philip Knight and in press releases issued by the company. The California Supreme Court ruled that the statements in question are commercial speech and therefore subject to federal regulation. The implications of this ruling are widespread because the case has exposed areas of corporate speech that were previously not subject to this level of regulatory scrutiny. In January 2003, the Supreme Court announced that it would hear an appeal in the case.

Unocal Corp. has tapped the firm to represent the multinational energy company in a suit alleging it participated in human rights violations against workers in Myanmar. In February 2003, attorneys at O'Melveny convinced the U.S. Ninth Circuit Court of Appeals to rehear the case after a panel of judges ruled that Unocal may have been involved in the abuses. As if that weren't enough to keep the appellate attorneys busy, the firm is also representing a large group of companies, including ExxonMobil, in an asbestos-related suit.

Newsworthy cases

In February 2003, the *Los Angeles Daily Journal* and the *San Francisco Daily Journal* proclaimed an O'Melveny victory one of the 10 top defense wins of 2002. In the case, in which the firm represented Tenet Healthcare, O'Melveny was able to disprove the claims of two of the hospital's founders that they'd been cheated out of stock options worth more than $20 million. The firm is also representing the former chief financial officer of the Rite Aid drugstore chain against charges brought by the U.S. Attorney's office and the SEC.

Of course, O'Melveny wouldn't be a true Los Angeles law firm if it didn't have its share of famous clients. O'Melveny's entertainment, sports and media practice dates back to the Golden Age of Hollywood when the firm represented such mega-stars as Jimmy Stewart, Jack Benny, Gary Cooper and Mary Pickford. Today, many of the practice's clients are multimedia conglomerates such as Fox, Time Warner and Sony. In one case that's sure to grab headlines, the firm is defending Time Warner against claims brought by Nancy Stouffer, who alleges that J.K. Rowling, author of the Harry Potter book series, actually stole much of the material from her 1984 children's book, *The Legend of Rah and the Muggles*.

Treasure Qwest

On the deal front, O'Melveny represented Qwest Communications in the sale of its telephone directory business for $7.05 billion, the largest leveraged buyout since RJR Nabisco's LBO back in the 1980s. The firm also continues its longstanding leadership position in representing senior lenders such as Deutsche Bank and Credit Suisse First Boston in complex credit transactions and restructurings. The merger with O'Sullivan significantly increased O'Melveny's profile in the private equity community, adding new clients such as JPMorgan Partners and Apollo Management.

Charity begins at O'Melveny

The firm has a long-standing commitment to giving back to the community. Its most visible programs are in the education arena. The firm awards eight college scholarships annually to students from O'Melveny Elementary School, a school the firm adopted, in addition to providing scholarships to students attending top law schools in Shanghai, and to Los Angeles Unified High School students via the Christopher Scholarship program, established in honor of the firm's prestigious senior partner, former Secretary of State Warren Christopher. The firm is also in the process of establishing a college scholarship program in partnership with the City of New York.

In March 2003, the firm helped secure a victory for legal aid programs across the country. O'Melveny, arguing before the U.S. Supreme Court on behalf of the Washington State Supreme Court, successfully argued that legal aid programs should be allowed to operate using interest earned on escrow accounts of the programs' clients. Walter Dellinger lent a hand to the University of Michigan by submitting an amicus curiae brief in support of the school's policy of considering race when making admission decisions. O'Melveny further strengthened its commitment to pro bono work with the addition of David Lash to the firm's litigation team. Lash will wear two hats; he will work with corporate clients while helping to coordinate the firm's pro bono efforts. Lash had previously served as executive director of Bet Tzedek, a California-based nonprofit that provides free legal services to elderly, disabled and low-income people.

In and out

The firm was forced to bid adieu to two of its most prominent international trade attorneys when they made the move to Wilmer, Cutler & Pickering in September 2002. But O'Melveny made a big hire of its own in March 2003 when Lawrence Nagin, a former general counsel at US Airways and United Air Lines, joined the firm as of counsel. Nagin's expertise in aviation law is particularly welcome at the firm right now, given the struggles facing the airline industry in the current economic climate. The firm has represented both airlines and airports in the past, most recently taking a lead role in advising US Airways and United Air Lines through labor law concerns in their respective Chapter 11 proceedings.

GETTING HIRED

Picky, picky

"With one or two notable exceptions, the firm is fairly strict about hiring only from top-10 law schools and only the top of the class. There is some deviation from this rule for laterals." "Lots of people with great grades still get dinged because of personality. We're very picky here and we're conscious of that," confides a litigation associate. Other insiders tell us, "An outgoing personality never hurts." Indeed, "grades and academic qualifications are just the beginning. There has to be a social fit or you're out." Hiring at O'Melveny's D.C. office "has become extremely competitive," says a Washingtonian. "Several current associates, including myself, have remarked that we don't think we would have been hired under the firm's current criteria," says a second-year associate. "The firm is looking for diversity and for people who are friendly and have interests other than the law," says an associate in the L.A. office. The firm tends to hire attorneys who "will fit into the laid-back and friendly atmosphere – as well as good lawyers."

An associate in the Tokyo office says, "Our office looks for the perfect candidate – someone with personality, excellent social skills, good grades from good schools and a clear reason for wanting to live overseas. Language skills are often a prerequisite for a foreign office position." A San

Francisco associate warns, "Don't even think about applying if you're not in the top 15 percent of your class." When it comes to the callback process, the emphasis is on "the interviewers really wanting to get to know the person" and determine "what it would be like to have that person as a colleague."

OUR SURVEY SAYS

Friendly, but in flux

Many insiders at O'Melveny say it's impossible to identify a firm-wide culture. "I don't think there is a firm-wide culture. Rather, there are sub-department cultures," says a San Francisco associate. This source continues, "Even within the corporate department here, there are different subcultures. Some partners are informative and approachable – though certainly demanding – while others can be difficult." "The firm tends to have a friendly atmosphere," says a senior associate, "although the changes that the firm has undergone in the past few years are making it a more competitive environment." In the opinion of an L.A. associate, the culture is "laid back and friendly, but people rarely socialize after hours." An officemate offers this perspective: "The culture here has always been friendly, but with a dose of old-fashioned formality befitting the firm's traditions." "Some lawyers like to socialize together outside of work," this source adds, "but unlike some places, that is not a requirement to fit in, just something that people genuinely enjoy." "As a result of the O'Sullivan merger, there really is not one culture. The O'Sullivan culture was laid back and friendly, but the O'Melveny culture tends to be more bureaucratic and rigid," says a corporate associate. A D.C. insider says, "Our office is not hugely social, but it is not stifling. It is intellectual but not uptight."

You call this a bonus?

Compensation at O'Melveny is "competitive with other major international law firms," associates report. "If you put in the hours, you will be rewarded," remarks one corporate associate, while another shrugs, "No complaints." "If you work hard you'll get a high bonus. If you work moderately, but do good work, you'll still be paid a lot. What more can you ask for?" asks a sixth-year associate.

However, several insiders have a bone to pick with O'Melveny regarding bonuses. "The constantly changing bonus structure is bewildering, opaque, and typically fails to meet the expectations that management created," a sixth-year insider states. An associate who has "no complaints" when it comes to base salary says the "fact that the bonus pool was shrunk in a year of record profits per partner was not received well" by other associates. One such attorney reports, "The firm justified lower bonuses by saying that the market wasn't paying any more but seemed to fail to account for the fact that we were working much harder than associates at other firms. Other firms may not have paid bonuses, but their associates also didn't have enough work to keep them busy." "The firm seems to be constantly restructuring its compensation system" is a complaint voiced by a number of associates.

No middle ground

Associates from a variety of practice areas report a "tremendous pressure to meet billable-hour requirements" as of late. "With the firm's emphasis on minimum billables, even if you don't have to spend 15 hours a day in the office, you can hardly enjoy your downtime because your bonus is at stake," complains a fourth-year. "I don't mind the long hours when it's busy, but when I'm here 12 hours to try to put up six billable [hours], it's frustrating," comments a real estate attorney. Says a sixth-year, "I remain troubled by the emphasis on hours, but I don't believe that things are different at any peer firms." Another associate groans about the difficulty of striking a balance in this economy. "Last year was a slow year overall and hours were low. As attractive as that sounds, it has its own stresses. Now that things have picked up, I'm spending my weekends and evenings in the office again. There just doesn't seem to be any such thing as a happy middle ground."

Some insiders are able to take the difficult hours in stride. "Working for any big firm means long unpredictable hours. People here expect sacrifices but understand when you need personal time," says a second-year. If the work is slow, "no one looks down on you for leaving early," this contact adds. A labor attorney informs us that "there is virtually no face-time requirement, and associates are judged not simply by the hours that they scribble on a timesheet, but by the quality of their work. That said," he continues, "the demands of our clients often require long hours. Fortunately, work seems to be distributed equitably." An associate in the New York office disagrees with that assessment, saying, "The firm needs to do a better job of spreading the work around." A first-year chimes in on this subject: "There doesn't appear to be any work coordination at all. One person could be very busy, while another is sitting around with nothing to do." For those who do find themselves working around the clock, "There is not a lot of emphasis placed on working in the office itself as opposed to telecommuting. This allows greater flexibility."

A dearth of screamers, throwers and voice-raisers

When it comes to the quality of working relationships between associates and partners, associates say, "It varies greatly." As one first-year tells it, "Some partners are amazingly helpful and respectful. Others can be disrespectful to junior people." Other associates acknowledge that there are a few partners in the firm who aren't always respectful or helpful. However, the majority of associates say the individual partners they work with regularly aren't among them. "From the very first day, what I had to say mattered here. Partners expect and cultivate opinionated associates," a third-year tells us. A fifth-year reports that the partners "treat me with tremendous respect. I remember a partner apologizing for needing me to work over Thanksgiving weekend on an emergency project." "Partners are generous, supportive, helpful, self-deprecating and genuinely nice. I haven't met any screamers, throwers or even partners who've raised their voices. The ones

I have worked with have been willing to stay as late as we have and have never dumped their work on us so they could go home early," shares a New York associate.

However, many of the same associates who say the partners are "open, friendly and available to answer questions" say they'd appreciate the partners being more proactive regarding mentoring and communication. A second-year opines, "Associates are treated with great respect when it comes to their work on legal matters. Associates' opinions regarding administrative and governance matters seem to be given less weight."

Plentiful pro bono

"The firm has a reasonably strong commitment to pro bono work," reveals a fourth-year. "All approved pro bono work – and approval does not appear to be a problem – counts toward annual minimum billable hours. There is no limit on the number of pro bono hours that will count toward billable hours." However, according to this source, "There is pressure to take on client billable hours that can interfere with the ability to actually get involved in the pro bono program."

Indeed, if associates have any complaints at all regarding pro bono, it's that they'd like the active support of partners regarding pro bono matters. "The firm as a whole has a huge commitment to pro bono work. This is, however, not entirely reflected in the New York office as much as in the L.A. office," says a Big Apple insider. An officemate reports, "The New York litigation department is so swamped right now that suggestions by associates to pursue pro bono opportunities are actively laughed at by partners, who are under tremendous pressure from firm management to raise per partner profits for the third year in a row – in a down economy!" A D.C. associate considers the firm's pro bono track record to be "pretty good," but feels "the initiative is all with the associates." There's "not much direct encouragement from above," this contact tell us, "but no discouragement either." "Actual support from partners in the D.C. office for doing pro bono has been weak. There is a new partner in charge of pro bono who seems more dedicated to leading by example." A Century City associate reports a very different experience: "They not only say you can do pro bono, but they encourage you to do so and provide you with the support you need."

Jones Day

North Point - 901 Lakeside Avenue
Cleveland, OH 44114-1190
Phone: (216) 586-3939
www.jonesday.com

LOCATIONS

Atlanta, GA • Chicago, IL • Cleveland, OH • Columbus,
OH • Dallas, TX • Houston, TX • Irvine, CA • Los
Angeles, CA • Menlo Park, CA • New York, NY •
Pittsburgh, PA • San Francisco, CA • Washington, DC •
Beijing • Brussels • Frankfurt • Hong Kong • London •
Madrid • Milan • Mumbai* • Munich • New Delhi* •
Paris • Shanghai • Singapore • Sydney • Taipei • Tokyo

Pathak & Associates, An Associate Firm

MAJOR DEPARTMENTS/PRACTICES

Business Practice
Government Regulation
Litigation
Tax

THE STATS

No. of attorneys: 2,000+
No. of offices: 29
Summer associate offers: 164 out of 178 (2002)
Managing Partner: Stephen J. Brogan
Hiring Partners: Patricia J. Villareal (Law School) and
James C. Hagy (Laterals)

BASE SALARY

Atlanta, GA; Cleveland, Columbus, OH;
Pittsburgh, PA
1st year: $110,000
Summer associate: $9,000/month (Cleveland,
Columbus and Pittsburgh); $8,500/month (Atlanta)

Dallas, Houston, TX
1st year: $115,000
Summer associate: $9,500/month

Chicago, IL; Irvine, Los Angeles, Menlo Park, CA;
New York, NY; Washington, DC
1st year: $125,000
Summer associate: $10,400/month

UPPERS

• Collegial co-workers
• Challenging and sophisticated work
• Solid training opportunities

DOWNERS

• Lack of mentoring/communication from partners
• No casual dress policy in some offices
• Secrecy regarding compensation

NOTABLE PERKS

• Free/subsidized parking (Dallas and Los Angeles)
• Moving expenses, plus movers who do the
  packing
• Twelve weeks maternity leave
• Annual retreats

THE BUZZ
WHAT ATTORNEYS AT OTHER FIRMS ARE SAYING ABOUT THIS FIRM

• "Big and powerful"
• "Breadth not depth "
• "The McDonald's of law"
• "Fighting the regional firm perception"

RANKING RECAP

Best in Practice

#4 - Antitrust

#6 - Bankruptcy/Corporate Restructuring

#10 - Litigation

Quality of Life

#2 - Part-Time/Flex-Time

#8 - Training

#15 - Retention

#17 - Best Firms to Work For

Best in Diversity

#16 - Diversity for Women

EMPLOYMENT CONTACT

Ms. Jolie A. Blanchard

Firm Director of Recruiting

Phone: (202) 879-3788

Fax: (202) 626-1738

E-mail: jablanchard@jonesday.com

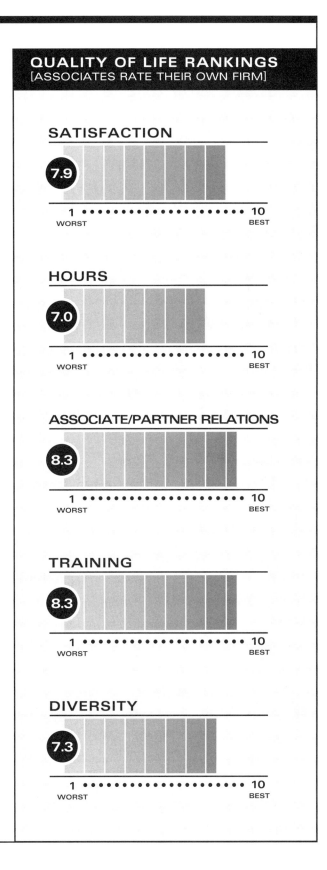

QUALITY OF LIFE RANKINGS
[ASSOCIATES RATE THEIR OWN FIRM]

SATISFACTION

7.9

1 WORST · 10 BEST

HOURS

7.0

1 WORST · 10 BEST

ASSOCIATE/PARTNER RELATIONS

8.3

1 WORST · 10 BEST

TRAINING

8.3

1 WORST · 10 BEST

DIVERSITY

7.3

1 WORST · 10 BEST

THE SCOOP

New York City may be the unofficial center of the corporate law universe, but with more than 2,000 attorneys in 29 worldwide offices, Jones Day is a star that continues to rise.

Midwest roots, worldwide presence

Jones Day has been a fixture in Cleveland since it was established in 1893. Local manufacturing and transportation companies were its first clients. Today, its major clients include RJR Nabisco, General Motors and Texas Instruments. Other clients include Eastman Kodak, Pfizer, Dell Computer Corp., Ernst & Young, Dow Corning, Foster's Brewing and Omnicom Group, a publicly traded marketing and communications company.

The firm rang in the new year with a new, streamlined name and a new managing partner. Known as Jones, Day, Reavis & Pouge since 1974, the firm took the step of officially shortening its name to Jones Day. The firm says the change wasn't spurred by any disregard for former name partners John W. Reavis and L. Welch Pogue. The shortened appellation is simply in keeping with the way the firm is popularly known throughout the legal and business communities. Former U.S. Deputy Assistant Attorney General Stephen Brogan is now the firm's managing partner, assuming the reins from Patrick McCartan, who is now a senior partner at the firm. Residing in the Washington, D.C., office, Brogan is the first Jones Day managing partner not based in Cleveland .

Movin' on up

Despite a climate of worldwide political and economic strife, Jones Day continues to expand internationally. In January 2003, the firm added a second German location with the opening of a Munich office. The new office specializes in German corporate transactions, including mergers and acquisitions, IT, biotechnology and intellectual property matters. The following month, Jones Day expanded its presence in London when it completed the acquisition of Gouldens, a practice with approximately 150 attorneys. (The firm is known as Jones Day Gouldens in London.) But that's not all. The firm has announced plans to establish an outpost in Beijing, which will be the firm's second Chinese office. The firm bolstered its Singapore practice in January 2003 with the addition of a partner from Orrick, Herrington & Sutcliffe and a team from Rajah & Tann, a local firm.

Jones Day will be making a few moves domestically, as well. The firm is planning to occupy approximately half of a new low-rise building in Columbus' Arena District. The Columbus, Ohio, office plans to give up its current space and move its 100 attorneys to the new building when it is completed in late 2004. Having been established just two years ago with 19 attorneys, the Houston office is already outgrowing its current space. The firm has signed on to move the Houston office to Calpine Center, a new 33-story high-rise, in November 2003. Attorneys in the Atlanta office are also slated to move into roomier digs during the first quarter of 2004.

High drama in the high court

Jones Day is playing a pivotal role in a U.S. Supreme Court case that could have large-scale ramifications for workers and employers. Jones Day is working on behalf of the state of Nevada, which was sued by a former employee who claims that by firing him, the state violated the Family and Medical Leave Act. Oral arguments have been given, and the court is expected to issue a decision on the case before July 2003.

Williams Communications has found out the hard way that going broke costs big money. Jones Day is the lead firm representing the cash-strapped communications concern in its bankruptcy. In the first five months of the proceeding alone, the company has run up a legal tab of $3.85 million. The firm is also representing National Century Financial Enterprises, a finance firm serving the healthcare industry, in its Chapter 11 bankruptcy proceedings.

Strength in numbers

With more than 860 attorneys, litigation is by far Jones Day's largest practice group; in fact it's the largest litigation group in the country. With all that muscle (and those brains) behind it, there's no wonder the group was named Litigation Department of the Year by *American Lawyer* in January 2002. A similar honor was bestowed upon the firm by U.K.-based legal publisher Chambers and Partners in June 2002. But it's not just the firm's litigators who are receiving notice. In July 2002, *Venture Reporter* ranked Jones Day third for top venture capital deals. This honor was due in part to the firm's work on behalf of clients Benchmark Capital and JP Morgan Partners.

Online retailer Amazon.com and Jones Day have a long-standing relationship. The firm has won 11 consecutive intellectual property cases for Amazon involving domain name disputes. As a result of Jones Day's most recent work for the client, three domain names containing "Amazon" were transferred to the company in March 2003. When Hughes Electronics agreed to be acquired by News Corp. in April 2003, Jones Day was part of the legal team advising Hughes. Partner Jonathan Rose has joined the legal team defending former HealthSouth CEO Richard Scrushy against charges of fraudulent accounting.

Lending a hand

Jones Day has an active pro bono practice. Through an affiliation with the Midwest Immigrant & Human Rights Center, the Chicago office is working on a number of cases for political asylum. One of the cases resulted in a victory in March 2003 for an Albanian woman from Kosovo who was about to be deported. Because of her involvement with Kosovo's underground government, the woman had been imprisoned and beaten and feared retribution if she returned to Kosovo. Attorneys in the firm's Washington office are administering the Children's Trust Fund. The endowment provides support to the children of astronauts killed in the Challenger and Columbia tragedies.

GETTING HIRED

Top lawyers wanted

"To get hired at Jones Day, you need to either be from a top-20 law school or be on law review at a lower-ranked school," a first-year tells us. "Candidates at the top of their class from third- and even fourth-tier law schools will be considered," but insiders say these candidates "must have exceptional academic qualifications." Says a senior associate, "We seek candidates with good grades – the range of 'good' can vary depending upon the law school attended – excellent writing skills and good communication skills. Since we interview candidates with very similar skills, the candidate's ability to interact with various individuals can distinguish this person from many others we interview." Jones Day "primarily recruits through an on-campus interview, followed by a callback to the office" that can last anywhere from half to a full day. "During the morning interview, the recruit meets with four lawyers and goes to lunch with at least two others. The afternoon interview includes dinner." "Jones Day can be extremely competitive in terms of lateral hiring. The firm not only looks for a strong academic background and lateral experience, but also for the type of person who will be willing to be a team player and be a self-starter, a combination that is not always easy to find." Ultimately, says a third-year, Jones Day's decision to extend an offer to a candidate comes down to deciding, "Will we like working with you?" FYI: "Recruiting is done on an office-by-office basis, but recommendations across offices do occur."

OUR SURVEY SAYS

Don't let the suits fool you

In the opinion of a second-year, Jones Day "is formal but not at all stuffy and very friendly. Lawyers socialize together both in and outside of work." A first-year tells us that the firm isn't nearly as formal as its dress code implies. "While we are required to wear suits and ties, you don't have to sit at your desk with your jacket on, and nobody is going to browbeat you if you're seen without a tie late at night. As far as socializing, I think that there are more casual get-togethers by younger attorneys, while older attorneys tend to have families and look to head right home after work." "Jones Day continues to be an oasis among law firms in New York," says a New Yorker. "The work is sophisticated and challenging, the hours manageable and the environment pleasant. When I get up each day, I actually look forward to going to work – not something many senior associates can say." "The client list is outstanding, and it is only outshined by the quality and skill of the partners here," says a Cleveland associate. What's more, says an Angeleno, "The work is challenging and cutting edge, and often very high profile."

Of course, not everyone feels the love. "For a firm that excels in so many crucial areas, it is remarkable that associates are given almost no feedback, good or bad, upon completion of even major projects, let alone on any regular sort of basis," sighs a frustrated second-year. However, notes this same source, "Because the firm's approach to most everything is hands-off, including mentoring and work assignments, the culture is fairly relaxed." "The downturn in the general economy has affected the amount and availability of work for junior associates. In these tight times, some partners and senior associates, in an effort to meet their own billable hour requirements, are more hesitant to pass work down the ladder," reveals a third-year. Nevertheless, this contact says, "The culture is one of my favorite things about my law firm. It is laid back and friendly." Says a Pittsburgh associate, "The people are wonderful and the pay is terrific, but incoming associates to this office should harbor no illusions that they will ever, ever get to court – even to present a simple motion."

Mystery money

Jones Day insiders around the world are grateful for their fat paychecks. "The compensation is more than fair, especially for the geographical area," says a Dallas associate. A Jones Day insider brags, "In Columbus, there's not a firm that pays any better." "This firm pays more than other local firms," another Columbus attorney agrees. "That being said," adds this contact, "there is considerable compression in the middle ranks of associates." But others in the Columbus office tell us, "When you adjust for the low cost of living in Columbus, the compensation is very nice," so much so that "many first- and second-year associates own homes." Likewise an Atlanta associate tells us, "I am very satisfied with my income." These opinions reflect those of the majority of associates surveyed.

But some insiders have a bone to pick with the firm. "Because salaries are not lockstep and are not disclosed, there is no basis for measuring how you are perceived and where you stand relative to your peers," reveals a third-year. This source elaborates: "The secret salary process remains a mystery overall. It would be helpful to know more clearly how pro bono hours and non-billable projects fit into the salary structure." "The compensation may be slightly lower in absolute dollars than at other firms of this size, but to work in a place that is both a highly reputable law firm and a downright pleasant place to work, this compensation has to be considered 'superior,'" explains a senior associate. "I feel like I'm paid very well. Our compensation system is based exclusively on merit, not hours, and generally operates very fairly," says a D.C. associate.

Time management for lawyers

It's hard to find a big-firm lawyer who gushes happily about his hours. Jones Day insiders don't gush. "All business lawyers spend too much time in the office," explains a New Yorker. "Jones Day is no exception. It's the main reason why most people are unhappy with the profession." "The office and firm have a tremendous amount of work available, and only the wary/diligent associates avoid the trap of frequent 200+-hour months." That being said, Jones Day-ers say the hours, while not nine to five, are manageable. "Keeping one's hours regularly at 170 to 200 per month is possible in this office but requires saying no to partners frequently and having to juggle partners'

needs and expectations with care," an Atlanta attorney informs us. For a Los Angeles attorney, "The workload is not so demanding that [working] consecutive high-hour weeks is required." "When Jones Day tells associates that the billable requirement is 2,000 hours, they mean it. Nobody has ever pressured me to bill more than 2,000 for the year, and I'm still on partnership track," a litigation attorney states.

"There is a lot of emphasis on meeting our budgeted hours, but if you are having a slow day, you can simply leave. There is no need to sneak out or be ashamed or anything like that," says a first-year. A senior associate has "found the firm to be very flexible regarding working from home and other alternative scheduling. I generally get in early and leave early – 6 p.m. – but bring a fair amount of work home with me. No one seems to have a problem with that, and it works for me." A litigation attorney agrees. "We are so connected at home that I do not feel the need to be here on weekends. It is very easy to access and work on documents and so on from home. This at least gives the illusion of not being chained to the desk."

Partners and associates: in it together

"My experience has been that most partners treat most associates with respect," says a seventh-year, "but there are exceptions, as there always will be." Partners "know the associates work hard and they value their contributions." "While the partners are clearly in charge, associates are treated as colleagues, not merely as grunts," says another contented source. "Partners are understandably demanding" and have "high expectations, but [they are] generally approachable, friendly people." In fact, a few insiders report that they have "supportive, friendly relationships" based on the attitude that partners and associates alike "are all in this together." "The expectation as to level of effort is high both for partners and associates," says a third-year, who adds, "There are no 'you get it done because I'm going home' games. If it's not done, both the partner and the associate will be there until it is." But associates say they wouldn't mind receiving more mentoring from the partners. "Partners can be so busy that they don't have as much time to spend mentoring associates as associates might like." Moreover, "the culture is somewhat guarded, in terms of flow of information from partners to associates," reveals a litigation attorney.

This old office

As can be expected of a large firm with many offices, the condition of the office space varies widely. "Jones Day D.C. just opened new offices on Capitol Hill in 1999 or 2000, and they're pretty awesome," says a first-year, whose "only complaint at the moment would be lack of space – it's getting a little cramped." A colleague tells us, "The offices are elegant and the views of the Capitol are incomparable." In the opinion of a very comfortable Atlanta associate, "The office's current digs are definitely posh and luxurious, though care has been given not to send the wrong message to clients, who ultimately pay for the luxury. We will be moving to new digs [in] our own building in the first quarter of 2004, with all new furniture, décor and so forth" and, "rumor has it, a gym."

Too bad Los Angeles associates can't say the same. Insiders say, "The office is not pretty. The lease has been 'about to run out' for four years now, so the firm has not invested in upgrading our facilities. The furniture is old and worn, and the carpet is tacked down in places." Not only that, "The furniture tends to be old, and the office space very poorly designed." In fact, according to one L.A. associate, "New carpeting was laid in some areas of some floors and seamed with the old carpeting, which it does not match." Nevertheless, she says the "lobby" and "views are impressive," and the "artwork is generally good." New Yorkers are satisfied, thanks to their recent move to new digs. "Office space has improved significantly," reports a New Yorker. "The offices are spacious and every associate has their own office – no sharing. When the space was being built, the firm solicited associate opinions on the office configurations, including desktop, filing and bookshelf space."

Hale and Dorr LLP

60 State Street
Boston, MA 02109-1816
Phone: (617) 526-6000
www.haledorr.com

LOCATIONS

Boston, MA (HQ)
New York, NY
Princeton, NJ
Reston, VA
Waltham, MA
Washington, DC
London
Munich
Oxford

MAJOR DEPARTMENTS/PRACTICES

Commercial
Corporate
Environmental
Government & Regulatory Affairs
Intellectual Property
Labor & Employment
Litigation
Private Client
Real Estate
Tax

THE STATS

No. of attorneys: 509
No. of offices: 9
Summer associate offers: 40 out of 40 (2002)
Managing Partner: William F. Lee
Hiring Partner: Daniel W. Halston

BASE SALARY

All domestic offices
1st year: $125,000 ($115,000 in Princeton)
2nd year: $135,000
3rd year: $145,000 ($155,000 in NY)
4th year: $155,000 ($165,000 in NY)
5th year: $165,000 ($175,000 in NY)
1st yr. jr. partner: $180,000 ($195,000 in NY)
2nd yr. jr. partner: $190,000 ($205,000 in NY)
3rd yr. jr. partner: $200,000 ($215,000 in NY)
Summer associate: $2,400/week

UPPERS

• Collegial, meritocratic culture
• New England prestige
• Superb training

DOWNERS

• Murky partnership track
• Erratic hours
• "Almost no" minority partners

NOTABLE PERKS

• Annual golf/tennis outing
• Friday happy hours
• Hale and Dorr fitness center (Boston)
• Twenty dollars for attending firm meetings

THE BUZZ
WHAT ATTORNEYS AT OTHER FIRMS ARE SAYING ABOUT THIS FIRM

• "Still the gold standard for New England"
• "A little old school"
• "Good Boston firm"
• "Stodgy white shoe"

RANKING RECAP

Best in Region
#2 - Boston

Quality of Life
#3 - Training
#8 - Offices
#9 - Pay
#9 - Retention
#13 - Best Firms to Work For
#14 - Selectivity

EMPLOYMENT CONTACT

Ms. Evelyn M. Scoville
Director of Legal Personnel
Phone: (617) 526-6590
Fax: (617) 526-5000
E-mail: evelyn.scoville@haledorr.com

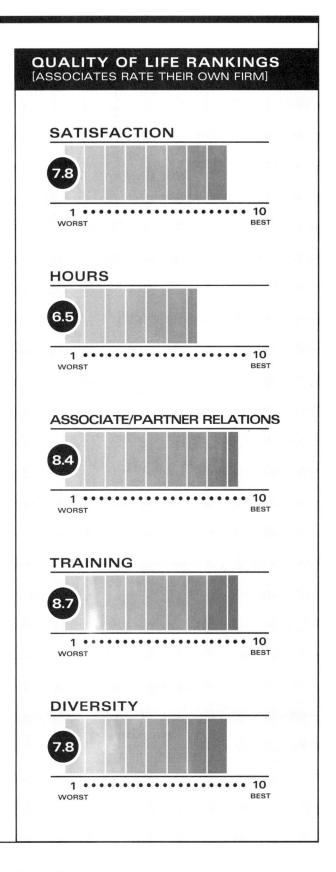

QUALITY OF LIFE RANKINGS
[ASSOCIATES RATE THEIR OWN FIRM]

SATISFACTION
7.8

HOURS
6.5

ASSOCIATE/PARTNER RELATIONS
8.4

TRAINING
8.7

DIVERSITY
7.8

THE SCOOP

An intellectual property leader and a New England institution, Boston-based Hale and Dorr has 500 lawyers in six U.S. offices and three overseas offices picked up from a joint venture with now-defunct Brobeck, Phleger & Harrison. The ampersand-less firm was one of the first to establish an intellectual property practice and has one of the largest litigation groups in New England.

A New England fixture

Big things were happening in Boston in 1918. The Boston Red Sox were in the middle of a championship season – their last to date – and Richard Hale and Dudley Dorr founded a law partnership along with a three other Boston lawyers. The next year the firm welcomed Reginald Heber Smith as managing partner. Smith had previously worked at the Boston Legal Aid Society and authored *Justice and the Poor*, the undisputed guide to legal aid work in the United States.

In 1954, Hale and Dorr attorneys represented the U.S. Army pro bono in the Army-McCarthy hearings, the congressional hearings into communist infiltration into the U.S. military. (Partner Joseph Welch is famous for asking Senator Joe McCarthy, during his questioning of Army witnesses, "Have you no sense of decency, sir? At long last, have you left no sense of decency?") Also representing the Army was Jim St. Clair. He left Hale and Dorr for one year in 1974 to represent President Richard Nixon during the Watergate scandal, for which his image graced the cover of *Time* magazine.

The firm opened its first satellite office, in Washington, D.C., in 1981. Two years later, Hale and Dorr opened its intellectual property practice, a staple of the firm since. In 1986, the firm represented the Boston Celtics in the team's public offering, the first by a sports team. In 1990, Hale and Dorr and Brobeck, Phleger & Harrison collaborated on the first independent law firm formed by two existing firms when they launched Brobeck Hale and Dorr in London. The collaboration expanded in 2001 with new offices in Oxford, England and Munich, Germany. (That expansion occurred as Hale and Dorr was growing in the U.S., adding offices in Reston, Va., New York, N.Y., Princeton, N.J. and Waltham, Mass.) In February 2003, Hale and Dorr took control of the European venture after Brobeck, Phleger & Harrison dissolved. Joe Pillman was named partner-in-charge of the European offices.

IP leader

Hale and Dorr's intellectual property group is celebrating its 20th anniversary in 2003 and is still going strong. The firm successfully represented Atrium Medical Corp. in a patent dispute with Genzyme Corp. Genzyme sued for $15 million in 2000, claiming that a chest-draining device Atrium manufactured infringed on Genzyme patents. In November 2002, a federal jury in Delaware found for Atrium. Hale and Dorr's litigation team was led by managing partner William Lee, who proved he still had his good stuff in getting the victory. Lee also prevailed in March 2003 for client RSA Security. Leon Stambler sued software maker RSA, saying that the firm's SSL (Secure Sockets Layer) version 3.0 infringed on three of his patents. (SSL is a common Internet security feature and is part of most browsers and servers.) A federal jury agreed with RSA and co-defendant VeriSign that SSL does not infringe on any of Stambler's patents. Alcon Laboratories used Hale and Dorr to press its case against Japanese firm Nidek Co. Alcon claimed that Nidek's laser eye surgery system infringed on 14 patents held by Summit Technology, which Alcon acquired in 2000. The jury sided with Summit and Alcon, ruling that Nidek violated the patents and awarding the U.S. firm $17.2 million.

The IP team added some muscle in July 2002. Eric L. Prahl joined Hale and Dorr as a senior partner from rival Fish & Richardson. The firm further raised its IP profile (and its Boston profile) by endowing an IP professorship at Harvard Law School. H&D gave $2.75 million to endow the Hale and Dorr Professorship of Intellectual Property Law in October 2002.

Corporate power

Hale and Dorr's corporate practice, like most other firms, has felt the pinch of recent economic hard times. The firm is still active in M&A, however, especially in the tech and health care industries, and handled over 100 M&A transactions worth approximately $10 billion. Hale and Dorr advised SkillSoft in its $413 million merger with SmartForce in September 2002. In July 2002, SilverStream called on Hale and Dorr when Novell purchased the tech firm for $221 million. H&D was counsel to Millennium Pharmaceuticals in its acquisition of COR Therapeutics. The $2 billion deal was announced in February 2002.

In 2002, Hale and Dorr handled 30 debt and equity offerings worth more than $5 billion. The firm handled a $300 million bond offering in December 2002 for PerkinElmer. In September 2002, Hale and Dorr acted as counsel to office supplies retailer Staples in its issuance of $325 million in bonds. Hale and Dorr acted as counsel to SRA International for the company's $103.5 million IPO in May 2002. A month earlier, the firm represented MSL in its $30 million stock offering.

GETTING HIRED

Gotta love Beantown

While law school, grades and experience are important factors in getting hired at Hale and Dorr, the firm also looks for individuals interested in its practice and location. "Having an interest in Boston is key," says one contact. "The firm recruits heavily from local schools. Candidates seem to be very well qualified academically and usually have worked on law review." "Hale and Dorr sifts through the larger number of highly accomplished candidates to select those people who have excellent interpersonal skills and who are likely to contribute in a positive way to the team atmosphere that is fostered here," says an associate. "Hale and Dorr hires law students into the

Hale and Dorr community, not into a law factory." Given the firm's IP practice and its work with tech firms and health care companies, it also helps if you've spent time in the lab.

"Top grades from a top law school will get you an interview but is no guarantee of a job offer, particularly in the corporate department," says one lawyer from that department. Dictators, villains and Satan need not apply. "The firm is really picky in looking for people that, well, aren't evil," says one angel.

No surprises

There are no surprises in the actual process. "The interview and callback process is much the same as other large firms – initial on-campus interviews, followed by callback interviews in the office with several attorneys," reports one contact. "The firm is very much open to having candidates who are offered a summer position return to the firm to meet with additional attorneys to answer questions." Don't sweat the callbacks too much. "Callback interviews are fairly laid back," says one insider. "People are mostly looking for whether the candidate is enthusiastic about the practice and someone you would want to work with."

OUR SURVEY SAYS

"Amazingly collegial"

Hale and Dorr inspires a lot of loyalty from its associates, probably because of a friendly culture. "The culture at Hale and Dorr is the best thing about the firm," gushes one source. "It is an amazingly collegial place. In spite of all the brilliant legal minds, there are very few egos and associates are given a lot of respect. I have never hesitated to raise a concern about a deal or a case with the senior partner in charge. I could not imagine a better large firm environment in which to practice." Though some might expect a firm with 85 years of experience to be a little stuffy or white shoe, insiders say that's far from the case. "The culture of Hale and Dorr is collegial and collaborative," says one associate. "Despite its excellent reputation, the firm is not stuffy or overly formal." Another insider agrees that any reputation for stuffiness is unearned. "Although Hale and Dorr has a reputation as being white shoe and stuffy, nothing could be further from the truth. While the attorneys are serious about their professionalism and are hard working, they are friendly, funny and social. They are dynamic people with many interests." That source continues: "I have met many of my closest friends in Boston at Hale and Dorr."

The collegial vibe doesn't mean Hale and Dorr can't get down to business. "Hale and Dorr appears to be pretty close to a pure meritocracy – a wide variety of personalities and styles are permitted as long as the work is done fast and without errors," says one source. "The culture is friendly but serious," says another insider. "People are friendly with one another, but everyone takes his or her job very seriously. The work comes first. However, people are very supportive of one another and always willing to lend a hand or provide guidance." Even clients get a sense of the balance between work and play. "The firm strikes a good balance of being professional on the one hand and also being laid back and friendly on the other," says one lawyer. "This culture extends beyond internal relationships to those with clients."

Ain't misbehavin'

For the most part, associates praise the partners at Hale and Dorr as mentors who treat them with respect. "On the whole, partners are fair and treat associates well," says one contact. "There are no yellers here." Some at Hale and Dorr swear they've never seen even a hint of misbehavior. "I have never seen a partner yell at or reprimand an associate," reports one source. "Partners treat associates as future colleagues, and many take a personal interest in mentoring associates informally and improving their experiences." That source may be unaware of a new trend. "The majority of partners with whom I work treat me with respect and value my opinions," says one associate. "There are always exceptions to the rule. The number of exceptions appears to have increased over the last couple years. I think this is a reflection of the amount of work in my department and the pressure on these partners." The poor economic conditions seem to have changed the dynamic. "Partners seem less sensitive to associate concerns and more willing to make unreasonable demands on associates given the current job market," says one lawyer. The firm's feedback system gives associates a chance to remedy many problems. "Hale and Dorr's upward evaluation process has helped to provide a forum through which some of the more abusive partners receive constructive feedback and suggestions for behavior modification."

Good pay, for Boston

Hale and Dorr associates are well compensated for their market, which is somewhat behind other cities. One associate reports that Hale and Dorr offers "standard big-firm pay," while another claims the compensation is "among the best in Boston." "Though base salary is similar to other Boston firms, bonuses are much better than those of competitors." The firm was surprisingly generous in 2002. "We received bonuses for 2002, which was a surprise to me given the economy and the situation of other law firms in the Boston area," says one contact. Others are just happy to be getting the big-firm paycheck, even if it comes with the big-firm life. "Pay is very good," says one attorney. "Although I think we're paid too well compared to the world at large, high compensation is a requirement in order to get anyone to live their lives around the clients' spontaneous needs." Some first-years feel a little left out. "The firm pays a bonus at the end of the year but skimps out before you join the firm. No advance, no interest-free loan. It makes doing anything the summer before joining difficult."

Gunning for 2,000

"There is a stated goal of 2,000 billable hours per year, but there are a few that believe that an associate should be billing a good deal more than that," remarks one insider. Indeed, the 2,000 hours target isn't the hard bare minimum that it often is at other firms, but associates are nonetheless strongly encouraged to hit that target. "Although [2,000 hours] is demanding, it is achievable and reasonable given the high level of associate compensation and the firm quality," says one insider. Don't worry about the dreaded face time. "As with all large law firms, billing minimums and targets are important," says one attorney. "However, I do not feel that this firm's billing expectations are out of line with other firms of equal caliber. Additionally, I have never felt any pressure to be in the office only for face time, which I know some associates at other firms do experience." Of course, the hours are often terribly erratic. "My work hours vary and, when I am not very busy, are not bad," says one source. "When I am busy, things are pretty insane, and all I do at home is shower and sleep." "The hours expected and put in are both very fair given the demands of a big-city practice," says one D.C. lawyer. "The firm encourages us to take all our vacation, and the senior associates and partners all do so. So long as you get your work done, the partners are very flexible about when you get it done. A workload coordinator ensures that associates get help when they are swamped or work when things slow down."

Associate boot camp

Insiders say that at Hale and Dorr, both formal training and informal mentoring are a priority. "Hale and Dorr provides a first-rate training program," says one insider. "However, it is the time that the senior associates and partners make during the course of the workday that is the most valuable training. Since most senior associates and partners view this as a part of their job at the firm, as an associate I do not feel uncomfortable using interactions with them as an opportunity to learn." The firm offers every kind of training opportunity. "The training is excellent," says one source. "From mock trials to deposition skills workshops, the firm offers a vast array of training opportunities. Sometimes it seems overwhelming, but most programs are very helpful."

First-years should be ready for indoctrination. "Training is of the highest priority at Hale and Dorr," says an associate. "From first-year corporate boot camp to mock negotiations and monthly training meetings, there is a strong emphasis on training."

Wanted: female corporate partners

Hale and Dorr's female associates seem to run into the same problems that occur at many big law firms. "There are a lot of women associates and not many women partners," reports one insider. "Still, I have never detected any hostility." The corporate department may have the most problems. "Women associates and junior partners are treated well, though numbers are still lagging in the senior partner ranks, particularly in corporate," says one lawyer from that department. Family may be an issue. One insider feels there are "too many women at the fifth- and sixth-year associate level who don't ever become partners, not because they could not, but because they are forced to choose between family and work and, at some point, make that choice in favor of family."

Insiders blame geography and demographics for a dearth of minority associates at Hale and Dorr. One insider observes that there are "not enough minorities here. Perhaps it's more a reflection on Boston. I do not believe that it has anything to do with the firm whatsoever." "There are few minority associates and almost no partners," sighs one source. "I have never detected any hostility, but neither is it a pressing issue in the firm's collective consciousness." One contact has a suggestion. "Although there are informal mentoring relationships, more structured mentoring programs for minorities and women would be helpful."

One Chase Manhattan Plaza
New York, NY 10005
Phone: (212) 530-5219
www.milbank.com

LOCATIONS

New York, NY (HQ)
Los Angeles, CA • Palo Alto, CA • Washington, DC •
Frankfurt • Hong Kong • London • Singapore • Tokyo

MAJOR DEPARTMENTS/PRACTICES

Banking • Capital Markets • Communications & Space •
Corporate • Employee Benefits • Environmental •
Financial Restructing • High Yield & Acquisition Finance
• Intellectual Property • Litigation • Mergers &
Acquisitions • Power & Energy • Project Finance •
Public Interest Law • Real Estate • Securitization • Tax
• Technology • Transportation Finance • Trusts &
Estates

THE STATS

No. of attorneys: 700
No. of offices: 9
Summer associate offers: 67 out of 71 (2002)
Chairman: Mel Immergut
Hiring Partners: Drew Fine, Jay Grushkin and Dan
Bartfield

BASE SALARY

New York, NY
1st year: $125,000
2nd year: $135,000
3rd year: $150,000
4th year: $165,000
5th year: $190,000
6th year: $205,000
7th year: $215,000
8th year: $225,000
Summer associate: $2,403/week

UPPERS

- Welcoming toward gays and lesbians
- Incredible views (NY)
- Sophisticated, high-level work

DOWNERS

- Lack of corporate work means smaller bonuses
- Few women role models/mentors
- Penny-pinching

NOTABLE PERKS

- In-firm subsidized cafeteria (NY)
- Four-weeks paternity leave
- Technology bonus
- Car rides home

THE BUZZ
WHAT ATTORNEYS AT OTHER FIRMS ARE SAYING ABOUT THIS FIRM

- "Cool younger associates and stuffy partners"
- "International"
- "Class act"
- "The Denny's of law"

RANKING RECAP

Best in Region
#12 - New York

Best in Practice
#4 - Bankruptcy/Corporate Restructuring
#6 (tie) - Technology/Internet/E-Commerce

Quality of Life
#14 - Offices

Best in Diversity
#19 - Diversity for Gays and Lesbians

EMPLOYMENT CONTACT

Ms. June Chotoo
Recruiting Coordinator
Phone: (212) 530-8322
Fax: (212) 822-5064
E-mail: Jchotoo@Milbank.com

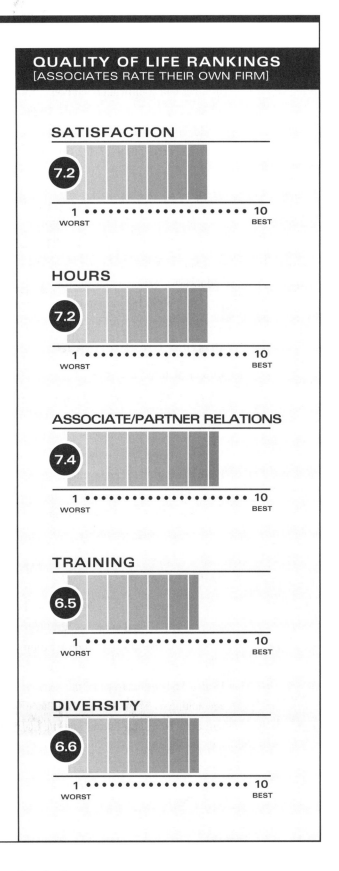

QUALITY OF LIFE RANKINGS
[ASSOCIATES RATE THEIR OWN FIRM]

SATISFACTION
7.2
1 • • • • • • • • • • • • • • • • • • • 10
WORST   BEST

HOURS
7.2
1 • • • • • • • • • • • • • • • • • • • 10
WORST   BEST

ASSOCIATE/PARTNER RELATIONS
7.4
1 • • • • • • • • • • • • • • • • • • • 10
WORST   BEST

TRAINING
6.5
1 • • • • • • • • • • • • • • • • • • • 10
WORST   BEST

DIVERSITY
6.6
1 • • • • • • • • • • • • • • • • • • • 10
WORST   BEST

THE SCOOP

Founded in 1866, Milbank, Tweed, Hadley & McCloy has always had an international bend. The firm has had significant operations in Asia since 1925, when Milbank worked on a bond issue with a Japanese utilities operation. Today, Milbank continues to be prominent in project finance, particularly in Asia, and boasts Asian offices in Tokyo, Singapore and Hong Kong. It's not all about the East, however; the firm is a big player on Wall Street as well.

Bali h'ai

In January 2003, the Indonesian government took another step toward privatizing its second largest telecommunications operation, PT Indonesian Satellite Corp. (otherwise known as Indostat) by choosing a winning bidder, Singapore Technologies Telemedia. Advising the government of Indonesia are none other than lawyers in Milbank Tweed's Singapore office. This is the largest privatization in Indonesian history to date; the winning bid was for US $630 million.

Justice for the media

Litigators in Milbank's Los Angeles office won a major victory for journalists everywhere in early 2003, forcing a settlement against the city of Los Angeles. The litigators worked with the American Civil Liberties Union on this case, which stemmed from an incident in which journalists covering the 2000 Democratic National Convention were assaulted with rubber bullets and batons as police dispersed a crowd outside the Los Angeles convention. The city and the Los Angeles Police Department, under the terms of the settlement, must recognize the right of journalists to cover public protests, even if police are ordered to disperse an unlawful assembly of protesters. The city of Los Angeles must also assign a press liaison to work with the media to establish designated viewing areas for protests.

Milbank star

Does the name William Webster sound familiar? Webster, who has held positions as a U.S. attorney and federal appeals court judge, has served the United States as both FBI director and head of the CIA. He also led a commission that investigated the IRS's treatment of taxpayers. In late 2002, Webster, after 11 years as a senior partner at Milbank, was once again called to serve the United States government, this time as the chair of the Securities and Exchange Commission's accounting oversight board. But the appointment proved controversial, because of both Webster's corporate board affiliations and the SEC's nomination process, and he returned to private practice a few weeks later.

High billing at Enron

The massive bankruptcy of Enron may not have brought glad financial tidings to Texans or energy consumers, but legal work on the complicated case has proved a financial boon for Milbank and other firms. A November 2002 invoice submitted by the firm brought the bill to $24.2 million owed to Milbank. Creditors are fretting about the high legal bills, which threaten to significantly reduce the value of Enron assets available. A court-appointed committee has called for fees claimed by Milbank to be reduced by 5.2 percent. (Milbank is by no means the highest Enron biller; that honor goes to Weil Gotshal & Manges.)

More to love in California

While some firms are fleeing Palo Alto, Milbank opened a new office there in May 2001, doubling its offices in California. (The firm already had a Los Angeles office.) The firm now boasts nine offices, four of which are located in the United States. The firm's other domestic offices are in New York and Washington, D.C.

Milbank's No. 1!

In terms of satellite syndicated loan transactions, that is. In October 2002, the firm was ranked numero uno by *Satellite Finance*, following a year in which Milbank closed four satellite deals valuing roughly $2.5 billion.

Dairy finds a home

The Dairy Mart chain of convenience stores went bankrupt in 2002 after years of non-fabulous performance. (Dairy Mart was once a chain of 1,400 stores, but, as of August 2002, operated a mere 450 stores. Most of its stores are located in Ohio and Kentucky.) The sole bidder and buyer of Dairy Mart was Couche-Tard, Canada's biggest convenience store chain. Couche-Tard will retain the majority of Dairy Mart's employees. Couche-Tard will be buying and operating the majority of those Dairy Marts, though some might be axed.

GETTING HIRED

Higher standards

Milbank, according to insiders, has used the rocky economy as an incentive to raise its standard for new associates ever higher. Says one associate familiar with the recruiting committee, "We have really tightened our standards within the last year. As a result, our summer program [in 2003] will be about half the size of last summer's program." Other insiders say that Milbank places an increasing emphasis on hiring associates with "Harvard and Yale" degrees. "The partnership has apparently decided to make getting a job here far, far harder than it's been in years past."

A top-notch degree isn't the only qualification Milbank seeks. One associate claims Milbank seeks "nicey-nicey, solid steady types. There is a lot of emphasis on social niceties." Says another associate, "I've seen [Milbank] turn down people who looked very good on paper but were lifeless in person. I think the attitude is that there are a lot of people who are capable of doing this work but they want to find people they can stand to work with, too." Warns another attorney, "Being able to fit in is important." So if you're "personable" and "well-adjusted," you'll have a clearer shot at entering the smaller Milbank associate classes.

OUR SURVEY SAYS

Friendly but distant

Insiders state that the internal culture at the firm "heavily depends on the group with whom one is associated." Some practices come in for praise; the intellectual property group, for example, is said to "rock." IP is "an extremely satisfying place to be, mostly because of the relationship between the people in the group," grins one insider. Corporate and leasing are also said to be particularly social. However, the firm is said to be "friendly but distant" overall. "Most people are not interested in talking about what you did over the weekend or anything like that. People want to get down to business, and [they are] friendly but professional. Lawyers socialize on more of a case-by-case basis, and many have families," says a New York associate. Another insider confirms that while "small groups do exist," "lawyers do not socialize after work as a general rule." "I like it this way," chirps one associate, "because you do not have to socialize to feel like you belong."

Professional partners

Milbank partners are said to be considerate and professional in their dealings at Milbank, though few associates term their relationships with partners particularly warm and fuzzy. Says one junior associate, "I've never been yelled at, but I've never been directly addressed by name either. They are fair but not friendly." A first-year associate begs to differ. "The partners that I have worked with have treated me with respect. They have had reasonable expectations of what I can do as a first-year. One in particular has always taken the time to explain things to me even when he's busy enough to work past midnight." A senior associate volunteers, "Many of the ogres have been put to pasture in the years I've been in service."

Great views, less fabulous color scheme

Milbank's New York office is known for its breathtaking views. "The views of the Statue of Liberty and Manhattan Island, looking north, are spectacular," marvels one associate in that office. New York associates have plenty of time to relish those magnificent vistas, since "all offices are exterior." As an added bonus, "Associates only share offices for their first year." On the downside, several associates take issue with the excessive use of beige in the New York office. "The décor is expensive," critiques one lawyer, "but everything is an ugly yellow beige that is a little oppressive on the eyes. The color scheme is totally monochromatic – orangey beige walls, rugs, offices, elevators, even the art on the walls." One beige lover defends the décor, insisting that "the office has some class, unlike some Midtown cubicle farms I've been to."

Ebbing hours, for some

Some associates have been working fewer hours - but they're not necessary happy about that fact. One corporate associate expresses dissatisfaction "because like many corporate associates, I billed very few hours [in 2002.] That led to a lower bonus. In fact, I understand that only one associate in the corporate finance group (consisting of about 80 attorneys) billed over 2,000 hours last year. We can't learn if we don't have deals on which to work." A project finance pro has had a somewhat different experience. "You have to work really hard when deals are hot or are closing. On the other hand, I have very little pressure to do any face time, and billing hours are not mentioned too many times except at bonus time." Litigators remain busy, and a senior litigator explains, "Generally, I am able to work late during the week and avoid weekend work except in emergency situations. Still, the late weekday hours are difficult." One insider claims Milbank "recently upped the minimum billable hours requirement to 2,100 hours."

Calling all mentors

Associates are critical of Milbank's record on the advancement of women, though most allow that the firm is making efforts to improve the situation of women at the firm. "There doesn't seem to be much of an advancement track for women at Milbank," states one woman associate. Only seven of the partners are women. The environment and culture are very male, and there are few female role models. The firm has admitted the problem but doesn't seem to know how to address it." Another associate with two X chromosomes theorizes, "The lack of female partners creates a lack of female mentors, and I suspect most of the female associates would say they have no mentor." One litigator points out that "there are no female partners in the litigation department in New York." Another associate says flex time is still hard to get; it's said to be "generally still frowned upon, and only new mothers seem to have a shot at it at all."

Other associates do see efforts being made. "Two female partners in one of the corporate departments try to have weekly women's lunches," says one insider. And one junior associate appears to be the beneficiary of a concerted effort by partners. "It's great to be a female here. All the senior attorneys and partners make an extra special effort to get to know the female associates," she says.

Caffeine-free perks

Milbank associates enjoy all the largesse of a major law firm. One insider cites some attractive perks. "We get typical large firm stuff – bar expenses and association fees are paid; cars home at

night; transit program and medical pre-tax spending program; 401(k); in-firm subsidized cafeteria; subsidized health club program; group lunches once a week; Super Bowl parties, golf outings and much more." Associates also "get four weeks of paternity leave" and "$2,000 in the first year as a technological bonus." Despite this luscious buffet of perks, one thing really sticks in the craw of Milbank associates – the removal of coffee machines. "We have to go to the 47th floor for coffee now because they removed the coffee machines on each floor," wails one java-addicted New Yorker. Other associates, however, suggest that "there seems to be a movement to bring [the coffee machines] back."

Mixed reviews on training

When it comes to training, Milbankers can't seem to agree. Some attorneys are impressed with the firm's commitment to training – " from the initial week-long training conference the firm schedules for its incoming first-years to its ongoing commitment to Continuing Legal Education Seminars." Others appreciate the informal training and mentoring that occurs between junior associates and their more senior counterparts and partners. "Most of my training has come from associates who I work with, and I feel that they usually take to time to teach me how to do things right," says one insider.

Still, others in the know express disappointment about the state of training at their firm. "Training? What training?" asks a corporate associate, while another insists that "partners give you no feedback." "Associates are tossed into the pool," explains a sixth-year associate, "and after a few months, the ones that drowned are fished out and fired."

A great record on gay and lesbian acceptance

Milbank has historically been one of the most welcoming firms towards gays and lesbians. That laudable legacy continues. Says one insider, "Milbank is very upfront about being proud of its history in extending health and insurance benefits to same-sex domestic partners. It is extremely welcoming of gay associates and partners." There are "partners and associates who are out and bring their partners to firm events," and one associate counts "at least four out partners."

"Associates are tossed into the pool, and after a few months, the ones that drowned are fished out and fired."

– Milbank associate

One International Plaza
Boston, MA 02110-2624
Phone: (617) 951-7000
www.ropesgray.com

LOCATIONS

Boston, MA (HQ)
New York, NY
San Francisco, CA
Washington, DC

MAJOR DEPARTMENTS/PRACTICES

Corporate
Creditors' Rights
Labor & Employment
Litigation
Private Client Services
Tax & Benefits

THE STATS

No. of attorneys: 500+
No. of offices: 4
Summer associate offers: 52 out of 52 (2002)
Chairman and Managing Partner: Douglass N. Ellis, Jr.
Hiring Attorney: Douglas H. Meal

All offices
1st year: $125,000
2nd year: $135,000
Summer associate: $2,400/week

UPPERS

- High compensation
- Superior training opportunities
- Major prestige

DOWNERS

- Poor communication from management
- Firm's size can impede getting to know co-workers
- Unpredictable hours

NOTABLE PERKS

- Stake in firm-sponsored investment fund
- On-site emergency daycare
- BlackBerry pagers
- High-speed Internet access at home

THE BUZZ
WHAT ATTORNEYS AT OTHER FIRMS ARE SAYING ABOUT THIS FIRM

- "Sophisticated Boston firm"
- "The stuffiest of the old school"
- "Everyone's from Hahvahd"
- "Good regional player"

RANKING RECAP

Best in Region
#1 - Boston

Quality of Life
#4 - Best 20 Law Firms to Work For
#5 - Training
#9 - Hours
#10 - Retention
#10 - Selectivity
#11 - Pay
#19 - Associate/Partner Relations
#19 - Satisfaction

Best in Diversity
#12 - Overall Diversity
#14 - Diversity for Minorities
#18 - Diversity for Women
#18 - Diversity for Gays & Lesbians

EMPLOYMENT CONTACT

Mr. Thomas A. Grewe
Director of Legal Recruiting
Phone: (617) 951-7239
Long Distance: (800) 951-4888, ext. 7239
Fax: (617) 951-7050
E-mail: hiringprogram@ropesgray.com

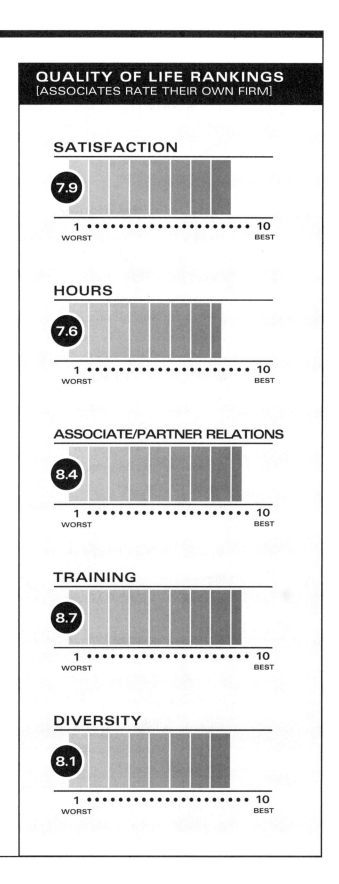

QUALITY OF LIFE RANKINGS
[ASSOCIATES RATE THEIR OWN FIRM]

SATISFACTION
7.9
1 WORST .... 10 BEST

HOURS
7.6
1 WORST .... 10 BEST

ASSOCIATE/PARTNER RELATIONS
8.4
1 WORST .... 10 BEST

TRAINING
8.7
1 WORST .... 10 BEST

DIVERSITY
8.1
1 WORST .... 10 BEST

THE SCOOP

When Harvard Law School grads John Codman Ropes and John Chipman Gray founded Ropes & Gray in Boston in 1865, they pledged to create a firm that would not only provide quality legal service to clients, but would also serve the interests of the community. Since that time, Ropes & Gray hasn't just upheld those ideals, it has done so while creating the second-largest firm in the city.

They're in the money

Ropes & Gray is frequently called upon to advise leaders in the financial industry. In particular, the firm is nationally renowned for its leveraged buyout practice, whose clients include Bain Capital and Berkshire Partners. In 2003, *The American Lawyer* ranked the firm No. 1 counsel for new mutual fund issues and No. 2 mutual fund counsel by value of client assets. But the firm isn't known only within financial circles. Ropes & Gray is a full-service practice counseling clients such as nationally and regionally known companies from a wide array of industry sectors. Firm clients include American Express, Gillette, Fleet Financial Group, Walco (a distributor of animal health care products) and Percardia (a biotechnology company that produces devices for heart surgery).

One of Ropes & Gray's burgeoning practice groups is intellectual property. In particular, the firm is seeing a growing interest on the part of clients in licensing their trademarked properties. Department head Ed Black told *The Boston Business Journal* in an April 2003 interview that the number of attorneys working on licensing matters for the firm has "probably doubled over the past three to four years" to its current number of 15.

In the public interest

Ropes & Gray was involved in a high-profile political battle involving the residency status of then-gubernatorial candidate Mitt Romney in the 2002 election. The residency status of the Republican candidate came under scrutiny when it was revealed that Romney was only a part-time resident of Massachusetts during 1999 and 2000. When members of the Democratic Party sought to void Romney's candidacy because of his part-time residency, the firm came to his aid. Not only did Ropes & Gray convince the state's election commission that its client did meet the Massachusetts residency requirement, but Romney then went on to win the governor's race.

While the publicity generated by the Romney case might be something of a novelty for the press-shy Ropes & Gray, the firm is no stranger to cases involving political and municipal entities. In October 2002, Ropes & Gray secured a favorable decision on behalf of two Oregon legislators who wanted the state to release detailed census data that reflect the presence of often under-counted groups. Ropes & Gray has also been working on behalf of the Massachusetts Port Authority in its longstanding fight to gain approval to build a new runway that could ease congestion at Boston

Logan International Airport. And the firm is representing the Nantucket Steamship Authority and the popular resort towns Martha's Vineyard and Wood's Hole in a dispute with the City of New Bedford regarding ferry service. In addition to litigating cases such as these, Ropes & Gray also serves as bond counsel for several cities, towns and school districts within Massachusetts.

R&G to the rescue

Governor Romney isn't the only governor counting on Ropes & Gray's legal expertise to help him out of a jam. New Hampshire Governor Craig Benson is a co-founder of telecom equipment maker Cabletron Systems (now known as Enterasys Networks). Investors are suing Benson and Enterasys, accusing the company of creating phony sales and revenues to hide losses. The case is pending.

Celebrated author and presidential historian Doris Kearns Goodwin turned to Ropes & Gray when *The Los Angeles Times* accused her of plagiarizing passages from the works of other writers for her book, *No Ordinary Time*. Attorneys at the firm conducted a thorough audit, examining each footnote in Goodwin's book, and announced that Goodwin had given proper credit to all her sources. In spite of the firm's assertion, Goodwin's reputation has taken a hit.

Introducing our new attorneys

In a first for Ropes & Gray, the firm acquired another firm, Bennett, Turner & Coleman, in June 2002. The 11-attorney firm specializes in regulatory law related to healthcare policy and approval of new foods and drugs. The Bennett Turner attorneys joined R&G's life sciences group, which advises biotechnology and pharmaceutical companies. And Ropes & Gray started off 2003 by making some high-profile hires to bolster key practice areas. The firm kicked things off in January with the addition of a seven-attorney team to the firm's private client group. The new attorneys previously worked at the now-defunct Hill & Barlow. The addition of the Hill & Barlow group reportedly increased Ropes' funds under management by nearly a half billion dollars. In February 2003, the firm brought in Adolfo Garcia from McDermott, Will & Emery to co-head its international practice group. The following month brought the addition of Laurel Fitzpatrick to the investment management group to manage the firm's hedge fund business. Finally, Paul Danello joined the firm's healthcare practice in April, leaving the U.S. Department of Health and Human Services. This just in: Ropes & Gray has gone a-courtin' again, this time with Reboul, MacMurray, Hewitt & Maynard, a New York-based firm with a top-notch private equity practice. The newly joined firms tied the knot in May 2003.

The spirit of giving

Ropes & Gray is actively involved in giving back to the community. The firm's pro bono committee reviews potential cases and makes assignments, and individual attorneys are welcome to call the committee's attention to cases in which they have a personal interest. Litigation attorneys are assigned annually to the Middlesex County district attorney's office, where they work on criminal appeals, and to the Political Asylum/Immigration Representation Project, where they assist poor immigrants who fear for their safety in their native countries.

GETTING HIRED

Top dogs

Insiders say Ropes & Gray is "probably the most selective large firm in Boston." The firm tries "to hire people at or near the top of their law school class who are also capable of contributing to a positive work environment." "The hiring criteria are rigorous and heavily weighted toward outstanding grades, but," reveals a corporate associate, "the firm has declined to extend offers to candidates with outstanding grades but underwhelming personalities." "To its great credit, Ropes has expanded the pool of schools where it recruits beyond New England and the traditional top 10." To be hired, you need to "demonstrate intelligence, a can-do attitude and a genuine interest in being a practicing lawyer." A fifth-year associate explains that the firm has "a very thorough interview/callback process. You meet many people at the firm." But the "questioning is not tough," this source says. A corporate associate tells us, "R&G is very particular about hiring people with a regional connection. They're almost obsessed with it." But according to a litigation associate, a "lack of a prior Boston connection is not a negative." "I think the firm is very concerned with hiring people who will fit in with the culture here," says a first-year, who adds, "They seem to hire more academic or bookish types." When it comes to lateral hires, one associate sees a trend. "There definitely seems to be an increase in the number of laterals that the firm has hired in the past years, especially in the New York and Washington, D.C., offices."

OUR SURVEY SAYS

Work hard, party if you want

Hardworking Ropes & Gray associates "want to come in, get work done and go home." That said, the attorneys at Ropes & Gray "seem to generally like working together and treat each other with consideration and respect. There are, of course, a few people who are considered difficult to work for, but they are the exception to the rule." "Ropes' reputation as a collegial but reserved place is probably well deserved. Though the attorneys here are very friendly and willing to answer any questions you may have, they tend to go their separate ways after hours," observes a first-year. "The firm is very friendly and collegial," a third-year tells us. "People tend to often stop to talk in the halls or in people's offices. Some lawyers socialize together, but many have families and lives outside the firm and choose to spend their free time with people outside of the firm." However, for those who aren't ready to go home at the end of the day, "the firm sponsors a number of teams" such as "ice hockey, basketball, softball" and "indoor soccer, which provide venues to allow lawyers and staff to socialize outside the office." Raves a very satisfied first-year, "This place is basically heaven. The partners are brilliant, there is no pressure to bill crazy hours, the salaries are reasonable and everyone works together."

Despite the words of praise, some associates are concerned that the R&G way of life will deteriorate as the firm gets bigger. A corporate associate who longs for the good old days confides, "The firm's culture is in flux, as it continues to grow very rapidly." "It used to be said that joining R&G is like joining a family. That's hard to say with a straight face these days, considering most of us don't know any of the numerous new laterals we've hired." "The firm seems to be increasingly cultureless," sighs a first-year. This contact adds, "Firm-wide events are rare, and many people don't know each other. It feels sort of generic – not too uptight, not too laid-back, not too friendly, not too unfriendly."

On the clock

Hours are long at R&G, but most associates believe it's "just the way it is" if you work for a major law firm. "There is little overt pressure to tally billable hours, but, this being a large firm with challenging work, there are still many times when I find myself working more than I'd like in an ideal world." A senior associate makes a familiar complaint: "It's not always the hours that are difficult; it's the unpredictability." "One week I'm bored. Then for the next three months, I can't leave the office it seems."

Some insiders think the hours are just fine. Says a litigation associate, "If you do the job, you go home, and no one looks at you funny if you are on the elevator at 4:40 in the afternoon." A senior associate reports similar experiences: "I have found that there is no premium on face time and in fact have been encouraged to get out of the office if I have slow times rather than logging hours [just] for the sake of being in the office." "People generally respect lines you can draw around significant personal time, such as dinner plans when family is in town, vacations and so on." But a fourth-year has had quite a different experience: "Face time is often the norm and expected, which has been quite disappointing." Another insider claims there is "too much emphasis on billing" and that "many times partners commit associates without asking about work schedules or other conflicts. They view personal conflicts as irrelevant."

Top dollar for a top firm

Ropes & Gray scores well when it comes to compensation, which insiders explain is "lockstep for the first three years." "No one, and I mean no one, in Boston makes more than we do," asserts a midlevel. "You hear the debates and read the guesses on chat boards, but based on my check, I know this is true." A corporate associate concurs: "Ropes is committed to paying top dollar in Boston." Likewise, a senior associate has no complaints, calling the compensation "very generous. Even in lean economic times," says this source, "the firm continues to pay substantial bonuses to

midlevel and senior associates." A D.C. associate says Ropes & Gray does not pay "highest total compensation in Washington, but" it does pay "perhaps the highest compensation per hour." According to a New York attorney, "Associates outside of the Boston office where the market base salaries are higher, such as New York, still get paid a base salary at the Boston market. However, total year-end compensation is comparable to the New York market."

Some insiders voice a few complaints. "Now that national firms have opened small Boston offices, Ropes is not the salary leader it claims to be. Nevertheless, the salary is generous," says a second-year. However, this source continues, "It is worth noting that first- through third-years do not receive bonuses, and no raises were given last year." A first-year, who nevertheless rated the firm 10 out of 10 on compensation, couldn't resist gossiping, "One problem for the incoming first-year associates was that the firm lowered its compensation without telling the first-years, so when the first-years arrived, they were making $10,000 less than anticipated." A classmate agrees that "Ropes did scale back the pay rates" but isn't very upset because "it's hard to complain too much about a six-figure salary."

Props to the partners

Insiders concede that "there are always some exceptions to the rule," but the vast majority of associates at Ropes & Gray give the partnership high marks. "Partners really seem to be interested in taking the time to act as mentors and teachers to young associates," a first-year shares. A third-year associate has found that "partners seem to value associates' contributions and respect the fact that people have outside commitments. Partners often thank associates for the work they do and express their appreciation when associates are working particularly long hours." Despite the high volume of praise, some associates express frustration over scheduling and the "lack of communication between partners and associates about the firm's direction." According to a litigation associate, "Partners almost uniformly respect the opinions of associates, but less often do they respect the associates' time." "Many associates," says a first-year, "complain that there is often not much feedback, positive or negative."

It takes a village

According to insiders, training is "one of the firm's highest priorities." An associate in the corporate department reports, "The training at Ropes is first rate, without question. The seminars are on helpful topics and conducted by individuals with experience in the field and with a desire to share their knowledge." A co-worker agrees: "Training as a matter of practical applicability is better than anywhere else, so far as I can tell from colleagues at other large firms." And the training doesn't stop after year one. "Even through midlevel years," remarks a sixth-year associate, "the commitment to training has been strong. Mentors are there if you seek them but are largely unnecessary. Most senior lawyers you work with go out of their way to train and pass on lessons from their experience." Insiders praise the firm's practice group lunches, which they say are great for "invaluable information that is directly useful to the practice of law." One newbie hints there can be too much of a good thing: "At times people have complained because there was too much training."

Staying put

Ropes associates are a fairly content bunch. "Retention seems no better or worse than [at] other large firms," they report. "Like any large firm, there is turnover," but "people rarely leave for other firms in town, however. They leave instead to pursue other interests, to live in different cities or to seek greater work-life balance than is possible in large-firm practice." "Our class is largely intact," says a sixth-year. A third-year observes, "The majority of associates leave of their own volition, under positive circumstances. The firm's policy is 'up or out,' but not that many people are let go in the first several years without serious performance issues." A senior associate shares this opinion of retention: "For a law firm, the retention here is great. People actually have a chance of making partner here."

Fried, Frank, Harris, Shriver & Jacobson

One New York Plaza
New York, NY 10004
Phone: (212) 859-8000
www.friedfrank.com

LOCATIONS

New York, NY (HQ)
Los Angeles, CA
Washington, DC
London
Paris

MAJOR DEPARTMENTS/PRACTICES

Antitrust • Bankruptcy & Restructuring • Benefits & Compensation • Corporate • Litigation • Real Estate • Securities Regulation, Compliance & Enforcement • Tax • Technology & IP • Trusts & Estates

THE STATS

No. of attorneys: 550
No. of offices: 5
Summer associate offers: 57 out of 59 (2002, NY, DC & LA)
Co-Managing Partners: Valerie Ford Jacob and Paul M. Reinstein
Hiring Attorneys: Howard B. Adler, David I. Shapiro and Steven J. Steinman (NY); Elliot E. Polebaum and Vasiliki B. Tsaganos (DC); Helen B. Kim and Ray LaSoya (LA)

THE BUZZ
WHAT ATTORNEYS AT OTHER FIRMS ARE SAYING ABOUT THIS FIRM

- "Powerhouse corporate"
- "At its prime in the 1980s"
- "Pro bono friendly"
- "Like a morgue"

BASE SALARY

New York, NY; Washington, DC
1st year: $125,000
2nd year: $135,000
3rd year: $150,000
4th year: $168,000
5th year: $190,000
6th year: $205,000
7th year: $215,000
8th year: $220,000
Summer associate: $2,400/week

Los Angeles, CA
1st year: $125,000
2nd year: $135,000
3rd year: $150,000
4th year: $165,000
5th year: $185,000
6th year: $195,000
7th year: $205,000
8th year: $220,000
Summer associate: $2,400/week

UPPERS

- Pro bono leaders
- Training opportunities "coming out of our ears"
- Accepting environment for gay attorneys

DOWNERS

- "Need more office space!"
- "Too many Friday-at-5:30 assignments"
- Hard to get the good assignments

NOTABLE PERKS

- Subsidized health club membership
- BlackBerries for midlevel and senior associates
- Weekly cocktail parties
- Firm picks up tab for monthly meal with your mentor

RANKING RECAP

Best in Region
#14 - New York

Best in Practice
#3 - Real Estate
#10 (tie) - Bankruptcy/Corporate Restructuring

Quality of Life
#11 - Training

Best in Diversity
#13 - Diversity for Minorities
#16 - Overall Diversity

EMPLOYMENT CONTACTS

New York
Ms. Elizabeth M. McDonald, Esq.
Director of Legal Recruitment
Phone: (212) 859-8621
E-mail: elizabeth.mcdonald@friedfrank.com

Los Angeles
Ms. Marian Wilk Gibbs
Recruiting Administrator
Phone: (213) 473-2049
E-mail: marian.wilk@friedfrank.com

Washington
Ms. Niki Kopsidas
Recruitment Manager
Phone: (202) 639-7286
E-mail: niki.kopsidas@friedfrank.com

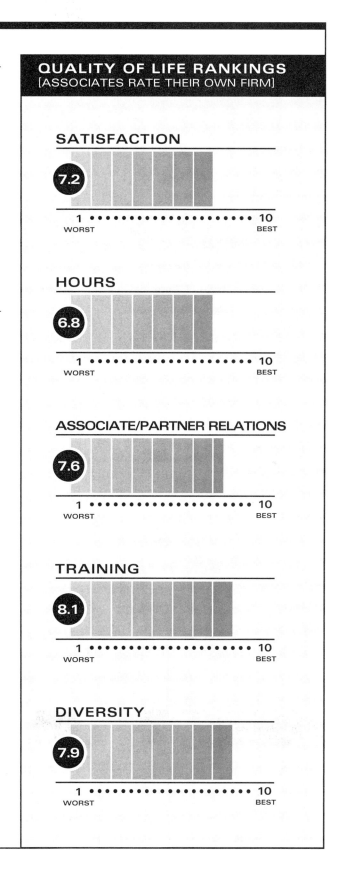

QUALITY OF LIFE RANKINGS
[ASSOCIATES RATE THEIR OWN FIRM]

SATISFACTION
7.2
1 WORST • • • • • • • • • • • • • • • • • 10 BEST

HOURS
6.8
1 WORST • • • • • • • • • • • • • • • • • 10 BEST

ASSOCIATE/PARTNER RELATIONS
7.6
1 WORST • • • • • • • • • • • • • • • • • 10 BEST

TRAINING
8.1
1 WORST • • • • • • • • • • • • • • • • • 10 BEST

DIVERSITY
7.9
1 WORST • • • • • • • • • • • • • • • • • 10 BEST

THE SCOOP

If you want to make it to the top, you have to pay your dues – and if anyone knows the meaning of dedication and commitment, it's the attorneys of Fried Frank. Over the last three decades, they've transformed Fried, Frank, Harris, Shriver & Jacobson into one of the major players in the arena of corporate law, especially when it comes to M&A.

Branching out

From its origins in New York in the late 19th century, Fried, Frank, Harris, Shriver & Jacobson assumed its present form in 1971 under name partners Walter Fried, Hans Frank, Sam Harris, Sargent Shriver and Leslie Jacobson. Hans Frank, a German law clerk who fled to America in 1933 after Hitler fired the nation's Jewish civil servants, remained with the firm until his death at the age of 90 in April 2002; Sam Harris had passed away nearly 20 years earlier. Fried, Shriver and Jacobson are all still with the firm in an of counsel capacity.

Fried Frank has always been at the forefront of expansion. Its Washington, D.C., office, established in 1949, was one of the nation's first law firm branch offices and today, with roughly 150 attorneys, is one of the largest; another office in Los Angeles balances out the firm's continental presence neatly. The London office, created in 1970, was likewise one of the first European offices of an American law firm. A Paris office joined it in 1993. Fried Frank also has a foothold in the Canadian legal market, thanks to a collaborative effort with Canada's largest law firm, McCarthy Tétrault, with which Fried Frank has had a twenty-year relationship. Dubbed the McCarthy/Fried Frank Alliance, the relationship facilitates a wide range of individual legal matters, particularly cross-border corporate transactions.

King of the hill

Fried Frank's D.C. office has a plethora of political contacts with both major parties. Name partner Sargent Shriver, related by marriage to the Kennedys, was a former Peace Corps director and ambassador to France. On the other side of the political spectrum, former partner William Howard Taft IV (his presidential namesake's great-grandson) is chief legal adviser to Secretary of State Colin Powell. Another former partner, Harvey Pitt, served just more than one turbulent year as the chairman of the Securities and Exchange Commission before controversy over his handling of appointments to the SEC's accounting oversight board led to an election-night resignation in November 2002.

Big money

In 2002, Fried Frank acted as legal advisers in two of the year's most prominent corporate transactions. *Institutional Investor* pegged the $5.3 billion acquisition of Rodamco North America NV by a consortium that includes Westfield America Trust, Simon Property Group and Fried

Frank's client the Rouse Company as its "Real Estate Deal of the Year." In the international capital markets arena, a $300 million senior note offering the firm orchestrated for Mexico's Grupo Televisa SA was dubbed the most significant corporate bond deal of 2002 by *Latin Finance* magazine.

Going for broke

Bankruptcy and restructuring deals can be delicate, complicated, protracted affairs, much like a [very expensive] game of pick-up sticks. Fried Frank excels in this arena, and it shows. In January 2003, *Investment Dealer's Digest* called the restructuring of NTL, one of Europe's largest cable companies, its "Overall Deal of the Year." The magazine enthused that it was the deal's "complexity" that made the restructuring "such a scene stealer."

The notable deal got going in February 2002, when Fried Frank began to work with NTL to restructure its debt. As the effort proceeded, Fried Frank lawyers represented an ad hoc committee of holders of more than half the company's $13 billion public debt. That gigantic amount of debt was eventually converted into equity in two new companies, NTL UK and Ireland, which would hold NTL's United Kingdom and Ireland assets, and the more snazzily named Euroco, which would hold NTL's continental European assets. Fortunately for NTL, while its holdings are primarily Eurocentric, it was listed on the U.S. stock exchanges and thus eligible to file Chapter 11. During the course of the Chapter 11 cases, Fried Frank lawyers represented the official committee of NTL's unsecured creditors. NTL triumphantly emerged from Chapter 11 on January 10, 2003. At the time of filing, NTL was one of the biggest Chapter 11 cases in history (in terms of the debt carried.) Since other stellar examples of Chapter 11 cases include Enron and WorldCom, it's clear that Fried Frank achieved an excellent result.

Litigation load

Fried Frank litigators are stepping up to the plate as well. The firm represents Martha Stewart Living Omnimedia and certain directors and officers (the ones who didn't have the company named after them) in a number of securities class-action and shareholder derivative lawsuits that have been filed in three states. In the first case to come up for decision, the firm successfully moved against consolidated derivative actions filed in New York state court.

The firm is currently defending CIGNA against seven putative federal securities class actions and two derivative suits. The suits were filed in late 2002 after CIGNA announced that its third-quarter and full-year earnings would be below initial projections due to the underperformance of its healthcare operations. The announcement drove down the company's stock and the lawsuits, accusing the company of making false statements to jack up its market price, inevitably followed.

A helping hand

Sometimes, a law firm can be a lonely and confusing place. To provide helpful, confidential answers to the many questions that puzzle associates, Fried Frank started the Office of Associate Affairs (OAA) in 1997. Headed by former practicing attorneys at the firm, OAA supports associates in the transition to firm life and in their professional development, serving as ombuds, counselors, facilitators and advocates. The office handles hardcore career questions as well as personal issues and has also developed programs in response to requests by associates, such as a management training program and a foreign language lunch club. For associates that prefer a more direct source of info, the firm assigns a junior and senior adviser to each new attorney.

Moving up the charts

Fried Frank is stuck on diversity – in a good way. The Spring 2002 issue of *Minority Law Journal* reports that the firm had a 7.5 percent increase in its minority attorney staff levels since 1998, the third-highest increase among all law firms included in the survey. Nearly a fifth of the firm's associates (and six partners) identified themselves in the survey as ethnic minorities. (Another minority attorney made partner after the survey was completed.) The firm sponsors fellowships for attorneys with the NAACP's Legal Defense and Educational Fund (LDF) and the Mexican American Legal Defense and Educational Fund (MALDEF), the latter of which recently re-elected Fried Frank partner Joseph A. Stern as its chair. After completing a two-year stint at Fried Frank and two years with either LDF or MALDEF, fellows can return to the firm as fully vested fifth-year associates.

Fried Frank also sponsors women's forums and recently appointed its first female head. Valerie Ford Jacob, who has run the capital markets practice since 1991 and has long served on the firm's governing committee, was elected co-managing partner in February 2003 along with management committee chair Paul M. Reinstein.

GETTING HIRED

Tighten up

Fried Frank has a yen for "serious academic types with personality," and "smart and quirky" attorneys with "interests outside of law." One source tells us, "The top law schools are well represented here, but there are plenty of very smart attorneys from other lower-tier schools." As at any law firm, a few duds manage to slip in. A first-year concedes, "A few lazy bones slipped in under the radar screen," but suggests repeat occurrences are "not likely to happen in the current economy." A junior associate in the real estate practice group suggests, "Some of the smaller practices are extremely selective."

A senior associate advises candidates, "Be cheerfully aggressive and self-confident in interviews." You can expect to meet with a partner during your on-campus interview and as many as five attorneys once you've been called back; a first-year cautions that they "seem to rely heavily on the interviews." A source observes, "Recruiting tries really hard to have candidates meet with attorneys in their areas of interest," and can arrange for interviews with minority and gay or lesbian attorneys at the candidate's request.

OUR SURVEY SAYS

One long party

Fried Frank associates are generally quite satisfied with life at their firm. Maybe that's because the vibe at the firm is one of acceptance and respect. "People's differences and eccentricities are more accepted" at Fried Frank, leading to "a weird hodgepodge of personalities" within the office walls. "The range of personal behavior that is acceptable is more broad" than at other firms, notes a third-year insider, but also "more restrictive. Verbally abusive behavior [is] not tolerated, [and] people generally treat each other with a baseline of respect." A newly arrived real estate attorney offers nothing but praise. "I hang out outside of work with the other junior associates on a regular basis, and my mentor and I make it to every mentor-mentee event," he declares. "The community atmosphere starts with the partners and senior associates, who eventually turn all discussion at department lunches to discussions about television." Another first-year chirps, "We celebrate each other's birthdays, and the turn-out at firm social events is pretty good."

Not everyone is a fan of the Fried Frank culture. "The work is boring, and the hours can be really long. People don't care about your other outside commitments," sighs an unsatisfied third-year associate. A newbie in the D.C. office remarks, "If you want to work at a firm where attorneys drop by your office to chat or to take you to happy hour, then Fried Frank is not the place for you."

Look before you leave

"Sometimes I find myself wishing I could go to sleep," says a cryptic first-year, "but I never find myself wishing I were dead." Other Fried Frank associates agree the hours, though they sometimes stretch "to the limits of human endurance," are "probably lower than most" comparable law firms. A third-year considers partners "conscientious about providing realistic deadlines, taking into account the private lives of associates. I rarely feel that stringent deadlines are imposed unless necessary." A senior associate adds, "I am given much latitude and am not constantly reminded of what needs to be done. In turn, I do not mind working harder to get it done because I am appreciated and treated professionally." Some folks, though, complain bitterly about the unpredictability of the hours. "It's either nothing to do or here until all hours of the night."

"Working from home is perfectly acceptable," confides one source. "Nobody seems to mind where you do the work as long as it is done well." A first-year associate adds, "The firm expects you to work hard when there is work to do and to meet deadlines, but if you have no work, then you should just leave." The only problem with that, say others at the firm, is that "work tends to come in the early evening or right before the weekend." "The associates here do not mind working hard," a second-year grumbles, "but they would appreciate some organization in the assigning process."

Fried Frank's recent switch to a merit-based bonus system after the first two years at the Washington, D.C., office "may push more associates into the office on weekends and later into the evenings," speculates one insider. "The jury is still out on whether the bonus system is a good or bad thing," says an eighth-year securities attorney. A junior associate confirms, "The attorneys that are the best do the lion's share of the work and the majority ride their coattails."

Partner pals

The partner/associate dynamic at Fried Frank "has always been fairly good," says a senior associate, "but has improved in recent years." "If there is work to be done," a junior associate says, "they make us do it but usually ask nicely." A fifth-year tax attorney finds his partners "treat me quite well, giving me days off after a grueling week." A third-year who calls the firm's partners "personable, gracious and appreciative" still observes, "I don't have tons of contact with them. I believe this is largely a function of the size and type of deals I work on, but there is also that benign neglect dynamic at work."

"Most partners treat associates fine, with a couple of glaring exceptions," says a senior corporate attorney. "The horrible ones are truly horrible and treat others with no respect," a third-year complains. "I haven't had occasion to work with the old-school, cranky types, but I hear there are a few," notes one first-year. Another adds, "Most partners really do try to treat associates with respect, in some cases despite their not-so-great personalities." And one other recent arrival says, "Many partners are very willing conversationalists and love talking with and advising associates." He continues, "The one partner I do work with always says thank you when I work with her. It goes a long way with me!"

Great learning curves

"There is always an opportunity to learn" at Fried Frank, with "tons of formal training" available every week. ("More training and CLE than I know what to do with," according to some associates.) Junior partners or midlevel and senior associates lead the courses ("which is, in itself, really good training"), and attendance is "strongly encouraged," even required for the most junior attorneys. "We all have CLE credit coming out our ears!" bursts one fifth-year. The firm may have a slight communication problem, however, as some associates appear to believe training stops after their first year; a second-year litigator who found the early training "outstanding" suggests "it seems to be almost non-existent after the first year," while another says "training has fallen off dramatically."

The firm also believes strongly in informal mentorship. "People don't just throw assignments at you without giving you context and precedent," a midlevel associate points out approvingly. "Most partners and senior associates will take time to explain assignments to you, knowing that the few minutes spent explaining will result in a better product." A junior associate reports, "I am learning at what I perceive to be an incredibly fast rate, and I judge that by comparing myself to peers at other large firms who sit on the other side of my deals. I am given as much responsibility as I can handle, and the level ramps up with each transaction."

Grappling with diversity

"At first, Fried Frank seemed to have everything a woman attorney could want," says a senior female associate. "But the reality is that it is nearly impossible for a woman who has had a child to succeed at the firm. Maternity leave effectively knocks you off partnership track." Others view the situation less starkly, and point to developments such as the revival of the firm's women's forum, further noting that new co-chair Valerie Ford Jacob had two children while she was an associate at the firm. But the concern is not unique among Fried Frank's women attorneys, many of whom believe, for example, that "mentoring suffers" due to the ongoing shortage of senior female associates. Conditions are "probably slightly better here than at most large firms," another source clarifies, "but there is still much room for improvement."

The perceived lack of mentorship also affects Fried Frank's efforts to build a diverse roster of minority associates, despite the strong advances noted above. "It is not clear why more diverse partners are not lateralled in as partners," comments one midlevel associate. "It would help because the firm will not be promoting too many diverse associates to partner because they all will have left due to the lack of mentoring." Firm leadership notes the increasing number of minority partners and suggests worries over mentorship will abate with time. For now, the firm seems to be doing a much better job of creating a "very accepting" environment where gay and lesbian attorneys are "respected and successful." One openly gay associate informs us, " I am pleased with the firm's acceptance and efforts to provide an open and welcoming work environment. Also, the firm has demonstrated a significant commitment to gay/lesbian public interest and pro bono work."

The leader in pro bono

"We don't just talk" about pro bono, brags a second-year, "we do." A senior associate in D.C. calls Fried Frank "the best firm for pro bono I've ever run across!" She adds, "This isn't just a lip service situation. There is a [D.C. jurisdictional] requirement to do 50 hours a year and the ability to do much, much more." One young corporate attorney calls the firm "the leader in pro bono" and declares, "That is one of the reasons I chose to work at this firm. They are dedicated to bettering the community." The firm dedicates senior attorneys to oversee pro bono efforts in D.C. and New

York, and "it's very easy and efficient to get an interesting pro bono assignment." A first-year proudly notes, "I have already completed two pro bono assignments in six months." The New York office has a rotating four-month externship for associates at the Community Development Project of the Legal Aid Society. Externs primarily advise Harlem-based micro-entrepeneurs on corporate, real estate, intellectual property and tax issues. Other pro bono externships are available for summer associates.

"We all have CLE credit coming out our ears!"

– Fried Frank associate

27 Morrison & Foerster LLP

425 Market Street
San Francisco, CA 94105-2482
Phone: (415) 268-7409
www.mofo.com

LOCATIONS

San Francisco, CA (HQ) • Century City, CA • Denver, CO • Los Angeles, CA • New York, NY • Northern Virginia, VA • Orange County, CA • Palo Alto, CA • Sacramento, CA • San Diego, CA • Walnut Creek, CA • Washington, DC Beijing • Brussels • Hong Kong • London • Shanghai • Singapore • Tokyo

MAJOR DEPARTMENTS/PRACTICES

Corporate Finance
Financial Services
Intellectual Property & Patent
International
Labor & Employment Law
Land Use, Environmental & Energy
Litigation
Real Estate
Tax & Estate

THE STATS

No. of attorneys: 995
No. of offices: 19
Summer associate offers: 57 out of 71 (2002)
Managing Partner: Keith C. Wetmore
Hiring Partner: James E. Hough

BASE SALARY

New York, NY; Tokyo; California offices
1st year: $125,000
Summer associate: $2,400/week

Denver, CO
1st year: $110,000
Summer associate: $2,000/week

Washington, DC
1st year: $125,000
Summer associate: $2,400/week

UPPERS

- Outstanding record on diversity
- Flexibility on work schedules
- Strong commitment to pro bono

DOWNERS

- "Lack of social opportunities between practice groups"
- Jumbled assignment system
- Long hours

NOTABLE PERKS

- Thursday night dinners (San Francisco)
- Friday happy hour
- Free BlackBerry

 THE BUZZ
WHAT ATTORNEYS AT OTHER FIRMS ARE SAYING ABOUT THIS FIRM

- "Incredible working environment"
- "Jumped the shark"
- "Key California firm "
- "Too dot-com"

RANKING RECAP

Best in Region
#4 - California

Best in Practice
#4 - Technology/Internet/E-Commerce
#6 - Intellectual Property

Quality of Life
#2 - Best 20 Law Firms to Work For
#3 - Satisfaction
#4 - Pro Bono
#5 - Associate/Partner Relations
#14 - Hours
#15 - Pay
#16 - Retention
#17 - Selectivity
#20 - Training

Best in Diversity
#1 - Overall Diversity
#1 - Diversity for Women
#2 - Diversity for Minorities
#3 - Diversity for Gays & Lesbians

EMPLOYMENT CONTACT

Ms. Jane Cooperman
Senior Recruiting Manager
Phone: (415) 268-7665
Fax: (415) 268-7522
E-mail: jcooperman@mofo.com

QUALITY OF LIFE RANKINGS
[ASSOCIATES RATE THEIR OWN FIRM]

SATISFACTION

8.5

1 • • • • • • • • • • • • • • • • • • • 10
WORST   BEST

HOURS

7.5

1 • • • • • • • • • • • • • • • • • • • 10
WORST   BEST

ASSOCIATE/PARTNER RELATIONS

8.7

1 • • • • • • • • • • • • • • • • • • • 10
WORST   BEST

TRAINING

7.9

1 • • • • • • • • • • • • • • • • • • • 10
WORST   BEST

DIVERSITY

9.0

1 • • • • • • • • • • • • • • • • • • • 10
WORST   BEST

THE SCOOP

You might not be able to pronounce their nickname without cracking a smile, but San Francisco-based Morrison & Foerster is a serious law firm unafraid to take risks. The firm also takes quality of life seriously and is known as a terrific place to work.

The name game

Although people started calling the firm "MoFo" as a joke, the abbreviated moniker has become a source of ironic pride, and even appears in the firm's official web address. The firm has actually gone through several name changes in its 120-year history. Thomas O'Brien and Alexander Morrison got the ball rolling in 1883 when they opened for business as O'Brien and Morrison. Constantine Foerster joined the firm seven years later and inspired the first iteration of "Morrison & Foerster" in 1892. He died a few years later, though, and the firm became Morrison & Cope. Ronald Foerster, Constantine's son, came aboard in 1916 and eventually got to change the firm's name back. But the firm would try out a few more names over the next half-century before returning to Morrison & Foerster once again. (And, no, we don't think people referred to it as MoFo in 1892.)

Morrison & Foerster is the largest law firm based in California, with seven offices in the state. It also has a substantial presence beyond the state line, with offices in New York, Denver and Washington, D.C., as well as international outposts in Beijing, Hong Kong, Singapore and Tokyo. The firm also has European offices in Brussels and London; a July 2002 merger with UK employment law specialisits Jones & Warner recently augmented the London branch.

What's on Wetmore's head?

MoFo has long positioned itself at the forefront of diversity and gay rights and practices what it preaches. In November 2000, the partners selected Keith Wetmore, formerly the managing partner of the San Francisco office, as the new chair. Wetmore became the second openly gay man to run a major law firm, and can frequently be seen around the office wearing his celebrated "Homo at MoFo" cap.

John Walker's blues

MoFo partner James Brosnahan offered his legal services to John Walker Lindh, the American Taliban convert who was captured in Afghanistan in late 2001, and helped Lindh negotiate his eventual plea bargain in July 2002, reducing the charges to illegally aiding the Taliban and weapons possession. But Brosnahan was operating as a free agent. Citing security fears, Morrison & Foerster insisted that its name not be used in conjunction with Lindh's defense.

Whiz kid

Like a lot of teenagers, Cole Bartiromo of Mission Viejo, Calif., has had his share of run-ins with the law. But Bartiromo wasn't involved in your usual juvenile delinquent shenanigans. MoFo attorneys have represented the 17-year-old in two securities fraud investigations by the Securities and Exchange Commission. The SEC had accused the youth of "pumping and dumping" – posting thousands of pseudonymous messages on online chat boards to drive up the value of his stock holdings. Bartiromo brought the latest inquiry to a close in June 2002, surrendering his $91,000 windfall to the SEC without admitting or denying guilt.

Fighting for her rights

When an Air Force Academy honor board investigated senior cadet Andrea Prasse for an alleged violation of the academy's honor code by cheating on an exam, she maintained that a vindictive fellow student had fabricated the charges against her. The honor board nevertheless found her guilty, raising the threat of expulsion just eight days before the dean's list student was scheduled to graduate. Her family retained Morrison & Foerster to represent her interests as Air Force officials investigated her accusations and mulled over how to deal with her conviction, which cannot be appealed. After months of deliberation, the Academy, which by now was facing numerous other complaints from female cadets concerning sexual harassment and rape by their classmates, ruled in February 2003 that Prasse would be allowed back on campus to serve six months of honor probation, after which she would receive her commission as a second lieutenant.

Gold medal performance

Morrison & Foerster scored a major victory in October 2002, edging ahead of competitors like Clifford Chance and Coudert Brothers to land an assignment as international counsel for the 2008 Olympics in Beijing. MoFo had previously advised the organizing committee for the Salt Lake City Games on licensing and entertainment contracts; this experience, combined with the firm's entertainment law expertise and Beijing presence, was viewed as a contributing factor in the firm's selection.

In another major international case, MoFo's Brussels office is advising an alliance of technology companies, including Sun Microsystems, AOL Time Warner, Eastman Kodak and Oracle, who filed a complaint with European regulators against Microsoft in February 2003. The Computer and Communications Industry Association claims that the release of Windows XP is yet another example of the software giant's stifling dominance of the computer industry, preventing competitors from introducing innovations in a wide range of electronic devices. The complaint came just as the European Commission's competition department was reaching the end of its five-year investigation of Microsoft's earlier business practices.

Pro bono giants

Lawyers from Morrison & Foerster assisted in the pro bono representation of three Salvadoran plaintiffs who had been detained and tortured by security forces in their homeland between 1979 and 1983. The MoFo attorneys collaborated with the International Human Rights Law Clinic of UC Berkeley's law school, Boalt Hall, in the federal civil trial, which resulted in a $54.6 million verdict in July 2002 against two retired Salvadoran generals who had commanded the torture squads. The two men were brought to trial under the terms of the Alien Tort Claims Act of 1789 and the Torture Victim Protection Act of 1992, federal laws which enable survivors of torture and other human rights abuses to sue the responsible parties, no matter where the crimes were committed, if they can be physically served with the lawsuit within the borders of the United States.

The firm is also providing legal representation for Hady Omar, a United States citizen of Middle Eastern descent who was detained by federal agents the day after the terrorist attacks on the World Trade Center and the Pentagon. Despite never being charged with any crime, Omar was secretly imprisoned for over two months in a maximum-security facility and denied his right to see an attorney for much of his incarceration. With the help of MoFo attorneys and the Lawyers Committee for Civil Rights, Omar is currently suing various employees of the former Immigration and Naturalization Service, the Bureau of Prisons and the Orleans Parish Criminal Sheriff's Office for violating his constitutional rights during his imprisonment. He is also pursuing a federal tort claim against the INS and the Bureau of Prisons.

Taking spam personally

When MoFo associates get bombarded with spam, they push back hard. The firm filed a lawsuit against e-mail marketer Etracks.com in February 2002, claiming that the company had sent them thousands of unsolicited bulk e-mails advertising the usual assortment of fantastic new mortgage rates, semi-professional pornography web sites and all-natural "enhancing" supplements. The firm accused Etracks of violating state laws against sending unsolicited e-mail and commercial advertisements via e-mail without identifying them as such in the subject line. The suit, which was later amended to include another spammer, Learn2 Corporation, seeks damages of $50 for each e-mail, up to $25,000 per day.

GETTING HIRED

Sharp minds, loose personalities

MoFo "seems to be interested in candidates from strong California law schools and schools with nationwide prominence," says one insider, as well as "top students from other law schools that specialize in a particular area of the law." Another source affirms the desire for "confident, down-to-earth, ethical lawyers who want to be involved in the pro bono legal community, have an intellectual interest in the law and are not afraid of hard work or science," given the firm's high concentration of technology clients.

"Stuffed shirts don't fit in here," a midlevel associate warns, and another tells us MoFo "is not an old boys' club at all." The firm seeks out "individuals with diverse and interesting backgrounds," and "extroverts tend to attract our attention." The firm has been "very selective" about candidates in recent years. "The candidates that I see are all top-notch in terms of experience and educational background," says one second-year associate. "Personality and fit within the firm culture and practice group can make the difference." A senior attorney agrees, "We look for someone who shares the same values – personal and professional."

OUR SURVEY SAYS

Intensely laid back

"A law firm is not a daisy farm," says a midlevel litigator, "but I think MoFo's as good a place to work as any firm and better than most." The office is "full of happy, well-adjusted lawyers" who "genuinely like each other" and "take their work but not themselves seriously." A second-year associate describes the environment in detail. "People in the firm maintain extremely professional relationships," she reports. "The attorneys are amicable but not necessarily social. Perhaps paradoxically, MoFo is simultaneously very laid back. It is a meritocracy devoid of conflict or office politics." But though "the focus is on the work, not on power and status," a midlevel associate reveals that "the hierarchy is felt in the way that decisions about work get made."

"Although market conditions have cast a shadow over the whole Bay Area market, we maintain a very laid-back and friendly firm culture," claims a fifth-year. "I often enjoy having lunch or coffee with my fellow associates and partners," another junior associate says. A senior litigator testifies, "I have many wonderful friends here, and I know most of the spouses and children of my co-workers in my department."

Partners who leave you alone

"I work with by far the nicest partners I have met at any firm," a midlevel associate reports. "The partners have been nothing short of amazing," agrees a sophomore. "I am given an exceptional amount of responsibility without the panopticon of micromanagement so rampant in big firms." An IP lawyer confides, "I could not ask for better guidance and support from the partnership. The door is always truly open within my practice group." The partnership, says one insider, "is one of MoFo's strong points," while a third-year suggests, "The partners here are terrific, down-to-earth people and excellent attorneys. They take an active role in associates' development."

Of course, not everyone thinks the MoFo partners are all that. "I've worked with a partner who is always willing to answer questions," says one first-year, "but then I've worked with partners I would never feel comfortable calling or e-mailing, who are really intimidating and actually seem to thrive on that." Some associates mention that partners "completely bungled the terminations of several associates by calling them performance-based when they were clearly market-driven, which caused great resentment among remaining associates."

Choosing to work hard

MoFo associates appear rather blasé about their hours. A fifth-year veteran finds his hours at MoFo "extremely humane." He advises, "To keep the partners really happy with you, 2,100 would more than do the trick, and in this market 1,900 is seen as a lot." Though some feel "pressure to bill in order to advance," most attorneys at the firm feel that they have control over their hours, enabling them to "work hard by choice, not under duress." Several cite scheduling arrangements that work to their advantage. "There are times when I spend far too much time working," one source reports, "but the firm is very flexible about whether this has to be in the office or not." A senior associate adds that "attorneys are understanding when family commitments require you to be away from the office during regular business hours." "I rarely work on weekends," says a second-year associate, "and when I do, I do so from home." A sunny first-year chimes in, "Sometimes the hours are long, but the work is so cool that staying here late doesn't bother me." And, brags a senior litigator, "I have an outside life, unlike my peers at other large firms."

Good for what you get

MoFo-ians are pleased with their hefty paychecks. "I can't believe how much I work," muses a first-year litigator, "but I really can't believe how much I get paid." Another associate agrees, "I don't think there are many attorneys in San Francisco who are paid more at my level." Others say MoFo is "not at the absolute top, but not that far behind." "We may not pay exactly market," says a seven-year veteran, but "because our firm culture is more laid back than other large firms, the slight dip in salary is well worth it." A less enthusiastic second-year finds fault with the "weak" productivity bonuses, which "do not provide much compensation for the extra hours." A colleague tries to put things in perspective: "We make a ridiculous amount of money," the young litigator observes. "Anyone who says otherwise is either greedy or subject to delusions of grandeur about their own worth."

Open arms

"Associates and staff alike realize that MoFo is a great place to work," says a third-year, "and they work hard to keep their jobs." A six-year veteran with the firm can boast, "My friends are the same people I met when I was a summer associate." Many associates do wind up leaving the firm after three or four years, but those who remain think that's partly because of the type of attorney MoFo hires. "Many associates here are interested in social justice or government work," observes one first-year. "They tend to stay for a few years and then move on to public interest jobs. I've noticed, though, that a lot of people leave for a couple of years and then come back." One of those "MoFo yo-yos" reports that the firm "welcomed me back with open arms" after a stint at a boutique firm. "I stayed friends with all my old colleagues at MoFo during the years I was gone," he adds.

Excellence in diversity

MoFo associates "can't imagine there's a firm that's better" when it comes to creating a "haven" for its gay and lesbian associates. From the head of the firm to the junior associates, "we have plenty of queer attorneys" and "the firm does not tolerate insensitivity on this issue." A gay second-year attests, "No one here has ever done anything that makes me feel uncomfortable or like an outsider."

One woman at the firm dubs the similarly strong commitment to female associates "MoFo's biggest strength." "MoFo has surpassed my expectations," says the second-year. "The firm has truly achieved gender equality." A member of the IP practice also believes "this firm offers a very supportive and welcoming atmosphere," adding, "I have never felt that being a woman meant that I was disadvantaged in any way." Women fill many management positions, and a senior male associate notes, "I have several women as mentors." Associates give the firm slightly lower marks for its track record with minority associates. While most admit the firm "encourages minority applicants," with one litigator calling MoFo "one of the most ethnically diverse places I've ever worked," others point to difficulties in keeping minority associates around. "The firm talks the talk," says one insider, "but does not necessarily walk the walk, particularly in offices outside San Francisco."

Pro bono champions

MoFo has a "well-deserved" reputation for being "very, very strong" on pro bono, and the associates agree "there is very little to hold you back" from such cases, with a "steady stream of e-mails" detailing new public service opportunities just about every day, and a mandatory pro bono assignment for all first-years. "Most everyone does pro bono," including the partners, and the work counts as billable hours for bonus assessment purposes. "Pro bono work provides me with more satisfaction than most other clients' projects," says one senior litigator. "I am happy not to be penalized for time spent on pro bono clients as opposed to the paying ones."

Dewey Ballantine LLP

301 Avenue of the Americas
New York, NY 10019
Phone: (212) 259-8000
www.deweyballantine.com

LOCATIONS

New York, NY (HQ)
Austin, TX
Houston, TX
Los Angeles, CA
Palo Alto, CA
Washington, DC
Budapest
Frankfurt
London
Prague
Warsaw

MAJOR DEPARTMENTS/PRACTICES

Bankruptcy • Capital Markets • Corporate • Energy &
Utility • Environmental • ERISA • Insurance •
Intellectual Property • International Trade • Investment
Management • Litigation • Mergers & Acquisitions •
Project Finance • Real Estate • Structured Finance •
Tax & Private Clients

THE STATS

No. of attorneys: 550
No. of offices: 11
Summer associate offers: 47 out of 50 (2002)
Chairman: Everett L. Jassy
Hiring Partner: James A. FitzPatrick, Jr.

BASE SALARY

All domestic offices
1st year: $125,000
2nd year: $135,000
3rd year: $150,000
4th year: $170,000
5th year: $190,000
6th year: $200,000
7th year: $205,000
8th year: $210,000
Summer associate: $2,403/week

UPPERS

- Laid back environment
- Lots of responsibility from the get-go
- Respected M&A practice

DOWNERS

- Inequitable work allocation
- Layoffs and office closing have affected morale
- Weak on diversity

NOTABLE PERKS

- Annual firm dinner at the Plaza
- Free dinners from SeamlessWeb ordering system
- Friday cocktail hour
- Profit-sharing program

THE BUZZ
WHAT ATTORNEYS AT OTHER FIRMS ARE SAYING ABOUT THIS FIRM

- "Silently gets the job done"
- "Vanilla BigLaw"
- "M&A group works really hard!"
- "Not what they used to be"

RANKING RECAP

Best in Region
#16 - New York

Quality of Life
#5 - Offices

EMPLOYMENT CONTACT

Ms. Nicole Gunn
Manager of Legal Recruitment
Phone: (212) 259-7050
Fax: (212) 259-6333
E-mail: db.recruitment@deweyballantine.com

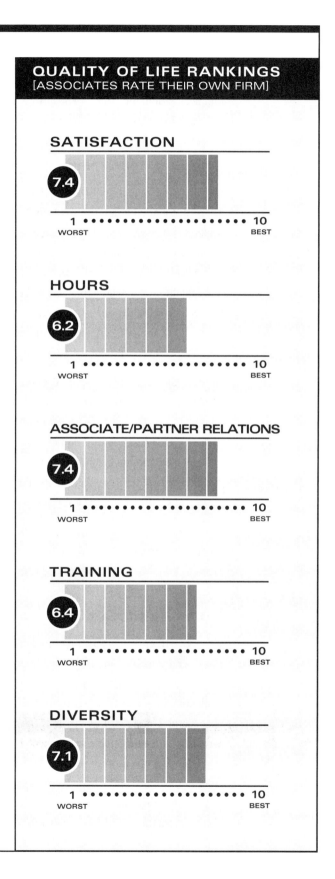

QUALITY OF LIFE RANKINGS
[ASSOCIATES RATE THEIR OWN FIRM]

SATISFACTION

7.4

1 • • • • • • • • • • • • • • • • • • 10
WORST   BEST

HOURS

6.2

1 • • • • • • • • • • • • • • • • • • 10
WORST   BEST

ASSOCIATE/PARTNER RELATIONS

7.4

1 • • • • • • • • • • • • • • • • • • 10
WORST   BEST

TRAINING

6.4

1 • • • • • • • • • • • • • • • • • • 10
WORST   BEST

DIVERSITY

7.1

1 • • • • • • • • • • • • • • • • • • 10
WORST   BEST

THE SCOOP

Dewey Ballantine is a leading New York firm with top-notch antitrust, corporate, tax and mergers and acquisitions practices. The firm, which has refused to take on tobacco companies as clients, has 550 lawyers in 11 offices: six in the U.S. and five overseas.

One firm, many names

In 1909, three recent graduates of Harvard Law School, Elihu Root Jr., Grenville Clark and Frances W. Bird, founded a law firm in New York. In 1913, Root, Clark & Bird (as the firm was known) took on two additional partners, Emory R. Buckner and Silas W. Howland, and the firm was reborn as Root, Clark, Buckner & Howland. The firm flourished in the 1920s, adding big-name clients like AT&T and the Guggenheim Brothers. The firm benefited from the presence of Elihu Root Sr., a Washington star who served as secretary of state (under William McKinley), secretary of war (under Theodore Roosevelt) and senator from New York (from 1909 to 1915). He won the Nobel Peace Prize in 1912. Another prominent name was Arthur A. Ballantine, a former solicitor of internal revenue, who put the firm's tax practice on the map.

In the 1950s, the firm welcomed Thomas Dewey aboard. Dewey served three terms as governor of New York and ran for president unsuccessfully in 1944 against Franklin Roosevelt and in 1948 against Harry Truman. That election is famous for the premature headline in *The Chicago Daily Tribune* "Dewey Defeats Truman." Early results had Dewey far enough ahead that the *Tribune* called the election in his favor; Truman pulled ahead after copies of the paper had gone out. That's not the firm's only connection to the New York State governor's office. Current New York Governor George Pataki is a former associate.

The firm added partners through lateral hiring in the 1980s and 1990s, building up its M&A, insurance, corporate and litigation practices. In October 1997, the firm took up its current name, Dewey Ballantine LLP. It was the 12th name change for what began as Root, Clark & Bird.

DB hit by tough times

Dewey Ballantine has taken its lumps in the current economic slump. The firm laid off a handful of associates in 2001 in New York, though the firm opened a Houston office in October of that year. In December 2002, the firm lost litigation counsel Sanford Litvack, who had joined Dewey Ballantine only a year earlier from Walt Disney Co., where he had served as vice chairman as well as general counsel. Litvack left Dewey for Los Angeles litigation boutique Quinn Emanuel Urquhart Oliver & Hedges. Vincent FitzPatrick, a prominent litigator who caused a big splash when he and seven other partners left White & Case for Dewey Ballantine in 1995, reversed his field in October 2002. Like a prodigal son, FitzPatrick (along with two other litigation partners, one of whom was an associate when he joined Dewey in 1995) returned to White & Case for that firm's international litigation capabilities. In January 2003, the firm announced it would shut its

Hong Kong office, home to seven lawyers. (The Hong Kong office closing led to a minor embarrassment for the firm. At the firm's annual dinner in late January, as detailed in a subsequent issue of *New York Law Journal*, several associates performed a parody song that included lyrics that some in attendance considered racially insensitive. Firm chairman Everett Jassy admitted to the publication that some of the lyrics were in poor taste, and the firm later issued both external and internal apologies.) Dewey lost partner Frank Morgan to client Coller Capital in April 2003. Morgan, who represented the private equity firm since its founding in 1990, was named head of Coller's brand-new New York office.

The firm has attracted some heavy hitters to build up several practice areas. In July 2002, Dewey Ballantine acquired the Warsaw office of Hunton & Williams, then snagged partner Geza Toth and four associates from the London office of Weil, Gotshal & Manges. Toth later set up a Frankfurt office for Dewey. The big score came in September 2002, when 11 partners from the intellectual property practice of now-defunct Brobeck, Phleger & Harrison, including Jim Elacqua, head of IP at Brobeck, defected to Dewey Ballantine. The 11 lawyers were spread out over Dewey Ballantine's Palo Alto, Washington, D.C., and Austin, Texas, offices. (Brobeck refugees founded the Austin office.) The mass exodus was a blow to Brobeck, which dissolved in early 2003 after more partner defections and financial problems. In April 2003, Dewey Ballantine welcomed David Grais as a partner. The litigator had been a partner and co-head of the insurance and reinsurance litigation practice group at Gibson, Dunn & Crutcher.

The chairman has turned on the "No Smoking" sign

Don't even think about lighting up anywhere near Dewey Ballantine. Former co-chairperson Joseph Califano Jr., was an anti-tobacco crusader, and the firm has refused to take on tobacco companies even long after he left the firm. (Califano was an associate at the firm before serving as a special assistant to President Lyndon Johnson and, later, as President Jimmy Carter's Secretary of the Department of Health, Education & Welfare. He returned to the firm as a partner from 1983-1992.) In fact, Dewey Ballantine represented health care company Blue Cross/Blue Shield in its quest for compensation for costs related to smokers' health problems. Dewey Ballantine won a $17.8 million verdict for Blue Cross/Blue Shield in June 2001. While the amount of the verdict was far less than the $800 million sought in the original complaint, Dewey Ballantine trumpeted the result as the first time an insurer had been repaid for health care costs by a tobacco company. (The firm was also pleased that the judge presiding over the case awarded Dewey Ballantine $38 million in legal fees.)

Big cases for a big firm

Dewey Ballantine lawyers have been in on some of the bigger recent cases. The firm's bankruptcy department is representing discount retailer Kmart. Dewey Ballantine partner Harvey Kurzweil is representing insurance firm Travelers Indemnity in its case against the leaseholders of the World Trade Center. Larry Silverstein, who held the lease for the buildings destroyed in the September

11 attacks, hopes to treat the collapse of each tower as a separate event, with separate insurance payouts. Travelers and other insurance firms want the attacks viewed as a single event with a single claim. The case is pending. Dewey Ballantine's M&A department was one of the top 20 law firms for 2002 in completed deals. In February 2003, Dewey Ballantine advised Irish Life & Permanent on the sale of its U.S. subsidiary Guarantee Reserve Life Insurance for $121 million.

GETTING HIRED

Top pedigree, top personality

Dewey Ballantine's recruiting process is typical of other big firms. One insider says the "interview and callback process is very thorough. I had plenty of time during both to find out all of the information I needed and to show my best side. The callback started with a meet-and-greet with a member of the recruiting department, which was helpful in guiding me through the rest of the day." Once you get to that meet-and-greet, the focus will be off your resume. "Once you get a callback it means they are really just looking at personality," says a contact. Where you went to school is very important. "The firm looks for candidates from top-25 law schools and the very top students at lower-tier schools." "People from Harvard can have an offer for the asking; people from New York School of Law have to be top-five in their class," reports one insider.

But Dewey Ballantine isn't just looking for law automatons. "The firm is looking for smart, independent, assertive people," says one associate. Successful candidates "must be intelligent and be able to think on your feet" and "must have a good sense of humor." Real people will get a second look. "Dewey Ballantine is looking for real people – not just resumes," says one attorney. "Real people who will work hard but also have lives outside of the firm. People who will think and learn while they do their work." Another source says the firm is looking for "highly qualified but normal nice people you enjoy spending you days with."

OUR SURVEY SAYS

Laid back culture, but it may be changing

Most Dewey Ballantine associates are pleased with the firm's culture, and "laid back" and "friendly" are the most common descriptive terms used by insiders. "The firm's culture is excellent," says one insider. "Staff and attorneys of all levels interact informally but very respectfully. The firm management rightfully prides itself on having created and maintained a very congenial workplace." There may be some bad apples, but that doesn't necessarily ruin the bushel. "I have always found Dewey Ballantine to be an extremely laid back, friendly environment," reports one associate. "It has a certain element of obnoxious personalities, which, given the sheer number of attorneys who work here, cannot be avoided. But those personalities are the exception, not the rule. While people socialize, and small pockets of close-knit friendships form, it is a firm that is generally respectful of an individual's personal and family life." "With the exception of a few partners and associates, the firm has a very friendly and informal environment," says another insider. "The firm encourages socializing outside of the office by sponsoring numerous sports teams and having firm-wide parties."

Of course, the firm isn't totally free of tension, and past layoffs may have hurt the culture. "The place is friendly enough on the basis of half-smiles and handshakes, but it's cynically collegial, like joining a social club where the only topic of conversation is the past, present and future dues payments," observes one source. At least one insider senses something different in the air. "I think this is a different firm than it once was," says one attorney. "There isn't enough work, but when there is, it is badly managed so you do nothing all day yet stay all night without anyone saying thank you or anyone caring you have given up your life and cancelled plans again."

Partner praise and pressure

Partners are a mixed bag, too; many are praised as treating associates well, while others seem to be less sensitive of associates' time and abilities. "Partners are very respectful, making you feel more like part of a team than a subordinate," gushes one insider. "They definitely pitch in and work as hard as the associates." They're not afraid to get toner on their hands, on rare occasion. "One partner went to the copy machine, punched in his codes and was making photocopies because I was so busy in a closing doing other things," continues that associate. "Partners have been known to, on more than one occasion, cancel vacations, even during the holidays," says another contact.

Associates in some departments feel pressure from the partners. "Litigation and M&A associates are abused. Some have no work while others are on track to bill 3,000 hours," sighs a corporate lawyer. "Other corporate associates are fairly well-treated." Some report feeling dehumanized. "Some partners are great, some just treat associates like pieces of meat." "I think partners used to treat people better but there are fewer senior associates and not enough work, so partners are nervous and so less friendly," says one lawyer. "Also, there is very little feedback on how you are doing."

Uneven hours, face time plague associates

Dewey Ballantine associates complain of "either too little or too many" hours. The work assignment system draws gripes, as does inconsistent and unpredictable scheduling. "Our group tends not to dispense assignments until late in the afternoon, which leaves one sitting around for most of the day," says a corporate lawyer. Complains one insider, "Consistent allocation of work is an issue." Insiders say it's difficult to predict how late you'll be at the office month-to-month or even week-to-week. "It's the roller coaster of a lot of work or none at all that is extremely frustrating," says one contact. Associates are also worried about face time. "I spend a lot of time with no work, but can't leave at 5 p.m. even if I have nothing to do," says one source. "Often I will do nothing all day and then get a pile of work at 4 p.m., or will get an assignment that is a rush for a week that we could have started working on earlier without being rushed."

"I deserve even more"

Despite taking home market pay, Dewey Ballantine associates have plenty of complaints about their compensation. "Like all firms, associates who work a lot of hours are not appropriately compensated at the end of the year," fumes one associate. "Of course, we are told that we are 'part of the long-term plans.' However, my bank will not lend to me based on that statement." Everyone acknowledges that they're taking home a lot; it's just that some feel it's not enough. "I get paid a lot, but I deserve even more," says one confident lawyer. "I'm good at what I do, damn it." Some New Yorkers feel they're being short-changed due to the costs of living in the Big Apple. "It's much harder to live on $125,000 in New York City than it is, say, in Austin, Texas," says one associate. "There needs to be some recognition of this by the firms. Even an additional $10,000 a year would really, really help. Rent is ridiculous and eats up almost half of my take-home pay each month."

Good training, but no spoon-feeding

Most insiders feel the training opportunities at Dewey Ballantine are "excellent. Even when I come onto a deal midway, I am told nearly all aspects of the deal. I have a good understanding of what I am learning and what, in the long term, I need to learn," says one corporate lawyer. Others from that department find formal training lacking but concede that partner and senior associates make up for it by mentoring those with less experience. "Partners and senior associates do a wonderful job of making themselves available for informal training and assistance, and there are a fair number of group-specific CLEs/training meetings. But at least in the corporate department there isn't as much formal training as I've heard is provided elsewhere," reports a Dewey corporate lawyer. Still, it isn't kindergarten, so don't expect to be treated like it is. Dewey Ballantine provides "exceptional training because you are thrown in with some guidance and expected to get it," reports one source. "If you prove competent, you will get a lot of responsibility. You will be helped but not babied."

Trouble moving up the ladder

Dewey Ballantine suffers from a common problem in the legal industry. "There are many women associates but few partners," reports one source. "This is partially due to the fact that there are few mentoring relationships while the men have developed close professional bonds." There are hints of problems. "The firm has historically been very good to women, relatively speaking, but that doesn't mean some crap doesn't get swept under the rug," says one contact. The firm handles specific complaints, which are "pursued aggressively, but no one is monitoring behavior or looking for problems," says an associate. It helps if you don't procreate. "As a woman I don't feel I am treated vastly differently, but it is clear by looking at senior people that one can't expect to have a family and become a partner."

Minority associates can face tough going as well. "Did you see the article?" asks one associate, referring to the embarrassing episode at the firm's 2003 dinner. "I wouldn't come here as a minority. Even if not a minority, it's pathetic that the firm let that song be used, and it's embarrassing and wrong." Some point the finger at firm policies or management. "There is no diversity/sensitivity training for attorneys or partners," complains one insider. "There is no clear person or committee responsible for complaints. Partners often handle complaints how they best feel they should be handled." The incident mobilized firm leadership into action, however, leading to a revised equal employment opportunity and prohibition of harassment policy as well as mandatory training for all personnel.

Mayer, Brown, Rowe & Maw

190 South LaSalle Street
Chicago, IL 60603-3441
Phone: (312) 701-7002
www.mayerbrownrowe.com

LOCATIONS

Charlotte, NC • Chicago, IL • Houston, TX • Los
Angeles, CA • New York, NY • Palo Alto, CA •
Washington, DC • Beijing* • Brussels • Cologne •
Frankfurt • London • Manchester • Paris • Shanghai*

Representative offices

MAJOR DEPARTMENTS/PRACTICES

Bankruptcy & Reorganization • Corporate & Securities •
Environmental • Employee Benefits • Finance •
Government Relations • Health Care • Intellectual
Property • Litigation • Real Estate • Regulated Industries
• Tax Controversy • Tax Transactions • Trust, Estates
& Foundations

THE STATS

No. of attorneys: 1,350
No. of offices: 13
Summer associate offers: 87 out of 90 (2002)
Chairman of the Firm: Tyrone C. Fahner
Managing Partner: Debora de Hoyos
Hiring Partnesr: J. Thomas Mullen (Chicago); Robert
Mendenhall (Charlotte); Terry Otero Vilardo (Houston);
Michael F. Kerr (LA); Kathleen A. Walsh (NY); John J.
Sullivan (DC)

BASE SALARY

**Chicago, IL; Los Angeles, CA; New York, NY;
Washington, DC**
1st year: $125,000
2nd year: $135,000
3rd year: $150,000
4th year: $165,000; $170,000 (NY)
5th year: $185,000; $190,000 (NY)
6th year: $195,000; $205,000 (NY)
7th year: $205,000; $215,000 (NY)
8th year: $225,000 (NY)
9th year: $235,000 (NY)
Summer associate: $2,400/week

Houston, TX
1st year: $125,000
Summer associate: $2,100/week

Charlotte, NC
1st year: $105,000
Summer associate: $2,000/week

UPPERS

- International growth
- Warm and fuzzy corporate culture
- Improved training

DOWNERS

- Few results from diversity efforts
- Unpredictable schedules
- Communication from management lacking

NOTABLE PERKS

- Monthly beer and pizza
- Free bagels and doughnuts
- Firm pays for BlackBerry service (but not devices)
- Excellent maternity and paternity leave program

THE BUZZ
WHAT ATTORNEYS AT OTHER FIRMS ARE SAYING ABOUT THIS FIRM

- "Fantastic Supreme Court practice"
- "Merger may have hurt them"
- "Impressively intellectual"
- "Sidley Lite"

RANKING RECAP

Best in Region
#3 - Chicago

Best in Practice
#7 - Real Estate

Quality of Life
#4 - Part-Time/Flex-Time

EMPLOYMENT CONTACT

See firm web site (www.mayerbrownrowe.com) for employment contacts in each office.

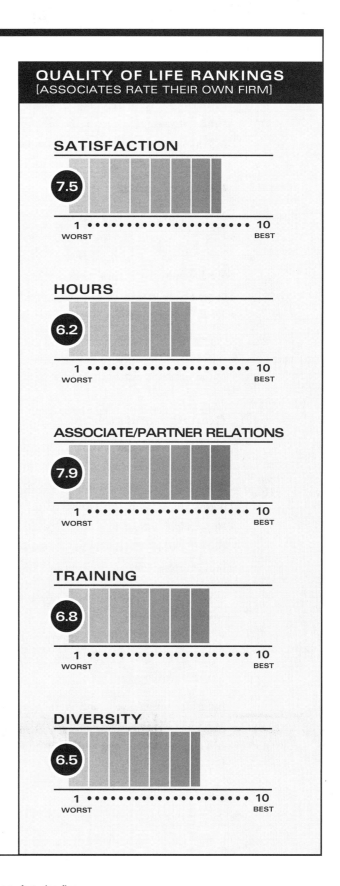

QUALITY OF LIFE RANKINGS
[ASSOCIATES RATE THEIR OWN FIRM]

SATISFACTION

7.5

1 WORST — 10 BEST

HOURS

6.2

1 WORST — 10 BEST

ASSOCIATE/PARTNER RELATIONS

7.9

1 WORST — 10 BEST

TRAINING

6.8

1 WORST — 10 BEST

DIVERSITY

6.5

1 WORST — 10 BEST

THE SCOOP

A 2002 international merger has created a trans-Atlantic law power. The product of the union between Chicago-based Mayer, Brown & Platt and London-based Rowe & Maw, the new Mayer, Brown, Rowe & Maw has 1,350 in lawyers in 13 offices. The firm also runs a legal consulting arm in Beijing and Shanghai and has a strategic partnership with a Mexico City law firm.

Chicago roots

Mayer, Brown & Platt traces its roots back to 1881, when Levy Nayer and Adolph Kraus founded a partnership. In its early years, the Chicago-based firm represented Windy City icons like Sears Roebuck and Continental Bank. The firm began expanding in the 1970s, opening offices in Washington, D.C., New York and London. From January 2001 to February 2002, the firm combined with Gaedertz in Germany, Lambert & Lee in France and Rowe & Maw (founded in 1895) in the United Kingdom, a move that created one of the world's largest law firms. Both firms were looking for greater reach. "We are doing this because of the needs of our client base, which is mostly international in scope," said Tyrone Fahner, chairman of the old Mayer Brown (as well as the combined firm), at the time of the merger.

Comings and goings

Since its merger, Mayer Brown has opened its doors to many high-profile lateral hires. In fact, 31 new lateral partners have joined the firm since January 2002. Mayer Brown was one of many firms that scooped up refugees from Brobeck, Phlegler & Harrison, the San Francisco-based firm whose dissolution in early 2003 shocked the legal world. New York partners Nigel Howard, head of Brobeck's information technology practice, and David Hudanish, Brobeck's lead outsourcing partner, joined Mayer Brown's IT/outsourcing group in February 2003. The two Brobeck stars brought along four other IT/outsourcing attorneys.

Mayer's antitrust group added Christopher Kelly, formerly of the Department of Justice's Antitrust Division, as a partner in the Washington, D.C., office, and DOJ antitrust lawyer, Michael Bodosky, as an associate. Loyola University Law School professor Spencer Weber Waller, author of *Antitrust and American Business,* recognized as a leading treatise in the field, joined the firm as special counsel.

But lateral hiring giveth, and lateral hiring taketh away. In December 2002, litigation partners John Miles and Marie Kidwell and five associates left Mayer Brown's London office for rival Hunton & Williams. Miles and Kidwell weren't exactly fixtures at Mayer Brown. The two had joined Mayer Brown & Platt from Denton Wilde Sapte just before the merger with Rowe & Maw.

Mayer Brown and the Supremes

Mayer Brown was one the first law firms to specialize in arguing cases in front of the U.S. Supreme Court, and has more than a dozen former Supreme Court clerks on its roster. The firm's appellate practice has argued more than 30 cases in front of the high court since 1995 – more than any other firm – and handles cases in appeals courts across the country.

The appellate practice welcomed a new star in January 2003. Joel Bertocchi, Illinois Solicitor General, joined the firm's Chicago office as a partner. Bertocchi had served as an assistant U.S. Attorney before becoming the Solicitor General, representing the state in civil and criminal proceedings.

Lawyers for bean counters

Mayer Brown has long been the firm of choice for the accounting industry, representing top names like Deloitte & Touche, Ernst & Young, KPMG and Grant Thornton. But it's worked the hardest for Arthur Andersen, the now-defunct giant that gave accounting a bad name due to its controversial work on behalf of clients such as Enron and Waste Management. Mayer Brown's corporate team advised on the worldwide divestiture of Andersen practice groups in spring 2002, negotiating and coordinating more than 50 separate transactions with consulting firms and Big Four accounting firms in the space of three months.

The firm's litigation team is trying to do what Saddam Hussein's Republican Guard couldn't: take on the Pentagon and live to fight another day. The firm represents 20 oil companies, including three of the world's four largest, in their bids to recover $2.5 billion in jet fuel underpayments by the Department of Defense since the 1980s. The suit says the Pentagon used its status as the world's largest purchaser of jet fuel improperly, forcing suppliers to pay less than market value for the stuff that makes bombers and fighters go.

Corporate power, and so on

The dot-com and economic crash of 2001 has brought a rash of lawsuits against investment banks and issuer companies for alleged rigging of stock offerings. Mayer Brown is one of the lead counsel in the largest securities class action to date, and they directly represent eight issuers against claims that investors were defrauded by artificial demand for stock shares created by underwriters and issuers. In April 2003, an appeals court upheld a $68 million verdict for Mayer Brown client LePage in its suit against office supplies maker 3M. A lower court had ruled that 3M violated antitrust laws by unlawfully stifling competition and forcing LePage out of the market for transparent tape.

Even in a down market, Mayer Brown's M&A practice is soaring, having jumped 18 places last year to No. 7 in the Thomson Financial list of completed mergers and acquisitions. Major recent deals include: Security Capital's $5.5 billion merger with GE Capital, the $2.6 billion acquisition of a new product line by Nestlé and Toronto-based Sherritt International Corporation's $1.2 billion acquisition of Calgary-based Fording Inc.

GETTING HIRED

Looking for winners

Potential Mayer Brown attorneys can expect the "same interview and callback process as other big firms." "Our firm basically interviews at the best law schools," says one associate, and the firm points out that it also interviews at local schools. The requirements are typical. "Mayer Brown, like the other big firms, likes the top candidates, and I think a big emphasis is placed on one's statistics, and particularly one's school," says one source. "The economy may have even ratcheted up the standards more." Another contact spells out the standards. "High GPA, law review and/or other activities and, depending on the practice group, prior work experience are all helpful."

Of course, the firm doesn't want misfits. "Though grades are always important, personality is also a key consideration," reports one insider. "Outside of the standard requirements of intelligence, good work ethic and so on, the hiring in my department also depends largely on whether the individual is liked." Most Mayer Brownies agree: an applicant "must have at least a minimum personality." Some departments are more selective than others. "Litigation is snobby about grades and school. Better have a federal clerkship," warns one litigator. "Other groups are selective, but not on those bases." The economy is making things tougher. "Because there are [fewer] jobs available than in years past, the hiring process has become more stringent," says one associate. "It is a supply and demand driven process."

OUR SURVEY SAYS

"We're talking about lawyers here"

Mayer Brown associates say the firm is a "civil and polite" place to work. "The culture is professional, cordial and collegial, with only rare exceptions," says one source. "Courtesy and team work are emphasized. There are lots of opportunities for lawyers to socialize for those that want to, but it is not required." "The culture at Mayer Brown New York is relatively laid back," says a senior associate. "Partners are extremely accessible, and their doors are almost always open. Associates are expected to work hard, but most of the partners make a point of showing their appreciation, whether through a drink after work, through dinner or lunch outings or by honoring associates' planned vacations or time to be spent with family." Some insiders feel there is a layer of formality, but it comes with the territory. "The culture here is on the whole pretty friendly, but, of course, a certain degree of uptightness is built into any firm," reports one lawyer. "I mean, my god, we're talking about lawyers here. We certainly don't sit around shooting the shit with partners or anything, but would you want to?"

"The culture may vary by department. The people I come in contact with seem very friendly but hardworking," according to one lawyer. "I socialize primarily with the other young lawyers in my department, or with other lawyers in my class." Others agree that your department can shape your Mayer Brown experience. "Culture varies from group to group," says one attorney. "Finance and litigation tend toward a boys' club atmosphere more so than corporate and other groups. Attorneys are generally friendly."

Friendly bunch of law geeks

If you thought law school was the end of your legal scholarship days, think again. "There are a lot of people here [who] really just love the law and stay current and engaged in recent Supreme Court and Court of Appeals decisions beyond those that affect their practices. So we're a friendly bunch of law geeks all working together," says one attorney. "It is a somewhat geeky place, full of law nerds," reports one nerd. "People are quite pleasant and friendly toward each other but don't tend to socialize outside of the office a huge amount."

Associates have warm feelings for Mayer Brown partners, who will give junior attorneys a chance to shine. "Most partners at Mayer Brown New York treat associates with great respect," says one associate. "The partners give associates high levels of responsibility in their cases, including significant client contact, very early on, at least where associates show an interest in increased responsibility." If you show that interest, you'd better come through in the clutch. "Partners generally treat associates well," reports one associate. "They are friendly and fairly reasonable. However, when they want something done, it had better be done well and done immediately."

Finally at the market

Mayer Brown has improved its compensation structure, much to the amusement of its associates. "This year, our bonus was at the higher end of comparable firms in the New York market," says one insider. "In prior years, the bonus was significantly lower than comparable firms." Others agree that the firm has recently paid more attention to the market. "While not historically the case, the firm currently seeks to match and on occasion exceeds the market," reports one lawyer. Associates are still reaping the benefits of the dot-com boom. "Can't complain at all," gushes one source. "Thank you, dot-commers!" That doesn't mean there aren't a few complainers. "Bonuses are lame – entirely based on hours, except for a discretionary bonus for extraordinary circumstances," says one contact. "Basic message to associates is that no one cares about quality of work."

The price of freedom

Associates at Mayer Brown spend time at the office, but no more so than other big-firm lawyers. Compared to a normal job, says one contact, "the hours are terrible." Compared to other big firms, however, "the hours are quite reasonable." The slumping economy has dragged down associate billables. "Although the past year was not as bad in light of the current economic climate, I have had numerous 2,400-plus billable years, which can be quite draining," reports one tired senior associate. "Because of the stagnant Wall Street environment, my hours have been unpredictable, and therefore I don't have a true sense of what the work flow would be in a more normal economy," says a corporate lawyer.

Mayer Brown is one of the few firms that practices a "free-market" work assignment system, where associates seek out cases rather than having work handed to them. The system has its advantages and disadvantages. "It is a so-called free market system here," reports one insider. "In other words, you can choose which partners and areas of specialty you are interested in working with. However, it is a 'swim or sink' approach, especially for junior associates because if fewer partners choose you to be their right hand, you will not meet the minimum 2,100-hour requirement." Watch out for case-hogs. "Because this is a free-market system and bonuses are driven by hours, there can be work distribution problems," complains a junior associate. "Senior and midlevel [associates] have [a] tendency to hog work in order to get maximum bonuses, often at the expense of juniors getting a sufficient workload." Many young attorneys share that feeling of helplessness. "I wish I had more control over my hours," sighs a second-year.

School is in session

Associates complain that training at Mayer Brown has been lacking, but the firm seems to have addressed that issue. "The firm has recently launched a variety of new training initiatives that seem very promising," says one source. While many praise the new system, informal training methods may be lacking. "The firm has implemented a new training program designed to give associates of all levels additional training," says one lawyer. "The firm hired a finance counsel whose part-time responsibilities include designing and implementing the training programs. Most of the training comes from hands-on experience, for which there is no real substitute. The firm may be a little guilty of not spending enough time with junior attorneys to ensure they're getting the maximum benefit from this type of training." Some feel the firm has been doing fine all along without classroom work. "Mayer Brown's corporate group provides the best training of all – trial by fire," reports one corporate associate.

'E' for effort

"I think historically the retention of women has been a problem," reports one Mayer Brown insider. "The firm is making efforts recently, including a seminar discussing issues facing women in the profession. I think mentoring can be better." The seminar gets good reviews. "[Mayer Brown] just sponsored a career symposium for women attorneys, which I thought was very helpful," says one female associate. Insiders appreciate the firm's outstanding maternity leave policy, but there is confusion about the firm's part-time program. Although one associate remarks, "The firm appears to be extremely flexible in permitting associates to work part-time," another complains, "The firm has taken some steps in the right direction, but there does not seem to be a well-articulated policy for part-time once a woman has a baby and how that affects her partnership chances." Generally murky partnership prospects draw the ire of female associates. "It is well known that the chances of a female associate in the New York office being promoted to partner anytime soon are slim to none," according to one source.

Mayer Brown is making improvements in minority hiring and retention, say insiders. "The firm has actively attempted to hire minorities, both at the associate and partner levels and has had some success. The need to remain committed to minority hiring continues," says one source. "I think we have tried to hire qualified minorities, but without a critical mass to begin with, it seems difficult to attract additional candidates," says another associate, singing a familiar refrain. Efforts are underway. "A committee of partners and associates oversees minority recruiting and retention, and the number of minorities has been steadily rising." The firm points out that 10 percent of the firm's associates in U.S. offices are minorities, and of the 123 students in the 2003 summer class, 34 (or 28 percent) are minorities.

Hogan & Hartson L.L.P.

555 Thirteenth Street, NW
Washington, DC 20004
Phone: (202) 637-5600
www.hhlaw.com

LOCATIONS

Washington, DC (HQ) • Baltimore, MD • Boulder, CO •
Colorado Springs, CO • Denver, CO • Los Angeles, CA
• McLean, VA • Miami, FL • New York, NY • Beijing •
Berlin • Brussels • Budapest • London • Moscow • Paris
• Prague • Tokyo • Warsaw

MAJOR DEPARTMENTS/PRACTICES

Antitrust • Communications • Community Services •
Corporate & Securities • Education • Energy •
Environmental • Financial Transactions • FDA •
Government Contracts • Health • Intellectual Property •
International Trade • Labor & Employment • Legislative
• Life Sciences • Litigation (Trial & Appellate) • Privacy
• Private Equity/Venture Capital • Project Finance •
Public Finance • Real Estate • Tax • Technology •
Transportation

THE STATS

No. of attorneys: close to 1,000
No. of offices: 19
Summer associate offers: 61 out of 66 (2002)
Chairman: J. Warren Gorrell, Jr.
Hiring Chair: Robert B. Duncan

BASE SALARY

Washington, DC
1st year: $125,000
2nd year: $135,000
3rd year: $150,000
4th year: $165,000
5th year: $180,000
6th year: $190,000
7th year: $200,000
8th year: $210,000
Summer associate: $2,400/week

UPPERS

- Meritocratic culture
- Respected lobbying practice
- Good family-friendly policies

DOWNERS

- Skimps on bonuses
- Still integrating recent mergers
- Mixed reviews on training

NOTABLE PERKS

- Annual tech allowance of $1,000
- Day care center
- Free coffee and doughnuts
- On-site cafeteria

THE BUZZ
WHAT ATTORNEYS AT OTHER FIRMS ARE SAYING ABOUT THIS FIRM

- "800-pound gorilla of the D.C. legal market"
- "Little fish"
- "Kinder, gentler law firm"
- "Good luck talking to a partner"

RANKING RECAP

Best in Region
#5 - Washington, DC

Best in Practice
#5 (tie) - Antitrust

Best in Diversity
#15 - Diversity for Women

EMPLOYMENT CONTACT

Ms. Ellen M. Purvance
Assoc. Recruitment & Professional Development Dir.
Phone: (202) 637-8601
Fax: (202) 637-5910
E-mail: empurvance@hhlaw.com

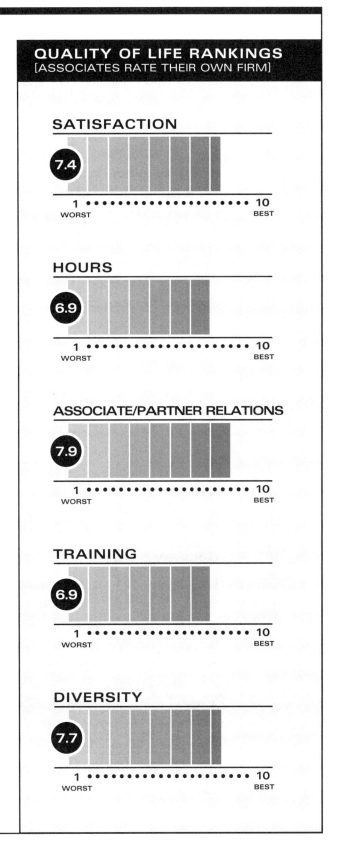

QUALITY OF LIFE RANKINGS
[ASSOCIATES RATE THEIR OWN FIRM]

SATISFACTION
7.4
1 WORST · · · · · · · · · · · · · · · · · · 10 BEST

HOURS
6.9
1 WORST · · · · · · · · · · · · · · · · · · 10 BEST

ASSOCIATE/PARTNER RELATIONS
7.9
1 WORST · · · · · · · · · · · · · · · · · · 10 BEST

TRAINING
6.9
1 WORST · · · · · · · · · · · · · · · · · · 10 BEST

DIVERSITY
7.7
1 WORST · · · · · · · · · · · · · · · · · · 10 BEST

THE SCOOP

Hogan & Hartson is the largest law firm in Washington, D.C., and one of the oldest, too. The firm began a rapid expansion in 1989 and now has nearly 1,000 lawyers in 19 offices worldwide covering four practice areas: business and finance, litigation, intellectual property and regulation.

A '90s boom

In 1904 trial attorney Frank Hogan started a law firm in Washington, D.C. Twenty-one years later, former Internal Revenue Service lawyer Nelson Hartson joined the firm. In 1938 Hartson became a full partner in the renamed Hogan & Hartson.

The firm developed prominent lobbying, tax and litigation practices over the years, but it wasn't until 1989 that Hogan & Hartson developed an international reputation. That year, Bob Odle, a former aide to Texas Congressman Sam Rayburn who had been with the firm since 1966, was elected the first managing partner in Hogan & Hartson's history. Odle initiated an impressive expansion that began in London in 1990. The next year, the firm added offices in Brussels, Belgium, Warsaw, Poland, Paris and Prague. Moscow and Budapest soon followed (1994 and 1996, respectively).

Hogan & Hartson waited until 1998 to open an outpost in New York. In April 2000, H&H merged with Davis, Weber & Edwards, a 45-lawyer litigation boutique with offices in New York and Miami. The New York team grew again in March 2002 when it absorbed Squadron Ellenoff Plesent & Sheinfeld, bringing the total H&H roster in that city to more than 125 attorneys. The union also boosted the Los Angeles team to more than 40 attorneys. The firm also picked up one of Squadron's biggest clients in News Corp., the media conglomerate owned by Rupert Murdoch. In August 2002, H&H opened a Beijing office, the firm's first foray into China.

Beltway insiders

Lobbying may be what Hogan & Hartson does best. The firm's legislative practice is full of Washington insiders. Robert Michel served 38 years as a U.S. representative from Illinois, including 14 years as House Minority Leader. John Porter was also elected to the House from Illinois, serving 21 years. David Skaggs spent 12 years as a U.S. Representative from Colorado. Partner Paul Rogers joined Hogan & Hartson's health policy group after 24 years as a representative from Florida. Clayton Yeutter served as U.S. Trade Representative (where he led the American team of negotiators on the historic U.S.-Canada Free Trade Agreeement, precursor to NAFTA) and Secretary of Agriculture and is of counsel in the firm's international trade practice group. Partner Loretta Lynch, who joined the firm in 2002, was appointed as a director of the Federal Reserve Bank of New York in March 2003.

Hogan in the court

The firm also takes pride in its litigation practice. The firm represented Twentieth Century Fox Home Entertainment, one of several defendants in a Texas antitrust suit accusing the major film studios of conspiring with Blockbuster Video to fix prices in the home video market and drive indie video retailers out of business. After the plaintiffs rested their case in June 2002, the court ordered a directed verdict, finding insufficient evidence of conspiracy and no evidence of causation for the allegations of price discrimination. A similar suit in California also went Hogan & Hartson's way by summary judgment in February 2003.

Hogan & Hartson won a $71 million verdict in April 2002 for opponents of Zimbabwe's ruling party, ZANU-PF, who charged the party with human rights abuses including torture, beatings and executions of dissidents. The case was heard in U.S. federal court under the Alien Tort Claims Act and the Torture Victims Protection Act, American laws designed to hold rogue regimes responsible for violations of international law and human rights. In another major human rights victory that month, H&H collaborated in a Tulia, Texas, court with the NAACP Legal Defense Fund and two other law firms to secure the potential vacation of 38 drug-related convictions based on the likelihood that the testimony of the sole witness, an undercover narcotics officer, was racially biased.

Trust in antitrust

Hogan & Hartson's antitrust practice boasts four partners who have served as commissioners or heads of industry sections at the Federal Trade Commission. Antitrust clients include British Telecommunications (in a joint venture with AT&T) and Netscape (when that firm gave testimony in the government's antitrust suit against Microsoft). The firm also represented Carnival in its proposed acquisition of competing cruise line P&O Princess, handling U.S. antitrust matters and coordinating other competition filings outside the United States and European Union.

Welcome to Hogan & Hartson

A number of attorneys have chosen Hogan & Hartson as their new home. Tom Strickland, a former U.S. Attorney for Colorado, joined the firm's Denver office as a partner in February 2003. That same month, Theodore J. Roper came on board as a partner in the firm's Los Angeles corporate practice, which also welcomed two former partners of the defunct firm of Brobeck, Phleger & Harrison: Paul Hilton in Denver and John E. Hayes, III, in Boulder. (The Denver office is on a roll; in March, it took on white-collar lawyer Daniel Shea as a new partner.) Experienced IP litigator Laurence H. Pretty joined Hogan & Hartson as partner practicing out of Los Angeles in December 2002, one month after H.P. Goldfield joined the firm as a senior international advisor. Goldfield served in several posts in the Reagan administration, including Assistant Secretary of Commerce and Trade Development and Associate Counsel to the President. In June 2002, William Thomson joined the firm's IP practice as a partner. Thomson had been chairman of the bioscience industry practice at McCutchen, Doyle, Brown & Enersen.

GETTING HIRED

Grades count – but not for jerks

Hogan & Hartson seeks law students from the top schools; grades and personality are key. "The firm looks for extremely strong candidates," says one associate. "Law review is helpful but certainly not necessary. One primary consideration is attitude. If you're brilliant but an arrogant jerk, you're not going to get hired. The firm puts a premium on both ability and personality." Clerkships can also get you in the door. "[Hogan & Hartson] definitely looks for the best and brightest," says a source. "The firm looks for those at the top of their class and prefers individuals who will be clerks or have clerked and those with journal experience. Having a good personality is also important."

The slumping economy is making it tougher to get hired at Hogan & Hartson. "The firm is becoming increasingly competitive in terms of hiring because it can be," reports one contact. "Some associates believe that the firm is showing its true colors in this economy – a preference for graduates from Ivy League law schools and other top-10 law schools." One attorney disagrees. "The firm still deludes itself into thinking it hires the crème de la crème from the true top-tier schools," this source claims. "I have not seen any resumes which blew me away, even in a bad economy."

OUR SURVEY SAYS

Good work begets respect

For the most part, associates at Hogan & Hartson find the culture welcoming. "The culture is laid back and, more importantly, a meritocracy," reports one insider. "Everyone is judged by the quality of their work, not by how they act or dress or look or suck up to the boss. Do good work here and you will be respected." The firm is the kind of place where lawyers become friends, though work obligations do limit interaction somewhat. "Associates definitely socialize together," says one contact. "The atmosphere is friendly, but like all big firms, lawyers are busy so lawyers tend not to take time to socialize outside their established group of friends." "Hogan & Hartson is generally laid back in terms of atmosphere, although it is understood that work comes first," agrees another lawyer.

The New York office is still sorting out the recent mergers, as attorneys from three different locations in the city were not brought together in one office until March 2003. "The firm culture for New York associates is schizophrenic," says one attorney based in New York. "There is a perceived culture gap not only between the D.C. home office, but also between the two smaller, New York firms (Davis Weber & Edwards and Squadron Ellenoff) which were merged into Hogan. There is not much interaction between these various camps. Relations are remote, almost frosty."

Another insider agrees, saying the culture at the firm's Big Apple satellite outpost is "confused due to the merger of Davis Weber several years back and Squadron Ellenoff last year. Overall, the firm culture is relatively laid back, polite and humane. D.C. influence makes it a little stiffer than I was used to as a former Squadron person."

It's the economy, stupid

In addition to merger issues, economic conditions may have altered the firm's atmosphere. "In the last 12-18 months, as the market has worsened, there has been a noticeable re-emphasis on bottom line issues and billable hours," gripes one insider. All told, there is some confusion among associates. "The firm seems to be trying to figure out whether the culture should be laid back or more formal," observes one contact. "I sometimes have to catch myself from acting too casually."

Few screamers, but not a total love fest

Hogan & Hartson associates agree that "associate/partner relations are a mixed bag" with many respectful partners, some tough cookies but few screamers. "The partners I work with give me great autonomy on the projects I work for and I feel treat me as an equal," says one source. "In addition to being impeccably professional, the partners with whom I have worked have been kind, constructive and very down-to-earth," concurs another associate. "I'm not sure about the other groups, but our group treats associates like chattel," says an IP lawyer. "No feedback, no idea of career progression, no communication and no feeling of being anything beyond a legal writing instrument." That's left some Hogan & Hartson associates feeling a little paranoid. "While relations are often good on the surface, there is a significant amount of duplicity on the part of the partners. People can be very nice to your face, but very quick to stab you in the back – even when there is no reason to do so. On the plus side, the percentage of screamers – partners who will fly off the handle – is fairly low."

Anger on paydays

Payday is not necessarily a happy day at Hogan & Hartson. "The compensation is already below-market in terms of base compensation, made worse by a stingy bonus policy," reports one insider. "Most associates earned either no bonus or a minimal bonus. The upper and middle ranges of each class year's bonus were contingent on unrealistically high billable hour requirements. What really angered associates was the lack of communication by firm management in announcing the bonus policy and salary structure for the upcoming year – and justifying the partial pay raises due to slow economic performance." (The firm insists that it "is competitive with other similarly situated firms in each place where we have offices.") H&H has a "dual-track" bonus system: associates can bill 1,950 hours and get a top bonus or 1,800 hours and get paid much less. "The bonus system stinks," growls one insider. "The firm screws you for working a lot when others aren't making their hours." A weak market has acted as a drag on bonuses, much to the chagrin of Hogan & Hartson associates. "The firm has stated that bonuses were lower because the market didn't demand that they pay higher bonuses – a comment that makes associates feel unappreciated and like the amount of your bonus is not your worth to the firm, but is what the firm feels it must pay to stay competitive." One insider offers a potential remedy. "In times such as these, I would like to see the firm include all pro bono hours in an associate's total billable requirement."

Balanced lives

Though many consider the two-tier salary system a drag, others insist the system "makes it possible for lawyers to balance their professional and personal lives." But even those insiders who think the system is a good one agree the application of the system is wanting. "There is resentment among the New York associates about the firm's disparate billable requirements for D.C. and New York associates. D.C. associates are offered a choice between a 1,950-hour or 1,800-hour track, while New York associates are held to a single 1,950-hour standard." Late nights and weekends are common, but some feel they're unnecessary. "The number of billable hours is manageable but deceiving," complains one contact. "Due to mismanagement of client expectations and the general lack of respect for personal lives, there are a lot of unnecessary late nights and work over the weekends." Still, the hours seem to be about on par with other big firms, with all the joy and pain that brings. "This is the Catch-22 of the law game," says one insider. "The more hours I work, the more I tend to like my job, since long hours usually means I've been staffed on an interesting project. At the same time, however, the long hours make me sad because I miss my family."

Life at H&H Academy

Hogan & Hartson offers the "H&H Academy" in Washington, D.C. Reviews are mixed. "Hogan & Hartson has an extensive on-site training program that is readily available," says one D.C. insider. "The programs they offer are well put together and useful. Most of the training is on the job, and the level of training you receive is incumbent on partner feedback, which varies greatly partner to partner." Criticism is more common outside of the home office. "The partners have a strong sink-or-swim attitude toward training," says a New York lawyer. "Within the New York office, there is no effort whatsoever to provide formal training opportunities. What's more disturbing is the disdain for which many New York partners hold the firm's formal H&H Academy training sessions." Some say the firm appears to be upping its commitment to training. "I think the firm is really just getting serious about formal training," says one source. "I've been lucky to have had several informal mentors who have taken responsibility for my development. Some haven't been so lucky."

Ladies' choice

Hogan & Hartson has little trouble recruiting and retaining female associates. "I have found this firm to be incredibly welcoming to women, and have had the pleasure of working with many female associates and partners since I started here," says one source. There may be fewer female partners, but the firm seems to be making an effort to keep women happy. In fact, the maternity policy at H&H is so good it seems women are getting pregnant just to take advantage of it. "The firm is great for women," says one insider. "You'd think pregnancy was the flu around here! Expectant mothers are in abundance."

According to Hogan & Hartson insiders, the firm is falling into the typical big-firm pattern with minority associates: a significant effort to recruit and retain minority attorneys without much result. One insider praises "improvement in recent years" but notes there's "still a long way to go." "Hogan & Hartson seems quite eager to promote diversity generally," reports one New York lawyer. "It is lagging a bit in the New York office." Insiders worry there "seems to be a dearth of minorities at the partnership level, and for some reason a lot of the minority associates leave before they even come up for consideration." The firm counters that it has a minority staffing level of 17 percent among U.S. associates (six percent among partners), and more than one-fifth of the last three summer asssociate classes have been minorities as well.

31

Willkie Farr & Gallagher

The Equitable Center
787 Seventh Avenue
New York, NY 10019-6099
Phone: (212) 728-8000
www.willkie.com

LOCATIONS

New York, NY (HQ)
Washington, DC
Brussels
Frankfurt
London
Milan
Paris
Rome

MAJOR DEPARTMENTS/PRACTICES

Bankruptcy
Corporate/Finance
Employee Benefits & Relations
Intellectual Property
Litigation
Real Estate
Tax
Trusts & Estates

THE STATS

No. of attorneys: 530
No. of offices: 8
Summer associate offers: 51 out of 51 (2002)
Chairman: Jack H. Nusbaum
Hiring Attorneys: Jeffrey R. Poss, Thomas H. Golden, William Gump and Loretta Ippolito

BASE SALARY

New York, NY
1st year: $125,000
2nd year: $135,000
3rd year: $150,000
4th year: $170,000
5th year: $190,000
Summer associate: $2,404/week

UPPERS

• "As laid back as it gets"
• Spacious, pleasant offices with great views
• No billable hours requirements

DOWNERS

• Over-market revenues, but mere market bonuses
• Unpredictable shifts in workload
• Cliquish social environment

NOTABLE PERKS

• Bagels every morning, cookies every afternoon
• Attorney lounge with flat-screen TV and DVD
• Dinners and car rides after 8 p.m.
• Subsidized gym memberships

THE BUZZ
WHAT ATTORNEYS AT OTHER FIRMS ARE SAYING ABOUT THIS FIRM

• "Soooooo nice"
• "Not the lifestyle firm they say they are"
• "Nurturing"
• "Mutton dressed up as lamb"

RANKING RECAP

Best in Region
#15 - New York

Best in Practice
#7 - Bankruptcy

Quality of Life
#13 - Offices

EMPLOYMENT CONTACT

Ms. Patricia M. Langlade
Recruiting Coordinator
Phone: (212) 728-8469
Fax: (212) 728-8111
E-mail: planglade@willkie.com

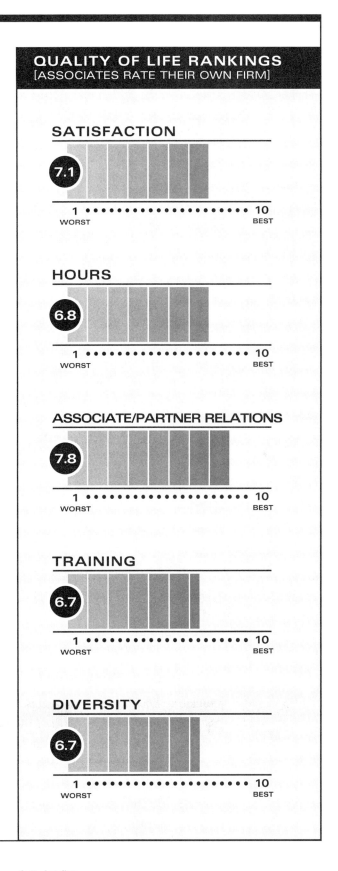

QUALITY OF LIFE RANKINGS
[ASSOCIATES RATE THEIR OWN FIRM]

SATISFACTION

7.1

1 WORST   10 BEST

HOURS

6.8

1 WORST   10 BEST

ASSOCIATE/PARTNER RELATIONS

7.8

1 WORST   10 BEST

TRAINING

6.7

1 WORST   10 BEST

DIVERSITY

6.7

1 WORST   10 BEST

THE SCOOP

Willkie Farr & Gallagher may have made a name for itself providing legal counsel to Donald Trump, but today its best-known client is probably billionaire New York City Mayor Michael Bloomberg. The firm has expanded its international clout in recent years with the addition of several European offices.

Business savvy, political sway

Willkie Farr & Gallagher was founded in 1899 in New York. In just over a century, the firm has grown to include more than 550 attorneys in eight offices, four of them established within the last three years. (Outposts in Frankfurt, Rome and Milan were established in 2000; the firm combined with Brussels-based Dieux & Associes in March 2002). It helped real estate tycoon Donald Trump restructure his holdings when he experienced financial difficulties, and represented brokerage firm Shearson Lehman throughout the 1980s; at one point, Shearson accounted for as much as one-third of the firm's business. Losing Shearson as a client forced Willkie to lay off 20 associates and prompted the partners to decree that henceforth no one client would account for more than 5 percent of the total workload. Two of its most prominent contemporary clients are Adelphia Communications, for whom Willkie is acting as counsel in bankruptcy proceedings, and Simon Property Group, whom the firm represents in their hostile bid to acquire Taubman Center.

The firm has had its moments of political prestige. Name partner Wendell Willkie was selected by the Republicans to run against FDR in the 1940 presidential election. The unlikely candidate, a lifelong Democrat until just months before his nomination, managed to capture nine states, including his native Indiana. More recently, former New York governor Mario Cuomo came to the firm after leaving office in 1995, and once told *New York Lawyer* magazine, "I never even considered any other firm." In August 2002, Cuomo was appointed by a federal judge to mediate a dispute among the parties in 27 asbestos lawsuits filed against Travelers Indemnity Co. and other parties. The plaintiffs, who number in the thousands, alleged that certain Travelers business practices entitle them to tort damages, while Travelers denied the allegations and further argued that the lawsuits have been enjoined under the terms of a separate settlement tied to the ongoing bankruptcy proceedings of the Johns-Manville Corporation.

Working for Mayor Mike

Willkie's association with Michael Bloomberg began several years ago, when his media company retained the firm to defend it – and Bloomberg himself – against charges of sexual harassment by former employees. The firm went on to provide counsel for Bloomberg on a variety of legal matters, including a 2001 case in which Bloomberg News reprinted a phony press release created by a disgruntled investor seeking revenge against Emulex when he lost money trying to sell the stock short. (The case was dismissed, as proof was not established that Bloomberg had fraudulent intent in distributing what it took to be an authentic document.) When Bloomberg was elected mayor of New York City, Willkie partner Benito Romano found himself in an unusual bind. Romano also works part-time on the city's Conflict of Interests Board, which had to sort through any potential conflicts raised by the billionaire mayor's holdings in companies that do business with the city. Romano's obvious conflict required him to recuse himself from the ongoing review process.

Steel driving men

Willkie serves as lead counsel to 17 nations that have been accused of dumping their steel products on the American market at artificially low prices. In August 2002 proceedings, the International Trade Commission offered temporary relief to those nations, when it denied the Commerce Department's efforts on behalf of the U.S. steel industry to get new tariffs imposed on cold-rolled steel, which is used to make automobiles and appliances. The ITC rejected the tariffs on the grounds that no conclusive proof existed that the low-priced foreign steel had adversely affected American steel producers.

Strike three, you're out!

Willkie partner Robert J. Kheel, the counsel to the office of Major League Baseball's commissioner, successfully faced down the heavy hitters representing former owners of the Montreal Expos in a federal racketeering lawsuit. The plaintiffs accused baseball commissioner Bud Selig and other league officials of cooking up a scheme with one-time Expos general managing partner Jeffrey Loria, who sold his stake in the team to buy the Florida Marlins. The parties allegedly schemed to run the Expos franchise into the ground to force dissolution or relocation to a potentially more lucrative market. (Maybe they got the idea after watching *Major League*.) The litigation was stayed in November 2002, when a federal court judge ruled the plaintiffs would have to resolve their differences with Loria before they could pursue any additional complaints against other parties.

Big on German telecom

In May 2002, Willkie's Frankfurt office won a landmark ruling before the German Regulatory Authority for Telecommunications and Post. Working on behalf of the German divisions of MCI Worldcom and UUNET, the firm had brought an action against Deutsche Telekom over its deliberate delay in providing telecommunications competitors with leased phone and data lines. In the most stringent ruling in the regulatory authority's history, Deutsche Telekom was ordered to make the lines available in a timely fashion and threatened with high fines if it continued to drag its feet in the matter.

Fresh off that victory, the Frankfurt office went on to represent several Internet service providers (ISPs) based in the German state of Northrhine Westfalia. The ISPs were fighting orders from Düsseldorf authorities to create filters blocking their customers from viewing certain web sites, many of which were owned and operated in the United States. The case is expected to set a precedent within Germany concerning the responsibility of ISPs and other access providers for third-party content.

GETTING HIRED

Levelheaded levity

"If there is one quality they look for more than anything else" at Willkie Farr, says one recent hire, "it is good judgment, which will come through in social as well as work settings." Other associates stress the importance of social compatibility as well, suggesting "the firm puts an emphasis on personality as much as possible" and seeks out "people who will be fun on a social occasion, but who will take their work seriously."

Although there's a "large Ivy League contingent," the firm "hires from around the country." Says one second-year associate, "If you went to a top law school or a lower-tier school and were on law review or had top grades, getting hired is not a problem." A first-year advises, "Interviewers tell it like it is around here and are mostly trying to determine if you fit the mold." Another recent hire recalls, "My interviews were extremely conversational and comfortable. I got a summer associate position through on-campus recruiting, and the whole process was very smooth."

OUR SURVEY SAYS

Intense but lively

"As big New York law firms go," a second-year associate reports, "Willkie is as laid back as it gets." The prevailing mood is "friendly and social but competitive." A first-year describes his coworkers as "the best kinds of people who go to law school: diverse interests, smart and still able to have a good time." A midlevel litigator admits, "Sometimes, the urgency of work can create an intense environment, but that is the exception, not the norm." A sophomore agrees, "People genuinely enjoy working together, and this creates a relaxed environment, even when the hours get long."

"All my professional relationships and personal relationships are extremely positive," says an enthusiastic first-year. "My best friends are at the firm, and I try not to date outside the firm. If the firm had a bar, lounge and restaurant I wouldn't have much reason to leave." But the "quirky" environment "can tend towards cliquishness" and, says a midlevel corporate attorney, echoing the observations of lawyers across the nation, "the atmosphere has been much less pleasant since the economy slowed down."

Getting along

"When the economy was good, associates were treated with a lot of respect," a midlevel corporate attorney recalls. But, says a senior associate, "the partners and very senior associates have become a lot more uptight and almost sneaky." A third-year describes "a handful of young corporate partners" who treat associates' complaints with a "get-used-to-it" attitude, but "the senior leadership among partners does not appear to subscribe to this view," he notes comfortingly. "I find the partners approachable, intelligent and very direct," a senior attorney states. "They are terrific attorneys, and it is an honor to be able to learn from them."

In addition to the many CLE seminars Willkie offers, "junior associates who show initiative are permitted to work above their level on deals," a midlevel associate reports. "Almost anyone here will take the time to review an assignment with you," a first-year says, "and you can never ask too many questions." Another rookie chimes in, " I have learned something new on every deal that I have worked on." But "the actual training any given associate gets varies significantly in practice," says a senior corporate attorney. "Uniformity could be improved."

"At least you're working with people you like"

"Too much to do, too many hours, too many nights and weekends," sighs an IP associate. "But what do you expect for what they pay us?" Indeed, many Willkie-ers say their hours are just plain overwhelming. But some admit it could be worse. One source says his hours are "better than many of my fellow associates both in my firm and at other firms. But the fact of the matter is that if something needs to get done and it needs to be done by Monday morning, you can expect to be here all weekend." Then again, asks a Willkie insider, "Who isn't working long hours? The best you can ask for is an environment that if you have to work late, at least you're working with people you like." Another sophomore associate has "enough ownership over my projects that I can manage my schedule in such a way that I can get out of the office when I need to," and several associates confirm partners are "respectful of your time." ("Vacations are sacrosanct," confides an insider.) And a first-year real estate attorney notes gladly, "When there is no work to do, it is 100 percent okay to walk out the door at 6 p.m."

Enough to get by

Willkie "pays what the top 10 percent pays after the other top 10 percent pays it," says a senior attorney at the firm. "Never more, never less." Associates firm-wide agree their salaries are "consistent with other New York firms." But, adds one first-year, "sometimes to the detriment of associates." It seems that, after a self-declared year of record revenues, Willkie's partners "followed the market instead of granting higher bonuses." A second-year litigator comments, "Everyone outside large New York law firms cannot believe that associates would complain about their compensation, but the fact is the partners are still making many times what any of the associates make, and the associates kill themselves for the partners." A senior corporate attorney

asks, "Why were bonuses less than the year before and not reflective of one of the greatest years at the firm? It is odd that the partners often forget who helps to earn the majority of the revenues."

Building diversity

Women are "more than welcome" at Willkie. "Incoming associate classes seem to have more women than men or are at least equal," observes a woman in her second year with the firm, while another source notes that female attorneys "dominate the associate ranks of the litigation department." One associate predicts, "The future of the firm is the rising ranks of women associates." But a woman who just arrived at Willkie says that while it may be "great in the hiring area," the firm "still feels like a boys' club." A midlevel corporate attorney confirms, "Women are constantly told that they are not aggressive and confident enough, even if they are good attorneys." Another young woman at the firm backs her up, observing, "Getting pregnant is a career ender." A male associate offers a potential explanation for the perceived lack of mentorship. "All of the female partners got to that point by being workaholics," he says, "and subscribing to the view that work at the firm comes first and everything else after that."

In contrast, the associates have little to say about Willkie's hiring and retention of minority associates, other than noting "the ranks are still somewhat homogenous" despite "consistent efforts." A senior corporate attorney addresses the problem: "Without a good base of minority partners," she muses, "or even senior associates for prospective associates to look toward, many interviewees are discouraged from coming here." Willkie's attorneys were equally tightlipped when it came to gays and lesbians; although they describe the firm as "open," it's also said "there aren't too many openly gay people around."

A room with a view

"It doesn't get any better" than Willkie's midtown Manhattan location, associates insist. "The offices are spacious and modern with lots of light" and "truly remarkable and impressive" interior design, not to mention "most of the floors have a very good view of Central Park." A midlevel associate exclaims, "I have more extra space in my office than my apartment." A second-year litigator rains on the parade, interjecting, "We seem to share offices much longer than my friends at other firms." And a newly arrived attorney finds it "embarrassing that our firm is notorious for being cheap about the small stuff." She explains, "Everybody gripes about the fact that there is only one water cooler in the entire office and that we are all dehydrated because Uncle Willkie is frugal."

"Tons of pro bono"

Willkie offers "tons of pro bono opportunities," including full-time externships in public interest law offices in New York. A pro bono coordinator sends out regular e-mails with potential new cases for associates. "One month I worked almost solely on pro bono," says an IP attorney, "and nobody said a word about it." Pro bono work is "not looked down upon" and counts towards billables. "We have taken on a tremendous amount of 9/11 cases," a second-year associate reports. Other insiders describe a laissez-faire attitude toward pro bono cases. "There is no affirmative push to work on pro bono matters," claims one source, "and I never hear partners discuss pro bono matters they're working on."

Clifford Chance LLP

200 Park Avenue
New York, NY 10166
Phone: (212) 878-8000
www.cliffordchance.com

MAJOR DEPARTMENTS/PRACTICES

Corporate Finance/Securities • Banking & Financial
Restructuring, including Project Finance • Financial
Products (including Derivatives and Structured Products)
• Litigation & Dispute Resolution (including Securities/
White Collar Crime, Antitrust, Intellectual Property,
Reinsurance, International Arbitration and Media/First
Amendment) • Mergers & Acquisitions (including Private
Equity and Corporate Technology) • Real Estate Finance

LOCATIONS

Los Angeles, CA • New York, NY • Palo Alto, CA •
San Diego, CA • San Francisco, CA • Washington, DC
• Amsterdam • Bangkok • Barcelona • Beijing • Berlin •
Brussels • Budapest • Dubai • Dusseldorf • Frankfurt •
Hong Kong • London • Luxembourg • Madrid •
Milan • Moscow • Munich • Padua • Paris • Prague •
Rome • Sao Paulo • Shanghai • Singapore • Tokyo •
Warsaw

THE STATS

No. of attorneys: 3,700
No. of offices: 32
Summer associate offers: 39 out of 39 (2002)
Managing Partner: John K. Carroll (The Americas)
Hiring Attorney: David Meister

BASE SALARY

New York, NY; Washington, DC
1st year: $125,000
2nd year: $135,000
3rd year: $150,000
4th year: $170,000
5th year: $190,000
6th year: $205,000
7th year: $220,000
8th year: $235,000
Summer associate: $2,404/week

UPPERS

• No more billable hours requirement!
• Glamorous, international atmosphere
• "Huge steps" taken to address concerns in associate memo

DOWNERS

• Little in the way of informal mentoring
• Lousy office space
• "Shameful" record regarding diversity

NOTABLE PERKS

• Two condos in Florida that associates can use for a week each year for free
• Munificent gym membership policy
• Generous technology allowance

THE BUZZ
WHAT ATTORNEYS AT OTHER FIRMS ARE SAYING ABOUT THIS FIRM

• "Didn't you get the memo?"
• "Innovative"
• "Solid and reliable"
• "McFirm"

RANKING RECAP

Best in Region
#20 - New York

Best in Practice
#6 - Antitrust

EMPLOYMENT CONTACT

Ms. Carolyn Older Bortner
Manager of Legal Recruiting
Phone: (212) 878-8252
Fax: (212) 878-8375
E-mail: Carolyn.bortner@cliffordchance.com

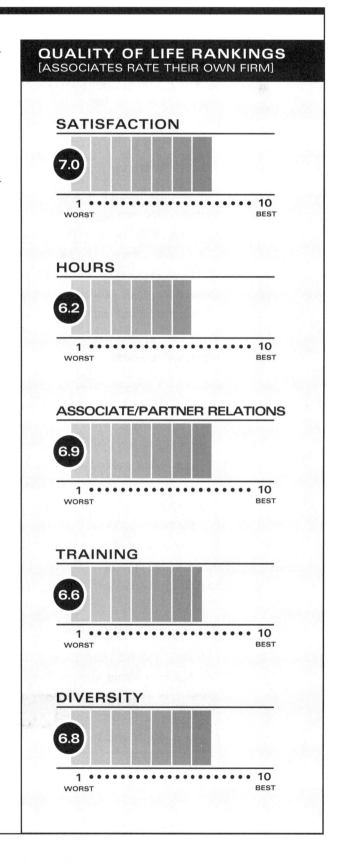

QUALITY OF LIFE RANKINGS
[ASSOCIATES RATE THEIR OWN FIRM]

SATISFACTION

7.0

1 • • • • • • • • • • • • • • • • • 10
WORST   BEST

HOURS

6.2

1 • • • • • • • • • • • • • • • • • 10
WORST   BEST

ASSOCIATE/PARTNER RELATIONS

6.9

1 • • • • • • • • • • • • • • • • • 10
WORST   BEST

TRAINING

6.6

1 • • • • • • • • • • • • • • • • • 10
WORST   BEST

DIVERSITY

6.8

1 • • • • • • • • • • • • • • • • • 10
WORST   BEST

THE SCOOP

Clifford Chance may have hit the news because of a scathing internal memo, but people in the know realize that the firm deserves to be known for much more than that. The global firm Clifford Chance is one of the largest law firms in the world and doesn't disguise its aims to be the most prestigious firm in the world as well.

To the top!

"We have not hidden in any way our ambition to be the world's premier global law firm," James Benedict, then managing partner of Clifford Chance's Americas operations, told *The American Lawyer* in 2002. And it looks like the firm is well on its way. This member of the "magic circle" of top London law firms was created in 1987 and was the largest firm in the United Kingdom at the time of its creation. Today Clifford Chance employs 3,700 lawyers worldwide and 650 in the United States alone. The firm has made strong inroads into the United States in the past few years and became the first major global law firm to expand into California in 2002.

Headin' West

One of the biggest stories in the world of law this last year was the bankruptcy and dissolution of Brobeck, Phleger & Harrison, once one of the West Coast's brightest legal lights. Clifford Chance had a tangential role in this legal drama. In May 2002, Brobeck ousted its former chairman, Tower Snow, while he was in discussions with Clifford Chance about taking a group of partners over to the firm. Two weeks later, Snow took the plunge, along with a group of 16 partners and approximately 40 associates. The move was a huge boost to Clifford Chance's plans to tap into the California legal market; the partners counted such California heavyweights as Cisco Systems and Sun Microsystems among their clients. The firm says those partners retained about 90 percent of their clients in the move to Clifford Chance. Clifford Chance subsequently opened its California offices in San Francisco, Palo Alto, Los Angeles and San Diego in July 2002. (Brobeck filed for bankruptcy in January 2003.)

An energizing deal

Clifford Chance put together a team from its Sao Paulo, New York, Washington, D.C., London and San Francisco offices to assist Petrobras, Brazil's largest provider of oil, gas and other energy products, in its acquisition of Perez Companc, the largest independently owned oil company in Latin America. The transaction, valued at $1.03 billion, was named M&A Deal of the Year by *Latin Finance Magazine*.

To Russia, with business development

In August 2002, Clifford Chance opted to move Michael Cuthbert, a senior banking partner, over to the firm's Moscow office. Along with the co-managing partners, Cuthbert will manage the strategic development of the office. Why the sudden interest in Moscow? The firm detects an increased interest in investments in Russia after a slow period following that country's economic collapse in 1998.

A memo-rable incident

After a shocked Clifford Chance came in dead last for associate satisfaction in *American Lawyer*'s annual associate survey, the firm asked its personnel committee to present some feedback from associates. The six New York-based associates on the committee took their task to heart – and then some. The committee members held a "town hall" meeting, commissioned a survey of firm associates and ultimately issued a memo to all of the firm's U.S. lawyers, outlining the grievances of Clifford Chance associates.

The memo went on to cite several areas of discontent at the firm. The first listed – and the grievance to attract the most subsequent attention from the media – was the billable-hour guideline of 2,420 hours per year to receive the maximum bonus, which included a 2,200 "hard billable" component and an additional 220 hours of "soft billable" hours "suggested." Associates were quoted in the memo as feeling that the soft billable contribution was "not actually counted in any meaningful way, but was rather a stick to coerce associates to do work for which they would receive no remuneration." The memo also stated that an associate suggested an hours-based incentive system could lead to overbilling. Other complaints focused on a somewhat murky assignment system, an inadequate review process, imperfect communications between associates and partners, a lack of support for pro bono work and insufficient training.

The memo caused a sensation; news reports tended to focus on associates' perception that they had to meet the billable guideline and the suggestion that meeting these perceived expectations could lead to inflated time recording by associates. The firm denied adamantly that it encouraged associates to pad hours. It also later confirmed that no clients had expressed serious concern about the memo, and that in fact clients were generally highly supportive. The firm subsequently set up a task force to address the concerns raised in the memo and scrapped its billable-hours requirement in December 2002. The firm has also restructured its assignment process, encouraged associates to do pro bono work and taken steps that have already fostered enhanced communication between partners and associates.

Loved by clients

Though Clifford Chance may not have come out on top of the above-mentioned associate survey, the firm did smashingly in another survey in 2002 – the annual survey of *Global Counsel* magazine, which surveys 5,000 companies for comments on law firms every year. The companies surveyed named Clifford Chance the best global law firm. The survey was published in November 2002. The firm was also the only law firm ranked in the PriceWaterhouseCoopers/*Financial Times* survey of most respected companies, ranking third in the financial services sector after Citigroup and AIG. Additionally, Clifford Chance was listed for the second year in a row among the "Firms with the Most Top 10 Rankings" in *The American Lawyer* 2002 Corporate Scorecard with seven top-10 rankings this year.

Tying the knot in Singapore

Clifford Chance is expanding in Asia as well as the United States. In November 2002, Clifford Chance entered into a joint partnership with Singapore's WongPartnership, one of the top five corporate law firms in Singapore. The partnership created a joint law venture dubbed Clifford Chance Wong. Several other JLVs have been created since the Singaporean government introduced new regulations in May 2000 allowing foreign firms to operate in the tidy city-state. Although JLVs don't have a fabulous track record in Singapore (two other JLVs, Shearman & Sterling Stamford and White & Case and Colin Ng & Partners, have dissolved since their creation), Clifford Chance is confident that the venture will succeed. The firm indicated to the *Business Times* of Singapore that it would work toward a merger with WongPartnership if Singapore regulations were to allow such a merger in the future.

Merrily hiring

Clifford Chance crooked its finger and lured George Schieren, head lawyer for Merrill Lynch's broker-dealer unit and a member of Merrill Lynch & Co.'s Executive Committee, to join its New York office in March 2003. Schieren is a securities litigation partner at Clifford Chance, where odds are he will defend Merrill Lynch once in a while. The firm also added two lateral M&A partners in 2002 – Brian Hoffman and Richard Pritz – and financial products partner Richard Coffman in addition to the group of partners in California.

GETTING HIRED

More and more selective

Clifford Chance is a firm that's quickly building its brand in the United States, and the hiring criteria reflect the firm's growing American prestige. "The firm, in an effort to boost its elite status, has become much more selective in the recruiting process," says one second-year associate. "If I interviewed with the firm today, I probably wouldn't get an offer." California-based associates claim that West Coast offices are especially selective.

An associate in the San Francisco office says that in the first first-year class after the office was created, "nine people were hired after over 500 resumes were collected and over 100 people interviewed." Confirms another associate, "We interview a lot of people and reject most of them for one reason or another." Not everyone is so selective in the callback: Some insiders say they look for candidates who are "nice to work with" and "not freaks" in the final interview.

The hiring process for first-year associates consists of an interview on campus, and, for candidates selected to continue to the next round, a half-day at a Clifford Chance office.

The firm is said to look at a "wide variety of law schools." Associates say that Clifford Chance adores "well-rounded candidates who are not only strong in their legal backgrounds but also in their ability to communicate effectively." Fluency in several languages doesn't hurt either, but is certainly not a requirement. Law students should know that "summer classes are small right now, and spots are only going to the people everyone really likes."

OUR SURVEY SAYS

The world of Clifford Chance, post-memo

Clifford Chance has focused on its internal culture since associate dissatisfaction was laid bare in the October 2002 memo. Insiders say they're seeing results in Clifford Chance's New York office. "Prior to the infamous memo, socializing was often limited to an attorney's departure gathering. Now, at least on a floor by floor basis, partners appear to be making an effort to at least appear more sociable," volunteers one New Yorker. Those looking for a social life will find one at Clifford Chance in New York. "There are always people to do things with outside of the office if you are so inclined, and it is an unwritten rule that work is not discussed during social activities," says one lawyer. One insider, however, comments that "the lack of a cafeteria or other meeting place" cuts down on workday camaraderie. This issue is being addressed: A cafeteria that seats several hundred is planned when the firm moves to the Deustche Bank building in the spring of 2004.

Despite the improvements, New York associates give Clifford Chance mixed marks for its internal culture. Several New York associates claim the atmosphere in the office is "cliquish, "political" and even "increasingly British." "The East Coast offices are struggling to transition from an uptight hierarchy to a more relaxed and friendly atmosphere," discloses one associate. A junior associate remarks, "The firm culture can be characterized as 'medium' uptight, although there is a fairly friendly environment and there is never the feeling that someone is looking over your shoulder." But that's not to say all New York associates are dissatisfied. A midlevel in the New York office reports, "Partners have made a clear effort to address associate concerns regarding mentoring, [the] assignment system and partner-associate relations. There is a real sense that the firm turned the corner and partners are focused on developing associates professionally, which makes for greater job satisfaction." A second-year tells us that the office is quite "friendly," although "culture varies from group to group." Additionally, this source says, "It is a very social place, and many lawyers here are friends and socialize outside of the office as well as in the office."

Clifford Chance's West Coast offices, according to insiders, possess a markedly different atmosphere. "The San Francisco office is very congenial and laid back. Everyone from partners to staff calls each other by their first name and there is an unspoken open-door policy. Many of the partners have been close friends for decades and the associates socialize occasionally. There is no pressure among the associates to socialize outside of work, although many do," says one Californian associate. Another speaks positively of the "feminine vibe" in the San Francisco office.

Raves another San Franciscan, "The partners in the San Francisco office care very much for the associates, and it is obvious in everything they do. The attorneys not only socialize with one another but also take a genuine interest in each other's lives outside work. From a partner throwing a baby shower for an associate, to everyone going out together after the Christmas party, we all enjoy working and socializing together. It makes for a positive work environment."

An hourly weight lifted

One of the major complaints in the October 2002 memo centered on the firm's billable-hours guideline. That standard has now been lifted, to the joy and relief of many Clifford Chance associates. Raves one midlevel insider: "Good work requires long hours at any firm, but I am much more inclined to work more efficiently now that the hours requirement is gone. The feeling, right or wrong, that being a merely acceptable associate meant 50 weeks of 50 billables each was, frankly, depressing. Now I believe that it's my work product, rather than pure time, that partners respect." Another insider reports receiving a bonus while billing far less than the previous 2,420 minimum. "I got a full bonus last year on under 1,300 hours. I think they were really serious about putting their reliance on billables behind them." The firm has taken additional steps to alleviate pressure on associates. An assignment partner in each group at the firm has "been assigned the task of staffing cases in an equitable way, balancing out hours, experience, and so on." These assignment partners meet regularly to ensure the firm is applying consistent and effective policies and practices.

The firm also makes it easy for associates to spend less time in the office – even if that doesn't mean working less. "Because of the firm's superior external networking access capabilities, we are able to work from home as if we are in the office," says a Californian associate. Clifford Chance is said to "aggressively distribute" fun networking technology like BlackBerrys and laptops.

Some insiders cite continued pressure to bill. "Although the firm has dropped the 2,200 [hours] requirement – a step in the right direction – I still feel pressure to work all the time. And often I do," laments one New York associate. Another insider notes that partners still appreciate high billers. "Partners have this strange grin on their faces when they see you toiling on their way home," reports one hard-working lawyer.

In general, however, Clifford Chance lawyers seem grateful for the lack of a billable-hours requirement and philosophical about their schedules. One newbie muses, "Some days I'm here until 5 p.m., other days until 5 a.m. It just depends. Typically, I am out on the elevator by 7:30

p.m. I've had to stay past midnight maybe 10 days since I've started working at Clifford Chance. The view on the hours depends on whether you are speaking from the point of view of a lawyer working in a big New York law firm, in which case these hours sound pretty manageable, or from the point of view of a typical working person, in which case staying past midnight may seem like a travesty."

Partner, partner

One source of complaint in the October 2002 memo was the treatment of associates by partners. Clifford Chance associates had plenty to say about this topic in our survey. In general, the news is good. "Partners have taken a huge step forward in addressing associates' concerns regarding partner-associate relations. Recent examples include allowing associates to take unpaid sabbaticals, assisting associates that relocate to other cities [through] alternative employment, if the firm does not have an office in that city and encouraging greater social interaction between partners and associates by sponsoring firm social gatherings," notes one associate. Another associate based in New York claims, "There is a real sense that the firm has turned a corner, and partners are focused on developing associates professionally, which makes for greater job satisfaction." Marvels one junior associate, "Things have changed a lot in the last year at the firm. Partners have stopped me in the hallways and introduced themselves."

Not all partners have assumed peachy attitudes since the memo was released. "Some partners are less friendly, more reclusive and at least one has a reputation that seems out of sync with the firm culture, but there is rarely, if ever, a problem between partners and associates." Some associates hold the depiction of partners in the memo to have been "an exaggeration."

Training too formal

Clifford Chance seems to be one of those rare law firms with excellent formal training but less than stellar informal training. (The reverse is normally the case.) "Partners call associates with an assignment," moans one associate, "and usually give little to no guidance let alone training. Associates are forced to train themselves through trial and error." "There is really no open-door mentoring policy," gripes another insider. On the other hand, "the firm has been making great efforts to institutionalize its training process, especially in the capital markets area. They have mandatory seminars for first-year associates, some advanced seminars and they bring in outside experts to train more senior lawyers on different topics." Another associate crows, "There's more training at this place than army boot camp. If you want to be trained, the opportunity is here. In particular, I attended the two-day Lawyers' Development Course for midlevels this past fall, and it was the best kind of on-the-job training that I have ever experienced or even heard of in a law firm setting." Training for all junior associates includes Financial Statement Basics, Ethics and Professional Practice and Presentation Skills. There is also a curriculum for senior associates that includes classes on client focus, advanced presentation skills and other custom training based on individual needs. Additionally, the litigation practice has introduced a training curriculum to support the entire career development cycle of litigation associates.

Perks are appreciated

Clifford Chance associates are pleased to discuss the array of perks they receive at the firm. "The gym membership program is outstanding – no initiation fee, 30 percent discount on monthly fee and then the firm pays for half of the lowered fee. Can't be beat," says one fit attorney. The firm also offers "free dinner for you and your significant other if you have the unfortunate pleasure of billing more than 250 hours in a month." The firm also possesses "two very nice condos in Florida that associates can use for a week each year for free." Those who think their salaries are the biggest perk are satisfied, though one insider carps: "[Clifford Chance is] usually late in announcing bonuses and don't pay bonus until mid-February, unlike other firms who pay it in December."

Trading spaces

Clifford Chance associates agree on one thing: Their office space is lousy. New York's offices come in for lots of criticism from associates who deplore their interior, windowless rooms. "You share an office your first two years, then move into an inside office with no window," grumbles one New Yorker. A junior associate waxes eloquent in his disdain of the sunless facilities. "To further cut off any chance of sunlight, the firm built suites so that when one is walking around the halls, the only sun one sees is a sliver of a sun ray that peeks through a partner's office." But associates shouldn't complain too much—great changes are on the horizon. The firm has already revised its policy on smoking in the office: As of March 30, 2003, all smoking in New York offices and work locations has been prohibited. Best of all, "We are moving to the Deutsche Bank building in May of 2004 and expect to have more room and more windowed offices there than we currently have," cheers an associate. London offices are termed "Spartan" and "filled with crap furniture." "Even partners share offices in London," remarks one insider in that office. (Firm officials remind us that it's a commonly accepted practice among firms in London for partners to share office space with trainee solicitors.) San Franciscan associates, meanwhile, recently moved into a "lovely" new office after an extended stay in a "less than stellar" rented space.

"We interview a lot of people
and reject most of them for
one reason or another."

– Clifford Chance associate

Boies, Schiller & Flexner LLP

333 Main Street
Armonk, NY 10504-1710
Phone: (914) 749-8200
www.bsfllp.com

LOCATIONS

Armonk, NY (HQ)
Albany, NY
Fort Lauderdale, FL
Hanover, NH
Hollywood, FL
Miami, FL
New York, NY
Oakland, CA
Orlando, FL
Palm Beach Gardens, FL
Washington, DC

MAJOR DEPARTMENTS/PRACTICES

Antitrust • Appellate • Arbitration • Business Crimes •
Class Actions • Commercial Litigation • Corporate •
Corporate Governance • Employment/FLSA •
Environmental • First Amendment • Health Care •
Intellectual Property • Internal Investigation •
International • Product Liability • Reorganization/Work-
outs • Securities

THE STATS

No. of attorneys: 170
No. of offices: 11
Summer associate offers: 12 of 13 (2002)
Managing Partners: David Boies, Donald L. Flexner and
Jonathan D. Schiller
Hiring Partners: Robin A. Henry (Armonk), Amy J.
Mauser and Carl J. Nichols (DC), Kirsten R. Gillibrand
(NY) and Mark J. Heise (Florida)

THE BUZZ
WHAT ATTORNEYS AT OTHER FIRMS ARE SAYING ABOUT THIS FIRM

- "David Boies is the man"
- "Top-heavy"
- "The place to be for high-profile litigation"
- "Don't believe the hype"

BASE SALARY

Armonk, NY
1st year: $138,000
Summer associate: $2,500/week (2L),
$2,100/week (1L)

UPPERS

- Cutting-edge, high-profile cases
- Immediate responsibility if you want it
- Casual atmosphere

DOWNERS

- "Opaque" bonus system
- Lack of formal training
- No pro bono program in place

NOTABLE PERKS

- Annual retreat now held at Atlantis (families included)
- Occasional happy hours
- Laptops for all associates

RANKING RECAP

Best in Region
#17 - New York

Best in Practice
#6 - Litigation
#9 (tie) - Antitrust

EMPLOYMENT CONTACTS

See list of hiring partners.

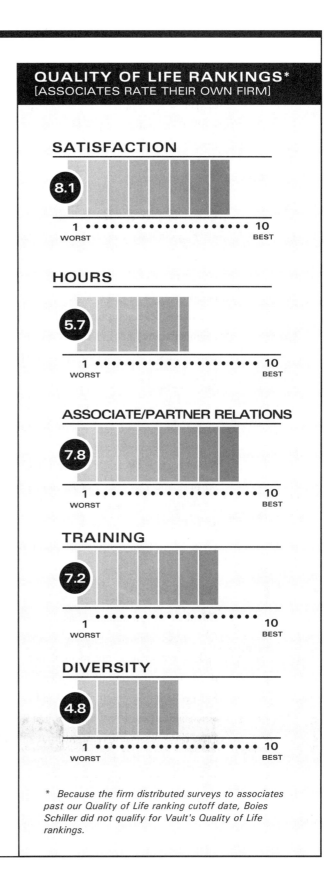

QUALITY OF LIFE RANKINGS*
[ASSOCIATES RATE THEIR OWN FIRM]

SATISFACTION

8.1

1 • • • • • • • • • • • • • • • • • 10
WORST   BEST

HOURS

5.7

1 • • • • • • • • • • • • • • • • • 10
WORST   BEST

ASSOCIATE/PARTNER RELATIONS

7.8

1 • • • • • • • • • • • • • • • • • 10
WORST   BEST

TRAINING

7.2

1 • • • • • • • • • • • • • • • • • 10
WORST   BEST

DIVERSITY

4.8

1 • • • • • • • • • • • • • • • • • 10
WORST   BEST

* Because the firm distributed surveys to associates past our Quality of Life ranking cutoff date, Boies Schiller did not qualify for Vault's Quality of Life rankings.

THE SCOOP

Boies, Schiller & Flexner LLP, already highly regarded for its expert handling of class-action lawsuits and complex commercial litigation, has developed a new strength in the post-Enron legal market: defending corporations accused of financial malfeasance. As always, the young firm's reputation rests largely on the laurels of superstar litigator David Boies.

Hotshot

Boies, Schiller & Flexner LLP was founded by one of the best-known and most sought-after attorneys in the country. After graduating magna cum laude from Yale Law School in 1966, David Boies moved to New York, signed up with tony Cravath, Swaine & Moore and made partner within six years. Boies made a name for himself with several high-profile cases. He successfully defended IBM over the course of a 13-year antitrust case, and represented CBS and Mike Wallace in a libel suit brought by retired army general William Westmoreland. He landed $200 million for Continental Airlines in a RICO suit against United and American Airlines, then counseled the FDIC during the savings and loan crisis and helped them get back $1 billion from junk bond king Michael Milken.

In 1997, Boies left Cravath and persuaded friend Jonathan Schiller, a powerhouse attorney in his own right, to start a new law firm with him outside Manhattan. (The firm's Armonk, N.Y., headquarters is located near Boies' Westchester home.) The firm has grown by leaps and bounds. Name partner Donald Flexner joined in 1999, bringing along blue-chip clients like Northwest Airlines and DuPont. Recent expansion by the firm in New York City, Miami and Oakland has come, in part, by means of swallowing up small firms like New York's Barrett Gravante Carpinello & Stern (20 attorneys in June 2000) and Florida's Zack Kosnitzky (30 attorneys in April 2002). Boies Schiller currently boasts more than 170 attorneys in 11 offices around the country.

In the news

David Boies' prominence has only accelerated since creating the firm that bears his name. The federal government hired him as special prosecutor to tackle the antitrust case against Microsoft, and he represented presidential hopeful and former VP Al Gore (free of charge) in the legal wranglings following the presidential election in 2000. More recently, the firm was involved in an independent investigation into the finances at Tyco International. Some suggested that Boies took a personal interest in the firm's handling of the investigation; shortly after Tyco hired the firm in June 2002, the word went out that Boies had been behind the ouster of the conglomerate's chief counsel, Mark Belnick, who Tyco officials publicly considered unwilling or unable to conduct a fair investigation into executives' use of corporate funds for personal gain.

From auction houses to modeling agencies

Boies Schiller has rapidly built a reputation for its ability to win big on behalf of class-action plaintiffs. The firm wrestled $512 million from Christie's and Sotheby's in settling an antitrust suit against the two auction houses, and made vitamin makers cough up $1.1 billion to resolve price-fixing charges. In July 2002, the firm filed another class-action suit on behalf of six fashion models. The models accuse eight top New York agencies of colluding for nearly three decades to fix their fees and charging twice the legal limit in commissions for lining up photo shoots and other services.

For the defense

Boies Schiller also works the defense side of the room. Hillenbrand Industries, the nation's largest maker of hospital beds, retained Donald Flexner in September 2002 to handle the appeal of a $173.6 million antitrust verdict against the company. Shortly thereafter, the firm was hired by NASCAR to fight off a lawsuit accusing it of monopolistic practices, particularly the refusal to grant one competitor-owned racetrack a date on the racing organization's Winston Cup Series schedule.

In the Fall of 2002, Qwest Communications called upon Jonathan Schiller to defend the telecommunications company against allegations of accounting fraud and corporate malfeasance. The case, which is pending, has become one of the largest putative federal securities fraud class actions and parallel lawsuits brought in multiple states. Schiller has also represented Qwest in related proceedings before the SEC, the House of Representatives Committee on Energy and Commerce and the House of Representatives Committee on Financial Services.

Health care

Boies Schiller scored another victory in December 2002 when pharmaceutical manufacturer Merck and its subsidiary, pharmacy-benefits manager Medco Health, agreed to a $42.5 million out-of-court settlement to shut down a lawsuit accusing Medco of overcharging its clients. (The settlement is subject to court approval.) Health plans and corporate employers rely on Medco to process prescription-drug claims and to negotiate pricing deals with drugstores and drug manufacturers. But, the lawsuit alleged, Medco was pocketing most of the savings for itself – and in some cases promoting higher-priced Merck drugs over competing medications. In addition to the cash award Boies Schiller negotiated for plaintiffs, the proposed settlement called for increased disclosure in Medco's business practices, including providing price comparisons on different medications to clients.

The firm wasn't as fortunate, however, in another health care case. In September 2002, a federal judge in Miami denied class certification in a group of lawsuits accusing five HMOs – Aetna, Cigna, Humana, Health Net and United Health Group – of restricting their subscribers' access to health care through fraudulent practices and racketeering against uncooperative physicians.

Into every law firm a little rain must fall

The fairness of Boies Schiller's compensation and partnership policies came under fire recently. In April 2002, the firm settled a discrimination lawsuit brought by two former associates who sued over alleged wage and sex discrimination. The settlement was essentially in the firm's favor, with payment to plaintiffs of only $37,500, rather than the $1 million each woman sought, and no admission of wrongdoing.

Later in the year, however, Boies Schiller got more of the wrong kind of publicity when the firm was accused of unethical conduct in a long-running dispute between two Florida lawn-care companies. A West Palm Beach attorney sought to have Boies Schiller removed from the case because, he alleged, David Boies held a stake in the company owned by client Amy Habie and had violated Florida's rules of ethical conduct for attorneys by paying for outside lawyers to represent Habie and her company. The motion was denied.

GETTING HIRED

Brush up on your conversational skills

"Only a few offers are given for the Armonk office," a senior associate at Boies Schiller advises, "in contrast to comparable Manhattan firms that may give over 80 offers." This litigator further cautions, "The firm has increasingly become more selective, searching for top-notch associates with extraordinary law school records and work experience." A midlevel associate in the D.C. office observes that "academic excellence is a requirement but is not sufficient by itself to get a candidate hired." Another insider says successful candidates "need to be independent and entrepreneurial with no fear of hard work."

"The quality of candidates I have seen are extremely impressive," gushes one attorney, while a fourth-year remarks, "The interview is critical." "The firm has interviewed many candidates who are superstars on paper, but if the applicant doesn't click with the interviewing partners, there is no way an offer is being extended. At the same time, candidates who are border-line on paper but excel in the interview are often offered positions."

OUR SURVEY SAYS

Loosen your tie

"Working in Armonk is phenomenal," says one associate at the home office. "There is no commute, or a reverse commute, and you are in a laid-back country environment in a state-of-the-art building which we just moved into. It's the type of place where you stroll into each other's offices to bounce ideas off each other." A midlevel associate in D.C. boasts, "I wear jeans to work and come and go as I please." (A fourth-year in New York City, however, describes that office as "far more formal.") "Everyone works very hard," one source says, "but the relationship between attorneys is laid back and friendly. It seems like everyone who is here wants to be with the firm." Another associate describes a "high-intensity atmosphere [that] is a function of workaholic lawyers who also want to spend time with their families."

Although "partners are often too busy to spend much time chatting," says a midlevel associate, they "seem to enjoy interacting with associates and encourage it." A senior associate reports that partners "do the same or similar work as associates when appropriate," and adds, "I feel that partners treat me more as a coworker than a subordinate." "This is not a hierarchical place," a colleague confirms. "Particularly since we work in teams, the partners tend to know the associates very well and are able to work closely with them and entrust them with greater responsibility."

Cutting-edge cases

"When you read the front page of *The Wall Street Journal* in the morning," brags a senior associate, "our cases are all over the front page." Another veteran insider backs him up, asserting, "If you want to litigate, this is the law firm for you." A fourth-year reports, "Even junior associates with initiative can do substantive work on important cases." A first-year agrees: "The junior associates here work hand in hand with the partners," he says, "and receive a tremendous amount of responsibility. You are treated as a lawyer, compared to other places where first-years spend the bulk of their time being treated as paralegals."

"If you can only learn in a classroom," warns a fourth-year, "do not come here." Boies Schiller doesn't hold hands, though some associates say they wish it would. "There is no formal training," sighs one associate, "and most partners are too busy to mentor anyone." Still, other associates say the cases they work on provide "the best hands-on training you can find." An associate fresh out of law school informs us, "I have learned more about being a lawyer in a month than some of my colleagues have in a year." A senior associate reveals, "There is more hands-on training here than at comparable firms because junior associates are sent to hearings and depositions early on and thus have the opportunity to gain responsibility quickly."

Phone it in

Associates at the firm that Boies built work hard. "The bad news is, with high-profile work the hours are demanding," says one Boies Schiller associate. "But the good news is, with an ultra-casual environment and laptops, work can be done from anywhere. Working from home is a non-issue and face time does not exist." Colleagues agree "the hours can be brutal" but also point out that they "have definitely been getting better." A junior associate observes, "Long hours have for the most part been a function of being a new firm with not enough people to do all the work. I wouldn't say we work harder than the average firm at our level." One freshman says, "I know that I am in the office as much as many of my friends at other firms with reputations for being more

relaxed. The difference is, when you come in you have work to do. So the billables can build themselves."

Casual minimalism

Boies Schiller's Armonk home office is "top notch," and was designed and built exclusively for the firm. Associates in various branch offices are also satisfied with their surroundings. "Our office space is unusual," says a senior associate in D.C. "I like it for the casual atmosphere it offers." An associate in Albany refers to the office there as "minimalist at best," but concedes, "Every associate gets her [own] office from day one." Space in the Manhattan office "is starting to be at a premium," says a fourth-year there, "but another floor is opening up very shortly."

Roll of the dice

The Boies Schiller associates we heard from gave their compensation wildly high marks. "To my knowledge," says one associate, "only Wachtell offers similar total compensation." But they admit the system that determines their bonuses is "opaque" and occasionally "frustrating." "One year you may do better than market," another associate reports, while "next year you may do well below." Although base salaries are "slightly lower" than the top law firms, the incentive bonuses, "linked directly with the amount of work done," can result in windfalls of $100,000 to $200,000 at year's end and, says one source, "even higher bonuses to associates who worked on successful contingency-fee cases."

"Because of the bonus system," a senior associate observes, "many choose not to spend significant time on pro bono." A junior colleague calls pro bono "the area that needs the most improvement" at Boies Schiller, adding, "I am hopeful that the firm will reach a point soon where there will be enough associates to do the paying work so that everyone will have the opportunity to participate in pro bono." One attorney who did work a pro bono case says the firm was "supportive," but notes, "There is no formal pro bono program, nor any specific encouragement."

Open to diversity

"Women are treated very well here," says a senior Boies Schiller associate, and a female colleague backs him up without reservation. "I was put on bed rest but wanted to keep working when I was pregnant," she recalls, "So the firm installed a wireless system in my house and let me work from home." She also appreciates the "liberal" maternity leave policy, which offers three paid months off (and more unpaid time if needed). "As a woman," says a source, "I have been given tremendous responsibility and have never been treated any differently than my male colleagues." A litigator in Albany says, "The firm heavily recruits women. Retaining women, especially until partnership, is difficult because of the time commitment of the job."

On other diversity fronts, "the firm is making tremendous strides," says one insider, "but has a ways to go in terms of attracting more minority candidates." And a sixth-year associate declares, "Sexual orientation is a total non-issue here. Tolerance abounds."

Akin Gump Strauss Hauer & Feld LLP

Robert S. Strauss Building
1333 New Hampshire Avenue, NW
Washington, DC 20036
Phone: (202) 887-4000
www.akingump.com

LOCATIONS

Albany, NY • Austin, TX • Chicago, IL • Dallas, TX •
Denver, CO • Houston, TX • Los Angeles, CA •
McLean, VA • New York, NY • Philadelphia, PA •
Riverside, CA • San Antonio, TX • Washington, DC •
Brussels • London • Moscow • Riyadh (affiliate)

MAJOR DEPARTMENTS/PRACTICES

Antitrust
Corporate
Energy, Land Use & Environmental
Financial Restructuring
Health Industry
International
Intellectual Property
Labor & Employment
Litigation
Public Law & Policy
Tax

THE STATS

No. of attorneys: 1,000
No. of offices: 16
Summer associate offers: 73 out of 83 (2002)
Chairman: R. Bruce McLean
Hiring Partner: Dennis M. Race

BASE SALARY

Washington, DC
1st year: $125,000
2nd year: $135,000
3rd year: $150,000
4th year: $160,000
5th year: $170,000
6th year: $185,000
7th year: $195,000
8th year: $200,000
Summer associate: $2,400/week

UPPERS

• Collegial atmosphere
• Early responsibility
• Washington connections

DOWNERS

• Controversial deferred salary system
• Formal training just getting off the ground
• Often unpredictable hours

NOTABLE PERKS

• Laptops
• Friday donuts and happy hours
• Longevity bonus for sixth-years
• Sports tickets

THE BUZZ
WHAT ATTORNEYS AT OTHER FIRMS ARE SAYING ABOUT THIS FIRM

• "Well-connected politically"
• "Boring"
• "Rising star"
• "They dream of prestige"

RANKING RECAP

Best in Region
#6 - Washington, DC

Best in Practice
#8 - Bankruptcy/Corporate Restructuring
#9 - Labor & Employment

EMPLOYMENT CONTACT

Ms. Erin L. Springer
Legal Recruitment Manager
Phone: (202) 887-4184
Fax: (202) 887-4288
E-mail: espringer@akingump.com

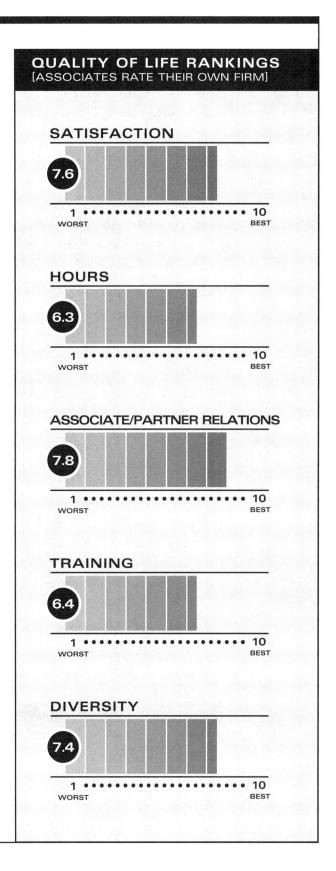

QUALITY OF LIFE RANKINGS
[ASSOCIATES RATE THEIR OWN FIRM]

SATISFACTION

7.6

1 WORST • • • • • • • • • • • • • • • • • 10 BEST

HOURS

6.3

1 WORST • • • • • • • • • • • • • • • • • 10 BEST

ASSOCIATE/PARTNER RELATIONS

7.8

1 WORST • • • • • • • • • • • • • • • • • 10 BEST

TRAINING

6.4

1 WORST • • • • • • • • • • • • • • • • • 10 BEST

DIVERSITY

7.4

1 WORST • • • • • • • • • • • • • • • • • 10 BEST

THE SCOOP

Akin Gump Strauss Hauer & Feld LLP, the quintessential Washington insider, is home to several politically connected lawyers. It's also a respected international firm with nearly 1,000 attorneys in 16 offices handling significant labor, litigation and corporate practices.

From Dallas to D.C.

Former FBI agents Richard A. Gump and Robert S. Strauss left the Bureau in 1945 to found Gump & Strauss in Dallas, Texas. The firm added two name partners in 1950, including Irving Goldberg, who later advised Lyndon Johnson on his transition to the presidency after the assassination of John F. Kennedy in 1963. In 1966 Goldberg was appointed to the U.S. Court of Appeals and Henry D. Akin joined the firm, which was renamed Akin Gump Strauss Hauer & Feld.

Akin Gump, built upon its established Washington connections by opening a D.C. office in 1971, the same year founding partner Bob Strauss was named treasurer of the Democratic Party. He was elected chairman of the Democratic National Committee the following year, then appointed U.S. special trade representative in 1977. Eleven years after receiving the Presidential Medal of Freedom, the nation's highest civilian award, he was named U.S. ambassador to Russia in 1992. In 1982 Vernon Jordan, Jr., President and CEO of the National Urban League and Executive Director of the United Negro College Fund, joined the firm as partner. Jordan would later become a household name through his role as adviser to a scandal-ridden President Clinton.

The firm expanded geographically in the 1990s, setting up in New York in 1993, Moscow in 1994 and London and Los Angeles in 1997. Former New York Congressman Bill Paxon came on board in 1999. Other federal bigwigs now at Akin Gump include Dan Glickman, Secretary of Agriculture under President Clinton, former 9th Circuit Judge William Norris and ex-Speaker of the House, Tom Foley. In April 2003, the firm entered into a strategic partnership with Bryant, Tipps & Malone, the law firm of J. Mark Tipps, former chief of staff to Senate Majority Leader Bill Frist. The two firms will collaborate on selected public policy and litigation matters.

World-wide lawyers

Akin Gump is a firm with international reach. The firm's 10-lawyer Moscow office handles energy and restructuring cases. (Akin Gump has a natural connection thanks to Bob Strauss's work as ambassador to Russia under the first President Bush.) The firm also has an affiliation with an office in Riyadh, Saudi Arabia, that handles securities and commercial transactions.

Litigation power

Litigation is one of Akin Gump's strengths, and the firm handles a variety of litigation cases, including antitrust matters, intellectual property, securities and white collar cases and appellate matters. In one of the largest antitrust verdicts in history, a federal jury returned a $173 million verdict in favor of an Akin Gump client, hospital bed manufacturer Kinetic Concepts, in September 2002.

Three months later, an appeals court upheld a September 2000 decision for Akin Gump client Coca-Cola in a lawsuit brought by rival PepsiCo. Pepsi challenged Coke's monopoly on soft drink contracts with food service vendors; the court determined Pepsi failed to prove the deals negatively affected consumers. Akin Gump's team was led by partner Jonathan M. Jacobson.

The firm also won a victory for SESAC, a musicians' rights organization, in November 2002. The lawsuit claimed that two Pittsburgh radio stations played songs by SESAC clients (including stars Bob Dylan and Neil Diamond) without authorization. A federal jury agreed with the organization and ordered WPNT, Inc., the owner of the two stations, to pay $1.2 million in damages. Though the award wasn't enough to generate headlines, the case was significant because it was the first jury trial for statutory copy infringement. Such cases had been handled by bench trials until a 1998 Supreme Court decisions ruled they were subject to jury trials.

The litigation practice got bigger in February 2003 with the addition of 17 lawyers from the Austin, Texas, office of Brobeck, Phleger & Harrison, the national law firm that closed down in early 2003. The group includes four partners, Steven M. Zager, Edward F. Fernandes, Paul R. Bessette and David P. Whittlesey, who will practice from Akin Gump's Austin and Houston offices.

Wheelin' and dealin'

Akin Gump's corporate practice handles investment funds, mergers and acquisitions, securities offerings and venture capital. The firm handled the historic first listing of a Russian company, the oil titan Lukoil, on the London Stock Exchange in the summer of 2002. In M&A, the firm handled the $524 million sale of 13 hotels for Wyndham International to Westbrook Partners in October. In February 2003, Akin Gump represented Houston-based Plains Exploration & Production Company in its $432 million acquisition of 3TEC Energy.

Akin Gump has long been recognized for its leading practice in hedge funds and other alternative investments. The firm currently represents 6 of the largest 10 hedge fund managers in the world (as ranked by *Institutional Investor*). The firm is also a leader in financial restructurings with clients that include bondholders in more than 80 major restructuring deals, like the creditors committee in the WorldCom bankruptcy, the largest corporate collapse in U.S. history.

Tech-pertise

No business fad gets past Akin Gump. The firm caught the technology wave in the late 1990s, opening "Akin Gump Technology Ventures," a tech specialty group that handles intellectual property, venture capital, M&A and public offering cases for tech firms. Akin Gump swallowed two IP boutique law firms in 1999 (one in Houston and one in Philadelphia) and opened an office

in Northern Virginia the following year. The firm's web site, www.akingump.com, won a Standard of Excellence WebAward from the Web Marketing Association in October 2002.

GETTING HIRED

Brush up your writing samples

Akin Gump is looking for a specific kind of lawyer. "I think the typical young associate is from a top 10-15 school, wrote on a journal and has better-than-average social skills," observes an insider. "We're very selective when it comes to recruiting," says one New York associate. "The firm looks for candidates with star talent combined with an easygoing personality." School or expertise in a specific practice area are determining factors. "There are plenty of people here from very prestigious law schools, and there are also people who were top students at less prestigious institutions that have noted reputations in a given area, such as environmental law," says one contact. "I was shocked at just how selective the litigation department is. Candidates that would be shoo-ins at my old firm are routinely shot down without a moment's hesitation," says one lateral litigator. "The litigation department is unabashedly committed to finding qualified people who would thrive in this environment. Bravo!"

Things may be getting tougher for slackers, so watch those grades. "The firm has recently changed its criteria for recruiting summer clerks with new, and higher, academic standards," says one associate. "We look for individuals with strong academic and writing skills," says a source. "We also look for individuals that are hardworking, dedicated, and enjoyable to be around." The writing sample is key. "A bad writing sample can kill you – no questions asked." That doesn't mean it's open seasons for stiffs. "They are extremely selective and look for people who are not only intelligent but will interact well with clients and other lawyers," says one attorney. It sounds tough, but "call backs are friendly and conversational," one Akin Gump associate assures us.

OUR SURVEY SAYS

The open-door firm

Most Akin Gump associates agree "the culture is laid back and very friendly." Accessibility and socialization are common. "You won't find too many closed doors as you walk through the halls – associates and partners are accessible," says one source. "Young associates hang out together frequently and have many spontaneous social functions." It's so social you won't even mind billing those long, big-firm hours – if Akin Gump associates are to be believed. "We are a firm where providing top-notch legal services to our clients is just as important as the camaraderie and congeniality among the attorneys," one insider enthuses. "This makes for a very comfortable environment where you can actually enjoy coming to work and billing long hours." "The firm is very laid back but also dynamic," explains a New York associate. "It's a fast-paced place that's still growing. The New York office was built by lateral hires and the firm – and all the employees appreciate that history and realize that they are in on the ground floor of a good thing."

The lovey-dovey theme continues, though not unabated. "With only a few exceptions, everyone from the mail guy to the partners are friendly and approachable," says a second-year. "When new attorneys start here the attorneys and many partners go out of their way to introduce themselves and make them feel welcome. The partners do not tolerate anyone, including themselves, being high-handed, condescending, etc." It won't be a frat-house: "For a New York office of a large law firm the culture is definitely less formal but not jocular or 'locker room informal,'" says a source. "People here are respectfully friendly." The firm may be taking a closer look at hours to the detriment of culture. "Although Akin Gump used to pride itself on a laid back, informal culture, in recent years, the firm has become extremely focused on billable hours," says one veteran attorney. "Partners only see a billable hours report each month, which excludes non-billable firm activities and pro bono time, and associates typically get a personal phone call in which they have to explain their hours if below a certain threshold." (Firm sources note that pro bono hours are treated the same as billable hours.)

Partners: the real Slim Shadys?

Akin Gump associates in general have good relationships with their bosses. "This inevitably varies from partner to partner," reports one insider. "Nevertheless, the vast majority of partners make an effort to be polite, and many of the partners have reputations for being great mentors. So far as I can tell, there are no screamers." If you like hip-hop, Akin Gump partners are off the hizzle. "How many partners can debate the influence of Eminem on pop culture and know what they are talking about?" asks one phat associate. "The youthful partners make practicing law as fun as it can be in a big firm setting. Partners and associates socialize outside the office although it is not a requirement in any way." Of course, every firm has its rogue element. "For the most part partners treat you with respect and are very interested in your development," says one insider. "However, the firm refuses to get rid of a few partners who are complete jerks and routinely mistreat everyone around them. The firm is willing to look the other way because these partners are usually rainmakers."

The new back-end scheme

In past years, Akin Gump associates lived in fear of the firm's back-end compensation scheme where approximately 10 percent of an associate's base salary was withheld until the end of the year and only paid out if the associate billed 2,000 hours. The scheme was not popular, and Akin Gump has made adjustments. "The firm changed it this year so that you get the money automatically if you stay through the year," reports one source. "So unless you are staying the entire year, you are earning less than you would at other firms in the city. And even if you do stay the entire year, you won't receive the [additional compensation] until the end of January of the next year. I don't understand why they just can't be like every other firm and give it to you up front."

Beyond this controversial arrangement (which doesn't apply in New York and Los Angeles), Akin Gump associates are satisfied with their compensation. "I feel very well, and competitively, compensated," says one associate. "I have no complaints as I am mindful that our compensation is not in proportion to the value we contribute to society," says another insider. Bonuses are an issue. "There is no monetary incentive to work more than 2,000 hours as the bonuses are sub-par," says one contact. (The firm disagrees, however, insisting its bonuses are "on par with other firms our size.") While the firm offers a longevity bonus for senior associates (it kicks in after six years), some associates in the D.C. office complain Akin Gump recently dropped the technology stipend it use to offer them.

Different departments, different schedules

Hours at Akin Gump are reasonable, but there can be marked differences between departments. "The hours are on par with most large law firms," reports one associate. "However, there is a real effort not to abuse associates. Most partners work as hard as, if not harder than, the associates." Litigation "has been incredibly busy the last three or four months," says one lawyer from that department. "This is probably a good thing considering the current economic climate. Nevertheless, something is wrong when the majority of associates are regularly staying past midnight and working through the weekends." Other departments complain of unpredictability. "Workflow in the corporate department can sometimes be very uneven: from four-alarm emergency projects on weekends to dead quiet for many days," says one source. Sometimes schedules are influenced by acts of Congress. "In government relations, we can predict our busy times according to the congressional schedule which allows me the ability to make vacation plans confidently," says a D.C. lawyer. "When Congress is in, we work very long hours; when they are out, days are more controllable."

A shifting, uncertain billable hours target is a source of complaint. "The hours are typical," says one associate. "However, the new problem is that our hour requirement just entered a vague area. Whereas 2,000 was the billable expectation before, now there is simply a rumor of expected hours in some sections being different from the hours being expected in other sections." "The unspoken, assumed pressure to bill hours is a burden at every top firm," observes one insider. "Here, certain groups like bankruptcy/financial restructuring are so busy that the vast majority of the group is billing 2,400 hours a year. Although the published billable hour requirement is 2,000, the vast majority of all attorneys here in New York, regardless of group bill a minimum 2,200. The good news on hours is that these high numbers mean we still have plenty of business in an economic down cycle and this firm is unlikely to lay off people."

Getting better at training

Akin Gump has traditionally been lacking in training, though insiders say the firm is making improvements. "Training generally has been on-the-job," says one source. "In response to the recognition of a need for more formal training, the firm has tried to implement a training program which is still in its early stages." Informal training is where it's at. "The formal training program is good but still developing," opines one insider. "More importantly, most partners take their role as teachers/mentors seriously and make an effort to teach by example." But you must seek out your mentor. "Mentoring opportunities are provided, but it takes a certain amount of proactive effort to obtain them." The firm reports that counsel (or senior associates) have had more formal training opportunities recently, including a firmwide retreat and seminars in each office.

Diversity efforts

The firm believes it has made great strides in bringing women's issues to the forefront. "The firm seems to be good on hiring, and is making an effort to improve mentoring," reports one contact. "Retention seems to be the challenge." Akin Gump is trying to meet that challenge. "We've developed a new Women's Forum to provide women with an avenue to come together and address common issues," says one associate. "It is new so we'll see how it goes." Another Akin Gump attorney says the creation of the Women's Forum "showed commitment on the firm's part to make sure that women's issues are being addressed." The firm reports that its women partners are working on a mentoring program as well.

A committee devoted to diversity issues is also up and running. "I think the firm is very conscious about issues concerning minority recruitment and retention, and has established a committee to address these problems," says one insider. It's had some success. "The firm is quite diverse with a number of represented minorities in both the associate and partner ranks," says one contact.

Cadwalader, Wickersham & Taft LLP

100 Maiden Lane
New York, NY 10038
Phone: (212) 504-6000
www.cadwalader.com

LOCATIONS

New York, NY (HQ)
Charlotte, NC
Washington, DC
London

MAJOR DEPARTMENTS/PRACTICES

Banking & Finance
Capital Markets
Corporate/Mergers & Acquisitions
Financial Restructuring
Health Care/Not-for-Profit
Insurance & Reinsurance
Litigation
Private Client
Real Estate
Tax

THE STATS

No. of attorneys: 502
No. of offices: 4
Summer associate offers: 68 out of 70 (2002)
Managing Partner: Robert O. Link, Jr.
Hiring Committee Chair: Paul W. Mourning

BASE SALARY

New York, NY; Washington, DC
1st year: $125,000
2nd year: $135,000
3rd year: $150,000
4th year: $170,000
5th year: $190,000
6th year: $205,000
7th year: $220,000
8th year: $235,000
Summer associate: $2,400/week

UPPERS

- Wall Street reputation goes back 200 years
- Great perks and fringe benefits
- Top-flight pay

DOWNERS

- Fractured firm culture
- Tough road to partnership
- Unpredictable schedules

NOTABLE PERKS

- "Mentoring budget" of $130/month for first-years
- Paid sabbatical after five years
- Tech goodies like laptops and BlackBerrys
- Massage therapists in office on pay day (DC)

THE BUZZ
WHAT ATTORNEYS AT OTHER FIRMS ARE SAYING ABOUT THIS FIRM

- "Very prestigious"
- "White shoe sweatshop"
- "Elite"
- "Worker bees"

RANKING RECAP

Best in Practice
#5 - Real Estate

EMPLOYMENT CONTACT

Ms. Monica R. Brenner
Manager of Legal Recruitment
Phone: (212) 504-6044
E-mail: monica.brenner@cwt.com

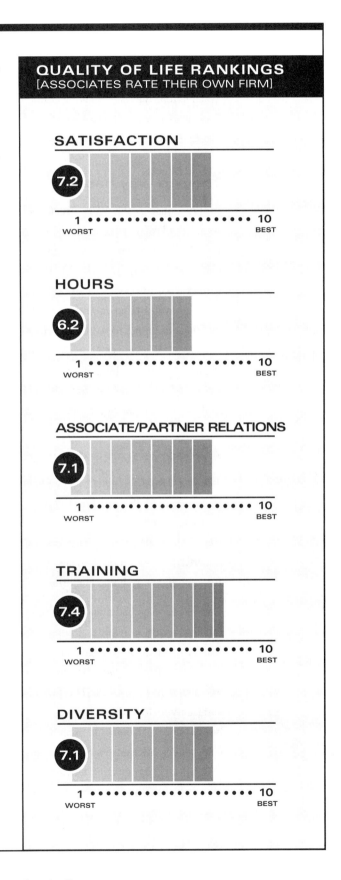

QUALITY OF LIFE RANKINGS
[ASSOCIATES RATE THEIR OWN FIRM]

SATISFACTION

7.2

1 •••••••••••••••••••• 10
WORST   BEST

HOURS

6.2

1 •••••••••••••••••••• 10
WORST   BEST

ASSOCIATE/PARTNER RELATIONS

7.1

1 •••••••••••••••••••• 10
WORST   BEST

TRAINING

7.4

1 •••••••••••••••••••• 10
WORST   BEST

DIVERSITY

7.1

1 •••••••••••••••••••• 10
WORST   BEST

THE SCOOP

Cadwalader, Wickersham & Taft LLP traces its roots back to the presidency of George W. – Washington, that is – making it one of the oldest continuous law practices in the United States. Cadwalader, known as a New York-based Wall Street firm, also has offices in Charlotte, N.C., Washington, D.C., and London.

They go way back

In 1792, just as the Wall Street area was becoming an important financial center, John Wells founded a law practice in lower Manhattan. Wells took on a partner, George Washington Strong, in 1818. Descendants of Strong took over management of the firm after his death in 1855 (Wells had died in 1823). In 1878, Charles Strong entered into a partnership with John L. Cadwalader, a former Assistant Secretary of State under President Ulysses S. Grant. Strong & Cadwalader was a legal innovator (Cadwalader notes that its predecessor was one of the first to offer paid associate positions as opposed to the unpaid legal clerkships that were once standard) and grew quickly. George W. Wickersham joined the firm in 1883 and later served as U.S. attorney general under President William Howard Taft. Henry W. Taft (the president's brother) joined the firm in 1889. Cadwalader continued its growth and innovation throughout the 20th century and became the first Wall Street law practice to add a female partner, Catherine Noyes Lee, in 1941.

A good year in a down year

The year 2002 was another banner year for Cadwalader in the field of commercial mortgage backed securities (CMBS), an area in which it has been long dominant. The firm was tops in both the issuer and underwriter counsel category, according to trade publication *Commercial Mortgage Alert*. Cadwalader was issuer counsel on 35 deals worth approximately $30 billion in 2002 and underwriter counsel on 24 deals worth over $19 billion. That was double the number of deals the firm completed in both categories in 2001.

Cadwalader also had a good year in mergers and acquisitions, despite the slump in the field across the legal industry in 2002. Cadwalader was eighth in M&A advisory in 2002 (according to market research firm Thomson Financial Securities Data), up from 45th in 2001. Much of that jump was due to the firm's work for pharmaceutical company Pfizer on its $62.5 billion acquisition of Swedish firm Pharmacia. The firm also helped Pfizer sell its Adams subsidiary, makers of Trident and Dentyne, to Cadbury Schweppes for $4.2 billion and counseled Skandia Insurance on the $1.26 billion sale of American Skandia to Prudential Financial. In a significant international deal, Cadwalader advised energy company AES Kelvin Power on the $329 million sale of Songas Limited in Tanzania. Cadwalader's M&A attorneys have also represented big names like Houghton Mifflin, Bear Stearns, Wakefern, Toys R Us and MediaOne.

Superstars

Cadwalader's M&A department is co-chaired by Dennis Block, dubbed a "dealmaker of the year" by *American Lawyer* and among the "Hot 100" by *The Lawyer* magazine in 2002. Christopher Kandel, a partner in the London banking and finance department, and Michelle Duncan, a restructuring and litigation partner in the London office, were also deemed hot enough to make the Hot 100 list. Gregory Markel, Cadwalader's litigation chair, is well known for representing banks, accounting firms and directors and officers in securities matters, while Christopher White, chairman of the firm's real estate department, is a preeminent force in real estate finance.

Going bananas

In a high-profile international win for Cadwalader's New York and London litigation teams, a London Commercial Court ruled in favor of Ecuadorian billionaire Alvaro Noboa in November 2002. Noboa was sued by two of his sisters, who claimed he gained control of the family banana business by fraudulent means. The court ruled that the sisters' claims were "brought dishonestly" and that their case was "inconsistent, lacking coherence and wholly unreliable." The judgment came just before Noboa lost a presidential election in Ecuador. The firm is also playing significant roles in most of the important and historic litigation of the day, including matters involving Enron, WorldCom and Tyco as well as IPO allocation and financial research litigations.

Legal Business honored the firm's London restructuring team, led by UK managing partner Andrew Wilkinson, as "Restructuring Team of the Year." Clients of the department, chaired by bankruptcy powerhouse Bruce Zirinsky, include bondholders of Telewest Communications, creditors of NTL and Barings and bankrupt companies such as Bradlees Stores, Casual Male and Enron.

Free lawyers

Mortgages worth less than $200,000 aren't usually the stuff of big-firm concern, but Cadwalader lawyers were celebrating such a small potatoes deal in October 2002. Associates at the firm took on a pro bono case for a Staten Island, N.Y., family that lost its concierge business in downtown Manhattan after the terrorist attacks of September 11, 2001. The firm was able to save the family from eviction three times, then worked to secure a loan for permanent housing for the family. In other pro bono news, Cadwalader is beaming with pride that the New York State Bar Association has bestowed upon litigation partner Debra Steinberg the 2003 President's Pro Bono Service Award.

Partner pick up

Cadwalader added partners to its litigation department in September 2002. Gregory Markel and Ronit Setton, formerly of now-defunct Brobeck, Phleger & Harrison, and Kenneth Pierce, formerly a senior vice president in the Insurance Products Group of investment bank Lehman Brothers, all

joined Cadwalader's New York office. Nancy Ruskin, of counsel at Brobeck, joined the firm as special counsel at the same time. Additional new partners include former U.S. Assistant Attorney General James Robinson and Michael Horowitz, a recent nominee to the United States Sentencing Commission. Both concentrate on business fraud and complex litigation at the firm.

GETTING HIRED

Big name school or bust

Cadwalader's recruiting process is standard: law school students are interviewed first on campus, then at the firm's offices. Don't expect an easy road. "Given that Cadwalader is a very prestigious law firm, it has been my experience that it is very competitive to get hired here coming straight out of law school," says one insider. The firm looks favorably on particular schools. "The firm increasingly stresses Ivy League or Chicago/NYU/Michigan-type schools and excellent grades," reports one associate. That doesn't mean those from other schools are frozen out, but it can be a tougher road. One attorney elaborates: "It seems like the firm is trying to recruit Ivy League students but still looks at second-tier schools as long as students are at the very top of the class."

"Regardless of what school you come from, the firm is concerned with your GPA," warns a source. But grades aren't everything. "The firm is looking to hire highly motivated, smart self-starters who also have the ability to mesh well with clients," claims one attorney. "[Candidates] will need to have proven themselves on both professional and personal levels," according to a second-year.

OUR SURVEY SAYS

Friendly, but fractured

In general, Cadwalader associates say the firm's culture is friendly and laid back. "This is not a formal environment," says one New York associate. "Partners and associates interact on a professional and relaxed basis, in both work and social environments." "Cadwalader is the type of firm that expects everyone to be professional and that the work product is the highest level," according to an insider. "However, this usually is done in a laid back, low key manner. The firm is a friendly place where people socialize together, but there is no pressure to do so." Associates are given the chance to succeed – but had better produce. "If you can do it, they let you do it," reports one lawyer. "But if you get the chance to do it, and you blow it, you can't do it anymore."

However, some Cadwalader attorneys feel the firm is balkanized. "The culture depends on one's practice group and office," according to a source. "Practice groups are highly integrated across offices, and closest personal relationships tend to be with people in one's practice group or related substantive areas of practice." This can be taken to the extreme. "Cadwalader is filled with diverse factions of partners, and if you work in Partner 1's group, Partners 2 and 3 generally are outwardly unpleasant to you," warns one associate.

As with the overall culture, opinions on partner/associate relations are mixed. "On the whole associates are treated well, and there is clearly a systemic effort to make this more consistent," reports one insider. "However, there are still enough unpleasant individual partners to make many average workdays less enjoyable than they ought, easily, to be." Relations between partners and their junior counterparts have improved, though. "Partners definitely treat associates better than they did a few years ago," says a source.

Don't make any plans you can't break

Cadwalader's associates work hours typical for big-firm lawyers. "I am very satisfied with my schedule," says one veteran associate. "We work hard, as we should at our level, but it's never mindless or unnecessary." "The firm is a high-billing place, and a premium is put on billing above 2,000 hours," says one attorney. "A typical day is about 12 hours in the office, with 15-20 not uncommon," says one New Yorker. "Weekend work is typical but more flexible barring a pressing deal." For some associates, the weekend is a rumor. "I cannot remember the last time I had an entire weekend off," complains one tired soul.

Unpredictable schedules are a sticking point. "It's not the year-end billables that kill you, it's the uncertainty of the schedule," says a source. "[You] can't even plan to be away over a weekend." It's not necessarily the firm's fault, but Cadwalader has made an effort to ease associate pain. "The hours can be quite long, but that is not really under the control of the firm, but simply the nature of the practice," observes one attorney. "We have the ability to work from remote locations outside the office via the Internet which has reduced the time that we need to be in the office considerably." Part-time schedules are available, if not always workable. "The partners in my department have been wonderful in helping to make my flex-time schedule work for me while still staffing me on exciting deals," says one insider impressed with the part-time life. Another complains, "While there is theoretical support for the concept of a part-time arrangement, it is not working so well in practice."

Top o' the market to ya

Cadwalader associates seem most happy on payday. "The firm is committed to matching the market, so at least I know that I will make as much as I would at any other firm," says one moneybags. Some complain the firm is watching time sheets closely. "Officially, there is no billable hours requirement but in reality bonuses are tied to hours you billed," reports one contact. That's a bone of contention. "Although it was not specifically stated that getting a bonus was tied to billable hours, many people who did not get bonuses were told that it was because their hours weren't high enough," claims one attorney. "We were not informed of this baseline threshold from the outset – only after the fact." (The firm, however, says its policy is clear: It expects a minimum

of 2,000 hours per year, including time spent on recruiting, pro bono, client development, article, speech and book preparation and training as an instructor.) The firm does have a healthy perks program. In addition to the usual goodies, like car service and meals for those working late, the firm gives associates tech goodies like laptops and BlackBerry pagers. Also, in the interest of fostering teamwork and professional growth, first-years are teamed with experienced mentors and given $130 a month to paint the town red.

A week at the Academy

Most associates agree training is a priority at Cadwalader. First-years spend a week at "Cadwalader Academy," and the firm has a mentoring program that's much loved. "[Cadwalader] really puts a lot of money and time into training its associates," brags one insider. "There are ample CLE programs offered firm wide and by practice area," says another lawyer. Litigation lawyers get some real-world experience. "We litigation first-years were given mandatory pro bono projects on which we are the lead counsel and have primary decision-making authority," says one contact. First- and second-year associates are paired off with an experienced associate or partner in a popular mentoring program that some say could be improved.

Taking the initiative

Some insiders complain about a perceived dearth of female partners, a situation Cadwalader has tried to address. "The women partners conduct the Women's Initiative meetings in New York several times a year – video-conferenced to other offices – that have been well-organized, thoughtful and candid presentations with very practical insights and suggestions based on their own experiences here," says one insider. Reviews are mixed. Some say it's "a great idea, but needs work" and that "many women find it patronizing." Another praises it, calling the Women's Initiative "a great opportunity for women at different stages of their career to talk to each other and get advice." Insiders also report the firm has tried to get more female representation on the firm management committee, although the firm points out that capital markets partner Anna Glick has been a member since 2001.

The firm confronts some familiar issues with regard to minority representation and promotion. "Like many of its peer firms, Cadwalader needs a lot of improvement in this area," says one contact. "However, discussions have begun to address these issues." Indeed, the firm reports it has launched a diversity awareness initiative and is now reaching out to traditionally black universities and BLSA. "The firm is receptive to new ideas, but they do not know what to do on this issue," observes another source. "Hiring is not as much of a problem as retention."

Cadwalader associates say the firm makes a welcoming environment for gay and lesbian employees. The firm is "surprisingly open for what seems to be a stodgy old place," according to one contact. "Bottom line: If you make them money and produce good work, your sexual orientation does not matter." Even though one associate claimed to be "unaware of any program here at Cadwalader for outreach to the gay and lesbian community," another said the atmosphere is "improving, and programs are in the works to continue improving." The firm notes its support of several organizations that seek to promote diversity, including the Lambda Legal Defense and Education Fund and the Lesbian and Gay Law Association of Greater New York (LeGaL).

36
PRESTIGE RANKING

King & Spalding LLP

191 Peachtree Street
Suite 4900
Atlanta, GA 30303-1763
Phone: (404) 572-4600
www.kslaw.com

LOCATIONS

Atlanta, GA (HQ)
Houston, TX
New York, NY
Washington, DC
London

MAJOR DEPARTMENTS/PRACTICES

Business Litigation • Construction & Procurement • Corporate & Finance • Employee Benefits & Executive Compensation • Energy • Environmental • Financial Restructuring • Financial Transactions • Food & Drug • Global Projects & Transactions • Government Practice • Governmental & Reulgatory • Health Care • Intellectual Property • International Trade & Litigation • Labor & Employment • Litigation - Special Matters • Litigation & Trade • Mergers & Acquisitions • Private Equity • Public Finance • Real Estate • Tax • Tort Litigation • Trusts & Estates

THE STATS

No. of attorneys: 700+
No. of offices: 5
Summer associate offers: 97 out of 122 (2002)
Chair: Walter W. Driver, Jr.
Hiring Committee Chairs: Richard A. Schneider (Atlanta); Kenneth S. Culotta (Houston); Douglas A. Bird (New York); Mark S. Brown (Washington)

BASE SALARY

Atlanta, GA
1st year: $100,000
2nd year: $105,000
Summer associate: $1,850/week

Houston, TX
1st year: $110,000
2nd year: $115,000
Summer associate: $2,100/week

New York, NY; Washington, DC
1st year: $125,000
2nd year: $135,000
Summer associate: $2,400/wk (NY);
$2,150/wk (DC)

UPPERS

• Prestigious reputation built on big-name clients
• Cordial work environment

DOWNERS

• Byzantine bureaucracy
• Doubtful partnership chances

NOTABLE PERKS

• Free Coca-Cola
• Annual mentors' spa weekend
• Attorney dining room (Atlanta)
• Your choice: laptop or BlackBerry

THE BUZZ
WHAT ATTORNEYS AT OTHER FIRMS ARE SAYING ABOUT THIS FIRM

• "Sophisticated and sharp"
• "Classic Southern sweatshop"
• "Atlanta's best"
• "Good ol' boys club"

RANKING RECAP

Best in Region
#1 - The South

Quality of Life
#12 - Training

EMPLOYMENT CONTACTS

Atlanta
Ms. Rebecca McClain Newton
Director of Recruiting
Phone: (404) 572-3395
Fax: (404) 572-5100
E-mail: rnewton@kslaw.com

Houston
Ms. Ann Harris
Recruiting Manager
Phone: (713) 751-3200
E-mail: aharris@kslaw.com

New York
Ms. Kristan A. Lassiter
Recruiting Manager
Phone: (212) 556-2138
E-mail: klassiter@kslaw.com

Washington
Ms. Kara O'Conner
Recruiting Manager
Phone (202) 626-2387
E-mail: koconnor@kslaw.com

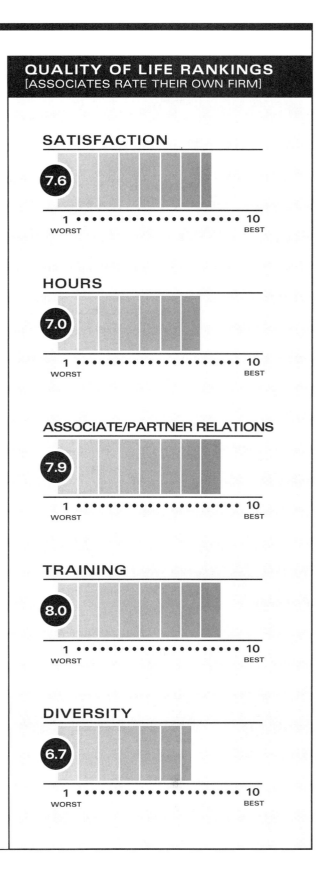

QUALITY OF LIFE RANKINGS
[ASSOCIATES RATE THEIR OWN FIRM]

SATISFACTION
7.6
1 WORST .... 10 BEST

HOURS
7.0
1 WORST .... 10 BEST

ASSOCIATE/PARTNER RELATIONS
7.9
1 WORST .... 10 BEST

TRAINING
8.0
1 WORST .... 10 BEST

DIVERSITY
6.7
1 WORST .... 10 BEST

THE SCOOP

Established in 1885, King & Spalding LLP maintains its Southern legacy but has evolved into a firm both international in scope and in high demand among the Fortune 100. Fellow Atlanta institution Coca-Cola relies on King & Spalding for legal counsel – and makes sure the firm never runs out of soft drinks.

We ain't just whistling Dixie

King & Spalding's practice has a breadth not typically associated with firms based below the Mason-Dixon Line. The firm excels in a wide variety of practice areas, including antitrust, appellate, intellectual property, business litigation, global projects and transactions, energy and employee benefits. Both multinational public corporations and small, private companies appear on King & Spalding's client roster, including such household names as Sprint, United Parcel Service, 3M, Delta Air Lines, ExxonMobil, General Electric and General Motors.

More than 700 attorneys call King & Spalding home, including former U.S. Senator Sam Nunn and Griffin Bell, a former judge who also served as attorney general under Jimmy Carter. Bell is considered something of a legend in Atlanta legal circles and continues to practice at the age of 84.

Smooth moves

Although King & Spalding has taken a cautious approach to expansion (the Atlanta location was its only office for nearly 100 years), the firm has established a pattern of growth that's impressive. The Houston office, for example, has swelled from three attorneys at its founding in 1995 to more than 70 today. King & Spalding opened its first international office in London at the start of 2003. The practice will focus primarily on international transactions, including those related to the former Soviet Union, the Middle East and Latin America. Four partners and two associates transferred to London to establish the new office. Another five partners not based in the city have committed to spending a substantial amount of time on cases originating in the London office. King & Spalding's Atlanta attorneys will have a new home in a few years, the firm having committed itself to a new 40-story midtown office tower overlooking the city's new symphony hall. The move is scheduled for 2006.

They make the deals

In September 2002, a team of King & Spalding attorneys assisted Sprint Corp. on the sale of its directory publishing business to R.H. Donnelly Corp. for $2.23 billion. Later that year, the firm advised client GE Power Systems on the $250 million acquisition of Osmonics, a developer of water purification and filtration technology. The firm kicked off 2003 by negotiating another large acquisition, this time on behalf of client Serologicals Corp., which will purchase life science research company Chemicon for approximately $95 million. King & Spalding helped negotiate a settlement on behalf of airport security firm International Total Services in February 2003. According to the terms, ITS, which has gone bankrupt, will pay its unsecured creditors 60.4 percent of the debt it owes. Atlanta-based biotechnology company CryoLife has retained King & Spalding to defend it in several shareholder class-action lawsuits and general corporate work.

King & Spalding represented former BellSouth Vice Chairman Gary Forsee in an employment dispute. When Sprint offered Forsee its leadership position, BellSouth argued that Forsee's contract stipulated he cannot work for a BellSouth competitor for 18 months after leaving the company. In February 2003, an Atlanta judge ruled that Forsee's non-compete clause was unenforceable. He is now chairman and CEO of Sprint.

Unquiet in the library

Board members of the Atlanta-Fulton County Library turned to the folks from King & Spalding to appeal a $16.6 million judgment levied against them in a reverse discrimination suit. Eight Caucasian librarians sued the county library system after they were transferred from the main library to smaller branches. The librarians say the transfers were racially based, while library officials say they were simply moved as part of a reallocation of personnel to meet the needs of various locations. The case is drawing heaps of attention, not only because of the reverse discrimination aspect, but also because legal legend Griffin Bell signed on to lead the board's appeal.

Running the numbers

K&S should be proud of the awards and accolades it has amassed from various legal media and community organizations. Fifty-one King & Spalding attorneys are listed in the 2003-2004 edition of *The Best Lawyers in America*. King & Spalding was among the top 10 firms receiving the most mentions by in-house counsel in *Corporate Counsel*'s 2002 "Who Represents America's Biggest Companies" survey.

The firm's gift of 500 used computers to various legal aid groups was recognized by the American Bar Association. Some of the firm's other ongoing pro bono activities include tutoring children in Atlanta, preparing meals for and providing legal services to the homeless in Atlanta and Washington, D.C., and renovating housing for the poor and elderly in Washington, Houston and New York.

GETTING HIRED

How 'bout those Braves?

"As the economy slows, we are more selective in hiring," King & Spalding associates tell us. "To do well as an associate here, one must be more than a great writer and researcher; the firm desires

strong personalities who relate well with and instill confidence in our sophisticated clients," explains a labor attorney. To nab an offer, a candidate should also be "well-rounded and have outside interests," but "the ultimate decision for hiring is based on how well the person would fit into the firm personally." According to a third-year, "The focus of the hiring committee is definitely shifting towards hiring associates with stronger academics – better grades and rank and top-10 schools." "Good credentials will only get you as far as the first interview. You have to display a little charm to claim your permanent chair," an attorney in the D.C. office tells us. "Tell them you love the Braves," jokes one Atlanta attorney before offering some serious tips: "I think that most callbacks get hired unless they are socially awkward or their references don't pan out. The perfect interviewee is a normal, nice person who just happens to be smart and hardworking." Another Atlanta lawyer believes the firm seeks to hire "the best and the brightest students from Mercer and the University of Georgia," while a New York associate reveals, "King & Spalding is very school-oriented in New York and hires from prominent southern law schools as well as Harvard."

OUR SURVEY SAYS

Southern manners

"Lawyers at K&S take their work seriously, but they do not take themselves too seriously," says one cliché-quoting insider. According to a Houston associate, "The associates are relatively friendly, but there is still quite a bit of competition, which the partners do nothing to dismiss." The good news, says this source, is "the number of screamer partners is low." "K&S has a very formal atmosphere," but "the culture of the firm varies from team to team," with some being "more uptight than others." "This conservatism manifests itself most notably in the refusal to surrender to casual dress." Yes, says an M&A attorney, "the culture is 'Southern formal,' and the attorneys here abide by the Southern rules of behavior. Although it is a formal atmosphere," this source adds, "I wouldn't classify it as uptight." To a Houston attorney, the "formality reflects the significance of the work we do and the seriousness with which we approach that work. And interpersonal relations are no more formal than elsewhere." King & Spalding is the type of place where "in the elevator, for example, a partner will say hi and talk to you, but only if there aren't other partners around," says a labor attorney. However, this lawyer says the behavior probably has less to do with snobbishness than the fact "that everyone is obsessed with networking at their level or above." "The Washington, D.C., office is exceptionally laid back. The people are both friendly and really interested in helping foster the careers of young attorneys." Although "lawyers socialize together," "they mostly stick to their own peer group," says an Atlanta attorney. "King & Spalding is a traditional firm," another Atlanta attorney tells us, "and with that comes some stuffiness," but it's not so bad "once you get past the suits."

A labor attorney is thrilled to be working on the type of matters "that probably would not be available to me at smaller firms." It's expected that "first-year associates at most firms end up doing a lot of document review." But, a source is thrilled to report, "I have been given amazing opportunities to do substantive legal work" outside of document review. An attorney in the same office reports a very dissimilar experience: "I'm not getting enough hands-on experience. Most of my first three years has involved document review, document review and document review. For the first couple of years, that was fine, but as a third-year, I need to be developing skills."

Southerners like money, too

Associates at K&S offer mixed reviews of their paychecks. Atlanta residents vent freely. "By the time associates in Atlanta reach the fourth or fifth year, the differences in the salary here and salaries in other cities is absolutely staggering." Another Atlanta associate fumes, "It makes no sense that the associates in the firm's home office make so much less than associates in all of the branch offices." A third-year says, "I think K&S should raise salaries in Atlanta to be commensurate with D.C. and New York rates, or at least closer to those rates." An insider attempts to cut the firm a little slack on the issue of varying salary levels among the offices. "The firm pays the same as the other Atlanta firms," she admits. "The low pay is more a symptom of what the market will allow in the South. But coming from an Ivy League school with a lot of loan debt, it really doesn't pay from a financial sense to work in the South where the pay is lower."

Other associates are a bit less brutal. A litigation associate observes, "Our bonus structure is tied to hours, which I believe is fair, but most other large New York firm's give boom-year bonuses without regard to hours. Such a bonus would certainly be appreciated here," says a New Yorker. A Washingtonian offers this mostly positive assessment: "I feel reasonably well compensated, although our bonus structure is far below market compared to top New York-based firms. But since the hours are pretty good, I can't complain." Associates gripe that their required time commitments to earn bonuses don't include "hours spent recruiting, pro bono or business development." However, reveals an insider, "High achievers are often compensated with a community service bonus, which rewards pro bono service." Several other attorneys confirm receiving bonuses for "non-billable contributions to the firm," so it seems it's not unusual for pro bono service to be rewarded even if it's not counted as billable time.

Six years to life

"Associates feel that there is no chance of making partner, so they are always looking for outside opportunities." Because King & Spalding's partnership track "is very much like a pyramid," an Atlanta attorney believes, "It is expected that numerous associates will leave before finishing their fifth and sixth years." People also leave "because working here opened up a great opportunity," or "they decide to live in a different town" or "don't like big-firm life." Among those in the D.C. office, "most leave for government opportunities" and "very few go to other firms."

A corporate attorney explains why associates feel the road to partnership is too long. For non-equity partnership "you are eligible and are voted on after your seventh year, the vote takes place in April of your eighth year and, if elected, you don't become a partner until January of the following year, the beginning of year nine." According to this source, "For equity, you have to wait two more years from the initial non-equity vote in April to put your name in the hat." Interestingly enough, other attorneys say there are a substantial number of K&S lifers. "The internal newspaper lists employee anniversaries, and it is not uncommon to see someone who has worked at the firm for 25 years or more, including staff." Then there are the members of the "grass-is-browner club – people who have left the firm and then returned." An insider observes that the firm has plenty of attorneys who fall into this category.

Respect goes a long way

"The level of personal involvement with associates varies from partner to partner. Some actually care about your professional development, while others just want the work to get done." One Atlanta insider says, "The associate/partner relationships are one of the very best qualities of K&S," while another says, "Overall, I've been very pleased with the way I'm treated by partners." New York partners "tend to go out of their way to thank you for the work that you do for them and are extremely respectful." "The bond between partner and associate is unprecedented. This is rewarding on a personal level, but also gives an associate easy access to the advice and guidance of the partners," shares an associate in Houston. A source whose interaction with the partners has always been respectful nonetheless feels "the most frustrating part of working with them is the lack of communication. For example, an assignment is completed and a partner is dissatisfied," but "news of this dissatisfaction" doesn't filter down to the associate until weeks or months later. A second-year tells us, perhaps a bit tongue-in-cheek, "Partners are always respectful, even when asking associates to give up a weekend."

Room to grow

A New York attorney gives us the lowdown on that office's soon-to-be available new space: "The firm has grown so fast, it outgrew the space. The firm has obtained leases on two more floors and is currently building out the spaces to King & Spalding standards, so that each associate may have their own office and members of all practice groups may be similarly located." Another Big Apple attorney says the "new space should improve things, but in the meantime, there are first-year associates in secretarial stations while some available space goes unused. An occasional painting 'touch-up' would also go a long way, both in offices and in common spaces." New York associates, eat your heart out: In Atlanta "everyone has their own office with a window from the first year." An Atlanta associate brags that King & Spalding has "the best building in Atlanta, although the firm recently announced plans to move to its own, new building in Midtown in 2006." "We moved into posh new offices in October 2001," beams a Houston attorney. "The art on the walls is modern, somewhat avant-garde."

"Partners are always respectful, even when asking associates to give up a weekend."

– *King & Spalding associate*

Paul, Hastings, Janofsky & Walker LLP

Paul Hastings Tower
515 South Flower Street, 25th floor
Los Angeles, CA 90071-2371
Phone: (213) 683-6000
www.paulhastings.com

LOCATIONS

Atlanta, GA
Los Angeles, CA
New York, NY
Orange County, CA
San Diego, CA
San Francisco, CA
Stamford, CT
Washington, DC
Beijing
Hong Kong
London
Tokyo

MAJOR DEPARTMENTS/PRACTICES

Corporate
Employment
Litigation
Real Estate
Tax

THE STATS

No. of attorneys: 840+
No. of offices: 12
Frim Chair: Seth M. Zachary
Recruiting Chair: Mary C. Dollarhide

BASE SALARY

California offices; New York, NY; Washington, DC
1st year: $125,000
2nd year: $135,000
3rd year: $150,000
Summer associate: $2,400/week

Stamford, CT
1st year: $112,500
2nd year: $121,500
3rd year: $135,000
Summer associate: $2,400/week

Atlanta, GA
1st year: $100,000
2nd year: $105,000
3rd year: $110,000
Summer associate: $2,400/week

UPPERS

- Cutting-edge work
- Relaxed working environment
- High salaries

DOWNERS

- Long hours
- Low bonuses
- Lack of partner/associate communication

NOTABLE PERKS

- Subsidized gym membership
- Free soft drinks and cappucino bars
- Emergency daycare
- Free lunch when working on Saturday

THE BUZZ
WHAT ATTORNEYS AT OTHER FIRMS ARE SAYING ABOUT THIS FIRM

- "Young and hip"
- "Bunch of workaholics"
- "Sophisticated"
- "Slaughterhouse"

RANKING RECAP

Best in Region
#9 - California

Best in Practice
#1 - Labor & Employment
#4 - Real Estate

EMPLOYMENT CONTACT

Mr. Anton Mack
Managing Director of Attorney Recruiting
Phone: (213) 683-5740
E-mail: antonmack@paulhastings.com

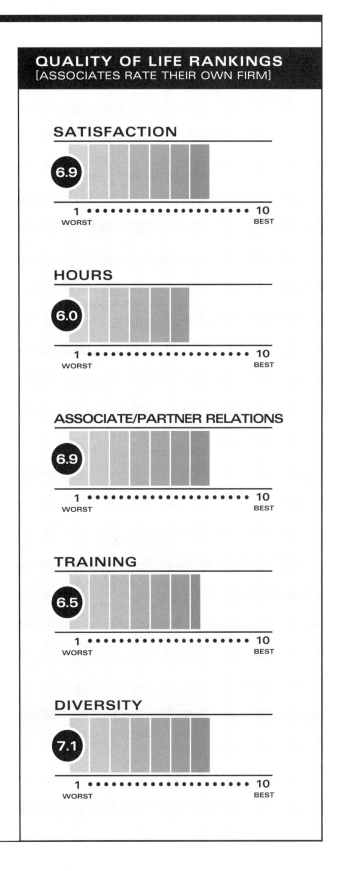

QUALITY OF LIFE RANKINGS
[ASSOCIATES RATE THEIR OWN FIRM]

SATISFACTION
6.9
1 WORST • • • • • • • • • • • • • • • • • 10 BEST

HOURS
6.0
1 WORST • • • • • • • • • • • • • • • • • 10 BEST

ASSOCIATE/PARTNER RELATIONS
6.9
1 WORST • • • • • • • • • • • • • • • • • 10 BEST

TRAINING
6.5
1 WORST • • • • • • • • • • • • • • • • • 10 BEST

DIVERSITY
7.1
1 WORST • • • • • • • • • • • • • • • • • 10 BEST

THE SCOOP

The antithesis of Hollywood attitude, Los Angeles-born Paul, Hastings, Janofsky & Walker LLP is too busy entering new markets and closing deals to seek out the spotlight. Though best known for its thriving labor and employment shop, the firm has a steadily increasing reputation in the areas of real estate, M&A and finance, and is strengthening its presence in the Asia-Pacific region.

California dreamin'

The firm traces its roots to Los Angeles, where Lee Paul and Robert Hastings teamed up with fellow Harvard-educated lawyer Leonard Janofsky in 1951. Eleven years later, tax specialist Charles Walker joined the team. The partners stayed pretty close to home when they set up their second office in Orange County, Calif., in 1974. Since then, they've ventured far and wide, opening offices in Atlanta, Washington, D.C., and four other U.S. cities. International expansion began in 1988 with the opening of the firm's Tokyo office. The opening of three other international offices followed.

Paul Hastings handles a variety of complex legal matters but is recognized for its expertise in corporate employment, real estate and tax law. President Gerald Ford named Charles Walker, who founded the firm's tax practice, assistant secretary of the U.S. Treasury for tax policy. Founder Leonard Janofsky has the distinction of being the first labor lawyer to become president of the American Bar Association. The firm is known for defeating motions for class-action certification in employment cases.

The Brobeck effect

Paul Hastings expanded its Asia-Pacific presence in a May 2002 merger with Hong Kong firm Koo and Partners and additions to the Beijing offices, with more expansion planned for the future. And, like several other firms, Paul Hastings seized the opportunity to snap up some top talent following the dissolution of Brobeck, Phleger & Harrison. To accommodate 31 new attorneys from Brobeck's San Diego office, Paul Hastings started a San Diego branch of its own in February 2003. After a few months in their old Brobeck digs, members of the firm's fourth West Coast office have recently moved into a brand-new space. Ten additional Brobeck attorneys were picked up to tackle commerical finance, real estate and securities litigation in other offices throughout the firm.

As the Brobeck refugees were getting settled, several long-time Paul Hastings attorneys from the Atlanta office were preparing to exit. Former partner R. Lawrence Ashe left the firm to open his own shop, taking four attorneys and a good-sized portion of his client list with him.

Numbers game

Major business and legal media have been taking notice of the firm's growth. In December 2002, *New York Lawyer* ranked Paul Hastings No. 9 on its list of the top 25 Manhattan offices of firms based outside New York, in terms of the number of attorneys in the office. That same month, the *Los Angeles Business Journal* ranked the firm No. 6 based on number of attorneys in Los Angeles County and No. 20 in Orange County. Meanwhile, the *Atlanta Business Chronicle* ranked the firm No. 12 for Atlanta. Chambers and Partners also ranked the firm's employment and real estate practices as the tops in California; the real estate practice is also No. 1 in New York with several partners earning high marks for their individual expertise.

A calling for telecom – and more

In addition to its core practices, the firm has developed a strong telecom practice that is frequently called upon to handle sales, acquisitions and joint venture projects. Early in 2003, Paul Hastings helped client Bresnan Communications Holdings complete the purchase of cable operations from Comcast Corp. A team of Paul Hastings attorneys guided Telkom SA through an initial public offering in March 2003. The company, which provides telecommunications services in South Africa, raised $475 million through the transaction.

The firm's litigation practice is emerging as an impressive force, adding nearly 50 new lawyers in the first few months of 2003. Paul Hastings litigators recently scored a big win for client Regent Hospital Products, defeating a plaintiff's $490 million claim over the manufacture and advertisement of surgical gloves. This verdict was named one of the year's top 10 by the *National Law Journal*. The firm also convinced a California judge to toss a $97.2 million claim in a fight between new and old owners of a pay phone company.

The firm has also been involved in some cases related to high-profile bankruptcies in the telecom industry. Wilmington Trust Co. tapped Paul Hastings to represent it during the bankruptcy of telecommunications provider Williams Communications Group. The Delaware-based bank, an unsecured creditor and bondholder of Williams, objected to Williams' reorganization plan.

It's in the bag

Attorneys at Paul Hastings should be sure to don their best duds for the Enzo Angiolini case. The firm is defending the clothing line and its parent company, the Jones Apparel Group, from a lawsuit brought by another designer. Celine, a division of LVMH, alleges that Enzo Angiolini illegally copied Celine's Boogie Bag, a handbag popular with the Hollywood set.

In December 2002, the firm advised health products retailer Vitamin Shoppe on its sale to Bear Stears Merchant Banking for $320 million. United Airlines hired Paul Hastings to help negotiate a December 2002 wage dispute with the airline's mechanics. The firm continues to work with United regarding salary issues related to its high-profile Chapter 11 bankruptcy filing.

Is the check in the mail?

The firm has recently found itself in a position it's unaccustomed to being in – that of plaintiff. Paul Hastings acted as counsel to the city of Tulsa, Okla., regarding a suit filed by black police officers against the city. Paul Hastings, which represented the city for about five months in 2001 and 2002 before withdrawing from the case, now says Tulsa still owes the firm for its work and has filed a suit to recover its fee.

GETTING HIRED

Let's see some energy!

"We need energetic and motivated attorneys who understand that the job involves long hours and high levels of stress," Paul Hastings attorneys tell us. Insiders also report "the firm's selectivity is becoming increasingly more stringent" and is "very focused on fit." Candidates should possess "the ability to take on tasks head on" and a personality "that will add to the pleasant atmosphere." The "firm hires from mid- to high-tiered law schools. Candidates from the higher tiered law schools – the Yales and Harvards – get away with a lower class ranking, top third to top half. Whereas candidates from other schools" may need to be in "the top 5 percent to top 25 percent of their class." "The callback process involves interviews with four to five attorneys here at the firm of all levels of seniority. Generally offers are made, if at all, several days after the interview."

OUR SURVEY SAYS

Many offices, many moods

Sources tell us the overall firm culture at Paul Hastings is difficult to define. "For a top-tier firm with high expectations, this is a remarkably humane place to work," an LA associate tells us. This source adds, "Although everyone is expected to do their share of work and to do good work, the overall culture is fairly relaxed. The partners and senior associates are generally available to assist with work, and there is no infighting among associates." An LA colleague shares, "A group of young associates often socialize together outside of work." However, a third associate from the City of Angels offers a completely different point of view: "There seems to be a real lack of bonding between attorneys. The associates and partners rarely have a chance to get to know the other attorneys outside their particular department." Another LA insider says, "The firm has a collegial atmosphere, although the recent decision to separate departments onto different floors has detracted from the unity of the firm as a whole."

Meanwhile, "the Stamford office is a perfect balance between having the finest clients and most challenging work while working in a relatively relaxed environment." Says another Connecticut attorney, "We come from a pretty wide background of schools, hometowns and so forth, and it is a comfortable place to work." An insider tells us the London office "has such a disparate collection of individuals that I feel there is no firm culture to speak of." An Atlanta associate finds the firm "a bit uptight and pretentious," although "overall, most of the lawyers are decent individuals." An associate in the New York office says, "The office culture is friendly, and attorneys – both partners and associates – will have lunch together and occasionally go out for drinks together."

Some think the culture varies widely from practice area to practice area. A midlevel associate describes the firm culture as a "sort of a continuum – with the free-wheeling, laid back, casual real estate department at one end" and the "conservative employment department at the other. Corporate and litigation fall somewhere in the middle."

Clock watchers

Overall Paul Hastings associates aren't very happy about the hours they keep and think the situation can be improved, even though long hours will always be a function of working at a top-tier firm. "The work hours are obscene," sighs one senior associate. One insider confides that the hours for litigation associates are "marginally better than at some of the comparable firms." The "employment folks work like galley slaves," though "they do get good experience and work on front-page cases." Some are better at managing pressure to work long hours than others. It's best to remember that "the work comes in waves, so you will have downtime again soon," says a wise first-year. "This place is a ghost town on Friday afternoons," an associate says of the Atlanta office. This source continues, "If you do not have work to do, you are not expected to waste your time sitting here on call. We all have lives outside the firm, and the partners really encourage a balanced lifestyle." But some colleagues disagree with that assessment. "I do not like feeling like I have to be here for face time when I'm not busy," says a midlevel. One attorney offers a somewhat sarcastic view of life at Paul Hastings. "Good news: Even in a terrible economy the firm has plenty of quality work available. Bad news: You are expected to work around the clock to get it done." A senior attorney tells us having a family "makes being here really painful. It's not so much the hours, it's the uncertainty and lack of control of your schedule." Others blame the long hours on inadequate staffing and poor planning. "The long hours in part reflect a lack of sufficient paralegal or other support that could help with some of the lesser involved issues."

Money isn't everything

An associate gripes that salaries in the Stamford office are "still behind other branches of the firm for no valid reason." Maybe this attorney should speak to the officemate who says his compensation is "way beyond expectations." According to another attorney, Paul Hastings "matches compensation of top-tier firms in each office's geographic location." Bonuses are "strictly hours based, which makes it impossible these days to get anything as a transactional associate. Other firms have more flexible systems," says an LA associate. Several colleagues agree, saying, "The salary is market, but the bonuses should be more generous to truly compete with other firms." Another lawyer in LA considers the pay "nothing extraordinary," but believes it to be "in line with our peers." "These days I am much less inclined to complain about compensation than I was a year or two ago," says a source who feels fortunate to have a job. A New York associate echoes those thoughts: "I feel especially fortunate in the current market," she says. A senior attorney reports being "totally satisfied with my salary. Generally, I'd prefer to be paid a little less and appreciated a little more." Another colleague "would prefer the option of taking a reduced salary in order to have a life and do some telecommuting."

How's your partner?

Treatment of associates "really varies among the partners." Some partners "are very kind and get along well with associates, and some do not manage these relationships well." "It seems to me," says an associate in the LA office, "that the relationships between partners and associates are great in real estate, OK in corporate and non-existent in employment and litigation." "There are partners who treat associates with tremendous respect. However, the firm and other partners do virtually nothing to police those others who abuse associates." "Most partners are a pleasure to work with, yet there are a few who can be abrupt and stubborn," shares a first-year. A litigation associate reports noticing "an improvement in the past year regarding the partners' interaction with associates." "While overall I think partners treat associates well," explains one senior associate, echoing the sentiments of many associates, "there is a definite lack of communication."

Mixed reviews on training

Associates give the firm mixed reviews when it comes to training. The "firm provides a lot of opportunities for training – in-house and by videoconference from other offices. Each associate is assigned to a mentor." However, "some mentor partners do a better job than others." A corporate associate reports that there are numerous CLE courses and the firm often "brings in outside people to give lectures on different topics. Computer training is always available," as well. "We have formal training sessions every two weeks," says an Atlanta associate. While an LA associate feels there is "more than enough training," an Orange County associate is less diplomatic, complaining of "too many worthless programs, such as the video conferencing and computer training, and not enough relevant ones, such as practice-oriented" training. "The formal training is usually not helpful. I find that it's more" helpful to get "on-the-job training. You learn by doing." An associate who disagrees about the abundance of formal programs says, "Any training associates get is on the job." This source adds, "There is very little mentoring and/or training from partners and senior associates despite firm lip service to the contrary." According to a first-year, "Although the firm offers plenty of training, all training is on your own time. This makes it difficult to take advantage of training opportunities. Budget relief for training during the first several years of practice would vastly improve training opportunities."

The other half

Associates give the firm cautious praise when it comes to its attitude toward women. "The women who are in partners do a lot to encourage and support other women in achieving their goals," says a newbie. A litigator in the Atlanta office reveals, "Our firm hires and promotes women at a very acceptable rate, but we have few senior women as mentors. There are no female partners in our department in this office. Nonetheless, I have received excellent mentoring from more senior female associates." A sixth-year associate sings a familiar tune: "Hiring is fine, but it is our retention, promotion and mentoring that is poor to nonexistent." Comments one female midlevel, "It is commonly believed that with few exceptions you essentially have to vow to not have children to make partner. Of course, you can have kids and tuck them in at night via your cell phone if you really want to." The firm counters that nearly 40 percent of its attorneys are women, quite a few of them partners, and that all three women promoted to the partnership ranks in 2003 had children.

Orrick, Herrington & Sutcliffe LLP

Old Federal Reserve Bank Building
400 Sansome Street
San Francisco, CA 94111-3143
Phone: (415) 392-1122
www.orrick.com

LOCATIONS

San Francisco, CA (HQ)
Los Angeles, CA
Menlo Park, CA
New York, NY
Orange County, CA
Pacific Northwest (Seattle, WA, & Portland, OR)
Sacramento, CA
Washington, DC
London
Milan
Paris
Tokyo

MAJOR DEPARTMENTS/PRACTICES

Bankruptcy & Debt Restructuring • Corporate •
Compensation and Benefits • Employment Law • Energy
& Project Finance • Intellectual Property • Litigation •
Mergers & Acquisitions • Private Finance • Public
Finance • Real Estate • Structured Finance • Tax

THE STATS

No. of attorneys: 650 +
No. of offices: 12
Summer associate offers: 31 out of 48 (2002)
Chairman: Ralph H. Baxter, Jr.
Hiring Attorney: Douglas Madsen

BASE SALARY

San Francisco, CA
1st year: $125,000
2nd year: $135,000
3rd year: $150,000
4th year: $165,000
5th year: $185,000
6th year: $195,000
7th year: $205,000
8th year: $215,000
Summer associate: $10,400/month

UPPERS

• Great partner/associate relationships
• Team spirit, including popular softball games
• Public finance superstars

DOWNERS

• "Creeping Dilbertization"
• Bonus linked to billables
• Sketchy support for flex-time arrangements

NOTABLE PERKS

• "Whiskeytown" bar in Menlo Park
• Concierge service
• Firm-sponsored breakfast and lunch ("The
  Trough")
• Profit-sharing program

THE BUZZ
WHAT ATTORNEYS AT OTHER FIRMS ARE SAYING ABOUT THIS FIRM

• "Fantastic bond lawyers"
• "Got too big too fast"
• "Associate-friendly environment"
• "The Cali firm that acts like a New Yorker"

RANKING RECAP

Best in Region
#7 - California

Quality of Life
#5 - Part-Time/Flex-Time
#8 - Pay
#14 - Retention
#16 - Best 20 Law Firms to Work For
#16 - Associate/Partner Relations
#17 - Satisfaction

Best in Diversity
#8 - Diversity for Gays and Lesbians
#14 - Overall Diversity

EMPLOYMENT CONTACT

San Francisco
Ms. Mireille Butler
Recruiting Administrator
Phone: (415) 773-5568
Fax: (415) 773-5759
E-mail: mbutler@orrick.com

Silicon Valley
Ms. Rebecca Whittall
Recruiting Manager
Phone (650) 614-7352
Fax: (650) 614-7401
E-Mail: rwhitall@orrick.com

New York
Ms. Francesca Runge
Recruiting Manager
Phone: (212) 506-3556
Fax: (212) 506-5151
E-mail: frunge@orrick.com

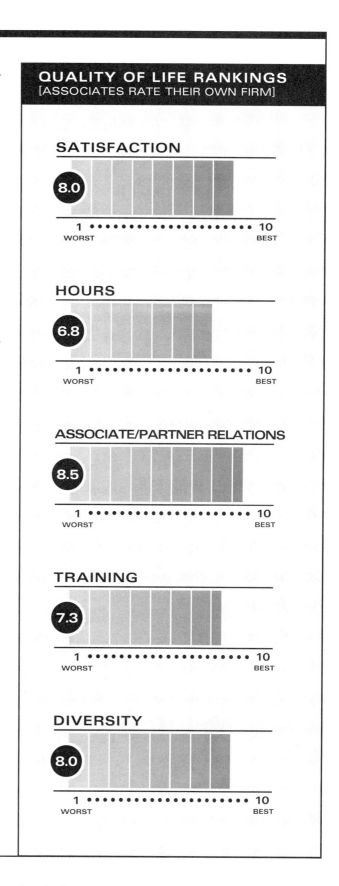

QUALITY OF LIFE RANKINGS
[ASSOCIATES RATE THEIR OWN FIRM]

SATISFACTION
8.0
1 WORST .... 10 BEST

HOURS
6.8
1 WORST .... 10 BEST

ASSOCIATE/PARTNER RELATIONS
8.5
1 WORST .... 10 BEST

TRAINING
7.3
1 WORST .... 10 BEST

DIVERSITY
8.0
1 WORST .... 10 BEST

THE SCOOP

Orrick Herrington & Sutcliffe LLP traces its roots back to Gold Rush-era San Francisco, but the firm has since developed firm footholds on the East Coast, as well as outside the United States. The firm is best known as a leader in the finance arena, but it dips into 14 other practice areas, including antitrust, intellectual property and litigation.

Lawyers by the Bay

Orrick's roots can be traced to the 1863 founding of the German Savings and Loan Society, which would later become part of the First Interstate Bank of California. The Society had as its general counsel John R. Jarboe, who became an authority on real estate law. In 1885 Jarboe founded Jarboe, Harrison & Goodfellow, the parent of modern-day Orrick Herrington & Sutcliffe. That partnership would dissolve in 1891, but W.S. Goodfellow soon got back in the game at Goodfellow & Eells. That firm hired William H. Orrick in 1910; George Herrington and Eric Sutcliffe would come on board by the early 1930s.

Over the years, Orrick Herrington & Sutcliffe in its various forms has helped build the business and physical landscape of San Francisco. The firm participated in the building of companies like the Pacific Gas & Electric Company and the Fireman's Fund Insurance Company, landmarks such as the Golden Gate Bridge and Candlestick Park (now 3Com Park) and BART (the Bay Area Rapid Transit System).

Around the world in 20 years

The firm expanded rapidly, doubling in size during the 1990s. The New York office, founded in 1984 with six lawyers, now houses nearly 200. The Los Angeles office, launched in 1985 with two attorneys, now employs 60. But Orrick's expansion hasn't been limited to the United States. In 1995 the firm opened its first overseas outpost in Singapore. (The firm eventually closed that office, a joint venture with local firm Rodyk & Davidson, in January 2003 due to a dearth of business.) In 1996 Orrick launched another Asian office in Tokyo; three years later that office entered into a joint venture with Tokyo-based Bengoshi Sho Kokusai Law Offices. A London branch which opened in 1998 has grown to 31 lawyers. In October 2002, after a long round of negotiations that included several U.S. competitors, Orrick acquired the Paris office of London-based Watson, Farley & Williams and its A-list client base, which includes Vivendi Universal, Renault, France Telecom and BNP Paribas. In April 2003, Orrick moved into Italy, scooping up the attorneys of Studio Associatio Legale Tributario, a Milan legal group formerly affiliated with Ernst & Young.

Money men

Orrick is perhaps best known for its public finance prowess; the firm boasts that it has been either bond counsel or underwriter's counsel on approximately 12 percent of all municipal bond issues over the past decade. Orrick was named Top Bond Counsel and Top Underwriters by *The Bond Buyer* in 2000 and 2001, and broke its record for bond business, serving as counsel for over 1,000 issues totaling $66 billion in 2002. *The American Lawyer* has honored Orrick attorneys as Dealmakers of the Year in the public finance sector. In 1999 department chair Roger Davis was the magazine's top dealmaker; partners Tom Myers and Eileen Heitzler were so feted in 2000 and 2002, respectively.

The firm's public finance work has included bonds based on future payments from tobacco lawsuits. Clients have included the state governments of Wisconsin, South Carolina and California, the City of New York and individual counties in New York and California. The firm also worked on the largest municipal finance deal in U.S. history, a $9 billion revenue anticipation note offering completed for the state of California in October 2002; a follow-on offering in November 2002 brought in another $3.5 billion for the Golden State. (Los Angeles-based law firm Curls, Brown & Duran acted as co-note counsel with Orrick.) The firm was part of a team selected by the California Controller's office in February 2003 to issue revenue anticipation bonds in anticipation of a budget deficit later in the year.

Lawyers for bankers

Orrick's private finance practice group is divided into three subgroups: private equity, commercial and institutional finance and bankruptcy and debt restructuring. The private equity group represents both fund investors and fund sponsors. Investor clients include the New York State Common Retirement Fund (Orrick's first private equity investor client in 1987), the Oregon Public Employees' Retirement Fund, CalPERS and TIAA-CREF. The firm's private equity fund sponsor clients include financial powerhouses like Goldman Sachs, Credit Suisse First Boston and American Century and venture capital investors such as Lucent Technologies. The firm's commercial and institutional finance attorneys have worked for a diverse array of clients. Fleet Capital, Bank of America, General Electric Capital Corp., Lucent Technologies and FINOVA Capital have all tapped the firm for secured and unsecured lending transaction. Banc of America Securities, Lucent and ABN AMRO Bank have availed themselves of Orrick's representation in lease financing transactions.

Bankruptcy clients include Reliance Insurance, Stone & Webster, Commodore Business Machines, the Los Angeles Kings of the National Hockey League, the Great Lakes Pulp & Fiber Company and Tri-Valley Growers. International bankruptcy clients have included the World Bank when that organization helped rewrite bankruptcy and insolvency laws in South Korea, the Kingdom of Thailand in the takeover of insolvent financial institutions, and the Republic of Ecuador in the restructuring of debt obligations.

Orrick in the court

In June 2001, Orrick's litigation department took a star turn in the biggest of legal venues – the U.S. Supreme Court. The firm represented the Mead Corp. in United States v. Mead Corp, a battle over tariffs. From 1989 through 1993, the Customs Service classified Mead's imported "day planners" as items not subject to a tariff. The Customs departments suddenly changed their classification and began levying a 4 percent tariff on the day planners. In June 2001, the Supreme Court ruled for the Mead Corp., saying that once the Secretary of the Treasury (whose office is charged with classifying which items are subject to tariffs) makes a decision, that decision stands unless the rules covering a product are changed by Congress or a change is made to the item.

The same month as Orrick's Supreme Court win, the firm suffered a litigation setback. An appeals court ordered a new trial in a copyright infringement case against Orrick client MP3.com. In November 2001, an appeals court rejected Orrick client Adchem's claim that punitive damages should not be awarded in an employment discrimination case.

Coming and going

Orrick is no stranger to the mad, mad attorney merry-go-round. In February 2003, four partners from the now-defunct Brobeck, Phleger & Harrison partners – James Baker, Grady Bolding, Frederick Holden, Jr., and Gregory Lemmer – went for greener, Orrickian pastures. Laurent Develle, a partner in White & Case's Tokyo office, joined Orrick in January 2003, while two partners (Christopher W. Wright and Laurie A. Smiley) and an associate (Eric Scott Carnell) joined Orrick's corporate and technology practice in Seattle from Cooley Godward.

Among those jumping the Orrick ship were partners Neal L. Wolf and Todd L. Padnos. The firm also bid adieu to Terrence McMahon (an intellectual property partner who left for McDermott, Will & Emery) and Barbara Caulfield (a litigator who went in-house at Affymetrix, Inc.).

GETTING HIRED

The new way

When it comes to hiring, Orrick is doing things a little different, say its associates. Prospective hires are screened by partners and associates at regional offices, "but the national leadership must also sign off on new hires." "The firm is becoming increasingly selective," according to one lawyer. "A central crew now screens all local office selections before offers are extended. This central crew has been accused of employing too many stereotypes and [trying] to discern from people's resumes and activities whether they are firm material or likely short-timers who really want to do public interest, criminal law or something else beyond the fold."

Not everyone is pleased with the new hiring process. "The firm has recently taken a step in the wrong direction where the focus is to hire candidates from Ivy League law schools, not the most qualified candidates," says one source. Orrick "is somewhat snobby about the law schools from which it will hire," concurs one attorney. "If a candidate has attended or does attend the 'right' law school, the candidate would have to work hard not to receive an offer." One source sighs, "I preferred when we recruited people we liked."

The new method isn't all bad. "The firm conducts at least two interviews of each applicant and attempts to have the applicant meet as many people in the respective practice group as possible," reports one insider. "Orrick definitely takes its time in making hiring decisions and looks for smart, motivated, diligent attorneys who are looking to build a career at Orrick." Despite the perceived new rules, "personality is extremely important." Be careful, Orrick wannabes. "I can't tell you how many otherwise qualified people get shot down because they submit a sloppy resume, cover letter or writing sample," warns one source. "All you need to do is spend some time on it, get feedback from your writing professor, put some effort into it. It's worth the time spent."

OUR SURVEY SAYS

Orrick's biggest asset

Orrick lawyers report a laid back, relaxed work environment. "The culture of Orrick is a highly prized asset of the firm," brags one insider. Another agrees, saying, "The atmosphere is very laid back and friendly." Don't worry about meanies. That associate says, "I'm not aware of any screamers or otherwise mean partners," and another happily reports that "ogres are not tolerated." Feel free to walk on in. "Doors are always open, and attorneys – partners and associates alike – are always willing to speak with you and answer questions," says one associate. "I'm not a tool in answering this," swears one tool. "I truly am happy with the work that I've been doing. I've been given significant responsibility in a range of difference cases, and I think that this is true for my colleagues."

"The firm's cultural values really come across in all activities," says one contact. "The firm emphasizes excellence and integrity, as well as mutual respect." The atmosphere carries over after-hours, that associate continues. "Lawyers do tend to socialize." The Menlo Park office, for example, will take you down to Whiskeytown. "It is common for attorneys and staff to congregate in our Whiskeytown Lounge for drinks and snacks on Friday afternoons," says one Silicon Valley associate. "There is also a monthly associates' lunch and many other little late-afternoon soirees and get-togethers on a fairly regular basis. Some attorneys also socialize with each other outside the office, although I'm not one of them." Bring your cleats and your glove – or at least your pom-poms – if you work in the Big Apple. "The softball team in the New York office is the pinnacle of the office's culture, says one New Yorker. "It is an institution and loved by players and non-players alike."

Partners and associates get along, according to Orrick associates. "Every partner I have worked with treats me with the utmost respect," says one lawyer. "I think it's a fundamental and unspoken condition for partnership in most cases." "This is the reason that I have remained at this firm – partners treat associates (and for that matter, everyone treats everyone else) with an extraordinary degree of respect," says one veteran. "Partners are accessible and tend to treat associates as valuable members of a team," gushes one source. "They are appreciative of effort and quality work product. They encourage associates to interact directly with clients and to assume a significant amount of responsibility on transactions."

Still busy

The downturn has affected Orrick, but its associates are still putting in time in the office. "We seem to be handling the downturn very well. My concern is overworking, not underworking," says one insider. Another source agrees: "I work a lot, but in these times, it's better to have a job in which I work a lot than no job at all." The firm has realistic targets, though. "Big firms are big firms, and they expect you to work hard," says one realist. "That said, they are very upfront with their expectations. If your yearly total begins with a '2' you generally have nothing to worry about." Another attorney elaborates. "Orrick's target for associates is nominally 1,950 or so, but the number everyone really aims for each year is 2,000. The firm won't complain if an associate bills 2,100-2,200. Anything above that, they say should be the exceptional case, as they don't want to see associates burn themselves out." Insiders are split about the firm's need for face time. "No one expects you to be here at night or on weekends unless you have something due," says one contact, but another complains, "There is incredible pressure to bill and put face time."

The firm seems to be lacking in part-time or flex-time arrangements. "Although I'm happy with my arrangement, I think it's hard to come by and is actively discouraged," says one part-timer. "Orrick tries to pay more than lip-service to flex-time working arrangements, and I can point to several of my colleagues who enjoy this benefit. But it is clear that Orrick would prefer we were all full-time," says one Orrick lawyer. Others are still more critical of the firm's stance. "The firm certainly doesn't go out of its way to encourage people to use the policy, and even locating a copy of the policy was cumbersome," reports one contact. "The partners are blatant about how they despise these alternative work schedules," says another source. At least one part-time associate feels supported, though. "I feel fortunate to have the opportunity to work at a prestigious firm on a part-time basis. On the whole, Orrick is very supportive of alternative work schedules."

Getting paid

In late 2002, Orrick adjusted its bonus structure, tying compensation strictly to hours. "The hours-based bonuses mean that if you had a grueling year, at least you were compensated for it and if you had a pleasantly light one, well, what the hell are you complaining about?" asks one Orrick associate. Another insider elaborates. "Like all big firms, our associate pay is lockstep by class. We have bonuses at 2,000, 2,100, 2,200 and I think 2,300 hours. I don't think we're the absolute top in the salary race, but we're close." That seems fine with most associates, even if some feel the firm pays too much attention to hours. "The firm pays commensurate with other big firms; the only negative is that bonuses are completely tied to hours," complains a source. "I have no issues with my base salary, but I don't think I'm worth what I'm paid," says one lawyer with low self-esteem. Another says, "We make so much money here, that sometimes you feel as if you'll never really earn what you make. God bless capitalism." Some scoff at rumors of a discretionary bonus. "While there theoretically is a discretionary bonus, few, if any, have ever seen it," says one source. "The discretionary bonus would more accurately be described as the elusive bonus," jokes another.

The perks are fairly standard, with tickets (in New York, for example, the firm gives out "damn fine Yankee tickets") and free food (catered lunches are nicknamed the "Trough"). The firm also offers a concierge service for dry-cleaning pickup, vacation planning and other personal errands.

School days

Opinions on the firm's training program vary. "Intensive in-house training occurs when one starts as a new attorney, and midlevel in-house training occurs periodically," states one associate. "During the last few months, we have instituted weekly litigation training sessions at lunch, which are mandatory for junior and midlevel associates and to which senior associates are encouraged to attend." "Orrick provides regularly scheduled training sessions for its associates and holds annual training sessions for its midlevel associates," another insider agrees. Others blast the firm's training efforts. "The firm thinks it does a great job of training associates, but in reality they do very little," fumes one insider. "Associates are not allowed to attend conferences or training sessions outside the office; everyone is so busy that there is no time for mentoring. Many associates worry that the firm is not creating a new generation of associates that are able to problem solve and think creatively."

Striving for diversity

According to its associates, Orrick has some of the typical big-firm problems with diversity issues. Most acknowledge the firm makes an effort to recruit and retain women and minorities, though some feel it doesn't always get results. "There are challenges in this area for all major law firms, but I believe Orrick goes out of its way to address the issues and is making real progress with gender diversity," reports one source. Another is more critical. "I think the firm is very open to hiring [and promoting] women. However, there is not any mentoring, and there are very few women partners or senior associates." Others concur that mentoring is an issue. "Generally the firm does a very good job of hiring women but only a good job of promoting or mentoring women," says one associate.

"The firm is receptive to the idea of diversity but needs to significantly improve in hiring, promoting, and mentoring minorities," criticizes one source. (Another balances that criticism by pointing out that the head of the Seattle office, Stephen Graham, is African-American.)

Morgan, Lewis & Bockius LLP

1701 Market Street
Philadelphia, PA 19103-2921
Phone: (215) 963-5000
www.morganlewis.com

LOCATIONS

Harrisburg, PA • Irvine, CA • Los Angeles, CA
Miami, FL • New York, NY • Northern Virginia
Palo Alto, CA • Philadelphia, PA • Pittsburgh, PA
Princeton, NJ • San Francisco, CA • Washington, DC
Brussels • Frankfurt • London • Tokyo

MAJOR DEPARTMENTS/PRACTICES

Antitrust • Bankruptcy • Business & Finance •
Employee Benefits & Executive Compensation • Energy
• FDA/Healthcare Regulation • Intellectual Property •
Investment Management • Labor & Employment Law•
Life Sciences • Litigation • Media • Mergers &
Acquisitions • Real Estate • Securities • Tax •
Technology

THE STATS

No. of attorneys: 1,167
No. of offices: 16
Summer associate offers: 52 out of 62 (2002)
Firm Chair: Mr. Francis M. Milone
Hiring Partners: Eric Kraeutler (Firm-wide); Coleen M.
Meehan (Philadelphia); Peter Buscemi & Thomas A.
Schmutz (DC); Christopher T. Jensen & Michele A.
Coffey (NY); Robert M. Brochin (Miami); John G.
Ferreira (Pittsburgh); Randolph C. Visser & Douglas
Rawles (LA); Howard Holderness (San Francisco)

THE BUZZ
WHAT ATTORNEYS AT OTHER FIRMS ARE SAYING ABOUT THIS FIRM

- "Philly power"
- "Smart not to merge with Brobeck"
- "Great reputation; good work product"
- "Haven't they fired everyone?"

BASE SALARY

Philadelphia, PA
Class of 2002: $125,000
Class of 2001: $130,000
Class of 2000: $130,000
Class of 1999: $135,000
Class of 1998: $140,000
Class of 1997: $145,000
Summer associate: $24,000/summer

Washington, DC
Class of 2002: $125,000-145,000
Class of 2001: $135,000-160,000
Class of 2000: $140,000-145,000
Class of 1999: $140,000-160,000
Class of 1998: $157,500-175,000
Class of 1997: $160,000-200,000
Summer associate: $25,000/summer

New York, NY
Class of 2002: $125,000
Class of 2001: $135,000
Class of 2000: $140,000-150,000
Class of 1999: $159,000-167,000
Class of 1998: $170,000-187,000
Class of 1997: $192,000-2000
Summer associate: $27,000/summer

UPPERS

- State-of-the-art Washington digs
- On the rise on the West Coast
- Reachable hours requirements

DOWNERS

- Murky partnership track
- Questionable commitment to part-time
- Screamers sprinkled in among partnership

NOTABLE PERKS*

- Free snacks and candy every afternoon
- Firm-sponsored socials, like black-tie dinner dance
- Weekly cocktail parties
- On-site gym (D.C. and Philadelphia)
Perks vary by office.

RANKING RECAP

Best in Region
#1 - Pennsylvania

Best in Practice
#4 - Labor & Employment

Quality of Life
#11 - Satisfaction
#14 - Training
#18 - Hours

EMPLOYMENT CONTACT

See www.morganlewis.com careers section for contacts in various offices.

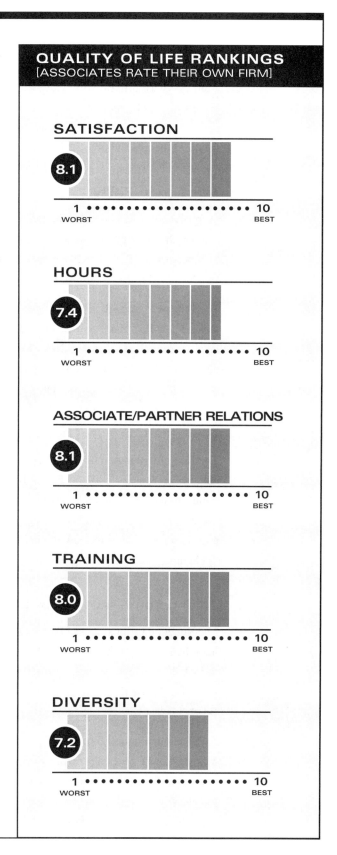

QUALITY OF LIFE RANKINGS
[ASSOCIATES RATE THEIR OWN FIRM]

SATISFACTION
8.1
1 •••••••••••••••••• 10
WORST   BEST

HOURS
7.4
1 •••••••••••••••••• 10
WORST   BEST

ASSOCIATE/PARTNER RELATIONS
8.1
1 •••••••••••••••••• 10
WORST   BEST

TRAINING
8.0
1 •••••••••••••••••• 10
WORST   BEST

DIVERSITY
7.2
1 •••••••••••••••••• 10
WORST   BEST

THE SCOOP

If size matters, then Morgan, Lewis & Bockius LLP matters a lot. The firm has more than 1,000 attorneys in 16 offices worldwide, with approximately 300 lawyers in legal hot spots New York, Washington, D.C., and Philadelphia, the only law firm to have such extensive coverage in all three cities. Recently, the firm expanded on the West Coast, too, with over 200 lawyers in California, thanks to the dissolution of Brobeck, Phleger & Harrison.

Starting in Philly

Morgan Lewis was founded in Philadelphia in 1873 by Civil War veterans Charles Eldridge Morgan, Jr., and Francis Draper Lewis. It took nearly 100 years before the firm opened an outpost in New York in 1972. Los Angeles soon followed (1976), then the firm went international, adding London (1981), Tokyo (1988), Brussels and Frankfurt (both in 1989).

The firm went through some changes, starting in 1999. A new management structure centralized power in the firm chair's office and created managing partners in charge of operations, practice and legal personnel. In October 2001, Morgan Lewis laid off 50 associates in the U.S. In a move designed to boost the firm's patent practice, Morgan Lewis acquired Hopgood Calimafde Judlowe & Mondolino, a 35-lawyer IP boutique firm based in New York, in December 2001.

D.C. flash

The firm's Washington office is a source of pride. Morgan Lewis moved into a new 14-story law complex in January 2002 on Pennsylvania Avenue, near the White House and the Capitol. The building has 46 conference rooms, a moot court room and a dining center overlooking the Washington Monument. (The dining center is especially popular on July 4th, when the firm holds a raffle for associates to view the annual D.C. fireworks display.) The building also has a funky "light tube," a 120-foot long pipe that brings natural light to the entire office.

Taking some, not all, of Brobeck

The Hopgood Calimafde deal didn't fulfill Morgan Lewis's appetite for expansions. The firm was identified as one of the suitors for Brobeck before it went bust. Brobeck, which had no choice but to look for a merger to save itself from post-dot-com collapse, was rumored to be in merger talks with D.C.-based Hogan & Hartson, but after that deal vanished, Morgan Lewis appeared to be Brobeck's last chance.

A full acquisition fell through, and Brobeck soon announced it would dissolve. In the aftermath, Morgan Lewis added 60 of the firm's partners on the West Coast and approximately 90 other attorneys. The new lawyers were added to Morgan Lewis's existing Los Angeles office, as well as three newly-created California offices in San Francisco, Palo Alto and Irvine. The hires bulked up eight different practice areas for Morgan Lewis, with much of the new blood joining litigation.

One of the 32 new litigation partners is Brock Gowdy, a 2002 recipient of a *California Lawyer* Attorney of the Year award.

More new blood in litigation

Morgan Lewis litigators in London scored a coup in August 2002, stealing partner Trevor Asserson, the head of litigation at rival Bird & Bird. The firm's Miami office added three new litigation associates in March 2003. Julie Russo left D.C.-based LeClair Ryan for Morgan Lewis; Coren Stern came from Winston & Strawn's New York office; Craig Leen left the Boston office of Skadden, Arps, Slate, Meagher & Flom.

Commitment to pro bono

The firm's pro bono practice and charity commitment have gotten noticed. The firm made a $50,000 contribution to the Support Center for Child Advocates in Philadelphia. Morgan put up matching funds for a total donation of $100,000 to the organization, which provides services, including legal representation, for abused and neglected children. In September 2002, Morgan Lewis associate Nora von Stange won the Abely Award, a pro bono award given by the Center for Battered Women's Legal Services, for her work on a complex, multi-jurisdictional child custody case. In March 2003, the firm was honored by Women In Military Service For America National Foundation for contributing over $1 million in legal services to the organization. In May 2003, two partners, J. Gordon Cooney, Jr. and Michael L. Banks, represented a man who was freed from death row after serving 18 years for a murder he did not commit. Morgan Lewis lawyers worked on this case pro bono for 15 years.

Morgan Lewis summer associates can take advantage of the Public Interest and Community Service (PICS), a pro bono program that allows law students to spend half the summer working at Morgan Lewis and the other half at a public interest or community service organization, earning the full summer stipend. Given that commitment to pro bono work, it's no surprise Morgan Lewis associates give the firm high marks for its pro bono program. "The firm is encouraging about pro bono work, allowing some pro bono work to count towards annual hours targets," says a senior associate at Morgan Lewis.

An army of litigators

Litigation is one of the firm's strengths; Morgan Lewis has over 600 litigators worldwide. Other key practice areas include intellectual property (160 lawyers), antitrust, business transaction and mergers and acquisitions (over 300 attorneys worldwide and over $150 billion in transactions completed in the last three years). Also, the firm is nationally recognized for its securities regulatory and life sciences practices.

GETTING HIRED

Study up

Thanks to the rough economy, Morgan Lewis can afford to be selective. "Our firm receives an overwhelming number of applications for each available position," reports one source. "The firm handles the screening and interview processes well. Candidates brought in to meet with members of a practice group are generally brought in to test the 'fit' with the group. Quality and germane experience for laterals is absolutely required." "Lately, the firm has moved towards hiring almost exclusively from the top 10 schools," observes one insider.

If you want in at Morgan Lewis, hit the books in law school. "The firm looks for highly qualified candidates, but does not limit itself to the Ivies. Those in the top 5-10 percent academically at second-tier schools will get a good look and personality counts for a lot." Another associate concurs. "[The firm] is only interested in candidates from top-tier law schools or from second-tier schools who were at the top of their class." Still, look alive during your interviews. "The firm's interview and callback process is very formal," says an associate. "We generally have a candidate spend a half day interviewing with us and let them know within a day or two if we are interested. We look for candidates that are intelligent, articulate, personable and will fit in with the firm culture."

OUR SURVEY SAYS

Formal, not white shoe

"The quality of life for an associate at Morgan Lewis is good," says one source. "I would say that the firm culture is friendly. I certainly would not characterize it as uptight. It is a notable characteristic of this firm that there don't seem to be a lot of shouters or yellers here, which is a valuable thing." "The firm's culture is very collegial," agrees an associate. The lovefest continues. "I find the work challenging and intellectually stimulating," enthuses one insider. "The attorneys I work with are bright, efficient, motivated and take a genuine interest in my professional development. The support staff performs its job adequately and in a timely manner. My colleagues are nice people."

The happy atmosphere permeates into associate/partner relations – for the most part. "We are treated like responsible and intelligent adults and are expected to act accordingly," says one lawyer. "In my experience the partners have always treated associates with great respect," another reports. "I am treated very well," says a senior associate. "However, I know of isolated instances where other associates are treated extremely poorly." On rare occasions, partners have been known to raise their voices. "I have seen a small number of senior partners berate and yell at associates and law clerks," says a contact. "The partners poorly communicate issues, comments, and information to associates," complains one attorney. "There is little partner/associate social interaction and partners often forget that associates have families and other obligations besides the firm."

Hours, yes. Face time, no

Morgan Lewis associates should be prepared to put in typical big-firm hours. One insider claims that "2,000 [billable] hours is the target" for associates, though insiders say the firm was flexible enough to drop the requirement down to 1,900 temporarily after the September 11, 2001 terrorist attacks and subsequent economic slump. That understanding on the part of the firm, as well as reasonable expectations on the part of Morgan Lewis associates, results in satisfaction with the amount of time spent at the office. "There is no doubt that I work a lot of hours as an associate here and that I would work much less in most other professions," says one associate. "Some weeks or months are especially grueling and my personal life suffers. But I choose to practice law in a large firm, and with the benefits come the hours. The hours I put in are no more than I anticipated." "The hours are not unreasonable – far from it, in fact – and most attorneys appreciate and respect the fact that people have lives outside of the office," agrees another contact.

"The hours are long but there is no face time requirement at all," says one associate. "No one cares when you come and go as long as the work gets done." Others agree Morgan Lewis "is a hard-working law firm but, except when deals are particularly active, late nights and weekend work are generally not necessary. It generally is possible to leave early if the deal load is light."

Matching, not making, the market

Most Morgan Lewis associates feel the firm's salary and bonus structure is fair, with the firm matching the market and following the lead of its competitors. "I feel my compensation is generally consistent with the best firms in the city," says one New York associate. "I don't think the firm strives to be the pacesetter in New York for associate salaries, but I don't think that is a negative as I think that the firm is more than competitive salary-wise." Associates in the City of Brotherly Love have a similar experience. "I feel that I am compensated at the top of the Philadelphia market and our system of guaranteed bonuses is nice," says one contact. "In 2002, the firm lowered the billable requirement (after the year closed, which was very nice) to allow more associates to receive bonuses." Another observes that the firm watches the market, and hopes the market trend is toward fatter associate paychecks. "The firm is committed to keeping compensation near the top of national levels and, in the Philadelphia region, at the top," gushes the Philly associate. "When Dechert raised first-year salaries last year, the firm matched it quickly. With any luck, the Dechert partners will splurge on associate compensation again this year!"

But 2,000 (as in hours) seems to be the magic number. "Our base salary contains a hold-back (guaranteed bonus) if you make 2,000 hours and receive a satisfactory evaluation," says one attorney. "This hold-back can range from $5,000 to $15,000. If you do not make your 2,000 hours, you do not even receive a discretionary bonus." The discretionary bonus is exactly that – meaning

some don't take home extra dough. "Bonuses are a little different than some other firms, as our bonuses are discretionary from one person to the next," reports one insider. "I think the system works in a very fair manner."

Comfortable spaces

Morgan Lewis' larger offices are deemed comfortable – especially Washington, where the firm recently opened a new building. But some critics knock what the firm does with its space. "The building facilities are very nice and the location is great," says a D.C. associate. "The individual offices are new but OK. The space is generally good, but I am not thrilled with the internal office configuration and furniture." "No one has to share an office," reports another Washington lawyer. "The office size is decent. The furniture could be improved." New York associates rave of a "fantastic class-A building with excellent city views," though "for some junior associates, the situation is cramped." In Philadelphia, "associate offices are larger than at most firms." And the firm management says the San Francisco, Miami and LA offices have outstanding views and comfortable spaces.

Top-notch training

"The training is top rate," says one associate, and most at Morgan Lewis agree. "There is a clear commitment to attorney development," that associate continues. "I appreciate the fact that Morgan Lewis is willing to devote so much time and resources to making sure that associates know what they are doing," says another source. The formal training structure is decentralized – each department has some flexibility in how it teaches its associates – but most departments get high marks. "My practice group has weekly training sessions for part of the year, as well as an annual three-day training session where all associates from all of the offices gather to train on a particular subject," says a junior labor lawyer. "They have done negotiation skills, taking and defending depositions, evidence issues, oral advocacy. I also get plenty of informal training from the partners I work with and through the early opportunities I have been given." An M&A associate says, "We have formal training programs at least two times a month. Most of these are very helpful. In particular, our training for first-year associates is exceptional." Speak up if you want to be taught. "There is as much training available as you want," says one source. "If you do not ask, however, you probably will not get those opportunities."

Mommy friendly?

Morgan Lewis insiders give the firm mixed reviews regarding its environment for female associates. Virtually all agree there's no bias in hiring or treatment, but some say the firm is lacking in female representation at higher levels. There's disagreement about how the firm's part-time program affects female partnership prospects. "The firm is terrific about accommodating women with part-time schedules and generally not taking them off a partnership track just for being part-time," says one insider. "Most of my women friends leave the firm or plan on leaving before they have children due to the part-time issue," another associate says. "The firm does not appear to be a mommy-friendly place to work. Hiring and promoting does not seem to be the big issue." Others are optimistic. "There could be more female partners, but I do not believe there is a true 'old boys network,'" says one source. "I think women will emerge in the partnership ranks in the near future." The firm points out that during the past five years, 26 percent of female rising partners were working on a reduced schedule when they were elected to the partnership.

The firm's efforts regarding minority recruiting and retention get higher marks. "The firm is very eager to hire and retain minorities," says one source. "I believe the firm is working to increase minority representation, through the summer associate class and otherwise," another insider observes.

Winston & Strawn

35 West Wacker Drive
Chicago, IL 60601-9703
Phone: (312) 558-5600
www.winston.com

LOCATIONS

Chicago, IL (HQ)
Los Angeles, CA
New York, NY
San Francisco, CA
Washington, DC
Geneva
Paris

MAJOR DEPARTMENTS/PRACTICES

Contracts
Corporate
Employment & Labor
Energy
Environmental
Government Relations
Intellectual Property & Technology
Litigation
Real Estate
Tax

THE STATS

No. of attorneys: 940
No. of offices: 7
Summer associate offers: 95 percent (2002)
Chairman: Gov. James R. Thompson
Managing Partner: James M. Neis
Hiring Chair: Julie A. Bauer
Associate Programs Chair: Paul H. Hensel

BASE SALARY

Chicago, IL
1st year: $125,000
2nd year: $135,000
3rd year: $150,000
Summer associate: $2,400/week

UPPERS

• High salaries and generous bonuses
• Magnificent offices
• Impressive pro bono commitment

DOWNERS

• Lack of communication from partnership
• Uneven training opportunities
• Long hours

NOTABLE PERKS

• Attorney dining room
• Bagels and donuts on payday
• Discounts for client merchandise
• Use of skybox for concerts and sporting events

THE BUZZ
WHAT ATTORNEYS AT OTHER FIRMS ARE SAYING ABOUT THIS FIRM

• "Perfection"
• "Conservative"
• "Rock solid"
• "All tobacco, all the time"

RANKING RECAP

Best in Region
#4 - Chicago

Quality of Life
#1 - Best 20 Law Firms to Work For
#1 - Associate/Partner Relations
#1 - Offices
#1 - Retention
#2 - Pay
#4 - Satisfaction
#5 - Pro Bono
#12 - Hours
#15 - Training

Best in Diversity
#1 - Diversity for Minorities
#7 - Overall Diversity
#19 - Diversity for Women

EMPLOYMENT CONTACT

Ms. Deborah S. Cusumano
Legal Recruitment Manager
Phone: (312) 558-6151
Fax: (312) 558-5700
E-mail: dcusumano@winston.com

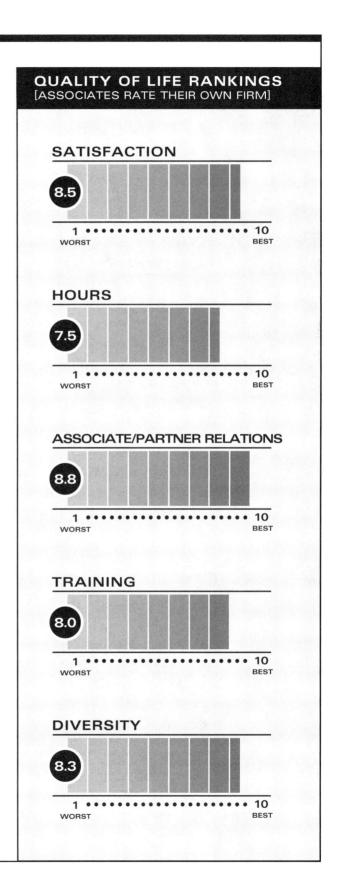

QUALITY OF LIFE RANKINGS
[ASSOCIATES RATE THEIR OWN FIRM]

SATISFACTION
8.5
1 WORST .... 10 BEST

HOURS
7.5
1 WORST .... 10 BEST

ASSOCIATE/PARTNER RELATIONS
8.8
1 WORST .... 10 BEST

TRAINING
8.0
1 WORST .... 10 BEST

DIVERSITY
8.3
1 WORST .... 10 BEST

THE SCOOP

Chicago-based Winston & Strawn, one of the country's oldest and largest law firms, celebrates its sesquicentennial in 2003. The firm, which excels in both litigation and corporate practices, puts its attorneys up in style, boasting some of the most attractive law offices in the United States.

Windy City institution

Prominent Chicago Democrat Frederick H. Winston established his law firm in 1853. By the time Silas Strawn came aboard 41 years later, the firm that became Winston & Strawn had one of the city's most powerful legal practices, with a client list drawing heavily upon the regional railroad and stockyard industries. The firm remained small throughout its first century of existence but has swelled to gigantic proportions in the last 15 years. In 1989, Winston conducted its first merger with a New York law firm, a process they would repeat a little over 10 years later. It also used a merger to bolster its strength in the Washington, D.C., legal market in 1990 and finalized plans to acquire the California boutique firm Murphy Sheneman Julian & Rogers in February 2003, augmenting its two-year presence in Los Angeles and creating a new outpost in San Francisco. Foreign offices in Geneva and Paris round out Winston's 800-plus-attorney roster, although the firm announced plans late in 2002 to add another office in London.

Winston is a high-powered firm that frequently attracts lawyers with political clout. Former Illinois Governor James Thompson joined the firm in 1991 and has served as its chairman since 1993. The firm's partners have even granted him two special extensions in order to allow him to continue running the firm beyond the original term limits of Winston's partnership agreement. The firm lured another powerful Republican to its Washington, D.C., office in February 2003, hiring Lee Johnson, the former chief of staff of the GOP's Senate caucus.

Playing with the big boys

Former federal prosecutor Dan Webb, who prosecuted Admiral John Poindexter for his role in the Iran-Contra scandal, heads Winston & Strawn's litigation practice. Since joining Winston, Webb has defended Phillip Morris in several class-action lawsuits (which led to a role as lead courtroom counsel for suits involving multiple tobacco companies), represented General Electric in a diamond price-fixing trial and signed on for the tail end of proceedings in Microsoft's federal antitrust case. He took on another A-list client in October 2002, when General Electric's former CEO, Jack Welch, tapped Webb to join the team of attorneys handling his drawn-out divorce proceedings.

In November 2002, the Hawaiian attorney general's office retained the firm to sue ChevronTexaco for more than $563 million. The state alleges that the oil company conducted a 30-year scam to avoid paying state taxes, buying barrels of crude oil at inflated prices through Indonesia. Winston will be working for Hawaii on a contingency basis and will cover its own expenses until the case is resolved.

Can I get fries with that?

Winston's attorneys helped bring an early end to the first round of a controversial lawsuit filed against omnipresent fast-food chain McDonald's, a firm client. The suit, filed on behalf of three children in the Bronx whose parents blame Mickey D's for their obesity and health problems, accused the restaurant of negligence for selling addictive food products with high cholesterol and fat levels and failing to adequately warn customers about the dangers of a steady diet of Happy Meals. A New York federal judge tossed the case out in January 2003, observing that the plaintiffs had failed to prove McDonald's advertising was deceptive and that most consumers knew fast food wasn't good for them. The judge did, however, leave room for the plaintiffs to replead their claim that McDonald's uses potentially harmful additives and processing techniques of which most of its customers are unaware. The amended suit is pending.

Close shave

Winston won a smooth legal victory when it represented Syndia Corp. in a patent infringement suit brought against Gillette. Winston's attorneys successfully argued that Gillette had violated Syndia's patents for coating razor blades with diamond-laced carbon (DLC), a process which enables the development of thinner and stronger blades. The jury awarded Syndia $10 million in damages for the infringement in its June 2002 verdict, and Winston's litigation team indicated that its client intended to seek injunctive relief against the future sale of Gillette products that use the DLC blades, including the Mach3 and Venus razors, unless the company agreed to pay a licensing fee to Syndia for continued use of the process. A settlement favorable to Syndia was reached in early 2003.

Corporate clout

Winston's strengths lie outside the courtroom, too. The firm's corporate and finance practices, primarily based in New York and Chicago, provide a wide range of transaction-related services to clients that include General Electric, Goldman Sachs, Motorola and UBS PaineWebber.

In early 2003, prominent local client Chicago Bridge & Iron Co.'s long-running dispute with the Federal Trade Commission came to a head. A little more than two years earlier, the company announced a deal to buy the water and engineered construction divisions of Pitt-Des Moines Inc. The two companies agreed to comply with an FTC request to delay the merger pending further review, but when they hadn't heard back from the commission by February 2001, they went ahead and closed the deal anyway. The FTC issued an administrative challenge to block the sale, arguing that it substantially lessened competition in several industrial markets. A two-month trial, during which Winston attorney argued on Chicago Bridge's behalf, concluded in January 2003, with a decision expected later in the year.

Promoting public service

Winston & Strawn encourages staff and attorneys to participate in pro bono activities and has had a full-time director of public interest law since 1999. The firm takes an especially active role in fighting death penalty sentences. In addition to litigating on behalf of several death-row inmates in Illinois, Winston has spent more than 2,000 attorney-hours working on the appeal proceedings of Eugene Clemons II, a mentally disabled Alabama man convicted of murder after initial representation by attorneys who offered no substantial defense. Winston's labors on the case have presented the court with compelling new evidence. The appeal is ongoing.

The firm also participated in the dramatic controversy over Illinois Governor George Ryan's desire to grant clemency to the state's death row inmates due to concerns about the possibility of wrongful convictions. The state's attorney general, a death penalty advocate, went to the Illinois Supreme Court in the fall of 2002 in an effort to block clemency for certain types of prsioners. Winston & Strawn prepared a brief on Gov. Ryan's behalf which led to the court's decision to decline consideration of the attorney general's challenge.

GETTING HIRED

Casual callbacks – but not too casual

"The interview process is very casual. Most attorneys just want to get a sense of your personality and demeanor as opposed to grilling you on academic credentials. That said, being too casual in an interview is definitely a turn-off. You still need to take it seriously and approach it as an exchange where people will carefully observe their impressions of you." "With the current economy," says a Chicago associate, "it appears that the firm is hiring candidates who are in the top 10 percent of their class, attend top-20 law schools and have work experience prior to attending law school." "You have to have good grades, but you also have to come across well in your interview. Even if you are the editor of the law review, you won't be hired here unless you can be articulate and personable." A second-year describes the "prototypical Winston lawyer" as someone who is "social, outgoing, has some interest in sports, has the ability to focus and work hard when necessary but lacks even the hint of arrogance." In the opinion of one midlevel, "being selected for the summer associate program is very tough. It is much easier to become an associate by means of the lateral pathway."

OUR SURVEY SAYS

Not nearly as stuffy as you'd think

A happy bunch, those Winston associates are. "I don't think I would be more satisfied at any other firm," muses one contented associate. Insiders characterize Winston & Strawn as "a work-hard, play-hard kind of place." "The firm has a reputation publicly as being stuffy, but the atmosphere is really very laid back once you're inside. The attorneys are very professional and serious about their work but, at the same time, very social once you get to know them in a professional environment," a real estate attorney tell us. Sure, "there are a few stiffs around here," says a third-year, "but there are also plenty of people who are a blast to hang out with." A fifth-year shares the best things about working at Winston & Strawn: The "people are very pleasant" and "it's a place you don't mind coming to in the morning."

The work is good, too, insiders say. "I find satisfaction in being challenged, and here I always have had as much responsibility as I can handle," shares a senior associate. A second-year has found that "the quality of work in my department, for my experience level, has been very good, challenging and varied." "Winston & Strawn has an excellent client base with interesting, high-profile cases. I get to work with smart people on challenging, important matters," brags a litigator. A corporate attorney is pleased to receive "substantial responsibility in cutting-edge deals, as well as the support I need from experienced, intelligent partners." At the same time, this source characterizes her department as "playful," adding, "There is lots of joking around intermixed with working hard." A second-year is impressed with the firm's prospects for the future. "Firm management is doing a nice job positioning Winston to compete in coming years." The "number of offices and associates continue to grow, and [the] presence of [the] firm continues to increase as we handle more complex and high-profile litigation and deals."

Long but flexible hours

Winston insiders tell us there's a lot of flexibility at their firm regarding hours. "There is no face-time requirement, sick day policy or vacation policy. All that matters is how many hours you bill. No one cares if you work from home. No one cares if you take December off because you've billed enough hours from January to November. No one cares if you work half days for three weeks straight because you've just come back to the office from an out-of-town trial." "While there are peaks and ebbs, the hours are very tolerable, relative to other big firms." "The hours are very manageable – 1,950 to get the top pay and 2,100 to qualify for a discretionary bonus. The bonuses were surprisingly excellent this past year, even for the 2,100 hour range, so it's worth it to go for the carrot," says a very happy senior associate. (The firm points out that some of those 2,100 hours can even be for non-billable work.) "It's a lot of hours. But that's what they pay us for," shrugs a first-year. "It spreads onto the weekends, which is sometimes annoying, but again, that's what they pay us for."

Winston & Strawn associates "can still have a life outside of the office, which is not necessarily the case at other large law firms." A litigation associate "appreciates that I can waltz in at 10:30 a.m. if I feel like it but still be recognized as a hard worker since in the end my hours are pretty good." But for another litigation associate, "It's a thrill and a rarity if you can leave before 7 or 8 p.m. or don't have to work on the weekends." Another attorney tells us, "Associates are sometimes in demand from many different partners, which makes it difficult to control the schedule." At the opposite end of the spectrum is a second-year who says, "While I have very little work and my billables are very low, I still have to be in the office 10-12 hours a day for face time."

Phat paychecks = fat wallets

Winston associates are delighted with their pay. There's only "one word to describe the salary and bonuses: phat!" "Law firm associates are overcompensated. But I'm not complaining," says a second-year. "Although I work hard and put in many hours, my current compensation very much exceeds any expectations I had when I joined the firm," says a very happy fifth-year. "The firm pays you to work hard and rewards you when you do." A litigation associate reports, "The firm is right on par with most [other firms] as far as salary. However, they really reward performance and hours with very generous bonuses." One associate confides, "There was some grumbling at the firm this year after bonuses were paid" because "the firm more or less caps its bonuses at 2,400 [hours]. Thus if you bill more than 2,400 hours, you make the same amount of money as someone who billed right at 2,400." This source concludes, "Other than this isolated example, most other associates are quite satisfied."

The many sides of training

Most Winstonites are pleased with the training at their firm. "There are frequent opportunities to participate in continuing legal education programs, both internally at the firm and outside." "The firm provides formal training sessions once a week for first-year transactional attorneys" in "real estate and corporate, which provides a great overview of many topics." A labor attorney tells us, "There is great training in my department, and terrific encouragement to attend trainings and seminars outside the firm as well." Some, however, are less than delighted. "In my department," says an IP attorney, "I have received no training or mentoring." A corporate attorney with no exposure to formal training says, "It is exclusively informal and takes the form of getting a lot of responsibility early on – the learn-by-doing approach." This source acknowledges that such a situation "can be scary," but says, "Partners are always available to provide advice." In the opinion of a senior associate, "We could always use more training. The laissez-faire approach causes a training shortfall, in my view." "While in-house training is minimal following the first year with the firm, they are becoming more liberal with allowing us to attend – and reimbursing us for – CLE courses that are relevant to current or prospective work." The firm just hired a new director whose sole function is to manage the training programs at the firm," so insiders expect "the number of training programs will increase as a result."

© 2003 Vault Inc.

A woman's job

On a whole, attorneys are pleased by the firm's efforts to hire and retain women, although some believe, "In terms of promotion, the firm needs improvement. However, there is a good balance of women among younger associates at the firm." "Some groups have better representation than others. While there are many terrific female income partners, the number at capital partner level still seems low." "From everything I have seen, there is a conscious effort to include women in the management of the firm," says a male associate in Chicago. Another male associate believes "Winston's diversity committee does a great job advocating for women here." A female attorney agrees, saying "Winston works hard to make things work out for women and mothers." However, others believe "the firm makes an effort to promote women, but does not seem to recognize the structural barriers women have to overcome."

Office envy

Almost without exception, Winston associates love their office space. Windy City attorneys brag that they have the "most beautiful law offices in Chicago!" "There's really no comparison to Winston's offices. They are refined, classy and functional," says a labor attorney, while another associate describes them as "very elegant." "We have the most beautiful and accommodating offices I have ever seen," muses another happy camper. Working in "gorgeous offices" with "great views" "really makes a difference during long days." Another Chicagoan concurs: "An elegant environment makes a difference." Attorneys in the D.C. office are looking forward to the day when they feel just as enamored with their offices as their Chicago colleagues. "The Washington office is old, run down and lacking in space. However, the firm is opening a new Washington office in the spring of 2005."

Proskauer Rose LLP

1585 Broadway
New York, NY 10036
Phone: (212) 969-3000
www.proskauer.com

LOCATIONS

New York, NY (HQ)
Boca Raton, FL
Los Angeles, CA
Newark, NJ
Washington, DC
Paris

MAJOR DEPARTMENTS/PRACTICES

Bankruptcy & Creditors' Rights
Corporate & Securitites
Employee Benefits & ERISA
Entertainment, Sports & Intellectual Property
Estates, Wills, Trusts & Probate
Health
Labor & Employment
Litigation
Real Estate, Environmental & Zoning
Tax

THE STATS

No. of attorneys: 590
No. of offices: 6
Summer associate offers: 79 out of 81 (2002)
Chairman: Alan S. Jaffe
Hiring Attorney: Julie M. Allen

BASE SALARY

New York, NY
1st year: $125,000
2nd year: $135,000
3rd year: $150,000
4th year: $165,000
5th year: $185,000
6th year: $195,000
7th year: $205,000
8th year: $210,000
Summer associate: $2,404/week

UPPERS

- Prestigious labor & employment, sports law groups
- It's fun to represent the rich and famous
- Supportive environment for gays/lesbians

DOWNERS

- Low marks for part-time policy
- Compensation lags for senior associates
- Retention issues for women and minorities

NOTABLE PERKS

- Department happy hours
- Professional back rubs
- The "world's greatest chocolate chip cookies"
- Yearly firm-wide gala in New York

THE BUZZ
WHAT ATTORNEYS AT OTHER FIRMS ARE SAYING ABOUT THIS FIRM

- "Many great lawyers have come from Proskauer"
- "Hi. We were cool in the '70s."
- "One of the best"
- "Proskauer Rose – we never close"

RANKING RECAP

Best in Region
#19 - New York

Best in Practice
#3 - Labor & Employment

Best in Diversity
#20 - Diversity for Gays & Lesbians

EMPLOYMENT CONTACT

Ms. Diane M. Kolnik
Manager of Legal Recruiting
Phone: (212) 969-5060
E-mail: dkolnik@proskauer.com

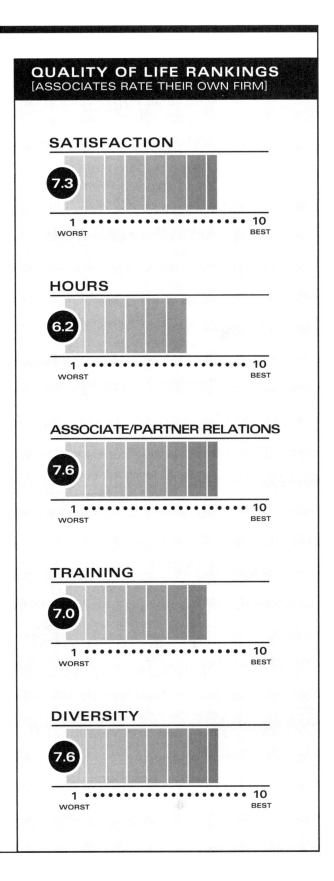

QUALITY OF LIFE RANKINGS
[ASSOCIATES RATE THEIR OWN FIRM]

SATISFACTION
7.3
1 WORST • • • • • • • • • • • • • • • • • • 10 BEST

HOURS
6.2
1 WORST • • • • • • • • • • • • • • • • • • 10 BEST

ASSOCIATE/PARTNER RELATIONS
7.6
1 WORST • • • • • • • • • • • • • • • • • • 10 BEST

TRAINING
7.0
1 WORST • • • • • • • • • • • • • • • • • • 10 BEST

DIVERSITY
7.6
1 WORST • • • • • • • • • • • • • • • • • • 10 BEST

THE SCOOP

Proskauer Rose LLP may be strongest in the labor and employment law department, but the firm is famous for its sports clients. Major League Baseball, the National Basketball Association and the National Hockey League are some of the sports giants that have used the firm's services. The firm has approximately 590 attorneys in five U.S. offices and a Paris outpost.

The family business

The first Rose in Proskauer Rose was William R. Rose, who founded a law practice in New York in 1875. He took on his friend Gibson Putzel as a partner three years later. When Putzel passed away suddenly in 1907, associate Benjamin G. Paskus became a partner in Rose & Paskus.

In 1911 Alfred R. Rose, William's son, joined the firm and became a partner in 1920 after a stint in the U.S. Navy during World War I. Alfred Rose had previously clerked at the law firm of James, Schell & Elkus where Judge Joseph Proskauer was a partner. In 1930 Judge Proskauer resigned his judgeship to go back to the lawyer life. Proskauer became the firm's leader; the name was changed to Proskauer, Rose & Paskus when he joined. It was changed again in 1942 to Proskauer Rose Goetz & Mendelsohn, and shortened to its current form in 1997.

A bunch of good sports

Proskauer Rose became one of the leading sports law firms in the mid-1970s. Although the firm was on the losing side of the famous Oscar Robertson case that brought free agency to the NBA, the league's mamagement, was pleased with the work of David Stern, the lead litigator on the case. Stern became in-house counsel at the NBA in 1978 and later commissioner. Gary Bettman, currently the NHL's commissioner, also got his start at Proskauer Rose.

The firm scored a big win in 2002. Proskauer was chosen over rival Morgan, Lewis & Bockius to represent Major League Baseball in labor negotiations with the Major League Baseball Players Association. The negotiations went well, for once. The two sides agreed to a deal and narrowly avoided a strike, the first time Major League Baseball was able to avoid a work stoppage through labor negotiation in 30 years of trying.

The National Football League selected Proskauer Rose and partner Joe Leccese for negotiations related to the building of a new football stadium in downtown Los Angeles. Proskauer has also represented the WNBA, Major League Soccer and teams such as the Minnesota Timberwolves (NBA) and the Montreal Expos (Major League Baseball).

Lights ... camera ... Proskauer!

The sporting world isn't the only arena in which Proskauer attorneys rub elbows with the rich and famous. The firm has an entertainment, media, information and technology practice that represents movie, music and other entertainment companies. In January 2003, Proskauer partner Charles Ortner was named national legal counsel for the National Academy of Recording Arts and Sciences. Ortner represents megastars like Madonna and Shania Twain and numerous music companies and record labels.

Partner Charles Sims represented the Motion Picture Association of America in a lawsuit against Eric Corley, the publisher of the hacker web site 2600, over the publication of DeCSS, the computer code that enables the copying of DVDs. A U.S. Circuit Court of Appeals ruled for the MPAA in December 2001. Sims also filed a brief on behalf of the Association of American Publishers and a group of artists, writers and composers in the much-watched Eldred vs. Ashcroft case. In January 2003, the U.S. Supreme Court ruled that a congressional act extending copyright protection by 20 years after the death of an artist was constitutional. Opponents of the law argued that the extension benefits entertainment companies at the expense of free speech; entertainment companies and artists claimed that the extension provided the original creators of the work and their descendents with increased fruits of their labor.

Proskauer suffered a setback for clients MGM, Universal and 20th Century Fox in an appeals court reversal in June 2002. The appeals court ruled that Sonicblue, Inc., a company that makes digital video recorders that allow users to skip commercials and share programming, would not be forced to collect customer data for movie studios concerned about copyright infringement.

The entertainment practice added a heavy hitter in November 2001. Howard Weitzman joined Proskauer's Los Angeles office after leaving technology start-up Massive Media Group. Weitzman has represented a bevy of celebrity clients including Michael Jackson, Magic Johnson, Ozzy Osbourne and O.J. Simpson. (Weitzman was the former football star's original attorney after O.J. was charged with murder, before he was replaced by the illustrious "dream team.")

Isn't it ironic?

It's pretty clear that Proskauer doesn't think singer Rod Stewart is sexy – unless they find not getting paid sexy. In September 2002, the firm sued the singer (whose hits include "Do Ya Think I'm Sexy?" and "Maggie May") for over $19,000 in unpaid legal fees. Proskauer had represented Stewart in a lawsuit filed by an interior designer who said Stewart hadn't paid up for work done on his estate. The firm negotiated a settlement in August 2002 but subsequently claimed – like the designer – that Stewart never paid his bill.

Lyon's share

In July 2002, six attorneys from Lyon & Lyon, a Los Angeles-based intellectual property boutique, defected to Proskauer. The six, led by partner James Shalek, joined just in time. Lyon & Lyon voted to dissolve a month later after partner defections and a failed merger deflated the firm.

Working on work

At Proskauer Rose, labor and employment is where it's at. Some of the firm's most high-profile cases in recent years have involved prestigious universities. Proskauer Rose successfully defended Yale University in 1997 in a lawsuit filed by graduate student teaching assistants seeking the right to organize a labor union. Three years later, the National Labor Relations Board ruled against a Proskauer Rose client in a similar matter, allowing New York University grad students to organize a union. The firm is representing Columbia University in a discrimination suit filed in March 2003. A former employee (ironically, the acting director of the school's Office of Equal Opportunity and Affirmative Action) claimed she was denied a promotion because she is an African-American female and charged that the university has a pattern of discrimination. The suit, which sought class-action status for all of Columbia's African-American employees, is pending.

Go for broke

Proskauer's bankruptcy practice covers all bankruptcy, insolvency and reorganization issues. Current cases include Superior Telecom and Lechters on the debtor side. The firm has represented creditors in a broad range of cases, including Alcatel, Scoreboard, Parklane Hosiery Company, Cibro Petroleum Products, Consolidated Steel, Berks Jewelers and Neptune World Wide Movers.

GETTING HIRED

Laboring to get into labor

Like most firms, Proskauer Rose's recruiting efforts start at the top, although "Proskauer is willing to branch out beyond the top-tier, Ivy law schools," reports one insider. "There are a fair amount of associates who did not graduate from top-tier schools. A significant percentage, though not majority, of the partners are non-Ivy graduates." Another associate agrees, saying that "aside from the top national schools, we recruit among the top students at regional schools" including Fordham, Brooklyn Law School, Seton Hall and Rutgers. Aggressiveness will not earn you any points. "We're looking for smart people who can do the job but are still kind of down-to-earth – not necessarily the Type-A personality," warns one mellow fellow. "A bad, ultra-competitive [personality] will sink you in the interview process regardless of paper credentials," agrees another source. Most concur that Proskauer's " interview process is pretty laid back, and most people they call back will get an offer."

Given Proskauer's pride in its labor and employment practice, it's no surprise insiders find that department a little more selective. "[The] labor department is very competitive," observes one labor lawyer. "Not all summers who want that department get it, even if they did good work." Another attorney in the same department says the firm is selective to a fault. "With respect to the labor department, they appear overly-selective, resulting in a shortage of associates," goes the complaint.

OUR SURVEY SAYS

Taking it easy

Most associates report satisfaction with the laid-back culture of Proskauer, which one source calls "the anti-white shoe firm." "The firm's culture is friendly, and while the firm is as big as other New York powerhouses, I do not think of it is as mean," says one associate. It's not all fun and games, of course. "The culture is generally quite friendly but definitely has an air of formality to it as well," observes a contact. "The younger lawyers seem to socialize together on a fairly frequent basis, for a large law firm, anyway."

"If you are slick, you will not be happy here," warns one associate. "Many of the attorneys are frumpy or have an individual sense of style, but none are in the cookie-cutter, slick attorney mode." That contact continues: "I think ranting and raving would be unacceptable. No one has shouted at me here." It seems variety is the spice of Proskauer life. "People seem to tolerate a variety of lifestyles and appearances within the range allowable at a 125-plus-year-old institution," says one third-year. "If you work hard when needed and have the ability to successfully complete a task, people will give you much leeway to be yourself."

The only consistent complaint about Proskauer's culture is one common to the legal industry – occasional run-ins with unreasonable partners. "Some partners are very nice," says one associate. "Some insist that lower level or midlevel associates deal with first-years. Some won't even acknowledge you are on the team." Although one contact thinks the partners at his firm are "generally fair," he goes on to say, "I don't always get the impression that they are really concerned with what type of experience I'm getting or how I am developing as a lawyer, as long as I bill the hours." When times get tough, things might get a little tense. "Most partners in my department are courteous to associates, although some will lose it when highly stressed, particularly if the associate has failed to anticipate issues [or] concerns," says one labor/employment associate. However, many agree that "we're all on the same team here, and the partners value our efforts and opinions. You won't hear any yelling in our hallways."

Gripes about money

Though Proskauer Rose doesn't lag the market significantly, there are a couple of recurring complaints about the compensation. "Our bonuses match the market but never make news," says a first-year. Geographic rivalries abound. "In the past there has been tension between the compensation of associates in the main office and Los Angeles, the largest satellite office," according to one West Coaster. "[It's] hard to understand how bonuses can be higher for associates

in New York when the Los Angeles office is the most productive." Other insiders, while not so quick to boast of their office's superiority, admit there seems to be some disparity. "I work in a national office, and we get paid OK for our geographic area," says a Newark lawyer. "However, the main office is less than 10 miles away and they make $30,000 more for doing the same work."

The firm usually approaches the market rate when it comes to junior associates, but compensation can start to lag for their more senior counterparts. "[The firm is] on par with their peer firms with respect to annual compensation for first- through third-years," says a fourth-year associate. "At the fourth-year level, there is a $5,000 gap. With respect to fifth-years and beyond, I assume that gap continues. With respect to bonuses, it is tied to hours and they are generally at market for the first-through third-year classes. I find that they consistently tend to make laterals take a step back in class year and salary, in an effort to lower costs."

Not chained to a desk

Proskauer associates seem resigned to the long hours inherent in law firm life. "Although the hours are longer than I would like, when you come to a law firm like this one, you expect to work long hours," says a contact. "We are considered 24/7 attorneys and always on call. I find that most senior attorneys and partners here are respectful of associates' need for downtime. But when push comes to shove, if you are needed, you work." Another lawyer concurs: "I haven't had many awful weeks yet, but when it's busy, it's very rough. I doubt it is any better at any other comparable firm." That source continues: "Bottom line: billing the target hours is very tough because you simply can't bill all of your time in the office, no matter how efficient you are." At least schedules are often predictable. "Although I work very long hours during the week, I am able to plan so that I have most weekends free," says one associate. "It would, however, be really nice to have a 9-to-6 job, but I don't view that as realistic in any law firm."

Part-time arrangements are rare and receive mixed reviews. "The part-time program is only for people with child care issues, and very few associates participate," says one lawyer. One lawyer who works full-time says, "From what I hear, part-time is never part-time. I know associates who work part-time, and all it basically means is that you have one day a week off." One complaint: "The flex-time program requires a higher proportionate hour commitment than that required for full-time associates."

Learning at the Proskauer Institute

Proskauer provides a week-long formal training program for new associates called the "Proskauer Institute" and a "unique" program in which junior associates shadow their more senior colleagues. "I am impressed by the Proskauer Institute training program, provided to all incoming first- and second-years in the fall, and the Proskauer in-house CLEs," says one associate. Others agree the training programs are helpful. "The Proskauer Institute is great, a week-long training program that ensures everyone has a solid level of training before they begin work," says a contact. Still, some say it's the informal mentoring that counts. "Training is rarely formal, but the on-the-job training is great," says one New Yorker. "I can go to partners with questions or steward things on my own when I am able."

The shadow program allows junior associates to tag along on cases and get billable hour credits at no extra charge to the client. "The firm's shadowing program is particularly useful and unique," says an associate. It's not perfect, of course. "There are some shadowing opportunities and things like that, but usually I don't go because it would mean I'd get behind in the rest of my work."

Retention problems?

Proskauer Rose attorneys report the typical big-firm diversity issues, though some feel the firm does better than most. "I think it could be better numbers-wise, but it doesn't seem nearly as bad compared to the situation at many other firms," says a source. "The number of women seems to dwindle when you look beyond the younger attorneys, though." The big-firm life may be to blame. "The firm is receptive to women, but there are few women partners in my department and the lifestyle they lead, which seems to involve tremendous sacrifice of time with family, is generally not perceived as the model to which others would aspire," reports one source. "As a result, many female associates opt out before they even come close to consideration for partnership."

Similar issues crop up in relation to minority associates. "I would love to see more people of color here, but I believe the firm works hard to recruit in this area," says one contact. "I think we're welcoming, but there aren't a whole lot of minority attorneys when you walk around here," another agrees. "They need to make a better effort to recruit minorities." "The racial diversity could definitely use a bolster," summarizes another associate. "I'm not sure if it's a large firm issue, or if it's more specific to this firm."

Insiders say the firm offers a welcoming environment for gays and lesbians. "The firm has several openly gay partners and associates, and I have not perceived any overt discrimination in this area," reports one associate. A gay associate in the New York office reveals, "This is a good place to be out. There is an expectation that gay/lesbian attorneys will be treated with respect that comes from the top. I was out from day one and have found the firm to be a great environment."

42

Cahill Gordon & Reindel LLP

80 Pine Street
New York, NY 10005
Phone: (212) 701-3000
www.cahill.com

LOCATIONS

New York, NY (HQ)
Washington, DC
London

MAJOR DEPARTMENTS/PRACTICES

Corporate
Litigation
Real Estate
Tax
Trusts & Estates

THE STATS

No. of attorneys: 245
No. of offices: 3
Summer associate offers: 43 out of 47 (2002)
Chairman: Immanuel Kohn
Hiring Partner: Roger Meltzer

BASE SALARY

New York, NY
1st year: $125,000
2nd year: $135,000
3rd year: $150,000
4th year: $170,000
5th year: $190,000
6th year: $210,000
7th year: $220,000
8th year: $230,000
Summer associate: $2,400/week

UPPERS

- Compensation matches top of market
- Famous First Amendment practice
- Free market system lets associates choose their assignments

DOWNERS

- Assignment system leads to hours disparity
- "Mud-like coffee"
- Virtually no formal training

NOTABLE PERKS

- Free cookies
- Matches law school donations
- Monthly happy hour

THE BUZZ
WHAT ATTORNEYS AT OTHER FIRMS ARE SAYING ABOUT THIS FIRM

- "Great First Amendment practice"
- "All dough, no know"
- "Better than most people recognize"
- "Better have an exit strategy"

RANKING RECAP

Best in Region
#18 - New York

EMPLOYMENT CONTACT

Ms. Joyce A. Hilly
Hiring Coordinator
Phone: (212) 701-3901
E-mail: jhilly@cahill.com

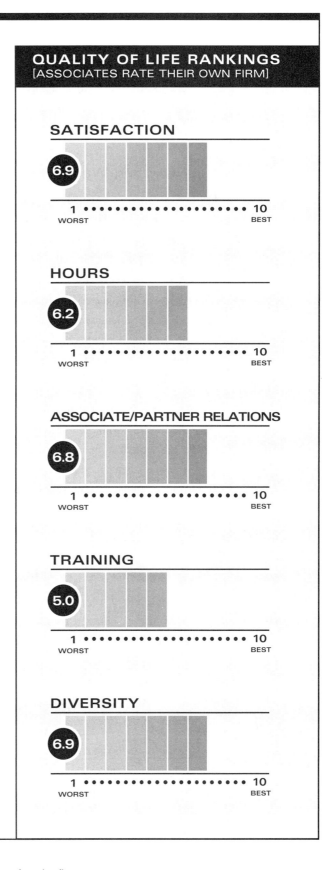

QUALITY OF LIFE RANKINGS
[ASSOCIATES RATE THEIR OWN FIRM]

SATISFACTION
6.9
1 • • • • • • • • • • • • • • • • • 10
WORST   BEST

HOURS
6.2
1 • • • • • • • • • • • • • • • • • 10
WORST   BEST

ASSOCIATE/PARTNER RELATIONS
6.8
1 • • • • • • • • • • • • • • • • • 10
WORST   BEST

TRAINING
5.0
1 • • • • • • • • • • • • • • • • • 10
WORST   BEST

DIVERSITY
6.9
1 • • • • • • • • • • • • • • • • • 10
WORST   BEST

THE SCOOP

With 245 attorneys in three offices (New York, Washington, D.C., and London), Cahill Gordon & Reindel LLP is strong in finance and corporate work (a historical strength), antitrust and litigation. The firm has argued several cases before the U.S. Supreme Court and counts First Amendment super-lawyer Floyd Abrams among its ranks.

Representing Wall Street since 1919

Cahill Gordon was founded in New York in 1919 and quickly built a respected finance and corporate practice. The firm began handling bankruptcy and reorganization clients during the Great Depression, and added a Washington, D.C., office in 1935. Under the leadership of former U.S. Attorney John T. Cahill, the firm became a top litigator, specializing in antitrust matters and, later, First Amendment cases. Cahill lawyers argued in front of the U.S. Supreme Court in cases like *National Broadcasting Co. vs. United States* (regarding the authority of the Federal Communications Commission) and *Times Picayune vs. United States* (a key antitrust decision). In a prominent First Amendment case, the firm represented the *New York Times* when the newspaper published the Pentagon Papers, top-secret government documents related to early U.S. involvement in Vietnam.

The firm has represented top investment banks since its inception. In the 1980s, the firm represented many Wall Street heavy hitters during a boom. When Wall Street stumbled in the late 1980s, the firm lost two clients to bankruptcy, including junk bond trader Drexel Burnham Lambert, which accounted for 25 percent of the firm's billings in 1988 and 1989. Cahill stayed the course and continues to represent some of the largest investment banks in the world such as Credit Suisse First Boston, Deutsche Bank, Goldman Sachs, J.P. Morgan Chase, Merrill Lynch, Citigroup, CIBC World Markets Corp. and UBS Warburg.

Defending the First Amendment

Cahill partner Floyd Abrams is a First Amendment celebrity, representing media companies and other organizations in free speech cases. In 1999 Abrams and Cahill partner Susan Buckley represented the Brooklyn Museum of Art against the City of New York and Mayor Rudolph Giuliani. Giuliani, who took umbrage to the Museum's controversial "Sensation" exhibit (especially a portrait of the Virgin Mary accessorized with elephant dung), served the institution with an eviction notice. Abrams and Buckley successfully staved off eviction. Abrams has also represented *Sports Illustrated* and *Time* magazines in libel cases.

Other well-known First Amendment/media clients include CBS (Cahill represented the network against charges by the estate of Rev. Martin Luther King, Jr., which claimed that the use of King's "I Have a Dream" speech infringed on the estate's rights) and CNN, for whom the firm has filed televised courtroom complaints (the network wanted to televise the 1998 impeachment trial of

President Bill Clinton and Supreme Court arguments in the 2000 presidential election) as well as assisting in an internal investigation into the reporting of a story charging the United States with using nerve gas against its own troops in the Vietnam War. The firm is also representing Senator Mitch McConnell, a Republican from Kentucky, in a challenge to the McCain-Feingold Campaign Finance Reform Act.

Corporate roots

Cahill's First Amendment work may get its name in the paper, but its corporate practice, a staple of the firm since its founding, does more to pay the bills. Cahill was part of a team that represented NBC in its $1.25 billion purchase of the Bravo cable television channel in November 2002. The firm represented pharmaceutical firm Accredo Health in its January 2002 purchase of the specialty pharmacy division of Gentiva Health Services.

M&A isn't the only corporate work for Cahill. The firm represented U.S.I. Holdings in its $90 million IPO in October 2002. Cahill was issuer counsel for Arch Capital in an April 2002 stock offering worth $165.8 million. Cahill performed the same function for Collins & Aikman Corp. in a $160 million offering in June 2002.

GETTING HIRED

More than grades

Applicants should know that Cahill has tweaked its hiring process. "The callback/interview process has recently changed," says a source. "In prior years decisions on candidates were made by one particular partner assigned to each school. Now there is an interview committee that makes hiring decisions." That committee may take a good, hard look at your transcripts. "In the past, Cahill has sought out a very particular type of person. Grades [were] far less important than personality and ability to work independently," reports one insider. "But I have heard that more emphasis is going to be put on grades going forward."

That's not to say the firm hasn't had its standards. Hiring at Cahill is "extremely competitive if you don't come from a national school. Still quite competitive even if you do," according to one associate. "[Cahill] generally hires B+ or better students from the top law schools," says one attorney. "However, it also hires top students from some of the lower-ranked, local law schools. As a result, it is not as competitive, on paper, as, say, Cravath or Davis Polk. However, it is a significantly smaller firm than most of its competitors, so it tends to be more selective in the sense of looking for the 'right fit.'"

OUR SURVEY SAYS

Law of the jungle

Cahill associates describe a "laissez-faire, live and let live" culture. "If you get your work done, people don't really care about when or how you do so," says one associate. "There are no rules at Cahill other than to do your work and do it well," says another contact. "There is no dress code, no face time, etc. As a result, the culture is very informal." "The culture here is at once entrepreneurial, traditional and laid back," agrees a veteran associate.

If you want the laid back life, you'd better get your work done. "Partners run the firm through fear of random firings," whispers one associate. "Reviews are annual, but firings are quarterly." (Other Cahill associates made the same suggestion, which the firm strenuously denies.) "There is no loyalty," that insider continues. "First-years have been fired less than six months in without being given a chance to prove themselves after making minor mistakes. Even top associates in a class are at risk of getting fired if they get on the bad side of the 'ax-loving' partners. The firm feels that they can get away with this culture of running the firm through fear because they pay market salaries and bonuses, and the economy is rough. When the economy turns, I wouldn't be surprised if the place cleared out and many of the top associates left for firms where associates are treated decently." Another lawyer agrees the firm's quick trigger results in damage to morale. "Job satisfaction is low," says one attorney. "Morale is bad since the last wave of firings... and the logic behind the dismissals becomes more opaque with each round."

Get your own work

Cahill hands out work assignments a little differently than most law firms. In Cahill's free market system, associates must seek out the cases or deals they want to work on, rather than be assigned work in a centralized system. While that system has its benefits – partners are responsible for making their cases attractive and keeping associates happy – there are critics. "While the firm maintains a free-market system, I believe it would manage better under a coordinated workload system that so many other firms use," opines one insider. "The lack of a central assigning system means that at the same time some associates are just sitting around doing nothing, others are up to their eyeballs in work," complains another source.

Hours at Cahill are typical, though some complain of unpredictability, face-time requirements and pressure from partners. "The actual number of hours is not too bad. It's the unpredictability and the expectation that you are on call 24 hours a day, seven days a week," says one lawyer. Another insider is more critical. "There is no guidance as to how many hours are acceptable, which was stressful last year when the majority of associates billed less than one would expect to bill at a large New York law firm," says that exasperated associate.

Partners are watching your billables, but not always in the way you'd think. "Many partners here are very billable hours conscious in two senses: they want your aggregate hours to be high, but individual partners want you to bill very lightly on the matters you're working on for them," says one source. "They don't want to have to chase their clients to pay huge legal bills. At Cahill, once a lawyer bills an hour, the partner in charge has no choice but to collect the fees related to that billable hour; they have no power to reduce the hours billed. As a result, associates are often saddled with the contradictory demands to bill lightly for individual partners but to have high overall billables."

Know your stuff

Insiders say Cahill offers "virtually no formal training. People are willing to teach if you ask them, but you must take initiative." "It's all on the job, baby," says one hip associate. "But I don't understand why anyone would have a problem with that. After three years of law school, do you really need someone to hold your hand as you write your first motion?" Another attorney says, "There is no codified, structured training that I'm aware of. All of my training is in the form of supervision and consultation, as close as I indicate a need for, on the matters I work on, in real time." That doesn't sit well with everyone. "Cahill is quite weak on training. I still cannot come up with a cogent list of skills I have picked up since beginning work here," says a junior associate. "Some partners are frustratingly reluctant to mentor associates. The problem is that associates who are paired with good liaison partners receive great mentoring, but the lion's share are not so lucky. There needs to be more uniformity in the level of training."

Paying up

Salary and bonuses at Cahill match the top of the market. "Salary and bonus are on par with other major New York law firms," says one attorney. "We are routinely told that we are being paid at the top of the market. That said, unlike other firms in the past two years, Cahill's profits per partner continue to soar, so one might expect associates to share in that more than associates at firms where profits are down." Some associates see a discrepancy. "That means that the partners are just lining their pockets even with the profits from the associates' hard work, but are using the recession to justify not having to share it with those associates," fumes one lawyer. Others bitch mildly that Cahill "will only match and never take the lead," a minor gripe considering the firm pays "the standard top bonus." "Bonuses are lockstep unless your hours are very low (about 1,750 or below)," according to one contact. "While the bonus was not tied to billable hours, anecdotal evidence indicates that certain associates had bonuses withheld, and of course others were fired before bonuses were distributed," says another associate.

Getting better on diversity

Cahill's diversity efforts seem to be working, according to insiders. "Cahill has been male-dominated, though this is perhaps changing," says one source. "Recruiting is increasingly even, and there have been at least two women made partner in the last four years – an apparent improvement for Cahill." "There is not the sense that women are treated differently in terms of who was going to make partner," according to an associate. "In terms of hiring and mentoring, I think women are treated exactly the same as men and are provided with the same opportunities for work and same level of responsibility." Others see equal treatment. "I don't think anyone gives a flying dustball whether you're a woman," cracks one lawyer. "They're interested in whether you're a good lawyer."

The firm's efforts at minority recruitment haven't yielded the same results, though insiders don't blame the firm. "There aren't too many minorities around, but I don't think that is the fault of the firm," says a lawyer. "My impression is that the firm would like to hire more minorities, but that it's a chicken and egg situation since minorities apparently assume that the firm must be hostile to them since there aren't too many of them." The perception of animosity is wrong, says an insider. "I don't sense hostility towards racial or ethnic minorities, but there are only a handful working here." "I don't think there is anything unwelcoming about Cahill, but there are a fairly small number of African-American associates and partners," agrees another source. There are some suggestions on how to overcome a lack of minority representation. "Cahill could use a greater emphasis on diversity when it comes to hiring minorities," says one associate.

Cookies and other perks

Some insiders term Cahill a "no frills place" compared to other law firms – but the evidence doesn't always bear that out. The firm offers "car service after 8 p.m., free dinners on weekdays after 7 p.m., free meals on weekends and paid bar membership," among other goodies. On the other hand, associates do not receive a technology stipend or a gym subsidy, as is the case at some other New York firms.

Cahill also offers a monthly happy hour ("weekly in the summer") and free cookies in the afternoon. Not everyone is delighted with the selection, however. Volunteers one cookie aficionado: "In recent months, the cookies have been sub-optimal, at best. Every once in a while, they throw in some half-coffee Double-Stuff Oreos, but for the most part, it's just stale Fig Newtons, and honestly, who likes those? Yesterday, I was pleasantly surprised by a few sugar wafers thrown into the mix. The cookies are clearly set out by someone who enjoys toying with associates, sometimes putting out a treat, sometimes leaving us stale junk. Don't get me wrong – I'll take it over nothing." The coffee also draws criticism; one insider terms it "mud-like."

"The lack of a central assigning system means that at the same time some associates are just sitting around doing nothing, others are up to their eyeballs in work."

– *Cahill associate*

43

Baker Botts L.L.P.

One Shell Plaza
910 Louisiana Street
Houston, TX 77002-4995
Phone: (713) 229-1234
www.bakerbotts.com

LOCATIONS

Houston, TX (HQ)
Austin, TX
Dallas, TX
New York, NY
Washington, DC
Baku, Azerbaijan
London
Moscow
Riyadh, Saudi Arabia

MAJOR DEPARTMENTS/PRACTICES

Antitrust • Bankruptcy & Insolvency • Corporate •
Energy, Oil & Gas • Entertainment, Media & Sports •
Environmental • Government Contracts • Intellectual
Property • International • Labor & Employment •
Legislation & Policy • Litigation • Real Estate • Tax •
Technology • Telecommunications • White Collar Crime

THE STATS

No. of attorneys: 660+
No. of offices: 9
Summer associate offers: 95 out of 111 (2002)
Managing Partner: Walter J. Smith
Hiring Partner: David Sterling (Houston)

BASE SALARY

Houston, TX
1st year: $110,000
2nd year: $114,000
3rd year: $121,000
4th year: $130,000
5th year: $140,000
6th year: $155,000
Summer associate: $2,100/week

UPPERS

• Supportive and respectful partners
• Strong pro bono commitment

DOWNERS

• Crackdown on hours
• Weak on diversity

NOTABLE PERKS

• Free parking
• Laptops and BlackBerry pagers
• Free snacks and late dinners
• Emergency backup childcare
• Subsidized gym membership

THE BUZZ
WHAT ATTORNEYS AT OTHER FIRMS ARE SAYING ABOUT THIS FIRM

• "Star of the Lone Star State"
• "Stodgy and conservative"
• "Extremely well-connected"
• "Democrats need not apply"

RANKING RECAP

Best in Region
#1 - Texas

Quality of Life
#13 - Associate/Partner Relations
#19 - Offices

EMPLOYMENT CONTACT

Ms. Melissa O. Moss
Manager of Attorney Employment
Phone: (713) 229-2056
Fax: (713) 229-1522
E-mail: melissa.moss@bakerbotts.com

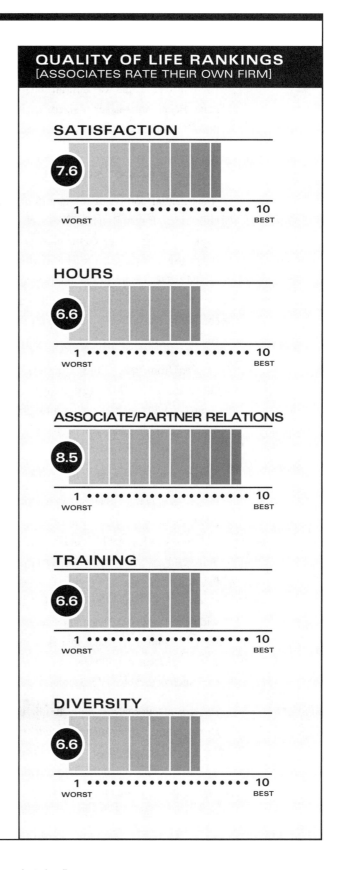

QUALITY OF LIFE RANKINGS
[ASSOCIATES RATE THEIR OWN FIRM]

SATISFACTION
7.6
1 WORST • • • • • • • • • • • • • • • • • 10 BEST

HOURS
6.6
1 WORST • • • • • • • • • • • • • • • • • 10 BEST

ASSOCIATE/PARTNER RELATIONS
8.5
1 WORST • • • • • • • • • • • • • • • • • 10 BEST

TRAINING
6.6
1 WORST • • • • • • • • • • • • • • • • • 10 BEST

DIVERSITY
6.6
1 WORST • • • • • • • • • • • • • • • • • 10 BEST

THE SCOOP

Baker Botts L.L.P. is the oldest law firm in Texas. When its founding partners created the firm in 1840, in fact, Texas was still an independent republic. And like a lot of things in the Lone Star State, Baker Botts is super-sized, with more than 660 attorneys in the United States, London and the oil-rich regions of the Caspian Sea and the Middle East.

Six degrees of separation from Dick Cheney

A substantial portion of the Houston-based law firm's business comes from the oil and energy industries. Baker Botts landed a prominent new client in 2002 when Halliburton, one of the world's largest energy companies, dropped its former primary outside counsel to sign up with Baker Botts. (These days, Halliburton may be best known as the place where VP Dick Cheney served as CEO in his pre-White House days.) Andy Baker, the partner who brought Halliburton to the firm, secured the deal by building upon a longstanding relationship with the company's general counsel. The alliance has already begun to pay off: In March 2003, the firm represented Halliburton in its sale of a UK-based flexible pipe-manufacturing subsidiary for $136 million.

Lawyers from Baker Botts' Houston headquarters represented Pennzoil-Quaker State when Shell Oil purchased it in March 2002 for $1.8 billion. In addition to creating the world's largest lubricant company, with the two leading brands of motor oil, the deal also included the Jiffy Lube chain, a former Pennzoil-Quaker State asset.

Media influence

Baker Botts is more than an energy firm; it also has prominence in the media industry. In March 2002, the firm provided counsel to YankeeNets LLC during its launch of the Yankee Entertainment and Sports (YES) cable television network, which will broadcast home games for the New York Yankees, New Jersey Nets and New Jersey Devils. That same month, when USA Network decided to sell its entertainment division to Vivendi Universal for $10.3 billion, Baker Botts was on hand to advise USA's majority shareholder, Liberty Media. A year later, the firm counseled presidential widow Lady Bird Johnson and the LBJ Holding Company in the decision to sell off the Johnson family's controlling stake in LBJS Broadcasting for more than $100 million. The sale, which affected six Austin radio stations, ended the family's 60-year presence in Texas media, which at its peak included cable TV systems as well as radio and TV stations.

Baker Botts also successfully fought off an antitrust suit filed against one of its clients, Hispanic Broadcasting Corporation. A federal district judge dismissed Spanish Broadcasting System's lawsuit in February 2003. The suit had alleged that HBC and one of its largest shareholders, Clear Channel Communications, had attempted to drive SBS out of business. In an unusually frank ruling, the judge found that the suit had simply been a frustrated attempt at revenge by SBS after merger talks between the two Spanish-language broadcasters failed.

Political punch

Baker Botts was one of the nation's largest corporate donors to George W. Bush's presidential campaign and participated in the legal battles following the disputed November 2000 election. It has established several powerful connections in the Bush administration. Stuart A. Levey and John P. Elwood received plum new assignments in the Department of Justice, while Kirk K. Van Tine became the Department of Transportation's general counsel. Partner Robert W. Jordan was appointed as ambassador to Saudi Arabia. Jordan had acted as Bush's attorney back in 1990, when the Securities and Exchange Commission investigated Bush's sale of his holdings in Harken Energy while he was on that company's board of directors. Although Bush's disclosure of the sale was filed nearly nine months late, the SEC cleared him of any wrongdoing. At the time, the SEC general counsel was James Doty, who recused himself from the investigation because, while a partner at Baker Botts, he had helped orchestrate Bush's purchase of the Texas Rangers. Doty returned to the firm in 1992. Another Baker partner with powerful connections to the first President Bush is former Secretary of State James A. Baker III, whose son James IV is a partner in the Washington, D.C., international practice group.

Corporate defense

One of the many corporate scandals of 2002 (albeit one of the lesser known) involved the indictment of four former Rite Aid executives on charges of fraud. Martin L. Grass, the pharmacy chain's former CEO and chairman, hired Baker Botts as his counsel, and the defense team, led by trial department head William H. Jeffress, Jr., promptly leapt into action. Baker's attorneys filed motions in August 2002 to have the judge presiding over the case dismissed for potential conflicts of interest. The judge recused herself in November; the trial of Grass and two co-defendants is expected to begin in June 2003.

The firm is also defending several corporations that have been sued over the use of corporate-owned life insurance (COLI), or "dead peasant" policies that allow corporations to receive benefits upon the death of their employees. (Taking out such a policy without the employee's knowledge is illegal in the state of Texas.) Dow Chemical is one of the firms that has retained Baker Botts to defend it in a dead peasant case; the class-action lawsuit accuses Dow of taking out policies on 21,000 employees without their consent. The firm is also involved in similar cases on behalf of SBC Communications and J.P. Morgan Chase.

Proud of pro bono

Baker Botts received the 2003 National Public Service Award from the American Bar Association's Business Law Section. The award recognizes the firm's ongoing participation in Texas C-BAR (Community Building with Attorney Resources), which provides legal assistance to non-profits working for and with low-income and disadvantaged communities. As a sponsor of Texas C-BAR since its founding in 2000, Baker Botts has helped several organizations, including Justice for Children, Texas Rural Legal Aid, and the La Gloria Development Corporation.

GETTING HIRED

Deep in the heart of Texas

While some associates at Baker Botts suggest the firm "is not super-elitist about which school you attended," a newly arrived attorney cautions plainly, "If you didn't go to an Ivy or a top-15 school, you better be in the top 15 percent of a law school in Texas." A midlevel associate confirms the preference for "highly qualified candidates with a Texas connection from the elite law schools," adding that the firm "also hires strongly from Texas and the University of Houston." Just about everybody agrees "you need to have the grades" if you want to catch a break in the firm's "competitive atmosphere." And one Washington insider confides, "I think the D.C. office is substantially more selective than the other offices, especially for litigation."

If you've got the academics down, "it is a matter of the attorneys here liking the person's personality and determining if they fit in." A junior IP attorney explains her interviewing strategy: "I expect a great deal from potential associates. They should not only be competent in what they have learned but also able to learn new things very quickly, have confidence in themselves and have the communication and presentation skills necessary to keep our clients happy." A first-year advises, "Expect a full afternoon or morning of interviews but also a nice lunch and dinner at one of Houston's nicer restaurants."

OUR SURVEY SAYS

Polite detachment

Associates say the "cordial, but not overly chummy" environment of Baker Botts offers "the perfect balance" between professional and laid back. The firm is "more laid back than its reputation would sometimes suggest," says one insider. "Pretty laid back for a conservative, Texas-based firm," a junior associate agrees. And associates in Austin and D.C. like to think they're a little more relaxed than their counterparts at other Baker Botts offices. "My husband and I socialize with other young associates," says one senior associate in Austin. (Not to be outclassed, a Houston litigator insists, "My spouse and I socialize extensively – almost exclusively – with my coworkers.") Others suggest the "courteous and old school" attorneys of Baker Botts do "very little mingling during working hours." A first-year bankruptcy associate reports, "Socializing among attorneys occurs mostly through formal firm functions, especially in the summer."

Pretty good for the market

Compensation at Baker Botts is "adequate, although not the highest in town," some associates suggest, with one junior litigator noting that "the bonus structure does not reflect the reality that associates increasingly bill well over 2,000 hours per year." Another attorney complains, "For the number of hours I work, I could get paid more at several firms in town." "They have cracked down on minimum hours," a third-year confides. "You work for every penny you get." But a young IP associate counters, "I am more than happy to be paid $20,000 less than I may have been at some other places when I have much greater job security." A first-year litigator feels "very well compensated," while a senior corporate attorney admits, "We're probably overpaid under current market conditions." Furthermore, says a midlevel associate, "This type of money in Houston goes a long way."

"The money is good," a litigator acknowledges, "but the hours will kill you." Another junior associate points out Baker Botts "is increasingly moving away from 2,000 billable hours per year toward 2,200 or more," while a sophomore grouses, "Work does not seem to be distributed evenly. Some associates are buried, and some are always trying to find work to do." But others find the work situation much less stressful. "I work plenty," a third-year admits, "but not as much as lots of other big firm associates." A midlevel tax attorney says, "I get to work very early each morning, but I am home for dinner with my family almost every night. And I rarely work weekends." An attorney in the D.C. office reports, "I have never had to cancel vacation plans, as all the partners I have worked with here are very understanding and supportive of outside plans." Even a first-year in the New York office finds the hours "very manageable."

Eager to please

Partners at Baker Botts "go out of their way to be respectful," and "the open door policy is very much observed." A third-year associate praises her bosses' "willingness to both compliment in a very specific manner and on a regular basis." A sophomore in the government regulation practice group emphasizes the opportunity for associates to anonymously critique their partners and sums up, "Some partners are wonderful to work with, and some are far from it." Another junior associate admits, "It would be hard to characterize an average. This really, really depends on the partner." Still, most feel the partners "are very understanding and accommodating."

You have learned well, grasshopper

When it comes to training at Baker Botts, opinions vary widely. "I clerked in three big law firms in Texas," a Baker Bottsian recalls. "The attorneys at Baker Botts are by far the most qualified and most well-trained attorneys I have worked with." The firm provides "excellent in-house training" with "open and liberal" access to CLE, as well as "a well-developed mentorship program" in the IP group. Even the junior associate who says "training has always been my biggest complaint" acknowledges the firm's newly implemented programs. "I have learned a lot on my first six months of being a lawyer," enthuses another first-year. But the "learn-by-doing environment" can be "both exciting and nervewracking." Observes one rookie real estate attorney, "Some partners teach more. Others give you an assignment and let you figure it out on your own." A first-year in the labor practice group warns, "You need more than just weekly CLEs. There needs to be more explanation of the forest and not just the trees – especially for new lawyers."

Strong but silent types

Baker Botts "is the most committed firm in Houston" when it comes to pro bono, according to its associates. "The firm does not advertise its pro bono activities," says a Dallas attorney, "but we do quite a lot." In addition to traditional pro bono, "we also try to do work areas that otherwise fall through the cracks." Once a pro bono case has been approved, time spent on the case applies to the firm's billable hours requirement. A few insiders, however, caution that "an associate who spends too much time on pro bono" may find those hours disallowed, no matter what the policy manual says.

Making headway

Although multiple sources insist there are no out gay or lesbian attorneys at Baker Botts' offices in D.C. or Dallas, a senior associate in Houston gladly informs us he has "no problems" in the firm's "very supportive environment." Another insider asserts, "If you can do your job, no one seems to care about your orientation." (Several insiders suggest it might be time to offer domestic partner benefits, though.) Associates are less enthusiastic about the firm's recruitment and retention of ethnic minorities. "We don't recruit at schools with large numbers of minorities, it seems," muses one insider. "I can count the number of minorities on one hand," claims one D.C. associate, with only slight exaggeration. A veteran attorney offers a blunt assessment of the whole diversity issue: "What will make women and minorities feel at home is if there are women and minorities in the firm, so the firm has to get over the hump of hiring a critical mass of them."

"Women are very welcome at the firm," a Baker Botts sophomore responds. "Whether they stay for more than two to three years is another question." A third-year adds, "Everything is great until you decide to have children." Even a first-year female attorney who believes Baker Botts "does a good job of hiring and mentoring women" warns, "The firm must adopt a part-time program for women with children, or it will continue to lose good attorneys." Another rookie, however, observes, "The real estate department is headed up by a woman, and all the associates in the Houston office are women." And though some women at the firm feel "you have to find your own mentor," a junior associate tells us, "I have found that the female partners really are willing to talk to you about almost anything."

"We desperately need new carpet"

A "top-rate firm" like Baker Botts "should have better aesthetics," grumbles a D.C. associate, who can't stand her office's "bland tan carpet and walls." New Yorkers may love their Rockefeller Center location, but the "recent renovations to the décor" are "just OK." In Austin, one insider reports, "associate and secretary comments were not considered to any large degree in recent renovations," resulting in a nice "but not incredibly functional" new space. A Houston associate calls the gold and brown color scheme "a throwback to the 1960s," and further observes, "The office chairs, which they will not update, are not very accommodating for even the average-sized woman." A first-year confirms, "The chairs they give you are backbreakers." Another Houstonian cries out, "We desperately need new carpet," while someone else claims there's "a strange barnyard odor" on the litigation floors. Still, associates say their actual offices, though "certainly not opulent," are "extremely spacious and well designed," and rejoice in "large windows" and doors that can close at the push of a button.

44

Baker & McKenzie

One Prudential Plaza
130 E. Randolph Street
Suite 2500
Chicago, IL 60601
Phone: (312) 861-8000
www.bakernet.com

LOCATIONS

Chicago, IL (HQ)

Dallas, TX • Houston, TX • Miami, FL • New York, NY
• Palo Alto, CA • San Diego, CA • San Francisco, CA •
Washington, DC • Toronto • 56 other offices worldwide
(34 countries + U.S. and Canada)

MAJOR DEPARTMENTS/PRACTICES

Banking & Finance • Corporate & Securities • E-
Commerce • Information Technology/Communications •
Intellectual Property • International Dispute Resolution •
International Trade • Labor, Employment & Employee
Benefits • Litigation • M&A • Major Projects/Project
Finance • Tax • Venture Capital

THE STATS

No. of attorneys: 3,273
No. of offices: 66
Summer associate offers: 16 out of 22 (2002)
Chairman of Executive Committee: Ms. Christine
Lagarde
Hiring Attorneys: Nam H. Paik (Chicago); John Flaim
(Dallas); David Brakebill (Houston); James Barrett
(Miami); Grant Hanessian (NY); Charles Dick (San
Diego); Peter Engstrom (San Francisco/Palo Alto);
Richard Slowinski (DC)

THE BUZZ
WHAT ATTORNEYS AT OTHER FIRMS ARE SAYING ABOUT THIS FIRM

- "Big. Really big"
- "Large, but not necessarily prestigious"
- "Fabulous international network"
- "McDonald's of the law firm world"

BASE SALARY

Chicago, IL
1st year: $125,000
2nd year: $130,000
Summer associate: $1,520/week

New York, NY; Washington, DC
1st year: $125,000
2nd year: $135,000

San Francisco, Palo Alto, CA
1st year: $120,000
2nd year: $120,000 - $135,000

San Diego, CA
1st year: $125,000

Dallas, Houston, TX
1st year: $110,000

Miami, FL
1st year: $95,000

UPPERS

- A "truly international" firm
- Relaxed culture
- "Recession-proof client base"

DOWNERS

- Dearth of training programs
- Hard-to-get bonuses
- Printers shared in Chicago office

NOTABLE PERKS

- Free Starbucks coffee
- Monthly firm socials
- July 4th party on terrace overlooking the White
  House (D.C. office)
- Weekly pizza nights

RANKING RECAP

Best in Region
#7 - Chicago

Best in Practice
#8 (tie) - Tax

EMPLOYMENT CONTACT

Chicago: Ms. Eleonora Nikol
Phone: (312) 861-2924
eleonora.nikol@bakernet.com

Dallas: Ms. Terry Deleon
Phone: (214) 978-3049
terry.a.deleon@bakernet.com

Houston: Ms. Nancy Rader
Phone: (713) 427-5009
nancy.a.rader@bakernet.com

Miami: Mr. Clement Noble
Phone: (305) 789-8908
clement.noble@bakernet.com

New York: Ms. Anne Zagorin
Phone: (212) 891-3573
anne.s.zagorin@bakernet.com

San Diego: Ms. Victoria Leach
Phone: (619) 235-7733
victoria.a.leach@bakernet.com

San Francisco/Palo Alto: Ms. Andrea Carr
Phone: (415) 984-3801
andrea.l.carr@bakernet.com

Washington, D.C.: Ms. Jane Lint
Phone: (202) 452-7024
jane.e.lint@bakernet.com

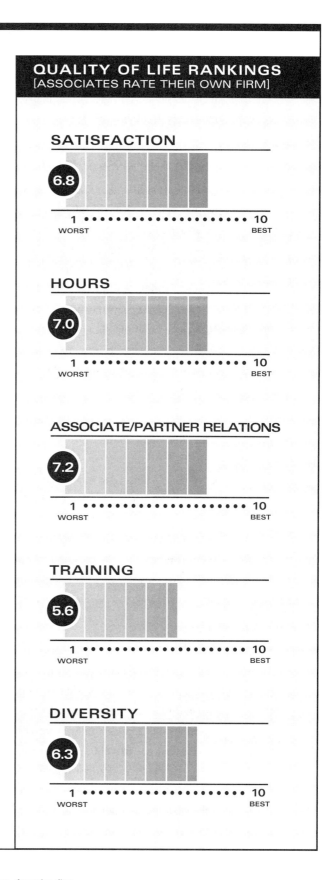

QUALITY OF LIFE RANKINGS
[ASSOCIATES RATE THEIR OWN FIRM]

SATISFACTION
6.8
1 WORST •••••••••••••••••••• 10 BEST

HOURS
7.0
1 WORST •••••••••••••••••••• 10 BEST

ASSOCIATE/PARTNER RELATIONS
7.2
1 WORST •••••••••••••••••••• 10 BEST

TRAINING
5.6
1 WORST •••••••••••••••••••• 10 BEST

DIVERSITY
6.3
1 WORST •••••••••••••••••••• 10 BEST

THE SCOOP

It used to be said that the sun never set on the British Empire. Now it's Baker & McKenzie that feels the sun's warm glow continually. This law giant bestrides the earth like a legal colossus, with more than 3,200 lawyers spread out among 66 offices in 36 countries.

Today Chicago, tomorrow the world

In 1949 Russell Baker founded a law firm in Chicago focused on international practice. His partner, John McKenzie, added tax expertise. The firm opened its first overseas office in Caracas, Venezuela, in 1955 (the first Latin American office for an American law firm). Baker & McKenzie moved into Washington, D.C. and Europe (Amsterdam and Brussels) two years later. New York and Zurich came the next year (1958). Important additions include London (1961), Paris (1963), Sydney (1964), Hong Kong (1974) and Moscow (1989). The firm moved quickly into Eastern Europe, opening seven offices in the former Communist bloc from 1990 through 1998. Baker & McKenzie hung out shingles for two additional European offices in 2002, opening in Bologna in April and Antwerp in July. In February 2003, the firm merged with Vienna, Austria-based Kerres & Diwok. That same month Baker & McKenzie opened its second office on mainland China in Shangai.

Baker & McKenzie has won its share of awards recently. London Managing Partner Russell Lewin won "Managing Partner of the Year" at the Legal Business Awards 2003. The firm won the first "Pro Bono Partner Award" from CorporateProBono.Org, a partnership between the American Corporate Counsel Association and the Pro Bono Institute at Georgetown University Law Center. The firm was honored along with Abbott Laboratories and the Midwest Immigrant & Human Rights Center for their collaboration on a program that assists Chicago-area immigrants in becoming U.S. citizens. Baker & McKenzie also picked up "International Practice of the Year" at the Australian Law Awards and "Antitrust Firm of the Year" from the *JUVE Handbook*, both in 2003. All those honors led to *mucho dinero* (as any of the firm's dozen Spanish-speaking offices might say): Baker & McKenzie pulled in $1.06 billion in revenues in fiscal year 2002.

Getting still bigger

Not content with being the world's biggest law practice, Baker & McKenzie has added numerous lateral hires around the world to strengthen specific practices. Domenico Mino Palumbo joined the Milan office as a partner and coordinator of the major projects practice group in September 2002. Baker & McKenzie's San Francisco office benefited from the sudden collapse of Brobeck, Phleger & Harrison in early 2003; in February, seven lawyers from Brobeck joined Baker & McKenzie's corporate practice. Partner Shane Byrne led the team, which included two other partners (Phillip Bush and Jason Kuhns) and four associates. Four more Brobeck refugees came to Baker & McKenzie the following month. Partner Gary Shapiro and associate Stuart Pixley were added to the firm's information technology and communications department while partner Michael Penner joined Baker & McKenzie's banking and finance team. Later that month, corporate and securities partner John Anzur completed the Brobeck exodus, and the firm's Brussels office welcomed Nina Niejahr as an associate in the firm's competition department. Niejahr previously toiled for Akin, Gump, Strauss, Hauer & Feld.

Financing the world

Baker & McKenzie's finance work has spanned the globe. In January 2003, the firm advised on a $4 billion equity offering for the Saudi Telecom Company. Riyadh-based Baker & McKenzie partner John Xefos led the transaction. Xerium, a Luxembourg-based paper company, tapped Baker & McKenzie for a $730 million recapitalization in March 2003. Partner Bernard Sharp was in charge of Baker & McKenzie's Xerium effort. In addition to representing issuers, Baker & McKenzie advises securities underwriters. Clients have included *über*-banks Goldman Sachs, Merrill Lynch, Credit Suisse First Boston, Lehman Brothers, Salomon Smith Barney, Bear Stearns and UBS Warburg.

The firm has approximately 600 lawyers worldwide who specialize in M&A advisory services. In January 2003, CapVis and Quadriga Capital used the firm's services for their investment in a management buyout of the Zellweger Uster Division from Zurich-based Zellweger Luwa. Martin Frey, a partner at Baker & McKenzie's Zurich office, led the legal team. Baker & McKenzie advised One Equity Group, a subsidiary of Bank One, in that company's acquisition of the MAUSER-Group, a Frankfurt packaging specialist. The deal, worth approximately $300 million, closed in March 2003. Frankfurt-based partner Dirk Oberbracht advised One Equity. The firm also advised the management of Vivid Imaginations, a London toy maker, on a leveraged buyout worth approximately $93 million. London-based corporate partner Jane Hobson advised the management team for Vivid, which holds U.K. licenses for toys based on *Spiderman*, *The Simpsons*, *The Lord of the Rings* and *X-Men*.

The firm's tax attorneys advise prospective mergers or acquirers on the tax implications of transactions. Baker & McKenzie tax partners Scott Brandman and Thomas May led a team that advised TMP, Inc. (owner of job web site Monster.com), on the spin-off of its eResourcing and Executive Search business units in October 2002.

Protecting helpless Microsoft

Baker & McKenzie's intellectual property department scored a victory for client Microsoft in Hong Kong. Able System Development, a Hong Kong computer firm, was found to be including versions of Microsoft's Windows programs on computers it sold in the 1990s. Baker & McKenzie partner (and head of the firm's Asian intellectual property group) Robert Arnold led the firm's efforts on behalf of Microsoft, which resulted in a multi-million dollar award for the software giant.

GETTING HIRED

The world is your oyster

Given Baker & McKenzie's massive size, it's natural for the firm's hiring needs and processes vary slightly by region. Baker & McKenzie's web site, www.bakernet.com, lists hiring contacts for every office. The firm offers 20 international clerkships to students interested in international law and two scholarships to law students looking to achieve specialist qualifications in the European Union. "The hiring process is very strange and depends largely on need," says one contact. An IP lawyer reports, "Some departments are much stricter regarding hiring requirements than other departments."

Both grades and personality are taken into account at Baker & McKenzie. "To its credit, the firm hires individuals with unique backgrounds and does not think first about whether a candidate's credentials will measure up in Martindale," reports one insider. "Strong academics are of course important, and weak students are generally not accepted for positions, but our firm does seem to hire individuals with something special to bring to the table above and beyond a stellar academic record." The firm takes its time when vetting candidates, maybe to its detriment. "I think that the partners look not only at performance, but also personality, when considering new hires," says a senior associate. "They want to make sure the person will fit in the firm's culture. Partners also look very, very closely at the firm's needs and economic factors before making a final decision. Sometimes, they even take too long to consider the new hire and miss the opportunity."

OUR SURVEY SAYS

Friendly but varied

Baker & McKenzie attorneys seem split on the firm's culture, with some describing a laid back environment and others sensing tension. Sheer size dictates that many types of personalities are in play, with differences frequently rooted in geography or practice area. "My firm's culture is very difficult to discern, which is a serious problem because it leads to lack of unity and cohesion among the lawyers," says one insider. "The firm is more a loose amalgam of sole practitioners than a true firm," reports another associate. "Partners tend to work with only a few associates each, therefore there is not a lot of unity among associates or practice areas." "Firm culture varies among offices and it can vary within the office depending upon with whom you are interacting," according to a source. "Some partners have excellent relationships with associates, and, while no one could call the atmosphere laid back even among the best of relationships, there are plenty of partners with whom one may have both professional and personal dialogue."

Others report that Baker & McKenzie is "relatively laid back, not formal" with a "good open door policy." One lawyer based in the firm's Chicago headquarters says, "The culture in the office is very pleasant. Almost all of the attorneys are well-balanced." Even the firm's good qualities can have their drawbacks. "The culture is laid back with an extreme amount of autonomy," says one attorney. "This is usually helpful in the good times, but in the bad times (like now) it can be very unnerving." The firm's global reach impresses some insiders. "Baker & McKenzie is a great unique institution," says a senior associate. "It's the only truly global firm, despite other's pretensions. Nevertheless, any institution so big is bound to have its good spots and bad spots."

There seems to be some tension between partners and associates. "It depends on the partner," reports one contact. "If you are lucky, you can work with partners who treat associates very well. Not everyone here is lucky." Some partners are just too busy. "The partners are not overtly hostile to associates," says one lawyer. "They are just much too busy to attend to the care and feeding of their associates." Some are just mean. A few partners "are generally taking advantage of the market and treating associates poorly," says one insider. "There seems to be almost glee in the misfortune of others."

"You mean people get bonuses?"

Baker & McKenzie associates are looking for their bonuses, and they've got to look hard. That leads to dissatisfaction with the firm's compensation. "Salaries (of associates) have been cut, raises are non-existent and bonuses are pipe dreams," reports one contact. "Bonuses are based on billable hours," explains a source. "The partners claim that merit bonuses are given out, but these are more figments of their imagination - carrots to be dangled to work on killer projects." "Our firm had a record year [in 2003] for revenue despite the economic downturn, and it was disappointing to some associates not to receive some token of extra appreciation, no matter how modest, at some point during the year," complains an associate. The policy hurts morale and has zapped motivation. "There is no real incentive to bill long hours because the compensation is laughable, while your time and personal sacrifices are great," fumes a source. Some insiders are so starved for bonuses they've forgotten what one is. "You mean people get bonuses?" asks one confused associate.

Time in the office

Hours at Baker & McKenzie are a little on the high side. "The hours required for the job are high," says one associate. "We do have high billable expectations and we are asked to perform substantial non-billable administrative, business development and professional development work as well which does not count toward minimum requirements. You are credited with 50 hours per year for pro bono work, but it would be nice if certain business development and professional development work was credited, too." The firm's billables requirement seems to be a suggestion. "The firm expects at least 2,000 hours but encourages much more," reports one source. "Last year my section was unusually slow due to the economy, so my hours worked were much less than in a typical year." Fluctuations can be a problem. "My experience is different than most others in the firm, I believe, in that my hours have been very boom (300 a month) or bust (less than 100)," says one lawyer. "My biggest problem with the hours here is that few people but the partners take vacation.

Officially, it is only three weeks. In practice, it can be much less." "The hours here are not bad," opines one lawyer. "However, the unpredictability of the emergency work here can really ruin your home and social life."

Training: you're on your own

Training doesn't seem to be a firm strength. Insiders complain of "very little, if any, actual training" though some feel informal and on-the-job training educates associates adequately. "My fellow first-years and I had little formal training from the firm," complains one young lawyer. "To figure things out I sometimes have to rely on the willingness of associates and partners to teach me. Fortunately they are often helpful." "We need improvement on the professional development and training front," offers one insider. "However, the firm recognizes this and has begun to implement professional development and training requirements on the individual offices to help improve the situation. Over the past year, we have had a number of office-wide training sessions on topics such as negotiation and dealing with difficult client situations." The firm has tried a mentoring program, but it's got its flaws. "The formal mentoring is a joke, and the program as it is set up formally is relatively useless for your professional development, as you are generally partnered with an attorney who is in an entirely different practice area," complains one lawyer. "Informally, if you ally yourself with the partners who do the work you are interested in, you can get some good opportunities." Some associates feel left behind. "The level of work I have been provided with is first-year work," gripes one non-first-year. "I have had little opportunity to write other than internal memos. I have had no deposition or courtroom experience. This is not adequate for a third-year lawyer."

Retention issues, except at the very top

"The firm does a great job with the hiring of women," reports one associate. "The problem lies in retention, quality of life and partnership issues as they relate to women." Things may be getting better, though, and the fact that Christine Legarde was elected chair in 1999 helps. "We have a substantial number of women associates," according to one source. "We have a growing number of women partners. Baker & McKenzie's chairman is a woman, one of the few law firm CEOs in the United States." "Baker & McKenzie attorneys show respect almost to the point of paranoia following a high-profile lawsuit against them a few years back," says one associate, referring to a sexual harassment suit from 1994.

Baker & McKenzie insiders report some problems with retention of minority associates. "We have very few minorities in this firm, and we need to improve our ability to attract and retain good minority candidates," says one contact. "However, I do notice and appreciate that the firm is trying in various ways, although they may not be too effective, to change our image and attract good first year and lateral candidates." One source has a theory. "[The firm is] better at hiring than they used to be, but promotion and mentoring is lacking." "There's not a lot of racial diversity," observes one insider. "It's certainly not a hostile work environment, just the luck of the draw type thing."

"[Baker & McKenzie] is the only truly global firm, despite other's pretensions. Nevertheless, any institution so big is bound to have its good spots and bad spots."

– Baker & McKenzie associate

Wilson Sonsini Goodrich & Rosati

650 Page Mill Road
Palo Alto, CA 94304-1050
Phone: (650) 493-9300
www.wsgr.com

LOCATIONS

Palo Alto, CA (HQ)
Austin, TX
Kirkland, WA
New York, NY
Reston, VA
Salt Lake City, UT
San Francisco, CA

MAJOR DEPARTMENTS/PRACTICES

Antitrust • Corporate & Securities • Employee Benefits & Executive Compensation • Environmental & Real Estate • Intellectual Property • Life Sciences • Litigation • Mergers & Acquisition • Patent Prosecution • Tax • Technology Transactions • Trademark & Advertising • Venture Capital • Venture/Investment Funds • Wealth Management

THE STATS

No. of attorneys: 593
No. of offices: 7
Summer associate offers: 31 out of 31 (2002)
Chairman: Larry Sonsini
Hiring Partners: Leo Cunningham, Matthew W. Sonsini and Jose Macias

BASE SALARY

Palo Alto, CA
1st year: $125,000
2nd year: $135,000
3rd year: $150,000
4th year: $165,000
5th year: $185,000
6th year: $195,000
7th year: $205,000
8th year: $215,000
Summer associate: $2,400/week

UPPERS

- High degree of independence
- Stimulating work (when you can get it)
- Relaxed vibe, casual dress, music in the office

DOWNERS

- "Constant wondering if you've billed enough hours"
- Frustration over handling of bonuses
- Disappearing perks

NOTABLE PERKS

- "Team-building" events among practice groups
- Participation in firm's investment fund
- Quarterly productivity bonuses
- Bar expenses

THE BUZZ
WHAT ATTORNEYS AT OTHER FIRMS ARE SAYING ABOUT THIS FIRM

- "The Wachtell of the West"
- "That's, like, so '90s""
- "Cutting edge"
- "Brother, can you spare a dime?"

RANKING RECAP

Best in Region

#10 - California

Best in Practice

#1 - Technology/Internet/E-Commerce

#9 - Intellectual Property

EMPLOYMENT CONTACT

Attorney Recruiting Department

Phone: 1 (888) GO2-WSGR

Fax: (650) 493-6811

E-mail: attorneyrecruiting@wsgr.com

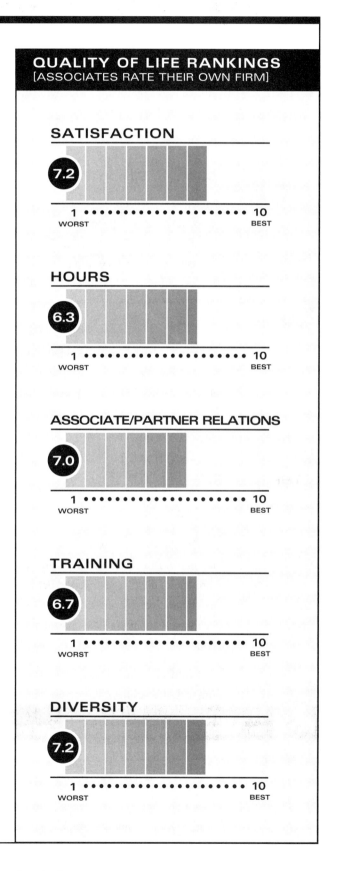

QUALITY OF LIFE RANKINGS
[ASSOCIATES RATE THEIR OWN FIRM]

SATISFACTION

7.2

1 WORST • • • • • • • • • • • • • • • • • • 10 BEST

HOURS

6.3

1 WORST • • • • • • • • • • • • • • • • • • 10 BEST

ASSOCIATE/PARTNER RELATIONS

7.0

1 WORST • • • • • • • • • • • • • • • • • • 10 BEST

TRAINING

6.7

1 WORST • • • • • • • • • • • • • • • • • • 10 BEST

DIVERSITY

7.2

1 WORST • • • • • • • • • • • • • • • • • • 10 BEST

THE SCOOP

Wilson Sonsini Goodrich & Rosati was in Silicon Valley long before other law firms - or most of America, for that matter - recognized the area's vast potential as a breeding ground for scientific and technological advancement. The young firm has a stellar reputation when it comes to IPOs, M&A and venture capital.

Sittin' in Silicon Valley

McCloskey, Wilson, Mosher & Martin was a California law firm that hung out its shingle in Palo Alto, the heart of Silicon Valley, in 1961. While other founding partners drifted away, John Wilson remained; Larry Sonsini, John Goodrich and Mario Rosati came aboard in 1966, 1970 and 1971, respectively, giving the firm its present name of Wilson Sonsini Goodrich & Rosati. Although John Wilson retired in 1983, he continued to serve as an advisor to the firm until shortly before his death in 1999. John Goodrich also retired in January 2002, after more than 31 years with the firm.

Larry Sonsini currently serves as the firm's chairman and played a very active role in Wilson Sonsini's advisement of Hewlett Packard during an internal challenge to its March 2002 merger with Compaq, as well as defending HP against a lawsuit filed by former director Walter Hewlett that accused CEO Carly Fiorina and other executives of rigging the shareholder election that narrowly approved the union of the two technology companies. In addition to serving on the firm's executive committee, Mario Rosati is the managing partner of a Wilson Sonsini spinoff, WS Investments, which has invested funds contributed by the firm's attorneys into a portfolio of emerging companies.

Legal backbone of the Internet

During the 1990s, Wilson Sonsini represented many of the companies whose products helped shape the modern Internet, including Infoseek, USWeb/CKS and Inktomi. The firm counseled Netscape throughout the five-year period between its IPO and its acquisition by American Online, and served as underwriter counsel to Yahoo! As recently as 2001, it remained the leader among law firms handling technology IPOs, participating in 13 of the year's 79 public offerings by American tech companies.

The firm's current client list includes more than 3,300 companies in the computer, semiconductor, Internet, life sciences and investment banking industries.

Skip to the good parts

Wilson represents Utah-based software developer ClearPlay in its ongoing battle with filmmakers and movie studios. The company has developed a program for DVD players that can automatically filter out objectionable scenes from movies while they play. Hollywood argues that the ability to strip a film of nudity, graphic violence and obscene language violates the director's artistic integrity, not to mention the studio's intellectual property rights. Wilson partner Andrew Bridges, who in 1999 successfully defended the makers of a popular portable MP3 player against a lawsuit by the Recording Industry Association of America, counters that ClearPlay's technology is no different than using the fast forward and mute buttons to control how you view a film in the privacy of your own home.

Fighting for justice

Wilson doesn't just handle technology cases. Since 1999, the firm has spent hundreds of pro bono hours assisting human rights activists at the Center for Justice and Accountability in a lawsuit against a former Chilean army officer. Retired major Armando Fernandez-Larios stands accused of participating in the "Caravan of Death," a Chilean torture squad believed to be responsible for the deaths of dozens of political prisoners during the reign of Augusto Pinochet in the 1970s and '80s. The suit, brought by surviving relatives of one of the Caravan's alleged victims, is scheduled for trial in mid-2003.

Bumps in the road

Unlike some firms that froze associate salaries at their 2001 levels, Wilson pledged in January 2002 to grant annual increases and continue to avoid the need to let go associates and staff. Eyebrows were raised, however, when the firm then proceeded to lay off several attorneys for "performance" reasons early in the year, and ultimately found itself forced by economic necessity to cut 100 support staffers from the payroll in August. At that time, the firm also announced that it planned to officially layoff additional associates in "underperforming" practice groups, but declined to specify how many. Some recent signs, however, indicate that the worst may be over: Wilson only promoted five new partners in 2001, but the following year a baker's dozen made the cut.

Picking up the pieces

When San Francisco-based Brobeck, Phleger & Harrison imploded just before the close of 2002, other law firms swooped in and scooped up former Brobeck attorneys and clients for themselves. Wilson took over much of the caseload from Brobeck's biggest client, Cisco Systems. The firm's Austin office also acquired four of Brobeck's Texas attorneys, including IP litigation partner Craig Tyler.

Lured by a combination of venture capital and cutting-edge research that seemed to mirror the early days of Silicon Valley, Wilson Sonsini established its Austin presence in 1999. Although other firms that had come prospecting in the Texas town found themselves forced to cut back in 2002 when the tech industry spiraled downward, Wilson held its ground, and even picked up its choice of attorneys from competitors. In addition to the Brobeck hire, the firm also brought in partners Brian Beard and Tony Allen, who had spent the last few years building one of the state's most lucrative technology practices under the auspices of Gunderson Dettmer Stough Villeneuve

Franklin & Hachigian. One strong sign of the firm's commitment to Austin: It was the only office specifically exempted from the August 2002 layoffs.

Wilson is also toughing out the blows to the tech sector in the Seattle area. Its office in Kirkland, Wash., snagged the managing director of the Venture Law Group's Pacific Northwest office for its own team in August 2002, along with another VLG partner. The acquisition bolstered Wilson's strength in a region where, by year's end, competing firms had dropped associates or, in the case of Cooley Godward, closed shop.

GETTING HIRED

Nice work if you can get it

"WSGR is firing more than it is hiring" these days, insiders at the firm agree, and "the only people who are left and the only people who are being hired are very high performers." A senior attorney confirms, "We haven't hired many lateral attorneys within the past two years and have significantly cut back our law school hiring." One associate muses, "I assume that only the New York top firms are more selective." But don't give up hope just yet. "If we're interested and you're qualified," an associate offers encouragingly, "there's no problem." (Going to the right school helps. A junior associate in the corporate practice group jokes, "I don't think they could get another Stanford associate if they tried.")

Wilson Sonsini "seeks strong personalities" with "excellent credentials and a confident, not arrogant, fun personality." IP attorneys are a particularly desirable commodity, especially if they have technology or science degrees. "A demonstratively entrepreneurial spirit goes a long way," advises one midlevel associate. "The Kirkland office is even more selective about personality," a senior attorney stationed in the Pacific Northwest claims, "whereas Palo Alto will take a smart jerk." A junior associate suggests, however, that, ultimately, "we look to hire sharp, well-qualified individuals with good personalities, the standard always being, 'Do you want to be at the printer for hours on end with this person?'"

OUR SURVEY SAYS

Looking for hours

"Even in an economic downturn," notes a senior WSGR attorney, "corporate and securities work is not a nine-to-five job." A midlevel associate concurs, "Even when we are not in the office, we seem to be on call 24 hours a day, seven days a week." The economic situation has, however, made many associates feel like they aren't getting enough good hours. "I feel underworked, under-utilized and mismanaged," sighs one beleaguered third-year. A sophomore associate complains,

"Sometimes I have to spend several hours in the office for each hour of billable time." A more experienced attorney remarks, "I've found that time spent on pro bono work and community/marketing activities has increased sufficiently such that the total hours I spend in the office hasn't really decreased all that much." Another second-year claims any problem individual associates may have with hours is manageable. "Autonomy is something you can expect here," she says, "and face time is not required."

Den of vipers or chillin' party?

"I really love this job," says one Wilsonian, "but I hate not knowing whether I will have it tomorrow." He's not alone: Many associates at the firm feel increased "pressure to produce" in the "increasingly competitive" setting a few have begun to think of as a "cutthroat" environment of "secrecy and backbiting." One unhappy associate explains the growing mood: "People hoard hours to try to avoid the axe, and the partners are so scared and greedy they've lost all concern for associates."

"In boom times," a second-year recalls, "it seemed that more people got together for social events, but that has slowed down." Another junior associate concurs that "outside of work, we tend to do our own thing," but suggests it's "because the Bay Area has so much to offer as far as outside activities." She, like many others, describes the Wilson Sonsini culture as "informal and friendly." Even attorneys in Washington D.C. refer to their office mindset as "very Cali." A second-year says, "I socialize on a regular basis with my co-workers and very much admire and enjoy the company of most of the people I work with." After all, another chimes in, "It's hard not to socialize together since you have a pre-selected pool of bright, talented and interesting people readily available."

Ready to do the right thing

"Pro bono is a strong firm value and has been since our firm was founded," says a second-year Wilsonian. All pro bono work counts toward billable requirements, and the firm has "no hourly caps" on how much you can do. "They're very supportive with any project I've ever wanted to work on," says one veteran associate, while a senior lateral notes approvingly, "The firm allowed me to bring in a longtime pro bono client from my previous firm." A midlevel corporate attorney reports, "The commitment level has skyrocketed with the increase in idle associates." But he's "not sure whether the levels could be sustained if we became busy again." Indeed, says a junior associate, "It is just difficult for associates to commit to non-billable work right now, when we need to be readily available for any billable work that may come in."

Bad form on bonuses

"I am pleased with my compensation given the state of the economy," says one Wilsonian, and others are inclined to agree. "I believe the firm is competitive with its Silicon Valley peers and just a notch below the New York-based law firms," states a senior corporate associate; another attorney

says he gets "the best compensation in Seattle," while a Utah associate is paid "well above the local market." But few are happy about the way Wilson Sonsini partners handled the bonus distribution at the end of 2002. "Many associates," says one source, "felt blindsided by the eligibility requirement announced after the year end." Others call the post hoc addition of an hours-based criterion "bad form" and ask, "Does that seem fair?" A third-year associate grumbles, "It's difficult to feel as though you're being compensated fairly when they announce criteria after the ability to achieve those criteria has passed."

Can't we all just get along?

"I think the partners here are very congenial and treat the associates with a significant amount of respect," says a longtime Wilson Sonsini veteran. Another associate amplifies, "The partnership is comparatively young, and it shows in their attitude. They are connected to associates, hear what associates have to say and make a sincere effort to address associates' concerns." But one attorney, while she agrees the firm's partners are "quite friendly and supportive," also points out they can be "a bit secretive." A midlevel associate concurs, observing that "the most common complaint" has been "that the partners do not communicate enough information to associates regarding the firm's financial performance and what that means for their jobs/salaries/bonuses." A third-year assesses the situation bluntly. "While they might be great people," she offers, "our partners are horrible, horrible, awful managers. They just don't know how to manage." The attitude is not uncommon at the firm; an experienced corporate attorney also feels "partners clearly see associates as disposable commodities. Personal relationships between partners and associates have become less meaningful as partners' draws have decreased." Another source suggests, "Candor and honesty are not high priorities in terms of partner/associate relations."

Training day

"I suppose with the economy down, there's more time to devote to training," says one freshman attorney, trying to look on the bright side of things. He, like other WSGR associates, describes the firm's formal training programs as "pretty extensive" and "very well-organized." Despite the "strong commitment," however, not everyone is impressed. While, as one veteran insider puts it, "an associate can easily satisfy his or her continuing education requirements without ever leaving the firm," opportunities for more direct experience and individual mentorship are often considered lacking. "Junior associates don't have much opportunity to work on transactions," says one source. "Training has improved lately," a senior litigator admits, "but the mentoring program is almost entirely based on who your partner mentor is." A third-year associate muses, "I'm not sure partners really put the emphasis on training that they should, or at least they don't particularly verbalize their expectations."

Dishing about diversity

Although some Wilson Sonsini associates believe "the partners have tried to hire a racially diverse set of first-years and laterals," even those who find the firm "very welcoming" say "there is not as much diversity as I think the firm would like." Insiders cite a strong contingent of Asian-American associates but hope for further improvements in the hiring and retention of African-Americans and Latinos. On a more upbeat note, one of the firm's openly gay associates told us, "I find the vast majority of my colleagues go beyond tolerance and are actually welcoming of the different experience I bring to the firm as a gay man."

Wilson associates don't perceive any great effort to improve its gender balance, but neither do they have particularly strong problems with the current situation. "I feel like I'm doing fine as a woman," says one senior corporate attorney, "but it's certainly nothing the firm is focused on." A woman in her second year says approvingly, " I've never felt anyone here discriminate, and there are some very powerful female partners with families here who are great role models for women in this profession." A first-year female attorney notes, however, that "some think that female associates as a whole get the short end of the stick or at least have to work harder to match the males." A senior litigator acknowledges "women get good assignments and their abilities are respected," but observes, "The price to be paid is putting up with juvenile, frat boy behavior from male partners, in the form of highly inappropriate comments that may be fine among men, but women do not want to hear." Another woman at the firm concurs, "There's still a feeling that men succeed here easier than women do."

Nowhere to run, nowhere to hide

"Obviously, in this economy most people stay here unless not given that option," says one senior WSGR associate. A bunch of people must be getting it; Wilson Sonsini associates gave their firm a less-than-average ranking when it came to retention and cite "significant turnover" within the last few years. "Many people have been asked to leave," says another senior attorney, "and others have opted for other career choices." Another insider adds, "Almost every single associate I know is actively looking for a job." A midlevel associate says, "There are definitely lots of associates that will leave for other opportunities," but also points out they got those opportunities "working here in the first place." Another associate shrugs, "In litigation, we seem to do as well as any other big firm, I suppose. There is always some attrition."

Fulbright & Jaworski L.L.P.

1301 McKinney, Suite 5100
Houston, TX 77010-3095
Phone: (713) 651-5151
www.fulbright.com

LOCATIONS

Houston, TX (HQ)
Austin, TX
Dallas, TX
Los Angeles, CA
Minneapolis, MN
New York, NY
San Antonio, TX
Washington, DC
Hong Kong
London
Munich

MAJOR DEPARTMENTS/PRACTICES

Admiralty • Corporate • Energy & Real Property •
Environmental • Health Law Administration & Litigation
• Intellectual Property & Technology • Labor &
Employment Law • Litigation • Public Law • Tax,
Trusts, Estates & Employee Benefits

THE STATS

No. of attorneys: 800 +
No. of offices: 11
Summer associate offers: 112 out of 155 (2002)
Executive Committee Chairman: Steven B. Pfeiffer
Hiring Committee Chairs: Gerry Lowry and Edward
Patterson

BASE SALARY

Houston, TX
1st year: $110,000
Summer associate: $2,100/week

UPPERS

- Reasonable hours
- Good litigation training program
- Major prestige in Texas

DOWNERS

- Not enough mentoring
- Below-market salaries
- Needs work in diversity

NOTABLE PERKS

- Subsidized parking (Houston)
- Weekly attorney lunches (D.C.)
- Cab rides home

THE BUZZ
WHAT ATTORNEYS AT OTHER FIRMS ARE SAYING ABOUT THIS FIRM

- "Texas at its best"
- "Overrated"
- "Killer litigation"
- "Good old boys at their worst"

RANKING RECAP

Best in Region
#3 - Texas

Quality of Life
#6 - Hours

EMPLOYMENT CONTACT

Ms. Katie Eleazer
Recruiting Coordinator
Phone: (713) 651-3715
Fax: (713) 651-5246
E-mail: keleazer@fulbright.com

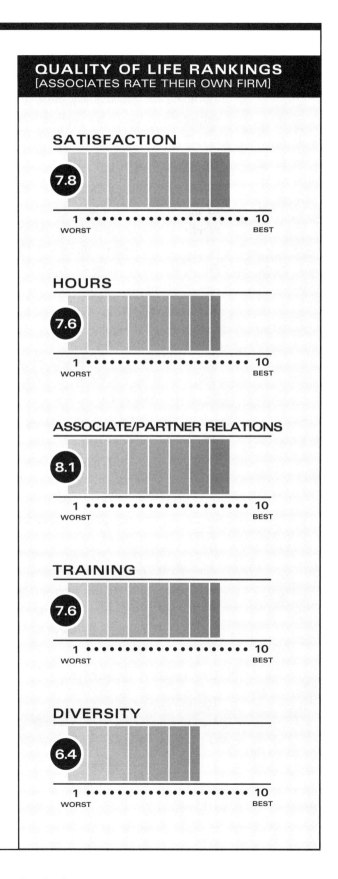

QUALITY OF LIFE RANKINGS
[ASSOCIATES RATE THEIR OWN FIRM]

SATISFACTION
7.8
1 WORST ● ● ● ● ● ● ● ● ● ● ● ● ● ● ● ● ● ● 10 BEST

HOURS
7.6
1 WORST ● ● ● ● ● ● ● ● ● ● ● ● ● ● ● ● ● ● 10 BEST

ASSOCIATE/PARTNER RELATIONS
8.1
1 WORST ● ● ● ● ● ● ● ● ● ● ● ● ● ● ● ● ● ● 10 BEST

TRAINING
7.6
1 WORST ● ● ● ● ● ● ● ● ● ● ● ● ● ● ● ● ● ● 10 BEST

DIVERSITY
6.4
1 WORST ● ● ● ● ● ● ● ● ● ● ● ● ● ● ● ● ● ● 10 BEST

THE SCOOP

Everything in Texas is big, right? Fulbright & Jaworksi LLP certainly is. After more than 80 years as one of the corporate and litigation stars of the Southwest, Fulbright & Jaworski just keeps getting bigger both in size and reputation.

From the panhandle to the Beltway

While working for a Houston law firm, R.C. Fulbright was approached by Anderson Clayton Company, the world's largest trader of cotton. Impressed with Fulbright's expertise in railway regulation, the company encouraged Fulbright to go into private practice. After partnering with litigator J.H. Crocker, Fulbright did just that, and Anderson Clayton became their first client. Fulbright's reputation as an expert in transportation and the country's post-World War I growth proved a fortuitous combination. The firm grew quickly and attracted talented attorneys, including John Freeman, who joined the firm in 1924. Freeman landed the firm's first big banking client, State National Bank. Freeman was also instrumental in expanding the firm's practice areas.

Because his practice focused on the transportation industry, Fulbright began spending more and more time in Washington, D.C. So in 1927 the firm opened an office in the District, making it the first firm to open a branch office in the capital. At the behest of Freeman and another partner, Leon Jaworski joined the firm after having beaten the other two attorneys in an appeal. Jaworski, who played a role in bringing leading oil industry clients like Exxon, Shell, Mobil and Texaco to the firm, became a name partner in the 1950s. He would later serve as a special prosecutor in the Watergate investigation.

New year, new leader

On January 1, 2003, Fulbright & Jaworski began a new era of leadership when Steven B. Pfeiffer took over the role of chairman and A.T. Blackshear Jr. stepped down after more than a decade at the firm's helm. Pfeiffer, who was previously partner in charge of the Washington, D.C., and London offices, specializes in corporate and international law. Blackshear remains at the firm and continues to practice in the tax department.

Continental champion

The firm is breaking new ground with its representation of Continental Airlines on a case involving deep vein thrombosis (DVT), a little known and potentially life-threatening medical condition that results in the development of blood clots. Long flights in cramped quarters are said to cause DVT, and airlines in recent years have come under scrutiny for not doing more to prevent passengers from developing the condition. The plaintiff in the Continental case, which is pending, claims DVT caused him to suffer a stroke during a flight. The firm is also representing insurance company

Farmers Group in a suit filed by the Texas state attorney general's office on behalf of policyholders in the state.

Fulbright answered the call when Richard Scrushy, founder and former CEO of healthcare services provider HealthSouth, was accused of insider trading and padding the company's balance sheet. Scrushy and HealthSouth remain under investigation by the Securities and Exchange Commission and the Federal Bureau of Investigation. A Fulbright attorney was part of the four-member legal team that secured a $61 million verdict on behalf of communications equipment maker Harris Corporation in an October 2002 patent infringement case. In July 2002, the firm won a summary judgment in favor of client Inforocket.com. The ruling found that Inforocket.com, operator of the Liveadvice.com web site, is not guilty of patent infringement as claimed by competitor Keen Inc.

New blood

With so many high-profile cases demanding so time, it's no wonder Fulbright enjoyed remarkable growth in 2002 and 2003. The firm added groups of attorneys to several of its offices. In January 2003, the firm announced that 19 new associates were joining its Houston office, with another eight signing on in Los Angeles. That same month, seven attorneys joined the San Antonio office, then seven in Dallas. In December 2002, the 11 attorneys of New York-based complex litigation firm Owen & Davis joined Fulbright & Jaworski.

Numbers game

Of the country's 200 leading law firms, BTI Consulting Group ranked Fulbright seventh in its 2003 Client Service Survey. Corporate counsel at Fortune 1000 companies were asked to rate the firms in 17 areas to determine the rankings. With M&A transactions totaling more than $2.4 billion, The firm also landed a spot on the *New York Law Journal*'s Top 50 M&A Law Firms list for deals completed in 2002. Fulbright & Jaworski captured the 17th spot on *Corporate Board Member* magazine's 2002 America's Best Corporate Lawyers list, based on a survey of in-house counsel and board members of public companies. Making the list was a feather in Fulbright's cap since it had not appeared the previous year. For the third straight year, the Houston Bar Foundation honored the firm's attorneys in that city for their work with the Volunteer Lawyers Program.

It's not just the firm that's receiving accolades; individual attorneys are receiving their share of recognition as well. Fulbright lawyers are among those deemed the best by national and local publications. A total of 70 attorneys from seven Fulbright offices are included in the 2002 edition of *The Best Lawyers in America*. The lawyers at Fulbright also received nine mentions in the 2002 edition of *Who's Who Legal*, one on *Minnesota Law & Politics*' 2002 Super Lawyers list, six in *Texas Lawyer*'s Go-To Guide for 2002 and two in *D Magazine*'s 2003 list of Best Lawyers in Dallas.

GETTING HIRED

What do you do besides eat, sleep and study?

"High grades are important, but the firm is also looking to hire associates who do more than just eat, sleep and study." Candidates should be "well-rounded individuals." Additionally "you must be able to carry on a conversation in a social setting in order to fit in. Other people will want to talk to you and to see what you are all about." "Having a friendly personality and pleasant disposition plays a big part, too." An Austin attorney says that office "is pretty selective and generally puts a big premium on the law school name. In-state students from schools besides UT will likely have a tough row to hoe getting in." According to a New York attorney, "The firm hires from all different schools, including the local New York schools that are not in the top tier." During the 2002 recruiting season, the firm conducted on-campus interviews at more than 30 law schools.

OUR SURVEY SAYS

Collegiality meets autonomy

Fulbright & Jaworski is "refreshingly collegial for a large, national law firm" where "people expect high-quality work from themselves and others, but do not act as if their talent gives them free rein to act like jerks." "The people at this office make working here a real pleasure," says an associate in the Los Angeles office. This source describes the LA attorneys as "very professional people with real and interesting lives" and "interesting personalities." Insiders say, "The New York office is very friendly and laid back." While several Houstonians describe the vibe in their office as "extremely laid back," at least one attorney has his own opinion about the various offices in the Lone Star State: "Houston is formal and stuffy. Dallas is as well, but not as much. Austin and San Antonio are more laid back and friendly." What "the people at Fulbright have in common is that they do not take themselves too seriously," reveals a Dallas lawyer. Although everyone in the office is concerned about producing high-quality work, they still manage to be "well rounded and appreciate the value of life outside the practice of law," this source adds.

A first-year reports, "The best part about Fulbright is its commitment to allowing young lawyers to have autonomy in their work. I am especially impressed that associates here do not get assignments, but rather get cases. Although the partner is primarily responsible for the case, the associate runs the day-to-day operations of each case, including making strategic decisions regarding the outcome of the case." This attorney has competition with a classmate over bragging rights for the best experience at Fulbright. "As a first-year associate I have already represented a client in court, had great contact with numerous clients and completed assignments in areas ranging from commercial litigation to white collar crime." A New York associate shares, "The work is okay, but it's certainly not cutting edge, and most of our clients are smaller companies. We represent very few large companies, and therefore we do not have exposure to that type of work." A midlevel who thinks highly of Fulbright's training program nonetheless offers this advice to law students and young attorneys who expect to work on big cases right away: "With the rates [law firms] are charging their clients, those clients are not going to accept young associates training on their cases. This reality is very apparent once inside a firm, and any representation to the contrary by a large firm should be taken with a grain of salt."

Time is on our side

According to one associate, the hours at Fulbright are "up and down but pretty reasonable overall." A litigation associate adds, "Our IT department works very hard to help attorneys be able to work from home in the evening or on the weekends or while traveling." Another attorney begs to differ. "I do wish the firm was more accepting of attorneys working from home on occasion. Working from home is discouraged here, even though we are all equipped with BlackBerries and can link to the firm's system from home." "The hours are a lot, but we are paid extremely well, so it seems fair," says a reasonable senior associate. "Partners don't seem to be picky at all about getting face time." A Washingtonian insists that the "place is pretty quiet by 6:30 each night." A Houston colleague concurs: "As long as you complete your assignments, you are free to come and go as you please." "Neither first-years nor second-years are required to bill a specified amount of hours in order to receive bonuses. Starting [in the] third year, the incentive-based bonus program begins, which is based upon the number of hours billed."

Money's not the most important thing in the world

Most insiders agree, "When it comes to compensation, it seems Fulbright is never at the head or rear of the pack." Associates differ, however, in how they feel about their paychecks. Says one associate, "This firm doesn't pay as much as the compensation leaders in the market, but the overall work environment more than compensates." A litigation associate is pleased with the compensation even though it is "at or maybe even slightly below market" because "when compared with the billable expectations, it is outstanding." Other coworkers agree with that assessment. "There are tradeoffs involved that to me more than make up for the slightly less-than-top-tier scale," says a third-year. A colleague contends that "a reasonable expectation of associate hours" and "an atmosphere that promotes taking the time to actually learn an area of the law, and more importantly, learn how to practice it well" are "more important" than bringing home a bigger paycheck. "Fulbright is a little behind the New York market, but it's still a lot of money," says a Big Apple attorney.

Some insiders, though, are steamed about their pay. According to a Houston source, "The compensation is basically the same as similar firms in the city, although it seems that we are slowly falling behind as other firms based in our city are slowly raising salaries. Partners already think we're overpaid, though, so expecting to get a raise is a waste of time." A New Yorker gripes, "Fulbright is not in the top of the market, but they seem to think that they are."

Mutual respect

Overall we have "excellent partner-associate relations," Fulbright associates say. Insiders report that "with a few rare exceptions, most partners treat the associates with great respect," "as apprentices and, at times, peers, as opposed to billing machines." "Partners go out of their way to be helpful and pleasant to associates." "While the partners demand quality work from the associates, they treat the associates respectfully and professionally." "Partners will joke around to make you feel comfortable," says one source, "but generally treat associates with a great deal of respect." Associates who would like to see improvement in this area voice their concerns. "This time last year the associate-partner relations were better than they are now," reveals a Houston associate. This source continues, "While it varies by department, partners are increasingly treating associates with less respect, relating to associates through egregiously passive-aggressive methods which show their lack of people-management skills and viewing associates more as billing machines." A senior associate believes that partners "seem to regard associates as overpaid and less competent than they actually are." "I think that most of the partners are respectful of the associates. However, there is a clear line between the two groups. For example, we don't go to lunch together and conversations are generally minimal," says a third-year.

Premium space

"Every associate gets their own very spacious office," beams a Houston attorney. Another Houston associate brags, "My office rocks. People come and visit me and can't believe I have such a great view!" "We could use better office furniture," says a reserved third-year, "but it's not bad." D.C. associates are treated to "well furnished" offices that are "very attractive and upscale." But the niceties don't end there. "All associates have offices with windows," "many overlooking Pennsylvania Avenue." They also have their "choice of laptop, desk top or sub-notebook computers." Even "clients have commented on how they enjoy spending time" in the firm's D.C. offices, according to one attorney. "Unlike the other Fulbright offices, the New York office décor is subpar at best for a major firm. Generally speaking, the carpet is drab and the furniture is not what you are used to seeing in any major firm." A corporate attorney adds, "The offices need better lighting, and there needs to be more of a commitment to maintaining cleanliness and not piling papers and boxes in hallways and common areas." Additionally, New York associates say they "need more conference rooms."

Top-notch training

Associates applaud Fulbright & Jaworski's "outstanding formal litigation training program, which includes assignment to a litigation mentor, requirements that must be met for taking depositions, writing motions and so on within a specified time frame, and a full mock-trial in Houston" at the end of an associate's first year. Another associate reports, "Fulbright has a new training program for corporate associates, including introductory accounting classes." A first-year associate wishes for "a little more hands-on training and mentoring of young attorneys." A second-year agrees, saying, "Informal opportunities are not very available unless you get to work with a partner who is interested in taking the time to do so." Additionally, some associates bemoan "the almost complete disregard for serious and effective mentoring."

McDermott, Will & Emery

227 West Monroe Street
Chicago, IL 60606-5096
Phone: (312) 372-2000
www.mwe.com

LOCATIONS

Chicago, IL (HQ)
Boston, MA
Irvine, CA
Los Angeles, CA
Miami, FL
New York, NY
Palo Alto, CA
Washington, DC
Düsseldorf
London
Munich

MAJOR DEPARTMENTS/PRACTICES

Antitrust • Communications & Technology • Corporate • Employee Benefits • Estate Planning • Health Law • Intellectual Property • International • Regulatory & Government Affairs • Tax • Trial

THE STATS

No. of attorneys: 950+
No. of offices: 11
Summer associate offers: 39 out of 42 (2002)
Chairman and Managing Partner: Lawrence Gerber
Hiring Attorney: Lydia R.B. Kelley

BASE SALARY

Most U.S. offices
1st year: $125,000
2nd year: $135,000
3rd year: $150,000
4th year: $165,000
5th year: $185,000
6th year: $195,000
Summer associate: $2,400/week

UPPERS

- Established tax practice, growing in IP
- Supportive and respectful partnership
- Early responsibility

DOWNERS

- Billable hours pressure in bad economy
- Impracticable part-time option
- Mysterious bonus structure

NOTABLE PERKS

- Bagel Monday (or Friday, depending on office)
- Up to $3,000 in moving expenses
- Weekly attorney dinners (some offices)
- Free parking (some offices)

THE BUZZ
WHAT ATTORNEYS AT OTHER FIRMS ARE SAYING ABOUT THIS FIRM

- "Venerable old Chicago firm"
- "Great firm, unless you're an associate there"
- "Getting better and better"
- "Too big, lost its focus"

RANKING RECAP

Best in Region
#5 - Chicago

Best in Practice
#7 - Tax

EMPLOYMENT CONTACT

Ms. Karen K. Mortell
Legal Recruiting Manager
Phone: (312) 984-7784
Fax: (312) 984-7700
E-mail: kmortell@mwe.com

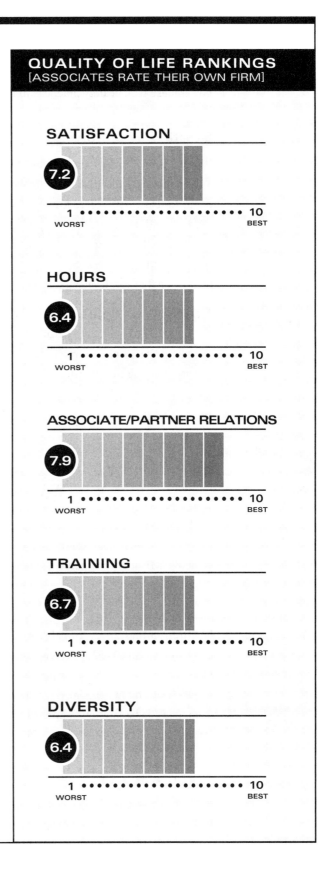

QUALITY OF LIFE RANKINGS
[ASSOCIATES RATE THEIR OWN FIRM]

SATISFACTION

7.2

1 10
WORST   BEST

HOURS

6.4

1 10
WORST   BEST

ASSOCIATE/PARTNER RELATIONS

7.9

1 10
WORST   BEST

TRAINING

6.7

1 10
WORST   BEST

DIVERSITY

6.4

1 10
WORST   BEST

THE SCOOP

With more than 950 lawyers in 11 worldwide offices, McDermott Will & Emery is an international powerhouse with healthy practices in tax, employee benefits and intellectual property.

Starting in Chi-town

Edward H. McDermott and William M. Emery founded McDermott, Will & Emery in Chicago as a tax practice. Howard A. Will joined the firm in 1941, starting the corporate practice at the re-dubbed McDermott Will & Emery. The firm would later add an employee benefits department (in 1954), a trial department (1961) and a health law department (1983). McDermott also expanded geographically, adding a Miami office in 1977 and a Washington, D.C., outpost in 1978. Los Angeles and New York came a decade later (1987 and 1988, respectively). The firm's first international office, London, opened for business in 1998.

McDermott's expansion has continued into the new millennium. The firm opened a Munich office in January 2002 with five partners from a German law firm; by the end of the year, a second German office would emerge in Düsseldorf. January also saw McDermott bid a fond farewell to Lithuania, as the firm transferred control of its office in Vilnius to the attorneys practicing there.

IP growth

The firm has aggressively expanded its intellectual property group recently, mainly through lateral additions of prominent IP attorneys. Edwin Wheeler, an IP lawyer with 20 years of experience, joined MWE's Palo Alto office in September 2002. Michael Oleinik was hired as an IP partner in Los Angeles in January 2003. Two months later, James Wolfson and Kenneth Korea came on board in Miami and Palo Alto, respectively. But the big news came that same month when the firm added Cathryn Campbell and Mauricio Flores, co-founders of an eponymous IP boutique, along with eight other IP attorneys, patent agents and scientific advisors from the firm.

McDermott handles IP clients in a broad array of industries, including life sciences, sports and technology, and *IP Worldwide* even named the firm a "Frequent Flier" in its annual survey of IP law firms in May 2002. In February 2003, a federal appeals court upheld a litigation victory for McDermott client Wesley Jessen Corp. The court upheld an earlier ruling that Bausch & Lomb infringed on Wessley Jessen's patent for silicone hydrogel materials in contact lenses. That same month, McDermott negotiated a settlement on behalf of Three Rivers Pharmaceuticals. Schering Corp. had filed a lawsuit claiming Three Rivers' generic version of the hepatitis C drug ribavirin infringed on several Schering patents.

Corporate work

The firm's M&A group has had its share of impressive deals. In July 2002, McDermott advised Schmalbach-Lubeca AO in the sale of its plastic container and closure business to Amcor Limited for $1.56 billion. In February 2003, McDermott represented Valassis Communications in its purchase of NCH Marketing Services for $60 million and Kellwood Company in a buyout of Briggs New York for an undisclosed amount. The month before that, the firm assisted Constellation Brands in acquiring BRL Hardy Limited, an Australian wine maker, for $1.4 billion. The firm advised Centerpulse on the sale of its cardiovascular medical devices division to Snia S.p.A. The $381 million deal closed in December 2002.

McDermott is also proud of its employee benefits practice, and trade groups recently honored several partners from this practice area. Paul M. Hamburger, a partner in the firm's Washington, D.C., office, was named a member of the National Advisory Committee for the Worldwide Employee Benefits Network in December 2002. Hamburger's colleague and officemate David Rogers was named to the BTI Client Service All-Star Team for Law Firms by benefits consultant BTI in January 2003. McDermott's employee benefits litigation team won a victory for its clients, four former officers of Avondale Industries. The plaintiffs, former employees of Avondale, claimed the four illegally sold off shares in the company's Employee Stock Ownership Plan, which they co-administered. McDermott won a complete victory for the four executives in February 2003.

Tax roots

McDermott, Will & Emery has stayed close to its roots in the tax arena. Thomas D. Sykes joined McDermott's tax department as a partner from a private practice in August 2002. Sykes had previously served as a trial attorney in the Department of Justice's tax division. Also in August 2002, Michael W. Gosk joined the firm's Palo Alto office as a partner. Gosk had been a tax partner at accounting firm KPMG. He joined a growing office; McDermott poached four more tax lawyers from rival Fenwick & West in March 2002.

Good deeds

McDermott is getting kid-friendly. The firm launched the "MW&E: Kids First Project" in December 2002. The project will allow lawyers in all of the firm's U.S. offices to work on behalf of education initiatives, including special education, school access and registration and eligibility for immigrant and undocumented children. It's not the first time McDermott has worked on education programs. The firm's lawyers and staff have tutored elementary school students for several years.

In a more traditional pro bono engagement, McDermott partner Michael Sommer represented Sami Leka, a Brooklyn pizza parlor worker convicted of murder in 1990. Sommer won a new trial for Leka after it was found that the prosecutor's office suppressed evidence that could have cast doubt on his conviction. The state later dropped the charges against Leka, and he was freed in January 2003.

GETTING HIRED

Don't be a jerk

"McDermott recruits at top 10 schools and from the top percentage of students at schools in each office's general region," says one insider. After an initial screening interview, prospective McDermott employees can expect a callback round that will include "interviews with three to five attorneys" say sources. "Getting a callback signals a high chance of getting an offer, but it is important to impress every attorney you meet during the callback interview," reports an associate. Insiders agree – don't be a jerk. "This firm truly wants people that have pleasant and friendly personalities and does not tolerate arrogance," warns a contact.

Other sources expand on what the firm looks for in an associate. "The firm is looking for candidates with proven academic abilities, an aptitude for rapid learning, excellent oral and written communication skills and independence in thought and work habits," says one associate. "I believe the firm is looking for people who we would like to work with who are professional and polished," observes a third-year. The economy is making things tougher. "It is getting harder to be hired as an associate," observes one insider.

OUR SURVEY SAYS

Culture by fiefdom

McDermott insiders describe a culture that varies greatly by department. At McDermott, it's "hard to get to know people." The culture is "formal but also very based on the individual 'fiefdom' that you are part of," remarks one associate. "The firm grew mostly through practice group acquisitions, so each practice group tends to maintain their own identity." For example, one attorney observes that "IP is more results-oriented, nuts and bolts, laid back, while some groups are formal, arrogant and condescending." "The 'going out of business sale' philosophy is very difficult to rationalize in light of the recent right-sizing in the corporate department," says an attorney in that department. "The firm had a banner year in 2002, and the corporate department associates are treated as though the firm was about to implode. In short, there is very little sense of security or appreciation."

Others paint a brighter picture. The "culture is friendly and cooperative," says a Chicagoan. "The culture at the firm and especially in the tax department is very friendly and laid back," says a happy tax lawyer. Another associate from that department says, "My practice group is friendly and down to earth." "The firm's culture is quite laid back for a large firm," says one Los Angeles associate. "The partners are informal and approachable."

However, many find some tension – or, at the very least, differences – between departments. "There are very clear lines marking the boundaries between many practice groups," says a second-year associate. "They are frequently territorial and possessive of anything falling within their area." That can affect the entire workplace. "The firm is full of cliques and frankly is unfriendly," says one source.

A few bad apples, but a good bunch

McDermott partners are considered, on the whole, respectful of associates. "The partners here are friendly, take the time to make sure associates are getting the feedback and training they need and seem to really appreciate the work the associates put in," says one glowing associate. "Generally the firm is not hierarchical, and the partners work just as hard as the associates," another contact agrees. Still, you might run into a few problems. "Partners generally treat associates well, but there are a few bad apples in the barrel," says one source. It's an observation backed up by another associate. "Most partners are relatively respectful in their dealings with associates, [while] others are notoriously less so."

You'll have a life

Insiders say the hours, "bane of all attorneys," are about average at McDermott. The firm sticks to a *de facto* minimum of 2,000 billable hours, though some say that minimum may be shifting. "Expectations as to hours at McDermott are reasonable," says one associate. "The official minimum is 2,000. Most associates try to bill more than that. However, associates that bill 2,000 are in good standing and on track for promotion." "McDermott places an enormous emphasis on billing 2,000 hours," says another source. "Because this year has been slow, it's been rather traumatizing for a number of associates because the work just hasn't been there, and they wonder what will happen when they don't make the required 2,000 hours." The firm makes no artificial demands on your time. "There does not appear to be any emphasis on face time," reports one attorney, "so if you are able to leave the office, that's fine, but when work needs to be done don't make other plans. However, the partners are good about not asking associates to cancel scheduled vacation unless absolutely necessary."

Opinions on the value of the firm's part-time program differ. "The firm was very open to a part-time schedule and offered it to me as an incentive to keep me from leaving," reports one associate who participates in the program. While that lawyer is clearly pleased, some are confused and skeptical. "While the firm pays great lip-service to the part-time option, in practice associates who take advantage of going part time are given less interesting work and are looked down-upon," says one source. "The firm should either stand behind its policy or get rid of it." Part-time programs are harder to come by in some departments. "Though we are told there is a firm flex-time policy, it has been suggested to me that such a policy would not work for litigation associates," says one litigator. "No associate in my group has ever tried it."

Mystery of the McDermott bonus structure

Some associates at McDermott are puzzled by their bonuses. "Base compensation is comparable to other top firms," reports one source. "The firm does not have or will not publicize a bonus scale. So every year what the bonuses will be is a big mystery." When the mystery is solved, most McDermott employees wind up near the market. "The firm tries to match the market rate for an associate," says one contact. "As a result of the time [it takes] to determine the market rate and the inherent institutional delays in the process, the firm seems to consistently lag behind others in salary increases and bonuses. To their credit, the firm has attempted to alleviate this lag by sometimes making raises retroactive." "McDermott is competitive with other big firms and better than most medium-size firms," observes one source. The firm's magic number – 2,000 – might not be so magic, according to some who suggest the firm isn't always generous when it comes to which hours count for bonus purposes.

Commitment to training

"The firm takes training very seriously," says one source. "On a weekly basis there are thorough and comprehensive training programs, either by partners or outside speakers. I have dozens of training volumes in my office. The firm is also very generous with supporting associates attending Bar Association and other training opportunities external to the firm. You just to have to ask." Many associates agree. "The firm has various in-house training sessions with the IP group and has training programs conducted at the firm by outside vendors," says an associate in that group. "However, it can be difficult to get the firm to pay for attendance at outside training courses."

Not everyone gives the firm high marks for training. "There is no training," sighs a Boston associate. Another insider insists the firm "could do much more in terms of getting practical, hands-on experience for associates." One lawyer remarks that "most learning still occurs on the job," and insists "that is not a bad thing." A fourth-year associate says, "There is currently not much emphasis on training, but they are working to develop more programs."

On diversity, effort, if not results

Most associates seem pleased with McDermott's diversity efforts even if, like a lot of firms, the results aren't always apparent. "McDermott can improve in this area, but it has taken many steps in the right direction and focused resources to improve minority hiring," reports one associate. "It seems that the firm strives for diversity but has trouble actually attaining it," says another lawyer. McDermott "is actively looking to recruit qualified minorities, but as of now the ranks are thin," according to one contact. Critics charge "McDermott fails to make this a priority," but the firm points out with understandable pride that one-third of its most recent incoming summer associate class was composed of minority law students.

A hazy part-time program is the biggest problem for female associates, according to insiders, who say the firm does a good job in hiring women. "Once the women are here the avenues for promotion are unclear, especially where the particular attorney has taken maternity leave or is on part-time status," reports one associate. "We could be better at making women partners, although we have more than several other firms," observes one source – and the firm reports that one such partner, Helen Friedli, was named head of the Chicago office in the spring of 2003. "There also seems to be some uncertainty among women associates as to how they will be able to balance childrearing and firm life. This tension is endemic to the 2,000-hour firms."

Munger, Tolles & Olson LLP

355 South Grand Avenue
35th Floor
Los Angeles, CA 90071-1560
Phone: (213) 683-9100
www.mto.com

LOCATIONS

Los Angeles, CA (HQ)
San Francisco, CA

MAJOR DEPARTMENTS/PRACTICES

Appellate
Bankruptcy & Restructuring
Corporate
Environmental
IP & Entertainment
Labor
Litigation
Real Estate
Tax
White Collar

THE STATS

No. of attorneys: 161
No. of offices: 2
Summer associate offers: 15 out of 16 (2002)
Co-Managing Partners: Robert K. Johnson and Greg Morgan
Hiring Attorneys: Lisa J. Demsky and Kelly M. Klaus

BASE SALARY

Los Angeles, CA
1st year: $125,000
2nd year: $135,000
3rd year: $150,000
4th year: $165,000
5th year: $185,000
6th year: $195,000
7th year and above: $205,000
Summer associate: $2,400/week

UPPERS

- Congenial vibe, markedly non-hierarchical and democratic
- Stellar pro bono commitment
- Firm contribution to 401(k) plan

DOWNERS

- Low marks for training
- Deficient in diversity
- "Egalitarian nature of the firm sometimes leads to inaction"

NOTABLE PERKS

- Firm lunches three times a week
- Free parking
- Weekly "sherry sips"

 THE BUZZ
WHAT ATTORNEYS AT OTHER FIRMS ARE SAYING ABOUT THIS FIRM

- "The best and the brightest attorneys"
- "Grade snobby, school snobby"
- "Supreme Court clerk haven"
- "Revenge of the nerds"

RANKING RECAP

Best in Region
#5 - California

Quality of Life
#2 - Selectivity
#9 (tie) - Associate/Partner Relations
#10 - Pro Bono
#18 - Retention

EMPLOYMENT CONTACT

Ms. Kevinn C. Villard
Director of Legal Recruiting
Phone: (213) 683-9242
Fax: (213) 687-3702
E-mail: villardkc@mto.com

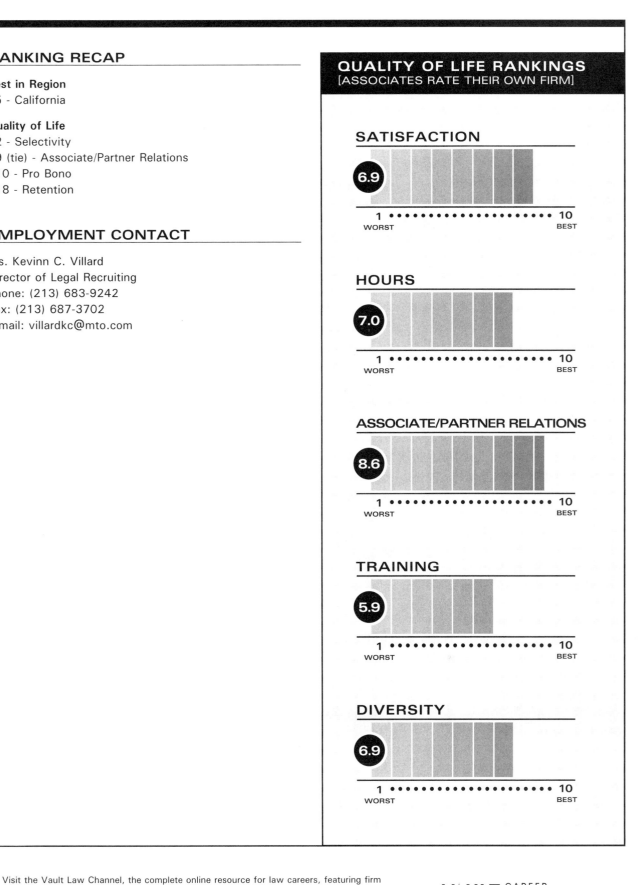

QUALITY OF LIFE RANKINGS
[ASSOCIATES RATE THEIR OWN FIRM]

SATISFACTION
6.9
1 WORST ••••••••••••••••••• 10 BEST

HOURS
7.0
1 WORST ••••••••••••••••••• 10 BEST

ASSOCIATE/PARTNER RELATIONS
8.6
1 WORST ••••••••••••••••••• 10 BEST

TRAINING
5.9
1 WORST ••••••••••••••••••• 10 BEST

DIVERSITY
6.9
1 WORST ••••••••••••••••••• 10 BEST

THE SCOOP

Munger, Tolles & Olson LLP has successfully disproved the idea that "bigger is better." With just 155 attorneys and a nearly 1:1 partner-associate ratio, the firm has remained committed to giving its attorneys hands-on experience commonly not found in larger, more bureaucratic firms.

On a mission

When the seven attorneys who founded Munger, Tolles & Olson established their practice in 1962, their goal was to create a firm run on democratic principles and staffed by the smartest, most talented attorneys available. More than 40 years later, those principles are still being practiced. At firm-wide meetings, all issues of major importance are discussed and voted on (new hires included), with associates and partners having equal voting power. The firm's size not only contributes to that spirit of democracy but also provides associates with opportunities to take on large amounts of responsibility early in their careers.

Not afraid to play with the big boys

The firm's size is surprising, considering the scope of its practice. Munger regularly advises clients regarding corporate finance, tax matters, mergers and acquisitions, environmental issues and bankruptcies and other financial transactions. But the firm is known primarily as a litigation shop, with some very impressive cases under its belt. The firm scored a major victory for its compatriots at law firm Kirkland & Ellis. As counsel to some of the partnerships allegedly used by Enron officials to doctor the energy company's books, K&E became entangled in Enron's bankruptcy woes. Munger Tolles represented the firm when investors named it as a party in a shareholder lawsuit. Munger was successful in getting K&E dismissed from the suit in December 2002 and promptly began defending another highly regarded firm, Sidley Austin Brown & Wood, against a suit filed by former Sidley clients. In a complex case involving several other defendants, Sidley has been accused of giving tax advice to plaintiffs who say the attorneys should have known their counsel was faulty. The firm is also representing telephone service provider Verizon Communications against a suit filed by Southern California residents alleging the phone carrier charged an equipment rental fee to customers who owned their phones. The suit was dismissed, but that dismissal was overturned in September 2002.

The firm represents Abbott Laboratories in a wide variety of matters, including antitrust and patent infringement matters. The firm successfully defended Abbott in the District of Delaware in 2002 in a patent infringement lawsuit brought by Novartis Pharmaceuticals concerning Abbott's generic Cyclosporin pharmaceutical formulation. Munger continues to represent Abbott on the appeal.

Friends of Warren

MTO has a longstanding relationship with Berkshire Hathaway. Founder Charles T. Munger and Berkshire Chairman Warren Buffet are old pals. Munger even left the firm to serve as Berkshire Hathaway's vice chairman. The firm represents the renowned investment company on a variety of matters, including all its acquisitions. One recent case is likely to make many a taxpayer giddy with excitement. The firm is representing Berkshire Hathaway as it sues the Internal Revenue Service for alleged erroneous interpretations of the U.S. tax code costing Berkshire $16.3 million in tax deductions. The firm also advised Berkshire on the February 2003 acquisition of Burlington, a textile manufacturer.

Munger is involved in what could prove to be one of the biggest Los Angeles real estate deals of the year. Munger client Pacific Realty is attempting to close on the Transamerica Center, a complex comprising three buildings that cover two blocks of downtown L.A., and convert the space into apartments. But as of January 2003, the company has been unable to raise the funds to complete the $88 million purchase. The San Diego Unified School District retained Munger Tolles in February 2003 to negotiate an agreement with an online educational services company.

That's show biz

Of course no L.A. practice would be complete without at least a few clients from the entertainment industry. The firm's clients include Universal Studios, ABC and the Los Angeles Avengers (the city's Arena Football franchise). Hollywood agent Michael Ovitz is a longtime client. Ovitz recently turned to the firm when a former employee of his former agency, Artists Management, sued the agent for wrongful termination in October 2002.

A helping hand

Pro bono is considered a vital element in the firm's overall practice. Munger works on a variety of individual cases, as well as with community-based nonprofit groups such as the Alliance for Children's Rights, California Lawyers for the Arts, the Society to Aid the Retarded and AIDS Project LA. In addition to such law-related service, associates also donate a percentage of their salaries to a fund that divides its assets among several charities. In March 2003, attorneys from the firm received a pro bono award from the ACLU Foundation of Southern California for their work on a First Amendment case involving the rights of gays and lesbians.

Our human resources

In January 2003, Greg Morgan replaced Ruth Fisher as co-managing partner. Fisher, whose practice focuses on mergers, acquisitions and other corporate financial matters, stepped down to work with clients full time.

GETTING HIRED

Strict scrutiny

"The typical process involves a screening interview, followed by an all-day callback interview, and then a thorough review of the candidate's qualifications." And when they say "thorough," boy do they mean it. "The firm scrutinizes everything: grades, experience, clerkships, maturity, interview performance and so on. It looks for candidates who have consistently demonstrated excellence in their past activities." The firm tends to hire "aggressive self-starters on law review, with one or more clerkships, at the top of their class at one of the top-five law schools in the country." Regarding the hiring process, the "biggest difference from other firms is that the entire firm reviews candidates' resumes, transcripts and interview results, then votes on whether to extend an offer. More than a handful of no votes means no offer." While one dumb answer in an interview doesn't necessarily spell doom for a candidate, an insider reveals, "Answers which show poor judgment or attitude problems may come out in only one interview during a day, but if they are considered sufficiently serious, that candidate will not get the 90+ percent of votes needed for an offer."

OUR SURVEY SAYS

If we've gotta work, we choose Munger

"Job satisfaction is all relative," says a well-adjusted corporate attorney. "I would rather be retired or independently wealthy, but since I am neither, at least I am at a place where the work is good, the pay is good and the atmosphere is good. Compared to life in other law firms, life is great." Most associates say they are satisfied with Munger life, and many say their colleagues make all the difference. "I wouldn't call Munger the social mecca of the working world," jokes a junior associate, "but I couldn't ask for better work colleagues." "Although there is not a great deal of socializing outside the office, the climate is very collegial. Attorney lunches three times a week provide an opportunity for the lawyers to get to know each other and to stay informed about each other's practice." In fact, a few associates feel there is "a little too much forced socializing." A junior associate elaborates: "Some of the more senior lawyers seem to think that this is extremely important, supposedly in the name of getting to know each other. But I find that those same people don't make an effort to get to know junior people at these events, and I do think that the initial effort should come from that side."

A senior associate describes what makes working at Munger interesting. "We primarily work on bet-the-company cases with the most intellectually demanding issues around. Associates are given tons of responsibility, and they are involved in the key decisions." A litigation associate tells us,

"If you're willing to assert yourself from the beginning as to what work you want to do and with whom and to some extent how much, you can have a lot of control over your own destiny here."

Pretty good hours

Like many associates, MTO insiders are somewhat ambivalent about their hours. "In general, I am happy with my hours," says a source. "When a deal is on, I work long hours, and when things are quiet, I leave early. Associates here have some control over their hours, and partners respect prescheduled vacations." Although "hours are reasonably heavy" at Munger, attorneys "can generally be home in the evenings and on weekends" if they are disciplined and efficient. An attorney on a part-time schedule believes the firm "has been committed to finding ways for me to continue to develop as a lawyer despite my part-time arrangement."

Lest this all sound too idyllic, Munger associates admit it's not all fun at the office. "My workload vacillates between a reasonable level and way too much. I am as much to blame for this as anyone else," confesses a senior attorney. A colleague concurs the long hours are a drag, saying, "Time management is the hardest part." Another insider says, "I feel I work just the right amount, and I'm told that it's enough. I just worry that someone will suddenly decide that it's not." One associate points out, "Munger is definitely a place where you can set your own hours within reason. But that doesn't mean you'll make partner."

Everyone's overpaid

"We are all overpaid, though so are associates at other top-tier firms," says a litigation associate. "The firm pays market rate in Los Angeles." "No matter how much one is paid," admits an associate, "you can always wish for more, but from a more objective perspective, it is hard to say that I am not paid well for what I do." Compensation at Munger is "less than Irell [& Manella], but the same as everyone else," explains an insider. "I do not feel underpaid," says an associate in the corporate department. "I have confidence in the associate compensation committee's perception of compensation at other firms and its willingness to adjust compensation so that it is consistent with the market." According to another attorney in the L.A. office, "Munger's base salary is competitive, but its bonus structure is slightly below market." Others describe hours as the nearly "exclusive basis for bonus," although the firm says it considers a number of other factors in determining bonuses, including quality of work.

No place like Munger

"MTO has far less associate turnover than other firms," insiders say. "There is some turnover, but overall many people have been here for a long time." "People often leave to do government work, especially the U.S. Attorney's Office. We occasionally lose people to smaller firms that provide more flexible work schedules," says a litigation associate. That really isn't too surprising, says a colleague, "given the caliber of the people here." Others suggest that while Munger has done fairly

well at retaining attorneys, retention could become a problem as the firm grows. One attorney offers this take on the issue: "It used to be that more people stayed, and there is no question in my mind that if the size of this firm continues to grow at the present pace that even more people will decide to leave. But we still do better than most firms."

Everyone in the pool

Munger associates give their firm low marks when it comes to training. "Training? What's that?" asks a cynical midlevel. "To succeed here," continues this source, "you need the ability to figure things out by yourself and the confidence to push forward without much guidance. If you need your hand held, you should go elsewhere." Says one associate, "You can get training if you pursue it, but mostly you learn by doing." In the opinion of a junior associate, "The biggest problem is busy partners with too little time for feedback and mentoring of associates. This problem is not unique to Munger, however." Another attorney makes the case for more informal training by partners. "Other than some NITA courses, training is pretty much on the job. What's difficult is that people seem to be critical of work that isn't up to our standards but are not really up to explaining what those standards are beforehand and giving guidance on how better to meet those standards in the future." According to another midlevel, there is "very little formal training, but the firm is aware of [this] deficiency and is looking at beefing it up." Other attorneys concede that Munger Tolles is a fairly "sink or swim environment," but don't seem to mind. "All of the training I have received has been on the job, but because I work very closely with the senior lawyers on my cases, I feel I have received extensive training in the best way possible - by seeing and doing." Says another, "We get plenty of on the job training, which in my opinion is the better sort. The firm has a 'see one, do one, teach one' mentality to training."

Diversity dilemma

Munger insiders say their firm needs improvement in the area of diversity. "We are making progress, but not enough. Like all major law firms, we have a long way to go," says a senior attorney. A San Francisco associate believes "the firm has made an effort to recruit and retain minorities, and we have some of the best minority lawyers in the country. It is hard to recruit minority lawyers to the firm, however, because there are few minority lawyers here. This gives the impression, however true or not, that the firm is unwelcoming to minority candidates."

A few associates share harsher opinions. "The firm is about average on racial/ethnic sensitivity but has a dearth of minority associates." This source continues, "There are two Hispanic associates, for example, in a firm with 160 lawyers in a city that is 50 percent Hispanic. Efforts to better the situation have so far proved to be nothing but window dressing." "The firm is like an ostrich with its head in the sand on this issue," sighs another frustrated attorney. A junior attorney offers some suggestions on how Munger Tolles can turn the situation around. The firm should try researching "what is attracting the best minority students to other firms." This contact thinks Munger "also should consider lateral hiring to improve minority presence in partnership ranks."

"To succeed here, you need the ability to figure things out by yourself and the confidence to push forward without much guidance."

– *Munger Tolles associate*

VAULT TOP 100

49

PRESTIGE RANKING

LeBoeuf, Lamb, Green & MacRae, L.L.P.

125 West 55th Street
New York, NY 10019-5389
Phone: (212) 424-8000
www.llgm.com

LOCATIONS

New York, NY (HQ)

Albany, NY • Boston, MA • Denver, CO • Harrisburg,
PA • Hartford, CT • Houston, TX • Jacksonville, FL •
Los Angeles, CA • Newark, NJ • Pittsburgh, PA • Salt
Lake City, UT • San Francisco, CA • Washington, DC •
Almaty, Kazakhstan • Beijing • Bishkek, Kyrgyzstan •
Brussels • Johannesburg • London • Moscow • Paris •
Riyadh, Saudi Arabia • Tashkent, Uzbekistan

MAJOR DEPARTMENTS/PRACTICES

Bankruptcy & Restructuring • Corporate • Energy •
Environmental, Health & Safety • Executive
Compensation, Employee Benefits & ERISA • Insurance
• Technology & Intellectual Property & Technology •
International • Litigation • Real Estate • Reinsurance •
Tax • Telecommunications • Trusts & Estates

THE STATS

No. of attorneys: 650
No. of offices: 24
Summer associate offers: 107 out of 181 (2002)
Chairmen: Steven H. Davis and Peter R. O'Flinn
Hiring Partner: William G. Primps

BASE SALARY

New York, NY
1st year: $125,000
2nd year: $135,000
3rd year: $150,000
4th year: $170,000
5th year: $190,000
6th year: $200,000
7th year: $205,000
8th year: $210,000
Summer associate: $2,404/week

UPPERS

- Competitive salaries
- International prestige
- Manageable, if unpredictable, schedules

DOWNERS

- Hazy partnership prospects
- Assignments sometimes lack diversity due to high volume of insurance work
- "Uptight" culture in New York

NOTABLE PERKS

- CLE and bar expenses paid
- Discounted gym memberships
- Moving expenses for first-years
- On-site dining room (in New York)

THE BUZZ
WHAT ATTORNEYS AT OTHER FIRMS ARE SAYING ABOUT THIS FIRM

- "Lots of insurance work"
- "Stuffy and white shoe"
- "Smart and capable"
- "The name is too funny"

EMPLOYMENT CONTACT

Ms. Jill Cameron
Legal Recruiting Coordinator
Phone: (212) 424-8266
Fax: (212) 424-8500
E-mail: jcameron@llgm.com

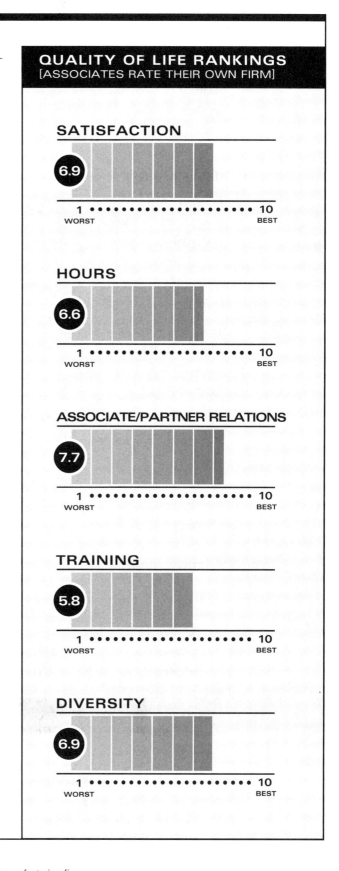

QUALITY OF LIFE RANKINGS
[ASSOCIATES RATE THEIR OWN FIRM]

SATISFACTION

6.9

1 • • • • • • • • • • • • • • • • • • 10
WORST   BEST

HOURS

6.6

1 • • • • • • • • • • • • • • • • • • 10
WORST   BEST

ASSOCIATE/PARTNER RELATIONS

7.7

1 • • • • • • • • • • • • • • • • • • 10
WORST   BEST

TRAINING

5.8

1 • • • • • • • • • • • • • • • • • • 10
WORST   BEST

DIVERSITY

6.9

1 • • • • • • • • • • • • • • • • • • 10
WORST   BEST

THE SCOOP

Founded in 1929, LeBoeuf, Lamb, Greene & MacRae, L.L.P. has built a multinational practice by focusing on three core industries: insurance, finance and energy. The firm has 650 lawyers in 14 locations in the U.S. and 10 overseas locations, including Moscow and cities in three other former Soviet republics.

You're in good hands

LeBoeuf's reputation has been built, in part, by its work in the insurance industry. One of the firm's oldest clients is venerable insurance giant Lloyd's of London. LeBoeuf's name graces the top of league tables in numerous insurance industry financial transactions. LeBoeuf was ranked fifth in overall insurance M&A deals in 2002, advising on 24 transactions worth $9.7 billion and first in M&A deals in 2002 in the property and casualty and life and health sector (seven deals worth $1.5 billion).

In a public relations win for the firm, LeBoeuf was tops among U.S. law firms in nominations to Euromoney Legal Media Group's "Guide to the World's Leading: Insurance and Reinsurance Lawyers" in November 2002. *Reaction* magazine named LeBoeuf "Reinsurance Law Firm of the Year" in 2002.

The firm added three lawyers to the insurance practice in December 2002, including two attorneys from Fulbright & Jaworski. On the minus side, three San Francisco partners in the firm's energy pracrice group left for Sonnenschein Nath & Rosenthal in January 2003. The energy group has been one of the firm's strongest in the 21st century, participating in and completing 22 industry-related M&A deals for $67.7 billion since 1999. (Only Skadden can claim as good a track record during the same period.)

Money guys

Corporate work goes way back for LeBoeuf; the firm has been working on corporate transactions since its founding in 1929. It handles M&A advisory, public and private securities offerings, private equity and venture capital, among other engagements. The firm can boast of handling M&A transactions worth $500 billion in the last three years. Recent securities clients include Scottish Annuity & Life Holdings (LeBoeuf advised on a secondary stock offering worth $109.5 million in April 2002), Montpelier Re Holdings (an initial public offering worth $190 million in October 2002), Safety Insurance Group (an IPO worth $72 million in November 2002) and Russian drug company Pharmacy Chain 36.6 (a private offering of 1.6 million shares in Europe in February 2003).

Bankruptcy at LeBoeuf is a growing business, and the firm has been taking on more and more high-profile engagements, representing Enron in its own bankruptcy as well as that of Pacific Gas & Electric. The firm represents Wachovia in the bankruptcies of USAir and United Airlines, and counsels Geneva Steel Holdings in Chapter 11 proceedings in Utah. Colorado-based e-book seller NetLibrary also tapped LeBoeuf for its Chapter 11 filing in early 2002. Partners Carl Eklund, Kenneth Cannon, Ralph Mabey and Stephen Jack McCardell were recognized by *Corporate Counsel* magazine as among the "Best Lawyers: Bankruptcy and Creditor-Debtor." The firm's bankruptcy practice grew by three in March 2003 when a trio of attorneys from Orrick, Herrington & Sutcliffe jumped ship. Neal Wolf and Todd Padnos joined LeBoeuf as partners while Brett Kitei came on board as an associate.

The London office also welcomed a new crop of corporate heavy hitters over the last year, adding partners Bruce Johnston (formerly of Weil, Gotshal & Manges), Keith Hughes (Paul, Hastings, Janofsky & Walker) and Lynn McCaw (Denton Wilde Sapte).

Court time

LeBoeuf's litigation practice is one of the cornerstones of its practice, with approximately 150 litigation attorneys worldwide. In addition to its core industries – insurance, finance and energy – the firm handles clients in the e-commerce, multimedia, manufacturing, retailing, health care, pharmaceuticals and real estate industries. In one prominent international case, the firm swiped a case from international rival Coudert Brothers. Maria Elena and Isabel Noboa replaced Coudert Brothers with LeBoeuf a few weeks before their lawsuit against their brother, Alvaro Noboa, went to trial in fall of 2002. The sisters were suing their brother, who was running for the presidency of their native Ecuador, over control of the family fruit company. LeBoeuf's clients lost, but they had the last laugh: Alvaro Noboa lost the presidential election the day after the ruling was announced in November 2002.

LeBoeuf scored a victory for watchmaker Swatch in December 2002. The Matterhorn Group sued Swatch for breach of contract, saying the timekeepers reneged on an agreement to let Matterhorn open as many as 30 Swatch stores in the U.S. John M. Nonna and Marc L. Abrams of LeBoeuf's New York office scored a near total victory for Swatch. Though plantiffs prevailed on three sub-claims, the decision, issued by the Southern District Court of New York, severely limited possible damages.

GETTING HIRED

Getting tough

Insiders report that LeBoeuf is tweaking its hiring process and "focusing more on a core group of elite schools." "[LeBoeuf] seems to be getting more and more competitive," according to one associate. "The range of law schools from which the firm recruits appears to be getting smaller." What schools are in favor? "They look at the big name East Coast schools and at the New York schools," says a source. When the firm does look beyond its A-list, it has a special candidate in mind. "[LeBoeuf] hires average students from top-tier law schools and top students from second-tier schools," observes one contact.

There are few surprises in the actual process. "For law students, different attorneys from the office interview on campus and then call back certain students for further interviews with at least three other attorneys – usually half a day total," according to one source. "For laterals, the hiring attorney usually reviews submissions either from recruiters or directly from the attorneys and determines whether to conduct a screening interview. If warranted, then additional callback interviews are set up, similar to that of law students." One lawyer isn't too pleased about the direction the firm is taking. "Too much emphasis has tended to be placed on grades and law schools," that insider opines. "What we need is energetic, well-adjusted people who are happy to be drawing a handsome salary in a down economy and aren't too proud to do the kind of work we have available. I believe, however, that we are moving away from what I view as silly standards with respect to grades and class rank." That contact offers the following advice: "The main thing that gets someone rejected is if they either have no interest in, or express reluctance about, the major areas of work available."

OUR SURVEY SAYS

A tale of two cultures

LeBoeuf associates tell of a culture that is more informal at branch offices than the New York headquarters. "The culture in the branch offices is friendly and professional," says an attorney at a U.S. satellite office. "Lawyers tend to socialize together. There is good camaraderie among the various offices, with the exception of the main office." A New Yorker agrees. "The culture is a tad uptight," says a Big Apple attorney. "There is no overt tension between the attorneys, and they conduct themselves politely and professionally, but the atmosphere is extremely chilly."

There are a handful of consistent complaints about the atmosphere at LeBoeuf. "Overall, the culture is polite and friendly," says a contact. "However, there is underlying competition among junior associates in the larger departments." Another warns prospective LeBoeuf associates not to "break the chain of command and go right to the source with assignments because you find that you step on the toes of more senior associates." Still another insider sees a difficult road to the promised land of partnership. "I'm concerned about the prospects for partnership here," says one forward-looking lawyer. "It seems that the criteria for making partner are not well-defined and may even be ad hoc from year to year. I believe that the vaunted premium on 'excellent lawyering' is disingenuous. It appears that excellent lawyers are routinely passed up. People with clients that generate big revenues are not."

However, associates say their relationships with partners have improved in recent years thanks to a significant effort on the part of the firm, though it's still a mixed bag, to some extent. One insider observes that "relationships vary greatly. Some partners really try to mentor junior associates." Another notices the improving trend. "It seems in the past year conditions have improved and the partners have been more cognizant of attending to associate needs, which is commendable," says a source. "A committee to raise associate concerns with the partnership has been quite effective," reports one attorney. "This committee takes the associate concerns seriously and follows up very well." That doesn't mean things are perfect. "There are some individual partners that have trouble interacting with associates. The firm should try to deal with these individual bad apples more effectively on a one-on-one basis."

Running with the pack

Associates agree that LeBoeuf is competitive with regard to compensation. "The firm tries to meet the market in terms of compensation," says one attorney. "It is never a market leader and tries to stay comfortably within the pack." "The base salary is at or near the top, and the bonus is reasonable in light of the hour requirements," another associate happily reports. "The firms that pay higher salaries require far more hours than they do here." Another satisfied lawyer reports opines that "for a billable hour requirement of 2,000, I feel our compensation is right at market level." In light of recent economic conditions, associates are happy to see such hefty paychecks. "I know this is a hot topic, but given this economy, anyone working at these wages must appreciate their salary and not take it for granted."

One compensation complaint is a hazy bonus structure. "Bonus criteria are a mystery," according to one contact. "The firm sets a billable hour requirement, but it is often not made known until after the year exactly what non-collectible matters will count as billable hours for bonus purposes." Another insider echoes that confusion, but does commend the firm for getting the money into associate hands sooner. "The firm would do well to establish some consistency in this area – as it stands, the bonus target is a constantly moving one, which is incredibly frustrating. The firm did, however, announce bonuses in the beginning of January and pay them quickly [in 2003]. Last year (2002) they weren't paid till March. This went a long way to make associates happy campers." Another happy camper says, "[LeBoeuf] has finally seemed to learn its lesson about giving timely bonuses."

All or nothing

Hours at LeBoeuf are reasonable, though some complain the firm is placing more demands on associates' schedules. Insiders also warn of varied and unpredictable hours. "The hours here are typical of other large firms, perhaps a little better," reports one source. "This used to be a quality of life firm. Now the firm has become fixated on billing. We're nicely compensated though." Another contact expounds on that: "Although LeBoeuf is sometimes dubbed a lifestyle firm, there is no question that those days are long gone. There is an increasing emphasis on the number of hours billed and low billers are definitely getting the message. Nonetheless, there still seems to be a great disparity among associates' hours – some are always here nights and weekends, while others are out the door nightly by 6:30." In the end, though most agree that "the 2,000 billable requirement is quite reasonable for a big firm."

"My hours are unpredictable and sporadic but could be worse," says a third-year. "The only annoying thing is not knowing if I will have my night or weekend free until the last minute, but I suppose that is true with any large firm in New York," says another attorney. "My workload falls within one of two extremes: absolutely nothing to do, or unreasonably busy," complains a legal veteran. "There is little predictability and steadiness to the work flow and as a midlevel associate, it is entirely out of your control."

Part-time schedules are accepted only sporadically. LeBoeuf "grant[s] part-time status only on a case-by-case [basis]," says one insider. "The office has never made clear under what circumstances they would grant such status." Some see it as an industry-wide problem. "I am disappointed that there are so few part-timers at LeBoeuf, which I attribute to unwillingness on the part of law firms to help make part-time arrangements work." One happy part-timer claims that "everyone I work with has accepted my reduced hours schedule."

Your LeBuddy at LeBoeuf

The quality and availability of training at LeBoeuf varies by department. "There is no training for first year litigators," says one associate in that department, a criticism the firm has addressed through the formation of a new litigation training program for its new arrivals. "This may be my sole area of true complaint with LeBoeuf," says one under-trained litigator. The firm is trying, though. "It's getting better slowly," reports one insider. "The firm has obviously made a commitment to better training, and it's starting to show." There's an informal mentoring program for junior associates dubbed "LeBuddy." It's not universally loved. "The informal LeBuddy mentoring program is a joke," growls one contact. "My LeBuddy, while a nice person, has absolutely no professional interests or goals in common with me." Another source says, "I think a mentor can only provide so much additional support."

Working on diversity

Insiders seem to agree LeBoeuf is "trying its best" to maintain a diverse atmosphere. That's manifested in visible efforts to recruit women and minorities, even if retention of said groups is occasionally lacking. "We have a great record for hiring female associates, but not a great record for promoting women to partnership," claims one lawyer; the firm points out that one-third of the New York partners are women. "The firm has excellent recruiting for women but only average retention of women," echoes another LeBoeuf lawyer. "I believe it is facing the same issues any other firm faces, with respect to the work/family balance." Ogres can be found, however. "In general, I would say that the many women attorneys who work here are well-respected and excellent at what they do," says a source. "It is possible, however, to run across someone who does not give women associates the respect they deserve and gives them secretarial work."

"LeBoeuf does not have a lot of minority attorneys," observes an insider. "I do believe, however, that they actively try to recruit and hire minorities." The numbers bear out the belief; 46 of the 155 associates, or 30 percent, in the New York office in 2002 were minorities. "The firm has done well with respect to hiring associates," says one lawyer, "but improvement is needed with respect to the partnership." Gay and lesbian attorneys seem to be doing OK. "A person's sexual orientation is irrelevant. People are not treated differently on this basis." Another insider observes that "some of the top attorneys at LLGM are openly gay or lesbian."

Chadbourne & Parke LLP

30 Rockefeller Plaza
New York, NY 10112
Phone: (212) 408-5100
www.chadbourne.com

LOCATIONS

New York, NY (HQ)
Houston, TX
Los Angeles, CA
Washington, DC
Beijing
London
Moscow

MAJOR DEPARTMENTS/PRACTICES

Bankruptcy • Corporate • Employment • Environmental
• Intellectual Property • Litigation • Products Liability •
Project Finance • Real Estate • Reinsurance/Insurance •
Tax • Trusts & Estates

THE STATS

No. of attorneys: 370
No. of offices: 7
Summer associate offers: 29 out of 29 (2002)
Managing Partner: Charles K. O'Neill
Hiring Partner: Vincent Dunn

BASE SALARY

New York, NY
1st year: $125,000
2nd year: $135,000
3rd year: $150,000
4th year: $170,000
5th year: $190,000
6th year: $205,000
7th year: $210,000
8th year: $215,000
Summer associate: $2,403/week

UPPERS

• Prestigious project finance group
• Respectful partnership; friendly culture

DOWNERS

• Not enough training (except in litigation)
• Unpredictable hours

NOTABLE PERKS

• Tech equipment at employees' disposal, e.g:
  BlackBerries, laptop computers on loan
• Free Starbucks coffee
• Online meal ordering service
• Generous subsidized gym membership

THE BUZZ
WHAT ATTORNEYS AT OTHER FIRMS ARE SAYING ABOUT THIS FIRM

• "Cool New York firm"
• "Forget about having a life at this place"
• "Project finance powerhouse"
• "One trick pony - tobacco"

RANKING RECAP

Quality of Life
#20 - Pay

Best in Diversity
#14 - Diversity for Gays and Lesbians

EMPLOYMENT CONTACT

Ms. Bernadette L. Miles
Director of Legal Recruiting
Phone: (212) 408-5338
Fax: (212) 541-5369
E-mail: bmiles@chadbourne.com

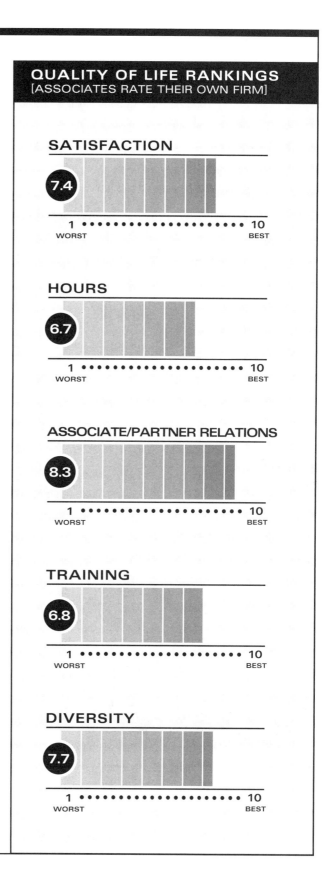

QUALITY OF LIFE RANKINGS
[ASSOCIATES RATE THEIR OWN FIRM]

SATISFACTION

7.4

1 •••••••••••••••••• 10
WORST   BEST

HOURS

6.7

1 •••••••••••••••••• 10
WORST   BEST

ASSOCIATE/PARTNER RELATIONS

8.3

1 •••••••••••••••••• 10
WORST   BEST

TRAINING

6.8

1 •••••••••••••••••• 10
WORST   BEST

DIVERSITY

7.7

1 •••••••••••••••••• 10
WORST   BEST

THE SCOOP

If you like smokin' and drinkin', you just might like Chadbourne & Parke LLP. Based in New York, the prestigious firm has courted controversy, representing tobacco companies and alcohol distributors in product liability cases. Chadbourne has approximately 370 attorneys in seven offices worldwide, 70 percent of whom are located in the firm's Rockefeller Plaza headquarters.

101 years of law

In 1902 Thomas Chadbourne moved his solo practice to New York. The Michigan native had practiced in Milwaukee and Chicago (where he had been a policeman) before moving to the Big Apple. Chadbourne's practice initially focused on business law, and Chadbourne himself owned a stake in New York City's subway and bus lines (privately held at the time). Among the firm's early clients were aviation pioneers Orville and Wilbur Wright; Chadbourne negotiated the sale of patents for the first pilots.

In 1924, Chadbourne, Babbit & Wallace (as it was then known) merged with Stanchfield & Levy. One of the partners in the new Chadbourne, Stanchfield & Levy was William Parke. When that partnership dissolved in 1936, Parke stayed on at the new Chadbourne, Wallace, Parke & Whiteside. The name was shortened to its current form in 1985.

Courting controversy

Chadbourne does not shy away from cases and clients others might view as controversial or potential sources of negative publicity. The firm has represented tobacco companies like Brown & Williamson in product liability cases and successfully defended booze maker Jim Beam in the first fetal alcohol syndrome lawsuit. Chadbourne also represented a nuclear bomb manufacturer in litigation claims filed by residents of the Marshall Islands stemming from hydrogen bomb tests in 1954. More recently, Chadbourne is representing Purdue Pharma, maker of pain medication OxyContin, in individual and class action suits in 23 states.

Project finance leaders

Not all of Chadbourne's clients incite such controversy. The firm's project finance group is considered one of the world's best; *Infrastructure Journal* rated Chadbourne third among global infrastructure mandates for law firms. The firm was first in geographic surveys of Americas and Latin America. In industry rankings, the firm was second in telecom and third in oil and gas. Engagements have included gas pipelines and power plants in Brazil and Argentina, power plans in India, Nepal, Pakistan and China, and numerous projects in former republics of the Soviet Union.

Chadbourne also handles project finance workout and restructuring engagements, a mix of project finance and bankruptcy law. The firm has represented lenders in the Orinoco Iron Project, a $1 billion Venezuelan iron project. The firm's clients include banks and lenders in the U.S., Europe and Asia; Chadbourne managed to get $300 million in payments for its clients. The firm has also represented lenders to Enron, the Houston energy company that has become synonymous with bankruptcy and accounting shenanigans. Chadbourne's Enron clients include St. Paul Fire and Marine, the Royal Bank of Scotland and Dresdner Bank. (The firm seems to have a knack for big-time bankruptcies; it's representing bondholders owed money by telecom firm Global Crossing.) More recent project finance clients include CDC Globeleq, which Chadbourne represented in its acquisition of electricity assets from AES Corp. in Africa.

GETTING HIRED

School matters

At Chadbourne, law school matters, as do grades. "Chadbourne only recruits from the *US News [& World Report]* top-15 law schools and some local New York law schools," observes one associate. Another insider concurs. "Chadbourne is looking for people with good grades at top schools or people with excellent grades from schools outside of the top-15 law schools." "It is all about grades here," says one smarty-pants. Some disagree, saying that while grades are (very) important, even brilliant misfits won't be welcome at Chadbourne. "I believe the firm is looking to hire people who are intelligent, ambitious and hardworking but also friendly and sociable," says one attorney. "Academic background is definitely important but so are intangible qualities like personality and life experiences."

"They're looking for nice, fun people who will do the work required but will not be unpleasant to be around late at night," according to one associate. "A sense of humor is important, I think." "The firm is looking for bright, team-oriented people who will be easy to work with," agrees another Chadbourne-ite. The actual process is standard. "The interview process consists of an on-campus interview with one person for 20 minutes," says an associate. There's also "a callback where you meet with four people for roughly half an hour each."

OUR SURVEY SAYS

The Chadbourne family

"Chadbourne is a friendly place and many associates find that they do socialize outside of the office," says one social butterfly. "One of my favorite things about Chadbourne is the laid back, informal, friendly yet professional atmosphere," says a second-year. "People are actually friends here, aside from being colleagues." Lace up your Nikes. The firm "is a fairly laid back place to work where people work hard and play hard," says one associate. "Junior associates tend to socialize together and genuinely like each other. It is not uncommon for a large group of associates to go out for drinks together or play basketball together on the weekends."

"The firm is quite laid back, particularly for an East Coast firm," says D.C. lawyer. "All of the lawyers get along quite well and when we do socialize together, we all seem to enjoy it." "For the most part, the firm's culture seems laid back," agrees another source. "I've made some good friends here, and lawyers do tend to socialize together."

Few screamers

Overall, associates are delighted with the treatment they get from Chadbourne partners, though a few are known as bad apples. "Partners seem to be making a committed effort – and are succeeding – in respecting associates' professional and private lives and rewarding good work and judgment," remarks one happy litigator. "I've always been treated with a great deal of respect by all the partners I've worked with," says one lucky associate. "You do hear of some partners who are not as respectful." Some partners like associates so much they can barely get things done. Remarks one lawyer, "The partners in my department have taken an active role in my development as an attorney. Additionally, it is fun working with them. It is not uncommon to spend the first five minutes of a meeting discussing family or weekend plans."

No pay leader, but not too shabby

Chadbourne associates aren't getting stiffed, but the firm is sometimes just below the market leaders when it comes to compensation. "Chadbourne tends to be a bit below the top-tier firms with respect to bonuses, if they can get away with it, but is never below market," says one source. "Regular compensation is equal to top-tier firms, and in some cases it is higher." It seems the longer an associate sticks around, the fatter the paycheck becomes, relative to other firms. "I am confident that Chadbourne management is committed to maintaining compensation levels equal to the top tier of New York law firms," states a fourth-year. "At the midlevel range, Chadbourne is actually a step ahead of most New York firms." There may be some lingering resentment left over from the late 1990s. "There is [an] underlying feeling that the partners begrudge us the salaries brought on by the dot-com boom," says one attorney.

Erratic but manageable hours

Reports one Chadbourne associate, "While like every other firm there are periods of intense hours, they have been few and far between. There is no need for face time, and if you are not busy you are encouraged to leave early." Others agree face time is not necessary. "Working less would be wonderful, but the culture is not one in which you have to be here if you don't have work to do," says a contact. "When I am busy, I am very, very busy. When things are slower, I can definitely take advantage of the slow time." At least one young lawyer is happy with the time spent at the office. "The hours are not bad at all," says that newbie. "Coming out of law school, I was worried about being a slave to a law firm. I found this to be untrue at Chadbourne. For the most part, if you work efficiently and wisely, you can bill a good number of hours and still get home at a reasonable hour. Late nights and weekends, though inevitable, tend to be the exception rather than the norm."

Some complain about the "feast or famine" nature of billables at Chadbourne. "Hours are erratic," says one source. "There are days where you will bill two or three hours followed by days where you will bill 14 and up." Many have similar experiences, though it seems 14-hour days are a rarity. "It ebbs and flows," shrugs one insider. "I've never been here past midnight, though." Another lawyer complains of "sporadic periods of extremely long hours and then almost nothing." As a result, "there is never a good time to take vacation."

Only litigators learn

Many Chadbourne associates complain of a dearth of training. "Chadbourne does not do a very good job of training new associates," gripes one insider. "Many of the high level associates and partners are not willing to take the time to train junior associates. But there are a few that are willing, and junior associates need to seek out these people." "The firm gives associates just enough training to make them useful for limited purposes but not enough to make people excellent lawyers," says a perfectly trained lawyer. It wasn't always this way. "At first, I received a lot of valuable training, but the training sessions have become almost nonexistent in the last year or so," says a senior associate.

Litigators appear to have hit the training jackpot. The firm has an "excellent training program for litigators," says one lawyer from that department. "Chadbourne has a good eight-week training program for litigation associates when you start at the firm and provides you with useful samples to use afterwards," says another litigator. "It would be helpful, however, to have some more advanced training courses as we progress."

Great location at 30 Rock

Chadbourne's New York offices are located at 30 Rockefeller Plaza, a major landmark of midtown Manhattan. "Thirty Rockefeller Plaza is a great location," says a senior associate. "Great views from all offices." First- and second-years in New York share offices, but there aren't many complaints. "I share an office as a first-year, but the space is still pretty large," says one associate. "Additionally, we just got new cutting-edge computer systems with flat screen LCD monitors." The space-starved will be glad to learn things might loosen up. "I understand that we are taking over more space in 30 Rockefeller Plaza, which will likely mean that associates will get their own offices sooner," reports one lawyer. D.C. associates say their space is "not overly luxurious but ample, and everyone has their own office," some with views of the Washington Monument.

Diversity efforts

Insiders say Chadbourne "is making an effort to recruit, mentor and retain women associates. For example, there are monthly women associate meetings that provide a forum for discussion and professional development." The firm's efforts get good marks. "[Chadbourne] is truly a wonderful place to work if you are a woman," says one female. "The women attorneys meet once a month to discuss issues that are particularly relevant to them. Additionally, the firm is very accommodating with part-time and flex-time arrangements, as they genuinely try to understand the conflicts that a lot of women struggle with as they try to balance work and family." The common complaint – common both to Chadbourne and the industry — is a tough road to the top. "Like most other large firms, there are few female partners," observes one contact. "Entering classes may be evenly split between men and women, but after a few years, many of the women have left the firm."

Minority attorneys face similar issues. "Our numbers reflect that we need a lot more diversity, particularly among African-American associates and partners. But I do not think this is due to a lack of effort on Chadbourne's part to recruit minorities and know that this is certainly not due to any reluctance to hire or promote minorities," according to one source. "Chadbourne seems very receptive towards improving racial diversity," says another insider. "As a minority myself, I have felt very comfortable working at Chadbourne. However, as is a problem with most firms, there are still very few minority attorneys at Chadbourne."

"It is not uncommon to spend the first five minutes of a meeting discussing family or weekend plans"

— *Chadbourne & Parke associate*

suit

THE VAULT 100:
FIRMS 51-100

Jenner & Block, LLC

One IBM Plaza
Chicago, IL 60611-7603
Phone: (312) 222-9350
www.jenner.com

LOCATIONS

Chicago, IL (HQ)
Dallas, TX
Washington, DC

MAJOR DEPARTMENTS/PRACTICES

Antitrust & Trade Regulation • Appellate & Supreme
Court Arbitration • Association Practice •
Bankruptcy/Corporate Restructuring • Class Action
Litigation • Commercial Law & Uniform Commercial
Code • Construction Law • Corporate & Commercial
Finance • Employee Benefits & Executive Compensation
• Environmental, Energy & Natural Resources • ERISA
Litigation • Estate Planning & Probate • Family Law •
Government Contracts • Health Care • Insurance
Litigation & Counseling • Intellectual Property &
Technology • Labor & Employment • Media & First
Amendment • Products Liability & Mass Tort Defense •
Professional Liability Litigation • Real Estate •
Reinsurance • Securities Litigation • Tax • Tax
Controversy • Telecommunications • Trade Secrets &
Unfair Competition • White Collar Defense & Counseling

THE STATS

No. of attorneys: 383
No. of offices: 3
Summer associate offers: 80 out of 88 (2002)
Chairman: Jerold S. Solovy
Managing Partner: Robert L. Graham
Hiring Attorney: Craig C. Martin

THE BUZZ
WHAT ATTORNEYS AT OTHER FIRMS ARE SAYING ABOUT THIS FIRM

- "Top, top notch"
- "Wants to be a 10, but just not there"
- "Heavy hitter litigators"
- "Sweatshop"

RANKING RECAP

Best in Region
#6 - Chicago

Quality of Life
#1 - Pro Bono
#10 - Best 20 Law Firms to Work For
#10 - Pay
#12 - Satisfaction
#18 - Training

Best in Diversity
#1 - Diversity for Gays and Lesbians
#2 - Overall Diversity
#3 - Diversity for Women
#9 - Diversity for Minorities

NOTABLE PERKS

- Reimbursement for montly BlackBerry fees
- Cab home after 7 p.m.
- Your own laser printer and laptop
- Subsidized gym membership

EMPLOYMENT CONTACT

Ms. Shannon Christopher
Manager of Legal Recruiting
Phone: (312) 923-2617
Fax: (312) 840-7616
E-mail: schristopher@jenner.com

BASE SALARY

Chicago, IL
1st year: $125,000
Summer associate: $2,403/week

THE SCOOP

Jenner & Block, LLC has spent just under 90 years building up one of the nation's top trial and appellate practices, and doubled the size of its corporate department in 2002 with a number of prominent hires. The firm has also greatly expanded its transactional practice, culminating in the handling of a $6.6 billion transaction for a Fortune 100 client, and picked up $1.6 million from Illinois in December after helping settle a complaint brought by four other Chicago firms over their fees for handling the state's suit against the tobacco industry (saving the state's taxpayers nearly $700 million in the process). Jenner appears frequently before the U.S. Supreme Court, arguing on behalf of telecom company NextWave in October 2002 and returning five months later to represent two men seeking to have a Texas sodomy law declared unconstitutional, then again on behalf of a Maryland death row inmate challenging his sentence on due process grounds.

GETTING HIRED

An "outstanding academic record" will help get you noticed by Jenner, but "strong commitment to public service" is also considered a crucial trait. "Clerkships are very important," advises a third-year, "as are top grades and law review experience." One litigator tells us, "If you have the grades or come from the right school, you'll get in. They don't care about personality." "Most associates are absolutely top-notch," so "the people who stand out are those with a unique background, an interest in pro bono work and an approachable manner."

OUR SURVEY SAYS

Thanks to nightly dinners and a regular Friday happy hour, "a significant number of firm attorneys socialize both in and out of work." One senior litigator suggests "either a sense of competitiveness or a hyperawareness of a perceived hierarchy" might cause an underlying tension beneath the cocktail chatter. Not so, counter colleagues, who feel "a remarkable combination of intellectual intensity and emotional support."

"Sophisticated legal practice is time consuming," but "so long as I have interesting work and good people around me," say Jenner associates, "working from 8 a.m. to 7 or 8 p.m. is fine." Insiders feel the firm is "very generous regarding salary" for junior and midlevel associates and report that, apart from "a handful of partners with incredibly unrealistic and perfectionist standards and deadlines," the firm's top dogs are "very respectful of associates and ready to help." "Everyone here takes pro bono very seriously," and that "strong commitment" is "one of our biggest selling points, if not our biggest." Jenner also gets high marks from within for its diversity efforts. "I feel completely comfortable with this office's treatment of women," says a third-year female associate, and insiders believe the firm is "absolutely improving" in its hiring of minority attorneys. Plus, gay and lesbian attorneys at the firm say they "couldn't ask for a better atmosphere."

Irell & Manella LLP

1800 Avenue of the Stars
Suite 900
Los Angeles, CA 90067-4276
Phone: (310) 277-1010
www.irell.com

LOCATIONS

Los Angeles, CA (HQ)
Newport Beach, CA

MAJOR DEPARTMENTS/PRACTICES

Alternative Dispute Resolution • Antitrust • Appellate •
Art • Aviation • Corporate Securities • Creditors' Rights
& Insolvency • Employee Benefits & Exec Comp •
Entertainment • Environmental • Insurance • Intellectual
Property • Labor & Employment • Land Use • Litigation
(including Entertainment, IP and Securities Litigation) •
Personal Planning/Trust & Finance • Real Estate &
Finance • Taxation • White Collar Criminal Defense

THE STATS

No. of attorneys: 240
No. of offices: 2
Summer associate offers: 26 out of 26 (2002)
Managing Partner: David Siegel
Hiring Chair: Laura W. Brill

RANKING RECAP

Best in Region
#6 - California

Best in Practice
#8 - Intellectual Property

Quality of Life
#4 - Pay
#8 - Selectivity

Best in Diversity
#5 - Diversity for Gays and Lesbians

NOTABLE PERKS

- Insurance premiums paid by firm
- $500 decorating allowance
- On-site gym
- Paid on-site parking
- Four weeks vacation for full-time associates

EMPLOYMENT CONTACT

Ms. Robyn Steele
Recruiting Administrator
Phone: (310) 277-1010
Toll-free: (800) 421-4502
E-mail: rsteele@irell.com

BASE SALARY

Los Angeles, CA
1st year: $130,000
2nd year: $135,000
3rd year: $150,000
Summer associate: $2,400/week

THE BUZZ
WHAT ATTORNEYS AT OTHER FIRMS ARE SAYING ABOUT THIS FIRM

- "Cool as hell"
- "Delusions of grandeur"
- "Excellent IP and corporate, laid back people"
- "Intellectual snobs"

THE SCOOP

Founded in 1941, Los Angeles' Irell & Manella LLP originally specialized in tax matters and today is a full-service law firm. Because other firms often turn to Irell & Manella when they have their own legal troubles, Irell refers to itself as the "lawyers' lawyers." But the firm may be best known for how its IP practice was born. Back in 1977, Mattel was facing a potentially disastrous patent suit regarding technology used in its hand-held video games. When a conflict of interest forced the toy maker's attorneys off the case, Mattel inexplicably turned to a first-year associate at Irell even though neither he nor the firm had any experience in IP litigation. The associate studied everything he could about patent law and technology and eventually prevailed in the case. IP soon became one of the firm's leading practice areas. And what became of Morgan Chu, that first-year associate? He just completed two three-year terms as co-managing partner of the firm.

GETTING HIRED

"Irell likes to hire very smart, well-credentialed individuals." Insiders say "only the best and brightest" receive offers, so candidates should possess "top grades, amazing credentials and a passion for working hard." Clerkships don't hurt either, especially for litigators. "The firm has pretty stringent grade cutoffs depending on where you go to law school," a midlevel reveals. In the opinion of an IP attorney, "If you come from one of the right schools, it's pretty easy to get hired. If you aren't from the perceived A-list schools, it's harder."

OUR SURVEY SAYS

Insiders report Irell & Manella is "laid back, professional, comfortable," "highly intellectual, a tad quirky" and "intense but informal." There's "not much of a social scene, although happy hours have improved over the last two years." A source reports that "the firm has become more and more focused on hours, and the stress to stay busy has caused more competition among associates." Some point to increased cost-consciousness and intensified "dissension among associates."

A happy first-year reveals, "Incoming first-years get a high summer stipend, get paid a larger salary than other firms in the city and get a larger bonus. You can't beat the pay." But another attorney confides, "Rumor has it that the firm is overhauling that past system, dumping associate profit-sharing and aligning associate compensation with Gibson, Latham and O'Melveny." Although overall compensation is high, many believe senior associates who participate in the profit-sharing plan are paid below-market base salaries. (The firm says compensation has recently been overhauled for senior associates, with base salaries increasing and associates no longer facing the downside risk of a pure profit-sharing model. Profitability will still be taken into account in setting total compensation.) Meanwhile, a litigation associate reports that associates can "just get the work done and go home. After you work a long case, you are expected to take a vacation."

Pillsbury Winthrop LLP

One Battery Park Plaza
New York, NY 10004
Phone: (212) 858-1000

50 Fremont Street
San Francisco, CA 94105
Phone: (415) 983-1000
www.pillsburywinthrop.com

LOCATIONS

Century City, CA • Costa Mesa, CA • Houston, TX • Los Angeles, CA • New York, NY • North County San Diego, CA • Palo Alto, CA • Sacramento, CA • San Diego, CA • San Francisco, CA • Stamford, CT • Tysons Corner, VA • Washington, DC • London • Singapore • Sydney • Tokyo

MAJOR DEPARTMENTS/PRACTICES

Antitrust • Bankruptcy & Creditors' Rights • Corporate, Securities & Finance • Class Actions • E-Commerce & Outsourcing • Emerging Companies • Employment & Labor • Executive Compensation & Benefits • Energy • Environmental & Land Use • Intellectual Property • International Transactions • Licensing, Technology & Trade • Life Sciences & Technology • Litigation • Media & Content • Real Estate, Project Development & Construction • Tax • Telecommunications

THE STATS

No. of attorneys: 767
No. of offices: 17
Summer associate offers: 44 out of 62 (2002)
Chairwoman: Mary B. Cranston
Managing Partner: Marina Park
Hiring Partners: David Crichlow and Courtney Lynch

 THE BUZZ
WHAT ATTORNEYS AT OTHER FIRMS ARE SAYING ABOUT THIS FIRM

- "Knowledgeable and capable"
- "Shadow of a number of firms' former selves"
- "My friends there love it"
- "Morale is hurting"

RANKING RECAP

Best in Region
#12 - California

NOTABLE PERKS

- Free dinners Monday through Thursday
- Bar fees
- BlackBerry pagers

EMPLOYMENT CONTACTS

Los Angeles & Century City
Ms. Mary Ellen Hatch
mhatch@pillsburywinthrop.com

New York
Ms. Dorrie Ciavatta
dciavatta@pillsburywinthrop.com

San Francisco
Ms. Sela Seleska
sseleska@pillsburywinthrop.com

See firm web site for employment contacts at other offices.

BASE SALARY

Various offices
1st year: $125,000
2nd year: $135,000
3rd year: $150,000
4th year: $165,000 ($170K - NY)
5th year: $185,000 ($190K - NY)
6th-8th years: $195,000

Houston, TX
1st year: $110-115,000
2nd year: $114-124,000
3rd year: $121-136,000
4th year: $130-150,000
5th year: $140-160,000
6th-8th years: $145-170,000

THE SCOOP

A result of the 2001 merger combining Pillsbury Madison & Sutro and Winthrop, Stimson, Putnam & Roberts, Pillsbury Winthrop LLP is a global giant with 17 offices. Pillsbury's newest office in Houston opened in January 2003 to serve clients in the energy, telecom, aerospace and financial sectors. Around the same time, Pillsbury took advantage of the dissolution of Brobeck, Phleger & Harrison and Skjerven Morrill and hired a total of 29 attorneys from the two firms. Recent deals include the successful defense of Bombardier in a patent infringement case seeking to enjoin the sale of its snowmobile skis, serving as underwriter's counsel to Merrill Lynch in a $250 million offering for National Fuel Gas Company and a $12.5 billion bond issue for the State of California. The firm has concluded a troublesome incident involving former partner Frode Jensen, who left the firm for Latham & Watkins, after which allegations of sexual harassment became public. Jensen sued Pillsbury for $45 million for defamation. The two sides settled the dispute in March 2003 for an unknown amount.

GETTING HIRED

"The firm has grown far more selective in its hiring since the recession," associates report. According to a litigation associate, "The firm tends to only interview people with high academic records. The firm is looking for first-years from the top of the class." But it takes more than brains to make the cut. "The firm is genuinely interested in finding people who fit in well with the group on a personality level. But they expect top-quality work, so you can't be a mental slouch," says a first-year. Candidates should be "very poised" and "confident."

OUR SURVEY SAYS

Insiders describe Pillsbury as a "friendly," "collegial, cooperative" firm that is "teamwork focused." An associate in San Francisco, typically considered a laid back town, says, "The firm presents itself as laid back but is truly quite conservative." A San Diego associate reports that "attorneys at the firm are uptight and running scared" because "the firm's profit priority overrules everything else," while another says it "is probably more casual and laid back than the firm as a whole." An associate in the Big Apple reports, "The laid-back culture of the past is giving way to the more aggressively profit-driven culture that is apparently becoming the norm at New York law firms." There is a 1,950-hour minimum, including pro bono, business development and special projects, with "generous automatic bonuses" for extra hours. "As with all big-firm law jobs, there is either too much or too little work." Many associates express frustration regarding the unspoken expectation to put in face time. Others insist partners encourage associates to "try to strike a balance between work life and personal life." Most associates are pleased with their pay, which is "near the top of the market." One attorney reports, "My salary is higher than any of my peers at other firms."

Alston & Bird LLP

One Atlantic Center
1201 West Peachtree Street
Atlanta, GA 30309-3424
Phone: (404) 881-7000
www.alston.com

LOCATIONS

Atlanta, GA (HQ)
Charlotte, NC
New York, NY
Raleigh, NC
Washington, DC

MAJOR DEPARTMENTS/PRACTICES

Antitrust • Bankruptcy • Capital Markets •
Environmental • ERISA • Fiduciary • Health Care •
Intellectual Property • International • Labor • Leveraged
Capital • Products Liability • Securities • Tax •
Technology • Trial & Appellate • Wealth Planning

THE STATS

No. of attorneys: 667
No. of offices: 5
Summer associate offers: 93 out of 105 (2002)
Managing Partner: Ben F. Johnson III
Hiring Partner: Jonathan W. Lowe

NOTABLE PERKS

- On-site gym, masseuse and day care (Atlanta)
- Friday happy hour
- Annual weekend retreat

THE BUZZ
WHAT ATTORNEYS AT OTHER FIRMS ARE SAYING ABOUT THIS FIRM

- "Tops in Atlanta"
- "Striving but still second tier"
- "Family friendly"
- "Middle child complex"

RANKING RECAP

Best in Region
#2 - The South

Best in Practice
#10 (tie) - Labor & Employment
#10 (tie) - Real Estate

Quality of Life
#2 - Retention
#6 - Satisfaction
#7 - Best 20 Law Firms to Work For
#10 - Offices
#14 - Associate/Partner Relations

Best in Diversity
#12 - Diversity for Minorities
#14 - Diversity for Women
#15 (tie) - Overall Diversity

EMPLOYMENT CONTACT

Ms. Emily S. Leeson
Director of Attorney Hiring & Development
E-mail: eleeson@alston.com

BASE SALARY

Atlanta, GA; Charlotte, Raleigh, NC
1st year: $100,000
2nd year: $105,000
3rd year: $110,000
4th year: $115,000
5th year: $122,000
6th year: $130,000
Summer associate $1,800/week

Washington, DC; New York, NY
1st year: $125,000
2nd year: $135,000
3rd year: $145,000 (DC), $150,000 (NY)
4th year: $155,000 (DC), $165,000 (NY)
5th year: $165,000 (DC), $190,000 (NY)
6th year: $175,000 (DC), $200,000 (NY)
Summer associate: $2,400/week

THE SCOOP

Alston & Bird LLP is one of the oldest and largest law firms in the Southeast, and it's rapidly assuming national prominence. Since landing the No. 36 spot on *Fortune* magazine's list of the "100 Best Companies to Work for in America" in 2000, the firm has continued to climb in the rankings, taking the bronze in 2003 with an impressive No. 3 ranking. Maybe that's why former senator and presidential candidate Bob Dole decided to join the firm in February (although his rumored $1 million-plus salary probably didn't hurt). The firm advised media conglomerate Bertelsmann on its acquisition of record label Zomba in 2002 and represented race car driver Dale Earnhardt's widow when she asked officials in Kannapolis, N.C., to stop using her husband's name and likeness to promote a memorial park without her permission.

GETTING HIRED

Alston & Bird's "strong and growing reputation makes it easier to be more selective" in its hiring these days, and "as a result, the firm gets pickier and pickier about grades." But the firm is "more likely to take a B+ student with amazing personal interaction skills than an A student with no ability to maintain a conversation." After meeting with two attorneys on campus, brace yourself for a half-day invite to the office of your choice; if you get called back, be ready to prove you have "the brains and the social skills to contribute to the firm culture."

OUR SURVEY SAYS

Insiders at Alston & Bird describe a "familial atmosphere where everyone works together as a team." Parents adore the subsidized day care center "a block from the office" and associates boast of such activities as "happy hours, bowling and ice cream socials." A veteran advises, "If you work hard, partners appreciate it and treat you very well." Some caution, though, that "the larger we've gotten, the more difficult it has been to continue the culture." "Make no mistake," a source advises, "this law firm is a business and the bottom line is hours." In recent years, "what was once the bonus target has become almost a minimal expectation." But "work hours have been very flexible." One associate marvels, "I have worked in the office on less than five weekends in the past two years."

Associates are more concerned about compensation. "Salaries are not the highest," and "the bonuses do not compare to bonuses that can be earned in other cities." "Minority recruiting efforts are taken seriously," though it "would be nice to mix it up more," especially in the branch offices. Gender equity, however, is "a point of strength and pride" at the firm. "Women are very involved in the firm," and female partners "are very interested in encouraging women to succeed." And with domestic partner benefits and a firm non-discrimination policy, Alston is "welcoming to gay men and lesbians with the talent to be here."

Kaye Scholer LLP

425 Park Avenue
New York, NY 10022-3598
Phone: (212) 836-8000
www.kayescholer.com

LOCATIONS

New York, NY (HQ)

Chicago, IL • Los Angeles, CA • Washington, DC •
West Palm Beach, FL • Frankfurt • Hong Kong • London
• Shanghai

MAJOR DEPARTMENTS/PRACTICES

Antitrust • Business Reorganization • Corporate &
Finance • Employment & Labor • Entertainment, Media
& Communications • Intellectual Property • International
• Legislative & Regulatory • Litigation • Product Liability
• Real Estate • Tax • Technology & E-Commerce •
Trust & Estates • White Collar Crime • Wills & Estates

THE STATS

No. of attorneys: 467
No. of offices: 9
Summer associate offers: 41 out of 41 (2002)
Chairman: David Klingsberg
Managing Partner: Barry Willner
Hiring Attorney: James Herschlein

RANKING RECAP

Quality of Life
#19 - Hours

NOTABLE PERKS

- 60 percent subsidy on laptop purchases
- Dinners and car rides after 8 p.m. (NY)
- Friday cocktail parties

EMPLOYMENT CONTACT

Ms. Wendy Evans
Director of Legal Personnel
Phone: (212) 836-8000
Fax: (212) 836-8689
E-mail: wevans@kayescholer.com

BASE SALARY

New York, NY
1st year: $125,000
2nd year: $135,000
3rd year: $150,000
4th year: $165,000
5th year: $186,000
6th year: $196,000
7th year: $205,000
8th year: $210,000
Summer associate: $2,410/week

THE BUZZ
WHAT ATTORNEYS AT OTHER FIRMS ARE SAYING ABOUT THIS FIRM

- "Friendly, lifestyle firm"
- "NYC sweatshop competing with Skadden for the reputation"
- "Phenomenal lawyers"
- "Macho and overbearing"

THE SCOOP

Although Kaye Scholer LLP is best known for over a half-century's worth of antitrust expertise, some of the firm's other specialties came to the fore in 2002. The firm's white-collar defense team, led by former federal prosecutor Paul Curran, picked up a client noted for its real-life white collars: the Roman Catholic Archdiocese of New York turned to Kaye Scholer for help defending itself in the widespread scandals involving sexual abuse by priests. The firm is also participating in one of the largest race discrimination class-action suits in American history, on behalf of more than 2,600 current and former African-American employees of hospitality services provider Sodexho.

GETTING HIRED

"The resumes of the summer applicants are replete with honors, accomplishments and awards," says a senior litigator at Kaye Scholer. "Intelligent people who are enthusiastic about the practice of law" have a great shot if they can convince the firm they'd make "interesting and diverse attorneys." A third-year notes encouragingly, "At the callback stage, the offer is the candidate's to lose." But another junior associate raises a potential red flag. "Candidates from second- and third-tier law schools, even if they are outstanding, don't always get a fair shake," she suggests. Other insiders agree Kaye Scholer "tends to stick to the top law schools" but insist the firm makes room for "students with good academic records."

OUR SURVEY SAYS

"From the 'Camp Kaye' summer associate program to Friday night cocktails, the firm has tried to institutionalize socializing among attorneys and a more relaxed atmosphere than at some other large firms." The attorneys are "smart people but not intellectual snobs" who "go out after work quite often" and enjoy a dress code so informal associates have been known to show up in the summer wearing sandals.

But a veteran litigator likens her job to "attending a school that does not give out grades." She explains, "After six years, I have absolutely no indication whether I will even be considered for partnership." Colleagues agree "some lack of communication" exists, and "older partners can be aloof," but suggest "younger partners are much friendlier" and "a good number of partners take a genuine interest in mentoring associates."

Kaye Scholer is "traditionally known for being on the cheaper side" and "doesn't give more than it has to," but does "keep up to par" with the competition. On the plus side, "the work day is one of the best I know of for firms in New York." An associate rejoices, "The partners don't work late unless they have to, so no one is calling you after 6:30 to give you more work."

VAULT TOP 100

56

PRESTIGE RANKING

Cooley Godward LLP

5 Palo Alto Square
3000 El Camino Real
Palo Alto, CA 94306-2155
Phone: (650) 843-5000
www.cooley.com

LOCATIONS

Palo Alto, CA (HQ)
Broomfield, CO
Reston, VA
San Diego, CA
San Francisco, CA

MAJOR DEPARTMENTS/PRACTICES

Antitrust/Trade Regulation • Complex Commercial
Litigation • Corporate • Credit Finance • Employee
Compensation & Benefits • Employment & Labor
Counseling Litigation • Immigration • Intellectual
Property Litigation/Patent/Trademark/Copyright • Life
Sciences • Mergers & Acquisition • Real Estate •
Securities Litigation • Tax • Technology • Transactions
• Venture Capital

THE STATS

No. of attorneys: 500
No. of offices: 5
Summer associate offers: 51 out of 54 (2002)
Chairman: Stephen C. Neal
Chief Operating Officer: Mark B. Pitchford
Hiring Committee Chair: John C. Dwyer

THE BUZZ
WHAT ATTORNEYS AT OTHER FIRMS ARE SAYING ABOUT THIS FIRM

- "Strong IP practice"
- "Coulda been a contender"
- "Back in the saddle again"
- "Too many layoffs!"

RANKING RECAP

Best in Region
#11 - California

Best in Practice
#2 - Technology/Internet/E-Commerce

Quality of Life
#9 - Training
#20 - Offices

NOTABLE PERKS

- Subsidized gym membership
- Stipend while studying for the bar
- Moving expenses
- Emergency daycare

EMPLOYMENT CONTACT

Ms. Jo Anne Larson
Director of Attorney Recruiting
Phone: (650) 843-5000
Fax: (650) 857-0663
E-mail: larsonja@cooley.com

BASE SALARY

Palo Alto, CA
1st year: $125,000
2nd year: $130,000
3rd year: $135,000
4th year: $150,000
5th year: $165,000
6th year: $185,000
7th year: $195,000
Summer associate: $2,400/week

THE SCOOP

Its representation of established and startup high-tech companies and ultra-relaxed, friendly vibe made Cooley Godward LLP the envy of other firms during the high-flying 1990s. But the firm has hit some rough patches since the tech boom went bust, including several rounds of layoffs. However sad such cost-cutting measures may seem, they have bolstered profits-per-partner, which reportedly have a number of East Coast firms eyeing Cooley as a potential merger partner. Although Cooley Chairman Stephen Neal says the firm favors a go-it-alone strategy, he hasn't ruled out a merger if the right firm comes along. One thing is clear: the turbulent economy hasn't diminished Cooley's ability to attract big-name clients. Pacific Gas and Electric has tapped the firm to lead its bankruptcy proceedings, and Cooley is counseling AT&T in a suit against Microsoft.

GETTING HIRED

If you're interested in joining Cooley, "you do not need to go to the best law school," says an associate, "but you have to have great grades and law review experience." The firm "looks to hire friendly, mature people with good attitudes." According to a Palo Alto associate, the firm prefers "people with real world experience who have sound judgment and know when to ask for help." A business and finance associate reports the firm is "just not hiring because there is not enough work." Because Cooley is "not hiring people in droves anymore," insiders say it has "become so selective that many of the people doing the recruiting, interviewing and hiring wouldn't qualify for callbacks."

OUR SURVEY SAYS

Insiders report the vibe at Cooley is "casual, friendly and relatively close knit," and the firm "recognizes the importance for people to have individual and personal lives." Sources appreciate the "interesting and varied" work. But some insiders reveal that morale at once-cheery Cooley has taken a hit because of the weak economy and layoffs. "Lawyers used to socialize together, but now you can't get anybody to show up at a happy hour," says one source. Others say the atmosphere has become more "uptight."

On the issue of pay, associates fall into two camps: those who are satisfied with the firm's "normal salary" and "strong bonuses,"and those who feel "compensation is below market." Many consider the bonuses "quite good," but say "the base salary is currently lagging competitors by a year." "The slowdown in business aside," says a corporate attorney, "the firm has done a nice job in managing costs while remaining competitive." According to a new associate, "There are a couple of Silicon Valley firms that pay slightly more than Cooley, but given the economic climate, the amount of pay is fantastic." The firm's training program is considered "extremely helpful." "There

Goodwin Procter LLP

Exchange Place
53 State Street
Boston, MA 02109
Phone: (617) 570-1000
www.goodwinprocter.com

LOCATIONS

Boston, MA (HQ)
New York, NY
Roseland, NJ
Washington, DC

MAJOR DEPARTMENTS/PRACTICES

Corporate
Environmental
ERISA & Employee Benefits
Estate Planning & Administration
Labor & Employment
Litigation
Real Estate
Tax

THE STATS

No. of attorneys: 470
No. of offices: 4
Summer associate offers: 36 out of 36 (2002)
Chairman and Managing Partner: Regina M. Pisa
Hiring Partner: Lawrence R. Cahill

RANKING RECAP

Best in Region
#3 - Boston

Quality of Life
#10 - Training
#14 - Pay

NOTABLE PERKS

- On-site emergency daycare
- Weekly lunches/happy hours
- Annual retreat with attorneys and families
- Car rides home

EMPLOYMENT CONTACT

Ms. Maureen A. Shea
Director of Legal Recruitment
Phone: (617) 570-1288
Fax: (617) 523-1231
E-mail: mshea@goodwinprocter.com

BASE SALARY

Boston, MA
1st year: $125,000
2nd year: $135,000
3rd year: $145,000
4th year: $155,000
5th year: $165,000
6th year: $180,000
7th year: $190,000
8th year: $200,000
Summer associate: $2,400/week

THE BUZZ
WHAT ATTORNEYS AT OTHER FIRMS ARE SAYING ABOUT THIS FIRM

- "Very respectable"
- "Stodgy white shoe"
- "Beantown power"
- "What if a fraternity opened a law firm?"

THE SCOOP

A fixture in Boston for more than 90 years, Goodwin Procter LLP has plenty to brag about. It was the first major firm to elect a woman to the dual role of chairman and managing partner. The firm reportedly picked up a hefty $5.8 million fee for representing well-known local company Arthur D. Little during its bankruptcy and ensuing asset auction and counts Harvard Bioscience and the Massachusetts Port Authority among its clients. Not one to shy from controversy, the firm has long served as national counsel for cigarette manufacturer Philip Morris, and is also advising the Archdiocese of Boston regarding the Catholic Church sex scandal.

GETTING HIRED

Insiders say getting an offer from Goodwin Procter has "definitely gotten more competitive over the last few years." "If a student goes to a school that is not ranked in the top five, his or her grades have to be pretty outstanding to get hired here," a source warns. The firm is "looking for smart, thoughtful, kind and social lawyers who write well, are quick to learn and are willing to work hard and as a team." It also seeks "people who we want to work with and would trust" working on highly confidential matters for clients. As for the interview process itself, it's fairly standard. "The firm conducts a 20-30-minute on campus interview, followed by a half-day callback. If you receive a callback interview, the offer is largely yours to lose," shares a corporate associate.

OUR SURVEY SAYS

"Overall, the firm provides a supportive professional environment and interesting work. Most partners and associates are friendly and pleasant to work with," remarks one associate. "The culture certainly varies by department, but I find it very friendly and laid back, yet still professional," says a labor attorney. One associate finds the firm's "commitment to meritocracy" waning recently "as the economic downturn has resulted in the performance review system being used to thin associate ranks."

Many associates aren't thrilled about the number of hours they work but realize "long hours are inescapable in this type of work." "Good planning and time management, which are not always easy for new lawyers, make it possible to leave before 7 p.m. each day and still take 90 percent of your weekends off," reveals a second-year. Insiders like that "the firm is very good about allowing people to work from home." The "1,850 minimum billable hours for bonus" is considered "totally reasonable," but the workflow is "often stop and go." "I feel that my compensation is very good and is about the norm for the Boston market," comments a third-year. Some sources are "disappointed that hours factor most heavily in determination of bonus, as opposed to quality of work and performance." Most agree with the senior associate who says, "Only a truly greedy capitalist would complain about Goodwin's associate salary structure."

VAULT TOP 100
58
PRESTIGE RANKING

Sonnenschein Nath & Rosenthal

8000 Sears Tower
Chicago, IL 60606
Phone: (312) 876-8000
www.sonnenschein.com

LOCATIONS

Chicago, IL (HQ)
Kansas City, MO • Los Angeles, CA • New York, NY •
San Francisco, CA • Short Hills, NJ • St. Louis, MO •
Washington, DC • West Palm Beach, FL

MAJOR DEPARTMENTS/PRACTICES

Antitrust, Franchising & Distribution • Corporate &
Securities • e-Business • Employee Benefits & Executive
Compensation • Energy • Environmental • Government
Contracts • Growth Companies • Health Care •
Insolvency, Bankruptcy & Reorganization • Insurance •
Intellectual Property & Technology • International •
Labor & Employment • Litigation & Business Regulation
• Media, Libel & First Amendment • Products Liability •
Real Estate • Taxation • Telecommunications • Trusts &
Estates • White Collar Criminal/Federal Regulatory

THE STATS

No. of attorneys: 640
No. of offices: 9
Chairman: Duane C. Quaini

RANKING RECAP

Best in Region
#8 - Chicago

NOTABLE PERKS

- Laptop computers
- Herman Miller Aeron chairs
- Late-night dinners

EMPLOYMENT CONTACT

Chicago
Ms. Barbara Petri
Recruitment Coordinator
Phone: (312) 876-8000
Fax: (312) 876-7934
E-mail: bpetri@sonnenschein.com

See web site for employment contacts in other
cities.

BASE SALARY

Chicago, IL
1st year: $125,000
Summer associate: $2,400/week

THE BUZZ
WHAT ATTORNEYS AT OTHER FIRMS ARE SAYING ABOUT THIS FIRM

- "Chicago powerhouse"
- "Cots for associates to sleep"
- "Scott Turow!"
- "No one is happy"

THE SCOOP

Closing in on its 100th anniversary, Chicago's Sonnenschein Nath & Rosenthal continues to be one of the Windy City's most competitive law firms. Its corporate client list includes McDonald's, General Electric and Sara Lee, while the real estate division handles deals for financial institutions like Prudential and Citicorp. The firm helped Rand McNally navigate its Chapter 11 proceedings in early 2003 and also advises the committee of unsecured creditors in the United Airlines bankruptcy. A 2002 merger with New York-based Rubin Baum amplified the firm's entertainment practice. The home office also picked up a high-flying new client in Boeing, which retained the firm shortly after relocating its corporate headquarters to Chicago and is defending Boeing in a wrongful death suit stemming from a crash. Scott Turow still drops in to handle commercial and white-collar criminal defense litigation when he isn't crafting his latest legal thriller.

GETTING HIRED

"The firm has gotten more competitive in the last few years," says an associate, and a senior attorney confirms "nearly all associates went to law schools ranked in the top 25." An insider disagrees: "I think that it should be a bit more competitive." One source says, "Only those that can maintain a sense of humor" make the grade, and "jerks are not allowed." The best advice current Sonnenscheiners have for preparing for interviews? "Know how to pronounce 'Sonnenschein,'" a senior IP attorney cautions. (It's SUN-en-shine, in case you were wondering.)

OUR SURVEY SAYS

Says one midlevel associate, "The attorneys who have spent their careers here and have been here for 20-plus years are quite friendly and social outside of the office, but that seems a part of the past." A veteran member of the IP team in Chicago insists his group "socializes a great deal," and associates in San Francisco say they get together outside the office, too. In LA, "everyone is treated with respect and professionalism" and "partners' doors are always open." One woman describes the firm as "a great place for women," although a colleague laments the presence of "few women partners, especially mentors, in the litigation department."

Insiders have little to say about hours. "The hours here are reasonable," shrugs an attorney. "Sometimes high, sometimes low." A point of contention among associates is the deferred compensation system, which asociates describe as "terrible." A litigator admits the system is "unique," but argues it isn't "wholly unfair. At such high salaries, it is important to pull your own weight." The deferred compensation system influences how associates view pro bono work. Associates need to spend a minimum of 100 hours on pro bono before they can apply that work toward their billable hours. Consequently, reports a source, "associates are wary of taking on pro bono cases. If you don't make your hours, you don't get the $25,000 the firm is holding on to."

Dechert LLP

4000 Bell Atlantic Tower
1717 Arch Street
Philadelphia, PA 19103-2793
Phone: (215) 994-4000
www.dechert.com

LOCATIONS

Philadelphia, PA (HQ)
Boston, MA • Harrisburg, PA • Hartford, CT • Newport Beach, CA • New York, NY • Princeton, NJ • San Francisco, CA • Washington, DC • Brussels • Frankfurt • London • Luxembourg • Paris

MAJOR DEPARTMENTS/PRACTICES

Business
Financial Services
Litigation
Tax

THE STATS

No. of attorneys: 770
No. of offices: 14
Summer associate offers: 57 out of 60 (2002)
Chairman: Barton J. Winokur
Hiring Partners: Timothy C. Blank & John V. O'Hanlon (Boston); David R. Kraus (Harrisburg); Katherine A. Burroughs (Hartford); Kurt C. Swainston (Newport Beach); Kathleen N. Massey (NY); Frederick G. Herold & Geraldine A. Sinatra (Philadelphia); Diane P. Sullivan & David A. Kotler (Princeton); Joseph B. Heil (San Francisco); Paul S. Stevens (Washington)

RANKING RECAP

Best in Region
#2 - Pennsylvania

NOTABLE PERKS

• Car rides home
• Overtime dinners
• Weekly happy hours
• Free legal services when buying a home

EMPLOYMENT CONTACTS

Firm-wide Associate Hiring Matters
Ms. Carol S. Miller
Director of Associate Administration
Phone: (215) 994-2147
E-mail: carol.miller@dechert.com

Summer & Entry-Level Assoc. Hiring - Philadelphia
Ms. Alberta Bertolino
Director of Associate Recruitment
Phone: (215) 994-2296
E-mail: alberta.bertolino@dechert.com

BASE SALARY

Boston, MA; Newport Beach, CA; New York, NY; Philadelphia, PA; Princeton,NJ; Washington DC
1st year: $125,000
Summer associate: $2,400/week

Harrisburg, PA
1st year: $93,000
Summer associate: $1,750/week

Hartford, CT
1st year: $100,000
Summer associate: $1,825/week

THE BUZZ
WHAT ATTORNEYS AT OTHER FIRMS ARE SAYING ABOUT THIS FIRM

• "Interesting work"
• "Didn't quite make it to the pinnacle"
• "Very congenial and great quality of life"
• "Stodgy"

THE SCOOP

With 14 domestic and international offices and strong litigation, mutual fund and M&A practices, Dechert LLP's reputation now extends well beyond its historic roots in Philadelphia. Dechert shocked many in the legal community when it announced first-year salaries in Philadelphia and Princeton would jump a whopping $20,000, to $125,000 beginning in early 2003. The fact that the firms's profitability has grown substantially over the last five years could explain the generosity. The firm has been retained for representations of major coprorate clients such as GlaxoSmithKline (Baycol products liability litigation), Delta Airlines (antitrust litigation), Citigroup (securities litigation and acquisition of Worldspan), Crown Cork & Seal ($3.2 billion refinancing plan), One Equity Partners (acquisition of Polaroid), Aetna and Starwood Capital (real estate financings) and Baxter, Pfizer and Wyeth (corporate work).

GETTING HIRED

"Dechert is one of the most selective firms in Philadelphia," insiders say. "Dechert wants to hire very bright students, typically from top national law schools or from the top of the class of local law schools," a fifth-year tells us. Additionally, the firm looks "for people who also have good interpersonal skills" and are "hardworking team players." A first-year observes that the firm "seems to like mature students, so lots of older/non-traditional students" have been hired in the past. This source adds, "There are lots of Ivy Leaguers, but some of the best new hires went to local schools at night while holding down a full time job and a family, too."

OUR SURVEY SAYS

Insiders say Dechert's culture is "socially laid back and nonjudgmental." "The firm isn't formal," says a Philadelphian, "but I wouldn't describe it as friendly, either. The attorneys are relatively serious about their work." Insiders say the Newport Beach office has a "generally a relaxed atmosphere," and the "partners are approachable, reasonable and easy to work with for the most part." In D.C., the "younger lawyers often socialize outside of the office." Dechert is "at or near the top of the associate pay scale in every market in which it is located," Indeed, most Philadelphia associates rave about Dechert's "amazing compensation package," although some point out that "bonuses can be stingy." Sources in some other locations share that last sentiment. "Associates have given up on receiving market bonuses here," sighs a frustrated New Yorker. D.C. associates say, "The firm is $20,000 behind other top firms." At least billable hour expectations are said to be "reasonable."

"Dechert offers several in-house training programs, into which it puts a substantial amount of time and effort," and "associates are assigned partner mentors." According to a first-year, the "formal training programs" "occasionally are so extensive that they start to get annoying."

Steptoe & Johnson LLP

1300 Connecticut Avenue, NW
Washington, DC 20036-1795
Phone: (202) 429-3000
www.steptoe.com

LOCATIONS

Washington, DC (HQ)
Los Angeles, CA
Phoenix, AZ
Brussels
London

MAJOR DEPARTMENTS/PRACTICES

Antitrust
Energy & Natural Resources
ERISA/Employment
International
Litigation
Tax
Technology
Transactions

THE STATS

No. of attorneys: 350
No. of offices: 5
Summer associate offers: 18 out of 18 (2002)
Chairman: J.A. (Lon) Bouknight, Jr.
Hiring Partner: Stephen A. Fennell

RANKING RECAP

Best in Region
#7 - Washington, DC

Quality of Life
#7 - Associate/Partner Relations
#15 - Satisfaction
#16 - Hours

Diversity
#6 - Diversity for Women
#11 - Overall Diversity
#15 - Diversity for Minorities

NOTABLE PERKS

- Box at the MCI Center
- Free lunch if you take out a new associate
- On-site gym
- Tenure awards beginning in third year at firm

EMPLOYMENT CONTACT

Ms. Rosemary Kelly Morgan
Director of Attorney Services & Recruiting
Phone: (202) 429-8036
E-mail: legal_recruiting@steptoe.com

BASE SALARY

Washington, DC
1st year: $125,000
2nd year: $131,000
3rd year: $138,000
4th year: $145,000
5th year: $155,000
6th year: $165,000
7th year: $172,000
8th year: $180,000
Summer associate: $2,400/week

THE BUZZ
WHAT ATTORNEYS AT OTHER FIRMS ARE SAYING ABOUT THIS FIRM

- "Good work, bright lawyers"
- "Mediocre reputation"
- "A good, solid, reputable firm"
- "Screamers galore"

THE SCOOP

Founded in 1913, the District of Columbia's Steptoe & Johnson LLP has seen a lot of action recently in the white-collar criminal defense department, counting the ex-CEO of WorldCom and former execs from Tyco, Rite Aid and Enron among its clients. The firm also represents 17 former American servicemen who filed a federal lawsuit against the government of Iraq and Saddam Hussein in April 2002. The servicemen are seeking $25 million each, plus a total of more than $300 million in damages, for their treatment while prisoners of war during the first U.S.-Iraqi conflict in 1991.

GETTING HIRED

Steptoe "wants a certain number of Ivy League students," and a senior source confirms the hiring process can be "a breeze for candidates from the right schools." But the firm "won't hire someone just to fill a hole," insists another veteran attorney. "The selectivity and care with which associates are chosen ensures that everyone is top quality on both academic and personal levels." A first-year recalls that "it took a lot of persistence to get hired," while a midlevel associate admits, "I probably would not have received an interview from this firm out of law school, but they gave me the opportunity to prove myself as a lateral hire. I'm grateful for that."

OUR SURVEY SAYS

"I didn't know that lawyers could be this nice to one another," marvels a senior associate. "Individual personalities" are "not only accepted but welcome" in Steptoe's casual dress environment. Remarks one first-year, "If I could count the number of happy hours I've been to since joining the firm..." The firm is committed to pro bono work, and associates can apply up to 100 hours of such work towards their hours target. A full-time pro bono coordinator helps, and the firm organizes six-month fellowships at Legal Aid for two associates each year. Some veteran associates suspect the enthusiasm has "waned a bit" given a recent emphasis on hours, but first-years can still boast about running their own pro bono cases.

The firm's billables requirement of 1,950 hours is "demanding but not difficult to meet" and can foster "a very comfortable lifestyle" for associates who manage their time effectively. Salaries are "not as high as some New York firms" and even "a bit below the top-paying D.C. firms," but the bonus system, which kicks in after 2,100 hours, "tends to make up" the difference. Insiders declare themselves "very impressed with the professionalism and respect" partners exhibit, and also appreciate that the firm is "good at not laying off people during temporary economic declines." Steptoe's Dupont Circle headquarters is "the best location in all of D.C.," and associates get their own office from day one. The building is "a little old and shabby," with little storage space. But the firm is planning a major overhaul to address such concerns. In the meantime, the interior is "a

1221 Avenue of the Americas
New York, New York 10020
Phone: (212) 610-6300

One New Change
London, UK EC4M 9QQ
Phone: +44 (0) 20-7330-3000
http://www.allenovery.com

LOCATION(S)

London (HQ) • New York, NY • Amsterdam • Antwerp
• Bangkok • Bratislava • Brussels • Beijing • Budapest •
Dubai • Frankfurt • Hamburg • Hong Kong •
Luxembourg • Madrid • Milan • Moscow • Paris •
Prague • Rome • Shanghai • Singapore • Tirana • Turin
• Tokyo • Warsaw

MAJOR DEPARTMENTS/PRACTICES

Antitrust • Banking • Derivatives • Employment
Environmental • International Capital Markets •
Litigation Project Finance • Real Estate • Securities •
Tax

THE STATS

No. of attorneys: 2,400
No. of offices: 26
Summer associate offers: 18 out of 18 (2002)
Managing Partner (NY): Mark Welling
Hiring Chair (NY): Marun Jazbik
Hiring Chair (London): Thomas Jones

RANKING RECAP

Quality of Life
#4 - Hours
#10 - Associate/Partner Relations
#11 - Retention
#20 - Best Firms to Work For

Best in Diversity
#9 - Diversity for Gays and Lesbians

NOTABLE PERKS

• London office has on-site pub
• five weeks paid vacation
• International offsite retreats

EMPLOYMENT CONTACTS

Ms. Elizabeth Papas, Legal Recruitment Manager
Phone: (646) 344-6633
elizabeth.papas@allenovery.com

Ms. Jennifer Thornton , Legal Recruitment Coordinator
Phone: (646) 344-6673
jennifer.thornton@allenovery.com

Ms. Nicola McNeill, U.S. Liaison Manager
Phone: +44 (0) 20-7330-2447
nicola.mcneill@allenovery.com

BASE SALARY

U.S. Law Group
1st year: $125,000
Summer associate: $2,403/week

THE BUZZ
WHAT ATTORNEYS AT OTHER FIRMS ARE SAYING ABOUT THIS FIRM

• "Best place to work in London"
• "All international transactional work"
• "Rising star"
• "A bit pompous"

THE SCOOP

Less than a decade after its founding in 1930, UK-based Allen & Overy became famous counseling the Duke of Windsor through his abdication of the British throne. The firm is best known today for its corporate practice, though it has recently added several new capacities to its New York office. The firm announced in June 2002 that it had hired lawyers from competing firms to head up new international real estate and antitrust practices in Manhattan. (A later strategic development jumpstarted a new U.S. litigation practice.). Meanwhile, the firm continues to nurture its international growth. A 2001 merger with a Belgian law firm added offices in Brussels and Antwerp, while a Shanghai outpost became a full-fledged branch office in 2002.

GETTING HIRED

"For people who want to work in London and have high quality work, there are few places to consider," so when A&O comes to recruit on American campuses, "students literally try to crash the interview sessions." The firm chooses associates carefully. "Candidates with second languages and who have lived and traveled abroad are most likely to be hired." The firm seeks "academic excellence [and] law school prestige" but "places equal if not greater emphasis on international experience, enthusiasm and personality." Some think the firm could screen more tightly. "We're good enough now," says a second-year. "It's time to be selective."

OUR SURVEY SAYS

The "tight-knit" U.S. law group in A&O's London office is "exceptionally casual," with "a bit of a party/hang out at the bar kind of atmosphere." Not surprising, since the firm has its own pub in the basement. A corporate attorney proposes, "I don't think any firm in this category can beat the relationships that our associates have with the partners, at least as a social matter."

"Many partners will apologize for making you work weekends," says one attorney, "and vacation is considered sacred." Attorneys' compensation "keeps pace with the New York market," but associates in London often find themselves on the wrong end of the exchange rate. "Although my salary theoretically went up by $25,000," gripes a third-year, "it hasn't actually gone up at all." The associates also hate the firm's policy of dropping the "cost-of-living" supplement after three years of employment. "One's cost of living in London does not dramatically decrease in one's fourth year," snaps a midlevel associate.

The firm's London office, across the street from St. Paul's Cathedral, is "a bit old and tattered, but [it] functions well enough," though not very gracefully, as "offices are showing signs of wear and tear and are quite cramped." "Swank" new digs should be ready by 2006. The New York office has already relocated, and associates there find "marked improvement" in their surroundings.

VAULT TOP 100

62

PRESTIGE RANKING

Fish & Neave

1251 Avenue of the Americas
New York, NY 10020
Phone: (212) 596-9000
www.fishneave.com

LOCATIONS

New York, NY (HQ)
Palo Alto, CA
Washington, DC

MAJOR DEPARTMENTS/PRACTICES

Intellectual Property • Litigation (Patents, Trademarks,
Copyrights, Trade Secrets, Licensing Disputes, Patent
Misuse, Antitrust Issues, Unfair Competition) • Patent
Prosecution & Interference Work • Trademark
Prosecution

THE STATS

No. of attorneys: 184
No. of offices: 3
Summer associate offers: 24 out of 24 (2002)
Managing Partner: Jesse J. Jenner

RANKING RECAP

Best in Practice
#2 - Intellectual Property

NOTABLE PERKS

- Keggers and "swank" holiday parties
- Partners might take you out for lunch
- Madison Square Garden sky box (NYC)

EMPLOYMENT CONTACT

Ms. Heather C. Fennell
Legal Recruitment Manager
Phone: (212) 596-9121
E-mail: hfennell@fishneave.com

BASE SALARY

All offices
1st year: $125,000
2nd year: $135,000
3rd year: $150,000
4th year: $165,000
5th year: $185,000
6th year: $200,000
7th year: $215,000
8th year: $230,000
Summer associate: $2,400/week

THE BUZZ
WHAT ATTORNEYS AT OTHER FIRMS ARE SAYING ABOUT THIS FIRM

- "IP gods"
- "Negative and unfulfilling work environment"
- "Best IP firm in the country"
- "Patent mill"

THE SCOOP

One of the nation's leading IP firms, Fish & Neave, founded in 1878, has counseled some of America's greatest inventors, including Alexander Graham Bell, Henry Ford, Thomas Edison and the Wright brothers. More recently, Fish & Neave helped Harrah's Entertainment settle a suit against a company accused of copying patented processes Harrah's had developed to guarantee slot machine bets. The firm also won a patent infringement case for Compaq in July 2002; the ruling resulted in a permanent injunction against eMachines which requires the company to remove the patented features from its personal computers, switch to Compaq's approved component suppliers or stop selling computers in the United States altogether.

GETTING HIRED

F&N "typically looks to hire lawyers with science or engineering backgrounds." It doesn't hurt to be "intelligent, quick to pick up new concepts and pleasant to work with." Candidates "must know that you want to specialize in patent law, preferably patent litigation." Although some insiders will tell you the firm "recruits only from top-notch programs," others suggest that "in terms of law school grades and pedigrees, we are much less selective than most big firms" if the candidate shows scientific aptitude.

OUR SURVEY SAYS

Fish & Neave's associates "generally dress casually, keep their doors open and often go out for happy hours together," but "the firm has grown a lot and feels much more Big Law than in the past." The vibe is "more uptight than a dot-com boom firm," but "more laid back than a big general practice firm." Sources on both coasts confide the interaction among attorneys is "very rigid with respect to seniority." Partners' treatment of associates is "a mixed bag, with most practicing benevolent indifference," though the better ones "give young associates a lot of responsibility."

F&N's compensation is "average for New York," but "bonuses have historically been below market." Insiders gripe about "poor first-year bonuses on record earnings" (and some say first-year associates didn't get bonuses at all). Although "everyone is working much harder and putting in many more late and weekend hours," most associates describe themselves as "happy with the pace." A midlevel associate, however, reports that partners demand more nighttime and weekend work than is strictly necessary. "Most people work pretty hard," says one source, "but there are slackers riding the system for the next year or two until they move elsewhere." A senior insider in Palo Alto admits the firm was "playing catch and release" with associates during the Internet bubble but suggests retention has improved "now that the economy's grown chilly." A New Yorker views the situation as a bit more stable, saying, "It still impresses that some associates remain into their ninth or tenth year here."

Howrey Simon Arnold & White, LLP

1299 Pennsylvania Ave., NW
Washington, DC 20004
Phone: (202) 783-0800
www.howrey.com

LOCATIONS

Century City, CA • Chicago, IL • Houston, TX • Irvine,
CA • Los Angeles, CA • Menlo Park, CA • San
Francisco, CA • Washington, DC • Amsterdam •
Brussels • London

MAJOR DEPARTMENTS/PRACTICES

Antitrust
Global Litigation
Intellectual Property

THE STATS

No. of attorneys: 570
No. of offices: 11
Summer associate offers: 26 out of 34 (2002)
Managing Partner: Robert F. Ruyak
Hiring Partner: Richard A. Ripley

RANKING RECAP

Best in Region
#9 - Washington, DC

Best in Practice
#2 - Antitrust
#5 (tie) - Intellectual Property

NOTABLE PERKS

- Attorney happy hours
- Practice group retreats
- Friday morning breakfast
- Profit sharing for senior associates

EMPLOYMENT CONTACT

Ms. Janet Brown
Manager, Attorney Recruitment
Phone: (202) 783-0800
E-mail: brownjanet@howrey.com

BASE SALARY

Washington, DC; Chicago, IL; California offices
1st year: $125,000
2nd year: $135,000
3rd year: $145,000 ($150,000 in CA)
4th year: $155,000 ($165,000 in CA)
5th year: $165,000 ($185,000 in CA)
6th year: $175,000 ($195,000 in CA)
7th year: $185,000 ($205,000 in CA)
Summer associate: $2,400/week (DC & IL)

Houston, TX
1st year: $115,000
2nd year: $123,000
3rd year: $132,000
4th year: $142,000
5th year: $152,000
6th year: $195,000
7th year: $205,000

THE BUZZ
WHAT ATTORNEYS AT OTHER FIRMS ARE SAYING ABOUT THIS FIRM

- "Great lawyers and versatile firm"
- "Bastard stepchild of former IP powerhouse"
- "Tops in antitrust"
- "Stupid summer program ruins reputation"

THE SCOOP

Howrey Simon Arnold & White LLP is the product of a January 2000 merger between Washington, D.C.-based Howrey & Simon and Houston-based Arnold White & Durkee. The new firm has honed respected practices in antitrust, global litigation and intellectual property law and boasts prestigious clients like Intel, Univision, Merck, 3M, Caterpillar, Monsanto, Ericsson, Samsung, Shell and Ford. Howrey lawyers have argued 50 cases in front of the U.S. Supreme Court. Nearly 570 attorneys practice in Howrey's 11 offices, which include eight in the U.S. and locations in Amsterdam, Brussels and London. The CapAnalysis Group, LLC supplements the practice groups by assessing complex financial, economic and environmental issues.

GETTING HIRED

Howrey's "Bootcamp" pairs law students with experienced lawyers as they try their hand at deposition practice, seminars and mock trial participation (following three weeks in the office of their choice). The program, a departure from the normal round of lunches, parties and outings for summer associates, has its proponents – and its critics. "I think the Bootcamp hurts recruiting and should be discontinued," says one associate. Good grades and motivation are key factors in getting hired. "The firm is looking for an intelligent, self-motivated, hardworking person who can work well under pressure to get the job done," reports one insider. Given the firm's narrow focus, "candidates have little chance of being interviewed and/or hired if they are not interested or experienced in intellectual property, antitrust or complex commercial litigation," warns one source.

OUR SURVEY SAYS

"In California [the firm] has a wonderfully pleasant work environment," says one West Coast lawyer. Washington is trying to catch up. "Although the firm is constantly trying to make the atmosphere more friendly, the culture remains a bit uptight," says a D.C. lawyer. Howrey lawyers appreciate the "great base compensation" but lament the "meager bonuses." "The bonus structure is too secretive," says a source. "There is a flat hours bonus for billing 2,100 hours, but anything below and anything above is determined on a case-by-case basis, which can be frustrating. Plus, it would be nice to get a huge bonus if you've worked tirelessly on a winning case, like other firms do."

Hours are typical of big-firm life. "When you have work, you stay as long as you need to," reports one associate. "Otherwise you can come and go as you please." The assignment system draws some complaints. "It isn't the hours that I dislike," gripes one associate. "It is the waiting around for an assignment with nothing to do for a week and then having something that requires 70 billable hours in five days."

Heller Ehrman White & McAuliffe LLP

333 Bush Street
San Francisco, CA 94104-2878
Phone: (415) 772-6000
www.hewm.com

LOCATIONS

San Francisco, CA (HQ)

Anchorage, AK • Los Angeles, CA • Madison, WI •
Menlo Park, CA • New York, NY • Portland, OR • San
Diego, CA • Seattle, WA • Washington, DC • Hong
Kong • Singapore

MAJOR DEPARTMENTS/PRACTICES

Antitrust & Trade Regulation • Corporate Securities,
M&A • Energy • Environmental Regulation & Litigation •
Financial Services • Information Technology • Insurance
Coverage • Intellectual Property Litigation • International
• Labor & Employment • Life Sciences • Patents &
Trademarks • Product Liability • Real Estate • Securities
Litigation • Tax

THE STATS

No. of attorneys: 635
No. of offices: 12
Summer associate offers: 28 out of 36 (2002)
Chairman: Barry S. Levin
Hiring Shareholders: Barbara Gregoratos & Michael
Rugen (San Francisco); Kyle Guse & Robert Hawk
(Silicon Valley); Stephen Goldberg (LA); Barry Tucker
(San Diego); Leif Ormseth (Northwest); Mark Vecchio &
Edward Joyce (NY); Kit Pierson (DC)

RANKING RECAP

Best in Region
#8 - California

Best in Diversity
#6 - Diversity for Gays and Lesbians
#19- Overall Diversity

NOTABLE PERKS

- $30,000 retention bonus paid into 401(k)
- Profit-sharing program
- Transit checks

EMPLOYMENT CONTACT

San Francisco
Mr. Craig Blumin
Professional Recruitment Manager
Phone: (415) 772-6591
Fax: (415) 772-6268
E-mail: cblumin@hewm.com

BASE SALARY

San Francisco, CA
1st year: $125,000
2nd year: $130,000
3rd year: $140,000
4th year: $150,000
5th year: $165,000
6th year: $175,000
7th year: $185,000
Summer associate: $2,400/week

 ## THE BUZZ
WHAT ATTORNEYS AT OTHER FIRMS ARE SAYING ABOUT THIS FIRM

- "Enlightened"
- "B-team"
- "A well-managed, nice place to work"
- "Nondescript"

THE SCOOP

San Francisco-based Heller Ehrman White & McAuliffe LLP has nearly 650 lawyers in 12 offices in the U.S. and abroad and affiliated offices in Milan, Paris and Rome. The firm has defended Visa, Microsoft, Philip Morris and 3M in antitrust actions, advised Washington Mutual in multi-billion-dollar mortgage securitizations; represented all Big Four accounting firms in securities litigation; and represented GMAC in insurance coverage issues arising from the World Trade Center terrorist attacks. Moreover, the firm was co-counsel to Northrop Grumman Corporation in the fourth-largest leveraged buy-out in history. In March 2003, the firm became embroiled in controversy when former client E-Compare alleged in a $200 million lawsuit that Heller Ehrman allowed a first-year associate to act as lead counsel on behalf of the now-defunct dot-com.

GETTING HIRED

Insiders say Heller Ehrman is selective to a fault in its associate hiring. "Only people from the most elite law schools with great grades need apply," says one source. Applicants need to be "really smart, possess a strong work ethic and have a realistic expectation of commercial litigation work. And they need to be a good team player who fits in the office." While grades may be the most significant factor, personality comes into play. "Once you've met the objective criteria, the firm looks hard at whether you'll fit in," says one insider. "The Heller Ehrman type tends to be extremely smart, but doesn't feel the need to let everyone know it. There's a strong emphasis on congeniality."

OUR SURVEY SAYS

Heller insiders describe the vibe as "laid back" and "friendly." Some, though, say the culture is in flux. "Once touted as a lifestyle firm, Heller associates now bill over the minimum [hours] required, simply because there is so much work to do. The increased workload has had a dampening effect on social activities and morale." More work means more hours – and more stress, for some. "Pressure has increased from gentle to firm to intense," says one contact. For some insiders, Heller Ehrman is paradise. "I love the firm's culture and don't know of another big firm I'd rather be at," gushes one source. Heller-ites have a lot to be thankful for in the compensation department, and most insist the salary is "competitive." Many, though, bemoan the firm's "back-end" compensation structure. "We are well compensated, but Heller back-ends our compensation to 2,000 hours, which means until 2,000 hours I am making substantially below market," reports one contact, though it seems like the economy never crashed for others: "Our salaries went way up with the dot-com boom in the Bay Area, and they've stayed up even through the bust and the layoffs at other area firms." The firm earns rave reviews when it comes to diversity. Says one insider, "You will not find a more welcoming or open firm, on every level."

2300 First City Tower
1001 Fannin Street
Houston, TX 77002-6760
Phone: (713) 758-2222
www.velaw.com

LOCATIONS

Houston, TX (HQ)
Austin, TX
Dallas, TX
New York, NY
Washington, DC
Beijing
London
Moscow
Singapore

MAJOR DEPARTMENTS/PRACTICES

Administrative/Environmental Law • Appellate •
Business & International • Corporate & Securities •
Employee Benefits & Executive Compensation •
Employment Litigation & Labor • Energy • Health •
Insolvency & Reorganization • Intellectual Property/
Technical Litigation • Litigation • Public Finance • Tax

THE STATS

No. of attorneys: 800 +
No. of offices: 9
Summer associate offers: 110 out of 131 (2002)
Managing Partner: Joseph C. Dilg
Hiring Partner: Thomas S. Leatherbury

THE BUZZ
WHAT ATTORNEYS AT OTHER FIRMS ARE SAYING ABOUT THIS FIRM

- "Top dogs in Texas"
- "Crooked E"
- "Still probably the best shop overall in Texas"
- "Cutting corners is not cutting edge"

RANKING RECAP

Best in Region
#2 - Texas

NOTABLE PERKS

- Annual "prom" in Houston
- BlackBerry pagers
- Free beverages
- Subsidized gym membership

EMPLOYMENT CONTACT

Ms. Patty H. Calabrese
Director of Attorney Employment
Phone: (713) 758-4544
Fax: (713) 615-5245
E-mail: pcalabrese@velaw.com

BASE SALARY

Houston, TX
1st year: $110,000
2nd year: $114,000
3rd year: $121,000
4th year: $130,000
5th year: $140,000
6th year: $145,000
7th year: $155,000
8th year: $160,000
Summer associate: $2,100/week

THE SCOOP

Founded in 1917, Vinson & Elkins L.L.P. is a Houston-based energy industry specialist. And when you think "Houston" and "energy," you think "Enron." V&E served as outside counsel to the now-defunct energy supplier, and former partner James V. Derrick, Jr., served as general counsel. The association has not brought the firm kudos. V&E is facing a class-action lawsuit by Enron shareholders unhappy with the firm's work for the company; former Enron officials have also been critical of V&E. The firm has vehemently denied wrongdoing and is contesting all legal action. Besides its energy group (which, Enron notwithstanding, is an acknowledged strength of the firm), V&E boasts a prominent lobbying practice, and White House Counsel Alberto Gonzalez is a former V&E attorney.

GETTING HIRED

V&E has the "usual interview and callback process typical of the large national firms." "Our firm generally looks to top-tier schools and individuals who are in the top 10-15 percent of their class, with the exception of graduates from University of Texas and University of Virginia, who generally are preferred," reports an insider. V&E "is very selective when deciding to grant initial interviews," says a contact. "Once you have received an initial interview, it is generally not too difficult to get a job." But study up. "The firm has strict GPA and school requirements. Also, the individual must have personality and other experience that adds value."

OUR SURVEY SAYS

The culture at V&E seems to be in flux. Reports one insider, "The historical firm culture, which prided itself on open communication, a laid-back atmosphere and a dedication to quality of life issues, has died off. What will emerge is not yet known." Not everyone agrees. "The culture is extremely friendly," says a first-year. "I was concerned that what I saw as a summer associate was a front, but people actually spend time together socially and seem to enjoy each other's company at work." But some find the firm has "a brutish dog-eat-dog culture." The economy may be to blame. "Lately there has been increasing attention to the bottom line," notes one attorney.

V&E historically had a lockstep compensation system with no hours-based bonuses; things are different now. One attorney says that "as associates become more senior, a greater percentage of the annual pay raise becomes end-loaded" in the form of bonuses. "Rumor has it that 2002 will be the last year of such bonuses and that the compensation system would be substantially revised." Some are wishing for "a bonus based on contribution to the firm rather than the set bonus we currently have." Insiders say the "hours are long, but generally flexible" and that "there really is not a need for face time here."

Riverfront Plaza, East Tower
951 East Byrd Street
Richmond, VA 23219
Phone: (804) 788-8200
www.hunton.com

LOCATIONS

Richmond, VA (HQ)
Atlanta, GA • Austin, TX • Charlotte, NC • Dallas, TX •
Knoxville, TN • McLean, VA • Miami, FL • New York,
NY • Norfolk, VA • Raleigh, NC • Washington, DC •
Bangkok • Brussels • Hong Kong • London • Singapore

MAJOR DEPARTMENTS/PRACTICES

Administrative Law • Antitrust • Commercial litigation •
Corporate & Finance • Energy • Environmental •
Intellectual Property • Labor • Litigation • Project
Development Finance & Leasing • Public Finance • Real
Estate & Land Use • Tax & ERISA • Technology

THE STATS

No. of attorneys: 850+
No. of offices: 17
Summer associate offers: 39 out of 55 (2002)
Chairman: Thurston R. Moore
Hiring Partner: David C. Landin

THE BUZZ
WHAT ATTORNEYS AT OTHER FIRMS ARE SAYING ABOUT THIS FIRM

- "Southern powerhouse"
- "Bum a smoke?"
- "Good work, good location, good history"
- "Old school southern, in a bad way"

RANKING RECAP

Quality of Life
#8 - Part-Time/Flex-Time
#12 - Pro Bono

Best in Diversity
#19 - Diversity for Minorities

NOTABLE PERKS

- Emergency child care (NY, Atlanta, DC)
- On-site gym (DC and Miami)
- Box seats at various sports venues
- Pre-tax transportation accounts

EMPLOYMENT CONTACT

Ms. Christine Tracey
Legal Recruiting Manager
Phone: (212) 309-1217
Fax: (212) 309-1100
E-mail: ctracey@hunton.com

BASE SALARY

**Atlanta, GA; Charlotte, Raleigh, NC; Knoxville, TN;
Norfolk, Richmond, VA**
1st year: $100,000 (plus $5,000 bonus in Atlanta)
Summer associate: $1,800/week

Miami, FL
1st year: $105,000
Summer associate: $1,800/week

Austin, Dalls, TX
1st year: $110,000 (plus $10,000 bonus)
Summer associate: $2,100/week

McLean, VA; New York, NY; Washington, DC
1st year: $125,000
Summer associate: $2,400/week

THE SCOOP

One of the Southeast's most prominent law firms, Hunton & Williams LLP hung out its shingle in Richmond, Va., in 1901, and now boasts 12 domestic offices after a 2002 merger with Texas-based Worsham, Forsythe & Wooldridge that added locations in Dallas and Austin. Although a ten-year venture in Warsaw ended in July 2002, a brand-new Singapore office replaced it a few months later. The firm has plenty of high-profile clients. In 2002, the firm successfully defended tobacco empire Philip Morris in a suit brought by a family that claimed cigarettes had caused one of its members to develop a fatal obstructive pulmonary disease. The firm also secured a major victory for Deutsche Bank Securities in a securities fraud case and had a similar case against client Circuit City dismissed with prejudice.

GETTING HIRED

Hunton & Williams is "very selective with a preference for the elite southern schools such as UVA and Washington & Lee," but "a solid transcript and personality will get you in the door from any number of quality law schools." The firm wants "gregarious and easygoing associates who are extremely intelligent and hard working." An associate warns, "Aggressive and competitive associates do not thrive here." But don't expect to hear back from the firm right away: "One of my few complaints about this firm is that it takes too long to respond about hiring," says a first-year. "Everyone I have spoken to has had the same experience."

OUR SURVEY SAYS

Associates describe Hunton & Williams as "the Disneyland of law firms," where "social events are just a regular part of life" and "there are always casual happy hours." The firm's atmosphere is "thoughtful with a bit of Southern charm." Currently "there is a move to revert to business formal attire from business casual," but the vibe is still "very congenial." A sixth-year tells us, "I not only want to work with the people here, but also want to spend time away from the office with them. They are not only my colleagues, but also my friends." A midlevel associate reports, "I used to tell recruits that face time is not important here, but now I think it is." While other insiders agree, several sources assure us that their hours are "completely reasonable" for a major law firm. "I work very hard during the week," reports one first-year, "but the weekends are my own."

The rank and file are somewhat less satisfied, however, with the compensation one senior associate dubs "at best average." And several at the firm gripe that bonuses are "doled out only to a chosen few selected through some mystical process never really explained." Associates "want more communication and input" in their relationships with partners, although many feel that within the firm's "very formal structure" they are treated with "nothing but great respect."

Holland & Knight LLP

Suite 100
2099 Pennsylvania Avenue
Washington, DC 20006
Phone: (202) 955-3000
www.hklaw.com

LOCATIONS

Atlanta, GA • Annapolis, MD • Bethesda, MD • Boston,
MA • Bradenton, FL • Chicago, IL • Fort Lauderdale, FL
• Jacksonville, FL • Lakeland, FL • Los Angeles, CA •
McLean, VA • Miami, FL • New York, NY • Orlando, FL
• Portland, OR • Providence, RI • San Antonio, TX •
San Francisco, CA • Seattle, WA • St. Petersburg, FL •
Tallahassee, FL • Tampa, FL • Washington, DC • West
Palm Beach, FL • Caracas* • Helsinki • Melbourne •
Mexico City • Rio de Janeiro • São Paulo • Tel Aviv* •
Tokyo
*Representative office

MAJOR DEPARTMENTS/PRACTICES

Corporate, Tax & Securities • Finance • Litigation •
Public Law • Real Estate, Environmental & Land Use •
Trusts & Estates

THE STATS

No. of attorneys: 1,241
No. of offices: 32
Summer associate offers: 54 out of 65 (2002)
Managing Partner: Howell W. Melton, Jr.
Hiring Attorneys: G. Richard Dunnells & Ruth L. Lansner

 THE BUZZ
WHAT ATTORNEYS AT OTHER FIRMS ARE SAYING ABOUT THIS FIRM

- "Cool Miami firm"
- "Well-documented problems"
- "High quality"
- "McLaw"

NOTABLE PERKS

- Domestic partner benefits
- 401(k) matching
- Pays for BlackBerry service

EMPLOYMENT CONTACT

Ms. Alida Coo-Kendall
National Recruitment Coordinator
10 St. James Avenue
E-mail: alida.cookendall@hklaw.com

BASE SALARY

Washington; McLean; Chicago; Los Angeles
1st year: $120,000
Summer associate: $2,200/week; $2,115/wk (LA)

Boston, MA
1st year: $115,000
Summer associate: $2,000/week

Ft. Lauderdale; Miami; West Palm Beach;
San Antonio; Seattle
1st year: $95,000
Summer associate: $1,600/week; $2,000/wk (San
Antonio); $1,650/wk (Seattle)

New York, NY
1st year: $125,000
Summer associate: $2,400/week

Atlanta, GA
1st year: $100,000
Summer associate: $1,750/week

Jacksonville; Lakeland;
St. Petersburg; Orlando; Tallahassee; Tampa
1st year: $77,000
Summer associate: $1,300/week

Portland, OR
1st year: $85,000
Summer associate: $1,400/week

THE SCOOP

After a solid decade of expansion, Holland & Knight LLP was one of many law firms that succumbed to economic pressure in 2002, cutting 60 attorneys and 170 other employees in May. The firm (still one of the ten largest in the United States) wasted no time bouncing back, though, announcing mergers in June with Chicago's McBride Baker & Coles and Seattle's Van Valkenberg Furber Law Group. The firm advocated on behalf of the *Orlando Sentinel* when the newspaper sought access to transcripts from a closed court hearing involving potential drug charges against Gov. Jeb Bush's daughter and recently launched a new practice group specializing in corporate governance. Looks like new managing partner Howell W. Melton Jr. will have plenty to keep him busy.

GETTING HIRED

It's important to show "a genuine interest in our firm, not just the prestige and compensation we offer," say sources. After receiving a callback invitation, candidates can expect to meet with anywhere from five to ten attorneys and be taken out to lunch and/or dinner. Insiders caution, "It is becoming increasingly difficult to join H&K, whether as a new lawyer or as a lateral hire." The firm's "extremely competitive environment" places great emphasis on academics. "Unless a prospect is in the top 5-10 percent of his or her class," says one associate, "there is little chance of receiving an interview." Others, however, insist "law school is not as important as whether you can manage your own time and produce high-quality work."

OUR SURVEY SAYS

Holland & Knight "is becoming increasingly more uptight," gripes a midlevel associate. A veteran attorney adds that the firm "used to be a quality of life firm in every sense of the phrase, but it has become a firm run entirely on profitability and billable hours." Associates describe their colleagues as "not only bright but congenial" and "consistently positive, even under pressure." Women attorneys "have a steadily growing presence in the partnership ranks," and "there are great mentoring opportunities" for younger female associates. The firm has also been "very aggressive in attempting to hire qualified minority candidates" and offers "extremely progressive" policies in support of its gay and lesbian associates, including domestic partner benefits for their companions.

"While most days are 12 hours long," says an insider, "rarely does it exceed the 13-hour mark." Many feel the work requirements are not "nearly as long as most other firms" and are "very flexible." Salaries have gotten "right up there with the other top firms," although the firm "had been behind the curve for a few years" and is "still a little short" in some markets. Associates are more concerned about bonus expectations being "hard to estimate" and a new multi-tiered compensation system that may fail to reward industrious associates who can't get enough work in their practice group.

Coudert Brothers LLP

1114 Avenue of the Americas
New York, NY 10036
Phone: (212) 626-4400
www.coudert.com

LOCATIONS

New York, NY (HQ)
Los Angeles, CA • Palo Alto, CA • San Francisco, CA •
Washington, DC • Almaty • Antwerp • Bangkok •
Beijing • Berlin • Brussels • Budapest* • Frankfurt •
Ghent • Hong Kong • Jakarta • London • Mexico City*
• Milan • Moscow • Munich • Paris • Prague* • Rome •
St. Petersburg • Shanghai • Singapore • Stockholm •
Sydney • Tokyo

* Denotes associates office

MAJOR DEPARTMENTS/PRACTICES

Corporate/Commercial • Energy & Natural Resources •
Entertainment & Media • Insolvency & Financial
Restructuring • Intellectual Property • Litigation/Dispute
Resolution • Real Estate • Tax • Telecommunications •
Technology, Internet & New Media

THE STATS

No. of attorneys: 650+
No. of offices: 30
Summer associate offers: 18 out of 18 (2002)
Chairman: David Huebner
Hiring Attorney: Edward H. Tillinghast, III

THE BUZZ
WHAT ATTORNEYS AT OTHER FIRMS ARE SAYING ABOUT THIS FIRM

- "Great hands-on international work"
- "Breadth, not depth"
- "Sophisticated practice"
- "Best days are behind them"

NOTABLE PERKS

- Friday happy hour
- Late night dinners and car rides
- Bar expenses

EMPLOYMENT CONTACT

Ms. Mary L. Simpson
Director of Legal Personnel
Phone: (212) 626-4400
Fax: (212) 626-4120
E-mail: simpsonm@coudert.com

BASE SALARY

New York, NY
1st year: $125,000
2nd year: $135,000
3rd year: $150,000
4th year: $170,000
5th year: $190,000
6th year: $200,000
7th year: $205,000
Summer associate: $2,400/week

THE SCOOP

From its humble beginnings in New York 150 years ago, Coudert Brothers LLP has expanded to over 650 attorneys in 30 cities around the globe. It was the first U.S. firm to open a European office, first to hang a shingle in the former Soviet Union and first into Beijing after the Communist takeover. Coudert's practice concentrates on corporate and commercial law for multinational clients, with particular expertise in project finance, telecommunications and trade regulation. In 2002, the firm advised the Russian government on the sale of its shares in LUKoil, the world's largest oil company, and were co-counsel in a successful multinational diversity jurisdiction case in the U.S. Supreme Court. Meanwhile, one of the firm's most famous counsel, former U.S. Senator Gary Hart, spent the early part of 2003 mulling over a potential third presidential campaign.

GETTING HIRED

Coudert is said to hire "from a broader range of schools than most big firms." The firm continues to attract "excellent candidates," says one associate, and "recent summer classes have been full of great students from great schools." A first-year associate reports that, no matter where you're from, "you need to be in the top of your class and have a demonstrated interest in international law." Other insiders also note the firm's "focus on things like relevant international experience and interests."

OUR SURVEY SAYS

Though outsiders might think of Coudert as "white shoe and uptight," associates find it "rather congenial and friendly." Partners and associates alike can be found at the New York office's "well-attended" Friday night cocktail parties. While "overall firm communication is very poor," associates tend to get on well with partners one-on-one. "They treat you with respect and really let you hit the ground running," a first-year beams. Associates have mixed feelings about their hours. Some say "the hours are much better than I expected them to be," while others complain they don't have enough work. "The minimum expected hours are low," says one insider, but partners still "expect us to bill what the other firms bill. And the hours just aren't there for the taking."

Compensation is another point of contention. First-years can take heart in the news that "Coudert's finally caught up with the big firms," with an opening salary of $125,000. But higher up the food chain, insiders claim, the firm is "always a little behind market," and "it would be nice to get a bonus that wasn't hours-based." Some, however, believe "satisfaction with the working environment more than makes up for the lower salary/bonus." Associates in Manhattan claim to have "one of the best views [of the city] imaginable."

Foley & Lardner

U.S. Bank Center
777 East Wisconsin Avenue
Milwaukee, WI 53202-5367
Phone: (414) 271-2400
www.foleylaw.com

LOCATIONS

Milwaukee, WI (HQ)

Chicago, IL • Denver, CO • Detroit, MI • Jacksonville,
FL • Los Angeles, CA • Madison, WI • Orlando, FL •
Sacramento, CA • San Diego, CA • San Francisco, CA
• Tallahassee, FL • Tampa, FL • Washington, DC •
West Palm Beach, FL • Brussels

MAJOR DEPARTMENTS/PRACTICES

Six departments (Business, Health, Intellectual Property,
Litigation, Regulatory, Tax/Individual Planning) divided
into more than 40 focused practice groups.

THE STATS

No. of attorneys: 946
No. of offices: 16
Summer associate offers: 67 out of 94 (2002)
Chairman: Ralf-Reinhard Boer
Managing Partner: Stanley Jaspan
Chair of Recruiting: E. Robert Meek

THE BUZZ
WHAT ATTORNEYS AT OTHER FIRMS ARE SAYING ABOUT THIS FIRM

- "King of the Midwest"
- "Meat grinder"
- "Lifestyle firm"
- "Lumbering megafirm that dominates smaller
  markets"

RANKING RECAP

Best in Practice
#7 - Intellectual Property

NOTABLE PERKS

- Bar expenses paid
- Free on-site gym (Chicago)
- Occasional sports tickets
- Weekly attorney lunches

EMPLOYMENT CONTACT

Ms. Kara E. Nelson
Director of Legal Recruitment & Development
Phone: (414) 271-2400
Fax: (414) 297-4900
E-mail: kenelson@foleylaw.com

BASE SALARY

Milwaukee, WI; Detroit, MI
1st year: $115,000*
2nd year: $120,000
3rd year: $125,000
4th year: $130,000
5th year: $140,000
6th year: $150,000
7th year: $185,000
8th year: $190,000
Summer associate: $2,100/week

All salaries listed are for non-IP associates.

THE SCOOP

Foley & Lardner is sized like a big-city legal machine, but it still has a midwestern soul. Founded in 1842, F&L has 1,000 lawyers in 16 locations, including its home office in Milwaukee. In May 2002, the firm launched an automotive industry team of 50 attorneys based, naturally, in Detroit. In March 2003, the firm announced the creation of a sports industry team. The 35-lawyer squad will serve clients such as Major League Baseball, NFL Properties, the Green Bay Packers, the Jacksonville Jaguars and the Milwaukee Bucks. But the practice will have to function without Ulice Payne. The Milwaukee Brewers named Payne (formerly managing partner of Foley & Lardner's Milwaukee office) president and CEO in September 2002.

GETTING HIRED

Although Foley & Lardner does visit many regional midwestern schools, it also interviews at many national schools, including several of the Ivies. Foley & Lardner is seeking "motivated learners with good grades, but no freaks." One associate says the firm seeks "only the best people," though another insists, "We're selective without being snobby." Some insiders point out that hiring is "even more demanding now that the market is bad."

OUR SURVEY SAYS

The culture at Foley & Lardner seems to be changing for the worse. "The firm has become very uptight and unfriendly," observes one associate. One senior associate notes, "When I joined, it was laid back but it is now quite a formal place." Concerns about the bottom line seem to be fueling the new atmosphere. Says one insider, "Everyone is stressed out because there is not enough work. Partners hoard work from associates so they can make their hours. Everyone is afraid of getting laid off." Partner paranoia seems to be widespread. It's as if the partners "are all afraid of getting the axe." Associates seem to get along. "People work well together."

The firm has an unpopular deferred compensation system where a portion of an associate's salary is held back until an hours threshold is reached. "The deferred compensation system is a joke," gripes one source. "The base pay ranks well below what other firms of this size pay, and the deferred nature of the hours bonus is terrible," fumes another associate. The bonus system hurts F&L's competitiveness. "Most large firms – if you hit your hours – also give a bonus on top of your salary that is not deferred compensation, so [Foley] is not truly on par with other peer firms," says one contact. Attorneys outside the Midwest feel shortchanged. "The pay might be good for associates in Oshkosh, but in LA it sucks," says one big-city lawyer. While insiders are pleased that F&L "has lower billing requirements than other firms of its size," there are issues with regard to scheduling. "There are problems regulating a steady stream of work," says one associate.

1201 Third Avenue
Suite 4800
Seattle, WA 98101-3099
Phone: (206) 583-8888
www.perkinscoie.com

LOCATIONS

Seattle, WA (HQ)
Anchorage, AK • Bellevue, WA • Boise, ID • Chicago, IL
• Denver, CO • Los Angeles, CA • Menlo Park, CA •
Olympia, WA • Portland, OR • San Francisco, CA •
Washington, DC • Beijing • Hong Kong

MAJOR DEPARTMENTS/PRACTICES

Business & Technology • Commercial Transactions •
Corporate Finance • E-Commerce • Energy •
Environmental/Natural Resources & Land Use •
Government Contracts • Labor & Employment •
Licensing • Litigation • Patent & Intellectual Property •
Personal Planning • Political Law • Product Liability •
Tax

THE STATS

No. of attorneys: 575
No. of offices: 14
Summer associate offers: 16 out of 21 (2002)
(Seattle/Bellevue only)
Managing Partner: Robert E. Giles
Hiring Partner: Steven Y. Koh

THE BUZZ
WHAT ATTORNEYS AT OTHER FIRMS ARE SAYING ABOUT THIS FIRM

- "Kinder, gentler law firm"
- "Coie? Fooey!"
- "Best in the West"
- "Get help, someone who knows what end is up"

RANKING RECAP

Best in Region
#1 - Pacific Northwest

Quality of Life
#17 - Hours
#20 - Associate/Partner Relations

NOTABLE PERKS

- Espresso machine, free sodas
- Free lunch with new associates
- Paid bar expenses
- Equity investment plan

EMPLOYMENT CONTACT

Ms. Laura MacDougall Kader
Lawyer Personnel Recruiter for Law Student Hiring
Phone: (206) 583-8888
Fax: (206) 583-8500
E-mail: lkader@perkinscoie.com

BASE SALARY

Seattle, WA*
1st year: $100,000 - 125,000
2nd year: $87,000 - 135,500
3rd year: $90,000 - 150,000
4th year: $93,000 - 165,000
5th year: $96,000 - 185,000
6th year: $110,000 - 195,000
7th year: $105,000 - 205,000
Summer associate: $2,000/week

1,800-2,000 hours. Bonus eligibility at 1,850 hours.

THE SCOOP

Founded in 1912 in Seattle, Perkins Coie LLP (that's 'Coo-ey') boasts a client list full of prestigious Seattle fixtures such as Boeing, Starbucks, Amazon.com and the Seattle Mariners, as well as tech giants like Adobe Systems and Yahoo! The firm has solid control of the Pacific Rim, with ten of its 14 offices on the West Coast or in Asia. But it also has its eye on the eastern United States. In September 2002, Perkins Coie opened a Chicago outpost, currently focusing on litigation, then shut down its Spokane, Wash., office a month later.

GETTING HIRED

Though Perkins Coie has consolidated its power in the Northwest, the firm recruits from major national law schools in addition to smaller, regional schools. "The hiring committee is looking for candidates from top-tier law schools with good grades and interesting backgrounds," says one Portland attorney. "The firm is very selective about hiring from in-state schools." A Seattle associate agrees: "While my sense is that the firm is only somewhat competitive for graduates of national law schools, it is very competitive for graduates of the more regional schools." Personality is important. "Of the people we have declined to give offers to, it's most often because we think there's a lack of fit with our culture," observes one source.

OUR SURVEY SAYS

Perkins Coie associates say their laid back, friendly culture is also "fast-paced and challenging – exactly what one would expect from a high-profile firm." The firm "bends over backwards to ensure a comfortable and collegial environment consistent with the values and lifestyle of the Northwest." Some feel the laid back feeling can be taken too far. "The culture in this office is too laid back," complains one San Francisco associate. "There are some of us who work very hard and love the job, and there are others who are allowed to underachieve and receive the same pay and job security." Partners "are as approachable, helpful and social as the associates. It really is a great group of people." Says one source, "Perkins truly is a team-oriented firm – from the top on down."

Perkins Coie's Northwest offices use a tiered compensation system based on 1,850, 1,900 or 2,000 hours, and your base salary is pegged to your productivity level. Most associates seem happy with the system and the paychecks they take home. However, one contact remarks, "The firm states publicly – in recruiting materials and at law schools – that its salaries are 'X' dollars, which is the 2,000 rate. The 1,850 rates are closer to the truth and are below market." Those sources living in cities with a low cost of living seem most pleased. "Considering cost of living, the compensation is great," says a happy Oregonian. Others think it all balances out in the end. "While the compensation in Seattle law firms tends to be lower than some cities, the lifestyle makes up for it."

Piper Rudnick LLP

203 North LaSalle Street
Suite 1800
Chicago, IL 60601
Phone: (312) 368-4000

901 Fifteenth Street, NW
Washington, DC 20005
Phone: (202) 371-6000
www.piperrudnick.com

LOCATIONS

Chicago, IL (HQ), Washington, DC (HQ)
Baltimore, MD • Boston, MA • Dallas, TX • Easton, MD
• Edison, NJ • Las Vegas, NV • Los Angeles, CA •
Miami, FL • New York, NY • Philadelphia, PA • Reston,
VA • Tampa, FL

MAJOR DEPARTMENTS/PRACTICES

Corporate & Securities • ERISA, Employee Benefits &
Executive Compensation • Finance • Franchise &
Distribution • Government Affairs • Intellectual Property
• International Commerce and Litigation • Labor •
Litigation • Private Client Services • Real Estate • Tax

THE STATS

No. of attorneys: 942
No. of offices: 13
Summer associate offers: 46 out of 56 (2002)
Chairpersons: Francis B. Burch Jr. and Lee I. Miller
Hiring Partners: Sally J. McDonald and James D.
Mathias

THE BUZZ
WHAT ATTORNEYS AT OTHER FIRMS ARE SAYING ABOUT THIS FIRM

- "Up and coming nationally"
- "Lackluster"
- "Enjoyable atmosphere"
- "Massive – no one knows each other"

RANKING RECAP

Best in Region
#9 - Chicago

Best in Practice
#2 - Real Estate

NOTABLE PERKS

- Review and bar exam costs covered
- Awards annual business scholarships for MBAs
- Pro bono bonus awards

EMPLOYMENT CONTACTS

Ms. Marguerite Strubing, Legal Recruiting Manager
Phone: (312) 368-8928
E-mail: marguerite.strubing@piperrudnick.com

Ms. Lindy Hilliard, Legal Recruiting Manager
Phone: (410) 580-4664
E-mail: lindy.hilliard@piperrudnick.com

BASE SALARY

Chicago, IL
1st year: $125,000
2nd year: $130,000-$135,000
3rd year: $140,000-$150,000
4th year: $150,000-$165,000
5th year: $160,000-$175,000
6th year: $170,000-$185,000
7th year: $185,000-$195,000
8th year: $190,000-$200,000
Summer associate: $2,400/week

Baltimore, MD
1st year: $115,000
2nd year: $120,000
3rd year: $125,000-$130,000
4th year: $135,000-$155,000
5th year: $145,000-$165,000
6th year: $145,000-$175,000
7th year: $155,000-$185,000
Summer associate: $2,200/week

THE SCOOP

The former Piper Marbury Rudnick & Wolfe just keeps getting bigger. Piper Rudnick announced a merger with the 80-attorney D.C.-based Verner Liipfert and a strategic alliance with the smaller Cohen Group (the latter led by former Secretary of Defense William Cohen), both in September 2002. In January 2003 Piper picked up 33 lawyers from Hill & Barlow to create a new Boston office. The expansions play to the firm's strengths in litigation and real estate while adding depth in lobbying and government regulation. Although Piper recently lost former Verner partner Bob Dole, he was soon replaced by another Republican heavyweight – retiring congressman Dick Armey, who signed up with Piper Rudnick in early 2003.

GETTING HIRED

Some associates suggest Piper Rudnick wants "solid candidates from national schools" and "only the very top candidates from local schools." But others tell us the firm "places far greater value on achievement, ability and the willingness to work hard than on where a candidate went to law school." One source says, "Writing ability is paramount," while another emphasizes that intellectual ability must be buttressed with "good social skills [and] personality." Hiring at other offices has grown "increasingly competitive," and with all the expansion, "the pedigree of the new associate may be changing."

OUR SURVEY SAYS

Piper Rudnick "is still trying to decide on a culture post-merger." Associates point to "a great feeling of optimism and promise" about the future. However, almost everyone points to a new emphasis on billable hours, though some insiders feel the firm may be getting ahead of itself. "Piper is not a sweatshop yet," says one insider, "but if they had enough work to give corporate associates, it probably would be." Colleagues agree the 2,000-hour minimum "can be a burden." Though some associates insist Piper is "serious about competing with the strongest firms in the country," most suggest their salary "consistently lags behind other top-tier firms." Associates are also bothered by a "sadistic ranking system" that determines individual annual raises, although some see signs of improvement.

Piper's commitment to pro bono is "singularly impressive." (Up to 100 pro bono hours can be applied to the billable hours requirement.) Litigators give high marks to their "top-notch" training, including annual trial advocacy retreats. In other departments, "the best training comes from quality billable work" and "significant responsibility and opportunities" given to lawyers "right out of the gate." "Minority recruiting has been very active," though "there is still work to be done on this front." An openly gay attorney told us he has "no problem" feeling accepted at the firm, but observed, "While they've got most of the policies right, they don't do much to publicize it."

Stroock & Stroock & Lavan LLP

180 Maiden Lane
New York, NY 10038-4982
Phone: (212) 806-5400
www.stroock.com

LOCATIONS

New York, NY (HQ)
Los Angeles, CA
Miami, FL

MAJOR DEPARTMENTS/PRACTICES

Capital Markets • Commodities & Derivatives • Energy •
Entertainment • ERISA & Employee Benefits • Financial
Services Litigation • Health Care • Insolvency &
Restructuring • Insurance • Intellectual Property •
Investment Management • Labor & Employment •
Litigation • Real Estate • Securities • Structured Finance
• Tax • Trusts & Estates

THE STATS

No. of attorneys: 345
No. of offices: 3
Summer associate offers: 29 out of 29 (2002)
Managing Partner: Thomas E. Heftler
Hiring Attorney: Ross F. Moskowitz

RANKING RECAP

Best in Practice
#8 - Real Estate

Quality of Life
#15 - Offices
#18 - Pro Bono

Best in Diversity
#17 - Diversity for Women

NOTABLE PERKS

- Annual firm-wide retreat
- Budget for tech expenses
- Weekly attorney lunches

EMPLOYMENT CONTACT

Ms. Diane A. Cohen
Director of Legal Personnel and Recruiting
Phone: (212) 806-5406
Fax: (212) 806-6006
E-mail: dcohen@stroock.com

BASE SALARY

New York, NY
1st year: $125,000
2nd year: $135,000
3rd year: $150,000
4th year: $170,000
5th year: $190,000
6th year: $205,000
7th year: $210,000
8th year: $215,000
Summer associate: $2,400/week

THE BUZZ
WHAT ATTORNEYS AT OTHER FIRMS ARE SAYING ABOUT THIS FIRM

- "Funny name, serious law firm."
- "Not a player"
- "Pro bono powerhouse"
- "Safety choice"

THE SCOOP

New York-based Stroock & Stroock & Lavan LLP specializes in corporate law, including finance, bankruptcy, intellectual property and litigation. The firm's clients include investment and commercial banks, insurance companies and tech firms. Bear Stearns, Goldman Sachs and JPMorgan Chase are a few large companies that have availed themselves of Stroock's services. In March 2001, the firm founded the Public Service Project, a pro bono program that focuses on matters such as disability rights, education and community economic development. The Firehouse Adoption program assists the families of police, fire and rescue workers who were killed or injured in the September 11 terrorist attacks. The Small Business Initiative provides legal services to small business in the World Trade Center area. The Stroock Spirit of New York fund was established soon after the attacks and provides direct financial assistance to those affected.

GETTING HIRED

"The firm hires primarily from NYU, Fordham, Colombia and Penn, with a sprinkling from Georgetown, BU and Cornell," reports one insider. "If you went to a top-five school, you'll get hired with B's," adds another source. "If you went to a second-tier school like Brooklyn or American you had better be in the top 1 or 2 percent." Don't sweat the interviews. "If you've made it that far, the attorney is just testing to see whether you would make a suitable workmate," says one associate. "A Stroock callback is not one that should strike fear in your heart."

OUR SURVEY SAYS

According to insiders, "Stroock is more laid back than most other New York law firms." Stroock folks are "friendly and outgoing and don't just go into their offices and hide." "[The firm] is laid back for a Wall Street law firm," says one attorney. "Everyone is very serious about their work, but it doesn't prevent them from stopping in the hallways to chat with each other, keeping their office doors open and getting together for drinks after work every so often." Bring your sense of humor. "The atmosphere is very friendly, often wittily sarcastic," observes one insider. Of course, not everyone feels the love; some insiders describe the vibe as "rather sterile" and "very stuffy."

"Compensation at Stroock is excellent," says one source. "Nobody who bills a good amount of hours will have any problem making exactly what the top firms pay." A senior associate describes a bonus "well in excess of what many of the other firms in New York" paid in 2002, yet the bonus policy draws ire from others. "The bonus system is very unclear, and even though it is based on merit, it seems to have more to do with favoritism," gripes one associate. "Relative to other large firms, the hours at Stroock are very reasonable," says an insider. "Billing 2,000 to 2,100 hours a year will permit you to advance, receive a very fair bonus and be well regarded in the firm." One junior associate worries about "not getting enough billable hours to justify my existence here."

Schulte Roth & Zabel LLP

919 Third Avenue
New York, NY 10022
Phone: (212) 756-2000
www.srz.com

LOCATIONS

New York, NY (HQ)
London

MAJOR DEPARTMENTS/PRACTICES

Business Reorganization
Capital Markets
Employment & Employee Benefits
Environmental Law
Financial Services
Intellectual Property
Investment Management
Litigation
Mergers & Acquisitions
Real Estate
Structured Finance
Tax
Trusts & Estates

THE STATS

No. of attorneys: 305
No. of offices: 2
Summer associate offers: 31 out of 31 (2002)
Executive Committee: Paul Roth, Martin Perschetz, Alan Waldenberg, Paul Weber and Marc Weingarten
Hiring Partners: Stephanie R. Breslow and Kurt F. Rosell

NOTABLE PERKS

- Alternative investment program
- Annual firm outing at Century Club
- BlackBerrys, Palm Pilots and laptops
- Gym discounts

EMPLOYMENT CONTACT

Ms. Lisa Drew
Director of Recruiting
Fax: (212) 593-5955
E-mail: lisa.drew@srz.com

BASE SALARY

New York, NY
1st year: $125,000
2nd year: $135,000
3rd year: $150,000
4th year: $170,000
5th year: $190,000
6th year: $205,000
7th year: $220,000
8th year: $230,000
Summer associate: $2,403/week

THE BUZZ
WHAT ATTORNEYS AT OTHER FIRMS ARE SAYING ABOUT THIS FIRM

- "Low visibility but excellent substance"
- "Tries, but hasn't risen to second-tier"
- "For T&E it's one of the best"
- "Good place for people who didn't make partner elsewhere"

THE SCOOP

Founded in 1969, Schulte Roth & Zabel LLP is counsel to the rich and famous. The firm's trusts and estates clients include the Lehmans, Toys R Us founder Charles Lazarus and billionaire George Soros. Name partner William Zabel is representing Jane Welch in divorce proceedings against her husband, former General Electric CEO Jack Welch. Besides helping the well to do, SRZ does corporate, litigation, tax, real estate, IP and employment and employee benefits work and represents 50 of the 100 largest hedge funds. The firm opened a London office in 2002, its first outpost outside New York, headed by founding partner Daniel Shapiro, a prominent hedge fund tax attorney. After adding 7 attorneys in London, the firm now has approximately 305 lawyers divided between its two offices.

GETTING HIRED

Schulte Roth insiders say the firm is looking for lawyers with the right personality. "The ability to joke and have fun," "work productively in a laid-back atmosphere" and "interact with interesting and diverse individuals are all qualities that are important in interviewing." SRZ recruiters take time "to really get to know candidates and take into account their personalities and what they can add to the firm," reports one contact. Don't be a jerk, warns one associate: "We tend to have pretty nice people working here, and if you're too uptight or cocky, go elsewhere."

OUR SURVEY SAYS

SRZ insiders say the firm "is very friendly, and people tend to be friends out of the office. The partners are very approachable and things are not very formal at all." The firm has "retained many of the best aspects of its culture as it has grown. It is energetic, entrepreneurial and personal in approach," says one source. But some departments aren't as happy as others. Says one lawyer, "Over the firm as a whole, the associates are reasonably happy. In the intellectual property group, the associates are uniformly furious with the lack of advance planning by the partners, the weekly catastrophes and 20-hour days required to clean them up, the overbearing work load, the lack of management support to provide resources to get the work done with anything other than associate labor." (The firm says it has begun addressing these concerns.)

Overall, SRZ insiders seem pleased with their work schedules, although "the hours can fluctuate tremendously." "Unless you make time for yourself, you'll realize you've spent the last couple of months in the office," remarks an associate. "I would be much happier here if I could work one less hour each day," wishes one insider. Compensation – specifically bonuses – is an issue. "Base compensation seems on par with other firms, but the firm recently screwed us big time on bonuses," fumes a source. "In a year where the firm made record profits, and we all worked record hours, the firm gave the same piddly bonuses as firms that had nowhere near the great year we did."

Testa, Hurwitz & Thibeault, LLP

125 High Street
Boston, MA 02110
Phone: (617) 248-7000
www.tht.com

LOCATION

Boston, MA

MAJOR DEPARTMENTS/PRACTICES

Business & Securities
Creditors' Rights, Business Restructurings & Bankruptcy
Employee Benefits & ERISA
Labor & Employment and Immigration
Litigation
Patent & Intellectual Property
Private Equity
Real Estate and Environmental
Tax
Trusts & Estates

THE STATS

No. of attorneys: 330
No. of offices: 1
Summer associate offers: 35 out of 47 (2002)
Managing Partner: William B. Asher, Jr.
Hiring Partner: Kenneth J. Gordon

RANKING RECAP

Best in Region
#5 - Boston

Quality of Life
#1 - Training
#7 - Pay
#14 - Pro Bono

NOTABLE PERKS

- State and patent bar expenses
- Concierge service
- Office decorating budget
- Emergency day care

EMPLOYMENT CONTACT

Ms. Judith A. St. John
Recruiting Administrator
Phone: (617) 248-7401
Fax: (617) 248-7100
E-mail: stjohn@tht.com

BASE SALARY

Boston, MA
1st year: $135,000
Summer associate: $2,400/week

THE BUZZ
WHAT ATTORNEYS AT OTHER FIRMS ARE SAYING ABOUT THIS FIRM

- "East coast VC king"
- "The partners lie about layoffs"
- "Good Boston firm"
- "Low morale"

THE SCOOP

Boston-based Testa, Hurwitz & Thibeault LLP specializes in counseling startup information technology and biotech companies and the venture capitalists and banks that fund them. The firm's bottom line has struggled along with the tech industry, causing it to shed 28 attorneys in 2002, as well as a dozen paralegals. The firm now has over 330 attorneys practicing in Boston, its sole location. Some sad news: the firm lost one of its founders, Richard Testa, in December 2002. Testa served as managing partner from the firm's founding in 1973 until 2001, when he became chairman.

GETTING HIRED

Insiders say "self-starters who are willing to work hard do best" at Testa Hurwitz. The firm seeks candidates with a "strong academic background. Sciences are a plus since Testa Hurwitz has a large and still expanding IP department." No geeks, though. "A good personality is key," says someone in the know. Insiders believe the new economic reality has affected the firm's hiring standards. "Hiring has slowed considerably at the lateral level, and standards are higher for summers given economic conditions," says one contact.

OUR SURVEY SAYS

Testa Hurwitz is filled with "mostly good, reasonable, friendly people." The firm culture is considered "fairly relaxed and friendly. Some partners seem to expect more formality in their dealings with associates than others, but overall it's a pretty collegial place." The economy has made some folks tense. Reports one insider, "Once very friendly and cooperative, people here are now a little uptight, which is probably attributable to most associates' concern with job security."

The firm's bonus structure is unusual: it doesn't have one. Rather than pay bonuses, which can create intra-firm competition and billable hours pressure, the firm pays higher base salaries. The solution "encourages team work and efficiency," says one efficient team player, but the hours can be tough. "It's slow now," says one attorney. "But when it's not, there's an absurd pressure to be available 24-7. Too many friends have had to give up vacations and other personal activities because of poor management on the part of partners." Some associates can't seem to get their schedules right. "Economic conditions and the cyclical nature of corporate practice mean that sometimes I wish I were busier and other times I am swamped," says one source, although he does add, "Overall, my hours have been reasonable."

TH&T wins high marks for its training. "Our training is far and away the best I have seen or heard of at any large firm," says one insider. "I find myself far ahead of my peers at other firms based largely on our training." "There is a real effort to empower and train associates," brags one insider.

Crowell & Moring LLP

1001 Pennsylvania Avenue, NW
Washington, DC 20004
Phone: (202) 624-2500
www.crowell.com

LOCATIONS

Washington, DC (HQ)
Irvine, CA
Brussels
London

MAJOR DEPARTMENTS/PRACTICES

Antitrust • Aviation • Construction • Corporate •
Energy • Government Contracts • Healthcare •
Intellectual Property • International • Labor &
Employment • Life Sciences • Litigation • Natural
Resources & Environment • Securities Regulation &
Enforcement • Tax • Telecommunications, Media &
Technology

THE STATS

No. of attorneys: 275
No. of offices: 4
Chairman: John A. Macleod
Hiring Partner: Kent R. Morrison

RANKING RECAP

Best in Region
#10- Washington, DC

Quality of Life
#6 - Pro Bono

NOTABLE PERKS

- Bar expenses paid
- "Cheap Booze" weekly happy hours
- Weekly practice group lunches

EMPLOYMENT CONTACT

Ms. Katherine A. Arnold
Assistant Director of HR for Attorney Recruiting
Phone: (202) 624-2729
Fax: (202) 628-5116
E-mail: karnold@crowell.com

BASE SALARY

Washington, DC
1st year: $125,000
2nd year: $135,000
Summer associate: $2,400/week

THE BUZZ
WHAT ATTORNEYS AT OTHER FIRMS ARE SAYING ABOUT THIS FIRM

- "Great litigation firm"
- "Nicknamed Cruel & Boring"
- "Great pro bono attitude"
- "More of a D.C. shop than anything else"

THE SCOOP

With 275 lawyers in four locations, D.C-based Crowell & Moring LLP is a politically connected firm with an international flavor. The firm is best known for its antitrust, litigation, tech and government contacts practices. In May 2001, the firm picked up 14 attorneys from D.C.-based IP boutique Evenson, McKeown, Edwards & Lenahan. C&M won a $341 million verdict from Iran on behalf of Terry Anderson, who was taken hostage and tortured there in 1979, and also represented victims of bombings of U.S. embassies in Nairobi in 1998 and Beirut in 1983. The firm also lobbied for passage of the Justice for Victims of Terrorism Act of 2000, a federal law that allows victims of terrorism to collect damages in the U.S. from foreign countries that support or aid terrorist acts.

GETTING HIRED

Landing a job at C&M "depends on the school you attend. This firm has certain feeder schools where we go year in, year out for candidates," reports an associate. "It seems that we are willing to make offers to anyone who attends some top five schools, even if they do not stand out among their peers and show little or no interest in actually coming to the firm." (The firm says its new hires in the last two years came from 40 different schools.) Personality counts. The firm is "looking for good attorneys who are also good people."

OUR SURVEY SAYS

Insiders agree C&M's culture is "informal" with a "friendly, team-work approach." One insider feels the "culture is the strength of the firm. Everyone works hard but in a laid back and friendly atmosphere. No screamers allowed." The firm's web site features rubber duck icons in an attempt to convey a fun-loving culture. Not everyone is buying it. "The firm is for the most part pretty laid back but is not nearly as cool as it is touted to be," says one source. Still, most feel C&M attorneys enjoy an environment of "casual professionalism."

The firm's hours are typically challenging. "Though [promoted] as a 'low mandatory billable' firm, the fact is that lately I'm billing hours comparable to any 'high billable' firm out there," complains an insider. C&M's pay is "pretty standard for the market," according to one source, though some disagree. Says one attorney, "There are other firms that are much more generous with associate bonuses, both in terms of criteria for receiving one and total dollar amount." Compensation at C&M is not lockstep after the second year, and "often junior lawyers are paid the same or more than more senior lawyers. The firm seems to be trying to fix that situation by early promotion of barely midlevel lawyers out of the associate ranks to the position of counsel." C&M is committed to training, but sources say informal methods are key. "The firm has undertaken initiatives to institute more formal training programs," says an insider.

Kirkpatrick & Lockhart LLP

Henry W. Oliver Building
535 Smithfield Street
Pittsburgh, PA 15222
Phone: (412) 355-6500
www.kl.com

LOCATIONS

Boston, MA • Dallas, TX • Harrisburg, PA • Los
Angeles, CA • Miami, FL • Newark, NJ • New York, NY
• Pittsburgh, PA • San Francisco, CA • Washington, DC

MAJOR DEPARTMENTS/PRACTICES

Corporate: Bankruptcy • E-Commerce • Employee
Benefits • Executive Comp. • Financing • Health Care •
Investment Management • Media/Entertainment • M&A
• Mortgage Banking • Real Estate • Securities

Litigation: Antitrust • Bankruptcy • Construction •
Employment • Environmental • Franchise • General
Commercial • Insurance Coverage • IP/Technology •
Media/Entertainment • Products Liability • Professional
Liability • Securities Fraud • Toxic Tort • White-Collar
Criminal

Tax/Trusts & Estates

THE STATS

No. of attorneys: 686
No. of offices: 10
Summer associate offers: 35 out of 41 (2002)
Chair: Peter J. Kalis

THE BUZZ
WHAT ATTORNEYS AT OTHER FIRMS ARE SAYING ABOUT THIS FIRM

- "Best in Pittsburgh with a great growth model"
- "Long way to go to play with the real big boys"
- "Friendly atmosphere"
- "Old school"

NOTABLE PERKS

- Firm 401(k) contribution
- Bar exam and review expenses
- Moving expense allowance
- Judicial clerkship bonus

EMPLOYMENT CONTACT

See www.kl.com for contacts in each office.

BASE SALARY

Boston, MA
1st year: $115,000
Summer associate: $2,200/week

Harrisburg, PA
1st year: $90,000
Summer associate: $1,700/week

Los Angeles, CA; Dallas, TX; Washington, DC
1st year: $110,000
Summer associate: $2,115/week (LA and DC),
$2,115/week (Dallas)

Miami, FL
1st year: $96000
Summer associate: $1,850/week

Newark, NJ
1st year: $102,000
Summer associate: $1,900/week

New York, NY
1st year: $120,000
Summer associate: $2,307/week

Pittsburgh, PA
1st year: $100,000
Summer associate: $1,920/week

San Francisco, CA
1st year: $125,000

THE SCOOP

Founded in Pittsburgh, Kirkpatrick & Lockhart LLP's practice is global in scope. Nearly 700 attorneys handle a wide range of corporate, litigation and regulatory matters from the firm's 10 offices, representing over half of the Fortune 100. K&L announced the launch of a homeland security practice in April 2003, which will assist companies in complying with new regulations established by the Homeland Security Act. This is the second new paractice group for K&L since 2001, when it started a food and drug practice out of its Washington, D.C., office. In the courtroom, K&L scored a victory for the Boston Police Department. In a March 2003 decision, an appeals court overruled a decision giving the court authority to monitor the department's hiring and promotion decisions.

GETTING HIRED

"The firm is not as uptight as many of its peers about the required qualifications," says a first-year. But a senior associate says a candidate's school still plays a large part in hiring: Kirkpatrick "generally focuses on 10 national, top-tier law schools and strong law schools in the area where respective offices are located. Quality students at those schools will get long looks from the firm. Students from other schools will have to make more of an effort." As for personality, insiders say the firm "looks for people who are self-assured and easy to talk to and whom we believe will fit in well at the firm." Good news: "Most summer associates are offered full-time positions."

OUR SURVEY SAYS

K&L "is trying very hard to maintain its laid back atmosphere despite its recent growth. There are always individual exceptions, but for the most part it's an open door atmosphere," a midlevel comments. Sources report that most K&L attorneys are "approachable and easy going." The firm "is not the most social place," a fourth-year concurs, and "thankfully it is not a place with lots of nights or weekends. They are also pretty accommodating about letting people work remotely." One insider complains the lack of a "system of workflow distribution causes a feast or famine workload situation, which is alternately frustrating and terrifying."

Work at K&L "ebbs and flows," making it "nearly impossible to meet minimum billable requirements some months and difficult to find free time other months," says one insider, while a senior associate expresses unease because there is "insufficient work to keep me busy, but I feel pressure to be present in the office 10 hours a day just in case." Associates report there are numerous "training programs set up and encouraged by the firm. However, not all are particularly helpful." Insiders appreciate that the firm "has implemented several formal mentoring programs assigning associate mentors and partner mentors." This "encourages forming informal mentoring relationships."

Greenberg Traurig, LLP

1221 Brickell Avenue
Miami, FL 33131
Phone: (305) 579-0500
www.gtlaw.com

LOCATIONS

Atlanta, GA • Boca Raton, FL • Boston, MA • Chicago,
IL • Denver, CO • Florham Park, NJ • Ft. Lauderdale, FL
• Los Angeles, CA • Miami, FL • New York, NY •
Orlando, FL Philadelphia, PA • Phoenix, AZ •
Tallahassee, FL • Tysons Corner, VA • Washington, DC
• West Palm Beach, FL • Wilmington, DE • Amsterdam
• Zurich

MAJOR DEPARTMENTS/PRACTICES

Antitrust • Appellate • Biotechnology • Business
Immigration • Corporate & Securities • Education •
Employee Benefits & Executive Compensation • Energy
& Natural Resources • Entertainment & Sports •
Environmental • ERISA • Financial Institutions •
Franchise & Distribution • Gaming • Golf & Resort •
Governmental Affairs • Government Contracts •
Healthcare • Insurance Coverage • Intellectual Property
• International • Labor & Employment • Land Use •
Litigation • Public Finance • Public Utilities • Real Estate
• Reorganization, Bankruptcy & Restructuring • Tax,
Trusts & Estates • Technology, Media &
Telecommunications • Transportation • Wealth
Preservation

THE STATS

No. of attorneys: 950
No. of offices: 20
Summer associate offers: 21 out of 22 (2002)
President and CEO: Cesar L. Alvarez
Chairman: Larry J. Hoffman
Hiring Attorneys: Stephen L. Rabinowitz, Richard J.
Giusto and Karl A. Freeburg

 ## THE BUZZ
WHAT ATTORNEYS AT OTHER FIRMS ARE SAYING ABOUT THIS FIRM

- "Moving up"
- "Bye bye, business casual"
- "Regional power that is expanding nationally"
- "The dollar store of big firms"

RANKING RECAP

Quality of Life
#7 - Satisfaction
#13 - Hours
#17 - Offices

Best in Diversity
#10 - Diversity for Minorities
#12 - Diversity for Women

NOTABLE PERKS *

- Profit-sharing program
- Free parking at many offices
- Firm-subsidized BlackBerrys and laptops
- Tickets to concerts and sporting events

* Perks vary by office

EMPLOYMENT CONTACT

*Atlanta, Boca Raton, Boston, Denver, Ft.
Lauderdale, Miami, Orlando, Tallahassee, West Palm
Beach, Wilmington:*
Ms. Janet McKeegan
Director of Recruitment
Phone: (305) 579-0855
E-mail: mckeeganj@gtlaw.com

See www.gtlaw.com for employment contacts for
other offices.

BASE SALARY

All offices
1st year: $85,000-$125,000, depending on
geographical location

THE SCOOP

A 950-attorney behemoth, Greenberg Traurig LLP is the first U.S.-based law firm to set up shop in the Netherlands, launching its Amsterdam office in 2003; an additional office in Zurich heralds the further European expansion. The Boston office is representing plaintiffs in nearly 300 lawsuits against the city's Roman Catholic archdiocese, which stands accused of covering up decades of sexual abuse by priests. Greenberg LA is counseling rockers Edgar and Johnny Winter in a lawsuit accusing a comic book company of misappropriating their likenesses for financial gain by creating mutant villains who look just like them. Meanwhile, the Atlanta office represents a full roster of musical stars, from B.B. King to Jimmy Buffett. In D.C., the distributors of Stolichnaya vodka and the African nation of Eritrea called upon the firm for lobbying assistance, as attorneys in Delaware worked with the unsecured creditors in the bankruptcy proceedings of dot-com casualty Napster.

GETTING HIRED

Greenberg Traurig is a "very competitive" environment; the firm "believes in very selected and targeted growth" and chooses its hires carefully. "Associates are hired to fill a specific need," advises a D.C. associate, "or join the firm along with a new partner or practice group." If you want to attract the firm's attention, "solid credentials and specialized experience" are essential. "Good writing and research skills" will also work in your favor, along with an "entrepreneurial approach." Should you get a callback, rest assured you won't be kept waiting, as insiders confide that "decisions are made quickly."

OUR SURVEY SAYS

With offices scattered across the country, it's hard to generalize about Greenberg Traurig's firm culture. Associates suggest "the smaller offices are more laid back," but ask around the larger outposts and you're likely to hear the firm is "uptight but pretends to be laid back." In New York, "the firm is moving toward more formality," and a recent decision to do away with casual attire leaves many associates seething. Greenberg "encourages hard work, long hours and a very high level of competence," but the firm's attorneys insist they have "very reasonable" time commitments within those guidelines. Associates get plenty of help and encouragement from the partners, who are "demanding yet fair" and "offer a lot of autonomy." Greenberg Traurig's geographical diversity is reflected in the differing opinions about the firm's compensation. Salaries are "very competitive" in Phoenix and "in line with other large Atlanta firms," but associates say the firm is "a bit below market" in D.C. and "used to be competitive with the other major Philadelphia firms, [but] now it is not." The bonus system has two components, one tied directly to billable hours and the other purely discretionary, perhaps fostering what one associate describes as "a sense that what you are paid can vary significantly from year to year."

Fish & Richardson P.C.

225 Franklin Street
Boston, MA 02110-2804
Phone: (617) 542-5070
www.fr.com

LOCATIONS

Boston, MA
Dallas, TX
Minneapolis, MN
New York, NY
Redwood City, CA
San Diego, CA
Washington, DC
Wilmington, DE

MAJOR DEPARTMENTS/PRACTICES

Appellate
Corporate & Securities
Entertainment & Media
International Regulatory Group
Litigation & Dispute Resolution
Patent Prosecution & Strategic Counseling
Trademarks & Copyrights
U.S. International Trade Commission Proceedings

THE STATS

No. of attorneys: 300 +
No. of offices: 8
Summer associate offers: 33 out of 38 (2002)
President: Peter J. Devlin
Hiring Principal: John F. Hayden

 THE BUZZ
WHAT ATTORNEYS AT OTHER FIRMS ARE SAYING ABOUT THIS FIRM

- "IP powerhouse"
- "Sweatshop that ruins associates' health"
- "Relaxed, cool place to work"
- "Overrated and cocky"

RANKING RECAP

Best in Region
#8 - Boston

Best in Practice
#3 - Intellectual Property

Quality of Life
#5 - Pay
#5 - Retention
#9 (tie) - Associate/Partner Relations
#9 - Satisfaction
#12 - Best 20 Law Firms to Work For

NOTABLE PERKS

- $500/year for attorney development/tech upgrades
- Huge discounts on client products (e.g., Bose speakers, See's candy)
- Gourmet coffee machines on every floor

EMPLOYMENT CONTACT

Ms. Jill E. McDonald
Firmwide Director of Attorney Hiring
Phone: (858) 678-5070
Fax: (858) 678-5099
E-mail: work@fr.com

BASE SALARY

All offices
1st year: $135,000
2nd year: $145,000
3rd year: $150,000
4th year: $160,000
5th year: $175,000
6th year: $180,000
7th year: $190,000
8th year: $195,000
Summer associate: $2,400/week (2L);
$2,200/week (1L)

THE SCOOP

Founded in 1878, Fish & Richardson P.C. is one of the country's oldest and largest firms specializing in patent and technology law. In May 2003 *IP Law & Business* named F&R the No. 1 patent defense litigation firm in the country and No. 2 overall among firms that handle the most patent litigation. In 2002 the firm's client Genzyme Corp. negotiated a settlement in a suit filed against Genentech for breach of a license agreement and patent infringement over a genetically altered clot-busting agent used to treat heart attack victims. The firm began 2003 with a handful of strategic expansions. It launched a media and entertainment section, Kneerim & Williams at Fish & Richardson (an in-house literary agency), and a white-collar, government and securities litigation section. The firm also expanded its corporate and securities group and helped Phillip Morris metamorphose into Altria Group.

GETTING HIRED

If you've studied electrical engineering, F&R would like to talk to you. In 2002, the firm offered signing bonuses starting at $50,000 to J.D.s with "double E" degrees. Sources emphasize that a tech background isn't the only way to get hired here. Candidates must be "quick on their feet and charismatic," and those with federal clerkships under their belts are viewed with particular favor. Still, looking good on paper offers no guarantees. "We even turn Order of the Coif circuit clerks from top ten schools away if their résumé doesn't smell right," warns a senior insider.

OUR SURVEY SAYS

F&R is "the ultimate in laid back and friendly, except when it comes to the quality of our work." The firm's offices provide a "relaxed atmosphere over a business-oriented topography." F&R attorneys "tend to be down-to-earth types, confident and not pretentious." A senior associate notes approvingly, "If you get in a bind, there are people who will go out of their way to support you." Others observe that the firm "seems to be moving into a more competitive stance" and has become "a drastically different place than it was two years ago."

"My hours are what I expected," says a first-year, "without the horror stories you always hear." Some are simply glad to have enough work in the current economy to necessitate the occasional late night at the office. Most insiders believe the firm offers a "superior base salary and bonus structure." One suggests, "Very few firms can compete, and among those that do, none offers a more livable firm culture." F&R partners are "true professional mentors" who "are not afraid to give credit and praise to associates." Although IP is "a mostly male-dominated world," women at F&R insist hiring is based solely on "qualifications, personality and potential" and add that they do not experience discrimination at the office. Associates also report the firm "appears to be openly receptive to minorities" and that sexual orientation is "just not an issue."

Patton Boggs LLP

2550 M Street, NW
Washington, DC 20037
Phone: (202) 457-6000
www.pattonboggs.com

LOCATIONS

Washington, DC (HQ)
Anchorage, AK
Boulder, CO
Dallas, TX
Denver, CO
McLean, VA

MAJOR DEPARTMENTS/PRACTICES

Administrative & Regulatory
Communications & Technology
Litigation & Dispute Resolution
Public Policy
Securities, Corporate Finance & Tax

THE STATS

No. of attorneys: 369
No. of offices: 6
Summer associate offers: 9 out of 9 (2002)
Chairman: Thomas Hale Boggs Jr.
Managing Partner: Stuart Pape
Hiring Partner: Darryl D. Nirenberg

THE BUZZ
WHAT ATTORNEYS AT OTHER FIRMS ARE SAYING ABOUT THIS FIRM

- "Powerhouse lobbying firm"
- "Old-school lobbying and three-martini lunches"
- "Politically connected"
- "Is it even a law firm anymore?"

RANKING RECAP

Best in Region
#8 - Washington, DC

Quality of Life
#10 - Satisfaction
#11 - Hours
#19 - Pro Bono

NOTABLE PERKS

- Subsidized gym membership
- "Third Thursday" cocktail parties
- Annual D.C. trip for associates in other offices

EMPLOYMENT CONTACT

Ms. Kara P. Reidy
Director of Professional Recruitment
Phone: (202) 457-6000
Fax: (202) 457-6315
E-mail: kreidy@pattonboggs.com

BASE SALARY

Washington, DC
1st year: $120,000*
2nd year: $125,000
3rd year: $135,000; $113,000
4th year: $145,000; $119,000
5th year: $155,000; $125,000
6th year: $165,000; $132,000
7th year: $175,000; $139,000
8th year: $185,000; $147,000
Summer associate: $2,300/week

Two-tier system - 1,900 billable track and 1,650 billable track (not available to first- and second-year associates).

THE SCOOP

The attorneys of Washington, D.C.-based Patton Boggs LLP are known as some of the Beltway's most well-connected lobbyists. Corporations and city governments alike rely on Patton Boggs' political juice, as in the case of the city of Los Angeles, which signed on with the firm in 2002 hoping its influence with Capitol lawmakers could lead to increased federal funding. A number of foreign countries also rely on the firm to represent their interests in Washington, including Angola, Mexico, Qatar and Saudi Arabia. And the firm boasts strong practices in litigation and securities law as well. In February 2003, the firm acquired the Dallas-based business and technology group of the now-defunct Brobeck, Phleger & Harrison, which specializes in advising emerging companies. Patton Boggs also maintains an active pro bono practice. In October 2002, the firm won a favorable ruling on behalf of a group of tenants living in a substandard D.C. housing complex.

GETTING HIRED

Patton Boggs "participates in on-campus recruiting, where candidates get 15- or 20-minute interviews, and then those who receive a callback interview come into the firm for a half day of interviewing with four or five attorneys, a mix of partners and associates." The "firm values self-starters," a fourth-year tells us. A first-year explains, "Personality is looked at as well as good grades. You won't get hired on grades alone. And a great personality can make up for average grades." Additionally, the firm "values individuals who have a strong sense of self, varied interests and very strong legal and writing skills."

OUR SURVEY SAYS

"The work is challenging, and the caliber of clients is very good. The reputation of the firm, particularly in D.C., is very good," says a happy fourth-year. A little friendliness means a lot. "Our firm is more laid back and friendlier than most," says a senior associate. "People actually stop and greet each other in the hallways on a regular basis!" Some attorneys say the Patton Boggs family isn't as close knit as it used to be. "Expansion over the last three or four years means that fewer people know each other, and that has an effect on the social atmosphere." Some associates seem to appreciate that the firm is "not very structured" because the "informal and loosely structured practice groups allow people to diversify their work."

"As long as you get your work done and make your hours for the year, no one is watching when you come and go," a first-year reports. "Lawyers get paid an extremely high amount of money," says a happy fifth-year, who adds, "I feel like, in comparison with other D.C. firms and the lifestyle I am able to lead, my compensation is very appropriate." While there are a number of associates who prefer fewer hours to higher salaries, most say they'd like more money and benefits. "Our

Bryan Cave LLP

One Metropolitan Square
211 North Broadway, Suite 3600
St. Louis, MO 63102
Phone: (314) 259-2000
www.bryancave.com

LOCATIONS

Chicago, IL • Irvine, CA • Jefferson City, MO • Kansas City, MO • Leahwood, KS • Los Angeles, CA • New York, NY • Overland Park, KS • Phoenix, AZ • St. Louis, MO • Washington, DC • Abu Dhabi, U.A.E. • Dubai, U.A.E. • Hong Kong • Kuwait City • London • Riyadh • Shanghai

MAJOR DEPARTMENTS/PRACTICES

Business & Transactional Counseling
Litigation & Dispute Resolution

THE STATS

No. of attorneys: 840 +
No. of offices: 18
Summer associate offers: 41 out of 45 (2002)
Chairman: Walter L. Metcalfe, Jr.
Hiring Chairs: John R. Haug (St. Louis); Robert M. Thompson (Kansas City); John R. Wilner (DC); Joel A. Levin and Elizabeth A. Bousquette (NY); David G. Andersen (LA); Steven H. Sunshine (Irvine); Carla A. Consoli (Phoenix)

RANKING RECAP

Quality of Life
#1 - Part-Time/Flex-Time
#20 - Hours

NOTABLE PERKS*

- Free parking
- Free cell phone and BlackBerry service
- New hire lunch program

* *Perks vary by office*

EMPLOYMENT CONTACT

See firm web site for employment contacts.

BASE SALARY

Irvine, Los Angeles, CA; New York, NY
1st year: $125,000
Summer associate: $2,400/week

Kansas City, St. Louis, MO
1st year: $85,000 (KC), $90,000 (SL)
Summer associate $1,500/week

Phoenix, AZ
1st year: $95,000
Summer associate $1,700/week

Washington, DC
1st year: $120,000
Summer associate $2,000/week

THE BUZZ
WHAT ATTORNEYS AT OTHER FIRMS ARE SAYING ABOUT THIS FIRM

- "Good real estate practice"
- "Not a big city firm"
- "Trying to be international, stress trying"
- "Disparity in work at different offices"

THE SCOOP

One of the 25 largest law firms in the country (and the one with the largest Persian Gulf presence of any U.S. law firm), St. Louis' Bryan Cave LLP was named one the 10 fastest growing firms of 2002 by *The National Law Journal*. In July of that year, Bryan Cave quadrupled the number of attorneys in its New York office and welcomed former New York City Mayor Ed Koch to the firm when it merged with Robinson Silverman Pearce Aronsohn & Berman. That same month, the firm announced that a team of six attorneys from local firm Thompson Coburn joined the St. Louis office. The firm received nearly $2.5 million in 2002 for advising two of the largest recent bankruptcies in the St. Louis area; solvent clients include Target, Anheuser-Busch and Ralston Purina.

GETTING HIRED

Looking to join the Bryan Cave team? Top grades are important, but a "winning personality will separate you from the pack." "I don't think Bryan Cave is looking to populate the office with all 4.0s from Harvard Law. They really do put an emphasis on the whole package," notes an associate. Still, keep in mind that "the hiring process is very competitive and it seems it is getting more competitive from year to year." Missouri fan? "With respect to the St. Louis office, commitment to the city/community is key, not only because the firm plays a big role in the community," but also because "the firm wants some reassurance that the potential hire" won't make tracks for a nearby Chicago firm at the drop of a hat (or a job offer).

OUR SURVEY SAYS

Insiders say Bryan Cave "strikes a good balance between being formal and still providing a casual, friendly work environment" and is "laid back, yet has a typical Midwestern work ethic." "From my experience," says an associate, "the culture at the offices which are the firm power bases tend to be more uptight. The smaller offices, like Kansas City, tend to be more relaxed." In the D.C. office, "many of the young lawyers socialize together in and out of work, both with other lawyers and with other employees of the firm." According to an attorney in St. Louis, "The atmosphere and culture are quite friendly and collegial."

Most associates seem content with their pay, though they wouldn't mind "a bit more room for discretionary bonus money at the end of the year and some room for differentiation amongst associates within the same class based upon performance." Partners are considered "very approachable and welcome questions or concerns." Partners "are more than willing to help out and teach," says one insider. Associates give the firm high marks when it comes to its part-time/flex-time program, raving that part-timers remain eligible for pro-rated bonuses and partnership.

Bingham McCutchen LLP

150 Federal Street
Boston, MA 02110
Phone: (617) 951-8000
www.bingham.com

LOCATIONS

Boston, MA (HQ)
Hartford, CT
Los Angeles, CA
New York, NY
San Francisco, CA
Silicon Valley, NY
Walnut Creek, NC
Washington, DC
London
Singapore

MAJOR DEPARTMENTS/PRACTICES

Corporate/M&A/Investment • Management • Estate
Planning • Finance/Banking/Project Finance/Real
Estate/Financial Restructuring • Litigation/Intellectual
Property/Antitrust/Environmental • Tax

THE STATS

No. of attorneys: 800+
No. of offices: 10
Summer associate offers: 77 out of 82 (2002)
Chairman: Jay S. Zimmerman
Vice Chairman: Donn P. Pickett
Hiring Attorney: Marijane Benner Browne

RANKING RECAP

Best in Region
#4 - Boston

Best in Practice
#10 (tie) - Bankruptcy/Corporate Restructuring

Quality of Life
#12 - Offices
#16 - Training

NOTABLE PERKS

- Emergency day care, domestic partner benefits
- Generous parental leave policy
- Subsidized gym membership, home computers
- Baseball tickets (Red Sox and Giants)

EMPLOYMENT CONTACT

Ms. Fiona S. Trevelyan, Esq.
Director of Legal Recruitment
Phone: (617) 951-8608
Fax: (617) 951-8736
E-mail: legalrecruit@bingham.com

BASE SALARY

Boston, MA
1st year: $125,000
2nd year: $130,000
3rd year: $135,000
4th year: $160,000
5th year: $180,000
6th year: $190,000
7th year: $200,000
Summer associate: $2,400/week

THE BUZZ
WHAT ATTORNEYS AT OTHER FIRMS ARE SAYING ABOUT THIS FIRM

- "Friendly, quirky"
- "Growing pains on acquired firms"
- "Rising star"
- "Needs to cement some kind of reputation"

THE SCOOP

Born of a high-profile merger between Boston's Bingham Dana and San Francisco's McCutchen, Doyle, Brown & Enersen in 2002, Bingham McCutchen LLP is one of the largest firms in the nation. Bingham may be best known for its global insolvency, antitrust and environmental practices, but its attorneys tackle everything from banking to IP law. The firm successfully represented consulting firm Bain & Co. in a $70 million lawsuit filed by a former Club Med CEO who accused a Bain director of conspiring to oust him. After six days at trial, a federal judge dismissed all claims against Bain. On the West Coast, the firm represented the NFL in 23 actions brought by the Oakland Raiders concerning the way the NFL governed and promoted itself. The team sought hundreds of millions in damages, but all but two of the causes of action were nixed by the court (and one of those is still a candidate for summary judgment).

GETTING HIRED

Bingham's expansion runs counter to the trend at other firms in Boston, many of which have laid associates off or shut down completely. The firm is said to be "more competitive than ever" since the merger, and some associates wonder if "the emphasis in what the new firm is looking for may be changing, enforcing grades rather than personality." (The firm does consider sense of humor when evaluating applicants, however.) Some say fit is as important as ever. "Bingham likes people who aren't plain vanilla smart," says a junior associate, "but people who have really well-developed communication skills and a warm feel to them."

OUR SURVEY SAYS

Bingham's West Coast associates are still trying to get their bearings in the post-merger environment. "It used to be more friendly and casual," several associates complain, kvetching that "partners and associates alike are being forced to follow countless new policies and procedures that make practicing law more difficult and much less pleasurable." Merger or not, many still think their colleagues "are the best thing about this firm." Back in Boston, associates find the office "a rather informal place, although sometimes intense," where attorneys are "mission-focused yet friendly and social." Expect "a close, warm, joking relationship" among junior associates.

Bingham's salaries are reportedly "competitive with the market and just went to lockstep." But some are worried about finding enough work to hit bonus requirements. Though it's "not a place that grinds you down, there is a lot of pressure to hit 2,000 hours and not always enough work." Moreover, "you never know when you arrive in the morning how late you may have to stay that night." Still, associates enjoy "tremendous" flexibility to work from home and "often ask each other what they're doing for the weekend, which seems to imply that most here expect to have [weekend plans]."

Fenwick & West LLP

Silicon Valley Center
801 California Street
Mountain View, California 94041
Phone: (650) 988-8500
www.fenwick.com

LOCATIONS

Mountain View, CA (HQ)
Boise, ID
San Francisco, CA
Washington, DC

MAJOR DEPARTMENTS/PRACTICES

Corporate
Employment & Labor
Intellectual Property
Licensing & Technology
Litigation
Mergers & Acquisitions
Tax

THE STATS

No. of attorneys: 280+
No. of offices: 4
Summer associate offers: 23 out of 28 (2002)
Chairman: Gordon Davidson
Hiring Attorneys: Shawna Swanson and Jeff Vetter

RANKING RECAP

Best in Region
#13 - California

Best in Practice
#3 - Technology/Internet/E-Commerce

NOTABLE PERKS

- One-week stay for two at firm's Hawaii condos
- Work enough hours, earn a weekend getaway
- Pet insurance
- Associate investment program

EMPLOYMENT CONTACT

Ms. Karen Amatangelo-Block
Attorney Recruiting Manager
Phone: (650) 335-4949
Fax: (650) 938-5200
E-mail: recruit@fenwick.com

BASE SALARY

All offices
1st year: $125,000
2nd year: $135,000
3rd year: $145,000
4th year: $160,000
5th year: $180,000
6th year: $195,000
7th year: $205,000
Summer associate: $2,400/week

THE BUZZ
WHAT ATTORNEYS AT OTHER FIRMS ARE SAYING ABOUT THIS FIRM

- "The incredible shrinking firm"
- "Solid Silicon Valley firm"
- "Conscious effort to make associates happy"
- "Another NASDAQ casualty"

THE SCOOP

Technology may be out of favor at many firms these days, but Fenwick & West LLP, founded in 1972, was a leading adviser to technology companies long before Silicon Valley became hip and has stayed true to its roots. Fenwick, which incorporated Apple Computer nearly 30 years ago, recently counseled networking giant Cisco on the acquisition of two companies, and is now squaring off against Research in Motion, the parent of the much-loved BlackBerry wireless e-mail provider. The firm represents Good Technology, a small, California-based company, in a suit accusing RIM of violating Good Technology's wireless e-mail patents. Fenwick holds the distinction of being the only law firm to appear four times in a row on *Fortune*'s 100 Best Companies to Work For list. Hey, how could attorneys not like a firm that provides pet insurance?

GETTING HIRED

"Fenwick is always very selective" when it comes to hiring, say insiders. The firm looks for candidates from "top schools and a few area schools. Now that the economy has tightened up, they're interviewing at fewer schools and really concentrating on candidates with excellent technical backgrounds, high grades," journal experience and so on. But a more senior associate has a different take on the firm's hiring criteria. "Judging from recent hires, the firm likes personable people. A personable candidate is more likely to get an offer than a highly credentialed candidate."

OUR SURVEY SAYS

Working at Fenwick is "truly fun" and "collegial." The "cooperative, supportive" and "easygoing" work environment leads to "minimal politics." "The firm's culture is almost too nice," reveals a San Francisco associate, "to the point where people are afraid to ask support staff to do essential tasks for fear of seeming mean." "Doors are always open and partners accessible," says a source. "Despite the poor economy, there is still a lot of exciting work going on here," a first-year happily reports. However, a couple of associates hint work could be more evenly distributed. Another insider is more blunt: Some "associates have taken to hoarding and stealing work because of the lack of interesting tasks," this insider alleges.

Insiders say the economic slump has its good points. "I have a life!" exclaims one insider, happy with the decreased hours. Still, the "slow economy means more hours spent chasing fewer billables," sighs a fourth-year, although others insist Fenwick "is not a lifestyle firm in the least" when it comes to hours. Associates say the firm's "do your work and go home" attitude eliminates the need for face time. And they give partners credit for being flexible about letting associates work from home whenever possible. California associates are pleased with new offices in downtown Mountain View (near Palo Alto). Says one attorney, "[The] new office is light and airy, plus the windows open." And attorneys in San Francisco are treated to "gorgeous views" everyday.

1155 Avenue of the Americas
New York, NY 10036
Phone: (212) 790-9090
www.pennie.com

LOCATIONS

New York, NY (HQ)
Palo Alto, CA
San Diego, CA (opening 2003)
Washington, DC

MAJOR DEPARTMENTS/PRACTICES

Intellectual Property and Industrial Property (divided into
three legal groups-Procurement, Litigation & Consulting)
with expertise in: Biotechnology • Pharmaceuticals •
Chemistry • Materials Technologies • Electrical
Engineering • Computer Science • Nanotechnology •
Internet & E-Commerce • Mechanical Technologies
•Trademark & Anticounterfeiting • Copyright & Unfair
Competition.

THE STATS

No. of attorneys: 195
No. of offices: 4
Summer associate offers: 26 out of 34 (2002)
Managing Partner: John J. Normile
Hiring Partners: Peter D. Vogl

RANKING RECAP

Best in Practice
#4 - Intellectual Property

Quality of Life
#19 (tie) - Pay

NOTABLE PERKS

- Cocktail parties
- Backup day care
- On-site gym (Palo Alto)
- Tickets to local sporting events
- Annual firm-wide black-tie dinner in NYC

EMPLOYMENT CONTACT

Ms. Annette I. Friend
Director of Recruitment & Professional Development
Phone: (212) 790-2930
Fax: (212) 699-0267
E-mail: afriend@pennie.com

BASE SALARY

All offices
1st year: $125,000
2nd year: $135,000
3rd year: $150,000
4th year: $165,000
5th year: $185,000
6th year: $200,000
7th year: $210,000
8th year: $220,000
Summer associate: $2,400/week

THE BUZZ
WHAT ATTORNEYS AT OTHER FIRMS ARE SAYING ABOUT THIS FIRM

- "Good IP firm"
- "Patent sweatshop"
- "If you do patent, do it here"
- "Not a player"

THE SCOOP

Founded in New York in 1883, Pennie & Edmonds LLP is one of the nation's largest intellectual property firms, with roughly 200 attorneys in four offices. It's also one of the fastest growing; the *National Law Journal* reported in 2002 that Pennie had expanded by 30 percent in the previous year – the largest increase for a firm not involved in a merger or acquisition. The firm won the largest pharmaceutical case in U.S. patent law history for Kremers Urban Development Co. in October 2002, convincing a federal district court judge that KUDCo's generic version of Prilosec, the second best-selling prescription drug in the U.S., did not infringe upon the patents held by the anti-ulcer medication's developer. The firm also scored a major Supreme Court victory in a case with implications for litigants who face a patent or other federal counterclaim to a civil action in federal or state court.

GETTING HIRED

"In normal times it's difficult to land a job at Pennie," acknowledges one senior associate. "The current economic and political climate make it even more difficult." According to its web site, Pennie looks for "superior law school credentials," as well as "broad-based experience including international exposure and foreign language ability." If you've landed an interview, rest assured that the hiring decisions are "based on personality and potential," as "most of the interviewers assume that you have the credentials on paper."

OUR SURVEY SAYS

Pennie & Edmonds "has changed significantly in the last two years" but is still "casual for a Manhattan firm." Associates sport "full-time business casual" and congregate at monthly cocktail parties. One source enthuses that "no one questions whether you come in late or leave early as long as you get your work done," but another describes "a sense of working in a fog" due to the lack of feedback from partners, who are otherwise "friendly and somewhat approachable."

Pennie's compensation "could be more," says one associate, but insiders are "grateful that it is not less." The workload is "comparable to other patent boutiques," and though "not as demanding as during the dot-com boom years, there is still plenty of work to keep you busy." First-years "are constantly worrying where their next project will come from," but at least they're "pleased not to be at the office for 12 hours consistently."

"About half of our lawyers are women," and though some suggest "it's pretty damn hard for a woman to make partner," others believe "women have a chance to excel." (The firm points out that two of its five most recent partners are women.) Sexual orientation is generally considered "not an issue," although a few gay and lesbian associates at the firm are "implicitly open."

Hughes Hubbard & Reed LLP

One Battery Park Plaza
New York, NY 10004-1482
Phone: (212) 837-6000
www.hugheshubbard.com

LOCATIONS

New York, NY (HQ)
Jersey City, NJ
Los Angeles, CA
Miami, FL
Washington, DC
Paris

MAJOR DEPARTMENTS/PRACTICES

Corporate
Corporate Reorganization
Employee Benefits
Financial Services
Intellectual Property & Technology
Litigation
Personal Affairs
Real Estate
Tax

THE STATS

No. of attorneys: 300
No. of offices: 7
Summer associate offers: 35 out of 35 (2002)
Chairwoman: Candace K. Beinecke
Managing Partner: Charles H. Scherer
Hiring Partners: George A. Tsougarakis and Carolyn B. Levine

NOTABLE PERKS

- Weekly attorney breakfast
- On-site cafeteria
- Weekly yoga class
- Subsidized gym membership

EMPLOYMENT CONTACTS

Lateral Hiring
Mr. Adrian Cockerill
Director of Legal Employment
Phone: (212) 837-6131
E-mail: cockerill@hugheshubbard.com

Law Student Hiring
Ms. Bianca Torres
Recruitment Coordinator
Phone: (212) 837-6131
E-mail: torres@hugheshubbard.com

BASE SALARY

New York, NY
1st year: $125,000
2nd year: $135,000
3rd year: $150,000
4th year: $165,000
5th year: $175,000
6th year: $180,000-$185,000
7th year: $170,000-$200,000
8th year: $190,000-$200,000
Summer associate: $2,403/week

THE BUZZ
WHAT ATTORNEYS AT OTHER FIRMS ARE SAYING ABOUT THIS FIRM

- "Great place to work"
- "Not the kinder, gentler firm it used to be"
- "Family friendly"
- "Slow death"

THE SCOOP

New York's Hughes Hubbard & Reed LLP has been well-known for its litigation work since it first hung out its shingle in 1937; founding partner Charles Evans Hughes, Jr., had earned his reputation as U.S. Solicitor General and as a partner at a previous firm established by his father. Hughes Hubbard expanded its white-collar criminal practice in New York with the addition of a team of five attorneys from Zuckerman Spaeder in January 2003. The firm secured a favorable verdict for client Magdalena Dabrowski in March 2003. Dabrowski, a former curator at the Museum of Modern Art, was sued by a German museum that accused her of conspiring to ruin the gallery's reputation in the New York arts community. Huges Hubbard is also working with lawmakers from Oregon who oppose a movement to overturn a state law legalizing assisted suicide.

GETTING HIRED

The "interview process was friendly and not intimidating – more like they just want to get to know you, not grill you on your legal knowledge." "If you go to a top-five law school, it is not hard" to get an offer from Hughes Hubbard, says a corporate associate. "If not, law review is a plus." "Good grades are an essential, but personality is also a huge benefit," insiders report. "We're looking for smart people who we think we would enjoy working with," a senior associate explains. According to a midlevel, "Candidates from lower-ranked schools or with less than stellar grades who hit it off with interviewers and make a strong impression can and do get offers."

OUR SURVEY SAYS

"I am challenged on a daily basis and receive regular positive feedback and constructive criticism from the partners for whom I work," raves an experienced litigation associate. Says another source, "The firm expects quality work from you, but people treat each other with respect and can be quite friendly." "I was pleasantly shocked to find that doing corporate work in a small firm does not mean the clients are less prestigious or less demanding," shares a corporate associate. Hughes "was originally billed as a lifestyle firm when we were recruited, which is a large part of why a lot of us came here, but they've been actively trying to get rid of that image and be as hardcore as the other New York firms."

"Compensation is pretty much top of the market for the first few years," reveals a midlevel. "It drops off somewhat for more senior associates." Hughes Hubbard "has a 1,950 minimum billable-hours requirement" for bonus purposes. Bonuses were either "good this year for those who billed a lot of hours" or "very frugal," depending on who's answering. "Pro bono is very much encouraged," Hughes Hubbard associates happily report. But they are disappointed the firm "does not count time spent on pro bono matters" toward bonuses until the total pro bono hours reach a certain threshold.

Gray Cary Ware & Freidenrich LLP

2000 University Circle
East Palo Alto, CA 94303
Phone: (650) 833-2000
www.graycary.com

LOCATIONS

Austin, TX
Golden Triangle, CA
La Jolla, CA
Palo Alto, CA
Sacramento, CA
San Diego, CA
San Francisco, CA
Seattle, WA
Washington, DC

MAJOR DEPARTMENTS/PRACTICES

Corporate & Commercial Disputes Litigation
Corporate & Securities
Labor & Employment
Licensing
Patent and Trademark
Patent, Copyright & Trademark Litigation
Real Estate
Tax
Trade Regulation & Consumer Liability Litigation

THE STATS

No. of attorneys: 405
No. of offices: 9
Summer associate offers: 30 out of 45 (2002)
Chairman: J. Terence O'Malley
Hiring Partner: Richard I. Yankwich

THE BUZZ
WHAT ATTORNEYS AT OTHER FIRMS ARE SAYING ABOUT THIS FIRM

- "Well thought of"
- "No job security"
- "Humane"
- "I'm melting!"

RANKING RECAP

Best in Region
#14 - California

Quality of Life
#12 - Retention
#12 - Associate/Partner Relations
#15 - Best Firms to Work For
#16 - Pay

Diversity
#8 - Diversity for Women
#15 (tie) - Overall Diversity

NOTABLE PERKS

- BlackBerrys, cell phones, other "mobile office" equipment
- Free use of home office equipment (fax/printer/copier)

EMPLOYMENT CONTACT

Ms. Leslie Colvin
Professional Recruiting Director
Phone: (650) 833-2000
Fax: (650) 833-2001
E-mail: lcolvin@graycary.com

BASE SALARY

All offices
1st year: $125,000
2nd year: $135,000
3rd year: $150,000
4th year: $165,000
5th year: $180,000
6th year: $195,000
7th year: $205,000
8th year: $215,000
Summer associate: $2,400/week

THE SCOOP

Gray Cary Ware & Freidenrich LLP was the result of a 1994 merger between a Palo Alto technology firm and a San Diego litigation star. The firm sports offices up and down the West Coast, as well as an outpost in the booming technology sector of Austin, Texas. In January 2002, it took a plunge even further eastward, absorbing the nine-attorney D.C.-based Blumenfeld & Cohen into its ranks. That same month, however, poor economic conditions caused the firm to lay off 46 associates and 68 other employees. Clients of the firm's IP division include Dr. Seuss Enterprises, and Gray Cary filed an amicus brief in *Eldred v. Ashcroft*, the 2003 Supreme Court case upholding congressional extensions on copyright protection to nearly a century after the author's death.

GETTING HIRED

Sources claim the jockeying for positions at Gray Cary has become "very competitive" as the firm has "fewer spots to offer and more candidates looking" to charm their way in. Consequently, "the firm tends to limit recruiting efforts to top-tier schools" and subjects candidates to an "exacting" pre-interview regimen so rigorous one senior associate wonders if the firm may "focus a bit too much" on academic pedigree. "Once you are in the door," says an insider, "your experience, presentation and personality become more important than academic performance." Other sources agree "intangibles" like "working style, ability to work with clients and ability to work within our culture" carry the most weight. "We don't want stuffy people," insists one associate.

OUR SURVEY SAYS

Attorneys at Gray Cary feel "ease and comfort" with each other, and there are "tons of fun conversations going on in the halls" during the day, though after-hours socializing seems to be infrequent. Some at the firm say they "used to socialize" before the layoffs but "the atmosphere is much more cutthroat" these days. One associate who admits "many of the fun things the firm offered have been reduced or eliminated" remains upbeat. "Overall," she says, "I still find it a pleasant place to work." Insiders confirm Gray Cary's attorneys "aren't working at the pace we were in 2000," but claim partners don't expect them to "blow the top off the benchmark billables." This may contribute to the warm regard with which associates hold the partners. "I've never seen a firm where partners are as open and down-to-earth as at Gray Cary," gushes one senior associate. "Partners take their mentoring role very seriously," reports another, "and are always willing to take time to help more junior attorneys with the learning process."

Gray Cary's "very competitive" salaries are "on par with the highest salaries in our geographic markets and likely the nation." Other sources grumble about the prolonged salary freeze that began in August 2001; although it is scheduled to be discontinued in the summer of 2003, "no one is confident that it will actually happen."

Dorsey & Whitney LLP

50 South Sixth Street
Suite 1500
Minneapolis, MN 55402
Phone: (612) 340-2600
www.dorsey.com

LOCATIONS

Anchorage, AK • Denver, CO • Des Moines, IA • Fargo,
ND • Great Falls, MT • Minneapolis, MN • Missoula, MT
• New York, NY • Palo Alto, CA • Salt Lake City, UT •
San Francisco, CA • Seattle, WA • Southern California
• Washington, DC • Hong Kong • London • Shanghai •
Tokyo • Toronto • Vancouver

MAJOR DEPARTMENTS/PRACTICES

Trial/Litigation Groups: Antitrust • Commercial/Contract
• E-Commerce • ENREG • ERISA • Estate & Trust •
Franchise • Indian & Gaming • IP • International • Labor
& Employment • Legislative • Patents • Securities •
Technology • Telecommunications • White Collar Crime

Business Groups: Bankruptcy • Broker-Dealer • Capital
Markets • Commercial & Banking • Emerging
Companies • Employee Benefits • Funds • Health •
Institutional & Corporate Trust • International • M&A •
Private Companies • Project Finance • Public Companies
• Public Finance • Real Estate • Securitizations • Tax,
Trusts & Estates • Technology • Telecommunications

THE STATS

No. of attorneys: 710
No. of offices: 20
Summer associate offers: 50 out of 73 (2002) (1Ls,
2Ls & 3Ls with clerkships)
Managing Partner: Peter S. Hendrixson
Hiring Partner: Holly S.A. Eng

THE BUZZ
WHAT ATTORNEYS AT OTHER FIRMS ARE SAYING ABOUT THIS FIRM

- "Solid Minnesota firm"
- "Regional firm trying too hard to be national"
- "Great atmosphere, brutal hours"
- "Obsessed with trying to be relevant"

NOTABLE PERKS

- On-site gym (Minneapolis)
- Six weeks paid maternity and paternity leave
- Free/pre-tax transit passes

EMPLOYMENT CONTACT

Ms. Kelsey Shuff
Manager of Lawyer Recruiting
Fax: (612) 340-2868
E-mail: shuff.kelsey@dorsey.com

BASE SALARY

Minneapolis, MN
1st year: $90,000
2nd year: $95,000
3rd year: $100,000
4th year: $105,000
5th year: $110,000
6th year: $115,000
7th year: $120,000
Summer associate: $1,750/week

New York, NY
1st year: $120,000
Summer associate $2,400/week

Seattle, WA
1st year: $95,000
Summer associate $1,750/week

Washington, DC
1st year: $105,000

THE SCOOP

Dorsey & Whitney LLP, the largest firm in Minnesota, has 20 domestic and international offices. Capitalizing on current events, the firm created an Iraq practice in April 2003, drawing upon the experience of attorneys in several practice groups, including energy, international affairs and construction. The firm recently added 18 attorneys to its Orange County office from the now-defunct Brobeck, Phleger & Harrison and six tax attorneys in London from PricewaterhouseCoopers' Landwell group. In 2002, Dorsey's Indian and Gaming group helped broker a $43 million deal that will enable four Native American tribes to build a Marriott hotel in Washington, D.C. It's not all fun and games, however; a decline in corporate work forced the firm to lay off 20 associates and contract attorneys at the end of 2002.

GETTING HIRED

"Grades are extremely important for those applying directly from law school. The firm is looking for articulate, intelligent individuals who can work on a team." According to one attorney, "the firm is extremely competitive as far as local firms go, but it really likes to hire people from big name schools." "Dorsey is becoming more and more selective," says a litigation attorney. Insiders say hiring varies by office. There are few to no positions available" in Seattle, an associate there warns. "In our office in Salt Lake, we are able to be extremely selective," an attorney reports.

OUR SURVEY SAYS

Dorsey's "midwestern mentality," promotes a "congeniality that is perhaps lacking at other large firms, and an emphasis on life outside of the office." The firm "pays little attention to the hierarchy when it comes to social interaction." "Things are still good, but they were much better when I first arrived," says a third-year. This source continues: "With layoffs, management changes, pay freezes and lack of work, morale is not that high." As the firm grows, insiders observe, "it is developing more of a big firm attitude."

The pay is "fabulous for this market but not comparable to East and West Coast markets, which is fine if we are not working those kind of hours," a Minneapolis attorney shares. Confides a Denver insider, "Associate compensation seems to be a notch below the biggest and best firms in the country, but considering the lifestyle [Dorsey] attorneys enjoy, it is a tradeoff most seem willing to make." Some associates still resent that "Dorsey instituted a pay freeze that prevented any upward movement in salaries despite the increasing profits awarded to partners." (It was lifted in 2002.) Dorsey's Minneapolis office recently moved into "wonderful" new digs, making associates in the other offices a tad jealous. "The common areas are nowhere near as nice as Minneapolis," a pouty D.C. associate says. In discussing the décor of the Seattle office, an associate says, "I would have rated it a '7,' but after I saw the décor in Minneapolis, I realized we had third-class furnishings."

Kelley Drye & Warren LLP

101 Park Avenue
New York, NY 10178
Phone: (212) 808-7800
www.kelleydrye.com

LOCATIONS

New York, NY (HQ)
Chicago, IL
Parsippany, NJ
Stamford, CT
Tysons Corner, VA
Washington, DC
Brussels
Hong Kong

MAJOR DEPARTMENTS/PRACTICES

Bankruptcy • Corporate • Employee Benefits •
Environmental • Labor • Litigation • Private Clients •
Real Estate • Tax • Telecommunications

THE STATS

No. of attorneys: 325+
No. of offices: 8
Chairman: John M. Callagy
Hiring Partner: Gregory M. McKenzie

NOTABLE PERKS

- BlackBerry pagers
- Late night car service (NYC)
- Free late-night dinners

EMPLOYMENT CONTACT

Mr. Randy J. Liss
Recruiting Coordinator
Phone: (212) 808-7721
Fax: (212) 808-7897
E-mail: rliss@kelleydrye.com

BASE SALARY

New York, NY; Parsippany, NJ; Stamford, CT;
Tysons Corner, VA; Washington DC
1st year: $125,000
2nd year: $135,000
3rd year: $150,000
4th year: $165,000
5th year: $180,000
6th year: $195,000
7th year: $205,000
Summer associate: $2,403.85/week

THE BUZZ
WHAT ATTORNEYS AT OTHER FIRMS ARE SAYING ABOUT THIS FIRM

- "Strong litigators"
- "Not a big player"
- "Well-regarded firm"
- "Anybody home?"

THE SCOOP

As clients go, it's hard to top Abraham Lincoln. Kelley Drye & Warren LLP, founded in 1836, once served as legal counsel to then-President Lincoln and today counts such corporate heavyweights as Union Carbide, DaimlerChrysler, Bacardi, Cigna, CSFB, Yahoo! and Six Flags on its client roster. The firm picked up an impressive assignment from J. P. Morgan Chase in 2002: handling the investment bank's Enron-related litigation after its original counsel was removed due to a conflict of interest. Kelley Drye helped settle J. P. Morgan Chase's legal dispute with 11 insurance companies over covering a $1.1 billion loss on trades between one of its banking subsidiaries and Enron. Under the terms of the January 2003 settlement, J. P. Morgan Chase will get roughly half of what it sought from its insurers.

GETTING HIRED

Associates at Kelley Drye describe the hiring process as "idiosyncratic." They insist "pedigree isn't too important" and say they recruit at schools "other firms would not even consider." During callbacks, "the focus is on whether the candidate is articulate and personable," due to the firm's "underlying soft spot for litigation skills and talkability." Be forewarned, says one source: "The firm hires very few entry level associates. Most hires are laterals with several years of experience."

OUR SURVEY SAYS

Kelley Drye attorneys in New York may not be big partiers ("When you don't need to work, you go home"), but some sources describe an "extremely cooperative, helpful, social and friendly" vibe. Chicagoans describe their office as "quite informal and friendly." Salaries at Kelley Drye are "slightly below the pace of other New York firms." Gripes one senior associate, "The maximum compensation is reached at only your seventh year." With a "much longer partnership track," compensation caps "considerably earlier than comparable firms." Furthermore, "bonuses are abysmal." "The firm no longer even maintains a pretense of competing with other firms in terms of bonuses," one source snaps. One sensible insider notes, "We do not receive the monster New York bonuses, but we do not work the monster New York hours either." Most associates consider the firm's billable hours target reasonable. They're "more disappointed about the lack of work available," especially since those who fail to bill 2,000 hours "simply do not get a bonus."

Although "there are some influential female partners and good role models and mentors," many female associates at the firm believe "there are no opportunities here if you are married, have kids or are of child-bearing age." (In fairness, one source did suggest "it is hard to be promoted – man or woman – in this firm.") Associates "have no doubt that the firm is and would be very welcoming of minority lawyers," but "they seem to disappear faster then they come." Gay and lesbian associates report their colleagues are "very friendly and accepting."

Shaw Pittman LLP

2300 N Street, NW
Washington, DC 20037
Phone: (202) 663-8000
www.shawpittman.com

LOCATIONS

Washington, DC (HQ)
Los Angeles, CA
McLean, VA
New York, NY
London

MAJOR DEPARTMENTS/PRACTICES

Corporate, Securities & Tax
Employee Benefits & Health
Energy & Environment
Financial Institutions
Government Contracts
Government Relations & Transportation
Litigation
Real Estate & Bankruptcy
Technology

THE STATS

No. of attorneys: 370
No. of offices: 5
Summer associate offers: 35 out of 43 (2002)
Managing Partner: Stephen B. Huttler
Hiring Partner: Thomas C. Hill

RANKING RECAP

Best in Region
#12 - Washington, DC

Best in Practice
#5 - Tech/Internet/E-Commerce

Quality of Life
#12 - Pay

NOTABLE PERKS

- Attorney lounge (Virginia office)
- Firm-provided laptops
- Monthly happy hours
- On-site gym

EMPLOYMENT CONTACT

Ms. Kathleen A. Kelly
Chief Recruiting Officer & Dir. Profess. Programs
Phone: (202) 663-8394
Fax: (202) 663-8007
E-mail: kathy.kelly@shawpittman.com

BASE SALARY

Washington, DC
1st year: $125,000
2nd year: $135,000
3rd year: $145,000
4th year: $155,000
5th year: $175,000
6th year: $185,000
7th year: $195,000
8th year: $200,000
Summer associate: $2,400/week

THE BUZZ
WHAT ATTORNEYS AT OTHER FIRMS ARE SAYING ABOUT THIS FIRM

- "Good government relations"
- "Have they finished laying everyone off yet?"
- "Great D.C. firm"
- "One step above oblivion"

THE SCOOP

Shaw Pittman LLP an bills itself as the place where "law, business and technology merge." They can throw government in as well, as the D.C.-based firm has a substantial government regulation practice, which features former Senator Connie Mack as a senior policy adviser. Because of its significant technology practice, which employs a third of the firm's 370 lawyers, the firm was not immune to the dot-com bust, laying off 19 attorneys in 2001. But they bounced back, merging with D.C.'s Fisher Wayland Cooper Leader & Zaragosa and LA's Klein & Martin. The firm is now eyeing new offices at home and abroad. (The firm already has a London outpost and four U.S. locations.) In early 2003, the firm elected Stephen B. Huttler managing partner, succeeding Paul Mickey.

GETTING HIRED

"In this depressed economy, it has become much more difficult to get hired here," says one associate. "Most recent summer associates have been from top-five law schools." Another insider agrees the economy has been a factor, but sees a few more law schools represented. "The firm is hiring a smaller number of summer associates and is concentrating more on the top-ten schools." The hiring process is standard – an hour-long interview with a partner, followed by four meetings at the callback round.

OUR SURVEY SAYS

Insiders say Shaw Pittman's culture is "not overly formal, but some groups are moving back in that direction." "In my practice group," says a litigator, "entry-level associates are given fairly substantive tasks and have significant direct contact with clients, opposing counsel and the courts." Some are enthused about the firm's atmosphere. "Pittman has a great culture. I have found the 'BS quotient' to be almost nonexistent." Hours are acceptable, with "enough to keep you busy, but most of us leave by 6:30 p.m. and work few weekends." They sometimes run hot and cold, though. "The firm does not do an effective job of spreading hours to underutilized associates," complains one source. Sometimes sleep is hard to come by. "Either I am in the office all day, stressing because I cannot find work, or I am working around the clock on high-stress jobs that needed to be done the day before when I receive the assignment and get an hour of sleep for weeks at a time," says a tired attorney.

Insiders are pleased on pay day. One lawyer says, "Compensation is on the high end of what firms pay in the D.C. area." The firm pays "market salary" and "acceptable productivity bonuses," although "discretionary bonuses are minimal." At Shaw Pittman, you'll learn as you go. "Training is mostly informal," although senior associates and partners "generally do a good job getting junior associates involved in all aspects of a project." The firm is "very supportive of sending associates to CLE programs of interest to the associates."

Finnegan, Henderson, Farabow, Garrett & Dunner, L.L.P.

1300 I Street, NW
Suite 700
Washington, DC 20005-3315
Phone: (202) 408-4000
www.finnegan.com

LOCATIONS

Washington, DC (HQ)
Atlanta, GA
Cambridge, MA
Palo Alto, CA
Reston, VA
Brussels
Taipei
Tokyo

MAJOR DEPARTMENTS/PRACTICES

Bio/Pharmaceutical
Chemical/Metallurgical
Electrical & Computer Technology
IP Specialties
Mechanical
Trademark & Copyright

THE STATS

No. of attorneys: 300+
No. of offices: 8
Summer associate offers: 18 out of 21 (2002)
Managing Partner: Christopher Foley
Hiring Partner: Michele Bosch

RANKING RECAP

Best in Region
#13 - Washington, DC

Best in Practice
#1 - Intellectual Property

Quality of Life
#6 - Retention
#6 - Training
#11 - Best 20 Law Firms to Work For
#18 - Selectivity
#19 (tie) - Pay

Diversity
#4 - Diversity for Women
#5 - Diversity for Minorities
#6 - Overall Diversity
#16 - Diversity for Gays and Lesbians

NOTABLE PERKS

- "Lots of free dinners"
- Annual firm outing
- Late-night car service
- Buy a cell phone, they pay for the minutes

EMPLOYMENT CONTACT

Washington, DC
Mr. Paul Sevanich
Attorney Recruitment Manager
Phone: (202) 408-4000
Fax: (202) 408-4400

THE BUZZ
WHAT ATTORNEYS AT OTHER FIRMS ARE SAYING ABOUT THIS FIRM

- "A top dog in IP"
- "Past its prime after tech bust"
- "Best IP firm in the land"
- "Needs a facelift"

Washington, DC
1st year: $125,000
Summer associate: $2,400/week

THE SCOOP

Finnegan, Henderson, Farabow, Garrett & Dunner L.L.P. may limit its practice to intellectual property law, but don't call it a "boutique." With more than 300 attorneys in eight offices worldwide, Finnegan is the largest IP firm in the United States and one of the busiest; a survey at the end of 2002 in *Corporate Counsel* magazine ranked Finnegan as the first firm Fortune 250 companies turn to when they need outside IP counsel. The firm serves corporate clients like 3M, Kraft Foods, Sony and Capital One and has appeared before the Federal Circuit Court of Appeals more than any other U.S. law firm. In March 2003, the firm successfully defended Verisign, which plays a critical role in maintaining the Internet's infrastructure, in a patent infringement lawsuit asserted against its communications security protocol.

GETTING HIRED

Insiders say "you've got to have a good technical background to be considered" at Finnegan, with a post-graduate degree in science or technology almost essential. In March 2003, the firm announced the creation of the Finnegan Henderson Diversity Scholarship, a $12,000 award for minority law students who aspire to a career in IP law. The scholarship also comes with a guaranteed offer for a summer associate's slot at one of the firm's domestic offices.

OUR SURVEY SAYS

Finnegan "promotes a friendly atmosphere" throughout its domestic offices. "The firm is not a party firm," says a first-year in D.C., "but everyone gets along with most everyone else." Other offices have a slightly more relaxed vibe: "Children and dogs are a major part of the office culture" in Palo Alto. The workday can be "long and tiring." A junior associate remarks, "You have a choice – you can do litigation and work an insane numbers of hours, or you can do [patent] prosecution and be more in control of your workload." Some put a different spin on the matter, claiming "it is more difficult to get hours for patent prosecution," and while other firms might recognize this and downgrade billables requirements accordingly, "not so at Finnegan." At least Finnegan's compensation has "consistently been extremely competitive."

Associates feel "very little barrier" between themselves and the partners. "I feel very comfortable in this environment," says a woman in her first year with the firm. Associates also give the firm high marks for its treatment of gay and lesbian attorneys. "I do not think this is an issue," one offers, and others confirm "sexual orientation does not appear to play any role at the firm in hiring, promotion and mentoring."

Choate, Hall & Stewart

Exchange Place
53 State Street
Boston, MA 02109
Phone: (617) 248-5000
www.choate.com

LOCATION

Boston, MA

MAJOR DEPARTMENTS/PRACTICES

Bankruptcy
Corporate
Environmental & Land Use
Health
Labor
Litigation
Patent
Real Estate
Tax
Trusts & Estate

THE STATS

No. of attorneys: 190
No. of offices: 1
Summer associate offers: 13 out of 14 (2002)
Managing Partners: William P. Gelnaw, Jr. and John A. Nadas
Hiring Partner: Mark D. Cahill

RANKING RECAP

Best in Region
#9 - Boston

NOTABLE PERKS

- Discounted gym memberships
- Annual golf and tennis tournament
- Domestic partner benefits
- On-site cafeteria

EMPLOYMENT CONTACT

Ms. Robin Carbone
Director of Recruiting
Phone: (617) 248-5000
Fax: (617) 248-4000
E-mail: rcarbone@choate.com

BASE SALARY

Boston, MA
1st year: $125,000
Summer associate: $2,400/week

THE BUZZ
WHAT ATTORNEYS AT OTHER FIRMS ARE SAYING ABOUT THIS FIRM

- "Hot Boston firm"
- "Fading Yankee glory"
- "Good place to work, friendly"
- "Stuffy, old school"

THE SCOOP

Choate, Hall & Stewart is a rarity in today's legal marketplace: a nationally recognized firm with strong corporate and litigation departments that prefers to remain close to home. Firmly committed to Boston, Choate seems content not to expand to other cities. Health care, intellectual property and real estate continue to be areas of strength and growth, and the firm's government enforcement and compliance group has been receiving notice lately, too. Some of Choate's clients include technology companies Teradyne, Data General and Analog Devices, fabric manufacturer Malden Mills and chemical maker Cabot Corp. Choate was the highest ranked Boston firm in American Lawyer Media's 2002 pro bono survey.

GETTING HIRED

Choate is "looking for smart, motivated people" who "present themselves as someone current lawyers would like to work with." "While obviously focused on a candidate's GPA and other academic credentials, Choate favors candidates who also have strong social skills," so "maturity, confidence and a sense of humor" will work to your advantage. "Personality is definitely the key ingredient at Choate. People with great resumes who aren't the right fit won't make the cut." Look for the firm's on-campus interviewers at Boston institutions such as Harvard and Boston University, and other nationally ranked schools like Columbia, Cornell and Stanford. The firm says it generally contacts candidates regarding callbacks within 48 hours of the on-campus interview.

OUR SURVEY SAYS

Choatians say their firm is "laid back," "informal and friendly." But some feel "the firm is more uptight" than it used to be, perhaps because folks are "more worried about hours" these days. "I don't see nearly as many associates in the cafeteria as I used to. They all eat at their desks now," sighs an associate. Despite the anxiety, associates and partners are getting along fine. "That partner-associate tension you hear about at other law firms?" Well, it's "nonexistent at Choate, Hall & Stewart," says an associate.

The consensus on training is that it's "great" early in the first year and then drops off "almost entirely." But a corporate associate happily reports, "The firm's structured training program has recently been revamped and improved, and we're expecting great things going forward." This source also tells us Choate "is trying to provide more organized, formal training to all levels of associates." When it comes to pro bono, Choate associates are confused. Some associates are reluctant to perform pro bono work, mostly because they say such work "does not count towards your hours." Other associates say this is false and add that "many young associates are involved" in pro bono cases. A litigation attorney considers Choate's pro bono program "great" because "pretty much anything gets approved."

Baker & Hostetler LLP

3200 National City Center
1900 East 9th Street
Cleveland, OH 44114-3485
Phone: (216) 621-0200
www.bakerlaw.com

LOCATIONS

Cleveland, OH (HQ)
Cincinnati, OH • Columbus, OH • Costa Mesa, CA •
Denver, CO • Houston, TX • Los Angeles, CA • New
York, NY • Orlando, FL • Washington, DC
International Affiliates:
Juarez, Mexico and Sao Paulo, Brazil

MAJOR DEPARTMENTS/PRACTICES

Corporate
Employment & Labor
Environmental
Intellectual Property
International
Litigation
Tax & Personal Planning

THE STATS

No. of attorneys: 526
No. of offices: 10
Executive Partner: Gary L. Bryenton
Hiring Partner: Ronald A. Stepanovic

NOTABLE PERKS

• Tickets to sports events (esp. in Cleveland)
• Practice group retreats

EMPLOYMENT CONTACT

Ms. Kathleen Ferdico
Attorney Recruitment and Development Manager
Phone: (216) 861-7092
Fax: (216) 861-6618
E-mail: kferdico@bakerlaw.com

BASE SALARY

Cleveland, OH
1st year: $105,000
Summer associate: $7,500/month

THE BUZZ
WHAT ATTORNEYS AT OTHER FIRMS ARE SAYING ABOUT THIS FIRM

• "Good regional firm"
• "Work farm"
• "Good work, especially First Amendment"
• "Average"

THE SCOOP

Founded in 1916, Baker & Hostetler LLP has expanded steadily outside its Ohio borders, adding its two latest offices in New York and Costa Mesa in 2001. The following year, the firm launched the employee relations consulting team BakerER, a natural outgrowth of the firm's established expertise in corporate law. Later in 2002, B&H represented SPX Corp. in its attempts to force Yahoo! to reveal the identities of two anonymous message board participants alleged to have revealed SPX trade secrets on the web. The firm is also the primary lobbyist for Major League Baseball in Washington, D.C., and recently stepped up to the plate to lobby Congress against intervening as team owners considered plans to eliminate unprofitable teams from the league.

GETTING HIRED

"Someone who wants sophisticated work but also wants a pleasant environment in which to work" should have no problem fitting in at Baker & Hostetler, suggest insiders. "It is probably easier to get hired if you attend a school with national recognition," say associates, and many insiders believe landing a job at B&H "has been getting much more competitive." The firm recruits heavily on campus – especially in the Midwest, but also at prominent schools near all of its offices – and follows up with a full day of interviews at the firm. Minority students at ten select law schools can also apply for the Paul D. White Scholarship, which includes a guaranteed summer clerkship.

OUR SURVEY SAYS

"I wouldn't want to be anywhere else," say several B&H associates. "Working in a large firm isn't always a picnic," an insider allows, "but the people here create an environment that is relaxed and fun." The firm has "no stiff hierarchy" and "most everyone gets along." Partners "are very willing to give informal training" as long as associates communicate what they need. Though one associate admits "you do hear sexist comments" occasionally, he and others firmly believe "women get a fair shake and a good opportunity to practice here." A Houston insider points out the office managing partner is a woman and the firm has "a number of" female partners besides.

Most B&H associates believe the firm offers them a competitive salary. "While I do believe it could be raised slightly throughout the associate levels," says one source, "I am aware the economy hasn't been stellar of late, and we are very well compensated." B&H insiders are also largely satisfied with the hours they work. In fact, some say in these tough economic times they could use more work, not less. The offices are comfortable, especially since "you have your own office from your first day." The Cleveland office may look "a little '70s" from the outside, but "the space overall is functional and clean." D.C. associates brag about "new furniture and very tasteful yet conservative décor."

Katten Muchin Zavis Rosenman

525 West Monroe Street
Suite 1600
Chicago, IL 60661-3693
Phone: (312) 902-5200
www.kmz.com

LOCATIONS

Chicago, IL (HQ)
Charlotte, NC
Los Angeles, CA
Newark, NJ
New York, NY
Palo Alto, CA
Washington, DC

MAJOR DEPARTMENTS/PRACTICES

Corporate • Customs & International Trade •
Entertainment • Environment • Financial Services •
Health Care • Intellectual Property • Litigation • Real
Estate • Sports Law & Sports Facilities • Tax • Wealth
Management

THE STATS

No. of attorneys: 600+
No. of offices: 7
Summer associate offers: 34 out of 37 (2002)
National Managing Partner: Vincent A.F. Sergi
Hiring Partners: Andy Small and Brian Richards

RANKING RECAP

Best in Region
#10 - Chicago

NOTABLE PERKS

- One-month sabbatical after five years of service
- Free coffee, bagels and soft drinks
- Discounted legal expenses, including home closing costs
- Subsidized cafeteria

EMPLOYMENT CONTACT

Chicago
Ms. Kelley Lynch, Director of Legal Recruiting
Phone: (312) 902-5526
E-mail: kelley.lynch@kmz.com

New York
Ms. Kim McHugh, Legal Recruiting Manager
Phone: (212) 940-6386

Los Angeles
Ms. Donna Francis, Legal Recruiting Manager
Phone: (310) 788-4766

Washington, DC
Ms. Judy Brown, Legal Recruiting Manager
Phone: (202) 625-3652

BASE SALARY

Chicago, IL
1st year: $125,000
2nd year: $130,000
3rd year: $142,000
4th year: $157,000
5th year: $170,000
6th year: $180,000
7th year: $190,000
Summer associate: $2,403/week

THE BUZZ
WHAT ATTORNEYS AT OTHER FIRMS ARE SAYING ABOUT THIS FIRM

- "Chicago giant"
- "Jury still out on the merger"
- "Well known, good work"
- "Everyone leaves"

THE SCOOP

Formed in March 2002 through a merger of New York-based Rosenman & Colin and Chicago-based Katten Muchin Zavis, KMZ Rosenman is one of the 100 largest firms in the country. While the merger was successful in helping the firm gain a foothold in the New York market, KMZR suffered an associate attrition rate of 33 percent, according to a survey by *The National Law Journal*. The combined firm has a strong presence in technology, corporate and entertainment law. Clients include Disney, Miramax, Showtime and *Simpsons* creator Matt Groening. The firm was the first in Illinois to hire a partner dedicated to working on pro bono matters full time, and KMZR continues to advise charities and individuals in the communities surrounding its offices. KMZR also sponsors community events, most notably the Making Strides Against Breast Cancer Walk.

GETTING HIRED

"Our firm is looking to hire bright, inquisitive associates who are outgoing, have exceptional communication skills and are eager to work hard and learn," an associate in the Chicago office informs us. According to a litigator, "We look to students coming out of the more prestigious schools but also seriously consider top students from local law schools." "We specifically try to avoid those who do not play well with others. This is the highest hurdle a candidate must pass to be competitive," a senior associate reveals. At the callback stage, candidates should expect to "meet with a combination of partners and associates." Often, would-be KMZR-ers will be interviewed by attorneys in departments about which they express an interest.

OUR SURVEY SAYS

Insiders at KMZR report, "The firm culture is professional, open and cordial," "aggressive" and "friendly, but not overly so." Some associates who characterize the firm as "generally laid back" caution it is becoming "more and more on edge and tense as the economic downturn continues." "Attorneys do not tend to socialize outside the office," "except for the Christmas party" and "occasional cocktail parties within the office." Associates brag about receiving "great responsibility and tons of client contact." "There is an overall 'get the deal done' mood here, which makes things fast-paced and interesting. Such work is more fulfilling because it feels like you are actually doing something." Some associates say "the workflow can be unreliable," but generally they are "satisfied with the number of hours" they spend at work. "When you're busy, it can be brutal," says a Chicago associate. "But there are down times when it's not expected that you show up to the office." Few at KMZR report problems meeting the 2,000 minimum billable hours requirement. "The firm does an excellent job at working with you so that you have access to the office from home. This technology allows me to work hard, provide solid client service and at the same time spend time with my family," shares a source.

Arent Fox Kintner Plotkin & Kahn, PLLC

1050 Connecticut Avenue, NW
Washington, DC 20036-5339
Phone: (202) 857-6000
www.arentfox.com

LOCATIONS

Washington, DC (HQ)
New York, NY

MAJOR DEPARTMENTS/PRACTICES

General Business
International
Litigation & Dispute Resolution
Public Policy
Regulatory
Technology

THE STATS

No. of attorneys: 275
No. of offices: 2
Summer associate offers: 16 out of 16 (2002)
Chairman: William R. Charyk
Hiring Attorney: Quana Jew

RANKING RECAP

Best in Region
#14 - Washington, DC

Quality of Life
#5 - Hours
#7 - Pro Bono
#8 - Associate/Partner Relations
#13 - Satisfaction
#18 - Best 20 Law Firms to Work For

Best in Diversity
#2 - Diversity for Gays and Lesbians
#3 - Overall Diversity
#5 - Diversity for Women
#7 - Diversity for Minorities

NOTABLE PERKS

- Friday happy hours
- Suite at the MCI Center
- Free on-site gym (D.C.)

EMPLOYMENT CONTACTS

Washington, DC
Ms. Amber Handman
Attorney Recruitment and Development Manager
Phone: (202) 857-6146
Fax: (202) 857-6395
E-mail: DCAttorneyRecruit@arentfox.com

New York
Ms. Kay Carson
Director of Administration
Phone: (212) 484-3900
Fax: (212) 484-3990
E-mail: NYAttorneyRecruit@arentfox.com

THE BUZZ
WHAT ATTORNEYS AT OTHER FIRMS ARE SAYING ABOUT THIS FIRM

- "Small but powerful D.C. firm"
- "Troubled"
- "Not sure about future direction"
- "Should be better known"

BASE SALARY

Washington, DC; New York, NY
1st year: $125,000
Summer associate: $2,300/week

THE SCOOP

Founded in Washington, D.C., in 1942, Arent Fox Kintner Plotkin & Kahn, PLLC has developed a strong reputation for its government relations and regulatory practices as well as IP, real estate and advertising law. The 275-lawyer firm sent two former employees to Capitol Hill in early 2003; Missouri Republican Jim Talent won a Senate seat while Democrat Chris Van Hollen became a U.S. Representative for Maryland. Meanwhile, two former senators, John Culver and Dale Bumpers, are on hand as counsel, as is Bonnie Campbell, a former Justice Department official in the Clinton administration. Firm clients have included governments, agencies or state corporations of a number of countries and global institutions including the World Bank, the Inter-American Development Bank and International Finance Corporation.

GETTING HIRED

"We get hundreds of resumes each month," says a senior insider at Arent Fox. Candidates who are invited to interview with the firm can expect to speak with four or five attorneys over the course of a single day. "Strong academics are a must," but sources insist the firm "does a good job of considering the candidate as a whole and not merely grades or scores." Insiders cite "personality, interests, diligence and friendliness" as important traits. The firm is said to seek attorneys who are "highly capable – cases are leanly staffed so associates get significant responsibility quickly."

OUR SURVEY SAYS

Arent Fox is a "good firm for those wanting to work in a large firm and yet have time to see the kids and/or the significant other." Associates say "hard work is encouraged" but so are "healthy working relationships," with strong attendance at weekly happy hours and additional socializing outside the office. Sources at the firm describe partners as "pleasant [and] eager to teach." First- and second-years aver, "Partners and associates bend over backwards to give advice and guidance." The firm's 1,900-hour billable hours minimum is deemed "favorable in comparison to other" firms, with bonuses tied to how much you work beyond that. "No one punches a clock around here," so if you need to leave, feel free.

Arent Fox pays less "for demanding less time," and that suits most insiders just fine. "I know I could go across the street and command a higher salary," states one, "but I also know that I would have to give up things that are more important." Still, a few malcontents grumble that their salary "is not keeping pace with the recent substantial increases in partner compensation." Just about everybody is committed to pro bono work, "from the chairman and managing partner on down." Up to 150 hours of pro bono counts towards hour requirements. Reports one associate, "You don't have to do anything to find a project. The firm comes looking for you to help out."

Mintz Levin Cohn Ferris Glovsky and Popeo, P.C.

One Financial Center
Boston, MA 02111
Phone: (617) 542-6000
www.mintz.com

LOCATIONS

Boston, MA (HQ)
New Haven, CT
New York, NY
Reston, VA
Washington, DC

MAJOR DEPARTMENTS/PRACTICES

Bankruptcy & Commercial
Biotechnology
Business & Public Finance
Communications
Employment, Labor & Benefits Immigration
Environmental
Health Care
High Technology
Immigration
Intellectual Property & Patent
Litigation
Real Estate
Tax & Trusts & Estates
Telecommunications

THE STATS

No. of attorneys: 502
No. of offices: 5
Chairman: R. Robert Popeo
Hiring Partners: Timothy J. Langella and Charles E. Carey

RANKING RECAP

Best in Region
#7 - Boston

Best in Practice
#6 (tie) - Technology/Internet/E-Commerce

NOTABLE PERKS

- Bar expenses
- Paternity leave
- On-site emergency daycare

EMPLOYMENT CONTACT

Ms. Claire N. Suchecki
HR Manager, Attorney Recruitment
Phone: (617) 348-1859
Fax: (617) 542-2241
E-mail: csuchecki@mintz.com

BASE SALARY

Boston, MA
1st year: $125,000
2nd year: $135,000
3rd year: $145,000
4th year: $155,000
5th year: $170,000
6th year: $175,000
7th year: $180,000
8th year: $190,000
Summer associate: $2,400/week

THE BUZZ
WHAT ATTORNEYS AT OTHER FIRMS ARE SAYING ABOUT THIS FIRM

- "Nice place to work"
- "They're hurting"
- "Respected, diverse"
- "Hello, layoffs"

THE SCOOP

Despite the decline of the tech sector, the expertise of Boston's Mintz, Levin, Cohn, Ferris, Glovsky and Popeo, P.C. continues to be in demand by clients such as Cablevision and America Online. But that doesn't mean the firm hasn't felt the economic pressure. In April 2003, the firm laid off approximately 40 employees, including eight attorneys. The cuts followed two rounds of layoffs in 2002 in which 17 attorneys were cut. That same month, managing partner Irwin Heller stepped down, handing over the reins to a team of four managing directors who will be supervised by President and Chairman R. Robert Popeo. A group of retailers, including CVS, Brooks Pharmacy and Shaw's Supermarkets are relying on the firm to help them fight a prescription drug tax imposed by the state of Massachusetts.

GETTING HIRED

"Academic performance matters" when it comes to hiring at Mintz Levin, "but drive, enthusiasm and overall likeability will seal the deal." The firm conducts interviews at several highly ranked East Coast schools, including Harvard, Boston University, Cornell and Georgetown. At callback interviews, candidates participate in "a series of 30-minute, one-on-one interviews with three to five Mintz Levin attorneys from a variety of practice areas," according to the firm's web site.

OUR SURVEY SAYS

Mintz Levin "is relatively laid back, with most people dressing casually. Doors are typically open, and people seem friendly and approachable." Insiders say the firm is "friendly," "entrepreneurial, collegial, frank" and "open." There is "some socializing," but "a lot of people" simply "go home to their families after work." An IP attorney informs us, "I've been given great control over the amount and type of work I receive," while another brags, "I've had the opportunity to handle and take to trial a number of cases." When it comes to pro bono, Mintz Levin is "one of the most active and supportive environments of all the big firms," says a first-year. According to a senior associate, "Virtually all legitimate pro bono proposals are approved for creditable/billable time."

Insiders lament the impact of the economy on Mintz Levin's culture. "In a bad economy that is showing no signs of recovery, people are on edge and continue to worry about additional layoffs," a Boston associate confides. Says another, "Morale among associates is very, very low. Most associates are paranoid that they're going to get laid off at any moment." A litigation associate concerned about succeeding at the firm while raising a family observes, "The firm is fairly diverse in terms of women, however male and female attorneys who take time off to have children seem to be penalized." "The mentoring of women by women is very good," though in the opinion of one female attorney, "the firm could do a much better job making life more manageable for women who are mothers."

Kramer Levin Naftalis & Frankel LLP

919 Third Avenue
New York, NY 10022
Phone: (212) 715-9100
www.kramerlevin.com

LOCATIONS

New York, NY (HQ)
Paris

MAJOR DEPARTMENTS/PRACTICES

Advertising
Antitrust
Appellate & Constitutional Litigation
Banking
Corporate
Creditors Rights & Bankruptcy
Employment & Labor
Intellectual Property
International
Land Use
Litigation

THE STATS

No. of attorneys: 260
No. of offices: 2
Firm Co-Chairs: Ezra G. Levin and Gary P. Naftalis
Hiring Partner: Barry H. Berke

NOTABLE PERKS

- Late-night dinners and car rides
- Reimbursement for computer purchases
- New business referral bonuses

EMPLOYMENT CONTACT

Ms. Pamela H. Nelson
Associate Director of Legal Recruiting
Phone: (212) 715-9213
Fax: (212) 715-8000
E-mail: pnelson@kramerlevin.com

BASE SALARY

New York, NY
1st year: $125,000
Summer associate: $2,404/week

THE BUZZ
WHAT ATTORNEYS AT OTHER FIRMS ARE SAYING ABOUT THIS FIRM

- "Quality mid-size firm"
- "Average"
- "Good work environment"
- "Wannabes"

THE SCOOP

Except for a small outpost in Paris, Kramer Levin Naftalis & Frankel has concentrated strictly on its midtown Manhattan office since opening shop in 1968. (However, the firm did expand its international reach in September 2002 through a strategic alliance with London-based Berwin Leighton.) The firm suffered some notoriety in 2002 in connection with the scandals at Tyco, one of its longtime clients, when it became known that one of the law firm's former partners was also a member of the conglomerate's board of directors – and had been compensated by Kramer Levin based in part by how much work Tyco sent the firm's way. In more upbeat news, the firm knocked Martina Hingis' multimillion-dollar lawsuit against Italian athletic shoemakers Sergio Tacchini out of the courts. Hingis had blamed Tacchini's products for the foot injuries that cut short her career.

GETTING HIRED

Kramer Levin recruits on law school campuses up and down the East Coast, plus inland excursions to Michigan and the University of Chicago. "At least in the litigation department, this firm emphasizes hiring former law clerks," offers one insider. If you make the initial cut, you'll be invited to the office for a half-day of interviews with attorneys from various practice areas, then taken out to lunch with two attorneys. Participants in the firm's summer program may find themselves playing a substantial role in pro bono cases under attorney supervision.

OUR SURVEY SAYS

The vibe is "cordial and respectful" at Kramer Levin, though pressure may be on the rise. The prevailing culture "used to be lifestyle," but "pressure to work longer hours is increasing." Still, sources suggest, the workload is "very manageable," and "people appreciate your hard work." They go on to say "most of the partners are extremely approachable." Though "the firm has recently begun instituting more formal training programs," training is largely informal, derived from "more responsibility on pro bono cases or smaller litigations." A senior associate reports, "Most cases are staffed 1:1, so there can be a significant opportunity for learning."

The firm has few female partners, but one associate suggests the situation is "a factor of women's choices not to be partner rather than the firm's decision." This source goes on to note the existence of "generous part-time work plans," in which other insiders observe many senior women associates at the firm participating. After your first year at Kramer Levin, you'll receive your own office with a window. Associates appreciate that, even if the space is "a little shabby" and decorated in "five shades of gray." They also note the firm's lease is about to expire, and hope the new space, when it comes, is "designed to be more efficient."

Thelen Reid & Priest LLP

875 Third Avenue
New York, NY 10022
Phone: (212) 603-2000

101 Second Street, Suite 1800
San Francisco, CA 94105
Phone: (415) 371-1200
www.thelenreid.com

LOCATIONS

Los Angeles, CA
Morristown, NJ
New York, NY
San Francisco, CA
Silicon Valley, CA
Washington, DC

MAJOR DEPARTMENTS/PRACTICES

Business & Finance • Commercial Litigation •
Construction & Government Contracts • Government
Affairs • Labor & Employment • Project & Asset
Finance • Real Estate • Tax, Benefits, Trusts & Estates

THE STATS

No. of attorneys: 421
No. of offices: 6
Summer associate offers: 29 out of 31 (2002)
Managing Partner/Chairman: Thomas Igoe, Jr.
Hiring Partners: Richard Lapping (San Francisco);
Sharon Carlstedt and Walter Godlewski (New York)

RANKING RECAP

Quality of Life
#6 - Offices

NOTABLE PERKS

- Paternity leave
- Bar review course and stipend while studying
- Domestic partner benefits
- Moving expenses

EMPLOYMENT CONTACTS

East Coast
Ms. Diane Amato
Attorney Recruiting Manager
Phone: (212) 603-2000
Fax: (212) 541-1518
E-mail: damato@thelenreid.com

West Coast
Ms. Holly Saydah
Attorney Recruiting Manager
Phone: (415) 371-1200
Fax: (415) 369-8794
E-mail: hsaydah@thelenreid.com

BASE SALARY

All offices
1st year: $125,000
2nd year: $125,000-$135,000
3rd year: $130,000-$150,000
4th year: $135,000-$165,000
5th year: $140,000-$185,000
6th year: $145,000-$195,000
7th year: $150,000-$205,000
8th year: $155,000-$210,000
9th year: $160,000-$215,000
Summer associate: $2,400/week

THE BUZZ
WHAT ATTORNEYS AT OTHER FIRMS ARE SAYING ABOUT THIS FIRM

- "Great place to work"
- "Second-tier"
- "Very gay friendly, super cool"
- "Overrated"

THE SCOOP

Thelen Reid & Priest LLP has carved a niche as legal advisers to companies in the infrastructure, utilities and construction industries. And the firm's litigation, tax and employment groups and growing entertainment practice make for an interesting mix. Clients include Calpine Corp. and the Bechtel Group. Had San Francisco won the coveted slot to represent the United States in the international competition to host the 2012 Olympic Games, Thelen Reid would have been poised to receive a surge of new Olympic-related work. The firm was one of the city's most loyal supporters, donating office space and attorney time to its bid to be named host city. As of April 2003, the firm has a new chairman at the helm: Thomas Igoe, Jr.

GETTING HIRED

As Thelen Reid's "profitability and reputation post-merger have evolved, the caliber of schools and candidates has evolved as well," insiders say. The firm, however, "still places a premium on a good fit, rather than swooning over a sterling resume or transcript." A "limited number of slots have made" the firm "very selective about the candidates" they accept. "Intelligent and hardworking but easygoing attorneys" who "are easy to work with" stand the best chance of receiving an offer. Says a first-year, "The firm has become much more selective in its law school hiring. The same is true of lateral hiring but might be attributable to the glut of unemployed lawyers in the area."

OUR SURVEY SAYS

"The firm is very laid back culturally, while at the same time people take their work and responsibilities to their clients very seriously." That's "the perfect combination in my book," says a fourth-year. "Thelen is a great place to work. It treats associates very well, both in terms of compensation and workloads," says a senior associate. There's quite a bit of "socializing in the halls but not a lot of socializing after work." "The firm asks you to work hard but does not sweat the small stuff like working from home once in a while," reports a New York associate. "The partners are very, very pleased if an associate bills 1,950," a San Franciscan reports. "If you work a lot of hours you can get a big bonus, but if you don't work a lot of hours, they won't show you the door," a midlevel tells us. A senior associate agrees, "While there is some pressure to meet your hourly minimums, there is not much pressure to work astronomical hours."

The firm's offices in New York, Los Angeles and Silicon Valley recently relocated, and associates are delighted with the new digs. Insiders say the offices are "impressive, functional and comfortable." Although New Yorkers gripe "the offices are smaller" than their previous space, they're impressed by the "state of the art technological capabilities." And their offices may not be brand-spanking new, but San Francisco associates are eager to report "the décor is outstanding."

Squire, Sanders, & Dempsey

4900 Key Tower
127 Public Square
Cleveland, OH 44114-1304
Phone: (216) 479-8500
www.ssd.com

LOCATIONS

Cleveland, OH (HQ) • Cincinnati, OH • Columbus, OH •
Houston, TX • Los Angeles, CA • Miami, FL • New
York, NY • Palo Alto, CA • Phoenix, AZ • San
Francisco, CA • Tampa, FL • Tysons Corner, VA •
Washington, DC • Beijing • Bratislava • Brussels •
Budapest • Hong Kong • Kyiv • London • Madrid •
Milan • Moscow • Prague • Rio de Janeiro • Taipei •
Tokyo

MAJOR DEPARTMENTS/PRACTICES

Business Law • Commercial Litigation •
Communications • Energy • Environmental Law •
General Practice • Health Care & Life Sciences •
Intellectual Property • International Business Law •
International Dispute Resolution • Labor & Employment
Law • Mergers & Acquisitions • Municipal Bond/Public
Authority Financing • Real Estate • Restructuring/
Bankruptcy • Securities Law • Tax Law

THE STATS

No. of attorneys: 750
No. of offices: 27
Summer associate offers: 31 out of 37 (2002)
Chairman: R. Thomas Stanton
Hiring Partner: Joseph M. Crabb

THE BUZZ
WHAT ATTORNEYS AT OTHER FIRMS ARE SAYING ABOUT THIS FIRM

- "Congenial atmosphere"
- "Run of the mill"
- "Good international coverage"
- "Struggling to get to the next level"

NOTABLE PERKS

- Donuts every Friday morning
- Bar review expenses

EMPLOYMENT CONTACT

Ms. Jane C. Murphy
Legal Personnel & Prof. Development Manager
Phone: (216) 802-7571
E-mail: jamurphy@ssd.com

BASE SALARY

Cincinnati, Cleveland, Columbus, OH; Phoenix, AZ
1st year: $110,000

**Los Angeles, Palo Alto, San Francisco, CA;
Washington, DC**
1st year: $125,000

THE SCOOP

Founded in 1890, Squire, Sanders & Dempsey has charted a path of steady growth. The firm has more than 750 attorneys in 27 locations worldwide, including a prominent practice in Eastern Europe and Russia. Recent clients include the official committee of Enron's unsecured creditors. Attorneys in the firm's Cleveland office executed a full court press against the Ohio High School Athletic Association. The OHSAA had revoked teenage hoops sensation LeBron James' amateur eligibility after he accepted some collectible jerseys as a gift from the owner of a local sporting goods store. Squire got James back in his uniform in time for the state championships.

GETTING HIRED

"Standards are high" at Squire, and one associate passes along rumors the firm "will turn down a candidate from a top-ten law school if they don't think the writing sample is up to par." Other sources confirm Squire "tends to favor candidates from very highly regarded law schools" with "an emphasis on prior judicial clerkships or significant writing experience." An insider in Phoenix considers Squire "the most competitive [in the city] with respect to hiring." A colleague there agrees, adding, "In this economy, only litigators are being hired." But, a midlevel associate stresses, "It's not a snobby place." As a lateral hire, he recalls, "they seemed to put far greater emphasis on my previous experience than on grades or the prestige of my law school."

OUR SURVEY SAYS

"Anything goes" at Squire, where "you are free to be yourself as long as you do the work and put in the time." Attorneys in offices out west suggest they are "much more laid back" than their Ohio counterparts, with one San Francisco associate revealing she and her colleagues "typically do lunch or midday coffee runs" together. It's not a party scene, though; the "quiet and somewhat intense" associates "skew nerdy" (at least in Cleveland) and "rarely socialize after hours." "Time demands are high" throughout the firm, and the "large billable requirement [2,000 hours] doesn't leave much time for anything else." Some suggest the problem isn't how much they're expected to work, but the "extremely slow workload" that makes meeting the goal difficult. Base salary is "highly competitive," though insiders bemoan the "minimal discretionary" bonuses.

Squire partners are "very respectful of weekend and evening plans and try not to overburden you if you let them know you have something coming up." But though everything is "smiles, smiles, smiles" around the office, at least one litigator worries his bosses are so civil "you'd never know if a partner was angry with you or dissatisfied with your work." One area in which associates greatly appreciate partner input is their on-the-job training. "I have received more training in my first year here than in three years at another firm," says one lateral hire. Another grateful attorney declares, "I've never been thrown into a situation I felt I wasn't prepared to handle."

McGuireWoods LLP

One James Center
901 East Cary Street
Richmond, VA 23219-4030
Phone: (804) 775-1000
www.mcguirewoods.com

LOCATIONS

Richmond, VA (HQ)
Atlanta, GA • Baltimore, MD • Charlotte, NC •
Charlottesville, VA • Chicago, IL • Jacksonville, FL •
New York, NY • Norfolk, VA • Pittsburgh, PA • Tysons
Corner, VA • Washington, DC • Almaty, Kazakhstan •
Brussels

MAJOR DEPARTMENTS/PRACTICES

Commercial Litigation • Corporate Services • Financial
Services • International • Labor & Employment •
Product Liability & Litigation Management • Real Estate
& Environmental • Taxation & Employee Benefits •

THE STATS

No. of attorneys: 542
No. of offices: 14
Summer associate offers: 21 out of 24 (2002)
Chairman: Robert L. Burrus, Jr.
Managing Partner: William J. Strickland
Hiring Attorney: Jacquelyn E. Stone

RANKING RECAP

Best in Diversity
#17 - Diversity for Minorities

NOTABLE PERKS

- Subsidized cell phone
- $1,000 CLE budget
- $10,000 bonus for JD/MBAs
- Flexible spending accounts

EMPLOYMENT CONTACTS

Ms. Ann McGhee
Attorney Recruiting Manager
Phone: (804) 775-7628
E-mail: amcghee@mcguirewoods.com

Ms. Dusti L. Plunkett
Attorney Recruitment Manager (Washington, DC)
Phone: (202) 857-1739
E-mail: dplunkett@mcguirewoods.com

BASE SALARY

Richmond, VA
1st year: $95,000
Summer associate: $1,800/week

THE BUZZ
WHAT ATTORNEYS AT OTHER FIRMS ARE SAYING ABOUT THIS FIRM

- "Competent lawyers, great offices"
- "Very old school and *very* Virginia"
- "Excellent firm"
- "Not prime time"

THE SCOOP

Founded in 1834, Virginia-based McGuireWoods LLP boasts 14 domestic and international offices. The firm's seven practice departments are augmented by McGuireWoods Consulting, a subsidiary that helps businesses and organizations influence policymaking. Some of the firm's major clients include Bank of America, CSX, DuPont and Dominion Resources. The firm recently assisted Dominion Virginia Power in reaching an agreement with the EPA and Department of Justice to improve air quality by settling allegations made as part of an EPA enforcement effort targeting coal-fired utilities for alleged violations of the Clean Air Act. In 2003, for the second year in a row, BTI Consulting Group recognized McGuireWoods as one of the nation's top 30 law firms for client service – the only law firm with the "best of the best" distinction in the client focus category.

GETTING HIRED

"If you've been given a callback, it's really about your fit with the attorneys and staff in the firm," says a McGuireWoods associate. A midlevel gives an example of how not to act during the interview: "I interviewed one lateral who had a great resume but got roasted because she came off as arrogant and a gunner. We really look for team players." When considering candidates, the firm looks at "school, grades, writing, personality" and that southern favorite, "common sense." Moreover, "maturity," "collegiality" and a "commitment to the geographic area" are important.

OUR SURVEY SAYS

Insiders say McGuireWoods' vibe is "typically southern: formal and reserved," yet "incredibly friendly and approachable." "Our office is laid back, but overall I think our relationships are somewhat formal, and lawyers do not tend to socialize with one another," a third-year observes, although another associate says, "The associates are a close-knit group and socialize often together, which makes it a fun place to work." A midlevel offers this assessment: "It really is like a dysfunctional family: well-intentioned, mostly, loves its members but unfortunately in the end is more concerned with its standing in the community. Plus, Dad has a tight grip on the wallet."

"The nice thing about this firm is that the stated billable-hour requirement is what they actually expect of you. They don't tell you to bill 1,950 with the unsaid expectation that you bill 2,100." A litigator adds that "bonuses are distributed after 2,000 hours." One associate believes corporate associates "are penalized for not having hours, when they don't have a lot of control over the situation" due to the dearth of work available. While most insiders think junior associates are paid well, especially "based upon a 1,950 hour requirement and the culture" at the firm, others say "the yearly raises for associates are not all that great." (The firm recently did away with lockstep salary increases for more senior associates.) However, attorneys at all levels note "arbitrary differences" in salaries "between smaller satellite offices and bigger offices."

Wiley Rein & Fielding LLP

1776 K Street, NW
Washington, DC 20006
Phone: (202) 719-7000
www.wrf.com

LOCATIONS

Washington, DC (HQ)
McLean, VA

MAJOR DEPARTMENTS/PRACTICES

Advertising • Antitrust • Aviation & Aerospace •
Bankruptcy • Business & Finance • Communications •
Education • Election Law • Employment & Labor •
Energy • Food & Drug • Franchise • Government Affairs
• Government Contracts • Health Care • Insurance •
Intellectual Property • International Trade • Litigation •
Postal • Privacy • White Collar Defense

THE STATS

No. of attorneys: 215
No. of offices: 2
Summer associate offers: 18 out of 18 (2002)
Managing Partner: Richard E. Wiley
Hiring Partner: Scott M. McCaleb

RANKING RECAP

Best in Region
#11 - Washington, DC

NOTABLE PERKS

- Drink up, the Tang's free!
- $500 annual technology allowance
- Pastries every Monday and Thursday
- Wine and cheese parties, group lunches

EMPLOYMENT CONTACT

Ms. Jill Bartelt
Attorney Recruitment Manager
Phone: (202) 719-7548
Fax: (202) 719-7049
E-mail: jbartelt@wrf.com

BASE SALARY

Washington, DC
1st year: $110,000; $125,000*
2nd year: $120,000; $135,000
3rd year: $130,000; $145,000
4th year: $140,000; $155,000
5th year: $150,000; $165,000
6th year: $160,000; $175,000
7th year: $170,000; $185,000
Summer associate: $2,400/week

*Two-tier salary structure based on 1,800 and
1,950 billable-hour benchmarks.*

THE BUZZ
WHAT ATTORNEYS AT OTHER FIRMS ARE SAYING ABOUT THIS FIRM

- "One of the best telecom firms"
- "Republican National Committee mouthpiece"
- "Better and better"
- "Pomposity at its finest"

THE SCOOP

D.C.-based Wiley Rein & Fielding LLP celebrates its 20th anniversary in 2003, capping off a second decade in which its attorney roster tripled in size. The 225-attorney firm has a stellar reputation in communications law, but also excels in insurance, government contracts and international trade law and beefed up its bankruptcy practice in the spring of 2002 by absorbing area firm Gold Morrison & Laughlin. In the courtrooms, Wiley Rein landed a major decision for Verizon Northwest, persuading a federal court to suspend Washington state laws banning companies from using "customer proprietary network information" to market new services to existing customers.

GETTING HIRED

"If you are a judicial clerk or attended Harvard," quips a senior associate, "welcome to Wiley." And he isn't kidding; if anything, "the firm is becoming even more selective, especially with regard to school snobbery." Regional recruiting is "limited," sources tell us, and "if you do not come from a top-rate school, you need to bring something unique to the table." What might that be? "Grades, grades, grades," or "very good people skills." Insiders also hint "strong interest in a particular practice group" will increase a candidate's chances.

OUR SURVEY SAYS

"If NPR were a conservative law firm," says one associate, it'd be Wiley Rein: "bright, friendly, not really outgoing." A senior associate describes how the firm "reflects the personality of chairperson Dick Wiley. It is a family-friendly place," this corporate attorney says, "where folks treat each other with respect, where the professional standards are very high and where we turn off the lights at a respectable hour in the evening."

Hours are "much better than I thought they'd be," admits a first-year. Wiley Rein offers a two-tier compensation structure and puts "very little pressure on new associates about hours." The firm's attorneys like the system, though one wonders "if the firm wouldn't rather have everyone on the upper track." Compensation is perceived as "right at the market" for D.C., though associates gripe about "pathetic" bonuses and the "opaque" criteria for their distribution. "If you want to work 2,500 hours a year," suggests one insider, "you will probably get a bigger bonus somewhere else."

Wiley Rein's downtown location "was premier D.C. office space in the 1970s," but "the building is really starting to show its age." But every first-year gets his or her own office and, says one, "I certainly would feel comfortable bringing a client here." Others support the firm's decision to "not try to impress people by the grandness of the office," a philosophy they view as putting more money in their own pockets.

Preston Gates & Ellis LLP

5000 Columbia Center
701 Fifth Avenue
Seattle, WA 98104-7078
Phone: (206) 623-7580
www.prestongates.com

LOCATIONS

Seattle, WA (HQ)
Anchorage, AK
Coeur d'Alene, ID
Orange County, CA
Portland, OR
San Francisco, CA
Spokane, WA
Washington, DC*
Hong Kong

* As Preston Gates Ellis & Rouvelas Meeds LLP

MAJOR DEPARTMENTS/PRACTICES

Corporate/Business • Employment & Labor • Environmental/Land Use • Litigation • Municipal • Public Policy • Real Estate/Bankruptcy • Technology & Intellectual Property

THE STATS

No. of attorneys: 424
No. of offices: 9
Summer associate offers: 14 out of 18 (2002)
Chairman: Richard Ford
Managing Partner: B. Gerald Johnson
Hiring Partner: Jamie D. Pedersen

THE BUZZ
WHAT ATTORNEYS AT OTHER FIRMS ARE SAYING ABOUT THIS FIRM

- "Very good Northwest firm"
- "Second fiddle"
- "The firm Microsoft built"
- "Dwindling player"

RANKING RECAP

Best in Region
#2 - Pacific Northwest

Quality of Life
#4 - Offices

Best in Diversity
#10 - Overall Diversity
#10 - Diversity for Women
#12 - Diversity for Gays & Lesbians

NOTABLE PERKS

- 401(k) match (except DC office)
- $1,200 technology allowance every two years
- Free Starbucks and soda, subsidized cafeteria
- Free transit pass/parking for midlevels and up

EMPLOYMENT CONTACT

Ms. Kristine Immordino
Director, Legal Recruiting
Phone: (206) 623-7580
Fax: (206) 623-7022
E-mail: krisi@prestongates.com

BASE SALARY

Seattle, WA
1st year: $95,000
2nd year: $100,000
Summer associate $1,900/week

THE SCOOP

Preston Gates & Ellis was formed through the merger of two revered Seattle firms in 1990 and carved a niche for itself as a premier source of legal advice for established and emerging tech companies while maintaining its more traditional practices in litigation, corporate, real estate, employment and environmental law. Though slow business forced the firm to close its Los Angeles office in August 2002, the firm anticipates continued growth and has been able to keep its revenues consistent. Preston is currently representing alternative newspaper publisher Village Voice Media in connection with potential antitrust violations in a deal struck with fellow publisher New Times Media. Other clients include Microsoft, the Bill and Melinda Gates Foundation, travel site Expedia.com, VoiceStream Wireless and Philips Oral Healthcare.

GETTING HIRED

"Preston looks for the top candidates and will not hire someone just to fill a slot," says a second-year. A first-year tells us, "It is quite difficult to come into Preston Gates as a first-year associate without some pre-existing connection to the Pacific Northwest." Preston Gates "employ[s] a rigorous selection process aimed not only at finding quality attorneys but also at finding individuals who share our priorities and will fit well in the firm's culture." The process is so rigorous that "fit with the entire group is necessary," a midlevel insists, "from partners to legal assistants."

OUR SURVEY SAYS

A litigation associate considers Preston Gates "the right blend of lifestyle [and] good, challenging work." "The firm also seems genuinely to care about its associates," a fourth-year adds. "I think I am extremely lucky to work at a firm where the partners are respectful to younger associates, the work is engaging and varied and I have genuine friends among my co-workers," raves a second-year. "To the rest of the world, the culture is laid back, but it's far more uptight on the inside," counters an associate in the business and finance group. A corporate insider worries "the economic climate in the Pacific Northwest has affected the culture a little."

The "work provides insufficient opportunity for involvement with sophisticated corporate finance work and minimal exposure to public clients with the exception of Microsoft," remarks a Seattle associate. Several insiders express worry that there's an "increasing emphasis to market, market, market, yet at the end of the year little value is placed" on the amount of time attorneys spend working on non-billable business development projects. "The salary is competitive for Seattle," say insiders, but, sighs a fourth-year, the city "is a relatively low-dollar market." However, some associates are content with lower salaries that give them more freedom than "higher paid associates who work all the time."

WHEN YOUR SOLE MISSION
IS TO BUILD ONE OF THE
MOST TRUSTED, DEPENDABLE
AND SUCCESSFUL LAW FIRMS
IN THE WORLD...
YOU TAKE IT PERSONALLY.

At Reed Smith, we foster an environment where personal growth is just as important as professional success. It's just one of the reasons why we attract some of the best and brightest talent in the world. For information about employment opportunities at Reed Smith, please visit our website www.reedsmith.com/careers.

ReedSmith

It's not just business. *It's personal.*℠

LONDON
NEW YORK
LOS ANGELES
SAN FRANCISCO
WASHINGTON, D.C.
PHILADELPHIA
PITTSBURGH
OAKLAND
PRINCETON
NORTHERN VA
WILMINGTON
NEWARK
MIDLANDS, U.K.
CENTURY CITY
RICHMOND
HARRISBURG
WESTLAKE VILLAGE

© Reed Smith LLP 2003
"Reed Smith" is a limited liability partnership formed in the state of Delaware.

THE BEST OF THE REST

Altheimer & Gray

10 South Wacker Drive
Chicago, IL 60606-7482
Phone: (312) 715-4000
www.altheimer.com

LOCATIONS

Chicago, IL (HQ) • San Francisco, CA • Springfield, IL •
Bratislava • Bucharest • Budapest • Istanbul • Kyiv •
London • Paris • Prague • Shanghai • Warsaw

MAJOR DEPARTMENTS/PRACTICES

Aircraft Leasing • Alternative Dispute Resolution •
Bankruptcy, Insolvency & Workouts • Civil Rights
Representation • Commercial Litigation • Construction
Litigation • Corporate Real Estate Services & Leasing •
Corporate Restructuring • Environmental • Executive
Compensation & Employee Benefits • Finance •
Government Procurement & Contracts • Government
Relations • Hotels, Leisure & Gaming • Insurance &
Reinsurance • Intellectual Property • Intellectual
Property Litigation • International Corporate •
International Real Estate • Internet/High Tech • Labor &
Employment • Land Use and Development Incentives •
Mergers & Acquisitions • Municipal Law • Patents •
Private Equity & Venture Capital • Public Finance • Real
Estate Litigation • Real Estate Transactions &
Development • Securities and Public Markets •
Securitization • Tax • Telecommunications • Wealth
Management • White Collar Criminal Defense

THE STATS

No. of attorneys: 320+
No. of offices: 13
Managing Partner: Jeffrey N. Smith
Hiring Partner: Bradley M. Falk

THE BUZZ
WHAT ATTORNEYS AT OTHER FIRMS ARE SAYING ABOUT THIS FIRM

- "Moderate-sized and sophisticated"
- "Many layoffs recently"
- "Good Chicago firm"
- "Nondescript"

NOTABLE PERKS

- Exercise room and equipment
- Bar expenses
- Free dinner in lunchroom on late nights
- Firm pays monthly BlackBerry fees

EMPLOYMENT CONTACT

Ms. Nancy P. Verheyen
Director of Legal Recruiting
Phone: (312) 715-4640
Fax: (312) 715-4800
E-mail: verheyenn@altheimer.com

BASE SALARY

Chicago, IL
1st year: $125,000
Summer associate: $2,400/week

Andrews & Kurth L.L.P.

600 Travis, Suite 4200
Houston, TX 77002
Phone: (713) 220-4200
www.akllp.com

LOCATIONS

Houston, TX (HQ)
Austin, TX
Dallas, TX
Los Angeles, CA
New York, NY
The Woodlands, TX
Washington, DC
London

MAJOR DEPARTMENTS/PRACTICES

Antitrust • Banking & Finance • Bankruptcy •
Biotechnology • Corporate & Securities • Intellectual
Property • Internet/E-Commerce • Labor & Employment
• Litigation • Mergers & Acquisitions • Project Finance •
Public Law • Real Estate • Tax • Trusts & Estates

THE STATS

No. of attorneys: 380
No. of offices: 8
Managing Partner: Howard Ayers
Hiring Partners: Jeffrey E. Spiers and Chanse McLeod

RANKING RECAP

Best in Region
#4 - Texas

EMPLOYMENT CONTACT

Ms. Kimberley Klevenhagen
Manager of Attorney Employment
Phone: (713) 220-4140
Fax: (713) 220-4285
E-mail: kimklevenhagen@akllp.com

BASE SALARY

Dallas, Houston, The Woodlands, TX
1st year: $110,000
Summer associate: $2,100/week

Washington, DC
1st year: $120,000
Summer associate: $2,300/week

THE BUZZ
WHAT ATTORNEYS AT OTHER FIRMS ARE SAYING ABOUT THIS FIRM

- "Strong corporate"
- "Cookie-cutter work"
- "Great people, great work"
- "Are they still around?"

Arter & Hadden LLP

1100 Huntington Building
925 Euclid Avenue
Cleveland, Ohio 44115-1475
Phone: (216) 696-1100
www.arterhadden.com

LOCATIONS

Cleveland, OH (HQ)
Columbus, OH
Dallas, TX
Dayton, OH
Irvine, CA
Los Angeles, CA
San Diego, CA
San Francisco, CA
Washington, DC
Woodland Hills, CA

MAJOR DEPARTMENTS/PRACTICES

Bankruptcy • Communications & Energy • Corporate &
Securities • Director & Officer Liability • E-Group •
Employment • Environment • Government
Affairs/International • Health Care • Intellectual Property
& Technology • Internet & E-Commerce Law • Real
Estate • Trial/Litigation • Trusts & Estates/Tax

THE STATS

No. of attorneys: 300
No. of offices: 10
Managing Partner: Mark S. Solomon
Hiring Partner: Eugene M. Killeen

NOTABLE PERKS

- Periodic catered breakfasts
- Bar expenses
- CLE expenses
- Beautiful office space

EMPLOYMENT CONTACT

Ms. Jill M. Filicko
Law Student Recruiting Coordinator
Phone: (216) 696-4886
Fax: (216) 696-2645
E-mail: jill.filicko@arterhadden.com

THE BUZZ
WHAT ATTORNEYS AT OTHER FIRMS ARE SAYING ABOUT THIS FIRM

- "Rising star"
- "Past its prime"
- "White-shoe Clevelanders"
- "Underwent a lot of highly publicized layoffs"

Ballard Spahr Andrews & Ingersoll, LLP

1735 Market Street, 51st Floor
Philadelphia, PA 19103-7599
Phone: (215) 665-8500
www.ballardspahr.com

LOCATIONS

Philadelphia, PA (HQ)
Baltimore, MD
Denver, CO
Salt Lake City, UT
Voorhees, NJ
Washington, DC
Wilmington, DE

MAJOR DEPARTMENTS/PRACTICES

Business & Finance
Financial Planning & Management
Litigation
Public Finance
Real Estate

THE STATS

No. of attorneys: 450
No. of offices: 7
Summer associate offers: 33 out of 33 (2002)
Philadelphia Managing Partner: Lynn R. Axelroth
Philadelphia Hiring Partner: Mark S. Stewart

RANKING RECAP

Best in Region
#3 - Pennsylvania

NOTABLE PERKS

- Free rides home if you work past 7 p.m.
- Free dinners if working late
- Bar expenses
- Happy hour every other Friday

EMPLOYMENT CONTACT

Ms. Jennifer L. Fallon
Recruitment Coordinator
Phone: (215) 864-8167
Fax: (215) 864-9184
E-mail: fallonj@ballardspahr.com

BASE SALARY

Baltimore, MD
1st year: $102,000
Summer associate: $1,900/week

Philadelphia, PA
1st year: $107,000
Summer associate: $2,000/week

THE BUZZ
WHAT ATTORNEYS AT OTHER FIRMS ARE SAYING ABOUT THIS FIRM

- "Solid Philadelphia firm"
- "Underpaid for the hours"
- "Family-friendly and diverse"
- "Unremarkable"

Blackwell Sanders Peper Martin LLP

Two Pershing Square
2300 Main Street, Suite 1000
Kansas City, MO 64108
Phone: (816) 983-8000
www.blackwellsanders.com

LOCATIONS

Kansas City, MO (HQ)
Edwardsville, IL
Omaha, NE
Overland Park, KS
Springfield, MO
St. Louis, MO
Washington, DC
London

MAJOR DEPARTMENTS/PRACTICES

Compliance
Corporate
Health Law
Labor & Employment
Litigation
Real Estate
Tax Law

THE STATS

No. of attorneys: 303
No. of offices: 8
Summer associate offers: 7 out of 8 (2002)
Chairman: Dave Fenley
Hiring Partner: Stephen Hill

NOTABLE PERKS

- Health enhancement program
- Free parking
- Weekend getaways
- Up to $2,500 moving expenses

EMPLOYMENT CONTACT

Ms. Marcia Cook, Esq.
Director of Client Development & Legal Recruiting
Phone: (816) 983-8931
Fax: (816) 983-8080
E-mail: mcook@blackwellsanders.com

BASE SALARY

Kansas City, MO
1st year: $80,000
Summer associate: $1,500/week

THE BUZZ
WHAT ATTORNEYS AT OTHER FIRMS ARE SAYING ABOUT THIS FIRM

- "Great Kansas City reputation"
- "Provincial"
- "Struggling for direction "
- "Surprisingly good attorneys"

Blank Rome LLP

One Logan Square
Philadelphia, PA 19103-6998
Phone: (215) 569-5500
www.BlankRome.com

LOCATIONS

Philadelphia, PA (HQ) • Allentown, PA • Baltimore, MD
• Boca Raton, FL • Cherry Hill, NJ • Cincinnati, OH •
Media, PA • New York, NY • Trenton, NJ •
Washington, DC (2 offices) • Wilmington, DE

MAJOR DEPARTMENTS/PRACTICES

Business Department: Business Tax • Emerging &
Closely Held Companies • Employment, Benefits &
Labor • Health Law • Intellectual Property & Technology
• Maritime • Private Client Group • Public Companies &
Capital Formation

Litigation Department: Commercial Litigation •
Corporate Litigation • IP Litigation • Matrimonial •
Products Liability/ Mass Torts/Insurance

Financial Services/Real Estate Department: Business
Restructuring & Bankruptcy • Financial Services •
Government Relations • Institutional Real Estate • Public
Finance • Real Estate Development

THE STATS

No. of attorneys: 450
No. of offices: 12
Summer associate offers: 20 out of 21 (2002)
Managing Partner & CEO: Fred Blume
Hiring Partner: Mary Ann Mullaney

THE BUZZ
WHAT ATTORNEYS AT OTHER FIRMS ARE SAYING ABOUT THIS FIRM

- "Regional strength"
- "Run-of-the-mill"
- "Solid reputation"
- "Stingy"

RANKING RECAP

Best in Region
#7 - Pennsylvania

Quality of Life
#20 - Retention

NOTABLE PERKS

- Bar expenses including CLE requirements
- Nice workout room in the office
- Private cafeteria and subsidized lunch
- Free lunch on Wednesday

EMPLOYMENT CONTACT

Ms. Donna M. Branca
Director of Attorney Relations
Phone: (215) 569-5751
Fax: (215) 569-5555
E-mail: branca@BlankRome.com

BASE SALARY

New York, NY
1st year: $125,000
Summer associate: $2,400/week

Philadelphia, PA
1st year: $105,000
Summer associate: $2,000/week

Bracewell & Patterson, L.L.P.

711 Louisiana Street, Suite 2900
South Tower Pennzoil Place
Houston, TX 77002-2781
Phone: (713) 223-2900
www.bracepatt.com

LOCATIONS

Houston, TX (HQ) • Austin, TX • Corpus Christi, TX •
Dallas, TX • Fort Worth, TX • Reston, VA • San
Antonio, TX • Washington, DC • Almaty, Kazakhstan •
London

MAJOR DEPARTMENTS/PRACTICES

Appellate • Bankruptcy/Creditors' Rights • Construction
• Corporate & Securities • Counter-Terrorism, Public &
Corporate Security • Election Law • Emerging
Companies • Employee Benefits • Energy •
Environmental • Finance • Government Relations,
Advocacy & Strategy • Hospitality • Insurance •
Intellectual Property • International • Internet, Telecom
& E-Commerce • Labor & Employment • Latin American
Business • Litigation • Manufacturing • Not-for-Profit •
Public Law • Real Estate • Regulated Industries •
School Law • Tax & Estates • Water Law • Wealth
Management

THE STATS

No. of attorneys: 350+
No. of offices: 10
Summer associate offers: 36 out of 54 (2002)
Managing Partner: Patrick C. Oxford
Hiring Partner: Jennifer W. Jacobs

RANKING RECAP

Best in Region
#5 - Texas

NOTABLE PERKS

- $1,200 allowance for schmoozing clients
- Bar and moving expenses
- Subsidized parking
- Free monthly lunches

EMPLOYMENT CONTACT

Ms. Jean P. Lenzner
Director of Attorney Employment
Phone: (713) 221-1296
Fax: (713) 221-1212
E-mail: jean.lenzner@bracepatt.com

BASE SALARY

Austin, Houston, TX; Reston, VA
1st year: $110,000
Summer associate: $2,100/week

Corpus Christi, San Antonio, TX
1st year: $100,000
Summer associate: $1,900/week

Washington, DC
1st year: $115,000
Summer associate: $2,100/week

THE BUZZ
WHAT ATTORNEYS AT OTHER FIRMS ARE SAYING ABOUT THIS FIRM

- "Good finance department"
- "Trying to play with the big boys"
- "Open to new areas, i.e. school law"
- "More hours than expected"

Brown Rudnick Berlack Israels LLP

One Financial Center
Boston, MA 02111
Phone: (617) 856-8200
www.brownrudnick.com

LOCATIONS

Boston, MA (HQ)
Hartford, CT
New York, NY
Providence, RI
Dublin
London

MAJOR DEPARTMENTS/PRACTICES

Banking & Finance
Consulting Group
Corporate
Government Relations
Health Care
Intellectual Property
International
Litigation
Real Estate

THE STATS

No. of attorneys: 213
No. of offices: 6
Summer associate offers: 8 out of 16 (2002)
Chairman: Andre C. Jasse
Hiring Partner: Michael R. Dolan

NOTABLE PERKS

- Paid bar membership
- Moving expenses
- Bar exam fees
- Emergency child care

EMPLOYMENT CONTACT

Ms. Linda Manning
Recruiting Coordinator
Phone: (617) 856-8316
Fax: (617) 856-8201
E-mail: lmanning@brbilaw.com

BASE SALARY

Boston, MA
1st year: $125,000
Summer associate: $2,403/week

THE BUZZ
WHAT ATTORNEYS AT OTHER FIRMS ARE SAYING ABOUT THIS FIRM

- "Solid firm"
- "Merger target"
- "First-rate shop"
- "Gobbling up everything along the way"

Buchanan Ingersoll Professional Corporation

One Oxford Centre
301 Grant Street, 20th Floor
Pittsburgh, PA 15219-1410
Phone: (412) 562-8800
www.buchananingersoll.com

LOCATIONS

Pittsburgh, PA (HQ)

Aventura, FL • Bryn Mawr, PA • Buffalo, NY •
Harrisburg, PA • Miami, FL • New York, NY •
Philadelphia, PA Princeton, NJ • San Diego, CA •
Tampa, FL • Washington, DC • Wilmington, DE •
Dublin • London

MAJOR DEPARTMENTS/PRACTICES

Bankruptcy • Biotech • Corporate & Institutional
Transactions • Commercial Litigation • FDA •
Government Contracts • Government Relations • Health
Care • Intellectual Property • Labor & Employment Law
• National Defense & Homeland Security • Non-
Traditional Couples • Real Estate • SEC • Tax

THE STATS

No. of attorneys: 350 +
No. of offices: 14
Summer associate offers: 26 out of 40 (2002)
President & CEO: William Newlin
Hiring Partner: Gregory A. Miller

RANKING RECAP

Best in Region
#8 - Pennsylvania

NOTABLE PERKS

- Bar expenses
- Free parking/mileage to and from hearings
- Pirates tickets
- On site attorney dining room

EMPLOYMENT CONTACT

Ms. Laurie S. Lenigan
Legal Recruiting Manager
Phone: (412) 562-1470
Fax: (412) 562-1040
E-mail: lenigansl@bipc.com

BASE SALARY

Philadelphia, PA
1st year: $105,000
Summer associate: $2,000/week (NY, DC,
Philadelphia, Princeton);
$1,950/week (Pittsburgh);
$1,750/week (Harrisburg);
$1,500/week (Miami);
$1,400/week (Tampa)

THE BUZZ
WHAT ATTORNEYS AT OTHER FIRMS ARE SAYING ABOUT THIS FIRM

- "Does great work"
- "Old school"
- "Decent, respectable firm"
- "Difficult personalities"

Cozen O'Connor

1900 Market Street
Philadelphia, PA 19103
Phone: (215) 665-2000
www.cozen.com

LOCATIONS

Philadelphia, PA (HQ) • Atlanta, GA • Charlotte, NC • Chicago, IL • Cherry Hill, NJ • Dallas, TX • Las Vegas, NV • Los Angeles, CA • Newark, NJ • New York, NY • San Diego, CA • San Francisco, PA • Seattle, WA • Trenton, NJ • Washington, DC • West Conshohocken, PA • Wichita, KS • Wilmington, DE • London

MAJOR DEPARTMENTS/PRACTICES

Business
Business Litigation
Insurance
Intellectual Property

THE STATS

No. of attorneys: 461
No. of offices: 18
Firm President and Chair: Patrick O'Connor
Firm Chairman: Steve Cozen
Hiring Partner: Marty Duffey

NOTABLE PERKS

- Bar expenses/CLE training
- Discounts on center city parking
- Associate happy hours
- Free lunches

EMPLOYMENT CONTACT

Ms. Lori C. Rosenberg, Esq.
Director of Legal Recruiting
Phone: (215) 665-4178
Fax: (215) 665-2013
E-mail: lrosenberg@cozen.com

BASE SALARY

Philadelphia, PA
1st year: $100,000
Summer associate: $1,923/week

THE BUZZ
WHAT ATTORNEYS AT OTHER FIRMS ARE SAYING ABOUT THIS FIRM

- "Laid back"
- "Great if you like slave wages"
- "Friendly"
- "More hours than it is worth"

Davis Wright Tremaine LLP

2600 Century Square
1501 Fourth Avenue
Seattle, WA 98101-1688
Phone: (206) 622-3150
www.dwt.com

LOCATIONS

Seattle, WA (HQ) • Anchorage, AK • Bellevue, WA • Los Angeles, CA • New York, NY • Portland, OR • San Francisco, CA • Washington, DC • Shanghai

MAJOR DEPARTMENTS/PRACTICES

Admiralty & Maritime • Aircraft Industry • Antitrust • Business & Corporate • China Practice • Communications, Media & Information Technologies • Construction & Government Contracts • Corporate Finance & Securities • Credit Recovery & Bankruptcy • Education • Emerging Business & Technology • Employment/Employee Benefits • Energy • Environmental & Natural Resources • Financial Institutions • Food & Agriculture • Health Care • Hospitality • Immigration • Intellectual Property • International Law • Internet & eCommerce • Legislation • Litigation • Municipal Finance • Real Estate & Land Use • Sports • Tax • Tax Exempt Organizations • Telecommunications • Trusts & Estates

THE STATS

No. of attorneys: 408
No. of offices: 9
Summer associate offers: 14 out of 17 (2002)
Managing Partner: Richard Ellingsen
Hiring Partner: Bergitta K. Trelstad

THE BUZZ
WHAT ATTORNEYS AT OTHER FIRMS ARE SAYING ABOUT THIS FIRM

- "Groovy Esq."
- "Forever Seattle's runner-up"
- "Interested in diversity and women's issues"
- "Better have an exit strategy"

RANKING RECAP

Best in Region
#3 - Pacific Northwest

Quality of Life
#3 - Hours
#15 - Associate/Partner Relations
#19 - Retention

NOTABLE PERKS

- Women-only and firm-wide retreats
- Lounge with coffee and soft drinks
- BlackBerry pagers

EMPLOYMENT CONTACTS

Ms. Carol Yuly
Recruiting Administrator, Seattle
Phone: (206) 628-3529
E-mail: carolyuly@dwt.com

Ms. Leslie Dustin
Recruiting Administrator, Portland
Phone: (503) 778-5243

BASE SALARY

Seattle, WA
1st year: $95,000
Summer associate: $1,538/week

Anchorage, AK
1st year: $80,000
Summer associate: $1,500/week

Los Angeles, CA
1st year: $102,500

Portland, OR
1st year: $85,000
Summer associate: $1,400/week

San Francisco, CA
1st year: $110,000
Summer associate: $2,115/week

Dickstein Shapiro Morin & Oshinsky LLP

2101 L Street, NW
Washington, DC 20037-1526
Phone: (202) 785-9700
www.legalinnovators.com

LOCATIONS

Washington, DC (HQ)
New York, NY

MAJOR DEPARTMENTS/PRACTICES

Antitrust • Bankruptcy & Creditors' Rights • Business
Crimes & Regulatory Enforcement • Business Litigation
• Communications • Complex Dispute Resolution •
Construction • Corporate & Finance • Energy & Natural
Resources • Financial Institutions & Real Estate •
Government Affairs • Government Contracts • Health
Law Services • Insurance Coverage • Intellectual
Property • International Transactions & Immigration •
Labor & Employment • Securities • Tax

THE STATS

No. of attorneys: 322
No. of offices: 2
Summer associate offers: 18 out of 19 (2002)
Managing Partner: Angelo V. Arcadipane
Hiring Partner: Howard S. Jatlow

RANKING RECAP

Best in Region
#15 - Washington, DC

NOTABLE PERKS

- Bar dues and exam fees paid
- 25-cent sodas
- Biannual "prom" dinner dance
- $10,000 referral bonus
- Emergency child care assistance

EMPLOYMENT CONTACT

Ms. Julie B. Miles
Phone: (202) 828-4851
Fax: (202) 887-0689
E-mail: MilesJ@dsmo.com

BASE SALARY

New York, NY; Washington, DC
1st year: $125,000
Summer associate: $2,400/week

THE BUZZ
WHAT ATTORNEYS AT OTHER FIRMS ARE SAYING ABOUT THIS FIRM

- "Family- and mom-friendly"
- "Tough hours"
- "Collegial"
- "Rambo-style litigators"

Drinker Biddle & Reath LLP

One Logan Square
18th & Cherry Streets
Philadelphia, PA 19103-6996
Phone: (215) 988-2700
www.drinkerbiddle.com

LOCATIONS

Philadelphia, PA (HQ)
Berwyn, PA
Florham Park, NJ
Los Angeles, CA
New York, NY
Princeton, NJ
San Francisco, CA
Washington, DC
Wilmington, DE

MAJOR DEPARTMENTS/PRACTICES

Business and Finance: Antitrust • Banking & Commercial Law • Communications Law • Corporate & Securities • Education • Employee Benefits • Gov't Affairs • Health Law • Intellectual Property • Investment Management • Public Finance • Real Estate • Tax • Workout & Bankruptcy

Litigation: Environmental • General Civil • Insurance • Labor & Employment • Products Liability • Professional Liability • White Collar/Corporate Investigations

Personal Law

THE STATS

No. of attorneys: 450 +
No. of offices: 9
Summer associate offers: 22 out of 27 (2002)
Chairman: James M. Sweet
Hiring Partner: William H. Clark Jr.

THE BUZZ
WHAT ATTORNEYS AT OTHER FIRMS ARE SAYING ABOUT THIS FIRM

- "Good local counsel"
- "Snobbish"
- "Philadelphia powerhouse"
- "Average"

RANKING RECAP

Best in Region
#4 - Pennsylvania

NOTABLE PERKS

- Free parking/taxi and dinner after 7 p.m.
- $7,500 stipend for first-years and judicial clerks
- Complimentary fitness center
- Firm-wide biweekly cocktail hour
- $10,000 federal judicial clerk bonus

EMPLOYMENT CONTACT

Ms. Maryellen Wyville Altieri
Director of Professional Recruitment
Phone: (215) 988-2663
Fax: (215) 988-2757
E-mail: maryellen.altieri@dbr.com

BASE SALARY

Philadelphia, PA; San Francisco, CA; Washington, DC
1st year: $125,000
Summer associate: $2,200/week

Florham Park, NJ
1st year: $110,000
Summer associate: $2,019/week

Duane Morris LLP

One Liberty Place, Suite 4200
Philadelphia, PA 19103-7396
Phone: (215) 979-1000
www.duanemorris.com

LOCATIONS

Philadelphia, PA (HQ) • Allentown, PA • Atlanta, GA •
Bangor, ME • Boston, MA • Cherry Hill, NJ • Chicago,
IL • Harrisburg, PA • Houston, TX • Miami, FL • New
York, NY • Newark, NJ • Palm Beach, FL • Princeton,
NJ • San Francisco, CA • Washington, DC •
Westchester, NY • Wilmington, DE • London

MAJOR DEPARTMENTS/PRACTICES

Commercial, Municipal & Affordable Housing Finance
Corporate
Employment, Benefits & Immigration
Energy
Estate & Asset Planning
Financial Products
Health Law
Intellectual Property
Real Estate
Reorganization & Financial Services
Tax
Trial

THE STATS

No. of attorneys: 500
No. of offices: 19
Summer associate offers: 16 out of 20 (2002)
Chairman: Sheldon M. Bonovitz
Hiring Partner: James J. Holman, Esq.

RANKING RECAP

Best in Region
#9 - Pennsylvania

NOTABLE PERKS

- Four weeks of vacation
- Flexible spending account
- Bar stipend
- Judicial clerkship bonus

EMPLOYMENT CONTACT

Ms. Peggy Simoncini Pasquay
Legal Recruitment Coordinator
Phone: (215) 979-1161
Fax: (215) 979) 1020
E-mail: simoncini@duanemorris.com

BASE SALARY

Philadelphia, PA
1st year: $105,000
Summer associate: $2,019/week

Washington, DC
1st year: $110,000
Summer associate: $2,115/week

Atlanta, GA
1st year: $100,000
Summer associate: $1,925/week

THE BUZZ
WHAT ATTORNEYS AT OTHER FIRMS ARE SAYING ABOUT THIS FIRM

- "Very nice people"
- "Average at best"
- "Up and coming"
- "Overextended"

Edwards & Angell, LLP

101 Federal Street
Boston, MA 02110
Phone: (617) 439-4444
www.edwardsangell.com

LOCATIONS

Boston, MA
Fort Lauderdale, FL
Hartford, CT
New York, NY
Providence, RI
Short Hills, NJ
Stamford, CT
West Palm Beach, FL
London (representative office)

MAJOR DEPARTMENTS/PRACTICES

Banking • Corporate • Financial Services • Insurance &
Reinsurance • Intellectual Property • Labor &
Employment • Litigation • Private Equity • Real Estate •
Securities • Technology Transactions

THE STATS

No. of attorneys: 316
No. of offices: 8
Summer associate offers: 11 out of 14 (2002)
Managing Partner: Terrence Finn

NOTABLE PERKS

- Paid maternity/paternity leave
- Domestic partner benefits
- Moving expenses
- Bar exam expenses

EMPLOYMENT CONTACT

Ms. Theresa M. Lenartowick
Recruiting Coordinator
Phone: (401) 276-6587
Fax: (401) 528-5835
E-mail: Tlenartowick@edwardsangell.com

BASE SALARY

Boston, MA
1st year: $115,000
Summer associate: $2,200/week

Fort Lauderdale, West Palm Beach, FL
1st year: $85,000
Summer associate: $1,600/week

Hartford, CT; Providence RI
1st year: $90,000
Summer associate: $1,700/week

New York, NY
1st year: $120,000
Summer associate: $2,300/week

Short Hills, NJ; Stamford, CT
1st year: $95,000
Summer associate: $1,800/week

THE BUZZ
WHAT ATTORNEYS AT OTHER FIRMS ARE SAYING ABOUT THIS FIRM

- "Good local firm"
- "Rhode Islandish"
- "Smart and sensible"
- "Regional sweatshop"

Epstein Becker & Green, P.C.

250 Park Avenue
New York, NY 10177
Phone: (212) 351-4500
www.ebglaw.com

LOCATIONS

New York, NY (HQ)
Atlanta, GA
Boston, MA
Chicago, IL
Dallas, TX
Houston, TX
Los Angeles, CA
Newark, NJ
San Francisco, CA
Stamford, CT
Washington, DC

MAJOR DEPARTMENTS/PRACTICES

Construction • Corporate & Securities • Employee
Benefits • Family Law • Government Contracts &
Technology • Health Law • Immigration Law • Labor &
Employment • Litigation • Personal Planning • Real
Estate

THE STATS

No. of attorneys: 340+
No. of offices: 11
Summer associate offers: 4 out of 4 (2002)
Managing Partner: George P. Sape
Hiring Partner: Dean L. Silverberg

RANKING RECAP

Best in Practice
#7 - Labor & Employment

NOTABLE PERKS

- Flexible spending account
- Pre-tax transportation plan

EMPLOYMENT CONTACT

Ms. Kalen T. Mikell
Recruitment and Training Coordinator
Phone: (212) 351-4500
Fax: (212) 661-0989
E-mail: kmikell@ebglaw.com

BASE SALARY

New York, NY
1st year: $95,000
Summer associate: $1,826/week

THE BUZZ
WHAT ATTORNEYS AT OTHER FIRMS ARE SAYING ABOUT THIS FIRM

- "Hard-working"
- "Unfriendly"
- "For a mid-sized firm, has held its own"
- "Second-tier"

Foley Hoag LLP

155 Seaport Avenue
Boston, MA 02210-2600
Phone: (617) 832-1000
www.foleyhoag.com

LOCATIONS

Boston, MA (HQ)
Washington, DC

MAJOR DEPARTMENTS/PRACTICES

Accountants Professional Liability • Administrative • Alternative Dispute Resolution • Banking • Bankruptcy, Reorganization & Workout Practice • Business • Business Crimes & Govt. Investigation • Business Litigation • Construction & Development Disputes • Corporate Finance/Securities • Corporate Social Responsibility • Education • Energy & Regulated Industries • Environmental • Govt. Strategies • Health Care • Immigration • Infrastructure & Transportation • Insurance • Insurance Litigation • IP • IP Litigation • International • Investment Management • Labor & Employment • Land Use & Development • Life Sciences • Litigation • M&A • Patent • Patent Litigation • Product Liability Litigation • Property Valuation Litigation • Real Estate • Securities & Corporate Disputes • Taxation • Technology Transfer & Licensing • Telecommunications • Trade Regulation • Trademark • Trusts & Estates • Venture Capital/Emerging Companies

THE STATS

No. of attorneys: 243
No. of offices: 2
Summer associate offers: 35 out of 38 (2002)
Managing Partners: Peter Rosenblum, Michele Whitham
Hiring Partner: John D. Hancock

THE BUZZ
WHAT ATTORNEYS AT OTHER FIRMS ARE SAYING ABOUT THIS FIRM

- "Intellectual place to work"
- "Not as good as it thinks it is"
- "Creative"
- "All sizzle, no steak"

RANKING RECAP

Best in Region
#6 - Boston

Quality of Life
#7 - Offices
#15 - Pro Bono

NOTABLE PERKS

- Bar expenses
- Free cafeteria dinners after 7 p.m.
- Parental leave policy
- Course tuition

EMPLOYMENT CONTACT

Ms. Dina M. Wreede
Dir. Legal Recruiting & Professional Development
Phone: (617) 832-7060
Fax: (617) 832-7000
E-mail: dwreede@foleyhoag.com

BASE SALARY

Boston, MA; Washington, DC
1st year: $125,000
Summer associate: $2,400/week

Gardere Wynne Sewell LLP

Thanksgiving Tower
1601 Elm Street, Suite 3000
Dallas, TX 75201
Phone: (214) 999-3000
www.gardere.com

LOCATIONS

Dallas, TX (HQ)
Austin, TX
Houston, TX
Washington, DC
Mexico City

MAJOR DEPARTMENTS/PRACTICES

Antitrust • Appellate • Bankruptcy • Corporate
Governance • Corporate Securities • Employee Benefits
• Energy • Environmental • Food & Beverage Industry •
Governmental Contracts • Health Care • Immigration •
Intellectual Property • Labor & Employment • Litigation
• Oil & Gas • Real Estate • Tax • Trusts & Estates •
White Collar Crime & Compliance

THE STATS

No. of attorneys: 290
No. of offices: 5
Summer associate offers: 25 out of 36 (2002)
Managing Partner: Steve Good
Hiring Partners: Randall L. Jones and Randy Ray

RANKING RECAP

Best in Region
#10 - Texas

NOTABLE PERKS

- Flexible compensation account
- Bar exam expenses
- Paid parking
- Moving expenses

EMPLOYMENT CONTACTS

Houston:
Ms. Sheri Green Howard
Director of Recruiting
Phone: (713) 276-5155
Fax: (713) 276-5555

All other offices:
Ms. Tammy Patterson
Dir. Recruiting & Professional Development
Phone: (214) 999-4177
Fax: (214) 999-4667
E-mail: tpatterson@gardere.com

BASE SALARY

Dallas, TX
1st year: $110,000
Summer associate: $2,100/week (2L);
$2,000/week (1L)

THE BUZZ
WHAT ATTORNEYS AT OTHER FIRMS ARE SAYING ABOUT THIS FIRM

- "Great atmosphere"
- "Middle of the road"
- "Rising star"
- "Big egos for no reason"

Gunderson Dettmer Stough Villeneuve Franklin & Hachigian, LLP

155 Constitution Drive
Menlo Park, CA 94025
Phone: (650) 321-2400
www.gunder.com

LOCATIONS

Menlo Park, CA (HQ)
Boston, MA
New York, NY

MAJOR DEPARTMENTS/PRACTICES

Corporate & Securities
Executive Compensation
Labor
Litigation
Mergers & Acquisitions
Tax
Technology, Intellectual Property & Corporate Partnering

THE STATS

No. of attorneys: 82
No. of offices: 3
Summer associate offers: 10 out of 12 (2002)
Managing Partner: Steve Franklin
Hiring Partner: Anthony J. McCusker

RANKING RECAP

Best in Practice
#6 (tie) - Tech/Internet/E-Commerce

NOTABLE PERKS

- Bar expenses
- Free dinners
- Ping pong and foosball tables

EMPLOYMENT CONTACT

Ms. Corinne Dritsas
Director of Legal Recruiting
Phone: (650) 463-5284
Fax: (650) 321-2800
E-mail: recruiting@gunder.com

BASE SALARY

All offices
1st year: $125,000
Summer associate: $2,400/week

THE BUZZ
WHAT ATTORNEYS AT OTHER FIRMS ARE SAYING ABOUT THIS FIRM

- "Quality attorneys"
- "Past its prime"
- "Thanks for the raises!"
- "Dot-com busted"

Haynes and Boone, LLP

901 Main Street, Suite 3100
Dallas, TX 75202-3789
Phone: (214) 651-5000
www.haynesboone.com

LOCATIONS

Austin, TX
Dallas, TX
Fort Worth, TX
Houston, TX
Richardson, TX
San Antonio, TX
Washington, DC
Mexico City

MAJOR DEPARTMENTS/PRACTICES

Antitrust • Appellate • Business Litigation • Business
Reorganization/Bankruptcy • Corporate Securities •
Employee Benefits/Executive Compensation •
Energy/Power • Environmental • Finance • Government
Contracts • Health Care • Immigration • Insurance •
Intellectual Property • International • Investment Funds
• Labor & Employment • Media Law • Mergers &
Acquisitions • Real Estate • Securities Litigation • Tax,
Business & Estate Planning • Venture Capital • White
Collar Criminal Defense

THE STATS

No. of attorneys: 415
No. of offices: 8
Summer associate offers: 59 out of 95 (2002)
Managing Partner: Robert E. Wilson
Hiring Partner: Taylor H. Wilson

RANKING RECAP

Best in Region
#6 - Texas

Quality of Life
#8 - Hours
#8 - Best Firms to Work For
#8 - Satisfaction
#13 - Pay

Best in Diversity
#8 - Diversity for Minorities
#18 - Overall Diversity

NOTABLE PERKS

- Firm-sponsored pizza lunches
- Four-month maternity leave
- In-house travel service
- Palm Pilots

EMPLOYMENT CONTACT

Ms. Stacey Yervasi
Fall Recruiting Coordinator
Phone: (214) 651-5438
Fax: (214) 200-0576
E-mail: stacey.yervasi@haynesboone.com

BASE SALARY

All offices
1st year: $115,000
Summer associate: $2,100/week

THE BUZZ
WHAT ATTORNEYS AT OTHER FIRMS ARE SAYING ABOUT THIS FIRM

- "Always well regarded"
- "Growing too quickly"
- "Family friendly"
- "Cheapskates"

Hinshaw & Culbertson

222 LaSalle Street, Suite 300
Chicago, IL 60601-1081
Phone: (312) 704-3000
www.hinshawculbertson.com

LOCATIONS

Chicago, IL (HQ) • Appleton, WI • Belleville, IL •
Champaign, IL • Crystal Lake, IL • Fort Lauderdale, FL •
Jacksonville, FL • Joliet, IL • Lisle, IL • Los Angeles,
CA • Miami, FL • Milwaukee, WI • Minneapolis, MN •
New York, NY • Peoria, IL • Phoenix, AR • Rockford, IL
• San Francisco, CA • Schererville, IN • Springfield, IL •
St. Louis, MO • Tampa, FL • Waukegan, IL •

MAJOR DEPARTMENTS/PRACTICES

ADR • Antitrust • Appellate • Bankruptcy • Business
Lit. • Commercial Lit. • Communications Technology •
Corporate Governance & Organization • Director &
Officer Liability • Employee Benefits • Environmental
Lit. & Regulation • Estate & Financial Planning • Family
Law • Fiduciary & Fidelity Bond • Financial Institutions •
Governmental Relations • Health Care • Insurance &
Reinsurance • Labor & Employment & ERISA • Not-For-
Profit Organizations • Product Liability • Professional
Athletics & Entertainment • Professional Liability • Real
Estate & Construction • School & Municipal • Surety
Bonds • Taxation • Tort Lit. • Transportation • Trusts &
Estates • White Collar Crime & Compliance

THE STATS

No. of attorneys: 400
No. of offices: 23
Summer associate offers: 10 out of 13 (2002)
Managing Partner: J. William Roberts
Hiring Partner: David R. Creagh

THE BUZZ
WHAT ATTORNEYS AT OTHER FIRMS ARE SAYING ABOUT THIS FIRM

- "Good reputation"
- "Boring insurance"
- "Good reputation"
- "Overworked and underpaid"

NOTABLE PERKS

- Associates get percentage of business
  brought into firm
- Free dinners after 7 p.m.

EMPLOYMENT CONTACT

Ms. Paula A. Dixton
Legal Recruitment Manager
Phone: (312) 704-3000
E-mail: pdixton@hinshawlaw.com

BASE SALARY

Chicago, IL
1st year: $90,000

Jackson Lewis LLP

One North Broadway
White Plains, NY 10601
Phone: (914) 328-0404
www.jacksonlewis.com

LOCATIONS

Atlanta, GA • Boston, MA • Chicago, IL • Dallas, TX
Greenville, SC • Hartford, CT • Long Island, NY • Los
Angeles, CA • Miami, FL • Minneapolis, MN •
Morristown, NJ • New York, NY • Orlando, FL •
Pittsburgh, PA • Sacramento, CA • San Francisco, CA •
Seattle, WA • Stamford, CT • White Plains, NY •
Vienna, VA

MAJOR DEPARTMENTS/PRACTICES

Employment, Labor & Benefits
Immigration Law

THE STATS

No. of attorneys: 360
No. of offices: 20
Managing Partner: William Krupman

RANKING RECAP

Best in Practice
#6 - Labor & Employment

NOTABLE PERKS

- Flexible spending programs
- Bar expenses
- Pre-tax transportation plan

EMPLOYMENT CONTACT

Ms. Terry Clifford
Director of Human Resources
Phone: (914) 328-0404
Fax: (914) 328-9096
E-mail: recruiting@jacksonlewis.com

THE BUZZ
WHAT ATTORNEYS AT OTHER FIRMS ARE SAYING ABOUT THIS FIRM

- "Family-friendly"
- "Union busters"
- "Tough as nails"
- "Employment factory"

Jackson Walker L.L.P.

901 Main Street, Suite 6000
Dallas, TX 75202-3797
Phone: (214) 953-6000
www.jw.com

LOCATIONS

Dallas, TX (HQ)
Austin, TX • Fort Worth, TX • Houston, TX •
Richardson TX • San Angelo, TX • San Antonio, TX

MAJOR DEPARTMENTS/PRACTICES

Appellate Practice
Bankruptcy
Business Law
Civil Trial Practice
Communications Law
Computer Law
General Practice
Health Care Law
Insurance Defense
International Business Law
Labor & Employment Law
Patent, Trademark, Copyright & Unfair Competition
Personal Injury
Product Liability Law
Real Estate Law
Regulatory & Legislative
Tax Law

THE STATS

No. of attorneys: 300 +
No. of offices: 7
Summer associate offers: 24 out of 34 (2002)
Managing Partner: T. Michael Wilson
Hiring Partner: David C. Myers

THE BUZZ
WHAT ATTORNEYS AT OTHER FIRMS ARE SAYING ABOUT THIS FIRM

- "Regional firm that pushes its attorneys hard"
- "Underrated""
- "Relaxed atmosphere"
- "Boring"

NOTABLE PERKS

- Associate home loan program
- Bar expenses
- Signing bonus

EMPLOYMENT CONTACT

Ms. Jacqueline L. Galli
Recruiting Coordinator
Phone: (214) 953-6000
Fax: (216) 953-5822
E-mail: jgalli@jw.com

BASE SALARY

Dallas, TX
1st year: $105,000
Summer associate: $2,100/week

Jenkens & Gilchrist, a Professional Corporation

1445 Ross Avenue, Suite 3200
Dallas, TX 75202-2799
Phone: (214) 855-4500
www.jenkens.com

LOCATIONS

Dallas, TX (HQ)
Austin, TX
Chicago, IL
Houston, TX
Los Angeles, CA
New York, NY
Pasadena, CA
San Antonio, TX
Washington, DC

MAJOR DEPARTMENTS/PRACTICES

Administrative • Antitrust • Bankruptcy • Construction
• Corporate & Securities • Criminal Law • Energy •
Environmental • ERISA • ESOP • Estate Planning •
Financial Institutions • Financial Services • Franchise &
Distribution • Health • Immigration • Intellectual
Property • International • Labor & Employment •
Litigation • Real Estate • Tax • Technology •
Transportation • White Collar

THE STATS

No. of attorneys: 600
No. of offices: 9
Summer associate offers: 44 out of 67 (2002)
Managing Partner: William P. Durbin
Hiring Partner: Robert W. Dockery

THE BUZZ
WHAT ATTORNEYS AT OTHER FIRMS ARE SAYING ABOUT THIS FIRM

- "Second-tier Texas"
- "Too big too fast"
- "Very impressive"
- "Troubled by defections"

RANKING RECAP

Best in Region
#8 - Texas

Quality of Life
#2 - Hours
#5 (tie) - Satisfaction
#6 - Best 20 Law Firms to Work For
#6 - Associate/Partner Relations
#17 - Pay

NOTABLE PERKS

- Bar expenses
- Regular CLE courses, as well as specialized practice group training (Lawyers College)
- Annual Halloween party for spouses and children
- Catered lunch on Fridays

EMPLOYMENT CONTACT

Ms. Lauren Sager
Law School Recruiting Contact
Phone: (214) 855-4500
Fax: (214) 855-4300

BASE SALARY

Austin, Dallas, Houston, San Antonio, TX
1st year: $110,000
Summer associate: $2,200/week

Los Angeles, Pasadena, CA; Washington, DC
1st year: $115,000
Summer associate: $2,400/week

Chicago, IL; New York, NY
1st year: $125,000
Summer associate: $2,400/week

Kilpatrick Stockton LLP

1100 Peachtree Street, Suite 2800
Atlanta, GA 30309-4530
Phone: (404) 815-6500
www.KilpatrickStockton.com

LOCATIONS

Atlanta, GA
Augusta, GA
Charlotte, NC
Raleigh, NC
Washington, DC
Winston-Salem, NC
London
Stockholm

MAJOR DEPARTMENTS/PRACTICES

Anti-Terrorism • Antitrust & Trade Regulation • Banking
& Finance • Biotechnology & Life Sciences • Business
Transactions • Construction Law & Public Contracts •
Corporate Finance & Securities • Customs • E-
Commerce & Internet • Employment & ERISA •
Environmental • Financial Restructuring • Franchising •
Government • Government Contracts • Health Care •
Infrastructure & Land Use • Insurance Coverage •
Intellectual Property • International • Investment
Management • Labor & Employment • Litigation • Real
Estate • Tax • Technology • Telecommunications •
Trusts & Estates • Utilities • White Collar Criminal Law

THE STATS

No. of attorneys: 441
No. of offices: 8
Summer associate offers: 24 out of 52 (2002)
Managing Partner: William H. Brewster
Hiring Chairman: Betty Wren

THE BUZZ
WHAT ATTORNEYS AT OTHER FIRMS ARE SAYING ABOUT THIS FIRM

- "Prestigious"
- "A lot of turnover"
- "Laid back"
- "Big law wannabes"

RANKING RECAP

Best in Region
#4 - The South

NOTABLE PERKS

- Bar expenses and moving expenses
- Friday happy hour
- Free parking (some locations)
- On-site wellness program
- Concierge service

EMPLOYMENT CONTACT

Ms. Lea W. Hughes
Recruiting Coordinator
Phone: (404) 532-6887
Fax: (404) 541-4668
E-mail: lehughes@KilpatrickStockton.com

BASE SALARY

**Atlanta, GA; Charlotte, Raleigh,
Winston-Salem, NC**
1st year: $100,000
Summer associate: $1,800/week
Summer associate: $1,700/week (Charlotte)

Washington, DC
1st year: $125,000
Summer associate: $2,200/week

Littler Mendelson, P.C.

650 California Street, 20th Floor
San Francisco, CA 94108-2693
Phone: (415) 433-1940
www.littler.com

LOCATIONS

Atlanta, GA • Bakersfield, CA • Chicago, IL •
Columbus, OH • Dallas, TX • Denver, CO • Fresno, CA
• Houston, TX • Las Vegas, NV • Los Angeles, CA •
Miami, FL • Minneapolis, MN • Newark, NJ • New
York, NY • Palm Desert, CA • Philadelphia, PA •
Phoenix, AZ • Pittsburgh, PA • Reno, NV • Sacramento,
CA • San Diego, CA • San Francisco, CA • San Jose,
CA • Santa Maria, CA • Seattle, WA • Stockton, CA •
Walnut Creek, CA • Washington, DC • Yakima, WA

MAJOR DEPARTMENTS/PRACTICES

Labor and Employment Law, including:
• Employment Litigation
• Employment Discrimination
• Labor
• Public Sector/Education Labor
• Other Administrative Labor Law

THE STATS

No. of attorneys: 400+
No. of offices: 29
Summer associate offers: 16 out of 18 (2002)
Managing Partner: Wendy L. Tice-Wallner

THE BUZZ
WHAT ATTORNEYS AT OTHER FIRMS ARE SAYING ABOUT THIS FIRM

- "Focused"
- "Stifling environment"
- "Great experience for young lawyers"
- "Hard to make partner"

RANKING RECAP

Best in Practice
#2 - Labor & Employment

NOTABLE PERKS

- Free parking (not for first-years)
- Moving expenses; bar review and exam fees
- Allowance for company store

EMPLOYMENT CONTACT

Ms. Karen R. Herz
Nat'l Manager, Recruiting & Profess. Development
Phone: (415) 433-1940
Fax: (415) 399-8490
E-mail: lawrecruit@littler.com

BASE SALARY

Atlanta, GA; Newark, NJ; Phoenix, AZ;
Pittsburgh, PA; Sacramento, CA
1st year: $90,000

Chicago, IL; San Diego, CA
1st year: $100,000
Summer associate: $1,850/week (Chicago)

Dallas, Houston, TX
1st year: $92,500
Summer associate: $1,650/week (Dallas)
Summer associate: $1,600/week (Houston)

New York, NY;Los Angeles, San Francisco,
San Jose, Walnut Creek, CA
1st year: $110,000
Summer associate: $2,000/week (San
Francisco)

Philadelphia, PA; Washington, DC; Seattle, WA
1st year: $95,000

Columbus, OH
1st year: $85,000

Denver, CO; Minneapolis, MN
1st year: $80,000

Locke Lidell & Sapp LLP

3400 J. P. Morgan Chase Tower
600 Travis
Houston, TX 77002-3095
Phone: (713) 226-1200

2200 Ross Avenue, Suite 2200
Dallas, Texas 75201-6776
Phone: (214) 740-8000
www.lockeliddell.com

LOCATIONS

Dallas, TX (HQ)
Houston, TX (HQ)
Austin, TX
New Orleans, LA

MAJOR DEPARTMENTS/PRACTICES

Corporate and Securities
Finance, Banking & Real Estate
Litigation
Public Law

THE STATS

No. of attorneys: 429
No. of offices: 4
Summer associate offers: 62 out of 84 (2002)
Managing Partner: Brian L. Goolsby
Hiring Partner: Stephanie Donaho

RANKING RECAP

Best in Region
#7 - Texas

NOTABLE PERKS

- Parking stipend of $165 per month
- Signing bonus
- Moving expenses
- Clerkship bonus

EMPLOYMENT CONTACT

Ms. Courtney O'Neil
Director of Recruiting
Phone: (713) 226-1425
Fax: (713) 223-3717
E-mail: coneil@lockeliddell.com

BASE SALARY

Houston, TX
1st year: $110,000
Summer associate: $ 2,100/week

THE BUZZ
WHAT ATTORNEYS AT OTHER FIRMS ARE SAYING ABOUT THIS FIRM

- "Solid"
- "Still working through merger"
- "Friendly for women"
- "McLaw, anyone?"

Lord, Bissell & Brook

115 South LaSalle Street
Chicago, IL 60603
Phone: (312) 443-0700
www.lordbissell.com

LOCATIONS

Chicago, IL (HQ)
Atlanta, GA
Los Angeles, CA
New York, NY
London

MAJOR DEPARTMENTS/PRACTICES

Appellate • Bankruptcy, Insolvency & Reorganization •
Banks & Financial Institutions • Business Litigation &
Arbitration • Construction • Corporate • Employee
Benefits & Executive Compensation • Environmental •
Health Care • Insurance • Intellectual Property &
Technology • Labor & Employment • Product Liability •
Real Estate • Tax • Transportation • Wealth
Preservation & Estate Planning

THE STATS

No. of attorneys: 325
No. of offices: 5
Summer associate offers: 18 out of 22 (2002)
Managing Partner: Daniel I. Schlessinger
Hiring Partner: David M. Agnew

NOTABLE PERKS

- Summer stipend while studying for bar exam
- London travel
- Bar and moving reimbursement
- BlackBerry pagers

EMPLOYMENT CONTACT

Ms. Kerry B. Jahnsen
Phone: (312) 443-0455
Fax: (312) 443-0336
E-mail: kjahnsen@lordbissell.com

BASE SALARY

Chicago, IL; New York, NY
1st year: $125,000
Summer associate: $2,400/week

Atlanta, GA
1st year: $100,000
Summer associate: $1,923/week

Los Angeles, CA
Summer Associate: $2,400/week

THE BUZZ
WHAT ATTORNEYS AT OTHER FIRMS ARE SAYING ABOUT THIS FIRM

- "Friendly place"
- "They invented stodgy"
- "Solid litigation firm"
- "Yellers"

Manatt, Phelps & Phillips, LLP

Trident Center
11355 West Olympic Boulevard
Los Angeles, CA 90064
Phone: (310) 312-4000
www.manatt.com

LOCATIONS

Los Angeles, CA (HQ)
Albany, NY • New York, NY • Orange County, CA •
Palo Alto, CA • Sacramento, CA • Washington, DC •
Mexico City • Monterrey

MAJOR DEPARTMENTS/PRACTICES

Antitrust • Banking • Bankruptcy & Financial
Restructuring • Corporate & Finance • Employment &
Labor • Energy & Natural Resources • Entertainment •
Government & Policy • Healthcare • Insurance •
Intellectual Property • Internet • International Trade &
Policy • Litigation • Non-Profit Organizations • Real
Estate & Land Use • Special Investigations/White Collar
Defense • Tax, Employee Benefits & Wealth
Management • Telecommunications • Venture Capital &
Technology • Manatt Jones Global Strategies, LLC
(Strategic consulting affiliate)

THE STATS

No. of attorneys: 325 (plus additional consultants)
No. of offices: 9
Summer associate offers: 5 out of 7 (2002)
Chief Executive & Managing Partner: Paul H. Irving
Hiring Partner: Keith Allen-Niesen

RANKING RECAP

Best in Region
#15 - California

NOTABLE PERKS

- Free parking and gym facilities (some locations)
- Pizza Wednesdays/doughnut Fridays
- Lots of CLE courses
- Tennis and basketball courts (LA)

EMPLOYMENT CONTACT

Ms. Kimberley A. Firment
Recruiting Manager
Fax: (310) 312-4224
E-mail: recruiting@manatt.com

BASE SALARY

Los Angeles, CA
Summer associate: $2,400/week

THE BUZZ
WHAT ATTORNEYS AT OTHER FIRMS ARE SAYING ABOUT THIS FIRM

- "Good lawyers, solid reputation"
- "A tough place to work"
- "Strong in entertainment"
- "Stifling, oppressive environment"

Nixon Peabody LLP

101 Federal Street
Boston, MA 02110
Phone: (617) 345-1000
www.nixonpeabody.com

LOCATIONS

Albany, NY • Boston, MA • Buffalo, NY • Hartford, CT • Long Island, NY • Manchester, NH • McLean, VA • New York, NY • Orange County, CA • Philadelphia, PA • Providence, RI • Rochester, NY • San Francisco, CA • Washington, DC

MAJOR DEPARTMENTS/PRACTICES

Bankruptcy & Reorganization • Business Litigation • Energy and Environment • Financial Services & Specialty Finance • Health Services • Insurance • Labor and Employee Benefits • Private Clients • Products Liability & Complex Tort • Public Finance • Real Estate • Technology and Intellectual Property

THE STATS

No. of attorneys: 600+
No. of offices: 15
Summer associate offers: 27 out of 29 (2002)
Co-Managing Partners: Harry P. Trueheart III and Nester M. Nicholas, Esq.
Hiring Partner: Jill K. Schultz, Esq.

RANKING RECAP

Quality of Life
#19 - Training

NOTABLE PERKS

- Signing bonus
- Matching 401(k)
- Firm pays for real estate attorney for first home

EMPLOYMENT CONTACTS

Boston, MA
Ms. Renée C. Vanna, Recruitment Coordinator
E-mail: rvanna@nixonpeabody.com

Long Island, NY
Ms. Theresa Donohue, Recruitment Coordinator
E-mail: tdonohue@nixonpeabody.com

New York, NY
Ms. Brenda K. Powers, Recruitment Coordinator
E-mail: bpowers@nixonpeabody.com

Rochester, NY
Ms. Karen E. Marr, Recruitment Administrator
E-mail: kmarr@nixonpeabody.com

San Francisco, CA
Ms. Valerie Lewis, Recruitment Coordinator
E-mail: vlewis@nixonpeabody.com

Washington, DC
Ms. Mieko I. Rechka, Recruitment Coordinator
E-mail: mrechka@nixonpeabody.com

All other offices
Ms. Layla Callahan, Recruitment Manager
E-mail: lcallahan@nixonpeabody.com

THE BUZZ
WHAT ATTORNEYS AT OTHER FIRMS ARE SAYING ABOUT THIS FIRM

- "Rising fast"
- "Stodgy"
- "Good work environment"
- "Wanna-be"

BASE SALARY

Boston, MA
1st year: $115,000
Summer associate: $2,050/week

Palmer & Dodge LLP

111 Huntington Avenue at Prudential Center
Boston, MA 02199
Phone: (617) 239-0100
www.palmerdodge.com

LOCATION

Boston, MA

MAJOR DEPARTMENTS/PRACTICES

Affordable Housing Finance • Antitrust • Bankruptcy, Reorganization & Workout • Biomedical • Business Law • Construction • Employee Benefits & Executive Compensation • Energy • Environmental & Land Use • Finance • Hospitality • Insurance • Intellectual Property • International • Internet/E-Commerce • Investment Management • Labor & Employment • Litigation • Patent • Private Client • Product Liability & Negligence Defense • Public Law • Public Offerings & Public Companies • Publishing & Entertainment • Real Estate • Schools & Colleges • Tax • Technology • Telecommunications • Transportation • Venture Capital & Private Equity •

THE STATS

No. of attorneys: 170 +
No. of offices: 1
Summer associate offers: 14 out of 14 (2002)
Managing Partner: Jeffrey F. Jones
Hiring Partner: Elizabeth P. Seaman

RANKING RECAP

Best in Region
#10 - Boston

Quality of Life
#3 - Offices
#17 - Associate/Partner Relations
#20 - Pro Bono

NOTABLE PERKS

- Bar expenses
- In-house cafeteria
- Generous family leave
- Friday cocktail receptions

EMPLOYMENT CONTACT

Ms. Katy von Mehren
Phone: (617) 239-0172
Fax: (617) 227-4420
E-mail: kvonmehren@palmerdodge.com

BASE SALARY

Boston, MA
1st year: $110,000
Summer associate: $2,115/week

THE BUZZ
WHAT ATTORNEYS AT OTHER FIRMS ARE SAYING ABOUT THIS FIRM

- "Strong local presence"
- "Precariously situated"
- "Very bright people"
- "Fading"

Pepper Hamilton LLP

3000 Two Logan Square
Eighteenth and Arch Streets
Philadelphia, PA 19103-2799
Phone: (215) 981-4000
www.pepperlaw.com

LOCATIONS

Philadelphia, PA (HQ)
Berwyn, PA • Detroit, MI • Harrisburg, PA • New York,
NY • Pittsburgh, PA • Princeton, NJ • Washington, DC
• Wilmington, DE

MAJOR DEPARTMENTS/PRACTICES

Antitrust • Appellate Practice • Bankruptcy &
Reorganization • Construction Law • Corporate &
Securities • Corporate Governance • Employee Benefits
• Energy Practice • Environmental Law • ERISA &
Employee Benefits • Executive Compensation • Family
Business • Financial Services & Banking • Franchising •
Government Regulation • Insurance & Reinsurance •
Intellectual Property • Health Care Services • Labor &
Employment • Litigation • Natural Resources • Retail
Industry • Sports Practice • Tax • Technology •
Transportation • Venture Capital • White Collar Criminal
Defense

THE STATS

No. of attorneys: 400
No. of offices: 9
Summer associate offers: 20 out of 25 (2002)
Managing Partner: Robert E. Heideck
Hiring Partner: Paul J. Kennedy

RANKING RECAP

Best in Region
#6 - Pennsylvania

NOTABLE PERKS

- Stipend for entry-level associates
- BlackBerry expenses
- Entrance fees for charity and community events
- Associates development lunch once a month

EMPLOYMENT CONTACT

Ms. Meg L. Urbanski
Director of Professional Recruitment
Phone: (215) 981-4991
Fax: (215) 981-4750
E-mail: urbanskim@pepperlaw.com

BASE SALARY

Berwyn, Philadelphia, Pittsburgh, PA; Princeton, NJ; Wilmington, DE
1st year: $105,000

Detroit, MI
1st year: $95,000

Harrisburg, PA
1st year: $90,000

THE BUZZ
WHAT ATTORNEYS AT OTHER FIRMS ARE SAYING ABOUT THIS FIRM

- "Competent"
- "Not a player"
- "Good, solid firm"
- "Questionable stability"

Powell, Goldstein, Frazer & Murphy LLP

191 Peachtree Street, NE, 16th Floor
Atlanta, GA 30303
Phone: (404) 572-6600
www.pgfm.com

LOCATIONS

Atlanta, GA (HQ)
Washington, DC

MAJOR DEPARTMENTS/PRACTICES

Antitrust & Consumer Protection • Bankruptcy &
Corporate Reorganization • Biotechnology & Life
Sciences • Business Transactions & Corporate Finance
• Commercial Lending • Corporate Compliance •
Employee Benefits & Executive Compensation •
Environmental • Financial Institutions • Financial
Products • Government & Construction Contracts •
Government Relations • Health Care • Homeland
Security • Immigration • Information Security & Privacy
• Intellectual Property • International • Labor &
Employment • Litigation • Public Finance • Real Estate •
Tax • Technology & E-Commerce • White Collar Crime

THE STATS

No. of attorneys: 293
No. of offices: 2
Summer associate offers: 30 out of 32 (2002)
Managing Partner: Armin G. Brecher
Hiring Partners: Todd E. Jones (Atlanta) and Richard A.
Medway (DC)

RANKING RECAP

Best in Region
#5 - The South

Best in Diversity
#7 - Diversity for Women
#9 - Overall Diversity
#13 - Diversity for Gays & Lesbians
#18 - Diversity for Minorities

NOTABLE PERKS

• Bar expenses for two states
• Annual $500 professional development fund
• Biannual associate retreat
• BlackBerry, laptop & home computer

EMPLOYMENT CONTACT

Ms. Jenny Wallace
Recruiting Manager
Phone: (404) 572-6782
Fax: (404) 572-6999
E-mail: jwallace@pgfm.com

BASE SALARY

Atlanta, GA
1st year: $100,000
Summer associate: $1,750/week

Washington, DC
1st year: $110,000
Summer associate: $2,115/week

THE BUZZ
WHAT ATTORNEYS AT OTHER FIRMS ARE SAYING ABOUT THIS FIRM

• "Prestigious in Atlanta"
• "Unimpressive"
• "Diverse, friendly, pleasant"
• "Lost crown-jewel trade department"

Reed Smith

435 Sixth Avenue
Pittsburgh, PA 15219
Phone: (412) 288-3131
www.reedsmith.com

LOCATIONS

Pittsburgh, PA (HQ) • Century City, CA • Falls Church, VA • Harrisburg, PA • Leesburg, VA • Los Angeles, CA • Newark, NJ • New York, NY • Oakland, CA • Philadelphia, PA • Princeton, NJ • Richmond, VA • San Francisco, CA • Washington, DC • Westlake Village, CA • Wilmington, DE • London • Coventry, UK •

MAJOR DEPARTMENTS/PRACTICES

Advocacy • Antitrust • Appellate • Associations • Banking • Bankruptcy & Reorganization • Benefits • Business Immigration • Communications • Competition • Construction • Consumer Financial Services • Corporate Services • Debt Recovery • E-Commerce • Energy & Natural Resources • Executive Comp. • Export, Customs, Trade • Financial Services • Fraud • French • Gov't Contracts & Relations • Health Care • Higher Education/K-12 • Homeland Security • Information Tech. • Infrastructure/Financial Solutions • Insurance/ Reinsurance • Insurance Cov. for Policy Holders • IP • Int'l Distribution • Investment Management • Labor & Employment • Life Sciences • M&A • Nonprofit • Product Liability • Project Finance/Public Finance • Real Estate • Risk/Liability • Securities • Tax • Tech. • Trusts & Estates • VC

THE STATS

No. of attorneys: 500+
No. of offices: 18
Summer associate offers: 56 out of 69 (2002)
Managing Partner: Gregory B. Jordan
Hiring Partner: Peter S. Clark II

THE BUZZ
WHAT ATTORNEYS AT OTHER FIRMS ARE SAYING ABOUT THIS FIRM

- "Family-friendly"
- "Style over substance"
- "Cool space practice"
- "Serious morale problems"

RANKING RECAP

Best in Region
#5 - Pennsylvania

NOTABLE PERKS

- Profit-sharing plan
- Well-funded 401k

EMPLOYMENT CONTACT

Ms. Lorraine Rivera Connally
Firmwide Director of Legal Recruiting
Phone: (412) 288-4194
Fax: (412) 288-3063

BASE SALARY

Philadelphia, Pittsburgh, PA;
Newark, Princeton, NJ; Falls Church, VA
1st year: $100,000
Summer associate: $1,923/week

Century City, Los Angeles,
Oakland, San Francisco, CA
1st year: $125,000
Summer associate: $2,400/week

New York, NY; Washington, DC
1st year: $110,000
Summer associate: $2,115/week

Schiff Hardin & Waite

6600 Sears Tower
233 South Wacker Drive
Chicago, IL 60606
Phone: (312) 258-5500
www.schiffhardin.com

LOCATIONS

Chicago, IL (HQ)
Lake Forest, IL
New York, NY
Washington, DC
Dublin

MAJOR DEPARTMENTS/PRACTICES

Antitrust
Bankruptcy
Construction
Corporate
Energy/Telecommunications & Public Utilities
Environmental
Estate Planning & Administration
Intellectual Property
Labor & Employment
Litigation
Product Liability
Real Estate
Securities
Tax

THE STATS

No. of attorneys: 300+
No. of offices: 5
Summer associate offers: 21 out of 23 (2002)
Managing Partner: Scott E. Pickins
Hiring Partner: Carol R. Prygrosky

THE BUZZ

WHAT ATTORNEYS AT OTHER FIRMS ARE SAYING ABOUT THIS FIRM

- "One of the better mid-size firms"
- "Low salaries"
- "Rising star, high quality"
- "B-team"

RANKING RECAP

Quality of Life
#1 - Satisfaction
#2 - Associate/Partner Relations
#3 - Retention
#17 - Pro Bono

Best in Diversity
#9 - Diversity for Women

NOTABLE PERKS

- Bar expenses for up to two organizations
- Workweek wine and cheese parties
- Bar exam stipend and moving expenses
- In-house travel agent
- Late evening dinner and cab reimbursement

EMPLOYMENT CONTACT

Ms. Lily Beltran
Law Student Recruitment Coordinator
Phone: (312) 258-4832
Fax: (312) 258-5600
E-mail: lbeltran@schiffhardin.com

BASE SALARY

All offices
1st year: $125,000
2nd-8th year: Individually set
Summer associate: $2,400/week

Sedgwick, Detert, Moran & Arnold LLP

16th Floor, One Embarcadero Center
San Francisco, CA 94111-13628
Phone: (415) 781-7900
www.sdma.com

LOCATIONS

San Francisco, CA (HQ)
Chicago, IL
Dallas, TX
Irvine, CA
Los Angeles, CA
Newark, NJ
New York, NY
London
Paris
Zurich

MAJOR DEPARTMENTS/PRACTICES

Antitrust • Bankruptcy • Business Litigation •
Employment & Labor • Environmental & Toxic Tort •
Intellectual Property • International • Product Liability •
Professional Liability • Real Estate • Safety

THE STATS

No. of attorneys: 335
No. of offices: 10
Summer associate offers: 5 out of 6 (2002)
Chairman: Stephanie A. Sheridan

RANKING RECAP

Quality of Life
#7 - Hours
#16 - Satisfaction
#20 (tie) - Offices

Best in Diversity
#10 - Diversity for Gays & Lesbians
#17 - Overall Diversity

NOTABLE PERKS

- Discounts on car purchases
- Happy hours
- Cell phone reimbursements
- Firm-wide Friday lunches

EMPLOYMENT CONTACT

Ms. Vicky Berry
Director of Attorney Recruiting
Phone: (415) 781-7900
Fax: (415) 781-2635
E-mail: vicky.berry@sdma.com

BASE SALARY

San Francisco, CA
1st year: $100,000
Summer associate: $1,925/week (firm-wide)

THE BUZZ
WHAT ATTORNEYS AT OTHER FIRMS ARE SAYING ABOUT THIS FIRM

- "Up and coming"
- "Sweatshop"
- "Solid"
- "Underpaid associates"

Seyfarth Shaw

53 East Monroe Street, Suite 4200
Chicago, IL 60603-5803
Phone: (312) 346-8000
www.seyfarth.com

LOCATIONS

Chicago, IL (HQ)
Atlanta, GA • Boston, MA • Houston, TX • Los
Angeles, CA • New York, NY • Sacramento, CA • San
Francisco, CA • Washington, DC • Brussels

MAJOR DEPARTMENTS/PRACTICES

Bankruptcy, Workouts & Business Reorganization
Business Immigration
Construction
Corporate
E-Commerce
Employee Benefits
Environmental Safety & Health
Government, Commercial & International Contracts
Intellectual Property
International
Labor & Employment
Litigation
Real Estate

THE STATS

No. of attorneys: 530
No. of offices: 10
Summer associate offers: 6 out of 6 (2002)
Managing Partner: J. Stephen Poor
Hiring Partner: James L. Curtis

RANKING RECAP

Best in Practice
#5- Labor & Employment

Best in Diversity
#20 - Diversity for Women

NOTABLE PERKS

• Free dinner Monday through Thursday

EMPLOYMENT CONTACT

Ms. Dawn M. Patchett
Legal Hiring Coordinator
Phone: (312) 739-6458
E-mail: dpatchett@seyfarth.com

BASE SALARY

Chicago, IL
1st year: $120,000
Summer associate: $2,300/week

THE BUZZ
WHAT ATTORNEYS AT OTHER FIRMS ARE SAYING ABOUT THIS FIRM

• "Good labor work"
• "One-trick pony"
• "Venerable old Chicago labor firm"
• "Mediocre"

Sheppard, Mullin, Richter & Hampton LLP

333 South Hope Street
Forty-Eighth Floor
Los Angeles, CA 90071-1448
Phone: (213) 620-1780
www.sheppardmullin.com

LOCATIONS

Los Angeles (2 offices) (HQ)
Costa Mesa, CA
San Diego, CA (2 offices)
San Francisco, CA
Santa Barbara, CA
Washington, DC

MAJOR DEPARTMENTS/PRACTICES

Corporate & Securities
Entertainment
Finance & Bankruptcy
Intellectual Property
Labor & Employment
Litigation
Real Estate
Tax & Estate Planning

THE STATS

No. of attorneys: 370+
No. of offices: 8
Summer associate offers: 19 out of 21 (2002)
Managing Partner: Guy N. Halgren
Hiring Partner: Robert E. Williams

NOTABLE PERKS

- Bar stipend
- Business casual attire
- Moving expenses
- Free parking

EMPLOYMENT CONTACT

Ms. Sally C. Bucklin
Manager of Attorney Hiring
Phone: (213) 617-4101
Fax: (213) 620-1398
E-mail: sbucklin@sheppardmullin.com

BASE SALARY

All offices
1st year: $125,000
Summer associate: $2,400/month

THE BUZZ
WHAT ATTORNEYS AT OTHER FIRMS ARE SAYING ABOUT THIS FIRM

- "Friendly"
- "Unimaginative"
- "Rising star"
- "In flux"

Shook, Hardy & Bacon L.L.P.

One Kansas City Place
1200 Main Street
Kansas City, MO 64105-2118
Phone: (816) 474-6550
www.shb.com

LOCATIONS

Kansas City, MO (HQ)

Houston, TX • Irvine, CA • Miami, FL • New Orleans, LA • Overland Park, KS • Tampa, FL • San Francisco, CA • Washington, DC • Geneva • London

MAJOR DEPARTMENTS/PRACTICES

Antitrust • Banking & Financial Services • Bankruptcy & Creditors' Rights • Business Planning • Commercial Law Commercial Litigation • Communications • Design & Construction • Employee Benefits • Energy • Environmental Law • ERISA Litigation • Estate Planning & Probate • Financing Transactions & Securities Offerings • Firm Services • Health Law • Insurance Litigation • Intellectual Property • National Employment Litigation & Policy • Privacy Statements • Products Liability Litigation • Public Policy • Real Estate • Tort • White Collar • Tax Controversy • Tax Planning

THE STATS

No. of attorneys: 600
No. of offices: 11
Summer associate offers: 21 out of 22 (2002)
Managing Partner: John F. Murphy
Hiring Partner: Steven D. Soden

NOTABLE PERKS

- Bar and moving expenses
- Profit-sharing
- Three-month mandatory sabbatical

EMPLOYMENT CONTACT

Ms. Jessica A. Baker, Esq.
Dir., Legal Recruiting & Professional Development
Phone: (816) 474-6550
Fax: (816) 421-4066
E-mail: jbaker@shb.com

BASE SALARY

Kansas City, MO; Tampa, FL
1st year: $83,000 (+ $5,500 stipend)
Summer associate: $1,550/week

Houston, TX
1st year: $110,000 (+ $10,000 signing bonus)
Summer associate: $2,100/week

Miami, FL
1st year: $105,000 (+ $5,500 stipend)
Summer associate: $2,000/week

New Orleans, LA
1st year: $80,000 (+ $5,500 stipend)
Summer associate: $1,500/week

San Francisco, CA
1st year: $125,000 (+ $6,000 stipend)
Summer associate: $2,400/week

Washington, DC
1st year: $120,000 (+ $6,000 stipend)

THE BUZZ
WHAT ATTORNEYS AT OTHER FIRMS ARE SAYING ABOUT THIS FIRM

- "Top litigators"
- "Big tobacco rules"
- "Hard-working lawyers"
- "One-dimensional"

The Vault Guide to the Top 100 Law Firms • 6th Edition
....
The Best of the Rest

Stoel Rives LLP

900 SW Fifth Avenue, Suite 2600
Portland, OR 97204
Phone: (503) 224-3380
www.stoel.com

LOCATIONS

Portland, OR (HQ)
Boise, ID
Sacramento, CA
Salt Lake City, UT
San Francisco, CA
Seattle, WA
Tahoe City, CA
Vancouver, WA

MAJOR DEPARTMENTS/PRACTICES

Business Services
Energy & Telecommunications
Litigation
Resources, Development & Environment
Technology & Intellectual Property

THE STATS

No. of attorneys: 370 +
No. of offices: 8
Summer associate offers: 17 out of 22 (2002)
Managing Partner: Stephen O. Kenyon
Hiring Partner: Stephen L. Griffith

RANKING RECAP

Best in Region
#4 - Pacific Northwest

NOTABLE PERKS

- Paid sabbatical
- Moving expenses, plus movers who do the packing
- Paid parental leave & domestic partner benefits
- Transportation subsidies

EMPLOYMENT CONTACT

Ms. Michelle Baird Johnson
Lawyer Recruiting Manager
Phone: (503) 294-9539
Fax: (503) 220-2480
E-mail: mbjohnson@stoel.com

BASE SALARY

Portland, OR; Salt Lake City, UT
1st year: $85,000
Summer associate: $1,500/week

Boise, ID
1st year: $72,000
Summer associate: $1,350/week

San Francisco, CA
1st year: $110,000
Summer associate: $1,800/week

Seattle, WA
1st year: $92,000
Summer associate: $1,850/week

THE BUZZ
WHAT ATTORNEYS AT OTHER FIRMS ARE SAYING ABOUT THIS FIRM

- "Among the best in the Northwest"
- "Struggling to be known"
- "Big fish in small pond"
- "Resting on its laurels"

Sutherland Asbill & Brennan LLP

1275 Pennsylvania Avenue, NW
Washington, DC 20004-2415
Phone: (202) 383-0100

999 Peachtree Street North
Atlanta, GA 30309
Phone: (404) 853-8000
www.sablaw.com

LOCATIONS

Washington, DC (HQ)
Atlanta, GA
Austin, TX
Houston, TX
New York, NY
Tallahassee, FL

MAJOR DEPARTMENTS/PRACTICES

Antitrust & Trade Regulation • Biotechnology & Life
Sciences • Business Restructuring & Bankruptcy •
Corporate • Dealer & Franchise Litigation • Employment
Litigation • Energy & Commodities • Environmental •
Financial Services • Health Care • Hospitality • IP •
International • Litigation • Professional Liability • Real
Estate • Securities Enforcement & Litigation •
Structured Finance • Tax • Technology •
Telecommunications • Timber & Forest Products

THE STATS

No. of attorneys: 329
No. of offices: 6
Managing Partner: James L. Henderson III
Hiring Partners: Richard G. Murphy Jr. (Washington)
and William G. Rothschild (Atlanta)

RANKING RECAP

Quality of Life
#8 - Retention
#15 - Hours

NOTABLE PERKS

- Breakfast and happy hour on Friday
- Moving expenses
- On-site massages
- Weekly attorney coffees

EMPLOYMENT CONTACTS

Washington
Ms. Melissa C. Wilson
Manager of Legal Recruiting
Phone: (202) 383-0100
Fax: (202) 637-3593
E-mail: mwilson@sablaw.com

Atlanta
Ms. Beth Miller
Manager of Legal Recruiting
Phone: (404) 853-8000
Fax: (404) 853-8806

BASE SALARY

Washington, DC
1st year: $110,000
Summer associate: $2,400/week

Atlanta, GA
1st year: $100,000
Summer associate: $1,750/week

THE BUZZ
WHAT ATTORNEYS AT OTHER FIRMS ARE SAYING ABOUT THIS FIRM

- "Very intellectual"
- "Tax nerds"
- "Good morale"
- Not big-time yet"

Swidler Berlin Shereff Friedman, LLP

3000 K Street, NW, Suite 300
Washington, DC 20007-5118
Phone: (202) 424-7500

405 Lexington Avenue
New York, NY 10174
Phone: (212) 973-0111
www.swidlaw.com

LOCATIONS

Washington, DC (HQ)
New York, NY

MAJOR DEPARTMENTS/PRACTICES

Washington only: Antitrust & Trade Regulation • E-Commerce Energy • Environmental • Franchising • Insurance Coverage • Intellectual Property • Telecommunications

All offices: Bankruptcy & Creditors' Rights • Corporate Government Affairs • Housing • Litigation • Mergers & Acquisitions • Public & Private Offerings • Real Estate & Structured Finance • Tax/ERISA • Venture Capital

THE STATS

No. of attorneys: 273
No. of offices: 2
Managing Partner: Barry B. Direnfeld
Hiring Partners: Brian W. Fiztgerald (DC) and Scott ZImmerman (NY)

NOTABLE PERKS

- Car service after 7 p.m.
- Bar expenses
- 12-week maternity leave, 4-week parental leave
- Free sodas and juice (DC)

EMPLOYMENT CONTACTS

Washington, DC
Ms. Kai Wilson
Recruiting Coordinator
Phone: (202) 424-7658
Fax: (202) 424-7664
E-mail: kewilson@swidlaw.com

New York, NY
Ms. Judith Abraham
Recruiting Manager
Phone: (212) 891-9325
Fax: (212) 891-9598
E-mail: jmabraham@swidlaw.com

BASE SALARY

Washington, DC
1st year: $125,000
Summer associate: $2,400/week

New York, NY
1st year: $130,000
Summer associate: $2,500/week

THE BUZZ
WHAT ATTORNEYS AT OTHER FIRMS ARE SAYING ABOUT THIS FIRM

- "Savvy attorneys"
- "Stodgy"
- "Good telecom practice"
- "Solid but uninspired"

Thompson & Knight LLP

1700 Pacific Avenue, Suite 3300
Dallas, TX 75201
Phone: (214) 969-1700
www.tklaw.com

LOCATIONS

Dallas, TX (HQ)
Austin, TX
Fort Worth, TX
Houston, TX
Algiers
Monterrey
Paris

MAJOR DEPARTMENTS/PRACTICES

Corporate & Securities
Corporate Reorganization & Creditors' Rights
Energy
Environmental
Finance
Government Relations & Public Policy
Intellectual Property
Labor & Employment
Real Estate & Banking
Tax Benefits & Estate Planning
Technology
Trials & Appellate

THE STATS

No. of attorneys: 347
No. of offices: 8
Summer associate offers: 39 out of 60 (2002)
Managing Partner: Peter J. Riley
Hiring Partner: M. Lawrence Hicks Jr.

RANKING RECAP

Best in Region
#9 - Texas

NOTABLE PERKS

- Moving expenses
- Signing bonus
- Graduation bonus
- Bar expenses

EMPLOYMENT CONTACT

Ms. Courtney L. Bankler
National Recruiting Coordinator
Phone: (214) 969-1379
Fax: (214) 969-1751
E-mail: courtney.bankler@tklaw.com

BASE SALARY

Austin, Dallas, Houston, TX
1st year: $121,500
Summer associate: $2,100/week

THE BUZZ
WHAT ATTORNEYS AT OTHER FIRMS ARE SAYING ABOUT THIS FIRM

- "Great regional firm"
- "Treading water"
- "Very Texan, very friendly"
- "B-list"

Troutman Sanders LLP

Bank of America Plaza
600 Peachtree Street, NE
Suite 5200
Atlanta, GA 30308-2216
Phone: (404) 885-3000
www.troutmansanders.com

LOCATIONS

Atlanta, GA (HQ)
McLean, VA
Norfolk, VA
Raleigh, NC
Richmond, VA
Virginia Beach, VA
Washington, DC
Hong Kong
London

MAJOR DEPARTMENTS/PRACTICES

Corporate
Finance
Litigation
Public Law (Regulatory)
Real Estate

THE STATS

No. of attorneys: 500+
No. of offices: 10
Summer associate offers: 47 out of 62 (2002)
Managing Partner: Robert W. Webb Jr.
Hiring Partner: John S. West

THE BUZZ
WHAT ATTORNEYS AT OTHER FIRMS ARE SAYING ABOUT THIS FIRM

- "Excellent firm atmosphere"
- "Stuck in place"
- "Southern hospitality"
- "Overrated"

RANKING RECAP

Best in Region
#3 - The South

Quality of Life
#1 - Hours
#4 - Retention
#14 - Best 20 Law Firms to Work For
#16 - Offices
#18 - Satisfaction

Best in Diversity
#6 - Diversity for Minorities

NOTABLE PERKS

- Three-month maternity leave
- Bar and moving expenses
- Braves' tickets in Atlanta office
- Summer associate & associate retreats

EMPLOYMENT CONTACT

Ms. Betsy Glass
Director of Recruiting
Phone: (404) 885-3000
Fax: (404) 962-6927
E-mail: betsy.glass@troutmansanders.com

BASE SALARY

Atlanta, GA
1st year: $100,000
Summer associate: $1,750/week

McLean, VA; Washington, DC
1st year: $120,000
Summer associate: $2,300/week

Richmond, Virginia Beach, VA
1st year: $90,000
Summer associate: $1,750/week

Venable LLP

1201 New York Avenue, NW
Washington, DC 20005
Phone: (202) 962-4800
www.venable.com

LOCATIONS

Washington, DC (HQ)
Baltimore, MD
Rockville, MD
Towson, MD
Vienna, VA

MAJOR DEPARTMENTS/PRACTICES

Advertising, Marketing & New Media • Banking &
Financial Services • Bankruptcy & Creditors' Rights •
Bioscience • Business Immigration/Transactions •
Commercial Litigation • Communications • Construction
• Copyright, Unfair Trade & Entertainment • Corporate
Defense/White Collar • Corporate Finance & Securities •
Corporate Governance & Investigations • Education •
Employee Benefits • Environment • Food & Drug •
Franchise & Distribution • Gov't Contracts • Health
Care • Homeland Security • IP Litigation • Int'l Trade •
Labor & Employment • Legislative & Gov't Affairs •
M&A • Nonprofit Organizations • Patent Prosecution •
Pharmaceuticals • Product Liability & Toxic Torts • Real
Estate • State & Local Government • Taxation • Trade
& Professional Associations • Trademark •
Transportation & Infrastructure • Trusts & Estates

THE STATS

No. of attorneys: 435
No. of offices: 5
Summer associate offers: 14 out of 21 (2002)
Managing Partner: James L. Shea
Hiring Co-Chairs: Thomas M. Lingan, David W. Goewey

THE BUZZ
WHAT ATTORNEYS AT OTHER FIRMS ARE SAYING ABOUT THIS FIRM

- "Cutting edge"
- "Overrated"
- "Fine litigators"
- "Has lost some luster"

NOTABLE PERKS

- Bar expenses
- Free taxi home if working late
- Moving expenses
- Happy hour after summer softball games

EMPLOYMENT CONTACT

Ms. Grace Cunningham
Director of Legal Personnel
Phone: (202) 962-4875
Fax: (202) 962-8300
E-mail: gcunningham@venable.com

BASE SALARY

Washington, DC
1st year: $125,000
Summer associate: $2,200/week

Baltimore, MD
1st year: $110,000
Summer associate: $2,000/week

Winstead Sechrest & Minick P.C.

5400 Renaissance Tower
1201 Elm Street
Dallas TX 75270-2199
Phone: (214) 745-5400
www.winstead.com

LOCATIONS

Dallas, TX (HQ)
Austin, TX
Fort Worth, TX
Houston, TX
Washington, DC
The Woodlands, TX
Mexico City

MAJOR DEPARTMENTS/PRACTICES

Banking & Credit Transactions
Bankruptcy
Corporate/Securities/Taxation
Environmental
Government Relations
Intellectual Property
Labor & Employment
Litigation
Public Law
Real Estate
Wealth Preservation

THE STATS

No. of attorneys: 332
No. of offices: 7
Summer associate offers: 17 out of 21 (2002)
Managing Partner: W. Mike Baggett
Hiring Partner: Wayne Bost

NOTABLE PERKS

- 401(k) matching plan and profit sharing
- BlackBerry pagers
- Paid parking

EMPLOYMENT CONTACT

Mr. Wayne Bost
Hiring Partner
Phone: (512) 370-2859
E-mail: AttorneyResume@winstead.com

BASE SALARY

Dallas, TX
1st year: $105,000
Summer associate: $2,100/week

THE BUZZ
WHAT ATTORNEYS AT OTHER FIRMS ARE SAYING ABOUT THIS FIRM

- "Probably the most up-and-coming firm in Texas"
- "Stodgy old men's firm "
- "Great place to work"
- "Overrated"

The Vault Guide to the Top 100 Law Firms • 6th Edition
....
The Best of the Rest

Wolf, Block, Schorr and Solis-Cohen LLP

1650 Arch Street, 22nd Floor
Philadelphia, PA 19103-2097
Phone: (215) 977-2362
www.wolfblock.com

LOCATIONS

Philadelphia, PA (HQ)
Cherry Hill, NJ
Harrisburg, PA
Newark, NJ
New York, NY
Norristown, PA
Wilmington, DE

MAJOR DEPARTMENTS/PRACTICES

Bankruptcy • Business Litigation • Communication •
Complex Fidelity/Liability Litigation • Corporate/
Securities • Employee Benefits • Employment Services •
Environmental Law • Estates & Trusts • Family Law •
Financial Services • Government Assisted & Affordable
Housing • Health Law • Intellectual Property &
Information Technology • Mortgage Credit Lending •
Real Estate • Securitiziation • Tax • Utility Regulation

THE STATS

No. of attorneys: 263
No. of offices: 7
Summer associate offers: 6 out of 8 (2002)
Chairman: Mark Alderman
Hiring Partner: Jodi T. Plavner

RANKING RECAP

Best in Region
#10 - Pennsylvania

NOTABLE PERKS

- Bar expenses
- Taxi vouchers or parking paid after 7 p.m.
- Free dinner after 7 p.m.

EMPLOYMENT CONTACT

Ms. Eileen M. McMahon
Director, Legal Personnel & Recruitment
Phone: (215) 977-2362
Fax: (215) 405-3962
E-mail: emcmahon@wolfblock.com

BASE SALARY

Philadelphia, PA
1st year: $107,000
Summer associate: $2,050/week

THE BUZZ
WHAT ATTORNEYS AT OTHER FIRMS ARE SAYING ABOUT THIS FIRM

- "Quality regional firm"
- "Impersonal"
- "Good people"
- "Low-end work"

Womble Carlyle Sandridge & Rice, PLLC

One West Fourth Street
Winston-Salem, NC 27101
Phone: (336) 721-3600
www.wcsr.com

LOCATIONS

Winston-Salem, NC (HQ)
Atlanta, GA
Charlotte, NC
Greensboro, NC
Greenville, SC
McLean, VA
Raleigh, NC
Research Triangle Park, NC
Washington, DC

MAJOR DEPARTMENTS/PRACTICES

Antitrust/Trade Practices • Bankruptcy & Creditors'
Rights • Business Litigation • Capital Markets •
Corporate & Securities • Economic Development •
Employee Benefits • Environmental Law/Toxic Tort
Litigation • Government Relations • Health Care •
Insurance, Governmental & Tort Litigation • Intellectual
Property • International • Labor & Employment • Patent
• Product Liability Litigation • Real Estate • Sarbanes-
Oxley • Tax • Technology & Commerce •
Telecommunications • Trusts & Estates

THE STATS

No. of attorneys: 450
No. of offices: 9
Chairman: Keith W. Vaughan
Hiring Partner: Ellen M. Gregg

NOTABLE PERKS

- Moving expenses
- Bar expenses
- Domestic partner benefits
- Judicial clerkship bonuses

EMPLOYMENT CONTACT

Ms. Cynthia K. Pruitt
Prof. Devevelopment & Recruiting Administrator
Phone: (336) 721-3680
Fax: (336) 721-3660
E-mail: cpruitt@wcsr.com

BASE SALARY

**Charlotte, Durham, Greensboro, Raleigh,
Winston-Salem, NC**
1st year: $90,000
Summer associate: $1,600/week

Atlanta, GA
1st year: $100,000
Summer associate: $1,750/week

Greenville, SC
1st year: $80,000
Summer associate: $1,450/week

McLean, VA; Washington, DC
1st year: $115,000
Summer associate: $1,875/week

THE BUZZ
WHAT ATTORNEYS AT OTHER FIRMS ARE SAYING ABOUT THIS FIRM

- "Solid"
- "Like a trip back to the fabulous fifties"
- "The best of the South"
- "All tobacco, all the time "

LEGAL
EMPLOYER
DIRECTORY

ARIZONA

Bryan Cave LLP
1 Renaissance Square
Two North Central Ave., Suite 2200
Phoenix, AZ 85004-4406
Phone: (602) 364-7400
Fax: (602) 364-7070
www.bryancave.com

Lynne L. Traverse

Manager of Legal Recruiting – Phoenix and Irvine
Phone: (602) 364-7000
Fax: (602) 364-7070
lltraverse@bryancave.com

CALIFORNIA

Bryan Cave LLP
120 Broadway, Suite 300
Santa Monica, CA 90401-2386
Phone: (310) 576-2100
Fax: (310) 576-2200
www.bryancave.com

Sheryl A. Jones
Manager of Legal Recruiting - Los Angeles
Phone: (310) 576-2303
Fax: (310) 576-2200
sajones@bryancave.com

Bryan Cave LLP
2020 Main Street, Suite 600
Irvine, CA 92614-8226
Phone: (949) 223-7000
Fax: (949) 223-7100
www.bryancave.com

Lynne L. Traverse
Manager of Legal Recruiting - Phoenix and Irvine
Phone: (602) 364-7400
Fax: (602) 364-7070
lltraverse@bryancave.com

Chadbourne & Parke LLP
350 South Grand Avenue
Suite 3300
Los Angeles, CA 90071
Phone: (213) 892-1000
Fax: (213) 622-9865
www.chadbourne.com

Jay R. Henneberry
Hiring Partner
Phone: (213) 892-1000
Fax: (213) 622-9865
E-mail: jhenneberry@chadbourne.com

Cooley Godward LLP
5 Palo Alto Square
3000 El Camino Real
Palo Alto, CA 94306-2155
Phone: (650) 843-5000
www.cooley.com

Ms. Jo Anne Larson
Director of Attorney Recruiting
Phone: (650) 843-5000
Fax: (650) 857-0663
E-mail: larsonja@cooley.com

Fenwick & West LLP
Silicon Valley Center
801 California Street
Mountain View, California 94041
Phone: (650) 988-8500
www.fenwick.com

Ms. Karen Amatangelo-Block
Attorney Recruiting Manager
Phone: (650) 335-4949
Fax: (650) 938-5200
E-mail: recruit@fenwick.com

Gibson, Dunn & Crutcher LLP
333 South Grand Avenue
Los Angeles, CA 90071-3197
Phone: (213) 229-7000
www.gibsondunn.com

Ms. Leslie E. Ripley
Director, Professional Development & Recruiting
Phone: (213) 229-7273

Gray Cary Ware & Freidenrich LLP
2000 University Circle
East Palo Alto, CA 94303
Phone: (650) 833-2000
www.graycary.com

Ms. Leslie Colvin
Professional Recruiting Director
Phone: (650) 833-2000
Fax: (650) 833-2001
E-mail: lcolvin@graycary.com

**Gunderson Dettmer Stough Villeneuve Franklin &
Hachigian, LLP**
155 Constitution Drive
Menlo Park, CA 94025
Phone: (650) 321-2400
www.gunder.com

Ms. Corinne Dritsas
Director of Legal Recruiting
Phone: (650) 463-5284
Fax: (650) 321-2800
E-mail: recruiting@gunder.com

Heller Ehrman White & McAuliffe LLP
333 Bush Street
San Francisco, CA 94104-2878
Phone: (415) 772-6000
www.hewm.com
San Francisco

Mr. Craig Blumin
Professional Recruitment Manager
Phone: (415) 772-6591
Fax: (415) 772-6268
E-mail: cblumin@hewm.com

Irell & Manella LLP
1800 Avenue of the Stars, Suite 900
Los Angeles, CA 90067-4276
Phone: (310) 277-1010
www.irell.com

Ms. Robyn Steele
Recruiting Administrator
Phone: (310) 277-1010
Toll-free: (800) 421-4502
E-mail: rsteele@irell.com

Latham & Watkins LLP
633 West Fifth Street
Suite 4000
Los Angeles, CA 90071-2007
Phone: (213) 485-1234
www.lw.com

Ms. Debra Clarkson
701 B Street, Suite 2100
San Diego, CA 92101
Phone: (619) 236-1234
E-mail: debra.clarkson@lw.com

Littler Mendelson, P.C.
650 California Street, 20th Floor
San Francisco, CA 94108-2693
Phone: (415) 433-1940
www.littler.com

Ms. Karen R. Herz
Nat'l Manager, Recruiting & Profess. Development
Phone: (415) 433-1940
Fax: (415) 399-8490
E-mail: lawrecruit@littler.com

Manatt, Phelps & Phillips, LLP
Trident Center
11355 West Olympic Boulevard
Los Angeles, CA 90064
Phone: (310) 312-4000
www.manatt.com

Ms. Kimberley A. Firment
Recruiting Manager
Fax: (310) 312-4224
E-mail: recruiting@manatt.com

McKenna Long & Aldridge LLP
444 South Flower Street
Suite 800
Los Angeles, CA 90071
Phone: (213) 688-1000
Fax: (213) 243-6330
www.mckennalong.com

Julie T. Inouye
Manager of Legal Recruitment
Phone: (213) 243-6148
Fax: (213) 243-6330
E-mail: jinouye@mckennalong.com

Number of Attorneys Firmwide: 368
Number of Attorneys in this Office: 52
Summer Associate Hires in this Office: 2 (2003)
Full-Time First-Year Hires in this Office: 2 (2003)
Lateral Hires in this Office: 0 (2003)
Summer Associate Salary (Weekly): $2,200
First-Year Associate Salary (Base): $125,000

Practice Areas
Litigation; Government Contracts; Corporate; Environmental
and Public Policy & Regulatory Affairs

Law Schools Firm Recruits From
Loyola of Los Angeles; Pepperdine; Southwestern; UCLA;
USC; Western Regional BLSA Job Fair

Firm Leadership
James Gallagher (Co-Chair); Clay Long (Co-Chair): Ray
Biagini (Co-Vice Chair); Jeff Haidet (Co-Vice Chair); Tom
Hall (Co-Managing Partner); and Tom Papson (Co-Managing
Partner)

Firm Description
Formed as a result of a merger in 2002, McKenna Long &
Aldridge LLP is a firm of more than 350 lawyers spread across
8 offices in the United States and Brussels, Belgium. The firm
is divided into six large departments: Litigation; Corporate;
Government Contracts; Intellectual Property and Technology;
Public Policy and Regulatory Affairs; and, Real Estate Finance
and Development. Each department is comprised of smaller
practice groups that provide a broad array of legal services to
our clients.

Morrison & Foerster LLP
425 Market Street
San Francisco, CA 94105-2482
Phone: (415) 268-7409
www.mofo.com
Ms. Jane Cooperman
Senior Recruiting Manager
Phone: (415) 268-7665
Fax: (415) 268-7522
E-mail: jcooperman@mofo.com

Munger, Tolles & Olson LLP
355 South Grand Avenue
35th Floor
Los Angeles, CA 90071-1560
Phone: (213) 683-9100
www.mto.com

Ms. Kevinn C. Villard
Director of Legal Recruiting
Phone: (213) 683-9242
Fax: (213) 687-3702
E-mail: villardkc@mto.com

O'Melveny & Myers LLP
400 South Hope Street
Los Angeles, CA 90071-2899
Phone: (213) 430-6000
www.omm.com

Ms. Jacqueline Wilson
Recruiting Administrator
Phone: (202) 383-5300
Fax: (202) 383-5414
E-mail: jwilson@omm.com

Orrick, Herrington & Sutcliffe LLP
Old Federal Reserve Bank Building
400 Sansome Street
San Francisco, CA 94111-3143
Phone: (415) 392-1122
www.orrick.com

San Francisco
Ms. Mireille Butler
Recruiting Administrator
Phone: (415) 773-5568
Fax: (415) 773-5759
E-mail: mbutler@orrick.com

Silicon Valley
Ms. Rebecca Whittall
Recruiting Manager
Phone (650) 614-7352
Fax: (650) 614-7401
E-Mail: rwhitall@orrick.com

New York
Ms. Francesca Runge
Recruiting Manager
Phone: (212) 506-3556
Fax: (212) 506-5151
E-mail: frunge@orrick.com

This Vault Legal Employer Directory is a special advertising section in the Vault Guide to the Top 100
Law Firms. For information on listing your firm in the directory, contact corporatesales@vault.com

VAULT CAREER LIBRARY   **643**

Paul, Hastings, Janofsky & Walker LLP
Paul Hastings Tower
515 South Flower Street, 25th floor
Los Angeles, CA 90071-2371
Phone: (213) 683-6000
www.paulhastings.com

Mr. Anton Mack
Managing Director of Attorney Recruiting
Phone: (213) 683-5740
E-mail: antonmack@paulhastings.com

Pillsbury Winthrop LLP
50 Fremont Street
San Francisco, CA 94105
Phone: (415) 983-1000
www.pillsburywinthrop.com

Los Angeles & Century City
Ms. Mary Ellen Hatch
mhatch@pillsburywinthrop.com

San Francisco
Ms. Sela Seleska
sseleska@pillsburywinthrop.com
See firm web site for employment contacts at other offices.

Quinn Emanuel Urquhart Oliver & Hedges LLP
865 S. Figueroa Street, 10th Floor
Los Angeles, CA 90017
Phone: (213) 624-7707
Fax: (213) 624-0643
www.quinnemanuel.com

Selene Dogan
Recruiting Coordinator
Phone: (213) 624-7707
Fax: (213) 624-0643
E-mail: selenedogan@quinnemanuel.com

Number of Attorneys Firmwide: 190
Number of Attorneys in this Office: 125
Summer Associate Hires in this Office: 22 (2003)
Full-Time First-Year Hires in this Office: 10 (2002)
Lateral Hires in this Office: 10 (2002)
Summer Associate Salary (Weekly): $2,400
First-Year Associate Salary (Base): $125,000

Practice Areas
All areas of business litigation

Law Schools Firm Recruits From
Harvard, Stanford, Boalt, UCLA, Yale, Columbia, UVA,
George Washington, Georgetown, University of Michigan,
University of Chicago, University of Pennsylvania, Duke

Firm Leadership
John B. Quinn (Managing Partner)

Firm Description
Quinn Emanuel Urquhart Oliver & Hedges is a firm of 190
lawyers with offices in Los Angeles, New York City, San
Francisco, Silicon Valley, Palm Springs, and San Diego. We
are the largest law firm in the United States devoted
exclusively to business litigation. Quinn Emanuel is one of
the few top tier firms that actually tries cases. We are in the
business of winning, and we do that spectacularly.

Quinn Emanuel Urquhart Oliver & Hedges LLP
201 Sansome Street, 6th Floor
San Francisco, CA 94104
Phone: (415) 986-5700
Fax: (415) 986-5707
www.quinnemanuel.com

Selene Dogan
Recruiting Coordinator
Phone: (213) 624-7707
Fax: (213) 624-0643
E-mail: selenedogan@quinnemanuel.com

shining lights.

The right talent in the right environment can work wonders. Just ask the associates of Edwards & Angell. When you join one of our offices, you'll focus on financial services, private equity and technology businesses. And you'll learn to guide clients through challenging problems, advise them on the best solutions and protect their interests in litigation, transactions and business operations. **Discover how to shine at www.EdwardsAngell.com.**

Edwards *&* Angell LLP

Guide. Advise. Protect.

more than 300 lawyers in

BOSTON | FT. LAUDERDALE | HARTFORD | NEW YORK | PROVIDENCE | SHORT HILLS, NJ | STAMFORD | WEST PALM BEACH | LONDON*

www.EdwardsAngell.com

*representative office

Quinn Emanuel Urquhart Oliver & Hedges LLP
555 Twin Dolphin Drive, Suite 560
Redwood Shores, CA 94065
Phone: (650) 620-4500
Fax: (650) 620-4555
www.quinnemanuel.com

Selene Dogan
Recruiting Coordinator
Phone: (213) 624-7707
Fax: (213) 624-0643
E-mail: selenedogan@quinnemanuel.com

Sedgwick, Detert, Moran & Arnold LLP
16th Floor, One Embarcadero Center
San Francisco, CA 94111-13628
Phone: (415) 781-7900
www.sdma.com

Ms. Vicky Berry
Director of Attorney Recruiting
Phone: (415) 781-7900
Fax: (415) 781-2635
E-mail: vicky.berry@sdma.com

Sheppard, Mullin, Richter & Hampton LLP
333 South Hope Street
Forty-Eighth Floor
Los Angeles, CA 90071-1448
Phone: (213) 620-1780
www.sheppardmullin.com

Ms. Sally C. Bucklin
Manager of Attorney Hiring
Phone: (213) 617-4101
Fax: (213) 620-1398
E-mail: sbucklin@sheppardmullin.com

Skadden, Arps, Slate, Meagher & Flom LLP
300 South Grand Avenue
34th Floor
Los Angeles, CA 90071
Phone: (213) 687-5000
Fax: (213) 687-5600
www.skadden.com

Kendall Nohre
Legal Hiring Administrator
Phone: (213) 687-5598
Fax: (213) 687-5600
E-mail: knohre@skadden.com

Number of Attorneys Firmwide: 1,729
Number of Attorneys in this Office: 114
Summer Associate Hires in this Office: 11 (2003)
Full-Time First-Year Hires in this Office: 13 (2002)
Summer Associate Salary (Weekly): $2,400
First-Year Associate Salary (Base): $140,000

Practice Areas
Banking & Institutional Investing; Corporate; Corporate Compliance; Corporate Restructuring; Litigation; Labor; Real Estate; Tax; ERISA

Law Schools Firm Recruits From
Boalt Hall, Chicago, Columbia, Georgetown; Harvard; Hastings; Loyola - Los Angeles; Michigan; NYU; Northwestern; Stanford; Texas; UCLA; USC

Firm Leadership
Rand S. April, Los Angeles Office Managing Partner

Firm Description
Since its opening in 1983, Skadden, Arps' Los Angeles office has become a dominant force in California. Our prominence is noted in publications, and our attorneys are recognized among the local legal community as a formidable, indigenous law firm. Unlike most local offices of national firms, virtually all of our work is generated by attorneys in L.A. We provide a structured series of training programs and send new associates for one week of training to New York. Summer associates participate in depositions, trial advocacy, writing and research, and corporate seminars.

Skadden, Arps, Slate, Meagher & Flom LLP
525 University Avenue
Suite 1100
Palo Alto, CA 94301
www.skadden.com

Leah Lovelace
Legal Hiring Manager
Phone: (650) 470-4500
Fax: (650) 470-4570
E-mail: pa/sfhire_@skadden.com

Number of Attorneys Firmwide: 1,729
Number of Attorneys in this Office: 70
Summer Associate Hires in this Office: 11 (2003)
Full-Time First-Year Hires in this Office: 8 (2002)
Summer Associate Salary (Weekly): $2,400
First-Year Associate Salary (Base): $140,000

Practice Areas
Alternative Dispute Resolutions; Antitrust; Banking and
Institutional Investing; Communications; Corporate
Compliance Programs; Corporate Finance; Corporate
Restructuring; Energy - Project Finance; Energy - Regulatory;
Environmental; Government Enforcement; Litigation; Health
Care; Intellectual Property and Technology; International
Trade; Investment Management; Labor and Employment Law;
Mass Torts/Insurance Litigation; M&A; Political Law;
Privatizations; Products Liability; Real Estate; Structured
Finance; Tax; Trusts and Estates; White Collar Crime

Law Schools Firm Recruits From
Boalt; Chicago; Columbia; Harvard; Hastings; NYU; Santa
Clara; Stanford; UCLA

Firm Leadership
Ken King, Managing Partner

Firm Description
The Palo Alto office of Skadden, Arps was opened in February
1998. This office represents clients in a wide range of
corporate and securities transactions. The work taken on by
our lawyers is varied and each associate works on matters in
different practice areas. The office has a very informal
atmosphere. The San Francisco office of Skadden, Arps
opened in 1987. Due to the relatively small size of the office,
we believe opportunities for development and expansion of
responsibility for associates early in their careers are plentiful.
Our attorneys handle a number of pro bono matters.

Thelen Reid & Priest LLP
101 Second Street, Suite 1800
San Francisco, CA 94105
Phone: (415) 371-1200
www.thelenreid.com

Ms. Holly Saydah
Attorney Recruiting Manager
Phone: (415) 371-1200
Fax: (415) 369-8794
E-mail: hsaydah@thelenreid.com

This Vault Legal Employer Directory is a special advertising section in the Vault Guide to the Top 100
Law Firms. For information on listing your firm in the directory, contact corporatesales@vault.com

VAULT CAREER LIBRARY

647

Townsend and Townsend and Crew LLP
2 Embarcadero Center
8th Floor
San Francisco, CA 94111-3834
Phone: (415) 576-0200
Fax: (415) 576-0300
www.townsend.com

Lindy Van der Reis, Esq.
Manager of Recruitment and Professional Development
Phone: (415) 576-0200
Fax: (415) 576-0300
E-mail: mhvanderreis@townsend.com

Number of Attorneys Firmwide: 151
Number of Attorneys in this Office: 65
Summer Associate Hires in this Office: 5 (2002)
Full-Time First-Year Hires in this Office: 4 (2002)
Lateral Hires in this Office: 4 (2002)
Summer Associate Salary (Weekly): $2,400
First-Year Associate Salary (Base): $125,000

Practice Areas
Patent Prosecution & Litigation; Trademark & Copyright
Prosecution & Litigation; Technology Licensing; Internet;
Antitrust; Complex Commercial Litigation

Law Schools Firm Recruits From
New York University; Columbia University; George
Washington University; Georgetown University; University of
California, Los Angeles; University of Southern California;
University of San Francisco; University of California,
Berkeley (Boalt Hall); Stanford University; University of
Pennsylvania; University of Texas; University of California,
Hastings; Santa Clara University; University of California,
Davis; University of Washington; University of Colorado;
University of Denver; Seattle University; Patent Law
Interview Program; San Francisco Intellectual Property Law
Association Job Fair

Firm Leadership
James G. Gilliland, Jr., Chairman; Susan M. Spaeth, Managing
Partner for Operations; Paul C. Haughey, Managing Partner
for Finance; Dennis Gavin, Executive Director

Firm Description
Townsend and Townsend and Crew LLP focuses on
Intellectual Property Law, teaming with corporations,
inventors, entrepreneurs, and scientists to protect their
innovative products and ideas. We offer a full range of
intellectual property services. Townsend has more than 150
attorneys, many of whom have advanced technical degrees and
extensive scientific and business experience.

Townsend and Townsend and Crew LLP
2175 North California Blvd.
Suite 625
Walnut Creek, CA 94596
Phone: (925) 472-5000
Fax: (925) 472-8895
www.townsend.com

Lindy Van der Reis, Esq.
Manager of Recruitment and Professional Development
Phone: (415) 576-0200
Fax: (415) 576-0300
E-mail: mhvanderreis@townsend.com

Townsend and Townsend and Crew LLP
379 Lytton Avenue
Palo Alto, CA 94301-1431
Phone: (650) 326-2400
Fax: (650) 326-2422
www.townsend.com

Lindy Van der Reis, Esq.
Manager of Recruitment and Professional Development
Phone: (415) 576-0200
Fax: (415) 576-0300
E-mail: mhvanderreis@townsend.com

Wilson Sonsini Goodrich & Rosati
650 Page Mill Road
Palo Alto, CA 94304-1050
Phone: (650) 493-9300
www.wsgr.com

Attorney Recruiting Department
Phone: 1 (888) GO2-WSGR
Fax: (650) 493-6811
E-mail: attorneyrecruiting@wsgr.com

ShawPittman LLP

Committed To Serving Out Clients And Our Community With Unparalleled Excellence And Enthusiasm In This Challenging And Exciting Global Legal Environment

If you are

- A highly successful law student
- A strongly motivated person
- Interested in assuming responsibility quickly
- Entrepreneurial in spirit and outlook
- Interested in working in a cooperative and collegial environment
- Committed to excellence

Then we want to talk to you about joining Shaw Pittman's 2004 Summer Program!

This year we will be interviewing at

Boalt Hall
Catholic University
College of William and Mary
Columbia University
Cornell University
Duke University
George Mason University

Georgetown University
George Washington University
Harvard University
Howard University
New York University
Stanford University
University of Chicago

University of Michigan
University of Pennsylvania
University of Virginia
Vanderbilt University
Washington and Lee University
Yale University

Come interview with us then. If we don't visit your law school, send us your resume.

We are proud to announce the Shaw Pittman summer public interest project.

In keeping with our long standing tradition and commitment to pro bono legal service, and as a Washington, D.C. "Pro Bono Firm of the Year," we offer the opportunity for highly qualified law students to divide their summer between Shaw Pittman and a public interest organization of their choosing.

For further information about Shaw Pittman or our recruiting program, please contact either:

Tom Hill
Chair, Attorney Recruiting Committee
Thomas.Hill@shawpittman.com

Kathy Kelly
Chief Recruiting Officer
Kathy.Kelly@shawpittman.com

WWW.SHAWPITTMAN.COM   WHERE LAW, BUSINESS & TECHNOLOGY CONVERGE

WASHINGTON, D.C.   NORTHERN VIRGINIA   NEW YORK   LOS ANGELES   LONDON

Winston & Strawn

333 South Grand Avenue

Los Angeles, California 90071-1543

Phone: (213) 615-1700

Fax: (213) 615-1750

www.winston.com

Lisa Kluck

Legal Recruiting Coordinator

Phone: (213) 615-1809

Fax: (213) 615-1750

Email: lkluck@winston.com

Winston & Strawn

101 California Street

San Francisco, California 94111-5802

Phone: (415) 591-1000

Fax: (415) 591-1400

www.winston.com

Lisa Kluck

Legal Recruiting Manager

Phone: (213) 615-1809

Fax: (415) 591-1400

Email: lkluck@winston.com

COLORADO

Townsend and Townsend and Crew LLP

1200 Seventeenth Street

Suite 2700

Denver, CO 80202-5835

Phone: (303) 571-4000

Fax: (303) 571-4321

www.townsend.com

Lindy Van der Reis, Esq.

Manager of Recruitment and Professional Development

Phone: (415) 576-0200

Fax: (415) 576-0300

E-mail: mhvanderreis@townsend.com

CONNETICUT

Brown Raysman Millstein Felder & Steiner, LLP

Cityplace II

185 Asylum Street, 10th Floor

Hartford, CT 06103

Phone: (860) 275-6400

Fax: (860) 275-6410

www.brownraysman.com

David E. Kuziak

Office Administrator

Phone: (860) 275-6400

Fax: (860) 275-6410

E-mail: hartfordinfo@brownraysman.com

DISTRICT OF COLUMBIA

Akin Gump Strauss Hauer & Feld LLP

Robert S. Strauss Building

1333 New Hampshire Avenue, NW

Washington, DC 20036

Phone: (202) 887-4000

www.akingump.com

Ms. Erin L. Springer

Legal Recruitment Manager

Phone: (202) 887-4184

Fax: (202) 887-4288

E-mail: espringer@akingump.com

Arent Fox Kintner Plotkin & Kahn, PLLC

1050 Connecticut Avenue, NW

Washington, DC 20036-5339

Phone: (202) 857-6000

www.arentfox.com

Washington, DC

Ms. Amber Handman

Attorney Recruitment and Development Manager

Phone: (202) 857-6146

Fax: (202) 857-6395

E-mail: DCAttorneyRecruit@arentfox.com

New York

Ms. Kay Carson

Director of Administration

Phone: (212) 484-3900

Fax: (212) 484-3990

E-mail: NYAttorneyRecruit@arentfox.com

Arnold & Porter
555 12th Street, NW
Washington, DC 20004
Phone: (202) 942-5000
www.arnoldporter.com

Ms. Lisa Pavia
Manager of Attorney Recruitment
Phone: (202) 942-5059
Fax: (202) 942-5999
E-mail: Lisa_Pavia@aporter.com

Bryan Cave LLP
700 Thirteenth Street N.W.
Washington, DC 20005-3960
Phone: (202) 508-6000
Fax: (202) 508-6200
www.bryancave.com

Christopher S. Manning
Manager of Legal Recruiting - Washington
Phone: (202) 508-6080
Fax: (202) 508-6200
csmanning@bryancave.com

Cadwalader, Wickersham & Taft LLP
1201 F Street, N.W. Suite 1100
Washington, DC 20004
Phone: (202) 862-2200
Fax: (202) 862-2400
www.cadwalader.com

Laura Griffith
Administrator
Phone: (202) 862-2366
Fax: (202) 862-2400
E-mail: laura.griffith@cwt.com

Chadbourne & Parke LLP
1200 New Hampshire Avenue, N.W.
Washington, DC 20036
Phone: (202) 974-5600
Fax: (202) 974-5602
www.chadbourne.com

Kenneth W. Hansen
Hiring Partner
Phone: (202) 974-5600
Fax: (202) 974-5602
E-mail: khansen@chadbourne.com

Covington & Burling
1201 Pennsylvania Avenue, NW
Washington, DC 20004-2401
Phone: (202) 662-6000
www.cov.com

Ms. Lorraine Brown
Director, Legal Personnel Recruiting
Phone: (202) 662-6200
E-mail: legal.recruiting@cov.com

Crowell & Moring LLP
1001 Pennsylvania Avenue, NW
Washington, DC 20004
Phone: (202) 624-2500
www.crowell.com

Ms. Katherine A. Arnold
Assistant Director of HR for Attorney Recruiting
Phone: (202) 624-2729
Fax: (202) 628-5116
E-mail: karnold@crowell.com

Dickstein Shapiro Morin & Oshinsky LLP
2101 L Street, NW
Washington, DC 20037-1526
Phone: (202) 785-9700
www.legalinnovators.com

Ms. Julie B. Miles
Phone: (202) 828-4851
Fax: (202) 887-0689
E-mail: MilesJ@dsmo.com

Finnegan, Henderson, Farabow, Garrett & Dunner, L.L.P.
1300 I Street, NW
Suite 700
Washington, DC 20005-3315
Phone: (202) 408-4000
www.finnegan.com

Washington, DC
Mr. Paul Sevanich
Attorney Recruitment Manager
Phone: (202) 408-4000
Fax: (202) 408-4400
E-mail: attyrecruit@finnegan.com

This Vault Legal Employer Directory is a special advertising section in the Vault Guide to the Top 100 Law Firms. For information on listing your firm in the directory, contact corporatesales@vault.com

VAULT CAREER LIBRARY

651

Hogan & Hartson L.L.P.
555 Thirteenth Street, NW
Washington, DC 20004
Phone: (202) 637-5600
www.hhlaw.com

Ms. Ellen M. Purvance
Assoc. Recruitment & Professional Development Dir.
Phone: (202) 637-8601
Fax: (202) 637-5910
E-mail: empurvance@hhlaw.com

Holland & Knight LLP
Suite 100
2099 Pennsylvania Avenue
Washington, DC 20006
Phone: (202) 955-3000
www.hklaw.com

Ms. Alida Coo-Kendall
National Recruitment Coordinator
10 St. James Avenue
Boston, MA 02116
Phone: (617) 523-2700
E-mail: alida.cookendall@hklaw.com

Howrey Simon Arnold & White, LLP
1299 Pennsylvania Ave., NW
Washington, DC 20004
Phone: (202) 783-0800
www.howrey.com

Ms. Janet Brown
Manager, Attorney Recruitment
Phone: (202) 783-0800
E-mail: brownjanet@howrey.com

McKenna Long & Aldridge LLP
1900 K Street, NW
Washington, DC 20006
Phone: (202) 496-7500
Fax: (202) 496-7756
www.mckennalong.com

Jennifer L. Semelsberger
Legal Recruitment Coordinator
Phone: (202) 496-7512
Fax: (202) 496-7756
E-mail: jsemelsberger@mckennalong.com

Number of Attorneys Firmwide: 368
Number of Attorneys in this Office: 104
Summer Associate Hires in this Office: 6 (2003)
Full-Time First-Year Hires in this Office: 3 (2003)
Lateral Hires in this Office: 4 (2002)
Summer Associate Salary (Weekly): $2,400
First-Year Associate Salary (Base): $125,000

Practice Areas
Litigation; Government Contracts; Intellectual Property &
Technology; Public Policy & Regulatory Affairs;
Environmental; Corporate; Real Estate Finance &
Development

Law Schools Firm Recruits From
Columbia; George Washington, Georgetown; Duke; Harvard

Firm Leadership
James Gallagher (Co-Chair); Clay Long (Co-Chair): Ray
Biagini (Co-Vice Chair); Jeff Haidet (Co-Vice Chair); Tom
Hall (Co-Managing Partner); and Tom Papson (Co-Managing
Partner)

Firm Description
Formed as a result of a merger in 2002, McKenna Long &
Aldridge LLP is a firm of more than 350 lawyers spread across
8 offices in the United States and Brussels, Belgium. The firm
is divided into six large departments: Litigation; Corporate;
Government Contracts; Intellectual Property and Technology;
Public Policy and Regulatory Affairs; and, Real Estate Finance
and Development. Each department is comprised of smaller
practice groups that provide a broad array of legal services to
our clients.

Patton Boggs LLP
2550 M Street, NW
Washington, DC 20037
Phone: (202) 457-6000
www.pattonboggs.com

Ms. Kara P. Reidy
Director of Professional Recruitment
Phone: (202) 457-6000
Fax: (202) 457-6315
E-mail: kreidy@pattonboggs.com

Porter Wright Morris & Arthur LLP
1919 Pennsylvania Ave., NW
Suite 500
Washington, DC 43215-6194
Phone: (614) 227-2000
Fax: (614) 227-2100
www.porterwright.com

David G. Zimmerman
Professional Personnel Coordinator
Phone: (614) 227-1907
Fax: (614) 227-2100
E-mail: Dzimmerman@porterwright.com

Number of Attorneys Firmwide: 277
Number of Attorneys in this Office: 20
Summer Associate Hires in this Office: 3 (2003)
Full-Time First Year Hires in this Office: 4 (2003)
Lateral Hires in this Office: 3 (2003)
Summer Associate Salary (Weekly): $1,730
First year Associate Salary (Base): $105,000

Practice Areas
Financial Institutions/Commercial Law; Business/Tax;
Energy/Environment/Government Affairs; Labor &
Employment; Litigation; Trusts and Estates; Real Estate

Law Schools Firm Recruits From
American University; Boston College; Capital; Case Western;
Catholic University; Chicago; Cincinnati; Cleveland-
Marshall; Columbia; Cornell; Dayton; Duke; George
Washington; Georgetown; Harvard; Howard; Illinois; Indiana
- Bloomington; Maryland; Michigan; NYU; Northwestern;
Notre Dame; Ohio State; Pennsylvania; Texas; Vanderbilt;
Virginia; Wake Forest; Washington & Lee; William & Mary;
Wisconsin

Firm Leadership
Robert W Trafford, Managing Partner

Firm Description
Porter Wright Morris & Arthur LLP is a major institutional,
multi-city law firm serving medium- to large-sized business
clients. We pride ourselves on the practicality, responsiveness,
and excellence of the services we have provided in meeting
the legal needs of our clients. Each of our six offices has a
need for bright, confident, energetic, and committed law
graduates to become a part of our growth into the future.

Shaw Pittman LLP
2300 N Street, NW
Washington, DC 20037
Phone: (202) 663-8000
www.shawpittman.com

Ms. Kathleen A. Kelly
Chief Recruiting Officer & Dir. Profess. Programs
Phone: (202) 663-8394
Fax: (202) 663-8007
E-mail: kathy.kelly@shawpittman.com

This Vault Legal Employer Directory is a special advertising section in the Vault Guide to the Top 100
Law Firms. For information on listing your firm in the directory, contact corporatesales@vault.com

VAULT CAREER LIBRARY

653

Skadden, Arps, Slate, Meagher & Flom LLP
1440 New York Avenue, NW
Washington, DC 20005
Phone: (202) 371-7000
Fax: (202) 393-5760
www.skadden.com

Kimberly C. Barry
Attorney Recruiting & Development Administrator
Phone: (202) 371-7730
Fax: (202) 371-7787

E-mail: kibarry@skadden.com
Number of Attorneys Firmwide: 1,729
Number of Attorneys in this Office: 248
Summer Associate Hires in this Office: 13 (2003)
Full-Time First-Year Hires in this Office: 12 First-Years; 9
Former Judicial Clerks (2002)
Summer Associate Salary (Weekly): $2,400
First-Year Associate Salary (Base): $140,000

Practice Areas
Antitrust; Banking/Regulatory; Communications;
Corporate/Securities; Employee Benefits; Energy;
Environmental; International Trade; Litigation; Political Law;
Restructuring; Tax; UCC

Law Schools Firm Recruits From
American; BC/BU/Northwestern in DC; Chicago; Columbia;
Cornell in DC; Duke; Emory in DC; George Washington;
Georgetown; Harvard; Harvard BLSA Job Fair; Howard;
Michigan; Mid-Atlantic BLSA; Mid-West/Cal in DC (UCLA,
USC, Minnesota, Iowa, Wisconsin, Tulane); NYU;
Northwestern; Penn; Stanford; UVA; Washington & Lee; Yale

Firm Leadership
Michael P. Rogan, DC Office Leader

Firm Description
Skadden, Arps has a full-service practice unmatched by any
other law firm in DC, because it combines both a transactional
DC and a national practice. The Firm has developed a
traditional DC practice in such diverse fields as
communications, energy, environmental, international trade,
legislation, litigation and political law. At the same time,
attorneys interested in antitrust, banking and institutional
investing, general corporate, corporate finance, corporate
restructurings, domestic and international project finance,
M&A and tax have the opportunity to engage in the kind of
transactional work that is ordinarily associated only with a
New York practice.

Steptoe & Johnson LLP
1300 Connecticut Avenue, NW
Washington, DC 20036-1795
Phone: (202) 429-3000
www.steptoe.com

Ms. Rosemary Kelly Morgan
Director of Attorney Services & Recruiting
Phone: (202) 429-8036
E-mail: legal_recruiting@steptoe.com

Sutherland Asbill & Brennan LLP
1275 Pennsylvania Avenue, NW
Washington, DC 20004-2415
Phone: (202) 383-0100
www.sablaw.com

Ms. Melissa C. Wilson
Manager of Legal Recruiting, Washington
Phone: (202) 383-0100
Fax: (202) 637-3593
E-mail: mwilson@sablaw.com

Swidler Berlin Shereff Friedman, LLP
3000 K Street, NW, Suite 300
Washington, DC 20007-5118
Phone: (202) 424-7500
www.swidlaw.com

Ms. Kai Wilson
Recruiting Coordinator
Phone: (202) 424-7658
Fax: (202) 424-7664
E-mail: kewilson@swidlaw.com

Venable LLP
1201 New York Avenue, NW
Washington, DC 20005
Phone: (202) 962-4800
www.venable.com

Ms. Grace Cunningham
Director of Legal Personnel
Phone: (202) 962-4875
Fax: (202) 962-8300
E-mail: gcunningham@venable.com

Wiley Rein & Fielding LLP
1776 K Street, NW
Washington, DC 20006
Phone: (202) 719-7000
www.wrf.com

Ms. Jill Bartelt
Attorney Recruitment Manager
Phone: (202) 719-7548
Fax: (202) 719-7049
E-mail: jbartelt@wrf.com

Williams & Connolly LLP
The Edward Bennett Williams Building
725 12th Street, NW
Washington, DC 20005
Phone: (202) 434-5000
www.wc.com

Ms. Donna M. Downing
Recruiting Coordinator
Phone: (202) 434-5605
E-mail: ddowning@wc.com

Wilmer, Cutler & Pickering
2445 M Street, NW
Washington, DC 20037
Phone: (202) 663-6000
www.wilmer.com

Washington, Baltimore and Tysons Corner
Ms. Mary W. Kiley
Lawyer Recruitment Administrator
Fax: (202) 457-4992
E-mail: JoinWCPLawyers@wilmer.com

New York
Ms. Marian Freed
Office Administrator
Fax: (212) 230-8888
E-mail: Marian.Freed@wilmer.com

Winston & Strawn
1400 L Street, N.W.
Washington, D.C. 20005-3502
Phone: (202) 371-5700
Fax: (202) 371-5950
www.winston.com

Victoria Rozanski
Legal Recruiting Manager
Phone: (202) 371-5896
Fax: (202) 371-5950
Email: vrozanski@winston.com

FLORIDA

Bilzin Sumberg Baena Price & Axelrod LLP
200 South Biscayne Boulevard
Suite 2500
Miami, FL 33131
Phone: (305) 374-7580
Fax: (305) 374-7593
www.bilzin.com

Jessica L. Buchsbaum
Personnel Manager
Phone: (305) 374-7580
Fax: (305) 374-7593
jbuchsbaum@bilzin.com

Number of Attorneys Firmwide: 75
Summer Associate Hires: 6 (2003)
Full-Time First Year Hires: 4 (2003)
Lateral Hires: 17 (2003)
Summer Associate Salary (Weekly): $1,730
First year Associate Salary (base): $105,000

Practice Areas:
Real Estate, Litigation, Land Use & Governmental Law,
Bankruptcy, Corporate & Securities, Commercial Finance, Tax
Trusts & Estates.

Law Schools Firm Recruits From:
Columbia, Florida, Georgetown, Harvard, Miami, NYU, Nova,
Pennsylvania, Yale, Miami Off-campus Job Fair.

Firm Leadership:
Alvin D. Lodish

Firm Description:
Bilzin Sumberg Baena Price & Axelrod LLP is a full service
law firm with 70 attorneys. The firm has extensive experience
in the areas of commercial real estate, corporate and securities,
restructuring and bankruptcy, land use/zoning and
governmental law, civil litigation and dispute resolution, and
tax, trusts and estates. The attorneys in the firm combine legal
expertise with business insight and innovative solutions in
handling complex matters and transactions and assisting
clients in achieving their objectives.

Greenberg Traurig, LLP
1221 Brickell Avenue
Miami, FL 33131
Phone: (305) 579-0500
www.gtlaw.com

Atlanta, Boca Raton, Boston, Denver, Ft. Lauderdale, Miami, Orlando, Tallahassee, West Palm Beach, Wilmington:
Ms. Janet McKeegan
Director of Recruitment
Phone: (305) 579-0855
E-mail: mckeeganj@gtlaw.com
See www.gtlaw.com for employment contacts for other offices.

Porter Wright Morris & Arthur LLP
5801 Pelican Bay Blvd.
Suite 300
Naples, FL 34108-2709
Phone: (239) 593-2900
Fax: (239) 593-2990
www.porterwright.com

David G. Zimmerman
Professional Personnel Coordinator
Phone: (614) 227-1907
Fax: (614) 227-2100
E-mail: Dzimmerman@porterwright.com

Number of Attorneys Firmwide: 277
Number of Attorneys in this Office: 12
Summer Associate Hires in this Office: 2 (2003)
Full-Time First Year Hires in this Office: 2 (2003)
Lateral Hires in this Office: 2 (2003)
Summer Associate Salary (Weekly): $1,730
First year Associate Salary (Base): $ 80,000

Practice Areas:
Financial Institutions/Commercial Law; Business/Tax; Energy/Environment/Government Affairs; Labor & Employment; Litigation; Trusts and Estates; Real Estate

Law Schools Firm Recruits From:
American University; Boston College; Capital; Case Western; Catholic University; Chicago; Cincinnati; Cleveland-Marshall; Columbia; Cornell; Dayton; Duke; George Washington; Georgetown; Harvard; Howard; Illinois; Indiana - Bloomington; Maryland; Michigan; NYU; Northwestern; Notre Dame; Ohio State; Pennsylvania; Texas; Vanderbilt; Virginia; Wake Forest; Washington & Lee; William & Mary; Wisconsin

Firm Leadership
Robert W. Trafford, Managing Partner

Firm Description
Porter Wright Morris & Arthur LLP is a major institutional, multi-city law firm serving medium- to large-sized business clients. We pride ourselves on the practicality, responsiveness, and excellence of the services we have provided in meeting the legal needs of our clients. Each of our six offices has a need for bright, confident, energetic, and committed law graduates to become a part of our growth into the future.

GEORGIA

Alston & Bird LLP
One Atlantic Center
1201 West Peachtree Street
Atlanta, GA 30309-3424
Phone: (404) 881-7000
www.alston.com

Ms. Emily S. Leeson
Director of Attorney Hiring & Development
E-mail: eleeson@alston.com

Ford & Harrison LLP

FORD & HARRISON LLP

1275 Peachtree St., NE
Suite 600
Atlanta, GA 30309
Phone: (404) 888-3800
Fax: (404) 888-3863
www.fordharrison.com

Wendi B. Fairchild
Director of Attorney Recruitment
Phone: (404) 888-3873
Fax: (404) 888-3863
E-mail: wfairchild@fordharrison.com

Number of Attorneys Firmwide: 140
Number of Attorneys in this Office: 50
Summer Associate Hires in this Office: 4 (2003)
Summer Associate Salary (Weekly): $1,600

Practice Areas
Labor & Employment (Defense)

Law Schools Firm Recruits From
University of Georgia; University of North Carolina; Mercer, Emory, Stetson; University of Florida, Florida State; University of Mississippi; Wake Forest; University of Memphis; Tulane; University of Alabama

Firm Leadership
Executive Committee; Management Group; Managing Partner in each office

Firm Description
Please visit our web site to learn more about our firm:
www.fordharrison.com

Kilpatrick Stockton LLP
1100 Peachtree Street, Suite 2800
Atlanta, GA 30309-4530
Phone: (404) 815-6500
www.KilpatrickStockton.com

Ms. Lea W. Hughes
Recruiting Coordinator
Phone: (404) 532-6887
Fax: (404) 541-4668
E-mail: lehughes@KilpatrickStockton.com

King & Spalding LLP
191 Peachtree Street
Suite 4900
Atlanta, GA 30303-1763
Phone: (404) 572-4600
www.kslaw.com

Atlanta
Ms. Rebecca McClain Newton
Director of Recruiting
Phone: (404) 572-3395
Fax: (404) 572-5100
E-mail: rnewton@kslaw.com

Houston
Ms. Ann Harris
Recruiting Manager
Phone: (713) 751-3200
E-mail: aharris@kslaw.com

New York
Ms. Kristan A. Lassiter
Recruiting Manager
Phone: (212) 556-2138
E-mail: klassiter@kslaw.com

Washington
Ms. Kara O'Conner
Recruiting Manager
Phone (202) 626-2387
E-mail: koconnor@kslaw.com

This Vault Legal Employer Directory is a special advertising section in the Vault Guide to the Top 100 Law Firms. For information on listing your firm in the directory, contact corporatesales@vault.com

VAULT CAREER LIBRARY

657

McKenna Long & Aldridge LLP
303 Peachtree St., NE
Suite 5300
Atlanta, GA 30308
Phone: (404) 527-4000
Fax: (404) 527-4198
www.mckennalong.com

Jennifer S. Queen
Director of Legal Recruitment & Professional Development
Phone: (404) 527-4139
Fax: (404) 527-4198
E-mail: jqueen@mckennalong.com

Number of Attorneys Firmwide: 345
Number of Attorneys in this Office: 149
Summer Associate Hires in this Office: 20 (2003)
Full-Time First-Year Hires in this Office: 10 (2002)
Lateral Hires in this Office: 8; 1 (2002; 2003)
Summer Associate Salary (Weekly): $1,500 (First-year); $1,750 (Second-year)
First-Year Associate Salary (Base): $100,000

Practice Areas
Litigation; Real Estate; Financial Restructuring; Mergers & Acquisitions; Corporate Securities; Tax & Employee Benefits/Trusts & estates; Technology; Sports & Entertainment; Environmental; Administrative/Regulatory/Government

Law Schools Firm Recruits From
Duke; Georgia; Harvard; Mercer; North Carolina; SE Minority Job Fair; Emory; Georgia State; Howard; Michigan; Virginia & SELPC

Firm Leadership
James Gallagher (Co-Chair); Clay Long (Co-Chair): Ray Biagini (Co-Vice Chair); Jeff Haidet (Co-Vice Chair); Tom Hall (Co-Managing Partner); and Tom Papson (Co-Managing Partner)

Firm Description
Formed as a result of a merger in 2002, McKenna Long & Aldridge LLP is a firm of more than 350 lawyers spread across 8 offices in the United States and Brussels, Belgium. The firm is divided into six large departments: Litigation; Corporate; Government Contracts; Intellectual Property and Technology; Public Policy and Regulatory Affairs; and, Real Estate Finance and Development. Each department is comprised of smaller practice groups that provide a broad array of legal services to our clients.

Powell, Goldstein, Frazer & Murphy LLP
191 Peachtree Street, NE, 16th Floor
Atlanta, GA 30303
Phone: (404) 572-6600
www.pgfm.com

Ms. Jenny Wallace
Recruiting Manager
Phone: (404) 572-6782
Fax: (404) 572-6999
E-mail: jwallace@pgfm.com

Sutherland Asbill & Brennan LLP
999 Peachtree Street North
Atlanta, GA 30309
Phone: (404) 853-8000
www.sablaw.com

Ms. Beth Miller
Manager of Legal Recruiting, Atlanta
Phone: (404) 853-8000
Fax: (404) 853-8806

Troutman Sanders LLP
Bank of America Plaza
600 Peachtree Street, NE
Suite 5200
Atlanta, GA 30308-2216
Phone: (404) 885-3000
www.troutmansanders.com

Ms. Betsy Glass
Director of Recruiting
Phone: (404) 885-3000
Fax: (404) 962-6927
E-mail: betsy.glass@troutmansanders.com

ILLINOIS

Altheimer & Gray
10 South Wacker Drive
Chicago, IL 60606-7482
Phone: (312) 715-4000
www.altheimer.com

Ms. Nancy P. Verheyen
Phone: (312) 715-4640
Fax: (312) 715-4800
E-mail: verheyenn@altheimer.com

Baker & McKenzie
One Prudential Plaza
130 E. Randolph Street
Suite 2500
Chicago, IL 60601
Phone: (312) 861-8000
www.bakernet.com

Chicago
Ms. Eleonora Nikol
Phone: (312) 861-2924
eleonora.nikol@bakernet.com

Dallas
Ms. Terry Deleon
Phone: (214) 978-3049
terry.a.deleon@bakernet.com

Houston
Ms. Nancy Rader
Phone: (713) 427-5009
nancy.a.rader@bakernet.com

Miami
Mr. Clement Noble
Phone: (305) 789-8908
clement.noble@bakernet.com

New York
Ms. Anne Zagorin
Phone: (212) 891-3573
anne.s.zagorin@bakernet.com

San Diego
Ms. Victoria Leach
Phone: (619) 235-7733
victoria.a.leach@bakernet.com

San Francisco/Palo Alto
Ms. Andrea Carr
Phone: (415) 984-3801
andrea.l.carr@bakernet.com

Washington, D.C.
Ms. Jane Lint
Phone: (202) 452-7024
jane.e.lint@bakernet.com

Hinshaw & Culbertson
222 LaSalle Street, Suite 300
Chicago, IL 60601-1081
Phone: (312) 704-3000
www.hinshawculbertson.com

Ms. Paula A. Dixton
Legal Recruitment Manager
Phone: (312) 704-3000
E-mail: pdixton@hinshawlaw.com

Jenner & Block, LLC
One IBM Plaza
Chicago, IL 60611-7603
Phone: (312) 222-9350
www.jenner.com

Ms. Shannon Christopher
Manager of Legal Recruiting
Phone: (312) 923-2617
Fax: (312) 840-7616
E-mail: schristopher@jenner.com

Katten Muchin Zavis Rosenman
525 West Monroe Street
Suite 1600
Chicago, IL 60661-3693
Phone: (312) 902-5200
www.kmz.com

Chicago
Ms. Kelley Lynch, Director of Legal Recruiting
Phone: (312) 902-5526
E-mail: kelley.lynch@kmz.com

New York
Ms. Kim McHugh, Legal Recruiting Manager
Phone: (212) 940-6386

Los Angeles
Ms. Donna Francis, Legal Recruiting Manager
Phone: (310) 788-4766

Washington, DC
Ms. Judy Brown, Legal Recruiting Manager
Phone: (202) 625-3652

Kirkland & Ellis
Aon Center
200 East Randolph Drive
Chicago, IL 60601-6636
Phone: (312) 861-2000
www.kirkland.com

Ms. Norah Faigen
Attorney Recruiting Manager
Phone: (312) 861-8532
Fax: (312) 861- 2200
E-mail: norah_faigen@kirkland.com

This Vault Legal Employer Directory is a special advertising section in the Vault Guide to the Top 100 Law Firms. For information on listing your firm in the directory, contact corporatesales@vault.com

VAULT CAREER LIBRARY

659

Lord, Bissell & Brook
115 South LaSalle Street
Chicago, IL 60603
Phone: (312) 443-0700
www.lordbissell.com

Ms. Kerry B. Jahnsen
Phone: (312) 443-0455
Fax: (312) 443-0336
E-mail: kjahnsen@lordbissell.com

Mayer, Brown, Rowe & Maw
190 South LaSalle Street
Chicago, IL 60603-3441
Phone: (312) 701-7002
www.mayerbrownrowe.com
See firm web site (www.mayerbrownrowe.com) for
employment contacts in each office.

McDermott, Will & Emery
227 West Monroe Street
Chicago, IL 60606-5096
Phone: (312) 372-2000
www.mwe.com

Ms. Karen K. Mortell
Legal Recruiting Manager
Phone: (312) 984-7784
Fax: (312) 984-7700
E-mail: kmortell@mwe.com

Piper Rudnick LLP
203 North LaSalle Street
Suite 1800
Chicago, IL 60601
Phone: (312) 368-4000
www.piperrudnick.com

Ms. Marguerite Strubing
Legal Recruiting Manager
Phone: (312) 368-8928
E-mail: marguerite.strubing@piperrudnick.com

Schiff Hardin & Waite
6600 Sears Tower
233 South Wacker Drive
Chicago, IL 60606
Phone: (312) 258-5500
www.schiffhardin.com

Ms. Lily Beltran
Law Student Recruitment Coordinator
Phone: (312) 258-4832
Fax: (312) 258-5600
E-mail: lbeltran@schiffhardin.com

Seyfarth Shaw
53 East Monroe Street, Suite 4200
Chicago, IL 60603-5803
Phone: (312) 346-8000
www.seyfarth.com

Ms. Dawn M. Patchett
Legal Hiring Coordinator
Phone: (312) 739-6458
E-mail: dpatchett@seyfarth.com

Sidley Austin Brown & Wood LLP
Bank One Plaza
10 South Dearborn Street
Chicago, IL 60603
Phone: (312) 853-7000
www.sidley.com

Ms. Jennifer C. Hernandez
Recruiting Manager
Phone: (312) 853-7495
Fax: (312) 853-7036
E-mail: jherna01@sidley.com

Skadden, Arps, Slate, Meagher & Flom
333 West Wacker Drive
Chicago, IL 60606
Phone: (312) 407-0700
Fax: (312) 407-0411
www.skadden.com

Lena Gonzales
Legal Hiring Coordinator
Phone: (312) 407-0909
Fax: (312) 407-0851

E-mail: legonzal@skadden.com
Number of Attorneys Firmwide: 1,729
Number of Attorneys in this Office: 184
Summer Associate Hires in this Office: 25 (2003)
Full-Time First-Year Hires in this Office: 22 (2002)

Practice Areas
Banking; Communications; Corporate; Corporate
Restructuring; Litigation; Mass Torts/Insurance Litigation;
Real Estate; Tax

Law Schools Firm Recruits From
Chicago, Chicago-Kent, IIT; Columbia, Depaul, Duke;
Georgetown; Harvard; Howard; Illinois; Iowa; Loyola-
Chicago; Michigan; North Carolina; Northwestern; Notre
Dame; Pennsylvania; Stanford; Washington University;
Wisconsin; Yale

Firm Leadership
Wayne W. Whalen, Chicago Office Leader

Firm Description:
The Chicago office offers a diversified practice. Major areas
of activity include negotiated acquisitions and leveraged
buyouts; contested takeovers; corporate restructuring; federal
income tax work; and litigation, among others. Opportunities
for development and expansion of responsibility for associates
early in their careers have been, and are expected to continue
to be plentiful. The goal of the summer program is to provide
a practical approach toward understanding what it is like to be
an attorney at Skadden, Arps. Our firm is committed to the
professional development and continued legal education of our
attorneys.

Sonnenschein Nath & Rosenthal
8000 Sears Tower
Chicago, IL 60606
Phone: (312) 876-8000
www.sonnenschein.com

Ms. Barbara Petri
Recruitment Coordinator
Phone: (312) 876-8000
Fax: (312) 876-7934
E-mail: bpetri@sonnenschein.com
(See web site for employment contacts in other cities.)

Winston & Strawn

WINSTON & STRAWN

35 West Wacker Drive
Chicago, Illinois 60601
Phone: (312) 558-5600
Fax: (312) 558-5700
www.winston.com

Deborah Cusumano
Legal Recruiting Manager
Phone: (312) 558-6151
Fax: (312) 558-5700
Email: dcusumano@winston.com

MASSACHUTTES

Bingham McCutchen LLP
150 Federal Street
Boston, MA 02110
Phone: (617) 951-8000
www.bingham.com

Ms. Fiona S. Trevelyan, Esq.
Director of Legal Recruitment
Phone: (617) 951-8608
Fax: (617) 951-8736
E-mail: legalrecruit@bingham.com

Bromberg & Sunstein LLP
125 Summer Street
11th Floor
Boston, MA 02110 -1618
Phone: (617) 443-9292
Fax: (617) 443-0004
www.bromsun.com

Ms. Roberta O'Brien
Human Resources Director
Phone: (617) 443-9292
Fax: (617) 443-0004
employment@bromsun.com

Number of Attorneys: 32
Number of Offices: 1
Summer Associate Hires in this Office (2003): 3
Full-Time First-Year Hires in this Office (2002): 2
Lateral Hires in this Office: (2002) 1
Summer Associate Salary (Weekly): $2019
First-Year Associate Salary (Base): $105,000
Chairman: Lee Carl Bromberg
Hiring Attorney: Joel R. Leeman

Key Facts
All attorneys at Bromberg & Sunstein LLP are immersed in the challenging and fast-paced world of intellectual property law. We represent nationally prominent clients in a wide range of industries. Our attorneys are comfortable working in the most sophisticated and advanced areas of science and technology. Our work environment emphasizes collegiality and the sharing of specialized knowledge and expertise across disciplines both to deliver outstanding services to our clients and to foster professional growth of our attorneys.

Brown Rudnick Berlack Israels LLP
One Financial Center
Boston, MA 02111
Phone: (617) 856-8200
www.brownrudnick.com

Ms. Linda Manning
Recruiting Coordinator
Phone: (617) 856-8316
Fax: (617) 856-8201
E-mail: lmanning@brbilaw.com

Choate, Hall & Stewart
Exchange Place
53 State Street
Boston, MA 02109
Phone: (617) 248-5000
www.choate.com

Ms. Robin Carbone
Director of Recruiting
Phone: (617) 248-5000
Fax: (617) 248-4000
E-mail: rcarbone@choate.com

Edwards & Angell, LLP
101 Federal Street
Boston, MA 02110
Phone: (617) 439-4444
www.edwardsangell.com

Ms. Theresa M. Lenartowick
Recruiting Coordinator
Phone: (401) 276-6587
Fax: (401) 528-5835
E-mail: Tlenartowick@edwardsangell.com

Fish & Richardson P.C.
225 Franklin Street
Boston, MA 02110-2804
Phone: (617) 542-5070
www.fr.com

Ms. Jill E. McDonald
Firmwide Director of Attorney Hiring
Phone: (858) 678-5070
Fax: (858) 678-5099
E-mail: work@fr.com

Foley Hoag LLP
155 Seaport Avenue
Boston, MA 02210-2600
Phone: (617) 832-1000
www.foleyhoag.com

Ms. Dina M. Wreede
Dir. of Legal Recruiting & Professional Development
Phone: (617) 832-7060
Fax: (617) 832-7000
E-mail: dwreede@foleyhoag.com

Goodwin Procter LLP
Exchange Place
53 State Street
Boston, MA 02109
Phone: (617) 570-1000
www.goodwinprocter.com

Ms. Maureen A. Shea
Director of Legal Recruitment
Phone: (617) 570-1288
Fax: (617) 523-1231
E-mail: mshea@goodwinprocter.com

Goulston & Storrs, PC
400 Atlantic Avenue
Boston, MA 02110
Phone: (617) 482-1776
Fax: (617) 574-4112
www.goulstonstorrs.com

Nancy Needle
Director of Legal Recruitment & Associate Development
Phone: (617) 574-6447
Fax: (617) 574-4112
E-mail: nneedle@goulstonstorrs.com

Number of Attorneys Firmwide: 164
Number of Attorneys in this Office: 160
Summer Associate Hires in this Office: 10 (2003)
Full-Time First-Year Hires in this Office: 5 (2003)
Lateral Hires in this Office: 30 (2002/2003)
Summer Associate Salary (Weekly): $2,400
First-Year Associate Salary (Base): $125,000

Practice Areas
Banking & Finance; Business Law & Corporate; Litigation;
Private Client & Trust Group; International; Real Estate;
Environmental; Tax; Technology

Law Schools Firm Recruits From
Boston College; Boston University; Columbia; Cornell
Georgetown; Harvard; Michigan; NYU; Northeastern;
Pennsylvania; Suffolk

Firm Leadership
Managing Directors: Douglas M. Husid; Kitt Sawitsky

Firm Description
Goulston & Storrs works hard to provide associates with the
opportunities and support they need to be successful. Our
steadfast commitment has not gone unnoticed. For the past
five years, Goulston & Storrs has been voted on of the top
firms in the United States at which to practice law in the
American Lawyer magazine's satisfaction survey of summer
and mid-level associates. Based on recommendations of
placement directors at top national law schools, the firm was
selected for inclusion in Kimm Walton's book, America's
Greatest Places to Work with a Law Degree. For more
information on our firm, please visit our web site at
www.goulstonstorrs.com.

Hale and Dorr LLP
60 State Street
Boston, MA 02109-1816
Phone: (617) 526-6000
www.haledorr.com

Ms. Evelyn M. Scoville
Director of Legal Personnel
Phone: (617) 526-6590
Fax: (617) 526-5000
E-mail: evelyn.scoville@haledorr.com

This Vault Legal Employer Directory is a special advertising section in the Vault Guide to the Top 100
Law Firms. For information on listing your firm in the directory, contact corporatesales@vault.com

VAULT CAREER LIBRARY   663

Mintz Levin Cohn Ferris Glovsky and Popeo, P.C.
One Financial Center
Boston, MA 02111
Phone: (617) 542-6000
www.mintz.com

Ms. Claire N. Suchecki
HR Manager, Attorney Recruitment
Phone: (617) 348-1859
Fax: (617) 542-2241
E-mail: csuchecki@mintz.com

Nixon Peabody LLP
101 Federal Street
Boston, MA 02110
Phone: (617) 345-1000
www.nixonpeabody.com

Boston, MA
Renée C. Vanna, Recruitment Coordinator
E-mail: rvanna@nixonpeabody.com

Long Island, NY
Theresa Donohue, Recruitment Coordinator
E-mail: tdonohue@nixonpeabody.com

New York, NY
Brenda K. Powers, Recruitment Coordinator
E-mail: bpowers@nixonpeabody.com

Rochester, NY
Karen E. Marr, Recruitment Administrator
E-mail: kmarr@nixonpeabody.com

San Francisco, CA
Valerie Lewis, Recruitment Coordinator
E-mail: vlewis@nixonpeabody.com

Washington, DC
Mieko I. Rechka, Recruitment Coordinator
E-mail: mrechka@nixonpeabody.com

All other offices
Layla Callahan, Recruitment Manager
E-mail: lcallahan@nixonpeabody.com

Palmer & Dodge LLP
111 Huntington Avenue at Prudential Center
Boston, MA 02199
Phone: (617) 239-0100
www.palmerdodge.com

Ms. Katy von Mehren
Phone: (617) 239-0172
Fax: (617) 227-4420
E-mail: kvonmehren@palmerdodge.com

Ropes & Gray
One International Plaza
Boston, MA 02110-2624
Phone: (617) 951-7000
www.ropesgray.com

Mr. Thomas A. Grewe
Director of Legal Recruiting
Phone: (617) 951-7239
Long Distance: (800) 951-4888, ext. 7239
Fax: (617) 951-7050
E-mail: hiringprogram@ropesgray.com

Testa, Hurwitz & Thibeault, LLP
125 High Street
Boston, MA 02110
Phone: (617) 248-7000
www.tht.com

Ms. Judith A. St. John
Recruiting Administrator
Phone: (617) 248-7401
Fax: (617) 248-7100
E-mail: stjohn@tht.com

MARYLAND

Miles & Stockbridge P.C.
10 Light Street
Baltimore, MD 21202
www.milesstockbridge.com
Phone: (410) 727-6464
Fax: (410) 385-3700

Randi S. Lewis, Esq.
Director of Diversity and Professional Development
Phone: (410) 385-3563
Fax: (410) 385-3700
E-mail: rlewis@milesstockbridge.com

Number of Attorneys Firmwide: 181
Number of Attorneys in this Office: 112
Summer Associate Hires in this Office: 10 (2003)
Full-Time First-Year Hires in this Office: 6 (2002)
First year salaries commencing Sept. 1, 2003: $102,000
Summer Associate Salary (Weekly): $1,825

Practice Areas
Business & Commercial Litigation, Labor and Employment Law, Products Liability, Mass Torts, Professional Malpractice, Insurance Regulation and Litigation, Commercial Real Estate and Finance, General Corporate, Mergers & Acquisitions, Securities, Immigration, International Child Abduction, ERISA and Benefits, Tax, Public and Corporate Finance

Law Schools Firm Recruits From
University of Maryland, University of Baltimore; Georgetown; George Washington; Duke; Emory; University of Virginia; William & Mary; Catholic; University of Pennsylvania

Firm Leadership
John B. Frisch, Chairman; John H. Murray, President; Jeffrey A. Seibert, Recruitment Committee Chair

Firm Description
Miles & Stockbridge is a regional law firm of approximately 180 lawyers. The firm's principal office is in Baltimore, Maryland and we have eight other offices in key locations in Maryland, the District of Columbia and northern Virginia. We are committed to providing comprehensive and sophisticated legal services to our clients while maintaining the informal friendly atmosphere that has characterized the firm since its formation in 1932. We represent clients in general civil matters involving a broad range of regional, national and international substantive legal issues.

Piper Rudnick LLP
6225 Smith Avenue
Baltimore, MD 21209-3600
Phone: (410) 580-3000
www.piperrudnick.com

Ms. Lindy Hilliard
Legal Recruiting Manager
Phone: (410) 580-4664
E-mail: lindy.hilliard@piperrudnick.com

MICHIGAN

Miller, Johnson, Snell & Cummiskey, P.L.C.
250 Monroe Avenue NW
Suite 800
Grand Rapids, MI 49503-2250
Phone: (616) 831-1700
Fax: (616) 988-1866
www.millerjohnson.com

Michelle D. Smith
Associate Recruitment and Development Manager
Phone: (616) 831-1866
Fax: (616) 988-1866
smithm@mjsc.com

Miller, Johnson, Snell & Cummiskey, P.L.C.
303 North Rose Street
Suite 600
Kalamazoo, MI 49007-3850
Phone: (269) 226-2950
Fax: (616) 988-1866
www.millerjohnson.com

Michelle D. Smith
Associate Recruitment and Development Manager
Phone: (616) 831-1866
Fax: (616) 988-1866
smithm@mjsc.com

MINNESOTA

Dorsey & Whitney LLP
50 South Sixth Street
Suite 1500
Minneapolis, MN 55402
Phone: (612) 340-2600
www.dorsey.com

Ms. Kelsey Shuff
Manager of Lawyer Recruiting
Fax: (612) 340-2868
E-mail: shuff.kelsey@dorsey.com

This Vault Legal Employer Directory is a special advertising section in the Vault Guide to the Top 100 Law Firms. For information on listing your firm in the directory, contact corporatesales@vault.com

VAULT CAREER LIBRARY

665

Leonard, Street and Deinard
150 South Fifth Street
Suite 2300
Minneapolis, MN 55402
Phone: (612) 335-1500
www.leonard.com

Ann Rainhart
Recruiting Manager
Phone: (612) 335-1763
Fax: (612) 335-1657
Ann.rainhart@leonard.com

MISSOURI

Blackwell Sanders Peper Martin LLP
Two Pershing Square
2300 Main Street, Suite 1000
Kansas City, MO 64108
Phone: (816) 983-8000
www.blackwellsanders.com

Ms. Marcia Cook, Esq.
Director of Client Development & Legal Recruiting
Phone: (816) 983-8931
Fax: (816) 983-8080
E-mail: mcook@blackwellsanders.com

Bryan Cave LLP
One Metropolitan Square
211 North Broadway, Suite 3600
St. Louis, MO 63102 - 2750
Phone: (314) 259-2000
Fax: (314) 259-2020
www.bryancave.com

Jennifer J. Sloop
Manager of Legal Recruiting - St. Louis
Phone: (314) 259-2617
Fax: (314) 259-2020
jjsloop@bryancave.com

Bryan Cave LLP
3500 One Kansas City Place
1200 Main Street, Suite 3500
Kansas City, MO 64105-2100
Phone: (816) 374-3200
Fax: (816) 374-3300
www.bryancave.com

Cristy M. Johnson
Manager of Legal Recruiting - Kansas City
Phone: (816) 374-3362
Fax: (816) 374-3300
cmjohnson@bryancave.com

Shook, Hardy & Bacon L.L.P.
One Kansas City Place
1200 Main Street
Kansas City, MO 64105-2118
Phone: (816) 474-6550
www.shb.com

Ms. Jessica A. Baker, Esq.
Dir., Legal Recruiting & Professional Development
Phone: (816) 474-6550
Fax: (816) 421-4066
E-mail: jbaker@shb.com

NEW JERSEY

Lowenstein Sandler PC

LOWENSTEIN SANDLER PC
Attorneys at Law

65 Livingston Avenue
Roseland, NJ 07068
Phone: (973) 597-2500
Fax: (973) 597-2400
www.lowenstein.com
Jane Thieberger
Director of Legal Personnel
Phone: (973) 597-6116
Fax: (973) 597-6117
E-mail: jthieberger@lowenstein.com

Number of Attorneys Firmwide: 204
Number of Attorneys in this Office: 191
Summer Associate Hires in this Office: 15 (2003)
Full-Time First-Year Hires in this Office: 15 (2002)
Lateral Hires in this Office: 30 (2002)
Summer Associate Salary (Weekly): $2,100
First-Year Associate Salary (Base): $95,000

Practice Areas
Corporate; Litigation; Environmental; Tax; Bankruptcy; IP;
Patent; Employment Law; Insurance; Securities Litigation;
Trusts and Estates

Law Schools Firm Recruits From
Boston College Law School Job Fair in NYC, Boston
University School of Law Job Fair in NYC, Cardozo School
of Law, Columbia University School of Law in NYC, Cornell
Law School Job Fair in NYC, Duke University School of Law,
Emory University School of Law Job Fair in NYC, Fordham
University School of Law, George Washington Law School
Job Fair in NYC, Georgetown University Law Center, Harvard
Law School, New York University School of Law, Rutgers
University School of Law-Newark, Seton Hall University
School of Law, University of North Carolina School of Law,
University of Notre Dame Law School, University of
Pennsylvania Law School, University of Virginia School of
Law, Massachusetts Law School Consortium, NJ Law Firm
Group Job Fair, Northeast BLSA Job Fair in NYC

Firm Leadership
Michael L. Rodburg (Managing Partner)

Firm Description
Lowenstein Sandler ranks first among New Jersey law firms
with the greatest number of corporate and tax attorneys listed
in the 2003-2004 edition of The Best Lawyers in America. The
firm is recognized in a diverse spectrum of legal practice
areas, including bankruptcy, business litigation, corporate,
environmental, tax, real estate, and trusts and estates.
Lowenstein Sandler has also emerged as New Jersey's premier
law firm in the 2003-2004 Chambers USA Guide to America's
Leading Business Lawyers.

NEW YORK

Allen & Overy
1221 Avenue of the Americas
New York, New York 10020
Phone: (212) 610-6300
http://www.allenovery.com

Elizabeth Papas
Legal Recruitment Manager
Phone: (646)344.6633
elizabeth.papas@allenovery.com

Jennifer Thornton
Legal Recruitment Coordinator
Phone: (646) 344.6673
jennifer.thornton@allenovery.com

Boies, Schiller & Flexner LLP
333 Main Street
Armonk, NY 10504-1710
Phone: (914) 749-8200
www.bsfllp.com

Hiring Partners
Robin A. Henry (Armonk)
Amy J. Mauser and Carl J. Nichols (DC)
Kirsten R. Gillibrand (NY)
Mark J. Heise (Florida)

This Vault Legal Employer Directory is a special advertising section in the Vault Guide to the Top 100
Law Firms. For information on listing your firm in the directory, contact corporatesales@vault.com

VAULT CAREER LIBRARY   667

Brown Raysman Millstein Felder & Steiner, LLP

BR⬤WNRAYSMAN

BROWN RAYSMAN MILLSTEIN FELDER & STEINER LLP

900 Third Avenue
New York, NY 10022
Phone: (212) 895-2000
Fax: (212) 895-2900
www.brownraysman.com
Wanda Woods
Legal Recruitment Coordinator
Phone: (212) 895-2000
Fax: (212) 895-2900
E-mail: legalrecruiting@brownraysman.com

Number of Attorneys Firmwide: 220
Number of Attorneys in this Office: 171
Summer Associate Hires in this Office: 8 (2003)
Full-Time First-Year Hires in this Office: 8 (2003)
Lateral Hires in this Office: 6 (2003)
Summer Associate Salary (Weekly): $2,212
First-Year Associate Salary (Base): $115,000

Practice Areas
Corp. & Securities; Technology; Media & Communications;
Outsourcing & Procurement; Real Estate; Intellectual
Property; Litigation; Labor & Employment; Trusts & Estates

Law Schools Firm Recruits From
BLSA; Boston College; Boston University; Brooklyn College;
Cornell; Columbia; Cardozo; Fordham; Georgetown; Harvard;
Howard; St. John's

Firm Leadership
Barry G. Felder, Esq., Hiring Partner

Firm Description
Over the past twenty-four years, Brown Raysman Millstein
Felder & Steiner has grown to more than 200 lawyers all of
whom possess a wide diversity of skills and experience to
service our continuously growing client base. Not only are we
a full-service firm with a wide diversity of work, but we are
also an entrepreneurial and growth-oriented firm that routinely
handles sophisticated work in an environment that is informal
and professional. The Firm seeks to avoid the unrelenting
pace associated with the New York legal community by
consistently maintaining an adequate level of associate
staffing. We actively recruit individuals who have the
intellect, initiative, interpersonal skills, maturity and
entrepreneurial drive that are the building blocks of the Firm's
success.

Bryan Cave LLP
1290 Avenue of the Americas
New York, NY 10104-3300
Phone: (212) 541-2000
Fax: (212) 541-4630
www.bryancave.com

Donna M. Harris
Manager of Legal Recruiting - New York
Phone: (212) 541-1114
Fax: (212) 541-4630
Donna.harris@bryancave.com

Cadwalader, Wickersham & Taft LLP
100 Maiden Lane
New York, NY 10038
Phone: (212) 504-6000
Fax: (212) 504-6666
www.cadwalader.com

Monica R. Brenner
Manager of Legal Recruitment
Phone: (212) 504-6044
Fax: (212) 504-6666
E-mail: monica.brenner@cwt.com

Cahill Gordon & Reindel LLP
80 Pine Street
New York, NY 10005
Phone: (212) 701-3000
www.cahill.com

Ms. Joyce A. Hilly
Hiring Coordinator
Phone: (212) 701-3901
E-mail: jhilly@cahill.com

Chadbourne & Parke LLP
30 Rockefeller Plaza
New York, NY 10112
Phone: (212) 408-5100
www.chadbourne.com

Ms. Bernadette L. Miles
Director of Legal Recruiting
Phone: (212) 408-5338
Fax: (212) 541-5369
E-mail: bmiles@chadbourne.com

Cleary, Gottlieb, Steen & Hamilton
One Liberty Plaza
New York, NY 10006-1470
Phone: (212) 225-2000
www.cgsh.com

Mr. Jaime E. Martinez
Manager of Legal Recruitment
Phone: (212) 225-3163
E-mail: jmartinez@cgsh.com

Clifford Chance LLP
200 Park Avenue
New York, NY 10166
Phone: (212) 878-8000
www.cliffordchance.com

Ms. Carolyn Older Bortner
Manager of Legal Recruiting
Phone: (212) 878-8252
Fax: (212) 878-8375
E-mail: Carolyn.bortner@cliffordchance.com

Coudert Brothers LLP
1114 Avenue of the Americas
New York, NY 10036
Phone: (212) 626-4400
www.coudert.com

Ms. Mary L. Simpson
Director of Legal Personnel
Phone: (212) 626-4400
Fax: (212) 626-4120
E-mail: simpsonm@coudert.com

Cravath, Swaine & Moore LLP
Worldwide Plaza
825 Eighth Avenue
New York, NY 10019
Phone: 212-474-1000
www.cravath.com

Ms. Lisa A. Kalen
Associate Director of Legal Personnel and Recruiting
Phone: (212) 474-3215
Fax: (212) 474-3225
E-mail: lkalen@cravath.com

Davis Polk & Wardwell
450 Lexington Avenue
New York, NY 10017
Phone: (212) 450-4000
www.dpw.com

Ms. Bonnie Hurry
Director of Recruiting & Legal Staff Services
Phone: (212) 450-4144
Fax: (212) 450-5548
bonnie.hurry@dpw.com

Debevoise & Plimpton
919 Third Avenue
New York, NY 10022
Phone: (212) 909-6000
www.debevoise.com

Ms. Ethel F. Leichti
Manager of Associate Recruitment
Phone: (212) 909-6657
E-mail: recruit@debevoise.com

Dewey Ballantine LLP
1301 Avenue of the Americas
New York, NY 10019
Phone: (212) 259-8000
Fax: (212) 259-6333
www.deweyballantine.com

Ms. Nicole Gunn
Manager of Legal Recruitment
Phone: (212) 259-7050
Fax: (212) 259-6333
E-mail: db.recruitment@deweyballantine.com

This Vault Legal Employer Directory is a special advertising section in the Vault Guide to the Top 100
Law Firms. For information on listing your firm in the directory, contact corporatesales@vault.com

VAULT CAREER LIBRARY   **669**

Dorsey & Whitney LLP
250 Park Avenue
New York, NY 10177
Phone: (212) 415-9200
Fax: (212) 953-7201
www.dorsey.com

Shell Zambardi
Recruiting Manager
Phone: (212) 415-9200
Fax: (212) 953-7201
zambardi.shell@dorsey.com

Number of Attorneys Firmwide: 753
Number of Attorneys in this Office: 79
Summer Associate Hires in this Office: 4 (2002)
Full-Time First-Year Hires in this Office: 5 (2002)
Lateral Hires in this Office: 4 (2002)
Summer Associate Salary (Weekly): $2,400
First-Year Associate Salary (Base): $125,000

Practice Areas
Our NY attorneys specialize in a full range of practice areas, including corporate law (e.g., M&A, securities, hedge funds, commodities and derivatives, commercial finance, project finance, securitization and tax), litigation and alternative dispute resolution (e.g., securities, banking, insurance, white collar defense, international arbitration, and labor and employment) and intellectual property (e.g., trademark, copyright and patent litigation and counseling).

Law Schools Firm Recruits From:
Dorsey accepts applications from students attending any law school. For a list of schools we visit for fall OCI, log onto our website at www.dorsey.com.

Dorsey is looking for students who have achieved academic excellence and possess superior writing and analytical skills, as well as having demonstrated leadership, responsibility and creativity as participants in their Universities and communities.

Firm Leadership
Pete Hendrixson, Managing Partner

Firm Description
Dorsey is one of the largest U.S. based international law firms. Our 700 plus lawyers are based in offices around the globe, but operate as one firm rather than as a collection of individual offices. Our NY office is at the center of the Firm's international practice and provides the best of all worlds: the resources of a large sophisticated global firm, the challenges of cutting-edge practice and a collegial atmosphere of a mid-size NYC firm dedicated to attorney development and world-class service for its US and foreign clients.

Epstein Becker & Green, P.C.
250 Park Avenue
New York, NY 10177
Phone: (212) 351-4500
www.ebglaw.com

Ms. Kalen T. Mikell
Recruitment and Training Coordinator
Phone: (212) 351-4500
Fax: (212) 661-0989
E-mail: kmikell@ebglaw.com

Fish & Neave
1251 Avenue of the Americas
New York, NY 10020
Phone: (212) 596-9000
www.fishneave.com
Ms. Heather C. Fennell
Legal Recruitment Manager
Phone: (212) 596-9121
E-mail: hfennell@fishneave.com

Fried, Frank, Harris, Shriver & Jacobson
One New York Plaza
New York, NY 10004
Phone: (212) 859-8000
www.friedfrank.com

New York
Ms. Elizabeth M. McDonald, Esq.
Director of Legal Recruitment
Phone: (212) 859-8621
E-mail: elizabeth.mcdonald@friedfrank.com

Los Angeles
Ms. Marian Wilk Gibbs
Recruiting Administrator
Phone: (213) 473-2049
E-mail: marian.wilk@friedfrank.com

Washington
Ms. Niki Kopsidas
Recruitment Manager
Phone: (202) 639-7286
E-mail: niki.kopsidas@friedfrank.com

Hughes Hubbard & Reed LLP
One Battery Park Plaza
New York, NY 10004-1482
Phone: (212) 837-6000
www.hugheshubbard.com

Lateral Hiring
Mr. Adrian Cockerill
Director of Legal Employment
Phone: (212) 837-6131
E-mail: cockerill@hugheshubbard.com

Law Student Hiring
Ms. Bianca Torres
Recruitment Coordinator
Phone: (212) 837-6131
E-mail: torres@hugheshubbard.com

Jackson Lewis LLP
One North Broadway
White Plains, NY 10601
Phone: (914) 328-0404
www.jacksonlewis.com

Ms. Terry Clifford
Director of Human Resources
Phone: (914) 328-0404
Fax: (914) 328-9096
E-mail: recruiting@jacksonlewis.com

Kaye Scholer LLP
425 Park Avenue
New York, NY 10022-3598
Phone: (212) 836-8000
www.kayescholer.com

Ms. Wendy Evans
Director of Legal Personnel
Phone: (212) 836-8000
Fax: (212) 836-8689
E-mail: wevans@kayescholer.com

Kelley Drye & Warren LLP
101 Park Avenue
New York, NY 10178
Phone: (212) 808-7800
www.kelleydrye.com

Mr. Randy J. Liss
Recruiting Coordinator
Phone: (212) 808-7721
Fax: (212) 808-7897
E-mail: rliss@kelleydrye.com

Kramer Levin Naftalis & Frankel
919 Third Avenue
New York, NY 10022
Phone: (212) 715-9100
www.kramerlevin.com

Ms. Pamela H. Nelson
Associate Director of Legal Recruiting
Phone: (212) 715-9213
Fax: (212) 715-8000
E-mail: pnelson@kramerlevin.com

This Vault Legal Employer Directory is a special advertising section in the Vault Guide to the Top 100
Law Firms. For information on listing your firm in the directory, contact corporatesales@vault.com

VAULT CAREER LIBRARY   671

Kronish Lieb Weiner & Hellman LLP

KRONISH LIEB
WEINER & HELLMAN LLP | K L W H

1114 Avenue of the Americas
New York, NY 10036-7798
Phone: (212) 479-6000
Fax: (212) 479-6275
www.kronishlieb.com

Tina F. Antonakakis
Director of Legal Recruitment and Professional Development
Phone: (212) 479-6000
legalrecruiting@kronishlieb.com

Number of Attorneys Firmwide: 110
Number of Attorneys in this Office: 110
Summer Associate Hires in this Office: 8 (2003)
Full-Time First-Year Hires in this Office: 5 (2003)
Lateral Hires in this Office: 6 (2002)
Summer Associate Salary (Weekly): $2,450
First-Year Associate Salary (Base): $125,000

Practice Areas
Litigation; Corporate; Bankruptcy; Tax; Real Estate; Trust & Estates

Law Schools Firm Recruits From
Boston College, Boston University; Columbia; Fordham; George Washington; Georgetown; Harvard; NYU; Rutgers-Newark; Penn

Firm Leadership
Alan Levine, Managing Partner

Firm Description
Kronish Lieb Weiner & Hellman LLP is a full service law firm that represents a diverse array of institutional and private clients from around the world. Kronish Lieb's clients range from large financial institutions and publicly-traded companies to entrepreneurial enterprises and individuals. Many of our clients come to the firm seeking specially skilled lawyers and creative advice. No single client or area of work dominates our practice.

LeBoeuf, Lamb, Green & MacRae, L.L.P.

125 West 55th Street
New York, NY 10019-5389
Phone: (212) 424-8000
www.llgm.com

Ms. Jill Cameron
Legal Recruiting Coordinator
Phone: (212) 424-8266
Fax: (212) 424-8500
E-mail: jcameron@llgm.com

Milbank, Tweed, Hadley & McCloy LLP

One Chase Manhattan Plaza
New York, NY 10005
Phone: (212) 530-5219
www.milbank.com

Ms. June Chotoo
Recruiting Coordinator
Phone: (212) 530-8322
Fax: (212) 822-5064
E-mail: Jchotoo@Milbank.com

Paul, Weiss, Rifkind, Wharton & Garrison LLP

1285 Avenue of the Americas
New York, NY 10019
Phone: (212) 373-3000
www.paulweiss.com

Ms. Patricia J. Morrissy
Legal Recruitment Director
Phone: (212) 373-2548
Fax: (212) 373-2205
E-mail: pmorrissy@paulweiss.com

Ms. Joanne Ollman
Legal Personnel Director
Phone: (212) 373-2480
Fax: (212) 373-2515
E-mail: jollman@paulweiss.com

Pennie & Edmonds LLP

1155 Avenue of the Americas
New York, NY 10036
Phone: (212) 790-9090
www.pennie.com

Ms. Annette I. Friend
Director of Recruitment & Professional Development
Phone: (212) 790-2930
Fax: (212) 699-0267
E-mail: staceyp@pennie.com

Pillsbury Winthrop LLP

One Battery Park Plaza
New York, NY 10004
Phone: (212) 858-1000
www.pillsburywinthrop.com

Ms. Dorrie Ciavatta
dciavatta@pillsburywinthrop.com
See firm web site for employment contacts at other offices.

Proskauer Rose LLP
1585 Broadway
New York, NY 10036
Phone: (212) 969-3000
www.proskauer.com

Ms. Diane M. Kolnik
Manager of Legal Recruiting
Phone: (212) 969-5060
E-mail: dkolnik@proskauer.com

Quinn Emanuel Urquhart Oliver & Hedges LLP
805 Third Avenue, 11th Floor
New York, NY 10022
Phone: (212) 702-8100
Fax: (212) 702-8200
www.quinnemanuel.com

Selene Dogan
Recruiting Coordinator
Phone: (213) 624-7707
Fax: (213) 624-0643
E-mail: selenedogan@quinnemanuel.com

Schulte Roth & Zabel LLP
919 Third Avenue
New York, NY 10022
Phone: (212) 756-2000
www.srz.com

Ms. Lisa Drew
Director of Recruiting
Fax: (212) 593-5955
E-mail: lisa.drew@srz.com

Shearman & Sterling
599 Lexington Avenue
New York, NY 10022
Phone: (212) 848-4000
www.shearman.com

Ms. Suzanne Ryan
Manager, Professional Recruiting
Phone: (212) 848-4592
Fax: (212) 848-7179
E-mail: sryan@shearman.com

Sidley Austin Brown & Wood LLP
787 Seventh Avenue
New York, NY 10019
Phone: (212) 839-5300

Ms. Shana Kassoff
Recruiting Manager
Phone: (212) 839-8600
Fax: (212) 839-5599
E-mail: skassoff@sidley.com

Simpson Thacher & Bartlett
425 Lexington Avenue
New York, NY 10017
Phone: (212) 455-2000
www.simpsonthacher.com

Ms. Dee Pifer
Director of Legal Employment
Phone: (212) 455-2687
Fax: (212) 455-2502
E-mail: dpifer@stblaw.com

Skadden, Arps, Slate, Meagher & Flom LLP
Four Times Square
New York, NY 10036
www.skadden.com

Carol Lee H. Sprague
Director, Legal Hiring
Phone: (212) 735-2076

E-mail: csprague@skadden.com
Number of Attorneys Firmwide: 1,729
Number of Attorneys in this Office: 831
Summer Associate Hires in this Office: 116 (2003)
Full-Time First-Year Hires in this Office: 113 (2002)
Summer Associate Salary (Weekly): $2,400
First-Year Associate Salary (Base): $140,000

Practice Areas
Antitrust; Corporate Restructuring; Banking; Corporate
Finance; M&A; Litigation; Mass Torts; Real Estate; Tax;
Intellectual Property

Law Schools Firm Recruits From
Albany, Boston University, Cardozo, Columbia, Cornell,
Duke, Georgetown, Harvard, Michigan, New York Law,
Stanford, UCLA, Virginia, Yale, Boalt Hall, Texas, Chicago

Firm Leadership
Robert Sheehan, Executive Partner; Howard Ellin, Hiring
Partner

Firm Description
New York is the headquarters of our broad-based national and
international practice. Skadden, Arps has 11 offices outside of
the United States, such as London, Paris and Tokyo. Our
clients are a substantial and diverse group that includes many
"Fortune 500" companies. We are engaged in more than 40
practice areas. In addition, we encourage pro bono work.
Associates are initially assigned to a particular department
based on their preferences and the Firm's needs. Thereafter,
we not only permit, but encourage our associates to work in
different practice areas.

This Vault Legal Employer Directory is a special advertising section in the Vault Guide to the Top 100
Law Firms. For information on listing your firm in the directory, contact corporatesales@vault.com

VAULT CAREER LIBRARY   **673**

Stroock & Stroock & Lavan LLP
180 Maiden Lane
New York, NY 10038-4982
Phone: (212) 806-5400
www.stroock.com

Ms. Diane A. Cohen
Director of Legal Personnel and Recruiting
Phone: (212) 806-5406
Fax: (212) 806-6006
E-mail: dcohen@stroock.com

Sullivan & Cromwell LLP
125 Broad Street
New York, NY 10004
Phone: (212) 558-4000
www.sullcrom.com

Ms. Nicole Adams
Assistant Manager of Legal Recruiting
Phone: (212) 558-3518
Fax: (212) 558-3588 FAX
E-mail: adamsn@sullcrom.com

Swidler Berlin Shereff Friedman, LLP
405 Lexington Avenue
New York, NY 10174
Phone: (212) 973-0111
www.swidlaw.com

Ms. Judith Abraham
Recruiting Manager, New York, NY
Phone: (212) 891-9325
Fax: (212) 891-9598
E-mail: jmabraham@swidlaw.com

Thelen Reid & Priest LLP
875 Third Avenue
New York, NY 10022
Phone: (212) 603-2000
www.thelenreid.com

Ms. Diane Amato
Attorney Recruiting Manager, East Coast
Phone: (212) 603-2000
Fax: (212) 541-1518
E-mail: damato@thelenreid.com

Wachtell, Lipton, Rosen & Katz
51 West 52nd Street
New York, NY 10019-6150
Phone: (212) 403-1000
www.wlrk.com

Ms. Elizabeth F. Breslow
Director of Recruiting and Legal Personnel
Phone: (212) 403-1334
Fax: (212) 403-2334
E-mail: recruiting@wlrk.com

Weil, Gotshal & Manges LLP
767 Fifth Avenue
New York, NY 10153
Phone: (212) 310-8000
www.weil.com

Ms. Donna J. Lang
Manager of Legal Recruiting
Fax: (212) 735-4502
E-mail: donna.lang@weil.com

White & Case LLP
1155 Avenue of the Americas
New York, NY 10036-2787
Phone: (212) 819-8200
www.whitecase.com

Ms. Dana E. Stephenson
Director of Attorney Recruiting & Employment
Phone: (212) 819-8200
Fax: (212) 354-8113
E-mail: recruit@whitecase.com

Willkie Farr & Gallagher
The Equitable Center
787 Seventh Avenue
New York, NY 10019-6099
Phone: (212) 728-8000
www.willkie.com

Ms. Patricia M. Langlade
Recruiting Coordinator
Phone: (212) 728-8469
Fax: (212) 728-8111
E-mail: planglade@willkie.com

Winston & Strawn
200 Park Avenue
New York, New York 10166-4193
Phone: (212) 294-6700
Fax: (212) 294-4700
www.winston.com

Lisa Soderberg
Legal Recruiting Manager
Phone: (212) 294-6815
Fax: (212) 294-4700
Email: lsoderberg@winston.com

NORTH CAROLINA

Cadwalader, Wickersham & Taft LLP
227 West Trade Street, 24th Floor
Charlotte, NC 28202
Phone: (704) 348-5100
Fax: (704) 348-5200
www.cadwalader.com

Emily Morrison
Manager of Associate Development & Recruitment
Phone: (704) 348-5238
Fax: (704) 348-5200
E-mail: emily.morrison@cwt.com

Womble Carlyle Sandridge & Rice, PLLC
One West Fourth Street
Winston-Salem, NC 27101
Phone: (336) 721-3600
www.wcsr.com

Ms. Cynthia K. Pruitt
Prof. Devevelopment & Recruiting Administrator
Phone: (336) 721-3680
Fax: (336) 721-3660
E-mail: cpruitt@wcsr.com

OHIO

Arter & Hadden LLP
1100 Huntington Building
925 Euclid Avenue
Cleveland, Ohio 44115-1475
Phone: (216) 696-1100
www.arterhadden.com

Ms. Jill M. Filicko
Phone: (216) 696-4886
Fax: (216) 696-2645
E-mail: jill.filicko@arterhadden.com

Baker & Hostetler LLP
3200 National City Center
1900 East 9th Street
Cleveland, OH 44114-3485
Phone: (216) 621-0200
www.bakerlaw.com

Ms. Kathleen Ferdico
Attorney Recruitment and Development Manager
Phone: (216) 861-7092
Fax: (216) 861-6618
E-mail: kferdico@bakerlaw.com

Jones Day
North Point - 901 Lakeside Avenue
Cleveland, OH 44114-1190
Phone: (216) 586-3939
www.jonesday.com

Ms. Jolie A. Blanchard
Firm Director of Recruiting
Phone: (202) 879-3788
Fax: (202) 626-1738
E-mail: jablanchard@jonesday.com

This Vault Legal Employer Directory is a special advertising section in the Vault Guide to the Top 100
Law Firms. For information on listing your firm in the directory, contact corporatesales@vault.com

VAULT CAREER LIBRARY

675

Porter Wright Morris & Arthur LLP
250 East Fifth Street
Suite 2200
Cincinnati, OH 45202-5117
Phone: (513) 381-4700
Fax: (513) 421-0991
www.porterwright.com

David G. Zimmerman
Professional Personnel Coordinator
Phone: (614) 227-1907
Fax: (614) 227-2100
E-mail: Dzimmerman@porterwright.com

Number of Attorneys Firmwide: 277
Number of Attorneys in this Office: 6
Lateral Hires in this Office: 5 (2003)
Summer Associate Salary (Weekly): $1,730
First year Associate Salary (Base): $80,000

Practice Areas
Financial Institutions/Commercial Law; Business/Tax;
Energy/Environment/Government Affairs;
Labor & Employment; Litigation; Trusts and Estates; Real
Estate

Law Schools Firm Recruits From
American University; Boston College; Capital; Case Western;
Catholic University; Chicago; Cincinnati; Cleveland-Marshall;
Columbia; Cornell; Dayton; Duke; George Washington;
Georgetown; Harvard; Howard; Illinois; Indiana -
Bloomington; Maryland; Michigan; NYU; Northwestern;
Notre Dame; Ohio State; Pennsylvania; Texas; Vanderbilt;
Virginia; Wake Forest; Washington & Lee; William & Mary;
Wisconsin

Firm Leadership
Robert W. Trafford, Managing Partner

Firm Description
Porter Wright Morris & Arthur LLP is a major institutional,
multi-city law firm serving medium- to large-sized business
clients. We pride ourselves on the practicality, responsiveness,
and excellence of the services we have provided in meeting
the legal needs of our clients. Each of our six offices has a
need for bright, confident, energetic, and committed law
graduates to become a part of our growth into the future.

Porter Wright Morris & Arthur LLP
Huntington Building 925 Euclid Ave.
Suite 1700
Cleveland, OH 44115-1483
Phone: (216) 443-9000
Fax: (216) 443-9011
www.porterwright.com

David G. Zimmerman
Professional Personnel Coordinator
Phone: (614) 227-1907
Fax: (614) 227-2100
E-mail: Dzimmerman@porterwright.com

Number of Attorneys Firmwide: 277
Number of Attorneys in this Office: 36
Summer Associate Hires in this Office: 6 (2003)
Full-Time First Year Hires: 3 (2003)
Lateral Hires: 5 (2003)
Summer Associate Salary (Weekly): $1,730
First year Associate Salary (Base): $100,000

Practice Areas:
Financial Institutions/Commercial Law; Business/Tax;
Energy/Environment/Government Affairs;
Labor & Employment; Litigation; Trusts and Estates; Real
Estate

Law Schools Firm Recruits From:
American University; Boston College; Capital; Case Western;
Catholic University; Chicago; Cincinnati; Cleveland-Marshall;
Columbia; Cornell; Dayton; Duke; George Washington;
Georgetown; Harvard; Howard; Illinois; Indiana -
Bloomington; Maryland; Michigan; NYU; Northwestern;
Notre Dame; Ohio State; Pennsylvania; Texas; Vanderbilt;
Virginia; Wake Forest; Washington & Lee; William & Mary;
Wisconsin

Firm Leadership
Robert W. Trafford, Managing Partner

Firm Description (75 words):
Porter Wright Morris & Arthur LLP is a major institutional,
multi-city law firm serving medium- to large-sized business
clients. We pride ourselves on the practicality, responsiveness,
and excellence of the services we have provided in meeting
the legal needs of our clients. Each of our six offices has a
need for bright, confident, energetic, and committed law
graduates to become a part of our growth into the future.

Porter Wright Morris & Arthur LLP
41 South High Street
Suite 2800
Columbus, OH 43215-6194
Phone: (614) 227-2000
Fax: (614) 227-2100
www.porterwright.com

David G. Zimmerman
Professional Personnel Coordinator
Phone: (614) 227-1907
Fax: (614) 227-2100
E-mail: Dzimmerman@porterwright.com

Number of Attorneys Firmwide: 277
Number of Attorneys in this Office: 185
Summer Associate Hires in this Office: 26 (2003)
Full-Time First Year Hires in this Office: 12 (2003)
Lateral Hires: 10 (2003)
Summer Associate Salary (Weekly): $1,730
First year Associate Salary (Base): $90,000

Practice Areas
Financial Institutions/Commercial Law; Business/Tax;
Energy/Environment/Government Affairs; Labor &
Employment; Litigation; Trusts and Estates; Real Estate

Law Schools Firm Recruits From
American University; Boston College; Capital; Case Western;
Catholic University; Chicago; Cincinnati; Cleveland-Marshall;
Columbia; Cornell; Dayton; Duke; George Washington;
Georgetown; Harvard; Howard; Illinois; Indiana -
Bloomington; Maryland; Michigan; NYU; Northwestern;
Notre Dame; Ohio State; Pennsylvania; Texas; Vanderbilt;
Virginia; Wake Forest; Washington & Lee; William & Mary;
Wisconsin

Firm Leadership
Robert W. Trafford, Managing Partner

Firm Description
Porter Wright Morris & Arthur LLP is a major institutional,
multi-city law firm serving medium- to large-sized business
clients. We pride ourselves on the practicality, responsiveness,
and excellence of the services we have provided in meeting
the legal needs of our clients. Each of our six offices has a
need for bright, confident, energetic, and committed law
graduates to become a part of our growth into the future.

Porter Wright Morris & Arthur LLP
One Dayton Center - One South Main Street
Suite 1600
Dayton, OH 45402-2028
Phone: (937) 449-6810
Fax: (937) 449-6820
www.porterwright.com

David G. Zimmerman
Title: Professional Personnel Coordinator
Phone: (614) 227-1907
Fax: (614) 227-2100
E-mail: Dzimmerman@porterwright.com

Number of Attorneys Firmwide: 277
Number of Attorneys in this Office: 18
Summer Associate Hires in this Office: 3 (2003)
Full-Time First Year Hires in this Office: 2 (2003)
Lateral Hires in this Office: 2 (2003)
Summer Associate Salary (Weekly): $1,730
First year Associate Salary (Base): $80,000

Practice Areas
Financial Institutions/Commercial Law; Business/Tax;
Energy/Environment/Government Affairs; Labor &
Employment; Litigation; Trusts and Estates; Real Estate

Law Schools Firm Recruits From
American University; Boston College; Capital; Case Western;
Catholic University; Chicago; Cincinnati; Cleveland-Marshall;
Columbia; Cornell; Dayton; Duke; George Washington;
Georgetown; Harvard; Howard, Illinois, Indiana -
Bloomington, Maryland, Michigan, NYU, Northwestern,
Notre Dame, Ohio State, Pennsylvania, Texas, Vanderbilt,
Virginia, Wake Forest, Washington & Lee, William & Mary,
Wisconsin.

Firm Leadership
Robert W. Trafford, Managing Partner

Firm Description
Porter Wright Morris & Arthur LLP is a major institutional,
multi-city law firm serving medium- to large-sized business
clients. We pride ourselves on the practicality, responsiveness,
and excellence of the services we have provided in meeting
the legal needs of our clients. Each of our six offices has a
need for bright, confident, energetic, and committed law
graduates to become a part of our growth into the future.

This Vault Legal Employer Directory is a special advertising section in the Vault Guide to the Top 100
Law Firms. For information on listing your firm in the directory, contact corporatesales@vault.com

V\ULT CAREER LIBRARY   **677**

Squire, Sanders, & Dempsey
4900 Key Tower
127 Public Square
Cleveland, OH 44114-1304
Phone: (216) 479-8500
www.ssd.com

Ms. Jane C. Murphy
Legal Personnel & Prof. Development Manager
Phone: (216) 802-7571
E-mail: jamurphy@ssd.com

OREGON

Stoel Rives LLP
900 SW Fifth Avenue, Suite 2600
Portland, OR 97204
Phone: (503) 224-3380
www.stoel.com

Ms. Michelle Baird Johnson
Lawyer Recruiting Manager
Phone: (503) 294-9539 / Fax: (503) 220-2480
E-mail: mbjohnson@stoel.com

PENNSYLVANIA

Ballard Spahr Andrews & Ingersoll, LLP
1735 Market Street, 51st Floor
Philadelphia, PA 19103-7599
Phone: (215) 665-8500
www.ballardspahr.com

Ms. Jennifer L. Fallon
Phone: (215) 864-8167
Fax: (215) 864-9184
E-mail: fallonj@ballardspahr.com

Blank Rome LLP
One Logan Square
Philadelphia, PA 19103-6998
Phone: (215) 569-5500
www.BlankRome.com

Ms. Donna M. Branca
Phone: (215) 569-5751
Fax: (215) 569-5555
E-mail: branca@BlankRome.com

Buchanan Ingersoll, Professional Corporation
One Oxford Centre
301 Grant Street, 20th Floor
Pittsburgh, PA 15219-1410
Phone: (412) 562-8800
www.buchananingersoll.com

Ms. Laurie S. Lenigan
Legal Recruiting Manager
Phone: (412) 562-1470
Fax: (412) 562-1040
E-mail: lenigansl@bipc.com

Cozen O'Connor
1900 Market Street
Philadelphia, PA 19103
Phone: (215) 665-2000
www.cozen.com

Ms. Lori C. Rosenberg, Esq.
Director of Legal Recruiting
Phone: (215) 665-4178
Fax: (215) 665-2013
E-mail: lrosenberg@cozen.com

Dechert LLP
4000 Bell Atlantic Tower
1717 Arch Street
Philadelphia, PA 19103-2793
Phone: (215) 994-4000
www.dechert.com

Firm-wide Associate Hiring Matters
Ms. Carol S. Miller
Director of Associate Administration
Phone: (215) 994-2147
E-mail: carol.miller@dechert.com

Summer & Entry-Level Assoc. Hiring - Philadelphia
Ms. Alberta Bertolino
Director of Associate Recruitment
Phone: (215) 994-2296
E-mail: alberta.bertolino@dechert.com

Drinker Biddle & Reath LLP
One Logan Square
18th & Cherry Streets
Philadelphia, PA 19103-6996
Phone: (215) 988-2700
www.drinkerbiddle.com

Ms. Maryellen Wyville Altieri
Director of Professional Recruitment
Phone: (215) 988-2663
Fax: (215) 988-2757
E-mail: maryellen.altieri@dbr.com

Duane Morris LLP
One Liberty Place, Suite 4200
Philadelphia, PA 19103-7396
Phone: (215) 979-1000
www.duanemorris.com

Peggy Simoncini Pasquay
Legal Recruitment Coordinator
Phone: (215) 979-1161
Fax: (215) 979) 1020
E-mail: simoncini@duanemorris.com

Kirkpatrick & Lockhart LLP
Henry W. Oliver Building
535 Smithfield Street
Pittsburgh, PA 15222
Phone: (412) 355-6500
www.kl.com
See www.kl.com for contacts in each office.

Morgan, Lewis & Bockius LLP
1701 Market Street
Philadelphia, PA 19103-2921
Phone: (215) 963-5000
www.morganlewis.com
See www.morganlewis.com careers section for contacts in various offices.

Pepper Hamilton LLP
3000 Two Logan Square
Eighteenth and Arch Streets
Philadelphia, PA 19103-2799
Phone: (215) 981-4000
www.pepperlaw.com

Ms. Meg L. Urbanski
Director of Professional Recruitment
Phone: (215) 981-4991
Fax: (215) 981-4750
E-mail: urbanskim@pepperlaw.com

Reed Smith
435 Sixth Avenue
Pittsburgh, PA 15219
Phone: (412) 288-3131
www.reedsmith.com

Ms. Lorraine Rivera Connally
Director of Legal Recruiting
Phone: (412) 288-4194
Fax: (412) 288-3063

Wolf, Block, Schorr and Solis-Cohen LLP
1650 Arch Street, 22nd Floor
Philadelphia, PA 19103-2097
Phone: (215) 977-2362
www.wolfblock.com

Ms. Eileen M. McMahon
Director, Legal Personnel & Recruitment
Phone: (215) 977-2362
Fax: (215) 405-3962
E-mail: emcmahon@wolfblock.com

TEXAS

Andrews & Kurth L.L.P.
600 Travis, Suite 4200
Houston, TX 77002
Phone: (713) 220-4200
www.akllp.com

Ms. Kimberley Klevenhagen
Phone: (713) 220-4140
Fax: (713) 220-4285
E-mail: kimklevenhagen@akllp.com

Baker Botts L.L.P.
One Shell Plaza
910 Louisiana Street
Houston, TX 77002-4995
Phone: (713) 229-1234
www.bakerbotts.com

Ms. Melissa O. Moss
Manager of Attorney Employment
Phone: (713) 229-2056
Fax: (713) 229-1522
E-mail: melissa.moss@bakerbotts.com

Bracewell & Patterson, L.L.P.
711 Louisiana Street, Suite 2900
South Tower Pennzoil Place
Houston, TX 77002-2781
Phone: (713) 223-2900
www.bracepatt.com

Ms. Jean P. Lenzner
Director of Attorney Employment
Phone: (713) 221-1296
Fax: (713) 221-1212
E-mail: jean.lenzner@bracepatt.com

This Vault Legal Employer Directory is a special advertising section in the Vault Guide to the Top 100 Law Firms. For information on listing your firm in the directory, contact corporatesales@vault.com

VAULT CAREER LIBRARY

679

Fulbright & Jaworski L.L.P.
1301 McKinney, Suite 5100
Houston, TX 77010-3095
Phone: (713) 651-5151
www.fulbright.com

Ms. Katie Eleazer
Recruiting Coordinator
Phone: (713) 651-3715
Fax: (713) 651-5246
E-mail: keleazer@fulbright.com

Gardere Wynne Sewell LLP
Thanksgiving Tower
1601 Elm Street, Suite 3000
Dallas, TX 75201
Phone: (214) 999-3000
www.gardere.com

Houston
Ms. Sheri Green Howard
Director of Recruiting
Phone: (713) 276-5155
Fax: (713) 276-5555

All other offices:
Ms. Tammy Patterson
Director of Recruiting & Professional Development
Phone: (214) 999-4177
Fax: (214) 999-4667
E-mail: tpatterson@gardere.com

Haynes and Boone, LLP
901 Main Street, Suite 3100
Dallas, TX 75202-3789
Phone: (214) 651-5000
www.haynesboone.com

Ms. Stacey Yervasi
Fall Recruiting Coordinator
Phone: (214) 651-5438
Fax: (214) 200-0576
E-mail: stacey.yervasi@haynesboone.com

Hughes & Luce, LLP

HUGHES·LUCE LLP
Know-how to win.

1717 Main St., Suite 2800
Dallas, TX 75201
Phone: (214) 939-5500
Fax: (214) 939-5849
www.hughesluce.com

Nancy Sloan
Director of Attorney Recruiting & Retention
Phone: (214) 939-5517
Fax: (214) 939-5849

E-mail: nsloan@hughesluce.com
Number of Attorneys Firmwide: 158
Number of Attorneys in this Office: 124
Summer Associate Hires in this Office: 24 (2003)
Full-Time First-Year Hires in this Office: 13 (2002)
Summer Associate Salary (Weekly): $2,100
First-Year Associate Salary (Base): $105,000

Practice Areas
Anti-Trust; Complex Commercial Dispute & Consumer Class Action Cases; Corporate Finance & Securities; Corporate Governance; Professional Defense; Bankruptcy & Business Reorganization; Environmental Team; Appellate; Home Building Industry; Internet/E-Commerce Deals; Insurance Industry; Intellectual Property; Income Tax; Labor/Employment; Outsourcing; Probate & Fiduciary Disputes; Private Equity; Protection Real Estate Rights; Real Estate Use & Development; Retail Industry Group; Technology Contracts & Licensing; Telecommunications Industry; Tax Incentives State & Local Projects; Tax Litigation; White Collar; Wealth Plan & Preservation/Trusts & Estates; Mergers & Acquisitions; Distressed Debt Group

Law Schools Firm Recruits From
Baylor, BYU, Chicago, Duke, George Washington, Georgetown, Harvard, Houston, Kansas, Michigan, Notre Dame, SMU, Southeastern Minority Job Fair, Stanford, Sunbelt Minority Job Fair, Texas, Texas Interview Program, Tulane, UC-Berkely, UC-Hastings, Vanderbilt, Yale

Firm Leadership
Robert H. Mow, Jr., Managing Partner

Firm Description
Being tops in our field is what Hughes & Luce is all about. Clients give us high marks for our service, and associates love our collegial atmosphere, ranking us first among big Texas firms as a place to work. From our Austin and Dallas offices, we represent a wide range of clients, including the blue chips of the Dow and the leaders of tomorrow. Our 160 lawyers enjoy the practice of law, and it shows.

Jackson Walker L.L.P.
901 Main Street, Suite 6000
Dallas, TX 75202-3797
Phone: (214) 953-6000
www.jw.com

Ms. Jacqueline L. Galli
Recruiting Coordinator
Phone: (214) 953-6000
Fax: (216) 953-5822
E-mail: jgalli@jw.com

Jenkens & Gilchrist, a Professional Corporation
1445 Ross Avenue, Suite 3200
Dallas, TX 75202-2799
Phone: (214) 855-4500
www.jenkens.com

Ms. Lauren Sager
Phone: (214) 855-4500
Fax: (214) 855-4300

Locke Lidell & Sapp LLP
2200 Ross Avenue, Suite 2200
Dallas, Texas 75201-6776
Phone: (214) 740-8000
www.lockeliddell.com

Ms. Courtney O'Neil
Director of Recruiting
Phone: (713) 226-1425
Fax: (713) 223-3717
E-mail: coneil@lockeliddell.com

Locke Lidell & Sapp LLP
3400 J. P. Morgan Chase Tower
600 Travis
Houston, TX 77002-3095
Phone: (713) 226-1200
www.lockeliddell.com

Ms. Courtney O'Neil
Director of Recruiting
Phone: (713) 226-1425
Fax: (713) 223-3717
E-mail: coneil@lockeliddell.com

Thompson & Knight LLP
1700 Pacific Avenue, Suite 3300
Dallas, TX 75201
Phone: (214) 969-1700
www.tklaw.com

Ms. Courtney L. Bankler
National Recruiting Coordinator
Phone: (214) 969-1379
Fax: (214) 969-1751
E-mail: courtney.bankler@tklaw.com

Vinson & Elkins L.L.P.
2300 First City Tower
1001 Fannin Street
Houston, TX 77002-6760
Phone: (713) 758-2222
www.velaw.com

Ms. Patty H. Calabrese
Director of Attorney Employment
Phone: (713) 758-4544
Fax: (713) 615-5245
E-mail: pcalabrese@velaw.com

Winstead Sechrest & Minick P.C.
5400 Renaissance Tower, 1201 Elm Street
Dallas TX 75270-2199
Phone: (214) 745-5400
www.winstead.com

Mr. Wayne Bost
Hiring Partner
Phone: (512) 370-2859
E-mail: AttorneyResume@winstead.com

VIRGINIA

Hunton & Williams LLP
Riverfront Plaza, East Tower
951 East Byrd Street
Richmond, VA 23219
Phone: (804) 788-8200
www.hunton.com

Ms. Christine Tracey
Legal Recruiting Manager
Phone: (212) 309-1217
Fax: (212) 309-1100
E-mail: ctracey@hunton.com

McGuireWoods LLP
One James Center
901 East Cary Street
Richmond, VA 23219-4030
Phone: (804) 775-1000
www.mcguirewoods.com

Ms. Ann McGhee
Attorney Recruiting Manager
Phone: (804) 775-7628
E-mail: amcghee@mcguirewoods.com

Ms. Dusti L. Plunkett
Attorney Recruitment Manager (Washington, DC)
Phone: (202) 857-1739
E-mail: dplunkett@mcguirewoods.com

WASHINGTON

Davis Wright Tremaine LLP
2600 Century Square
1501 Fourth Avenue
Seattle, WA 98101-1688
Phone: (206) 622-3150
www.dwt.com

Seattle
Ms. Carol Yuly
Recruiting Administrator
Phone: (206) 628-3529
E-mail: carolyuly@dwt.com

Portland
Ms. Leslie Dustin
Recruiting Administrator
Phone: (503) 778-5243

Perkins Coie LLP
1201 Third Avenue
Suite 4800
Seattle, WA 98101-3099
Phone: (206) 583-8888
www.perkinscoie.com

Ms. Laura MacDougall Kader
Lawyer Personnel Recruiter for Law Student Hiring
Phone: (206) 583-8888
Fax: (206) 583-8500
E-mail: lkader@perkinscoie.com

Preston Gates & Ellis LLP
5000 Columbia Center
701 Fifth Avenue
Seattle, WA 98104-7078
Phone: (206) 623-7580
www.prestongates.com

Ms. Kristine Immordino
Director, Legal Recruiting
Phone: (206) 623-7580
Fax: (206) 623-7022
E-mail: krisi@prestongates.com

Townsend and Townsend and Crew LLP
Two Union Square
601 Union Street, Suite 5400
Seattle, WA 98101-2327
Phone: (206) 467-9600
Fax: (206) 623-6793
www.townsend.com

Lindy Van der Reis, Esq.
Manager of Recruitment and Professional Development
Phone: (415) 576-0200
Fax: (415) 576-0300
E-mail: mhvanderreis@townsend.com

WISCONSIN

Foley & Lardner
U.S. Bank Center
777 East Wisconsin Avenue
Milwaukee, WI 53202-5367
Phone: (414) 271-2400
www.foleylaw.com

Ms. Kara E. Nelson
Director of Legal Recruitment & Development
Phone: (414) 271-2400
Fax: (414) 297-4900
E-mail: kenelson@foleylaw.com

LONDON, UK

Allen & Overy
One New Change
London, UK EC4M 9QQ
Phone: +44 (0) 20-7330-3000
http://www.allenovery.com

Nicola McNeill, U.S. Liaison Manager
Phone: +44 (0) 20-7330-2447
nicola.mcneill@allenovery.com

LEGAL
RECRUITER FIRM
DIRECTORY

REIGN ENTERPRISES

Legal Staffing

Dedicated to serving the staffing needs of the legal community

Noel H. Gordon
Chairman and CEO

Twenty Nassau St., Suite 200, Princeton, NJ 08542
Tel: (609) 688-9898 • Fax: (609) 688-1898
noel@reignenterprises.com • www.reignenterprises.com

Arizona

Phyllis Hawkins & Associates, Inc.

105 East Northern Avenue
Phoenix, AZ 85020
Phone: (602) 263-0248
Fax: (602) 678-1564
www.azlawsearch.com

Phyllis Hawkins
President
Phone: (602) 263-0248
Fax: (602) 678-1564
phassoc@qwest.net

California

Garb Jaffe & Associates Legal Placement, LLC

Garb Jaffe & Associates

2001 Wilshire Boulevard, Suite 510
Santa Monica, CA 90403
Phone: (310) 998-3388 | **Fax:** (310) 998-3392
www.garbjaffe.com

Eve Jaffe, Esq., President
Phone: (310) 998-3388
evejaffe@garbjaffe.com

Garb Jaffe & Associates Legal Placement LLC was founded in 1992 and specializes in placing both partners and associates within law firms and corporations in Southern California. We work with virtually every law firm in Southern California that utilizes the services of legal recruiters. Almost all of our recruiters are attorneys that graduated from top law schools and practiced law in Southern California.
One reason clients come to Garb Jaffe & Associates, and also provide frequent referrals, is due to our commitment to excellence and ethics. We have offices in the Los Angeles and Orange County/San Diego areas.

JM Associates

JM ASSOCIATES
Client-Centered Marketing Programs
Consulting · Retreats · Training

2222 Martin
Suite 255
Irvine, CA 92612
Phone: (949) 260-9200 | **Fax:** (949) 260-0940
www.jmassociates.com

Diane Rifkin, Head of Recruiting
Phone: (949) 260-0945
drifkin@jmassociates.com

Since 1988, JM Associates has assisted attorneys with full time placement, achieving career success and satisfaction beyond their expectations. More than 98% of our placements have withstood the test of time because we listen, communicate, and work tirelessly to create the perfect match. As a member of the National Association of Legal Search Consultants (NALSC), we subscribe to a stringent code of ethics that guarantees our candidates strict confidentiality, dignity and respect. JM Associates' Head of Recruiting, Diane Rifkin, was elected to the Board of Directors of NALSC and serves on the Ethics Committee.
Learn more by visiting www.jmassociates.com.

The Vault Legal Recruiter Directory is a special advertising section in the *Vault Guide to the Top 100 Law Firms*.
For information on listing your firm in the directory, contact H.S. Hamadeh, Esq. at hshamadeh@staff.vault.com.

VAULT CAREER LIBRARY   **685**

Kass-Abell & Associates, Inc.

10780 Santa Monica Blvd.
Suite 200
Los Angeles, CA 90025
Phone: (310) 475-4666 | **Fax:** (310) 475-0485
www.kassabell.com

Peter J. Redgrove, President
Phone: (310) 475-4666
attyplcmnt@kassabell.com

Kass Abell & Associates has 22 years of experience successfully conducting searches for corporate law departments and law firms in California. Our team of experienced recruiters take great pride in representing the needs of clients and candidates in an ethical and professional manner. Peter Redgrove's reputation as a leader in the IN-HOUSE sector is widely acknowledged. Our LAW FIRM representation includes leading firms in Los Angeles, Orange County, San Diego, San Francisco and Silicon Valley.The success of Kass Abell is based on our caring Commitment to every search we undertake.

We are a founding member of NALSC.

Katharine C. Patterson Consulting, Inc.

235 Montgomery Street
Suite 1850
San Francisco, CA 94104
Phone: (415) 398-2622 / (800) 248-6556 (U.S. Toll Free)
Fax: (415) 391-2826

Katharine C. Patterson, President
Phone: (415) 398-2622
gneisserperson@msn.com

Reece Legal Search, Inc.

ATTORNEY SEARCH CONSULTANTS

555 W. Fifth Street
Suite 3100
Los Angeles, CA 90013
Phone: (213) 996-8585 | **Fax:** (213) 996-8579
www.reecelegalsearch.com

Carl D. Reece
info@reecelegalsearch.com

Number of Recruiters/Consultants: 3
Domestic office locations: Los Angeles
Date founded: 1999
Percentage of Business Devoted to Placing Attorneys: 100%
% of Placements Law Firm vs. Corporate Legal Departments:
80% Law Firm and 20% In-House

Firm description: Carl D. Reece, the firm's founder and principal, has been a legal recruiter since 1987. He has placed associates and partners at premier national and boutique law firms and Fortune 500 companies globally. His clients have expertise in a wide array of practice specialties, including banking, bankruptcy, corporate securities entertainment, finance, intellectual property and real estate law.

Before establishing RLS in 1999, Mr. Reece was a senior attorney search consultant with a nationally recognized recruiting firm based in Los Angeles. He has been a contributing panelist and seminar moderator at numerous industry conferences. Most recently, he was a guest lecturer at the University of Southern California School of Law. He is currently Co-President of the National Association of Legal Search Consultants (NALSC).

The Vault Legal Recruiter Directory is a special advertising section in the *Vault Guide to the Top 100 Law Firms.*
For information on listing your firm in the directory, contact H.S. Hamadeh, Esq. at hshamadeh@staff.vault.com.

VAULT CAREER LIBRARY   **687**

Russo & Fondell, Inc.

RUSSO & FONDELL, INC.
ATTORNEY SEARCH CONSULTANTS

190 N. Canon Dr., Suite 300
Beverly Hills, CA 90210
Phone: (310) 277-1717 | **Fax:** (310) 277-3777
www.russofondell.com

Joan Fondell or Mary Jo Russo, Principals
info@russofondell.com

In a survey of top law firms in California, Russo & Fondell. Inc. received highest praise, recognized as Headhunters Extraordinaire and was rated one of California's top legal recruiting firms. Russo & Fondell is considered a leader in the placement of Associates, Partners and Counsel in law firms and corporations. The firm strictly adheres to NALSC's Code of Ethics.
The two principals, Mary Jo Russo and Joan Fondell, have a combined 41 years of legal recruiting experience. They have extensive contacts throughout California and nationwide and have developed outstanding relationships with law firms and corporations. Their professionalism is measured by the trust and respect of their clients and candidates.

Seltzer Fontaine Beckwith

2999 Overland Avenue, Suite 120
Los Angeles, CA 90064
Phone: (310) 839-6000
Fax: (310) 829-4408

www.sfbsearch.com
Madeleine Seltzer or Valerie Fontaine
Partners
Phone: (310) 839-6000
info@sfbsearch.com

Swan Legal Search

Swan Legal Search
SLS
Attorneys Helping Attorneys

11500 W. Olympic Boulevard
Suite 370
Los Angeles, CA 90064
Phone: (310) 445-5010 | **Fax:** (310) 445-0621
www.swanlegal.com

Delia K. Swan, Esq., Owner, Recruiter
info@swanlegal.com

Swan Legal Search is ranked by the Los Angeles and San Francisco Daily Journals (California Law Business section) as one of California's "Top Ten" legal recruiting firms for the placement of partners, associates, groups of attorneys, and firm mergers. Our success is a direct reflection of the commitment, accountability and integrity brought in to each search. Comprised of former practicing attorneys, Swan Legal Search understands what makes an attorney successful, as well as what law firms and in-house legal departments seek. Swan Legal Search conducts business throughout California, including Los Angeles, Bay Area, Orange County and San Diego. We work in all practice areas, including intellectual property, antitrust, bankruptcy, environmental, corporate,

litigation, ERISA, labor & employment, real estate, banking and tax.

The SLS team consists of former lawyers:

- Delia Swan (1990 J.D., University of Southern California)
- Claudia Trevisan (1992 J.D., Loyola Law School)
- Elise Lau (1993 J.D., Hastings College of the Law)
- Melinda Adams (2000 J.D., University of Michigan Law School)

Our recruiters are known for their extensive knowledge of the California market. SLS maintains the highest standards of confidentiality and ethics, and is a member of both the National Association of Legal Search Consultants (NALSC) and the Better Business Bureau. We have an unprecedented passion for facilitating a "fit" on both a personal and professional level. Our information technology is the most advanced in the industry, and enables us to respond quickly with the right candidates and opportunities. We are committed to our attorney candidates' careers and have a genuine desire to develop and maintain long-term relationships.

Without exception, attorneys placed by SLS enthusiastically endorse us for the individual care they received, and for the career-enhancing positions they obtained through our efforts. For references, job listings, and representative clients, please review our website at www.swanlegal.com.

Wolk Associates

11601 Wilshire Boulevard
5th Floor
Los Angeles, CA 90025
Phone: (310) 575-1863 | **Fax:** (310) 456-7232

Marilyn Wolk, President
mwolk@earthlink.net

For over 15 years, Wolk Associates has handled permanent and contract placements with prestigious regional and national firms. Seventy percent of its business is from placing individual partners, associates and groups in law firms, and thirty is from placing in-house counsel, including general counsel. The firm places lawyers in all specialty areas, including bankruptcy, corporate, entertainment, environmental, intellectual property, internet and multimedia, labor, litigation, real estate, securities, tax and trust and estate. The firm works on retained exclusive partner and group searches, and in-house corporate counsel searches. Wolk Associates provides consulting services and general information about the legal marketplace and also provides outplacement services.

The Vault Legal Recruiter Directory

is a special advertising section in the *Vault Guide to the Top 100 Law Firms*. For information on listing your firm in next year's directory, or our legal recruiting directories in other Vault law guides, contact H.S. Hamadeh, Esq. at hshamadeh@staff.vault.com.

Vault Law Career Guides include:

- **Vault Guide to Top 100 Law Firms**
- **Vault Regional Law Firm Guides (New York, Washington, DC, Boston, Chicago, Texas, etc.)**
- **Vault Practice Area Guides (Corporate, Litigation, Labor & Employment, Bankruptcy, etc.)**

District of Columbia

Garrison & Sisson, Inc.

GARRISON & SISSON, INC.
ATTORNEY SEARCH CONSULTANTS

1156 15th Street, N.W.
Suite 502
Washington, DC 20005
Phone: (202) 429-5630 | **Fax:** (202) 659-2028
www.garrison-sisson.com

Charles W. Garrison or Martha Ann Sisson, Partners
g-s@garrison-sisson.com

Garrison & Sisson, Inc., serves a diverse client base in all substantive areas of legal practice and at all levels of experience. Clients include global, national and regional firms, as well as national specialty law firms, which all share the objective of recruiting the most capable and qualified attorneys. Garrison & Sisson assists law departments of emerging growth and Fortune 500 corporations to recruit lawyers who possess the requisite legal skills and value the importance of advancing the business needs of their companies. The firm recruits lawyers for business and management consulting, government relations, trade and accounting firms and professional associations.

GroupMagellan Attorney Placement

1050 17th Steet N.W.
Suite 600
Washington, DC 20036
Phone: (202) 325-0606 | **Fax:** (202) 625-03155
www.groupmagellan.com

Tom Goldstein, Esquire, President, Career Counselor
tom@groupmagellan.com

Professional and experienced career counseling for positions at the partner, of counsel, and associate levels. Call or email us for confidential career counseling and job placement. We place candidates in top law firms and companies in the Washington, D.C. metro and Boston, Massachusetts metro areas. Questions about trends in the job market, and non-profit or Capitol Hill careers are also welcome. Staffed by attorneys, and founded by Yale law school graduate and former Skadden Arps associate.

The Vault Legal Recruiter Directory is a special advertising section in the *Vault Guide to the Top 100 Law Firms*.
For information on listing your firm in the directory, contact H.S. Hamadeh, Esq. at hshamadeh@staff.vault.com.

VAULT CAREER LIBRARY   **689**

Florida

Hertner, Block & Associates, Inc.

Hertner, Block & Associates, Inc.
Legal Search Consultants

15485 Eagle Next Lane
Suite 110
Miami, FL 33014
Phone: (305) 556-8882 | **Fax:** (305) 556-5650
www.legalrecruiting.com

Herbert H. Hertner, President
hertner@bellsouth.net

Hertner, Block & Associates, Inc. (HBAI) was founded in 1984 to service the legal staffing needs for partners, associates and mergers of law firms, in addition to, general counsel and staff counsel for corporations. HBAI has concentrated its efforts in the state of Florida, but has developed a network of leading search firms in all major cities in the United States. HBAI is a member of the National Association of Legal Search Consultants (NALSC), a national organization committed to upholding the highest ethical standards in the legal search field.

Phillips & Juarez Legal Consultants

10364 Triple Crown Avenue
Suite 100
Jacksonville, FL 32257
Phone: (904) 260-2929 / 888-710-6565 (U.S. Toll Free)
Fax: (202) 478-0445
www.legalonesearch.com

Donald E. Phillips
dep@legalonesearch.com

Our firm represents highly qualified and accomplished attorneys in their confidential efforts to explore new affiliations. We place associate and partner level individuals in law firm and in-house opportunities. While the majority of our efforts focus on the Washington, DC metro and Florida markets we have successfully completed projects in many of the world's major economic and legal centers. Additionally, we offer specialized consulting services in law firm development through practice group and firm mergers.

During the 1st quarter of 2003 our accomplishments have included:

- Development of a Government Contracts discipline for a top 100 ranked law firm
- The addition of a Corporate Practice to the Washington, DC office of a top 100 ranked law firm
- Placement of a Labor & Employment Partner with an "old line" 300 +/- Attorney law firm

Georgia

BG Search Associates

1040 Crown Pointe Parkway
Suite 300
Atlanta, GA 30338
Phone: (770) 804-0355 | **Fax:** (770) 804-0123
www.bgsearch.com

Barbara Goldman, President
Phone: (770) 804-0355
bgoldman@bgsearch.com

Hughes Consultants

hughes CONSULTANTS

The Bitmore
817 West Peachtree Street, Suite 208
Atlanta, GA 30308
Phone: (404) 879-5070 | **Fax:** (404) 879-5075
www.hughes-consultants.com

Melba N.G. Hughes, President
inquiry@hughes-consultants.com

Hughes Consultants is dedicated to serving the search and consulting needs of the legal community. With over 40 years of cumulative experience, our staff has the knowledge and the expertise to uncover the best opportunities in the marketplace. We fill positions nationally from associates to partners, from staff attorneys to general counsels. Our clients are a diverse group of law firms and corporations many of whom are ranked among the AmLaw 100 and Fortune 500 corporations. We strive to be an invaluable resource to each candidate and company we serve and pride ourselves on making the perfect match.

Illinois

Haydon Legal Search

HAYDON
LEGAL
SEARCH

5225 Old Orchard Road, Suite 8
Skokie, IL 60077 (Chicago area)
Phone: (847) 965-8222 | **Fax:** (847) 965-1447
www.haydonlegal.com

Meredith Haydon, Principal
haydonlegal@aol.com

Meredith Haydon has specialized in permanent attorney search and placement since 1979. She established her own recruiting firm in 1988 and provides recruitment services to many prominent Chicago-area corporations and law firms, frequently on an exclusive-assignment basis.

With 24 years in attorney search, Meredith Haydon makes available to clients and candidates her extensive knowledge of and experience with Chicago's legal community and is recognized for outstanding service to attorneys at all levels. Member, NALSC since 1990. Please visit our website (www.haydonlegal.com) for a list of representative clients.

McCormack Schreiber Legal Search Inc.

150 North Wacker Drive
Suite 2950
Chicago, IL 60606
Phone: 312-377-2000 / 866-819-4091 (U.S. Toll Free)
Fax: 312-377-2001
http://www.thelawrecruiters.com

Amy L. McCormack and Gay R. Schreiber, Principals
info@thelawrecruiters.com

McCormack Schreiber Legal Search Inc., with its 7 attorney recruiters, is the largest all attorney search firm in Chicago. McCormack Schreiber specializes in the placement of associates and partners at large, midsize and boutique law firms, and in-house counsel of all levels at regional, national and international corporations. McCormack Schreiber also participates in acquisitions and transfers of practice groups, and in law firm mergers. The principals and recruiters at McCormack Schreiber have over 60 years of combined experience as practicing attorneys and as legal recruiters. McCormack Schreiber is a member of the National Association of Legal Search Consultants, and all inquiries to McCormack Schreiber will be kept strictly confidential.

Vera L. Rast Partners, Inc./VLRPI

2 North LaSalle Street
Suite 1808
Chicago, IL 60602
Phone: (312) 629-0339 | **Fax:** (312) 629-0347
www.vlrpilegalsearch.com

Vera Rast, President
vlrpi@vlrpilegalsearch.com

Looking for a legal position? Need a change of venue?

Find your dream career opportunity on the Vault Law Job Board. Featuring hundreds of top positions throughout the U.S. and Canada.

Positions for all positions, including:

- Associate
- Partner
- Paralegal
- In-house Counsel

Positions in all practice areas, including

- Corporate
- Intellectual Property
- Labor/Employment
- Litigation
- Real Estate
- Tax
- Trusts & Estates

Go to law.vault.com

The Vault Legal Recruiter Directory is a special advertising section in the *Vault Guide to the Top 100 Law Firms.*
For information on listing your firm in the directory, contact H.S. Hamadeh, Esq. at hshamadeh@staff.vault.com.

 **V**AULT CAREER LIBRARY   **691**

Massachusetts

Bickerton & Gordon, LLC

60 State Street, Suite 700
Boston, MA 02109
Phone: (617) 371-2929 | **Fax:** (617) 371-2999
www.bickertongordon.com

Brion Bickerton; Richards Gordon, Principals
info@bickertongordon.com

One of the nation's leading legal recruitment firms for corporations and law firms since 1988. Rated the #1 legal search firm for 5 consecutive years by the Massachusetts Lawyers Weekly, B&G is headed by a former General Counsel and law firm partner. Concentration on New England-based clients but searches also nationwide.

General Counsel and Partner Searches • Chief Patent and patent personnel searches • Associate and Staff Attorney Searches • Temporary and Permanent Placement

Past searches include: General Counsel (Fortune 100 to start-ups); Associate placements at wide range of corporate firms; Chief Patent, patent attorneys and tech specialists in all industry areas; Partner placements with portables ranging $500K - $5 + million.

New England Legal Search

280 Commonwealth Ave.
Suite 304
Boston, MA 02116
Phone: (617) 266-6068 | **Fax:** (617) 266-8510
www.newenglandlegalsearch.com

Linda J. Kline, Dee B. McMeekan, Managing Directors

New England Legal Search, founded in 1982, is the region's oldest attorney recruiting firm. Comprised of three full-time recruiters, all attorneys, we focus exclusively on the permanent placement of attorneys with law firms and corporations. Our legal experience, the depth of our knowledge of legal careers, and our commitment to and reputation for exceptional client service have enabled us to become the leading legal recruiter in the region. NELS is a Founding Member of the National Association of Legal Search Consultants and managing director McMeekan has served as its Vice President and Board member.

New Jersey

E M Messick Legal Recruiting & Consulting

E · M · MESSICK
LEGAL RECRUITING & CONSULTING

444 Washington Blvd.
Suite 2331
Jersey City, NJ 07310
Phone: (201) 386-9484 • **Fax:** (253) 660-2326
www.emmcjob.com

Edna Messick, President
info@emmcjob.com

E M Messick Legal Recruiting & Consulting, Legal search and consulting firm, places corporate counsel, partners and junior/senior-level associates in major corporations and international law firms worldwide. The firm specializes in the placement of diverse candidates in the areas of Banking, Bankruptcy, Corporate, Corporate Securities, Mergers and Acquisitions, International Finance, Structured Finance, Project Finance, Intellectual Property, Tax, ERISA, Real Estate, Litigation and Labor and Employment. Consulting services are also available for firms contemplating mergers and practice group acquisitions.

Myra Binstock Legal Search

Myra Binstock Legal Search
Associates
Partners
Mergers

121 Squire Hill Road
Upper Montclair, NJ 07043
Phone: (973) 783-6006
Fax: (973) 783-0037
www.myrabinstock.com

Myra Binstock, President
Phone: (973) 783-6006 • **Fax:** (973) 783-0037
myrab2@aol.com

Myra Binstock Legal Search is a goal-oriented search firm whose principal is dedicated to hands-on counseling and personal involvement in introducing those people who will work best together. Whether the applicant is an entry-level attorney or a seasoned professional, each is given ample time and attention to productively focus on their career path. Myra is a former paralegal whose own career includes years both as an administrative assistant to an Appellate Division Judge and sole paralegal for a Fortune 100 corporation. She understands the working environment of companies and law firms, and knows how to match the right person to the job.

Hughes Consultants

The Bitmore
817 West Peachtree Street, Suite 208
Atlanta, GA 30308
Phone: (404) 879-5070 | **Fax:** (404) 879-5075
www.hughes-consultants.com

Melba N.G. Hughes, President
inquiry@hughes-consultants.com

Hughes Consultants is dedicated to serving the search and consulting needs of the legal community. With over 40 years of cumulative experience, our staff has the knowledge and the expertise to uncover the best opportunities in the marketplace. We fill positions nationally from associates to partners, from staff attorneys to general counsels. Our clients are a diverse group of law firms and corporations many of whom are ranked among the AmLaw 100 and Fortune 500 corporations. We strive to be an invaluable resource to each candidate and company we serve and pride ourselves on making the perfect match.

Oliveras & Company, Inc.

1605 John Street
Suite 119
Fort Lee, NJ 07024
Phone: (201) 947-6662
Fax: (201) 947-5934
www.oliverascoinc.com

Wendy Oliveras, President and CEO
Phone: (201) 947-6662
wo@oliverascoinc.com

Oliveras & Company, Inc. ("OC") is a full service professional attorney search firm specializing in the recruitment of intellectual property attorneys, partners, practice groups, and IP and general firm mergers and acquisitions. Recruitment services are also provided for all legal and administrative support staff, including all Human Resources positions. OC's clientele includes law firms, in-house legal departments, and corporations, most of whom have domestic and international presence. OC is unique in that it brings over 22 years of hands-on experience in the legal, intellectual property and recruitment industries. Other specialized services include Career Planning and Development Services.

Reign Enterprises

REIGN ENTERPRISES
Legal Staffing

Twenty Nassau Street
Suite 200 C
Princeton, NJ 08542
Phone: (609) 688-9898 • **Fax:** (609) 688-1898
www.reignenterprises.com

Noel H. Gordon, Chief Executive Officer
jobs@reignenterprises.com

Reign Enterprises LLC dedicates itself to serving the staffing needs of the legal community. The members of the company have over 30 years of legal and staffing experience. With a large and diverse network of contacts, combined with a sophisticated and extensive data base, we are able to offer contract, temporary, temp-to-hire attorney, paralegal or legal professional placements. We specialize in diversity candidates and providing antitrust, trademark, employment, and products liability staffing services to law firms, corporations and government agencies.
Reign Enterprises specializes in providing excellent temporary or contract legal talent to law firms, corporations and government agencies primarily in New York, New Jersey, Delaware and Pennsylvania, but also throughout the United States and United Kingdom.

The Vault Legal Recruiter Directory

is a special advertising section in the *Vault Guide to the Top 100 Law Firms*. For information on listing your firm in next year's directory, or our legal recruiting directories in other Vault law guides, contact H.S. Hamadeh, Esq. at hshamadeh@staff.vault.com.

Vault Law Career Guides include:
• **Vault Guide to Top 100 Law Firms**
• **Vault Regional Law Firm Guides (New York, Washington, DC, Boston, Chicago, Texas, etc.)**
• **Vault Practice Area Guides (Corporate, Litigation, Labor & Employment, Bankruptcy, etc.)**

The Vault Legal Recruiter Directory is a special advertising section in the *Vault Guide to the Top 100 Law Firms*.
For information on listing your firm in the directory, contact H.S. Hamadeh, Esq. at hshamadeh@staff.vault.com.

VAULT CAREER LIBRARY   **693**

TAKE this JOB and LOVE IT.

Whether you are exploring new challenges or a lifestyle change, striving for a broader client base or refocusing your career path, Conduit can provide you with the resources and personalized attention to meet your professional goals. Our goal is to find a match that best meets your professional objectives.

Connecting people to jobs.

full service legal search

www.conduitrecruiting.c

New York

Ann Israel & Associates

ANN ISRAEL & ASSOCIATES
CONSULTANTS TO THE LEGAL COMMUNITY

The Crown Building
730 Fifth Avenue, Suite 900
New York, NY 10019
Phone: (212) 333-8730 | **Fax:** (212) 765-4462
www.attorneysearch.com

Ann Israel, President
aisrael@annisrael.com

Ann Israel & Associates dedicates itself to serving the search and consulting needs of the global legal community. With a large and diverse network of contacts, along with one of the most sophisticated and extensive databases known in the legal search profession, we offer a broad range of recruiting and consulting services.

Ann Israel is the immediate Past President of the National Association of Legal Search Consultants (NALSC) and a member of the Board of Directors since 1981. Ann writes a weekly advice column called, "Advice for the Lawlorn." Please visit the column at www.nylawyer.com/lawlorn; we encourage you to submit questions.

Conduit Recruiting Corp.

conduit

145 West 45th Street
8th Floor
New York, NY 10036
Phone: (212) 768-2121 | **Fax:** (212) 768-2821
www.conduitrecruiting.com

Mark P. Arrow, President
arrow@conduitrecruiting.com

Rethink the possibilities!

Conduit Recruiting Corp. is a leading legal recruiting firm that places legal professionals with national and international law firms and corporations. Each Conduit client and candidate benefits from our commitment to personalized attention, customized searches and innovative technology - the cornerstones of our business. We are dedicated to fostering partnerships with our clientele to ensure mutually beneficial matches. With our dynamic client base and access to high-caliber candidates, Conduit connects people to jobs.

Gardiner Simpson Legal Search, Inc.

10 Park Avenue
New York, NY 10016
Phone: (212) 779-1125 | **Fax:** (212) 696-4524

Donna Hurry, Managing Director
Phone: (212) 779-1125
dhurry@garsim.com

Greene-Levin-Snyder LLC

greene
levin
snyder
llc

150 E. 58th Street
16th Floor
New York, NY 10155
Phone: (212) 752-5200 | **Fax:** (212) 752-8245
www.glslsg.com

Karin L. Greene, Alisa F. Levin, Esq., Susan Kurz Snyder, Esq., Principals
search@glslsg.com

Greene-Levin-Snyder conducts exclusive searches for General Counsel, partners, in-house counsel and associates of all levels in every practice area. The firm also places lawyers in business and quasi-business positions. Clients include domestic and international law firms of all sizes as well as financial institutions, media and entertainment companies, and a broad variety of other corporations. Many of our twelve search professionals are former practicing attorneys who, combined, have over five decades of legal search expertise. Our search consultants work in teams to ensure that clients receive the full benefit of our collective knowledge and experience. The firm provides placement as well as career counseling and strategic planning services. Member NALSC

The Vault Legal Recruiter Directory is a special advertising section in the *Vault Guide to the Top 100 Law Firms.*
For information on listing your firm in the directory, contact H.S. Hamadeh, Esq. at hshamadeh@staff.vault.com.

V/\ULT CAREER LIBRARY **695**

J. Smith Associates, Inc.

420 Lexington Avenue
Suite 1708
New York, NY 10170
Phone: (212) 867-9203 | **Fax:** (212) 867-9219
www.smithcounsel.com

Judith E. Smith, President
Phone: (212) 867-9203
info@smithcounsel.com

Klausner Group, Ltd.,The

TheKlausnerGroup

45 West 45th Street
New York, NY 10036
Phone: (212) 557-5800 | **Fax:** (212) 557-3833
www.klausnergroup.com

Morley Klausner, President
mklausner@klausnergroup.com

We are staffed with a top-notch team of attorneys and professional consultants whose goal is to be fully acquainted with the hiring requirements for our clients as well as the long-term personal and professional goals of the attorneys we represent. Each consultant focuses on the placement of attorneys who specialize in a particular area of the law. Additionally, each counselor concentrates on a defined geographic region. Thus, the counselors develop an expertise in their specific marketplace. This structure uniquely positions us to provide the intimate contacts of a local recruiter with the network of a national enterprise.

Klein Windmiller, LLC

Klein Windmiller
Legal Search Consultants

230 Park Avenue
10th Floor
New York, NY 10017
Phone: 212-808-3038 | **Fax:** 212-808-4082
www.kwrecruit.com

Marlene Windmiller, Esq. or Nancy Klein, Esq., Principals
mw@kwrecruit.com or nk@kwrecruit.com

Klein Windmiller, LLC is a global attorney placement firm with offices in New York and San Francisco. Our focus is a more personalized approach toward legal placement. With a staff composed of four attorney recruiters and two professional consultants, we work in teams to offer candidates the benefit of our combined knowledge and responsive service. We conduct searches for general counsel, partners, in-house counsel and associates of all levels in every practice area. Our clients include domestic and international law firms, investment banks and a variety of financial and consumer products companies.

Lexolution, LLC

Lexolution LLC

330 Madison Avenue
9th Floor
New York, NY 10017
Phone: 212-653-0845 | **Fax:** 212-377-2001

1776 I Street, N.W.
Washington, DC 20006
Phone: 202-756-4874 | **Fax:** 202-756-1583
www.lexolution.net

Scott Krowitz, Nora Plesent, Dick Osman, Karen Stempel, Principals
jobs@lexolution.net

Lexolution, LLC is a leading contract legal staffing firm in the New York and Washington, DC metropolitan regions. Founded by accomplished attorneys who practiced at leading law firms, Lexolution provides top attorney and paralegal talent to law firms and corporations in all practice areas. Lexolution makes the effort to identify and recruit the very best person for every job, often providing creative solutions for difficult staffing situations. Temporary staffing can be the best way to manage personnel costs for: large document production projects; corporate and real estate due diligence projects; maternity or extended leave coverage; unique brief or other non-recurring legal writing projects; as well as for special situations requiring outside legal expertise.

The Vault Legal Recruiter Directory is a special advertising section in the *Vault Guide to the Top 100 Law Firms.*
For information on listing your firm in the directory, contact H.S. Hamadeh, Esq. at hshamadeh@staff.vault.com.

VAULT CAREER LIBRARY   697

Michael Lord & Company

245 Fifth Avenue, Suite 901
New York, NY 10016
Phone: 646-258-1761 | **Fax:** 212-689-4975
http://www.mlordco.com

Michael Lord, Principal
michael@mlordco.com

With offices in Manhattan and Fairfield County, CT, Michael Lord & Company provides responsive and resourceful recruiting for large national law firms, mid-sized firms, and scores of boutique firms. The company also places attorneys in investment banks and hedge funds. Prior to founding his firm, Mr. Lord worked at one of New York's veteran attorney placement firms. He is active in the NALSC, the Real Estate Board of New York, the NY Bar Association, and has lectured on attorney placement at a seminar sponsored by Salomon Smith Barney. Mr. Lord holds a JD from Syracuse where he was Executive Editor of the Syracuse Law Review, and a BA from Emory where he played varsity tennis. Before entering the legal search field, Mr. Lord spent nearly a decade as an attorney with law firms in NY and CT. Earlier, he was deputy finance director for Robert Abrams' U.S. Senate campaign and had been with the CHD Public Relations firm.

Sivin Tobin Associates, LLC

516 Fifth Avenue, 14th Floor
New York, NY 10036
Phone: (212) 573-9800 | **Fax:** (212) 573-6122
www.sivintobin.com

Eric Sivin or David Tobin, Principals
info@sivintobin.com

The two principals of Sivin Tobin have an aggregate of over 35 years of legal recruiting experience. Over that time frame, they have placed a myriad of lawyers at firms and companies throughout the US and internationally. Many of those attorneys have risen to senior positions in their organizations, providing Sivin Tobin with a range and breadth of contacts throughout the legal community which is second to none. The firm's leading position in partner and practice group movement also enables it to work on associate positions which other firms do not have access to, enhancing its service in that area.

The Legal Recruiters Inc.

THE LEGAL RECRUITERS INC

275 Madison Avenue, Suite 612
New York, NY 90013
Phone: (212) 856-4412 | **Fax:** (212) 880-4246
www.thelegalrecruiters.com

Muriel Holland, President
vault@thelegalrecruiters.com

Placing attorneys since 1990 in corporations, financial institutions and law firms, in legal, quasi-legal and non-legal positions.

Placement specialties: corporate/securities (with a sub-specialty in structured finance, structured products, and securitization), international, banking/bank regulatory, M&A, tax, ERISA, labor/employment, intellectual property, insurance, and environmental.

In-house clients include financial conglomerates, bulge bracket investment banks, commercial banks, rating agencies, credit enhancers, broker/dealers, hedge funds, issuers, consulting firms, and manufacturing/consumer products.

Law firms, both domestically and internationally; ranged from small to large NYC-based to branches and boutiques, and non-US based firms; placements concentrated in the tristate area, but extends coast-to-coast and throughout Europe and Asia.

Toby Spitz Associates Inc.

TOBY SPITZ
ASSOCIATES, INC.

110 E. 59th Street
29th floor
New York, NY 10022
Phone: 212-319-0990 | **Fax:** 212-319-1555
www.jdsearch.com

Toby Spitz, President
TobySpitz@jdsearch.com

Toby Spitz Associates Inc., successor to Corporate Counsel Search, Inc. founded in 1982, places full-time attorneys in law firms and corporations. We also facilitate mergers of law firms and partner groups. Five of our seven recruiters are attorneys who practiced in law firms and in-house. Each recruiter works in a specialized area of the law so that he or she is familiar with the hiring needs and qualifications for attorneys in the particular specialty. We place in all practice areas, with an emphasis on corporate, litigation, intellectual property, regulatory, labor, real estate, tax and benefits. Further information about Toby Spitz Associates, Inc. is available at www.jdsearch.com.

The Vault Legal Recruiter Directory is a special advertising section in the *Vault Guide to the Top 100 Law Firms*.

For information on listing your firm in the directory, contact H.S. Hamadeh, Esq. at hshamadeh@staff.vault.com.

VAULT CAREER LIBRARY **699**

WiseCounsel LLC

767 Third Avenue, 24th Floor
New York, NY 10017
Phone: (212) 588-9600 | **Fax:** (212) 355-5983
www.wise-counsel.com

Karen L. Frankel, President
kfrankel@wise-counsel.com

WiseCounsel LLC is a woman-owned NY based legal recruiting firm founded by Karen L. Frankel in May 2000. WiseCounsel offers its legal and corporate clients a creative mixture of permanent, temporary, and blended recruitment options. We provide entry level to high level Attorneys, Paralegals, and Financial Professionals. We are former attorneys and paralegals with over 20 years of recruiting experience. We represent law firms and corporations nationwide. Our state-of-the art database enables us to identify the most qualified attorneys and paralegals for all your legal hiring needs. Additionally, we provide consulting services with respect to all aspects of staffing for both law firms and corporations.

Pennsylvania

Carpenter Legal Search, Inc.

One Oxford Centre Suite, 3030
301 Grant Street
Pittsburgh, PA 15219-6401
Phone: (412) 255-3770 | **Fax:** (412) 255-3780
www.carpenterlegalsearch.com

Lori J. Carpenter, President
lcarpenter@carpenterlegalsearch.com

Carpenter Legal Search, Inc. was established to satisfy the increasing need for strategic, well defined search services in today's dynamic legal market. Our clients comprise a diverse field ranging from Fortune 500 corporations to closely held businesses and internationally recognized law firms to prominent regional law firms. Whether you are searching to join a law department or another law firm, or creating an in-house legal department, adding partners or associates, building a new practice area, or opening additional offices, CLS provides strategic consulting services to identify the foremost opportunities or candidates to meet your needs.

Abelson Legal Search

Attorneys & Paralegals, Permanent & Temporary

1700 South Market Street
Suite 2130
Philadelphia, PA 19103
Phone: (215) 561-3010 | **Fax:** (215) 561-3001
www.abelsonlegalsearch.com

Cathy Abelson, President
abelson@abelsonlegalsearch.com

Since 1990 Abelson Legal Search has provided cost and time-efficient legal recruiting to law firms and corporations throughout the country, with an emphasis in PA, NJ, and DE. Our skilled professionals combine modern technology and old-fashioned commitment to guarantee personalized attention to every permanent or temporary attorney and paralegal placement. Working with law firms of every size and description, corporations ranging from Fortune 100 to start-ups, and many types of financial institutions, Abelson Legal Search has a well-earned reputation for integrity and productivity. Member NALSC.

The Vault Legal Recruiter Directory is a special advertising section in the *Vault Guide to the Top 100 Law Firms*.

For information on listing your firm in the directory, contact H.S. Hamadeh, Esq. at hshamadeh@staff.vault.com.

V∧ULT CAREER LIBRARY **701**

Sacks Legal Search

271 Henley Road
Wynnewood, PA 19096
Phone: (610) 649-5539
Fax: (610) 649-2635
www.sackslegalsearch.com

Sabrina J. Sacks, Esq., President
ssacks@sackslegalsearch.com"

Sacks Legal Search is led by Sabrina J. Sacks, a licensed attorney with extensive experience placing attorneys in permanent positions with law firms and corporations in the PA/NJ/DE area and nationwide. Specializing in providing the personalized, efficient attention necessary to help both lawyers searching for new opportunities and law firms or corporations seeking new talent, SLS places associates and partner level attorneys at internationally recognized, national, regional and boutique law firms and companies nationwide, and handles law firm acquisitions and mergers. A member of the National Association of Legal Search Consultants, we pride ourselves on achieving client satisfaction through principled, discreet, resourceful, timely and cost-effective service which is custom-tailored for our individual clients.

The Vault Legal Recruiter Directory

is a special advertising section in the *Vault Guide to the Top 100 Law Firms*. For information on listing your firm in next year's directory, or our legal recruiting directories in other Vault law guides, contact H.S. Hamadeh, Esq. at hshamadeh@staff.vault.com.

Vault Law Career Guides include:
- **Vault Guide to Top 100 Law Firms**
- **Vault Regional Law Firm Guides (New York, Washington, DC, Boston, Chicago, Texas, etc.)**
- **Vault Practice Area Guides (Corporate, Litigation, Labor & Employment, Bankruptcy, etc.)**

Tennessee

AMERICAN Legal Search, LLC

209 10th Ave South, Suite 428
Nashville, TN 37203
Phone: (615) 251-9600 | **Fax:** (415) 532-1641
www.americanlegalsearch.com

Joe Freedman, CEO
joe@americanlegalsearch.com

AMERICAN Legal Search, LLC is a full-service national legal search firm. Before launching AMERICAN, our executive management team founded and built one of the largest privately held legal search firms in North America. From law firm mergers and practice group acquisitions to permanent search and contract staffing, AMERICAN's principals have been serving the legal communities throughout the country for more than a decade.

AMERICAN operates three core business divisions:
1. Assist law firms with firm mergers, practice group acquisitions and expansions into new cities.
2. Placement of associates and partner-level lawyers with law firms and corporations on a permanent basis.
3. Placement of contract (temporary) attorneys for specific projects.

Looking for a legal position? Need a change of venue?

Find your dream career opportunity on the Vault Law Job Board. Featuring hundreds of top positions throughout the U.S. and Canada.

Positions for all positions, including:
- Associate
- Partner
- Paralegal
- In-house Counsel

Positions in all practice areas, including
- Corporate
- Intellectual Property
- Labor/Employment
- Litigation
- Real Estate
- Tax
- Trusts & Estates

Go to law.vault.com

The Vault Legal Recruiter Directory is a special advertising section in the *Vault Guide to the Top 100 Law Firms*.
For information on listing your firm in the directory, contact H.S. Hamadeh, Esq. at hshamadeh@staff.vault.com.

V\ULT CAREER LIBRARY   **703**

Canada

ZSA Legal Recruitment Limited

20 Richmond Street East
Suite 315
Toronto, Canada M5C 2R9
Phone: 416-368-2051 • **Fax:** 416-368-5699
www.zsa.ca

Christopher Sweeney, President
info@zsa.ca

ZSA Legal Recruitment is Canada's leading and only national legal recruitment firm. With offices in Vancouver, Calgary, Edmonton, Toronto, Ottawa and Montreal, we are uniquely positioned to serve the legal recruitment needs of both law firms and corporations across Canada. ZSA provides its services to a broad range of domestic and international clients including the largest law firms and global corporations to sole practitioners and start-up companies. Our unparalleled success to date is the result of both our pioneering "selection" or non-headhunting-based recruitment strategy, and our single-minded focus of meeting the demands of our clients. Our services range from recruiting partners, associates, and general counsels/assistant general counsels to paralegals/law clerks, and legal assistants. Both lawyers and support personnel can be supplied on either a permanent or a temporary basis.

The Vault Legal Recruiter Directory

is a special advertising section in the *Vault Guide to the Top 100 Law Firms*. For information on listing your firm in next year's directory, or our legal recruiting directories in other Vault law guides, contact H.S. Hamadeh, Esq. at hshamadeh@staff.vault.com.

Vault Law Career Guides include:

• Vault Guide to Top 100 Law Firms
• Vault Regional Law Firm Guides (New York, Washington, DC, Boston, Chicago, Texas, etc.)
• Vault Practice Area Guides (Corporate, Litigation, Labor & Employment, Bankruptcy, etc.)

Intellectual Property

Janet Zykorie Legal Search, Inc.

INTELLECTUAL PROPERTY ATTORNEYS
Founded in 1985
P.O. Box 20709
New York, NY 10025
Phone: (212) 362-1709

Janet Zykorie, President
Phone: (212) 362-1709

JANET ZYKORIE LEGAL SEARCH, INC. specializes in the recruitment and placement of patent, trademark, and copyright attorneys nationwide. INTELLECTUAL PROPERTY ATTORNEYS, PARTNERS, IN-HOUSE COUNSEL, PARTNER GROUPS, ASSOCIATES.

AWARDED HIGHEST RATING
"The time spent in finding the proper 'marriage' of attorney and prospective firm or corporation is unusual, refreshing, and simply unparalleled," rhapsodized one candidate in Chicago. Another added, "Of about 20 head-hunters I used, Janet Zykorie was the most professional and most dedicated."
"Rating Recruiters 1989"
– The American Lawyer.

William K. McLaughlin Associates

William K. McLaughlin Associates
Executive Search–Patent Attorneys

P.O. Box 10308
Rochester, NY 14610-0308
Phone: 1-800-728-1964 • **Fax:** 1-800-342-7486
http://www.wkmclaughlin.com

William K. McLaughlin, President
information@wkmclaughlin.com

For over 38 years, William K. McLaughlin Associates has assisted patent attorneys in finding positions with the leading law firms and corporations throughout the United States. Our telephone number, 1-800-PAT-1964 represents Bill McLaughlin's first patent placement with another recruiting firm, and two years later he started his own search firm in 1966. As of May 2003, we have received the resumes of over 21,000 patent attorneys, and our list of placements numbers in the thousands. We have developed contacts and clients with General Counsels, Chief Patent Counsels and partners in most major law firms. Visit our web site for over 150 pages of detailed job openings that are updated daily.

APPENDIX

Alphabetical List of Law Firms

Firms by Main Offices

ARMONK, NY

Boies, Schiller & Flexner LLP 342

ATLANTA, GA

Alston & Bird LLP 494
Kilpatrick Stockton LLP 614
King & Spalding LLP 366
Powell, Goldstein, Frazer & Murphy LLP 622
Troutman Sanders LLP 633

BOSTON, MA

Bingham McCutchen LLP 548
Brown Rudnick Berlack Israels LLP 597
Choate, Hall & Stewart 566
Fish & Richardson P.C. 542
Foley Hoag LLP 606
Goodwin Procter LLP 500
Hale and Dorr LLP 258
Mintz Levin Cohn Ferris Glovsky and Popeo, P.C. . . .574
Nixon Peabody LLP 619
Palmer & Dodge LLP 620
Ropes & Gray 274
Testa, Hurwitz & Thibeault, LLP 534

CHICAGO, IL

Altheimer & Gray 590
Baker & McKenzie 430
Hinshaw & Culbertson 610
Jenner & Block, LLC 488
Katten Muchin Zavis Rosenman 570
Kirkland & Ellis 162
Lord Bissell & Brook 617
Mayer, Brown, Rowe & Maw 308
McDermott, Will & Emery .454
Piper Rudnick LLP 528
Schiff Hardin & Waite 624
Seyfarth Shaw 626
Sidley Austin Brown & Wood LLP 202
Sonnenschein Nath & Rosenthal 502
Winston & Strawn 398

CLEVELAND, OH

Arter & Hadden LLP 592
Baker & Hostetler LLP 568
Jones Day 250
Squire, Sanders & Dempsey 580

DALLAS, TX

Gardere Wynne Sewell LLP 607
Haynes and Boone, LLP 609
Jackson Walker L.L.P. 612
Jenkens & Gilchrist, A Professional Corporation 613
Locke Liddell & Sapp LLP .616
Thompson & Knight LLP 632
Winstead Sechrest & Minick P.C. 635

HOUSTON, TX

Andrews & Kurth L.L.P. 591
Baker Botts L.L.P. 422
Bracewell & Patterson, L.L.P. 596
Fulbright & Jaworski L.L.P. 446
Locke Liddell & Sapp LLP .616
Vinson & Elkins L.L.P. 516

KANSAS CITY, MS

Blackwell Sanders Peper Martin LLP 594
Shook, Hardy & Bacon L.L.P. 628

LONDON, UK

Allen & Overy 508

LOS ANGELES, CA

MENLO PARK, CA

MIAMI, FL

MILWAUKEE, WI

MINNEAPOLIS, MN

NEW YORK, NY

PALO ALTO, CA

PHILADELPHIA, PA

Ballard Spahr Andrews & Ingersoll, LLP 593
Blank Rome LLP 595
Cozen O'Connor 599
Dechert LLP 504
Drinker Biddle & Reath LLP 602
Duane Morris LLP 603
Morgan, Lewis & Bockius LLP 390
Pepper Hamilton LLP 621
Wolf, Block, Schorr and Solis-Cohen LLP 636

PITTSBURGH, PA

Buchanan Ingersoll, Professional Corporation 598
Kirkpatrick & Lockhart LLP 538
Reed Smith 623

PORTLAND, OR

Stoel Rives LLP 629

PROVIDENCE, RI

Edwards & Angell, LLP 604

RICHMOND, VA

Hunton & Williams LLP 518
McGuireWoods LLP 582

SAN FRANCISCO, CA

Heller Ehrman White & McAuliffe LLP 514
Littler Mendelson, P.C. 615
Morrison & Foerster LLP 292
Orrick, Herrington & Sutcliffe LLP 382
Pillsbury Winthrop LLP 492
Sedgwick, Detert, Moran & Arnold LLP 625

SEATTLE, WA

Davis Wright Tremaine LLP 600
Perkins Coie LLP 526
Preston Gates & Ellis LLP .586

ST. LOUIS, MO

Bryan Cave LLP 546

TAMPA, FL

Holland & Knight LLP 520

WASHINGTON, DC

Akin Gump Strauss Hauer & Feld LLP 350
Arent Fox Kintner Plotkin & Kahn, PLLC 572
Arnold & Porter 218
Covington & Burling 138
Crowell & Moring LLP 536
Dickstein Shapiro Morin & Oshinsky LLP 601
Finnegan, Henderson, Farabow, Garrett &
Dunner, L.L.P. 564
Hogan & Hartson L.L.P. 316
Howrey Simon Arnold & White, LLP 512
Patton Boggs LLP 544
Shaw Pittman LLP 562
Steptoe & Johnson LLP 506
Sutherland Asbill & Brennan LLP 630
Swidler Berlin Shereff Friedman, LLP 631
Venable LLP 634
Wiley Rein & Fielding LLP 584
Williams & Connolly LLP .186
Wilmer, Cutler & Pickering 226

WHITE PLAINS, NY

Jackson Lewis LLP 611

WINSTON-SALEM, NC

Womble Carlyle Sandridge & Rice, PLLC 637

About the Authors

Brook Moshan Gesser

Brook Moshan Gesser is the senior editor at Vault. She holds a JD from the Fordham University School of Law and a BA in English from Vassar College. Before joining Vault, she was a prosecutor for the New York City Law Department.

Marcy Lerner

Marcy Lerner is the vice president for content at Vault. She holds a BA in history from the University of Virginia and an MA in history from Yale University.

Tyya N. Turner

Tyya N. Turner worked at several publishing companies, including Pocket Books, McGraw-Hill and Miller Freeman, prior to joining Vault. She is a graduate of Howard University.

Ron Hogan

Ron Hogan is a freelance writer currently based in New York. He also publishes the popular literary web site Beatrice.com.

Use the most **targeted** job search
tools for lawyers on the Internet.

Vault's Law Job Board and VaultMatch™ Resume Database

■ **Law Job Board**

The most comprehensive and convenient
job board for legal professionals. Target
your search by practice area, function, and
experience level, and find the job openings
that you want. No surfing required.

■ **VaultMatch™ Resume Database**

Vault takes match-making to the next level:
post your resume and customize your
search by practice area, trial experience,
level and more. We'll match job listings
with your interests and criteria and e-mail
them directly to your in-box.

> the most trusted name in career information™

Find out more at
www.law.vault.com